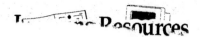

Learning Resources

D1356784

00113639

Deadly Embrace

DEADLY EMBRACE

Morocco and the Road
to the Spanish Civil War

SEBASTIAN BALFOUR

KINGSTON
LEARNING
RESOURCES
CENTRE
COLLEGE

OXFORD
UNIVERSITY PRESS

OXFORD

UNIVERSITY PRESS

Great Clarendon Street, Oxford OX2 6DP

Oxford University Press is a department of the University of Oxford.
It furthers the University's objective of excellence in research, scholarship,
and education by publishing worldwide in

Oxford New York

Auckland Bangkok Buenos Aires Cape Town Chennai
Dar es Salaam Delhi Hong Kong Istanbul Karachi Kolkata
Kuala Lumpur Madrid Melbourne Mexico City Mumbai Nairobi
São Paulo Shanghai Singapore Taipei Tokyo Toronto

with an associated company in Berlin

Oxford is a registered trade mark of Oxford University Press
in the UK and in certain other countries

Published in the United States
by Oxford University Press Inc., New York

© Sebastian Balfour 2002

The moral rights of the author have been asserted
Database right Oxford University Press (maker)

First published 2002

All rights reserved. No part of this publication may be reproduced,
stored in a retrieval system, or transmitted, in any form or by any means,
without the prior permission in writing of Oxford University Press,
or as expressly permitted by law, or under terms agreed with the appropriate
reprographics rights organization. Enquiries concerning reproduction
outside the scope of the above should be sent to the Rights Department,
Oxford University Press, at the address above

You must not circulate this book in any other binding or cover
and you must impose this same condition on any acquirer

British Library Cataloguing in Publication Data

Data available

Library of Congress Cataloging in Publication Data

Data available

ISBN 0–19–925296–3

1 3 5 7 9 10 8 6 4 2

Typeset by Hope Services (Abingdon) Ltd
Printed in Great Britain
on acid-free paper by
Biddles Ltd.,
Guildford and King's Lynn

KINGSTON COLLEGE LEARNING RESOURCES CENTRE	
Class No.	949.081 BAL
Acc. No.	0011 3639
Date Rec.	12/02
Order No.	LD

We will encircle Africa with our arms, that daughter caressed by the sun, who is the slave of the Frenchman and should be our wife.

Juan Donoso Cortés (1809–53)

Acknowledgements

DURING THE FIVE years of research and writing that led to the production of this book, I have incurred many debts of gratitude. The vast majority of people whom I approached for advice or whom I came across in the course of my research shared their knowledge and gave their advice unstintingly.

My warmest thanks go to my colleague Professor Paul Preston, who has always been the major inspiration for my research. He suggested I should tackle the theme in the first place and throughout he has given me support and perceptive advice. It was on the basis of his recommendation that I was awarded two research grants by the Cañada Blanch Foundation. I also benefited from the shrewd comments of another colleague, Professor Dominic Lieven, who generously gave his time to read an earlier version of the manuscript

Among those people who helped my research in Spain, I am indebted to the family of José Enrique Varela, the Marqués de Varela de San Fernando, for making the Varela archive available, and in particular to Casilda Güell who helped me in the search for material in the archive of her great-uncle. I would also like to thank Diego Hidalgo for allowing me to look at his father's archive in Madrid, Colonel Eduardo Bravo Garrido for granting me the right to consult the archives of the Servicio Histórico Militar, and Comandante Ruiz for giving access to the Fernández Silvestre documents. General Rafael Casas de la Vega gave me the benefit of his advice and contacts, enabling me to meet and interview two veterans of the colonial war. Ignacio Ruiz Alcaín, of the Archivo Central of the Ministerio de la Presidencia, provided me with valuable documents and communicated his passionate interest in the colonial history of Morocco, and Antonio González Quintana, Co-ordinator of the military archives of the Ministry of Defence, gave me advice about the location of military sources. I was pleased to make contact with the descendants of General Alberto Castro Girona, in particular his nephew Marcial Castro Sánchez. My only regret is that our efforts to retrieve the General's documents proved fruitless.

I am also indebted to the Dirección General de Relaciones Culturales y Científicas del Ministerio de Asuntos Exteriores for a two-month research grant for foreign Hispanists in 2000 and to the British Academy for a research grant in the Humanities in the same year. I was also the beneficiary throughout the period of my research of an annual research grant from the Department of Government of the London School of Economics and Political Science.

In my search to locate veterans of the colonial war in Spain, I am very grateful to the organizers of the Programa LUAR of Galician Television, María

Pires Silva and Marina Alexey Laptera, and the people in Galicia who responded to an appeal for information in LUAR programme. Similarly, I want to thank the organizers of the radio programmes *El Complot dels Oyents* and *La Nit dels Ignorants*, both broadcast on Catalunya Radio, as well as the *Diari de Tarragona* for making appeals for veterans to come forward and for the resulting contacts in Catalonia. I am deeply grateful to the interviewees and their families in all parts of Spain (see the Appendix) and to those who contacted me with information, such as Joan Sardiña Alcoberro, Ricardo Lareo Rodríguez, Josefina Barreiro Águila, Rosa María Alonso Pérez, Antonio Fernández Gómez, Carmen García, María del Rosario Ruiz, Xoan Guitián, Ernesto López Naveiras, and Fernando Llauradó. I also wish to thank my friends from the University of Santiago de Compostela, Isaura Varela González and Pilar Cagaio Vila, and in particular Carmen Fernández Casanova, who kindly accompanied me on a tour of interviews of veterans in Galicia who responded to the television appeal.

To all those who received me in their homes or in public spaces in Catalonia, Galicia, and Madrid and spoke about their personal histories or those of their fathers, I am immensely indebted and feel privileged to have known them.

On the theme of toxic gas, I am grateful to Angel Viñas, Morten Heiberg, and Jean-Marc Delaunay for unreservedly sharing their information with me. George O. Bizzigotti of Mitretek systems gave useful advice about toxic gas and Geoffrey Miller from Australia provided me with sources about their carcinogenous effects. Peter Eliot, of the Department of Research and Information Services of the Royal Air Force Museum, kindly provided me with feedback about bomb-firing mechanisms.

I want also to thank Colonel Eduardo Álvarez Valera for his expert advice at the beginning of my research in the Servicio Histórico Militar, José Pettenghi for giving an interview and providing copies of articles on his experience of the Civil War, Roberto Muñoz Bolaños for his useful suggestions about Chapter 4, and Pablo La Porte for his fruitful collaboration over several years as research assistant and co-author of an article, and for his feedback about some of the text. Among the many other people who helped my research in Spain, I wish to mention (in no particular order): Vicente Camarena, Alberto Carrillo, Ana Cristina Pérez Rodríguez, Sara Lorenzo, Xavier Canalis, Carlos Díez, Pedro Fusté Salvatella, Lucas María Oriol y Urquijo, Vicente Fernández Riera, Sr Mascort, José Luis Villanova, Francesc Xavier Puig Rovira, Francisco Espinosa Maestre, Angeles González Fernández, Enric Olivé, Ama Imet Laiti, Gabriel Riera Barreiro, Enrique Carabaza Bravo, Eloy Martín Corrales, Pablo Manuel Rosser Limiñana, Diego Camacho (Abel Paz), Miguel Alonso Baquer, Victor Morales Lezcano, as well as my friends and fellow historians José Álvarez Junco, María-Jesús González Hernández, Enrique Moradiellos, Josep Benaul Berenguer, and Montserrat Guibernau. In London I benefited from the advice of Francisco Romero Salvadó, Gerald Howson, Rosa Balfour, and Gerry Tannenbaum. I do not need to stress that any errors of fact or interpretation are my exclusive responsibility.

In Morocco my thanks go to all those who gave me advice and gave up their time to help me, in particular Ilyas Elomari, his brother Samir, who drove me to Anual and Ben Tieb, and to all those in the Association for the Defence of the Victims of Toxic Gas in Morocco whom I was lucky enough to meet, in particular Souhaila Riki. I am very grateful to those members of the Association in Al Hoceima (such as the Vice-President Aziz Benazouz of the organization in Morocco) who took me to Ajdir and the villages nearby on which many tons of mustard gas were dropped during the colonial war. I was privileged to meet some of the survivors of this war as well as the descendants of the muhayeddin who had fought in it. During an earlier trip to north-west Morocco I was fortunate to meet many people with personal or historical knowledge of the colonial war, such as the historian Mohammad Ibn Azzuz Hakim and the Chauen justice of the peace Ali Raisuni. But I am above all indebted to Mustapha El Merroun of Tetuan, who worked as a research assistant for me and read several chapters of my manuscript. His meticulous and unconditional research in Tetuan and Ceuta prised open documents that would have been difficult to obtain otherwise. He also created the opportunity for numerous interviews with Moroccan veterans of the colonial and Civil War in which he acted as interpreter. As with the veterans of north-east Morocco, it was a great honour for me to meet these men and I was particularly moved by the interview granted to me on his deathbed in Tetuan in 2000 by a veteran of both wars. I am also grateful to the Ministry of the Interior in Rabat for granting me permission to carry out research in Morocco. The publisher and author wish to acknowledge the help of Peninsula in processing many of the illustrations in this book.

My daughters Rosa and Marianna were a constant source of encouragement even though they saw less of me than I and they would have liked because of the time I had to devote to research. But it was my wife Graínne above all who had to put up with my physical and emotional absence when I was abroad doing research or when I was so absorbed in the making of this book that I must have seemed another being in another time and place. For her love and support, I am most grateful.

Preface

THE CENTRAL EPIC of twentieth-century Spain was the colonial war in Morocco and the Civil War. Spain undertook a colonial mission in northern Morocco at the beginning of the century that appeared to offer some compensation for the loss of its overseas colonies in 1898 and promised to raise it to the status of other European powers. But it was sucked into a colonial war from 1909 that led to a succession of military disasters resulting in dictatorship and the fall of the monarchy in 1931. The experience of that war politicized many of the Spanish conscripts who were mobilized to fight for a cause they barely understood. It also created a brutalized and interventionist officer elite, which rose in revolt against the Republic in 1936. Without the intervention of the colonial army, backed by the military force of Hitler and Mussolini, the coup would have failed. The so-called Army of Africa crossed the Straits of Gibraltar with a mission to destroy the internal enemy and transform a decadent Spain from outside. The self-appointed agents of Spain's purification were those officers who had fought and won a colonial war, and that war inspired their initial strategy and tactics in the Civil War. The regime installed by Franco also derived its mythological and ideological underpinning from the colonial experience.

Despite the huge literature both wars have attracted, no serious study has been made of the links between them. The war in Morocco itself has generated dozens of volumes, from the panegyrical, self-exculpatory accounts of right-wing military protagonists to the anti-war, autobiographical novels of middle-class conscripts who fought there against their will. Yet all of them give at best only glimpses of the war and at worst a complete distortion of the nature of the encounter between Spaniards and Moroccans. The Civil War, for its part, has given rise to more volumes than any other event or historical process in Spain's history. Yet the influence that the colonial war had on its genesis and development has received attention only in the broad narratives of twentieth-century Spanish history. This fracture between the literature of the two wars is no doubt due partly to traditional demarcations of theme and chronology. The colonial war ended in 1927 and the Civil War began in 1936 after five eventful years of the Republic that have absorbed the interest of historians.

This book, therefore, is the first overarching study of the colonial war and the Army of Africa in the Civil War. It attempts to fill the many gaps in the existing bibliography and to challenge some of its hypotheses, in particular with reference to the colonial war. The vast number of texts on the issue deal only with specific conjunctures and the conclusions they draw are very limited. Apart from the links between the colonial war, the Civil War, and the

Dictatorship of Franco, the book examines identity, racism, and images of the enemy in both wars as well as the divisions and cultures within the colonial army. It also looks at the conditions in which the soldiers fought and suffered and spent their leisure and how this affected their culture in the long term. An attempt is made also to evaluate the experience of the northern Moroccan people under Spanish rule.

The area that has been explored least in the literature of the colonial war is the chemical offensive launched by the Spanish army against Moroccans, using large quantities of mustard gas. This book offers the first detailed evidence of the use of chemical bombs by the Spanish air force and artillery based on research in the military archives in Spain, France, and Britain. Interviews with Moroccans who suffered its effects were recorded and incorporated into this analysis. Prima facie evidence about its cancerous effects on the Moroccan population and about its degradation of the environment is discussed. The Spanish state has never admitted to the use of chemical weapons and the fact is virtually unknown in Spain even to this day, while the Moroccan state has made strenuous efforts to prevent the news from surfacing, mainly in order to avoid worsening its relations with Spain.

This book also seeks to locate Spanish colonialism within a wider context of colonial experiences, in particular British, Italian, and French. Spanish bibliography on the colonial war is notoriously self-absorbed. The myth dominating much of Spanish historiography until recently, that Spain was an exceptional case, needs debunking also in relation to its colonial rule in Morocco. Spain's military disasters and its brutal treatment of those who resisted its penetration were matched by those of other European powers, including the most powerful, Great Britain. Both the British and the Italians suffered major colonial disasters at the end of the nineteenth century, and the French established the precedent of total war against colonies as early as 1845 in their military offensive in neighbouring Algeria. Amongst other such comparative themes, the book also endeavours to compare the experience of Spanish soldiers in the nightmarish conditions of the Moroccan war with that of soldiers in the First World War.

As readers will surmise, this book does not fall easily into any of the traditional categories of historiography. If it can be called a military history at all, it belongs to the relatively recent school of New Military History, which draws inspiration from different disciplines, from the traditional *histoire bataille* through political, cultural, and social history to the *histoire de mentalités*. These different approaches are driven by the search to understand not just tactics, training, and hardware but the myths that inform war, as well as the everyday life of the soldiers and the impact of war on society.

The structure of the book was shaped, almost without any other possible design, around these axes. I had intended to weave thematic analysis into chronological narrative but some themes imposed themselves to such an extent that I felt I could only do justice to them in separate chapters. Themes only briefly touched on in the narrative-based Part I are developed more fully in the thematic Part II. The reader hoping to find systematic treatment of issues such as military logistics or Moroccan society will need to be patient in the hope that these expectations will be met in the course of the book, from different angles and at different points in the narrative.

Like all historical projects depending on a search for sources, this has been for me a journey into the unknown filled with exciting discoveries and prolonged frustrations. Like the Civil War, the colonial war has been subject to a conspiracy of silence, in particular over the use of chemical weapons. The so-called 'pacto del olvido' or pact of forgetfulness that was supposed to be the price of democracy twenty-five years ago has helped to keep many of the sources locked up. Books and articles still appear that conspicuously omit reference to dramatic events or details known to their authors. Many of the leading protagonists or their families still cling on to documents that would help the historian to understand the past better, long after blame or guilt could be an issue. Some archives open to researchers have been emptied of their polemical documents, which have either been hidden or destroyed. Another archive, the enormous Archivo General de la Administración, houses documents dating from the first half of the 1930s that have not yet been sorted and therefore are unavailable to the researcher.

The contrast with the state of public archives in Russia could not be greater. The archives of the Soviet Union became available for consultation at the end of 1991, immediately after the dissolution of the communist state. In Spain, official documents more than seventy years old that should be available under current legislation cannot yet be consulted in public archives. The result is that the historian of twentieth-century Spain has to rely on conjecture and surmise for many questions. I have made it clear throughout when I have done so. My hope is that this publication may help to flush out some of the hidden documents, even if the bearer of new information is set to refute some of my conclusions.

The information I have gleaned comes from five years of intensive research in public and private archives in Spain and military and diplomatic sources in Britain and France. I have also conducted numerous interviews with protagonists of the colonial and Civil War in both Spain and Morocco. In Spain, surviving veterans of the colonial war were located after appeals over radio and television and in the press. The organizers of the LUAR programme on Galician national television fitted me in for an appeal for veterans between go-go dancers and a quiz programme. In Morocco, interviews were conducted in Arabic (with an interpreter) with veterans of the colonial war who fought on both sides, others who fought in the Spanish Civil War, and with the survivors of the chemical offensive.

The most important source on which this book relies is the military archive in Madrid, the Servicio Histórico Militar. There, hundreds of thousands of documents of the colonial war, most of which have been microfilmed, are stored in its precincts. As far as I am aware, this valuable archive has not undergone any purging, but a full perusal of its contents would be a lifelong project and many of the valuable documents I came across there were found by sheer persistence and luck rather than as a result of detailed classification.

It will be obvious from the above that the themes examined in the book, as well as the hypotheses drawn and the choice of the book's structure, are very personal. Especially where new ground is being explored, the compass and the record of the journey are highly individual. But as any historian should, I have tried to be scrupulous in balancing the evidence. However uncomfortable it may make some people, I trust they will recognize the care I took. I hope too that the reader will derive some of the enjoyment I experienced during that journey without the frustrations that went with it.

Contents

List of Illustrations

The author and the publishers are very grateful to Rosa Ros Amador and to Jordi Carulla for kind permission to reproduce illustrations from their collections. All possible efforts were made to contact the copywright owners of two other illustrations for permission to reproduce them.

List of Maps

PART I

The Colonial Embrace

CHAPTER ONE

The Invasion of Morocco

THE LAST STAGE in the colonization of Africa in the late nineteenth and early twentieth centuries, otherwise known as the Scramble for Africa, transformed not just the new subjects of colonial rule but the colonizers themselves. Colonial expansion was not a one-sided affair. While Africans individually and collectively attempted to resist the invaders, many others collaborated in the invasion. Some sought to share power with the colonizers; others hoped to achieve the modernization of their countries by co-operating with the new powers. In that collaboration, accommodations were made and complicities created that transformed the identity of both. It was not just a political, cultural, and economic experience. It was also a sexual encounter. Rape and sexual exploitation were common forms of racist domination by the invaders, but there were frequent sexual liaisons between the colonizer and the colonized that could generate affection across racial barriers and modify behaviour and identity on both sides.[1] Indigenous resistance against European penetration also inflicted frequent disasters on the colonial powers, sometimes so severe that governments and systems of government were overthrown. So while Africa was transformed by colonial invasion, European history was rewritten by contact with Africa.[2]

One of the characteristics of this reshaping of Europe was the emergence of European elites based in the colonies that challenged or adopted a critical stance towards their governing circles. The Spanish case is the most extreme example of a growing colonial identity at odds with the metropolis. The thread linking all the chapters of this book is the formation of an interventionist Spanish military elite through the experience of colonial war in Morocco. This first chapter will briefly examine the European invasion of North Africa in the first decade of the twentieth century, consider the effect this had on Moroccans, and look more closely at the dominant role played by the Spanish military in that invasion.

For Spain, the colonial adventure in twentieth-century Africa began in 1908. Ten years after the 1898 Disaster, the year of Spain's defeat in the

---

[1] Ronald Hyam, *Empire and Sexuality: The British Experience* (Manchester, Manchester University Press, 1990).

[2] David Levering Lewis, *The Race to Fashoda: European Colonialism and African Resistance in the Scramble for Africa* (London, Bloomsbury, 1988), 11.

Spanish–American War, when it lost the last remnants of its old empire, Spanish troops began to invade Morocco from Spain's two historical enclaves on the north Moroccan coast. Their first operation was to occupy a rudimentary port 19 kilometres south of the enclave of Melilla in north-east Morocco. The action began at six in the morning of 14 February. Two companies and a brigade of soldiers on disciplinary charges set sail from Melilla in a gunboat and a mailship. At dawn, in heavy rain and cold winds, four landing boats plunged through rough sea towards land and Spanish soldiers leapt into the water up to their chests to reach the shore.

The military engagement that followed was an orchestrated charade. The dominant sharif (chief) in the area, El Rogui, put up a token resistance to persuade his fellow countrymen that he was opposed to the Spanish incursion into their land. His horsemen galloped about firing wild shots, while the Spanish let off a few bursts of machine-gun fire and cannon-shot from the gunboat. Without loss on either side, the troops moved into the port and hoisted the Spanish flag on the small warehouse.[3]

The operation marked the beginning of the invasion of Morocco by the Spanish army, which would eventually occupy its entire northern region and stay there until 1956. It was not directed against the sultan, though neither he nor his government was consulted. Nor was it directed against his opponent, the pretender to the throne, El Rogui. Nor was it, at least at that stage, the action of an expansionist power. Rather, it was the consequence of an international obligation undertaken by Spain.

The new venture in Morocco was a direct result of the insecurity felt by the Spanish political elites after the Spanish–American War. Spain had lost the scattered possessions of its once extensive empire after colonial wars in Cuba and the Philippines had turned into a disastrous military confrontation with the United States. Remaining aloof from the system of international relations in the last quarter of the nineteenth century, Spain had relied fatally on dynastic and religious connections to protect its colonies from foreign predators.[4] After the Disaster, Spain had sought to reinsert itself securely into the changing network of international alignments in order to protect its metropolis and islands and enclaves from the increasing competition between the Great Powers.[5]

From a policy of international withdrawal, Spain moved to an active search for allies and treaties. This quest was helped by Spain's very weakness in the aftermath of the war, which had given rise to fears among European powers

[3] Estado Mayor Central del Ejército, *Historia de las campañas de Marruecos* (Madrid, Servicio Histórico Militar, 1947–81), ii. 20; Gabriel de Morales, *Datos para la historia de Melilla* (Melilla, n.p., 1909), 369–71.
[4] Sebastian Balfour, *The End of the Spanish Empire 1898–1923* (Oxford, Oxford University Press, 1997) = *El fin del Imperio español (1898–1923)* (Barcelona, Crítica, 1997).
[5] For a fuller treatment of Spanish foreign policy in the post-Disaster period, see Sebastian Balfour, 'Spain and the Great Powers in the Aftermath of the 1898 Disaster', in id. and Paul Preston (eds.), *Spain and the Great Powers in the Twentieth Century* (London, Routledge, 1999).

that a competitor amongst them might gain some advantage. France was particularly worried about its security if Spain reached agreement with another power which would compromise the status quo over the Spanish port of Ceuta on the Moroccan coast opposite Gibraltar, and that of Mahon in Menorca astride French maritime routes between Algiers, Oran, Corsica, and Toulon.[6] Spanish–British relations were still tense because the British government had informally sided with the United States during the Spanish–American War, hindering the passage of a third Spanish fleet through the Suez Canal on its way to the theatre of war in the Far East. During the engagement Spain had fortified its defences in Algeciras opposite Gibraltar, giving rise to further tensions that persisted after the war.[7]

The main focus of colonial competition between the European powers was the partition of the Dark Continent. The scramble for African colonies since the 1870s had led to intensive negotiations between them. Germany, a new and aggressive international actor, was muscling in on spheres traditionally regarded as belonging to the Old Powers. Britain and France had begun to settle their differences after the latter withdrew from east Africa and the Nile in 1898. In subsequent negotiations, the French agreed to confine their colonial ventures in Africa mainly to Algeria, Tunisia, and Morocco.[8] For all their growing rapprochement, Britain was anxious to keep the French from encroaching as far as the northern coast of Morocco, from where they might challenge Britain's control of the Straits of Gibraltar and the route to the British Empire in India and the Far East.

Having signed a treaty with Spain in 1900 recognizing the latter's possessions of Guinea and the western Sahara opposite the Canary Islands, France sought, in secret negotiations two years later, to woo it into a new alliance that might strengthen its own position vis-à-vis Britain. In these talks, France offered to share spheres of influence in Morocco in the knowledge that French colonial expansion in the area would be little hindered by a weakened Spain.[9] The Spanish government withdrew from the negotiations out of fear of British displeasure. Unknown to Spanish policy-makers, however, Britain had been holding secret talks with France in which she had secured the assignation of a sphere of influence for Spain in northern Morocco as a buffer against French expansion towards the coast opposite Gibraltar.

It was German ambitions in North Africa above all that brought about a Franco-British rapprochement. In negotiations leading to the Entente

---

[6] *Documents Diplomatiques Français* (Ministère des Affaires Étrangères), vol. XX, Doc. 2, 2ème série, p. 196 (25 Sept. 1902).

[7] Rosario de la Torre, *Inglaterra y España en 1898* (Madrid, 1988).

[8] G. P. Gooch and Harold Temperley, *British Documents on the Origins of the World War, 1898–1914*, vol. 1, *The End of British Isolation* (London: HMSO, 1927), Docs. 157–235, pp. 132–93.

[9] *Documents Diplomatiques Français*, Doc. 333, pp. 197–9. The 1902 draft treaty between France and Spain was first published in 1912 in the *Diario de Sesiones del Congreso de los Diputados* (henceforth DSCD) for 26 Nov. 1912 (Apéndice).

Cordiale of 1904, in which the Spanish government was not invited to take part, it was agreed that Spain should be given a sphere in northern Morocco. Having settled the matter with Britain, France reduced the area it had proposed to concede to Spain in 1902 by almost 50 per cent. In a subsequent Franco-Spanish treaty, Spain accepted a sphere of influence covering barely a fifth of Moroccan territory, some 22,000 square kilometres.

The land awarded to Spain as a sphere of influence was dominated by the Rif Mountains, a great limestone mass rising from the Mediterranean coast and stretching some 300 kilometres along the width of the narrow horizontal strip. Reaching heights of 2,500 metres, the mountainous range forms a natural barrier between Europe and Africa and, with the Sahara, separates most of Morocco from Algeria and the rest of the Magreb. To the south of the sphere the mountains give way to valleys and crests before reaching the French zone, while in the west they rise to dramatic heights, punctuated by deep valleys scored by torrential rivers, and then fall away into the plains on the Atlantic coast. The terrain varies dramatically, from the many forested slopes of the mountains in the south and west to the bushes and olive trees of the Mediterranean fringe and the barren peaks and sparse valleys of the eastern Rif.

The climate is also subject to extremes. In most of the western and southern strip the rainfall in winter is heavy and increases the rush of the streams and rivers swollen by snow that run down to the sea or into the French zone, while in the east it is often unreliable, threatening the harvests. During the summer the heat and lack of rain in the east dry up the riverbeds and crack the parched earth. Temperatures can plunge to well below freezing during all seasons except the summer, even in the valleys, and can rise to unbearable heights in the summer.

Together with its largely primitive trails and tracks, this was not the most propitious terrain for the military operations of even the most accomplished colonial power. France, on the other hand, had awarded itself not only the vast majority of Moroccan territory but also the most fertile and peaceful part. Thousands of square kilometres of its rich agricultural land were watered by rivers that ran down from slopes of the Rif and Atlas mountain systems. Apart from the mountain tribesmen of the Atlas and the southern Rif, the inhabitants of the French area of influence were largely obedient to the sultan and his government.

The Spanish area was inhabited mainly by Berber tribes, who distinguished themselves from neighbouring Arab tribes by their language rather than their ethnicity, but who shared Islam as a common religion with the Arabs. With the rest of the indigenous inhabitants of Spain's sphere of influence, they numbered some three-quarters of a million people in 1904. For all their reputation as uncontrollables, the Berber tribes of the mountains maintained contacts with the sultan's government and paid their taxes or tribute through their tribal leaders. The sultan's forces had little control over law and order in the heart-lands of the Rif, but revolts occurred only sporadically when the balance of power within the area or between Rif tribes and the central authority was dis-rupted. Far from being the lawless and impenetrable wilderness painted in some hyped-up Spanish accounts, most of the Rif was connected to the rest of Morocco through trade routes and regional markets.[10]

In a secret clause of the Franco-Spanish Treaty of 1904, France and Spain awarded themselves the freedom to intervene in their spheres of influence if the Moroccan state failed to maintain order or showed 'persistent impotence', or if the maintenance of the status quo became impossible. France had already begun to invade Morocco from its base in Algeria to stop the frequent raids into its colony by Moroccan border tribes. Under its new commander, Lyautey, the French colonial army in northern Africa was transformed into an efficient fighting force manned mainly by so-called native troops from different parts of the French Empire. Unconnected with the local population either by kinship or religion, these contingents had the added advantage of being more able than European troops to cope with the harsh environment of much of Morocco. The policy of peaceful penetration advocated by the Quai d'Orsay had given way by 1904 to a predominantly military strategy of conquest, after Lyautey, backed by the French colonial party, had persuaded the French gov-ernment that it was the only solution to the increasing anarchy in Morocco caused by colonial penetration.[11]

German pressure against French expansion in North Africa led to the inter-national Conference of Algeciras in 1906, in which Germany found itself fur-ther isolated by the Franco-British alignment. The resulting treaty stipulated that Morocco should remain open to international trade and that the sover-eignty of the sultan should be guaranteed. France and Spain were entrusted by the thirteen participating powers with the task of ensuring that the Moroccan state, the Mahkzen, held sway in their respective spheres. What this task entailed would be interpreted differently by the French and Spanish govern-ments. A year later, in the Cartagena Pact of 1907, Spain was tied into the Entente by the signing of a mutual guarantee between Britain, France, and Spain against German expansion in North Africa. In Morocco itself, the main effect of the Algeciras Treaty was the disintegration of the authority of Sultan Abdel Aziz, who had put his signature to the treaty under pressure from the Great Powers. The rapid invasion into Morocco of European diplomacy and business stirred up a new holy war against the Christian.

Thus, it was above all Spain's sense of strategic insecurity following the Disaster of 1898 and the increasing competition between the European Powers that led it to take on a role in Morocco on their behalf. Some of the Spanish

---

[10] David Seddon, *Moroccan Peasants: A Century of Change in the Eastern Rif 1870–1970* (Folkestone, Dawson, 1981), 45.

[11] Douglas Porch, *The Conquest of Morocco* (London, Jonathan Cape, 1982).

policy-makers were aware of the potential costs and the risks involved. Shortly after his government fell in 1902, the premier responsible for withdrawing from the secret talks with France, Francisco Silvela, declared, 'we should banish from our thoughts the idea that the situation in Morocco . . . represents profit and wealth for us, when, on the contrary, it is the source of poverty, sterility, and stagnation for Spain, and we accept it and we have to maintain it merely to avoid worse ills of a political and international nature'.[12]

The oft-premier and leader of the Conservatives after Silvela, Antonio Maura, made an even more pessimistic analysis of the potential risks involved in Spain's new international commitment. In a letter to his minister of foreign affairs written in his usual rolling prose, he described Morocco as a 'variegated and contradictory multitude of dispersed, unattached energies without organic solidarity and without even a regular and stable bond . . . political life in Morocco . . . is all asymmetry and uncertainty'.[13] Yet publicly he insisted that Spain had a mission of peace in Morocco and, referring to the new sphere of influence assigned by the Great Powers, 'was disposed to defend, whatever the cost and if it became necessary, the integrity of her territory in Morocco . . .'.[14]

In contrast to the Conservatives, rooted still in a policy of international abstentionism, the Liberals were receptive to the European currents of colonial expansion. However, an influential body of opinion they could not ignore was arguing that in the aftermath of the Disaster Spain's resources should be devoted to internal regeneration. As a result of the human cost of the colonial and Spanish–American wars, it was also widely acknowledged that any new venture entailing a military call-up would be deeply unpopular. At a time when social protest was beginning to escalate, the stability of the Spanish state might be in jeopardy.

Another lobby closer to ruling circles was calling for the peaceful commercial penetration of Africa as a means of regenerating Spain. Just as the Franco-Prussian War of 1870 had generated an enthusiastic movement in France for colonial acquisition, so the loss of its American empire boosted the influence in Spain of proponents of neo-colonial expansion who had been increasingly active in the last quarter of the century.

Some of the leading Liberals were also businessmen keen to exploit the opportunities for investment in Morocco. Behind them were business lobbies seeking new markets to make up for the loss of the protected colonial markets.[15] A questionnaire distributed by the Ministry for Commerce in 1906 revealed some enthusiasm amongst Chambers of Commerce, public-sector

[12] *Artículos, discursos, conferencias y cartas* (Madrid, Mateu Artes Gráficas, 1922–3), iii. 115.

[13] José Manuel Allendesalazar, *La diplomacia española y Marruecos, 1907–1909* (Madrid, Ministerio de Asuntos Exteriores, 1990), 80.

[14] In a speech in the senate quoted in the *Diario de Barcelona*, 27 Nov. 1907.

[15] *Diario Mercantil*, 25 Dec. 1898 and 8 Jan. 1899, *El Trabajo Nacional* (mouthpiece of the Catalan *Foment*), 5 Aug. 1898 and 30 Jan. 1902, *La Vanguardia*, 27 Oct. 1904. See also Archivo Romanones (AR), Leg. 53 no. 55 (2).

bodies, banks, professional associations, mining, shipping, and fruit companies and so on, for commercial expansion into Morocco, backed by state aid.[16] The intellectual and political proponents of closer relations with Morocco of the nineteenth century had been overtaken by commercial and industrial interests of the early twentieth. The organic intellectuals of the Spanish–Moroccan business lobby were adamant that neo-colonial expansion into Africa was a 'work of civilization' entailing no loss of sovereignty on the part of the Sultanate.[17] What was less openly articulated was the likely cost to the Spanish Exchequer of the subsidies required by businesses venturing into Morocco and the infrastructural work—roads, railways, and ports—necessary for their success. It was taken for granted that most sensible Moroccans would appreciate the benefits of Spanish commercial penetration into their country.[18]

Another lobby pushing for a different kind of action in Morocco was military opinion. In the immediate aftermath of the loss of its empire, the Spanish colonial military had been deeply embroiled in the problems of repatriation, recompense, and adjustment to life in the metropolis. The defeat had left them with a bitter grievance. They had fought to defend the last remnants of the empire and believed that they had been sacrificed by the regime and betrayed by fickle public opinion. Much of their time was taken up with defending the army and navy against accusations of incompetence and cowardice. Their alienation from civil society was intensified by the rapid growth of left wing, anti-military movements in the first decade of the new century. In the absence of a modern police force, the military were used to quell the growing social unrest. The bond that had linked the army and the urban populace in the first half of the previous century was now dissolving.

The rise of regional nationalism in the first years of the new century was also seen by many officers as a challenge to the integrity of the nation. In their own self-image, it was the military that had created the modern state in Spain, and it was their duty to defend it against the forces of national dissolution.[19] Officers stationed in Barcelona ransacked the offices of two Catalanist newspapers in 1905 and the government responded by giving military courts extensive powers over civilian affairs. The new law marked the return of the army as a political force.

During the last quarter of the nineteenth century, the army had withdrawn to its barracks after decades of political intervention. But in its new role in the first decade of the century as defender of law and order and centralism, it began to shed the progressive and republican tendencies of the nineteenth century to embrace an increasingly anti-democratic ideology. The combined

---

[16] Ministerio de Fomento, *Expansión comercial de España en Marruecos* (Madrid, 1906).

[17] Real Sociedad Geográfrica de Madrid, *Exposición al Excm Sr. Presidente del Congreso de Ministros*, 30 Apr. 1904, in Archivo de la Fundación Antonio Maura Montaner (AFAMM), Fondo Documental, Mortera, Caja 4; Gonzalo de Reparaz, *Política de España en Africa* (Madrid, Calpe, 1907).

[18] See Ch. 7 for further treatment.   [19] See Balfour, *The End*, ch. 6.

effect of the loss of empire and the growth of new social forces as a result of the accelerating process of modernization shifted the bulk of military opinion away from the progressive tendencies of the previous century towards a range of traditional and new rightist ideologies.

The transformation of military thinking in Spain was part of a Europe-wide reaction against the certainties of nineteenth-century liberal positivism. One of its features was the adoption of new vitalist currents influenced by Nietzsche. The French model of the citizen army, so important in nineteenth-century Spain, was giving way in some military circles to the Prussian model of an elitist professional army whose strength lay in moral and spiritual values allied to military science.[20] In the post-Disaster period, however, the army was in no condition to wage war in any theatre. It was made up of 529 generals and 23,767 officers (though many were on the reserve list) for 110,926 troops. There was thus, for those on active service, a general for every 340 soldiers and an officer for every seven.[21] During the first decade of the new century half of the military budget was consumed by pay, in contrast to the French, who devoted only a sixth of their budget to salaries. The result was that the Spanish army was seriously underequipped.

On the eve of the first serious colonial battle of the twentieth century in 1909, the military boasted sixty divisional generals for an army of 111,435 soldiers. In comparison, the British army had thirty-four divisional generals commanding a total of 374,000 troops. Even more significant was the fact that, as the colonial war grew more serious, the metropolitan army continued to consume the lion's share of an already inadequate budget. Military expenditure rose from 218 million pesetas in 1909 to 627 million for a similar period in 1920–1, when the colonial army had begun its most serious military campaign to date. Of these 627 million pesetas, the army in Spain absorbed 480 million, that is to say, 76.55 per cent of the total. Yet the condition of the metropolitan army was such that, when the military disaster of July 1921 occurred in Morocco, there was not one division in Spain that was available immediately for action.[22]

Nevertheless, the potential of a new area of colonial activity after the loss of the overseas colonies awakened the military appetite. Morocco had a mythical resonance for the army and conservative sections of Spanish society. The medieval Reconquest against the Moorish infidel had spread across the Straits of Gibraltar into northern Africa by the end of the fifteenth century. The Papal Bull of 1457 had given the Church's blessing for the conquest of Islamic territories by Spain, while Isabel the Catholic's will enjoined her successors to carry

[20]   Robert Geoffrey Jensen, 'Intellectual Foundations of Dictatorship: Spanish Military Writers and Their Quest for Cultural Regeneration, 1898–1923', Ph.D Diss., Yale University, 1995. For further discussion, see Ch. 6.

[21]   *Anuario Militar, 1900* (Ministerio de la Guerra, Madrid, 1900).

[22]   Juan Pando, *Historia Secreta de Annual*, 2nd edn. (Madrid, Temas de Hoy, 1999), 77–80.

on the struggle against the infidel. But Spain's early conquests in Morocco had been gradually whittled down over the next few centuries to a few enclaves. Morocco had been the scene of two military victories in the nineteenth century. After harassment by tribesmen of two of these enclaves on the coast, Ceuta and Melilla, the Spanish army had marched out in 1859 to seize Tetuan and bomb Tangier, forcing the sultan to accept humiliating terms for peace in the following year.

The unwitting desecration of a holy tomb by labourers in Melilla in 1893 provoked a new uprising by tribesmen. A detachment of Spanish troops was surrounded and many of its soldiers killed, including their general. A military offensive against the local tribes led to a new treaty in 1894, in which the Moroccan state committed itself to maintain order in the area surrounding Melilla while Spain agreed to respect the integrity of Morocco. The two military engagements became mythologized in Spanish nationalist discourse as a new model of the qualities of the Spanish race and its inherent military attributes. After the loss of the old empire in the Americas, expansion in Morocco came to epitomize 'an advantageous compensation for past disasters' in keeping with Spain's 'historic and geographical destinies'.[23]

Thus national security, investment potential, and the reaffirmation of military pride became the contradictory impulses of Spanish colonialism. This was in contrast to Italy's expansion into Libya at the beginning of the twentieth century. The Italian search for a new colony was rationalized above all by internal demographic pressure that led its leaders to see the new colony as a promised land for its agricultural labourers, a space in which Italy's emigrants would remain Italian rather than become American or Argentinian.[24]

The Spanish military's new opportunity for action in northern Africa, however, was heavily circumscribed by Spain's international obligations. The military daily newspapers were impatient at the constraints imposed by the Treaty of Algeciras on the army's freedom of action. 'The Spanish army,' an editorial of a military newspaper complained, 'in its role as police or security, will enter Morocco . . . with a Maüser in one hand and an olive branch in the other; not as representatives of the Motherland, but as agents of the Sultan; not as conquerors, but as guarantors of the sovereign independence of the [Moroccan] empire.'[25] According to military opinion, the treaty exposed Spain's weakness in the struggle of nations. 'Because we are weak, we have to content ourselves with the crumbs of a feast which should be for us alone.' What had been Spain's 'birthright', expansion into Morocco, had been sold 'for a mess of

[23] 'La cuestión marroquí. España dormida', *Correo Militar*, 21 May 1900; 'Francia y Alemania en Marruecos', *El Ejército Español*, 3 Feb. 1910.

[24] Claudio G. Segrè, *L'Italia in Libia. Dall'età Giolittiana a Gheddafi* (Milan, Feltrinelli, 1978), originally published in English as *The Fourth Shore: The Italian Colonization of Libya* (Chicago, University of Chicago Press, 1974), 28–43.

[25] 'La chilaba triste', *La Correspondencia Militar*, 2 Apr. 1906.

pottage'.[26] Whatever the limitations of Spain's role, the army had to prepare for its task of policing northern Morocco, according to another paper. If it was not ready, a new military disaster might occur.[27]

The military and commercial lobbies wielded considerable influence but they did not dictate the government's strategy. The two main parties of the Restoration state, a system resting on patronage and a fictitious electoral contest, had to satisfy a variety of constituencies. They were thus relatively impermeable to the influence of individual lobbies. Indeed, diplomatic correspondence reveals the driving-force of Spanish foreign policy in Morocco to be Spain's search to fulfil her international commitments.[28] But both the government and the military commanders in Morocco entrusted with carrying out its policy were faced with an excruciating dilemma. The sultan's authority had never held sway in most of the area Spain was meant to oversee from within the Spanish enclaves. What little remained was crumbling under the impact of the penetration of European capital and French territorial encroachments. The military could not act as surrogate policemen for the sultan. To restore his authority meant Spain intervening directly in her sphere of influence, apparently in contravention of international treaties.

On the other hand, a pragmatic acceptance of *de facto* power also meant failure to fulfil the obligations of these treaties. Moreover, it entailed establishing amicable relations with chieftains responsible for levels of abuse and corruption against their own people that were unacceptable to European sensibilities. The unarticulated gut reaction of the military was to respect neither diplomacy nor local power but march in and restore order. These dilemmas were at the heart of Spain's problems in Morocco.

Spanish colonial officers had a model of military intervention close at hand. In the huge French sphere of influence in Morocco, the growing resentment against foreign invasion was beginning to take its toll of European residents. Until 1904 the French Ministry of Foreign Affairs under Théophile Delcassé had championed a policy of peaceful encroachment. But the terms of the Algeciras Treaty could be interpreted as a licence for military penetration. Attacks on French citizens in Morocco following the signing of the treaty led the colonial party in France to push for armed intervention.

They had a new instrument for military action in Morocco. The ambitious and talented French officer Hubert Lyautey had arrived in 1903 to take charge of the headquarters of the French Army in South Oranais near the undefined frontier between French Algeria and Morocco. In the space of four years he had transformed a bureaucratic military force into an efficient fighting unit of

[26] 'Mirando al exterior', ibid., 16 Mar. 1906.

[27] 'La Conferencia de Algeciras. Después de la conferencia', *El Ejército Español*, 26 Apr. 1906.

[28] See e.g. President Maura's letter to the governor-general of Melilla, General Marina, on 23 Dec. 1908 in *Documentos presentados a las Cortes en la legislatura de 1911 por el Ministro de Estado (D. Manuel García Prieto)* (henceforth *Libro Rojo*) (Madrid, 1911), no. 435, anejos, pp. 166–8.

professional soldiers from different parts of the French Empire. No longer bound by the antiquated rules of nineteenth-century military engagement, the new army specialized in the tactics of counter-guerrilla insurgency adapted to the conditions of campaigns in Morocco.[29] Determined to stop raids by Moroccan tribes into Algeria, Lyautey had sent troops into southern Morocco in June 1904 and persuaded the French government to establish a permanent base there.

A rebellion in southern Morocco and the murder of a French doctor in Marrakesh in March 1907 gave the French government the excuse for further military intervention long demanded by the colonial party, though government spokesmen were careful to declare that it would be only provisional. Four months after the French military occupation of the rebellious region, a fresh incident led to a new military encroachment by the French. The killing by Moroccans of nine workers working for the French in Casablanca on 30 July was answered by the devastating shelling of the Arab quarter by a French warship. The action led to widespread looting and atrocities by Moroccans against men, women, and children in the nearby Jewish quarter. France asked Spain to contribute to a joint expeditionary force but the new president, Antonio Maura, turned down the request on the grounds that such action would arouse further hostility and disrupt the commercial life of the whole region.[30] French troops landed in the port of Casablanca and proceeded to carry out a massacre of Moroccans. Delcassé's policies now lay in ruins and the French felt they had little option but to consolidate direct rule over their part of Morocco.[31]

Although there is no evidence of the influence of French military actions, there can be little doubt that they strengthened the spirit of armed interventionism among Spanish colonial officers. Thus equipped with a model of military efficacy drawn from the hegemonic power in the area, they felt justified in moving beyond the cramped confines of their enclaves. The action of 14 February 1908 that began this narrative signified the first triumph in the Spanish sphere of the military over the diplomatic thesis, though like its French counterpart the government represented the occupation as a temporary measure. Despite Spain's misgivings, it was accepted by the international community. Neither Sultan Abdel Aziz nor his successor exercised control over their north-eastern territory. The pretender to the throne, El Rogui, falsely claiming to be the lost son of a former sultan, had mobilized tribes in the area and defeated the Moroccan government forces in December 1902. Since he controlled a vast swathe of territory, the Spanish authorities had had little option but to do business with him while at the same time they were under an obligation to ensure the Sultan's ascendancy. For the time being the Spanish government had taken on board the contradiction between constitutional and *de facto* powers.

[29] Porch, *The Conquest*, 129–30.   [30] *British Documents*, part 1, vol. 28, doc. 214, p. 335.
[31] Charles-André Julien, *Le Maroc face aux impérialismes 1415–1956* (Paris, Editions JA, 1978), 72.

In situ, this contradictory policy was much more difficult to carry out. The commander of Spain's troops in Morocco, General José Marina, a leading figure among the enlightened Spanish military Arabists of the new century, saw Spain's mission as a civilizing one, to be achieved through peaceful penetration. He devoted much effort to making friends with the neighbouring tribes while continuing to deal with their enemy, El Rogui. He also went to some lengths to recognize the different cultures in the area. During Ramadan, Marina gave orders for cannon-fire to signal the beginning and the end of the fast and banned the traditional anti-Jewish demonstrations of the Christian celebration of Holy Saturday.[32] This search for neutrality frequently meant interceding with the pretender when he overstepped the mark in his attacks on other tribes loyal to the sultan. But Marina's ability to maintain order from across the border was coming under increasing strain.

Before the occupation of the port, the Spanish army had made a brief incursion onto Moroccan soil on 29 January 1908 to protect the retreat of the sultan's bedraggled and abandoned troops (and their harem) besieged by El Rogui's forces. The occupation shortly afterwards was intended also to ensure order in the area by preventing the renewal of a lucrative operation controlled by French–Belgian interests which had been smuggling arms to El Rogui through the port. The fact that the Spanish authorities failed to consult the Moroccan government beforehand was a token of the extent to which they had begun to see themselves as a substitute for the Moroccan state, though they diplomatically assured the Sultanate that it was only a temporary occupation.[33] A third incursion took place on 12 March to occupy nearby Moroccan territory to secure peace in the area surrounding Melilla. Marina had felt this necessary because his policy of gaining sympathy among as many tribes as possible had won the local tribes away from El Rogui's sphere of influence. Without the protection of government troops, they were exposed to his reprisals against pro-sultan tribes.[34]

Marina's strategy thus undermined El Rogui's power and encouraged local opinion unsympathetic to European penetration. One of the pretender's supporters and chieftain of a tribe near Melilla had begged Marina not to go ahead with the occupation. He could not persuade his own people to accept it because they would think their land had been sold to Spain. He said he felt like a grain of wheat caught between two stones and waiting to be ground.[35]

It was above all the invasion of European capital into the Spanish zone of influence in Morocco that destabilized the area. Besides fulfilling its inter-

---

[32] Morales, *Datos*, 383.   [33] *Libro Rojo*, doc. 6, p. 5 and doc. 33, pp. 18–19.
[34] The Cabo de Agua occupation was also designed to make life easier for the small Spanish garrison on the Chafarinas Islands nearby whose soldiers had to cross to the mainland to buy provisions from the Quebdanis: Allendesalazar, *La diplomacia*, 149; Morales, *Datos*, 372–3.
[35] Manuel Galbán Jiménez, *España en Africa. La Pacificación de Marruecos* (Madrid, Imprenta del Servicio Geográfico de Marruecos, 1965), 29.

national commitment to maintain order in north-east Morocco, the Spanish government hoped thereby to create the conditions for the attraction of Spanish investment to the area. In the neo-colonialist discourse of the time, trade would benefit everyone, from businessmen to the Moroccans themselves. In the aim of enticing investment to the north-east, Marina could count on the pretender's search for money. El Rogui was not averse to European penetration, because it held the promise of profitable business deals. French and Spanish business agents had noted the potential for the mining of iron ore, copper, lead, and other minerals in the area under his control. Samples of iron ore from the mountains not far from Melilla had been analysed and found to be rich in content and easily mineable.

A race took place between rival European interests to gain the right to exploit these deposits. Various expeditions had been sent to acquire contracts to do so. A French company registered in Spain struck a deal with the chieftain to exploit both the lead and iron-ore deposits in the area for 400,000 pesetas. A further expedition by Spanish rival interests was organized to obtain a new contract from El Rogui. Arranged by the Jewish businessman David Charbit, already established as the chieftain's agent in Melilla, it set out on 20 November 1907 on behalf of a newly established company whose capital came from important business interests in Spain.[36]

An unpublished report on the expedition paints a vivid European picture of the meeting of two different cultures.[37] Having obtained military authorization to move into El Rogui's territory, Charbit's expedition was escorted to his headquarters by the Pretender's own troops. Arriving there before another rival expedition showed up, the six-member team and their servants set up camp but were forced to plead for a different site because they had been located by a ditch into which El Rogui's people deposited faeces and animal corpses. In their first meeting with the leader, they were clearly impressed but also puzzled by his attire. Besides his jellaba, he was wearing white leather gloves, boots made of red morocco leather lined with silver, a red silk handkerchief, and a silver-plated pistol. In his hands he held a rosary and a large pencil.

Among the gifts the Spaniards had brought were a gramophone and records. They had also brought thousands of 5-peseta pieces as a downpayment to El Rogui if the deal went ahead. As part of the ceremony preceding the bargaining, the Spaniards wound up the gramophone and played the Spanish Royal March, to which El Rogui appeared to listen with pleasure. They also presented him with a photograph of the king and played records of

---

[36] Ibid., 13–14; María Rosa de Madariaga, *España y el Rif. Crónica de una historia casi olvidada* (Melilla, La Biblioteca de Melilla, 2000), 125–9; Victor Ruiz Albéniz, *La campaña del Rif. La verdad de la guerra* (Madrid, n.p., 1909), 11–12.

[37] Jacobo Butler, 'Yo negocié con el Rogui las minas del Rif', cyclostyled document in García Figueras archives, Biblioteca Nacional, n.d.

Spanish and Arab songs. If the Spaniards found Moroccan culture somewhat strange, it must have been equally bizarre for Moroccans to listen to a European military march.

Before they could begin discussing the deal, El Rogui left with his men to fight tribes loyal to the Sultan. The expedition witnessed their return and their inhuman treatment of prisoners. In a further audience, the writer was struck by El Rogui's 'intellectual and speculative sharpness'. The appearance of the rival expedition delayed further negotiation and Charbit's team was forced to pay for several intermediaries among El Rogui's chiefs. They finally obtained his signature, apparently in pencil and virtually illegible, for the right to exploit local iron-ore mines in exchange for 20 per cent of the mining profits, with advance payments every three months of 125,000 pesetas. The deal thus annulled the contract with the French company, which was left with the nearby lead mines. On their return to Melilla, the Spanish drew up a contract and made another trip to get a final signature. Work on both iron-ore and lead mines and the building of a railway to bring personnel to the mines and carry the minerals back to Melilla began in the spring of 1908. Presumably without Marina's consent, the Spanish company agreed that El Rogui could use the rail and trains to transport his own troops in his fight with other tribes in the area.[38]

The dealings of European businessmen with such a flamboyant imposter no doubt put Marina under some strain, though he was a decided advocate of opening the interior of Morocco to commerce. More seriously, the invasion of European capital into the Rif dislocated relations amongst the tribes that lived in the areas surrounding the mines. The problem was not just that El Rogui was opening the doors for the penetration of foreigners of a different religion, but that he was keeping the profits for himself. He was also looking for new areas of mining wealth to sell to the foreigner and made violent incursions into the territory of surrounding tribes. Also, private deals were being made elsewhere in the region between European speculators and tribal chieftains for the rights to exploit mines at prices that varied enormously. In the scramble for mining concessions, the Liberal statesman Count Romanones and his brother had struck a number of cheap deals, often behind the back of the Spanish authorities. In contrast to the high sums of money exchanged for mining concessions from El Rogui, they had bought plots of land judged to be rich in minerals for paltry sums of money.[39]

In an immensely poor region like the Rif, the sudden and unequal inflow of money and work opportunities exacerbated the divisions between the tribes. The subsequent appearance of machines, railways, and large numbers of foreigners constituted an invasion of their land and culture. It was also seen as a

---

[38] Galbán Jiménez, *España en África*, 15.

[39] From between 3,000 and 7,000 pesetas: Archivo del Banco de España, Sociedad de Minas del Rif, legajo 1. At the beginning of 1908 the two groups merged to form the Compañía Española del Rif.

threat to their religion. The jihad against the Spanish some fourteen years previously had been provoked merely by work to extend Melilla's fortifications that had disturbed a holy shrine. The potential for such desecrations now seemed far greater.

The descent into war between Spain and the tribes surrounding Melilla was thus the result of disruptive commercial and political penetration. The arms trade in the last decade of the nineteenth century and the invasion of mining interests in the first decade of the new century had upset the balance between tribes. The French and the Spanish policy of divide and rule in Morocco further undermined the system of coalition or *leff* amongst tribes, which had served to maintain some degree of order in the Moroccan hinterland. The local tool of conflict resolution, a fine imposed on an individual or group of individuals by village or tribal authorities such as the *Jema'a*, was weakened by Spanish intervention. The result was an increase in feuds and vendettas and the emergence of new petty tyrants.[40] This was a common effect of colonial intrusion in other parts of Africa. Traditional patterns of interaction among different ethnic or tribal groups were upset when colonial powers sought to alter the balance of power by fostering intermediaries.[41]

On the other hand, where a chieftain was unrecognized by the Sultanate, Spain sought to replace him. The Spanish policy of encouraging tribes loyal to the sultan helped to undermine El Rogui's power. A Spanish doctor in one of the mines, Ruiz Albéniz, a notable Arabist and a proponent, along with the mining companies, of a neo-colonialist strategy of not interfering with the existing balance of power in the Rif, complained that the governor general's policy had destabilized the whole area. 'There was no power in the Rif other than that of El Rogui, and we set out to destroy it and support something that was fictitious, anarchic, without responsibility: that of the kabyles [or tribal groups].'[42]

The first attack against the mines took place in October 1908, forcing the fifty or so Spanish workers there to flee to El Rogui's headquarters, where the chieftain provided them with an escort to Melilla. The mines were sacked, moving the pretender to seek out and punish the perpetrators from the nearby tribes. El Rogui had frequently resorted to violence to assert his authority. He also liked to remind the Spanish that he exercised effective control in his area of domination by sending them macabre tokens of his hegemony. After seizing

[40] Madariaga, *España*, 273–5; J. David Seddon, 'Local Political and State Intervention: Northeast Morocco from 1870 to 1970', in Ernest Gellner and Charles Micaud (eds.), *Arabs and Berbers: From Tribe to Nation in North Africa* (London, Duckworth, 1972), 109–33.

[41] Thus, for example, French colonialism on the Ivory Coast: Timothy C. Weiskel, *French Colonial Rule and the Baule People: Resistance and Collaboration 1889–1911* (Oxford, OUP, 1980), 210–14.

[42] Victor Ruiz Albéniz *Ecce homo: las responsabilidades del desastre* (Madrid, Biblioteca Nueva, 1922), 24; also, Ruiz Albéniz, *La guerra*, 29–30. The author explains also that the Spanish authorities refused him permission to treat any of the pretender's followers and blocked the passage of a consignment of food for the chieftain through the port of Restinga. For a similar analysis, see Galbán, *España en África*, 25–8.

some of those apparently guilty of the action against the mining companies, he sent thirty-two decapitated heads to Melilla to persuade the Spanish authorities that work on the mines could begin again. Instead, they insisted that all the tribes had to give their consent first.[43]

In a further blow to the pretender, his troops were refused permission by Marina to proceed directly into the territory of a neighbouring tribe to impose financial contributions on the chieftain. An attempt by the Spanish mining company to provide El Rogui with ammunition so that he could continue to protect the mining and railway works was blocked by the Spanish High Command.[44] Retreating before the gathering uprising against him, El Rogui was forced by the end of 1908 to abandon the area and withdraw southwards with his declining number of followers to his headquarters in the French sphere of influence. Before he left, he sent a letter to the Spanish authorities declaring: 'My departure will cost Spain many thousands of millions of pesetas and streams of blood and tears. Poor Spain!'[45]

In his absence, the prevailing anarchy in the area convinced Marina that there was no other option but decisive military intervention to restore order and allow the mines to start work again. Maura was sympathetic and asked Marina to make a formal request for more troops and war matériel. But he urged him to await the policy of the new sultan, who had ousted his brother as part of a rebellion in central Morocco, analogous to that of the Rif, against his collaboration with Europe.[46] Faced by an increasingly impatient military lobby, and by pressure from France after a French expedition had attempted to reach the mines without permission, Maura's government finally agreed at the end of May 1909 to a limited military protection of the works.[47]

In successive telegrams to the minister of foreign affairs, Marina warned of increasing agitation amongst the Moroccan tribes for action against the mines. Only the absence of many of the local men, who were working on the harvest in Algeria, was holding up an attack. Three days before the first assault Marina warned the government that the threat was now serious.[48] What followed was by no means a 'predictable tragedy', as many critics of the government were to argue. Both government and military knew that military conflict was likely and they prepared for it. However, they failed to take into account the nature of the enemy and the special conditions in which that war would be fought.

In the vacuum of power after El Rogui's flight, a new chieftain, El Sharif Mohammad Amzian, had emerged in the Rif calling for violent resistance against the Spanish. His was not an exclusively religious movement. Under the banner of a jihad he managed to assemble the different protests against the

[43] Ruiz Albéniz, *Ecce Homo*, 22–24.   [44] Galbán, *España en Africa*, 26–7.
[45] Ruiz Albéniz, *Ecce Homo*, 12.   [46] *Libro Rojo*, no. 435, anejos pp. 166–8.
[47] Ibid., 251; Germain Ayache, *Les Origines de la guerre du Rif* (Paris, Publications de la Sorbonne, 1981), 140–1.
[48] *Libro Rojo*, no. 619, p. 260, no. 628, p. 266, and no. 640, p. 270.

effects of Spanish penetration. Spanish sources later calculated that he had gathered together some 5,000 warriors.[49] Before June 1909 the Spanish garrison in Melilla numbered 5,700 officers and soldiers. Marina started to deploy a detachment of these troops to protect work on the railway between the mines and Melilla. On 9 July Spanish workers constructing a railway bridge along the line were attacked; six were killed and another injured, while the remainder escaped on the train that had brought them to the site. While his detachment moved quickly to the area, Marina mobilized the Melilla garrison, which had been training for military action for some time, and marched out with most of the troops to drive away the attackers with few losses to either side. Marina also ordered a naval bombardment of coastal villages on 13 July in the area supposedly dominated by the Moroccan resistance movement. The Spanish government, conscious of its negative international impact, called a halt to any further shelling.

As the soldiers were deployed in the area around the mines from 9 July they were subject to repeated guerrilla harassment. Fresh troops from the metropolis were immediately mobilized for action in Morocco, and the first contingent set sail from Spain. The war was deeply unpopular in Spain. Reservists, drawn from the poorer classes who could not pay the sum of money required for exemption from military service, and who had never expected to have to do it at all, were forced to abandon their families and jobs. The Disaster of 1898, the injustices of the ensuing demobilization, and the conviction amongst many that soldiers were being sent merely to defend the mining companies, led to vociferous protests at the ports and stations of embarkation. Such was the strength of feeling against the conflict in Barcelona, the most politicized city in Spain, that an anti-war strike was declared on 26 July by militant metalworkers. Their action triggered a week of rioting, later called the Tragic Week (*Semana Trágica*), that brought into play a range of different grievances against the establishment, in particular the Church.[50]

Not unexpectedly, many of the troops that arrived in Morocco were hardly prepared for the extraordinary conditions of warfare in the Rif. Some were sent into action almost immediately, after spending two days travelling by train through Spain and twelve hours on a rough crossing to the port of Melilla. Insufficient training and lack of incentive among the soldiers hardly made for an efficient army. In addition, the officers had an inadequate knowledge of the terrain and tended to use inappropriate textbook strategy. There were many

---

[49] The following details of the war, though not the analysis, are drawn mainly from: Estado Mayor Central del Ejército, *Historia*, vol. 2; Carlos Hernández Herrera and Tomás García Figueras, *Acción de España en Marruecos* (Madrid, n.p., 1929–30), vols. 1 and 2; Capitán Eduardo Gallego Ramos, *La campaña del Rif (1909): orígenes, desarrollo y consecuencias* (Madrid, n.p., 1909); Enrique López Alarcón, *Crónica de un testigo: Melilla 1909. Diario de la guerra escrita durante las operaciones militares en el Rif* (Madrid, Hijos de R. Álvarez, 1911).

[50] Joan Connelly Ullman, *The Tragic Week: A Study of Anticlericalism in Spain, 1875–1912* (Cambridge, Mass., Harvard University Press, 1968); Balfour, *The End*, ch. 4.

veterans of the 1895–8 colonial campaigns amongst them, but in the new theatre of operations the experience of counter-guerrilla warfare in Cuba and the
Philippines had to undergo major adjustments.

The most important differences as far as military tactics was concerned
were the terrain and the weather. The Rif, as the etymology of the name exem-
plifies, is a rugged land of high mountains and deep valleys, 'a constant dislocation of terrain,' as the doctor in the mines, Ruiz Albéniz, wrote, 'made up
here of a mountain peak, there a whole mountain range, beyond that a hill,
and everywhere a broken terrain, a mad geological configuration'.[51] The climate was one of harsh extremes. In the mountains, the temperature could rise
to 50 degrees during the day and plummet to below zero at night. Water,
vegetation, and wood were sparse, forcing campaign troops to carry all their
supplies with them.

Another problem for the occupying army, not unlike the conditions of the
Cuban campaign, was that it could never be sure who the enemy was until it
was too late. A General Staff report stated: 'The absence of a regular and
defined enemy, for the struggle is against the tribes of the territory in which
combat is taking place and even against others who have joined up, makes it
difficult to determine which inhabitants are hostile and which are peaceful,
and diminishes the result of victorious combats . . .'[52] The ruthless strategy in
the Cuban campaign of forcing the civilian population into concentration
camps to clear the countryside of support for the freedom-fighters was not an
option available to the Spanish commanders in Morocco, both for logistic reasons and because of Spain's international commitments.

In certain circumstances, the Rif tribesmen were among the most accomplished guerrilla fighters in the world, equivalent in some respects to the
Gurkha warriors of Nepal. Skilled horsemen and mountaineers, they could
survive for days carrying only figs, bread, and ammunition in the hood of their
jellaba. Their religion assured them that if they died fighting the infidel they
would go to paradise. They evaded frontal attacks and fought in small groups.
Neither artillery nor cavalry nor fixed bayonet charges were very effective
against them. Spanish troop movements and convoys of supplies were almost
always vulnerable to their ambushes. They could track the enemy unseen all
day, hiding amongst rocks and behind undergrowth waiting for an opportunity
to shoot. As an observer of the 1909 war wrote: 'As they have no positions to
defend, no town to guard, no forts to garrison, convoys to escort, provisions to
bring, works to carry out, and as in addition they know the land like the back
of their hand and are operating in their own territory, they can move about
with extraordinary ease knowing only too well that their spies won't betray
them and that their own people in the rearguard run no risk.'[53] They did have

[51]   Ruiz Albéniz, *La campaña del Rif. La verdad de la guerra* (Madrid, n.p., 1909), 71.
[52]   Estado Mayor Central del Ejército, *Enseñanzas de la campaña del Rif en 1909* (Madrid, n.p., 1911), 11.
[53]   Augusto Riera, *España en Marruecos. Crónica de la campaña de 1909* (Barcelona, Maucci, 1909).

settlements and fields to defend, and these would present the Spanish army with targets, but their overall mobility was not thereby significantly impaired. Ruiz Albéniz calculated that each Rif guerrilla was worth a hundred Spanish soldiers.[54]

There were other circumstances in which the traditional military culture of the tribesmen worked to their disadvantage. Concerted resistance to armed penetration across tribes was extremely difficult to achieve because of the fragmentation of social structure. Moreover, tribal alliances were fragile and the leaders of a jihad were forced to make messianic appeals to muster a collective response always conditioned by pragmatic considerations.[55] War was traditionally a means for one tribal leader to assert hegemony over another and for the individual to acquire loot, and often both these mechanisms had to coincide. Combining to halt the invasion of a foreign army, on the other hand, posed almost insuperable problems of supplies, weaponry, ammunition, and above all discipline. The Rifian guerrillas were highly skilled at harassing an army as it advanced. Following up a victory over a conventional force, though, required the sort of co-ordination they sorely lacked. The rifles that tribesmen possessed were more effective for sniping than for pitched battles. The best-armed amongst them owned a Maüser 93 rifle that they had acquired through trade or war loot. Others possessed older rifles that needed repeated, time-consuming reloading.

In the Spanish military discourse of the time, the Rifians' tactics could be seen as treacherous. Far from absorbing the lessons of the colonial wars of 1895–8, in which modern guerrilla and anti-guerrilla warfare was put into practice, Spanish military writers continued to appeal to nineteenth-century values of honour, chivalry, and outmoded rules of engagement. A populist, myth-making account of the 1909 military campaign described the Rifian warriors thus: 'When they want to they accept battle, or seek it out; but when they don't want to, they run away and flee in disorder without fear that their honour might suffer, because they do not know what honour is. They only know about fighting with advantage, and treachery is their only advisor.'[56] Even the more enlightened officers and observers of the military campaign, who favoured commercial over military penetration, evidently failed to understand that European civilization was not generally welcome among the population.[57] Ignorance of what drove the Rifians to fight was exacerbated by the prevailing racism among most Europeans. Contemporary Spanish pictures of

---

[54] Ruiz Albéniz, *La campaña*, 72.

[55] Amal Vinogradov and John Waterbury, 'Situations of Contested Legitimacy in Morocco: An Alternative Framework', *Comparative Studies in Society and History*, 13: 1 (1971), 32–59.

[56] Riera, *España*, 66.

[57] e.g. the infantry officer Federico Pita in his *La acción militar y política de España en Africa a través de los tiempos* (Madrid, Revista Técnica de Infantería y Caballería, 1915), and Ruiz Albéniz, *La campaña*.

the Moroccan Other, similar to the racist imagery of other colonial powers, were tinged with nineteenth-century romantic projections.[58]

Quite apart from ignorance of the enemy and problems of logistics, Spain's government and her military had not caught up with changing technology and the consequent transformation of the tactics of warfare. Some military regulations still dated from the pre-1898 period and were only slowly being over-hauled. New Infantry Regulations had been approved less than nine months before the 1909 campaign began, and were unlikely to have been fully in place by then. Military tactics had not been fully revised to take into account the new weapons the army was acquiring on the international market.[59] The training of reservists was inadequate and many of them had long forgotten its basic principles. The law of recruitment mobilized individuals from different parts of Spain with no apparent rationale. The disciplinary brigade of soldiers on charges that took part in the first actions on Moroccan soil in 1908 and in the offensive of 1909, suffered frequent desertions, showed little discipline in its use of ammunition, and was notorious for its behaviour in the rearguard. In general, the Spanish army betrayed little preparation for counter-guerrilla warfare.[60]

In the events leading to the so-called 'Disaster of the Wolf Ravine', or Barranco del Lobo, on 27 July, two incidents that took place four days earlier illustrate the shortcomings of Spanish military preparations. A column had set out at night to reach before dawn the heights of a mountain from where Moroccan guerrillas had been directing lethal fire every day at Spanish convoys carrying provisions to troops in advanced positions. With only a rough and inaccurate drawing of the area to guide him, the colonel and his men got lost and found themselves at another position already secured by Spanish troops. When light came, the Moroccans were able to fire on a mass of Spanish soldiers gathered together in a small space. According to one account, the colonel exclaimed, 'Follow me if you're a man!' and charged into the open with a number of officers and men, . . . only to be cut down after a few paces by Moroccan bullets.

Later that day, another column made up of troops who had just arrived from Catalonia halted by a ruined Moroccan dwelling to eat their cold rations. The commander, believing they had left the combat zone, wanted his exhausted troops to eat and rest after their long journey and a full day's campaign. Without adequate cover, and leaving many of their rifles in a pile, they sat down on the ground. As they ate, guerrillas stole up on them and started shooting them down. Many of the soldiers ran off without their arms and others were killed, including their commander and several officers.[61]

[58] For further discussion of the Moroccan Other see Ch. 7.
[59] General de Torcy, *Los españoles en Marruecos en 1909* (Madrid, Adrian Romo, 1911), 210–11.
[60] Estado Mayor, *Enseñanzas de la campaña del Rif en 1909.*
[61] Hernández Herrera and García Figueras, *Acción de España,* ii. 68–70.

It was above all lack of knowledge of the complex topography of the Rif that led to the Disaster of the Barranco del Lobo. No study had been made of the area and no proper map existed. The result was a simple error of direction that led to the deaths of many Spanish soldiers. During the previous night, some 300 metres of the railway line leading to the mines had been ripped up and damaged by tribesmen. Marina sent out two columns, one to protect the repair of the line and another, led by General Pintos, to prevent the enemy from leaving the valleys nearby where they were supposed to be gathered. Pintos himself, along with one of the brigades of his column, had arrived in Morocco only two days before. His expedition set off for the foothills of the Gurugú mountain range. In the midday light the terrain leading to them seemed a large sloping plain, whereas it was in fact rugged land scored with deep gullies leading to ravines. Although their advance had been preceded by artillery bombardment by both campaign pieces and the long-range guns in nearby Melilla, they found themselves under deadly fire as they laboriously crossed the rough terrain. Grouped in too dense a formation, they began to suffer substantial losses.

As they approached the Barranco del Lobo ravine, Pintos divided the column into two. The right-hand column managed to reach a hill to the right of the ravine. Disregarding Marina's instructions, Pintos led the left column towards the ravine and was killed by a sniper as he sat to rest on a rock. The column that penetrated into the Barranco del Lobo began to be hit by fire from above, in front, and from both sides. Most of the officers were shot dead. The troops retreated in disorder, leaving behind the dead and wounded as well as the mules carrying ammunition. In the action the Spanish army suffered over a thousand casualties, of which around 180 were fatal (casualties on the Moroccan side are unknown). In order to make known his anger over Pintos's action, Marina refused to attend his funeral.[62]

The disaster had the paradoxical effect of mobilizing support in Spain for army action in Morocco. More effectively than a victory, the spectacular defeat strengthened solidarity towards the military among the middle and upper classes. Proper war, with a suitable number of heroic deaths, brought passion and drama to daily life in the peninsula. The facility to evade military service by making a payment to the state was suspended on 4 August. In a blaze of publicity, some young aristocrats volunteered to serve in Morocco with the troops. The disaster also gave a new sense of identity and self-righteousness to officers and many troops stationed in Morocco. Expanding operations gave officers the opportunity for rapid promotion and the award of medals for

---

[62] Ruiz Albéniz, *La campaña*, 73. There is some polemic over whether Pintos obeyed or disobeyed Marina's instructions. For the view that he was simply following orders, see Roberto Muñoz Bolaños, 'La campaña de 1909', in José Luis de Mesa *et al.*, *Las campañas de Marruecos 1909–1927* (Madrid, Almena, 2001), 31–8.

courage. What had started out as a police operation to protect the mines now turned into a war of revenge against 'barbarian' tribes.

Rather than risking their lives to prop up a corrupt and collapsing empire or to protect the interests of rich speculators, the military now felt at last that they were defending national pride.[63] The outrage over Spanish casualties in the Barranco del Lobo strengthened the latent racism against Arabs. Marina was obliged to issue an order for local inhabitants friendly to Spain to be accompanied by a two-man military escort when they made their way about Melilla. Ruiz Albéniz met a Moroccan acquaintance of his who had fought on the Spanish side in the campaign and who found on his return to Melilla from battle that a relative of his and several other Moroccans had been badly beaten up by Spanish soldiers.[64]

For Marina and probably most of his officers, further military expansion into Spain's sphere of influence beyond the outposts established in 1908 was long overdue. He was insistent that the positions the army was now occupying should be permanent. In a confidential letter to the Minister of War on 15 July, eleven days before the disaster, he had written: 'Even disregarding the protection of the mine works, the main positions we are occupying have immense importance for the expansion of Spain and her influence in this region . . . it is right that I should point out this importance, so that what is provisional should become permanent in the future, for this represents so much for Spain.'[65] For military colonial opinion, the battle in the Barranco del Lobo sanctioned the penetration of the army into areas from where the enemy operated. Especially since their losses on 27 July, the Moroccan fighters now evaded any direct confrontation with Spanish columns and instead confined their actions to assaults on outposts and convoys.

During a two-month halt to operations, and with a steady stream of reinforcements and supplies from Spain, Marina assembled a well-equipped expeditionary force. By mid-September it numbered around 40,000 men. While the troops were largely confined to Melilla, Spanish artillery and naval guns had kept up a daily barrage of the ravines that the troops would soon be crossing.[66] On the Moroccan side, the new leader Mohammad Amzian had emerged in the course of 1909 among the anti-Rogui allies to lead the jihad against Spain, and he profited from the lull in fighting to recruit more fighters.

Operations by Spanish columns to forestall a jihad were a source of preoccupation for the government, for the harsh methods considered necessary by the military augured badly for future relations with local people. The Maura government was keen to hide the brutality of Spanish occupation from civilian eyes at home. The minister of war requested Marina in future 'not to allude in

---

[63] 'Momentos de expectación' and 'Política africanista: la empresa de ahora', *El Ejército Español*, 5 and 7 Aug. 1909; 'Homenaje al ejército', *La Correspondencia Militar*, 22 Jan. 1910.

[64] Ruiz Albéniz, *La campaña*, 61 and 64.   [65] Estado Mayor, *Historia* (Apéndice), 335.

[66] Hernández Herrera and García Figueras, *Acción de España*, ii. 74.

reports to the destruction of houses and the devastation of fields, recommending to the commanders of columns that in the use of coercive methods against the tribes they adopt military exigency as a norm, avoiding any act of destruction that does not have this necessity as its cause, respecting as far as possible the cattle, seeds, and farming implements, which should be impounded and retained.' The gap between mission and reality was full of wishful thinking. The minister went on to state: 'The pacifying and civilizing mission carried out by our troops should not be marked by ruin, as far as possible, so that the path of reconciliation of minds is left open. We should not have to deal with irreconcilable people, but on the contrary we must lay the basis for friendly relations in the future.'[67]

Yet after the July disaster such niceties were far from the military mind. This was reflected in an earlier telegram sent on the same day to Marina by the same minister to the effect that the very success of pacification might lead to a suspension of the offensive before it got under way, which would cause great disillusion both in the public and amongst the military, who were keen to subjugate the Rifians. In a further example of the contradictions in which Maura's government now found itself, he also warned that Marina should not publicly state that rebellious tribes had submitted to Spanish troops since this would give the impression that Spain had replaced the authority of the sultan, which, of course, she had been doing for at least a year.[68]

On 20 September Marina's offensive was launched on several fronts.[69] Accompanied by artillery and guided by a reconnaissance balloon, units of infantry and cavalry moved out of advanced positions into territory controlled by the Rif tribes under Amzian. The tribesmen put up a fierce resistance, but by 27 September units had reached the Barranco del Lobo, where they found the remains of the bodies of the troops killed two months earlier, which were sent to Melilla for burial. Mt. Gurugú above the ravine was also occupied, and in an almost theatrical ceremony the Spanish flag was planted at the summit.

These military successes were enthusiastically celebrated in Spain. Several battlefield events, such as the Gurugú flag-planting, became myths of Spanish courage. A further epic story was the action of Corporal Noval. Captured by the Moroccans, he was told to lead them at night to a Spanish position where they could surprise the sentries. But Noval apparently cried out to the sentries to fire and he was shot along with his captors. Such heroic events raised hopes that the war was coming to an end. The government's lifting of restrictions and announcement of the opening of parliament encouraged these hopes. A final push was made in November. Several chiefs who had supported Mohammad Amzian sued for peace and the offensive was finally declared at an end. The repatriation of troops was staged over the following six months. Out of a total

---

[67] Ibid., vol. 2, appendix, docs. XIX and XX, 15 Sept. 1909, pp. 347–8.   [68] Ibid.
[69] The following account is drawn from a number of sources, including a semi-official account by Gallego Ramos, *La campaña* and Hernández Herrera and García Figueras, *Acción de España*, vol. 2.

of 42,000 soldiers who had been mobilized since July, 20,000 were left to occupy the conquered region. This area covered some 17,000 square kilometres outside the Melilla frontier.[70]

The 1909 campaign was the catalyst of the Army of Africa. It had been a tough apprenticeship for serving officers in gaining an understanding of the peculiar conditions of warfare in the Rif. There was a renewed awareness of the disadvantages of using Spanish troops doing military service for action in the harsh environment of the Moroccan countryside, in a war to which they felt little commitment. Once again the crucial distinction observed in the Spanish–Cuban war between counter-guerrilla professionals and columns of peasant boys doing military service had become all too apparent. The royal order of August 1909, which had opened the ranks to volunteers, had injected militancy into the campaign army. More importantly, as in the colonies of other European powers, the use of irregular native troops had been highly effective. Spanish military officers, like the politicians themselves, were always looking over their shoulder at the French model just a few miles away in Algeria and Morocco.

The French colonial army under Lyautey had become an efficient and ruthless military machine, relying to a great extent on its mercenary colonial troops. Unlike the Spanish native troops, however, France could draw its mercenaries from other parts of the French Empire such as Senegal, while Spain had to rely on local troops to fight against local enemy. Spain's military command in Morocco had begun to recruit mercenaries from neighbouring tribes to fight against Moroccan resistance. They were good fighters like their enemy and knew the land. These would soon form the core of new regular native troops called the Regulares. Before the 1909 campaign, a small force of native police had been created and soon two nuclei were set up on a more permanent basis in the area along with a Native Office. In December they were enlarged to form a full company of native police, capable of operating in other areas under Spanish control.[71]

Many lessons were also learnt regarding military strategy and tactics. A report by the General Staff published in 1911 made a number of unsurprising recommendations based on the experience of the campaign.[72] Shelling by artillery and ships was seen to have been highly effective in cowing the enemy, though not in inflicting heavy casualties because of their mobility. The thorough training of the troops in appropriate skills was essential. Their diet needed to be improved: rather than the heavy doses of rice which they had consumed during the 1909 campaign, they should have lighter and richer food. Oddly to our contemporary tastes, biscuits were recommended as the most useful source of nutrition during operations.

---

[70] Hernández Herrera and García Figueras, *Acción de España*, ii, 88.
[71] Javier Ramos Winthuyssen, *Tropas indígenas y Ejército Colonial* (Seville, n.p., 1921), 41 and 51–2.
[72] Estado Mayor, *Enseñanzas*, 15–320.

As for strategy, according to the report, the army needed to follow up victories rather than retreat to rest. Mobility was vital. The column under a permanent commander should be the main unit of operation and small mobile companies should protect main columns on all sides. Marches should be short. Columns should only go through passes when the heights above were secured. The tactic of enveloping the enemy through lateral movements was far preferable to frontal assault. Infrastructure such as road-building and sanitation needed improving. The adoption of new technology in telecommunications, military hardware, and hygiene was also urged. Many of these recommendations, however, were likely to cost the sort of sums the hard-pressed Spanish governments were hardly inclined to approve, given the continued unpopularity of the war and the fierce demands on the Exchequer from domestic sources, including the metropolitan army.

The 1909 campaign also forged a new colonial identity amongst veterans of the previous colonial wars, and among younger, ambitious officers who relied on military action for the advancement of their careers because they were insufficiently well connected in Spain. The harsh landscape of the Rif, the tough conditions of the campaigns, and the ruthless character of battles helped to shape a sense of identity far removed from the culture of the metropolitan garrison where routine and bureaucracy reigned. It was characterized by elitism, a scorn for the softness of civilian life, and, by extension, of garrison life, and an increasing disdain for civilian government.[73] This self-perception of a unique identity was encouraged by mainland publicity for the defeats and victories, and the wealth of promotions and medals that followed the campaign. The disaster of the Barranco del Lobo alone gave rise to sixty-one promotions.

Understandably, officers in Spain felt put out since they were not given similar opportunities for rapid promotion. One of the daily newspapers for officers launched a campaign at the end of the war arguing that promotion should be based not on the number of casualties but on merit.[74] Why else would the defeat of 27 July be rewarded by so many medals when the successful action of 9 July, when the Rif aggressors were driven away from the railway with few losses, earned none at all?[75] Gonzalo Queipo de Llano, a veteran officer of the Cuban campaign now based in Spain, wrote two open letters in the newspaper arguing for a closed military scale.[76] A rival military newspaper rose to the

---

[73] See Ch. 6.

[74] 'Sobre la propuesta del 27 de julio', *La Correspondencia Militar*, 23 Dec. 1909; the point was repeatedly argued in the paper throughout December and into January 1910. The question had already aroused much polemic in the military press in April and May 1906.

[75] Joaquín Llorens, 'Los ascensos por méritos de guerra', ibid., 30 Dec. 1909.

[76] Ibid., 31 Dec. 1909 and 1 Jan. 1910. The paper also campaigned against the minister of war for allegedly promoting his relatives and friends. For an interesting analysis see a report from the British ambassador in Madrid to the minister of foreign affairs, Lord Grey, in *British Documents*, part 1, vol 28, doc. 47, 14 Jan. 1910.

defence of the promotions system and attacked the campaign.[77] Small demonstrations followed, and the debate became especially heated when the government fined Queipo de Llano and the editor of the newspaper, and arrested a military MP for supporting them. The growing cultural cleavage between colonial officers and military circles in Spain was now intensified by a professional dispute.

Yet even among colonial officers a fissure began to emerge regarding the nature of military occupation in Morocco. The government's precepts about respect for Moroccan society and for its structures of local power were backed by enlightened colonial military opinion. The General Staff report on the role of the military in Morocco insisted that the army was there to enable the Moroccans to rise from barbarism to civilization. Alongside civilian authorities, its function was to oversee the opening of commerce, the building of roads, hospitals, and first-aid centres, and so on throughout the Spanish sphere of influence. The 'natives' had to be treated with a 'nobility of sentiment'. Force should only be used if all other means of persuasion failed; that is, peaceful penetration should always be attempted first. Prisoners should be treated correctly. The army should also respect property and customs and pay the right sums for all goods purchased from local people.[78] Such an approach was backed by two generations of colonial officers.

Though this sort of discourse was obligatory in official settings, in private many colonial officers felt differently. After the 1909 disaster in particular, military instinct was to march into Morocco and break some heads. A new spirit of interventionism in politics was in any case evident after the events in Spain of 1905–6. Impatience with the government's supine policies in Morocco overflowed after July 1909. One of the main mouthpieces of these sentiments was the military paper *El Ejército Español*. Its editorials pushed for military action in Morocco before anything else and whatever the circumstances. In the typically florid language of the time, it declared: 'Weapons plough the virgin soil so that agriculture, industry, and mining might blossom there, so that paths are opened up that become the arteries of commerce.'[79] An army enthusiast himself, the young king encouraged this militarism. After the first action on 9 July he sent a telegram of congratulations to Marina that went far beyond the ritual language of compliment. 'The first act of war waged in my reign has filled me with pride. The great hopes I have placed in the Army and in the future of the Motherland have been fully borne out.'[80]

[77] 'Sobre recompensas', *El Ejército Español*, 24 Dec. 1909, and 'Movimiento de escalas', ibid., 11 Feb. 1910.

[78] Estado Mayor, *Enseñanzas*, 15–320.

[79] 'Política africanista. La empresa de ahora', 7 Aug. 1909.

[80] M. García Álvarez and A. García Pérez, *Diario de las operaciones realizadas en Melilla a partir del día 9 de julio de 1909* (Toledo, n.p., 1909), 6.

Among many colonial officers, militarism was accompanied by racism towards Moroccans. Ignorant, primitive, fanatical, barbaric, and infantile, they needed the heavy hand of the army to convince them of the value of European civilization.[81] Racism, imperialism, and militarism were therefore important components of a new right-wing culture within the military. Taking the Prussian military as its model, it celebrated the priority of character and energy of leaders over rules and tactics. Unlike other strands of right-wing opinion, this culture did not sympathize with the conservative clerical establishment and rejected religion as a motive for Spain's colonial advance in Africa. In the words of the military newspaper, Isabel la Católica's testament meant merely 'fisticuffs for faith against the infidel', while the army's role was to bring civilization in all its forms.[82]

Both enlightened and militaristic opinion shared a common distrust of neo-colonialism. Officers serving in Morocco had had to risk their lives for the sake of the mining elites, who had been quite happy to do deals with local chieftains behind their back. In contrast to the mining barons, the more progressive business circles in Catalonia and Madrid were still calling for peaceful, commerce-led penetration into North Africa. The earnest neo-colonial discourse of liberal businessmen and intellectuals of the Africanist lobby was greeted with derision by the right-wing military press. Most of them were, according to a military newspaper: 'Exhibitionists, who come more out of a desire to show off than to contribute to the greater glory of the Motherland . . . Military victory is the cutting edge of the victory of commerce and of industry.'[83]

Thus armed with a sense of moral justification and the nucleus of a more professional colonial army, the Spanish military were poised for further expansion into the Moroccan empire. The new military operations would bring them into collision with Moroccan opponents more formidable than those they had previously encountered. Unlike the experience of the French in their Moroccan sphere or the British in Egypt and India, the Spanish had to deal with tribes, fractions of tribes, and chieftains without the benefit of an indigenous hierarchy of power and clientelism. With considerably fewer resources than other colonial powers, Spain began to face resistance that was far more complex and difficult to handle than that of her rivals. Accommodation with local chieftains increasingly broke down as it became clear that Spain was neither respecting their sphere of influence nor bringing the advantages some of them had expected. The British Raj, in contrast, had brought technology to

[81]   e.g. Narciso Gibert, *España y Africa* (Madrid, n.p., 1912), 20; Un Africanista más, *La guerra y el problema de Africa. Unas cuantas verdades* (Burgos, n.p., 1914), 1–88; Fernando de Urquijo, *La campaña del Rif en 1909. Juicios de un testigo* (Madrid, n.p., 1910), 248. For further analysis, see Ch. 7.

[82]   Modesto Navarro, 'De táctica', *El Ejército Español*, 20 Jan. 1908. See also Carlos Blanco Escolá, *La Academia General Militar en Zaragoza (1928–31)* (Barcelona, Labor, 1989).

[83]   *El Ejército Español*, 'El Congreso Africanista', 15 Dec. 1909.

India and created a host of collaborators. When its power was challenged, it had responded by making the sort of political concessions Spain could not afford and most Spanish colonial officers did not want.[84]

---

[84]   Lawrence James, *Raj: The Making and Unmaking of British India* (London, Abacus, 1997), 417–36.

CHAPTER TWO

Calm Sea and Furious Wind

THE SCRAMBLE FOR African possessions among European colonial powers followed a competitive logic that overtook previous rationalizations of colonialism, such as the generation of growth in Third World dependencies or the
protection of weak client states. By the end of the first decade of the twentieth
century, most of Africa had been carved up. Under the impact of this colonial
expansion, the Sultanate began to disintegrate and France and Spain were
positioning themselves to take it over by one means or another in order to
secure or assert their international status. Outright resistance against
European penetration in Africa became less common at the beginning of the
new century, although there were sporadic revolts in the first decade against
the British, Germans, and Portuguese in different parts of the continent. The
same people who had first resisted colonial invasion continued to work for their
independence even as they collaborated with the invaders and learnt from the
technology the Europeans brought with them.[1] This chapter will look at the
contradictory responses of local leaders to this invasion in Morocco in the second decade, as well as the changing culture within the Spanish colonial army
in its continuing efforts to grapple with indigenous resistance.

The war of 1909 had cleared the path for Spanish military expansion into
the empire. Over the next two years Spanish troops penetrated far into
Moroccan territory from almost all directions of the compass. For the Spanish
government, the operations responded to two distinct rationales. It was keen
to subdue the last resistance against commercial penetration, but it also
wanted to stake Spanish claims against those of the French in the approaching
partition of the crumbling Moroccan Empire.[2] For most colonial officers, on
the other hand, the military operations had one purpose only, which was to
take over militarily that part of Morocco assigned to Spain merely as a sphere
of influence. They could not openly express their support for expansionism
because to do so would be to break military discipline. But amongst themselves, they were clear that peaceful penetration had failed and many parts of

---

[1] D. K. Fieldhouse, *The West and the Third World: Trade, Colonialism, Dependence, and Development*
(Oxford, Blackwell, 1999), 27–8; Lewis, *The Race*, 230.
[2] This was made clear at the time to the British foreign minister in a conversation with the Spanish
ambassador: *British Documents*, part 1, vol. 28, doc. 85, p. 208. As Liberal president in 1913, Count
Romanones confirmed to General Alfau, commander of the north-west region, that this had been the
purpose of the military expansion; ARAH, Archivo Romanones 6 (2)/8 (30).

Morocco had succumbed to anarchy and rebellion. The sultan exercised little control over his Empire. Only military occupation could restore order and pave the way for 'civilization'.

The actions of the French Army of Africa strengthened this conviction. Increasingly ignoring the Algeciras Pact, the French military, with the blessing of their government, were moving into their own sphere and taking control of the sultan's forces.[3] They were also stealthily penetrating the Spanish zone, threatening its trade routes into the interior, and through their Moroccan agents campaigning against Spain amongst the more independent tribes in the mountains.[4] To the Spanish military, sitting back and complying with the hitherto passive policy of the political elites amounted to the surrender of 'Spanish Morocco'. Protecting Spain's strategic interests was more important than the mission of civilizing the backward. In the military discourse of the time, possessing colonies was a measure of the strength of the nation and a means of safeguarding its integrity. A military newspaper declared,

the whole nation should perish before tolerating the occupation by another people, another power, of a single inch of land on the northern coast of Morocco . . . because that occupation would entail not only the dishonour of the Fatherland but the future loss of nationality . . . [it would be] total ruin for Spain if France—as she longs for and desires—takes possession of that piece of coast, enclosing us within the Pyrenees and her dreamed of Empire in Morocco in order to destroy completely our strategic position in Europe.[5]

The French military relief in May 1911 of Fez, the capital of Morocco besieged by rebels, gave the excuse for the Spanish occupation a month later of the Atlantic coastal town of Larache in the far south west of the Spanish sphere. The nascent colonial party in Spain had persuaded the Liberal president, José Canalejas, to intervene directly in Morocco against his political beliefs. The most prominent advocate of intervention was the young King Alfonso XIII who was in close communication with his colonial officers in Morocco.[6] The overt justification for military action was the threat to the lives and property of the small Spanish colony in the area. In private, Canalejas argued that the French action had stoked up the rebellion against Europeans, and Spain had the right, according to the secret clause of the Franco-Spanish Treaty of 1904, to intervene to restore order. Thus, in correspondence with Maura he insisted on the legitimacy of a temporary police operation. Maura's

---

[3] In a letter to his minister of foreign affairs, the French ambassador to Spain calculated that the number of French officers attached to the sultan's mehallas had quadrupled by 1911 and that effectively the French military had taken control of the Moroccan army: *Documents diplomatiques français*, 2ème série, vol. XIII, doc. 253, pp. 479–82.

[4] Cándido Pardo González, *Al servicio de la verdad* (Madrid, n.p., 1930), 146.

[5] 'La obra de un ex-ministro', *La Correspondencia Militar*, 9 June 1911.

[6] The French ambassador noted the king's passionate concern about French encroachment in Morocco in a conversation with the monarch in early 1911: *Documents Diplomatiques Français*, Doc. 137, pp. 237–40.

reply reveals the deep reluctance of sections of Spain's political elite to get sucked into the Moroccan maelstrom. Any further territorial expansion, he insisted, would damage Spain's interests.[7]

The French and Spanish actions sparked off an international crisis, as Germany responded to the violation of the Algeciras Pact with characteristic heavy-handedness by sending a gunboat to Agadir in July 1911. Franco-German tensions were temporarily eased when, in the bilateral treaty of the same year, drawn up without consulting Spain, the French conceded a huge slice of her colonial possession in the Congo in exchange for a free hand in Morocco. Without the counterbalance of Germany, Spain would now have to rely on British mediation to brake French expansionism, just as she had done, with dubious results, in 1904. The temptation to expand further into Morocco, the unmistakable programme of the Spanish colonial military, became even more difficult to resist.

Occupation of the western area brought Spanish military officers into direct contact with the remarkable leader of the Beni Arós tribe, the sharif Muley Ahmed el Raisuni. Raisuni was a descendant of the patron saint of Morocco, Muley Idris, and therefore part of the theocratic aristocracy exempt from the sultan's taxes and immune to prosecution by the local tribunals of justice. According to some sources, his family had lost much of its wealth after it was attacked by a rival sharifian family. As a result, Raisuni had given up his ambition to be a Moroccan justice of the peace, to devote himself to banditry to restore his family's fortunes. Imprisoned in appalling conditions by Sultan Mulay Abdel Aziz in 1895, and only released in 1900, Raisuni emerged during the first decade of the new century as the most powerful leader in the northwest at a time when the Sultanate was disintegrating.[8] After attempting to crush him, the sultan was forced to recognize his authority by giving him an official position representing the Moroccan state in the area.

As had become the custom in much of northern Morocco by the end of the nineteenth century, Raisuni had enriched himself on the proceeds of banditry against his fellow Moroccans and against European residents alike. The British diplomats Walter Harris and Sir Harry McLean, as well as the Greek-American millionaire Ion Perdicaris (accompanied by his English son-in-law), were all separately kidnapped near Tangier by Raisuni. They each spent a few days in captivity in his headquarters in the mountains before being released for substantial ransoms and all manner of concessions (and after Theodore Roosevelt had sent two cruisers to Moroccan shores to ensure Perdicaris's release).[9]

[7] Duque de Maura and Melchor Fernández Almagro, *Por qué cayó Alfonso XIII*, 2nd edn. (Madrid, Ambos Mundos, 1948), 187 and 192.

[8] Abdel Aziz Khallouk Temsamani, *País Yebala: Majzen, España, y Ahmed Raisúni* (Granada, Editorial Universidad de Granada, 1999).

[9] Ibid.

Raisuni treated his Moroccan prisoners with less regard and maintained his power by savage repression and extortion. Much of his wealth was also raised through taxing villages in the areas he controlled by military force. Representatives of tribes under his rule wrote to the military governor of Ceuta saying they preferred to become Spanish citizens rather than suffer Raisuni as the sultan's governor.[10] Yet, for all his depredations against his fellow countrymen, Raisuni became identified with the struggle to defend Islam against the Christian penetration of Morocco. Against Sultan Abdel Aziz's apparent aping of European values, Raisuni raised the banner of Moroccan traditionalism.[11]

Raisuni's immediate interlocutor with Spain's occupation forces was Lieutenant-Colonel Manuel Fernández Silvestre, who had been named commander-in-chief of the forces shortly after they landed at Larache. Born in Cuba, like many other colonial officers, in 1871 (possibly in the same year as Raisuni), Silvestre was a veteran of the colonial war in Cuba of 1895–8. As a young lieutenant he had been severely wounded in a cavalry charge against the Cuban freedom-fighters. Posted to Spanish Morocco in 1904, he then headed a Spanish military mission to Casablanca in 1908 whose objective, as part of the Algeciras agreement, was to help the French train the native Moroccan police force.[12] Silvestre was a bluff, impetuous cavalry officer with a bristling handlebar moustache, impatient with the ambivalence and prevarications of diplomacy. Attached to the king's court after his mission in Casablanca, he had come to the attention of Alfonso XIII because they shared a passion for Spain's supposed African vocation. His appointment as Commander of the Spanish forces was due largely to the king's intervention.[13]

The dealings between Raisuni and Silvestre were emblematic of the encounter between two very distinct cultures: those of the mountain people of northern Morocco and the Spanish colonial military, and beyond that, those of the Maghreb and Europe. Seated on a carpet opposite the Spanish officer, the astute, massive Raisuni, bearded, hooded, and bloated by dropsy, listened and agreed to the requests made by his counterpart. Like El Rogui, Raisuni appeared to welcome the presence of Spanish troops in the area.[14] Indeed, without his acquiescence Spanish troops could not have landed in Larache. In two earlier interviews with the Spanish envoy in Tangier, Raisuni had expressed his anger against the French for their constant agitation against him, and had suggested that the Spanish were softer and easier to get on with than the French.[15] His opposition to France had encouraged the British to extend

[10] BN García Figueras Archive (GF), *Raisuni*, caja 10, leg. 12, 13 Apr. 1909.
[11] Ibid., leg. 12–13.
[12] Details of Silvestre's background from *Legado Manuel Fernández Silvestre* (Servicio Histórico Militar).
[13] Pando, *Historia*, 54.   [14] BN GF *Raisuni*, caja 10, leg. 6.
[15] Marqués de Villasinda to the minister of foreign affairs, 11 Aug. 1911 in BN GF *Raisuni*, caja 10, leg. 8.

their protection to him. By appearing to agree with the Spaniards, he hoped to have a free hand in his area of influence.

For his part, Silvestre was expected by the Spanish authorities to negotiate a *modus vivendi* with Raisuni that would ensure Spanish control of the crucial western part of Spain's sphere without any further significant military occupation. Silvestre had clearly learnt from Spain's mistaken strategy in the Rif in 1907–9 that he had to work with the *de facto* power in the area rather than try to supplant it. Raisuni's negotiating skills were such that he managed for several months to persuade Silvestre of his pro-Spanish feelings. As international negotiations began in early 1912 to replace the spheres of influence in Morocco with a fully fledged Protectorate, Silvestre nominated Raisuni as his choice for the caliph representing the sultan in the future Protectorate's Spanish sphere.[16]

However, Silvestre soon discovered that Raisuni had no intention of keeping his word. He continued, through the use of force, to raise the taxes he had agreed to end; he failed to withdraw his troops into the interior; he persisted in the acquisition of land through illegal means; and he had secret dealings with German companies. According to Silvestre, Raisuni's protestations of support for Spain were in fact, 'the cloak under which he may hide a policy of obstruction towards our work, although I am more inclined to believe that it responds to the fact that he has not found amongst the kabyles (or tribes) sufficient support to carry out a policy of intransigence towards us . . .'[17] But neither was Silvestre being honest to the Moroccans about Spanish intentions. He was in touch with local anti-Raisuni chieftains, ostensibly to organize a concerted campaign against Raisuni. In fact he was also seeking to occupy their land.[18]

Silvestre was also shocked by Raisuni's treatment of prisoners. In his prison at his headquarters at Arcila, Raisuni kept ninety-eight of his Moroccan enemies chained up in appalling conditions, forty of them on the same chain.[19] While he had been prepared to accept differences of culture, Silvestre could not tolerate the injustices that had become endemic partly as a result of the crumbling of the Sultanate order. Like many other colonial officers, Silvestre went to Morocco convinced that part of his mission there was to instil European civilization amongst semi-civilized tribes, by one means or another. His experience of France's harsh colonial methods in Casablanca had convinced him of the need for resolute action.[20] The continued indulgence of the

---

[16] Raisuni's skills were such that he convinced many Spaniards of his benevolent feelings towards Spain: Rafael López Rienda, *Frente al fracaso. Raisuni. De Silvestre a Burguete* (Madrid, Sociedad General Española de Librería, 1923), 65; Tomás Maestre, *El problema de Marruecos. Polémica periodística* (Melilla, el Telegrama del Rif, 1914), 21–3.

[17] Letter from Silvestre to Villasinda, 2 Oct. 1912, BN GF *Raisuni*, caja 10, leg. 6.

[18] Telegram of 6 Sept. 1911 to the minister of foreign affairs quoted in Mohammad Ibn Azzuz Hakim, *Sharif Raisuni and the Armed Resistance in Northern Morocco* (in Arabic) (Rabat, Sahel, 1981), 31–2.

[19] Letter from Silvestre to the Spanish Government, 24 Jan. 1913, SHM R1014.

[20] Un Africanista más, *La guerra y el problema de África. Unas cuantas verdades por un Africanista más* (Burgos, n.p., 1914), 50–1.

government and the diplomats towards Raisuni's barbarities deeply offended the military man and increased his distaste for politicians.[21]

A more urgent consideration for Silvestre was that Raisuni's persistent violation of their agreements was undermining his own authority. In a letter to the Spanish envoy in Tangier, he complained about 'the scorn Raisuni feels for me and the poor state of my authority, which I cannot impose within the framework of compromises and prudence in which I am supposed to operate, but have to resign myself to let him do whatever he wants, with the consequent and hardly favourable judgements about our tacit, humble, and servile acquiescence in his acts shared by Moors of all classes when commenting on our, for them, inexplicable passivity'. Raisuni's lack of 'respect and obedience' towards Spanish rule could only be overcome by 'the virility typical of a nation which, moved always by a paternalist spirit, will spare no measures, however violent, to extirpate the causes opposed systematically to the implantation of the new regime and the implementation of the high mission with which we have been entrusted'.[22] Virility, violence, paternalism, and high mission were all terms encapsulating the self-image of the traditional Spanish colonial officer.

Nevertheless, the government was well aware that confronting Raisuni meant stoking the fires of Moroccan resistance to Spanish penetration. However distasteful the contact with the mountain chief was, a policy of compromise was unavoidable, because while the campaign in the east continued there were neither the resources nor the public support for a fresh war in another part of Morocco. The differences between Silvestre and the government typified the fissure between the colonial military and civilian rule that had grown since 1909. Raisuni neatly summed up Silvestre's restless and forthright personality in their last meeting. No doubt the interview was subject to much reconstruction afterwards, but Spanish accounts agree on the substance of his comments. In the original version, he was supposed to say to Silvestre: 'You and I together make the storm; you are the furious wind; and I am the calm sea. You arrive and blow irritatedly; I become agitated, stir and break out in foam. There you have the storm. But between you and me there is a difference; I, like the sea never move from my place, and you, like the wind, are never in yours, in one place alone.'[23]

Without consulting the government, Silvestre proceeded to occupy Raisuni's headquarters, free his prisoners, and disband his troops in Arcila on 30 November 1912. The Spanish government, deeply concerned that his actions might harm delicate negotiations with the French over the shape of the coming Franco-Spanish Protectorate, forced Silvestre to back down once again. As part of its efforts to win over the Moroccan elites to Spanish colonial

---

[21] Letter from Silvestre to Villasinda on 6 Dec. 1912 in BN GF *Raisuni*, caja 10, leg. 6 and to Alfau on 9 Apr. 1913 in ibid., caja 9, leg. 4, exp. 3.

[22] Ibid., 6 Dec. 1912. Most Spanish reports referred mistakenly to Raisuni as Raisuli.

[23] Manuel L. Pichardo Ortega, *España en Marruecos. El Raisuni* (Madrid, n.p., 1917), 112.

rule, the government also attempted unsuccessfully to entice Raisuni to Spain with his retinue, to have an interview with the king. Silvestre finally lost patience, occupied Arcila once again, liberated Raisuni's prisoners, and seized his family as hostage. When he was ordered to retract, Silvestre resigned. In a letter to the minister of war on 5 February, he wrote, 'I prefer to sacrifice my dearest hopes as a military man rather than back a policy I consider mistaken'.[24] Pressure from the government induced him to remain. Raisuni's family was released. But continued negotiations for a settlement led nowhere, and a new Spanish protégé was named as caliph of the Spanish Protectorate in April 1913. Raisuni withdrew into the mountains to begin war against the Spanish.[25] Advocates of military occupation could only have felt vindicated.

In view of the approaching redefinition of the colonial spheres of influence, the government was sympathetic to the expansionism of the military because it wished to stake out its claims in Morocco against those of the French. In these operations, Spain's political leaders were now willing to give full backing to the shelling of civilian targets. In the colonial wars waged by European powers in the new century, killing civilians was no longer a serious moral issue, especially since the French had set the trend in Casablanca in 1907. Indeed, as early as the 1840s France had waged total war against all the Algerian partisans of Abdel Kader, destroying their crops and animals and killing men, women, and children.[26]

What posed a greater problem were Spanish casualties and the mounting costs of operations that were turning into a protracted campaign. The Moroccan fighters seldom sought direct engagements with Spanish troops. They simply fell back when the enemy advanced in order to regroup and attack the vulnerable parts from the side or in the rearguard, making intelligent use of the terrain. The Spanish military conundrum was that no advance was of any value unless it led to occupation, but the front was too broad and the number of troops too few for such a strategy. They were well aware of Lyautey's dictum that an expedition not followed by occupation left 'a memory as fleeting as that of the wake of a ship crossing the sea'.[27] For their part, the Rifians were clearly familiar with a vital principle of guerrilla warfare against a stronger enemy, formulated decades later by the Vietcong general Vo Nguyen Giap: if the enemy masses his forces he loses ground; if he scatters he loses his strength. It was a contradiction the Spanish high command would fail to overcome during the next ten years.

The fortuitous death in action in May of the main leader of the resistance in the east, Mohammad Amzian (clutching a Mauser, with a pistol in his belt and

[24] *Historia de la campañas*, ii. 886.

[25] J. Causse, 'Le Remplacement de general Alfau et la campagne du Djebala', *L'Afrique Francaise*, 9: 8 (Aug. 1913), 330–1.

[26] Bruce Vandervort, *Wars of Imperial Conquest in Africa 1830–1914* (London, UCL, 1998), 68.

[27] *La Correspondencia Militar*, 11 Sept. 1911.

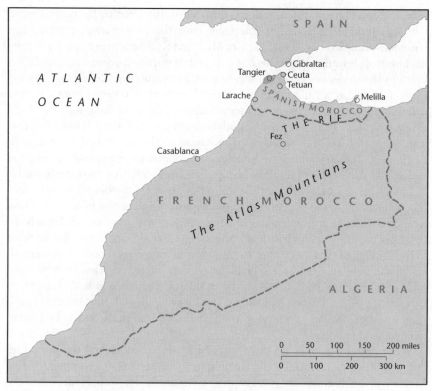

MAP 1   Spanish and French Protectorates in Morocco 1912

a rosary and a copy of the Koran in his jellaba), brought concerted resistance against Spanish penetration in the east to an end. The Kert riverbed remained, for several years, the natural frontier between the pacified and unpacified regions of the eastern part of the Spanish sphere, across which the 'untamed' tribes continued to make brief and bloody incursions.

The virtual collapse of the sultan's order in Morocco led to the Treaty of Fez on 27 November 1912, whereby the international community agreed to transform the French and Spanish spheres of influence into a Protectorate. The creation of protectorates was the means by which colonial powers propped up their client states when they were in danger of collapsing. They did so professedly to defend the traditional authorities and extend European civilization. But the very weakness of these states derived above all from the penetration of European colonial interests and the competition between them. Behind the façade of an indigenous state, the colonial powers took over trade, foreign policy, and internal and external security. Where that state was no longer appropriate, such as the Khedive dynasty under the British Protectorate in Egypt in 1914, the colonial powers simply dismantled it.

Officially Spain was co-protector of Morocco, but in practice it sublet its area from France because negotiations with the Moroccan government were always conducted through the French authorities. Ostensibly, the colonial administrative structure was designed to complement that of the sultan's government in order to strengthen it. In reality, the two colonial powers were now in charge. The sultan's representative in the Spanish part of the Protectorate was a caliph who had to be selected from amongst his numerous extended families. But the sultan could choose from only two candidates previously selected by the Spanish High Command. Likewise, the sultan's government in the Spanish Protectorate was largely picked by the Spanish embassy in Tangier. Thus, both the caliph and his administrators were expected to collaborate with the colonial power, but neither had any authority amongst Moroccans.

The weakness of Spanish colonial rule was largely a consequence of the weakness of the Sultanate. There was no effective hierarchy of power in Morocco that the Spanish could use to their advantage. This was the considered view of the first Spanish high commissioner, General Alfau, who was at the apex of Spanish military and civilian organization. It was also recognized in the Treaty of Fez itself, because it invested both he and the French high commissioner with the power to intervene in the Moroccan administration if they so chose. The quality of candidates for the position of caliph chosen by Spain and the sultan can be gathered from Alfau's comment about the first of the sultan's representatives in the new order, 'a beardless, fat, and apathetic young man'.[28]

Unlike its French equivalent, where civil and military affairs were separate, the Spanish Protectorate was run almost entirely by the military. The area was divided into three High Commands, Melilla, Ceuta, and Larache. Beneath them, administration outside the occupied towns was run by the Service of Military Intervention, manned by officers and ultimately responsible, like their superiors, to the Ministry of War. The army was entrusted with the bulk of work: day-to-day security operations, contacts with tribes, collection of taxes, and law and order. Civil affairs in the relatively small occupied areas were organized into three departments—native affairs, finance, and economy and communications—and staffed both by officers and by civilians employed by the Ministry of the Interior but also directly responsible to the military High Command.[29]

As a blueprint it was an orderly model but in execution it suffered from major flaws. The Spanish Treasury was far too weak to fund both military

[28] In a telegraphic exchange with the minister of war, General Luque, on 12 June 1913 in Archivo Romanones (AR), leg. 17, carp. 4 (1).

[29] Hernández Herrera and García Figueras, *Acción de España*, ii. 56–71; Ramón Salas Larrazábal, *El protectorado de España en Marruecos* (Madrid, Mapfre, 1992).

operations and infrastructural investment in Morocco, all the more so because there was no popular support and little elite backing for colonialism amongst Spaniards. Colonial administration required skilled and experienced officers, but very few Spanish officers spoke either Arabic or the local dialect, shelja, and many were imbued with an instinctive racism towards Moroccans or at best a heavy-handed paternalism.[30] Least of all did they understand the role they were supposed to carry out as supposed guardians of the Moroccan order. After a tour of the Spanish Protectorate in July 1913, a Liberal MP reported that 'the functionaries and authorities named and established there by the Spanish Government haven't a clue what the Spanish Protectorate is, with the result that they all operate as if the mission of Spain and her agents was to govern and administer directly, as if they were exercising sovereignty'.[31]

A third problem was demarcating authority at each level of administration. The high commissioner received orders from both the Ministry of War and the Ministry of State, with the result that there was much duplication. A royal decree of April 1913 also complicated matters by giving the commanders of the military regions the autonomy 'necessary for the better execution and fulfilment of the functions they have been assigned'.[32] This power made some sense in a country where communications hardly existed, but it was to cause grievous problems in the future. The problem of defining the line of command was exacerbated by the king's desire to intervene in military affairs as the nominal head of the armed forces. Another royal decree of 14 January 1914 gave him the right to communicate directly with officers without consulting either the government or the military hierarchy.[33]

Tetuan, a holy city for the Moroccans, became the capital of the Spanish Protectorate. For Spain, Tetuan also had a strong historical resonance. In the Spanish–Moroccan War of 1859–60, Spanish troops had conquered the city, only for the British to insist on their immediate withdrawal. Its renewed occupation was seen by the Spanish colonial military as a historical task left unfinished. Alfau had prepared the invasion of the city with great care, going as far as concealing the objective of his operations from his own officers. The local pasha had been won over by various inducements, including one of the many Spanish decorations. The Spanish government got cold feet at the last minute, but Alfau had reassured ministers that their occupation would not provoke the townspeople.[34] Spanish troops entered the city on 18 February 1913 without a shot being fired. Alfau had issued orders that the soldiers should not stop in

[30] The commander of the Melilla region, General Gómez-Jordana, complained in 1913 that the Spanish officers commanding native police 'lacked the preparation to carry out such a delicate service': SHM R266, leg. 117, carp. 4. For further discussion of racism amongst officers see Chs. 6 and 7.

[31] AR leg. 17, carp. 9 (3).

[32] Real Orden del Ministerio de Guerra relativa a las atribuciones militares del Alto Comisario, 24 April 1913 in *Acción de España*, 70–1.

[33] SHM R273, leg. 124.

[34] Larios, *España en Marruecos*, 69; *Heraldo de Madrid*, 10 Feb. 1913; SHM R1014.

front of mosques, nor stare at the women, nor do anything that might upset local religious customs. He made the mistake, however, of escorting the new caliph into the city, thereby reinforcing the impression that he was a Spanish puppet.[35]

Although welcomed by many of its citizens, the occupation of the holy city fired up the anger of nearby Moroccan chieftains.[36] The most decided opponent of Spain was the sherif Mohammad Ben Sidi Lahsen, who masterminded the creation of military brotherhoods funded by the tribes to oppose any further Spanish expansion. When exhorted by the caliph to sit down and negotiate with the Spanish, he replied that he had no confidence in them. 'They are not like the English or like the French who respect our religion and our customs in Egypt just as in Algeria or Tunisia. The Spanish respect nothing and hate our religion. Never speak to us of peace. Nobody wants to hear the word. From El Hauz to the Rif we are all prepared for the holy war and we will triumph with the help of God.'[37]

As the first high commissioner, Alfau was forced to seek the creation of a security cordon around the city stretching 8 kilometres on all sides. The degree of resistance by the local inhabitants and the resulting toll of casualties on either side took him and his advisers by surprise. Spanish encroachment was firing up the anger of many local inhabitants, not least because it disrupted their traditional trading routes and was beginning to undermine the local economy. It also became clear that Raisuni, for all his pro-Spanish protestations, was joining the agitation in order to avoid becoming marginalized in the new jihad. Alfau's request for a further 10,000 soldiers to add to the 10,000 already on duty in the area aroused the anger of the minister of war, who accused him of inconsistency and lack of foresight.[38] Once again, the scale of problems faced by the colonial army had been underestimated.

Alfau liked to think of himself as an enlightened colonialist who preferred to use the carrot rather than the stick.[39] Like so many of his colleagues in the years to follow, Moroccan insurgency led him increasingly to rely on the stick. Those who opposed the Spanish advance were treated savagely. The consequence was the increasing brutalization of Spanish colonial officers. Adopting an old custom in Morocco, Alfau resorted to the beheading of prisoners to instil fear. A brief exchange recorded in the transcript of a telegraphic communication reveals the growing brutality among colonial officers that has been concealed ever since in official or semi-official accounts. Speaking with the minister of war in June 1913, Alfau remarked: 'It is very useful to decapitate the

[35] Causse, 'Le Remplacement', 332–3.

[36] According to Alfau in a telegram to the minister of state, most of the Tetuan population went into the streets to greet the Spanish troops, including many women, 'a rare thing given their religion': AFAMM leg. 387/22.

[37] Khallouk Temsamani, *País Yebala*, 89.   [38] AGA M156, exp. 4; AR leg. 17, carp. 4 (1).

[39] In his suave dealings with journalists, he liked to stress the point: e.g. Larios, *España en Marruecos*, 69.

Moors for the moral effect it has on the masses, but it is best not to say that we agree to it.' General Luque replied: 'That sort of severity seems insignificant to me, so you can decapitate all the Moors you want, but our civilization does not allow us to make it public, so you can tell it to me and on this matter I shall conceal the truth.'[40]

Luque's comment reveals the growing gap between the practice of colonialism and the notional standards of civilized behaviour accepted in the metropolis. Colonial officers would increasingly feel alienated from Spanish opinion which criticized them for taking the necessary measures, however unpalatable, to bring civilization to the semi-savage cultures. Indeed, civilization became the rationalization for uncivilized behaviour. Spain was in Morocco, according to this thinking, through the divine law of history. Only idealists or the faint-hearted could expect progress to be peaceful. The advance of civilization was inexorably marked by blood.[41] The assumption was that the Moroccans who opposed Spanish penetration should be killed for the good of Morocco.

This rationalization of brutality had been common amongst colonial powers for at least 60 years. The strategy of total war against anti-colonial resistance, for example, had been adopted by the French would-be conqueror of Algeria, General Thomas-Robert Bugeaud in the 1840s. Justifying his asphyxiation by smoke of 500 Arab men, women, and children, he had said, 'Far from being ineffective or dangerous, such liquidations would finally convince the natives that they had no choice but "to accept the yoke of conquest".' Similarly, the German general appointed to crush the Herero revolt in German South-West Africa in 1904, Lothar von Trotha, had stated in a letter, 'I know the tribes of Africa. They are all alike. They only respond to force. It was and is my policy to use force with terrorism and even brutality. I shall annihilate the revolting tribes with streams of blood and streams of gold. Only after a complete uprooting will something emerge.'[42]

Alfau's inability to restore order in the outskirts of Tetuan led to increasing doubts within the government and doubts amongst his military colleagues. The resistance against the Spanish had led Alfau to extend his operations along the supply routes between Tetuan, Ceuta, Larache, and Tangier. At strategic points above these roads, after numerous clashes with the local muhayeddin, he began to build small forts that would be permanently occupied. The toll of dead and wounded resulting from the enemy's tactic of isolated and multiple ambushes began deeply to concern public opinion in Spain.

The assassination on 12 November 1912 of the outstanding reformist leader of the Liberals, Canalejas, removed Alfau's boss and let in the wily Liberal of the old school, Count Romanones, as the new president. The count had different plans for Morocco. One of his many eccentric ideas, eventually

---

[40] AR leg. 17, carp. 4 (1).   [41] 'Agresiones de los moros', El Ejército Español, 6 June 1913.
[42] Both quotes from Vandervort, Wars, 68 and 198.

discarded, was that the state should pay a private company to raise an army of mercenaries to replace the conscript troops that were doing so badly in Morocco.[43] Popular opposition to the dispatch of further troops compounded the problem. Romanones admitted in private that he was conscripting soldiers from different provinces 'in order not to draw attention too much in each'.[44] His instructions to Alfau were impeccably correct according to the terms agreed by the European powers. The high commissioner should seek no further expansion and work with local authorities, because 'the indigenous authority is that which should function, directed and counselled by the agent of the protecting state'. Properly trained colonial officers should know the habits, customs, and feuds of the 'natives'. Exquisite tact was necessary, backed by financial handouts to chieftains and jobs on the public works. Any transgressions should be punished immediately and harshly in accordance with the French model, but the repression should be carried out by the sultan's troops.[45]

Romanones made clear his impatience with Alfau's inability to carry out these precepts in a letter to the king on 7 July 1913. Alfau's '24,000 troops' were too many for a police operation and too few for the punishment and destruction of the rebels. As high commissioner, Alfau had failed, according to the president, both in his military and civil functions.[46] But in response to Romanones's impatience, Alfau complained that the reinforcements he was being sent from Spain were of no use to him. His officers were having to sacrifice themselves to make up for the poor quality of the soldiers, who were reluctant even to fire a rifle. A field battery that accompanied the new recruits was in such a bad state that it had to be withdrawn from the battlefield for repairs.[47] But some of Alfau's subordinates made a scathing criticism of his military strategy. A staff officer serving in Morocco wrote to an MP friend that Alfau's continuation of war when he should be governing the peace was criminal. '[W]hile Alfau and Silvestre are those who represent Spain there will be no peace or hope.'[48]

However, like many of his predecessors and successors, Romanones was inconsistent over Moroccan strategy. His government approved of a plan to invade one of the most restless areas in the Protectorate by landing troops in the Bay of Al Hoceima.[49] This bay would become the focus of countless blueprints for the suppression of Moroccan dissidence until the landing was finally carried out in 1925. The plan was suspended in the summer of 1913 when

[43] Pando, *Historia*, 64–5 (from AR leg. 17).   [44] AR leg. 6 (2) /8 (30).
[45] Ibid.   [46] AR leg. 6 (1), carp. 1.
[47] Telegram from Alfau to Romanones, 28 June 1913, in AR leg. 17, carp. 3 (8).
[48] Letter of 9 Aug. 1913 from General Servando Marenco, head of the General Staff in Ceuta, to Pedro Rodríguez Borbolla, MP for Seville: AR leg. 6 (2), carp. 8 (17). Alfau's own commander-general in the Ceuta region, General Menacho, had made his opposition to his operations outside Tetuan clear to the government. For the serious divergence between Alfau and Menacho, see letter from the minister of war to Alfau, 5 July 1913, in AR carp. 8 (9). For Berenguer's criticism see AR leg. 58, carp. 4.
[49] Telegram from High Commissioner Berenguer to the minister of state, 3 Dec. 1921, AGA caja M7 81/03.

Raisuni's growing restlessness diverted attention away from the eastern zone. Having replaced Alfau with General Marina in August 1913, Romanones advocated the continued cleansing of the area around Tetuan and an even more hazardous military operation into Raisuni's heartland through the international enclave of Tangier.[50]

In fact, the conundrum of keeping the peace and maintaining the façade of Moroccan authority repeatedly frustrated the neo-colonial intentions of politicians and inclined them towards the aggressive colonialism increasingly espoused by the military in the Protectorate. One of the exceptions amongst the officers was the new high commissioner, Marina, veteran of the 1909 campaign and an enlightened Arabist. As commander-general of Melilla he had banned the traditional anti-Jewish ceremonies of Easter Saturday in deference to the many local Jews, and, as we have seen, had marked the dawn and sundown of every day of the Muslim Ramadan with an artillery salvo. He had also reached a peace agreement with leaders of the Anjera tribe, who occupied one of the most strategically sensitive areas in north-western Morocco between Ceuta and Tangier.[51]

The lesson Marina had learnt from the 1909 experience was that the local balance of power had to be respected. In the western part of the Protectorate, that meant bringing Silvestre to heel and enticing the ambiguous Raisuni back into the Spanish fold. The former would claim, from his own experience, that Raisuni was an unavowed, implacable enemy of Spain. Silvestre's own officers believed that the chieftain was subverting Spanish efforts to win over the tribes, particularly through the medium of his go-between, the rich and influential local notable Sidi Ali Ben Ahmed Akalay, who had been in contact with Marina and foreign embassies in Tangier. The high commissioner was convinced Akalay was pursuing terms of peace between Spain and Raisuni. He had thus issued him with a safe-conduct pass to enable him to get through Spanish lines. Silvestre's officers in the native police headquarters were working closely with a bitter local rival of Raisuni. With a handful of his men, they intercepted Akalay and his servant on 12 May 1915 and murdered them, throwing their bodies into a stream and burning Marina's pass. The bodies reappeared further down stream at the mouth of the river and were fished out by Moroccan fishermen.

Silvestre's first reaction was to defend his men. Marina steamed to Larache on a warship and ordered the immediate arrest of those implicated in the murders.[52] A military investigation found Silvestre's three officers guilty but sen-

[50] Letter to Antonio Maura, 13 Aug. 1913, AR leg. 35 (16).

[51] Letter for the king's information on 19 Aug. 1914 from the Tangier Spanish Legation in Archivo General del Palacio Real (AGPR), caja 15599/16. For the Jewish and Muslim ceremonies, see Morales, *Datos*, 383.

[52] 'Mediación de Alí Alkalai: asesinato', BN GF *Raisuni*, caja 9, leg. 4, exp. 5, 1915; letter from General Marenco to Romanones AR leg. 58, carp. 2 (2); Pando, *Historia*, 66–7.

tenced them to light jail terms. The whole matter was hushed up, and a year later they were secretly released. There is no evidence to suggest that Silvestre had approved of the action; indeed, given his sense of military propriety, he is unlikely to have sanctioned it. However, there can be little doubt that his enmity towards Raisuni and the belligerent and racist culture of his head-quarters deeply influenced those serving under him. Silvestre's feelings towards his enemy can be gauged by his letter to Alfau, in which he stated that 'everything that smells of the influence of such an odious personage should be drowned in blood, if necessary'.[53] The captain who led the action against Akalay wrote to Silvestre after his imprisonment that the general was the 'only man who had found the formula for extending our civilization without the need to approach the Moors with charity or bribery but . . . by treating them as an inferior race, a race led and guided through teaching towards our heights'.[54] With customary ambiguity, the government, now under Conservative administration, resolved the dispute over military strategy in Morocco by dismissing both Silvestre and Marina whilst simultaneously awarding them the highest military decorations. Silvestre was appointed aide-de-camp to the king, and Marina was posted to the Ministry of War.

The new high commissioner, Francisco Gómez Jordana, a short, tubby, and engaging man, was a disciple of Marina. As such, in the eyes of the uncom-promising colonialist wing of the military, he was yet another advocate of 'charity and bribery'. As commander-in-chief of the Melilla region under Marina, Jordana had been tough on abuses committed by his own soldiers against Moroccans.[55] But he had also brought some order into his zone by multiplying the number of native police. With government agreement he had tried to win over tribes by loaning them seeds and accepting repayment in kind, with the result that many Rifians were able to stay in their villages in win-ter rather than migrate to Algeria for work. He had also set up a committee of Moroccans to oversee the protection of Muslim cemeteries and sanctuaries, and had created an Arab school in Melilla.[56]

During his period of office as high commissioner between 1915 and the end of 1918, Jordana made tireless efforts to pacify the tribes opposed to Spanish presence by combining the stick and the carrot. He was in any case under strict instructions from the government to maintain the status quo in Morocco so as not to upset the balance of power in northern Africa during the First World War. The French had withdrawn many of their troops to fight on the Western Front, and the Germans had redoubled their efforts to gain allies amongst

---

[53] 9 Apr. 1913 in BN GF *Raisuni*, caja 9, leg. 4, exp. 3.
[54] SHM Legado Manuel Fernández Silvestre, carp. 4 (quoted in Pando, *Historia*, 68); Un Africanista más, *La guerra*, 50–1.
[55] SHM R251, carp. 7.
[56] Teniente General Gómez-Jordana Souza, Conde de Jordana, *La tramoya de nuestra actuació en Marruecos* (Madrid, Editora Nacional, 1976), 23–4.

Moroccan chieftains such as Raisuni. With the Spanish consul in Tangier and other enlightened colonial officers under his command, such as his replacement in Melilla, General Luis Aizpuru, Jordana set about winning support from Moroccans by providing work, free grain, and medical surgeries, and protection for the crops of pro-Spanish groups. He approached tribal chieftains and offered them regular payments and other forms of support. The Office of Native Affairs was strengthened and officers were encouraged to cultivate local tribes by attending key social events, such as weddings and circumcisions. The network of tribes or fractions of tribes receiving money from Spain in exchange for information and military support was extended.[57]

But Jordana was also prepared to bear down on any opposition to Spanish hegemony. The most important military campaign of his period as high commissioner was in the rugged Anjera region in the northernmost part of the Protectorate in 1916, where he employed 20,000 soldiers to quell unrest exacerbated by German agents, and to establish new defensive positions. He used tribal divisions and blood-feuds among Moroccans to mobilize pro-Spanish tribal groups against those who were not collaborating. The latter were fined or their land was occupied by Spanish troops. Their houses were burnt down, their crops destroyed, and they were prevented from sowing seed. The result was often starvation. Another policy used to some effect was the elimination where possible of the *haqq* fine, a system designed by the tribes to regulate feuds at all levels. Without this form of primary justice, Moroccans were more likely to turn against each other than against the Spanish.[58] For enlightened colonialists such as himself, the combination of reward and punishment was seen as the necessary contradiction of progress.

Another of Jordana's problems was dealing with the abuses committed by his own men. Military secrecy and the tacit agreement by most of the press to refrain from criticizing the behaviour of officers meant that we have only occasional and confidential references to these abuses. Allowing for some exaggeration from anti-military sources, it is clear that verbal abuse of Moroccans and Jews by Spanish officers was common and that occasionally it turned to physical violence, especially when officers got drunk. It appears also that some officers stole beams, doors, windows, and tiles from Moroccan and Jewish homes to build their own houses in Tetuan. Corruption was rife in the garrison towns. For example, officers compensated for their relatively low salaries by setting up businesses, some of which were rewarded by exclusive contracts to supply the Spanish colonial administration, thereby destroying local services or industries.[59] Jordana was hardly in a position to change the culture of nepotism and

---

[57] Madariaga, *España*, 397–8.

[58] Evidence of Lt.-Col. Riquelme to the Comisión de Responsabilidades in *De Anual a la República. La Comisión de Responsabilidades* (Madrid, Javier Morata, 1931), apéndice, p. 137; *Boletín Oficial de la zona del Protectorado Español* (henceforth BOZPEM), 1916 and 1917; *El Telegrama del Rif*, 22 Nov. 1918.

[59] AR 58 37(1). For further discussion of these abuses see Ch. 8.

patronage so typical of Spain, but he clearly tried hard to stamp out racist violence against Moroccans. For all his efforts, the abuses continued and their effect must have turned even the most sympathetic Moroccans against Spain.

The Moroccan collaborators of the Spanish were not all guided solely by money or the search for protection against their internal enemies. A number of them believed that co-operation with Spanish colonialism was more fruitful for Morocco than opposition. Spain might bring some of the benefits of modernity to a poor and semi-feudal society without imposing direct rule, unlike the French in their sphere of Morocco. As long as Spain did not encroach any further into their territory, modernization might eventually create the basis for the independence of the Rif.

The outstanding modernizers in the Rif were the influential family of the Abdel Krims, who belonged to the large tribe of the Beni Uriaghel. The father, Sidi Abdel Krim el Khattabi, was a notable Islamic judge in the town of Ajdir who had established close contact with the Spanish authorities. He was rewarded by substantial and regular payments and military decorations for himself and his family. His two sons both benefited from the family's collaboration. The younger one was given a grant to study mine engineering in Madrid, while the elder, who like his father had become an Islamic judge, was given a job as editor of the Arabic section of the Melilla Spanish paper, *El Telegrama del Rif*, and as instructor of Arabic to Spanish colonial officers. In that post he became a close collaborator of one of the most active and enlightened of Jordana's officers of the native police, José Riquelme.

The Abdel Krims also profited from the sale of mining and oil exploration rights in their lands to European companies. Those profits would in due time be used to finance a rebellion against the Spanish when, under new colonial administration, they began to invade the Rif.[60] The family had become so intimately identified with Spanish colonial rule that they had been forced to flee to the Spanish-held island off Al Hoceima, and their house was burnt down and several of their relatives killed. Yet their co-operation with the Spanish was driven by pragmatism. Their heart was with the Moroccan resistance against colonial penetration, but their mind counselled the advantages of collaboration. A letter from Mohammed Ben Abdel Krim to his father on the occasion of Mohammad Amzian's death in 1912 reveals his sadness at the death of an outstanding muhayeddin, but in it he advises his father to demonstrate 'ostensible courtesy' by congratulating the Spanish on their victory.[61]

Relations between the Spanish authorities and the Abdel Krims became problematic at the beginning of the First World War. During the 1911 Agadir crisis, the elder son, Mohammed, had become known to the French authorities when he wrote virulently anti-French and pro-German articles in the *El*

[60] Galbán, *España*, 41–97.
[61] The letter is quoted in full in Madariaga, *España*, 403–4. Madariaga vividly describes the tragic side of their pragmatic collaboration as that of the 'face' and the 'mask'.

Telegrama del Rif. The Abdel Krims' pro-Central Powers alignment in 1914 was due not only to their opposition to French imperialism in North Africa but also to their support for Turkey in the war, a support shared by most Muslims in the Mediterranean. Even before war broke out, German agents had been active in Spanish Morocco, seeking to encourage pro-German and anti-French sentiments. Their activity during the war disrupted relations with Spanish authorities by providing alternative sources of money, goods, and arms. As a consequence, the opponents of Spanish rule began to bind together. Abdel Krim later confessed that he had held negotiations with a German agent in 1914 who promised to finance an uprising against the French.[62]

Mohammed Abdel Krim was interviewed in 1915 by the head of the local Office of Native Affairs and openly declared his detestation of the French and his desire for the independence of the Rif. Well aware that Spain was a minor power in international relations, Abdel Krim offered a deal in which the Spanish could keep a small part of the Protectorate in exchange for acceding to the creation of a Republic of the Rif. No doubt fearing French reaction to the Abdel Krims' pro-Central Powers activities, Jordana ordered the arrest of the head of the family, but in his place Mohammed Abdel Krim was detained in September by a reluctant Riquelme and imprisoned. Four months later he tried to escape from his cell down a rope provided by his followers. The rope snapped and he fell and broke a leg, an injury which left him permanently lame.[63] Abdel Krim's experience was unlikely to have made him enamoured of the Spanish authorities, but he continued to maintain for several more years a pragmatic policy of collaboration with them, despite intense harassment by other tribes or fractions of tribes.

Jordana's relations with Raisuni were even more difficult. The Spanish government had insisted on a rapprochement with the chieftain after the rupture over Akalay's murder. But Raisuni's ambiguous collaboration with the Spanish army was causing him problems with his own people. An example of the volatility of their relations was the affair in February 1918 over three Spanish civilians who made a living selling drink and other goods to the military columns. They were caught by Raisuni's people burning wood for charcoal beyond the agreed front line and therefore damaging local property. No doubt to impress his followers, Raisuni threatened to withdraw to his mountain stronghold and break relations with Spain; the matter was settled by a humble apology on the part of Jordana.[64]

---

[62] In his subsequent trial Abdel Krim was acquitted, thanks in part to the support he received from Riquelme, who was acting as his defence lawyer in the military court: Madariaga, *España y el Rif*, 415. See also J. Roger-Matthieu (ed.), *Mémoires d'Abd-el-Krim* (Paris, n.p., 1927), 60–1. See also Cándido Lobera, 'La derrota de los Centrales y las cábilas marroquíes', *El Telegrama del Rif*, 7 Dec. 1918.

[63] Roger-Matthieu (ed.), *Mémoires*, 86–7; evidence of Riquelme to the Comisión de Responsabilidades in *De Anual*, apéndice, 117–18; Ayache, *Les Origines*, 217–19.

[64] SHM caja 52/6.

By the summer of 1918 Raisuni was threatening to start war again. At the same time, the high commissioner was under intense pressure from some of his own officers to bring to an end the 'humiliating' compromises with the chieftain.[65] In a last attempt at reconciliation, he sent a top-flight delegation to see Raisuni, including the Spanish consul in Tangier and the manager of the Spanish company responsible for the exploitation of Moroccan agricultural land. Raisuni agreed to continue his collaboration in exchange for further arms, munitions, and money, including 1 million pesetas-worth of shares in the company. The manager also arranged for a dentist to be transported with his dentist's chair to treat Raisuni in his mountain retreat, and the chieftain's son was invited to Ceuta with his retinue of soldiers to travel on the new railway. The Spanish government agreed to pay Raisuni the money but decided against giving him arms and munitions, on the grounds that he might use them against his Moroccan rivals in the French protectorate.[66]

Deeply frustrated by repeated concessions to the 'enemy', many Spanish colonial officers grew restive. Their contempt for the government in Spain turned into anger when it caved in to the revolt by metropolitan officers for equal pay and promotion for those on active service in Morocco and those living quiet lives in the mainland garrisons or at home. The rebellion of the so-called Juntas de Defensa in June 1917 came behind a wave of labour agitation throughout Spain sparked by the hardship caused by wartime inflation. It also coincided with the revolt of the Catalan bourgeoisie and middle-classes against the political system of the Restoration after the government had imposed new taxes on industry. The government was forced to resign and the new Liberal administration gave in to the demands of the officers, instituting a closed-scale system of promotion based exclusively on length of service, and abolishing the generous bonuses awarded to officers on campaign in Morocco. The effect on the Army of Africa was devastating. The reforms embittered colonial officers not just against the Restoration system but against their own fellow officers in the metropolis. They could not easily express their anger in public, but others did it for them. *El Telegrama del Rif* launched a passionate defence of the colonial officers, 'enthusiastically giving up their youth on behalf of our Protectorate until one day they look around them and, seeing themselves alone, without incentives, without justice being done to their deeds, perhaps passed over [in promotions] by favouritism, give up and turn into furious critics of our action'.[67]

Six days after the editorial appeared, Jordana wrote a long and impassioned letter to the new prime minister of yet another Liberal government, Count Romanones, in which he listed the grievances of the Army of Africa. One of the most serious problems he faced was the military reform of 1917. As a result

---

[65] 'Raisuni', BN García Figueras Archive, doc 6/12.   [66] Ibid.
[67] 'Al margen del problema de Marruecos', 12 Nov. 1918.

of this reform there was little demand among officers for posts that used to be highly coveted, such as in the Native Troops. This indicated that nobody wanted to serve in Morocco, and that those who came did so out of obligation, and from the moment of their arrival thought only of their departure. 'There are very few who go as far as to expose their lives in combat and submit themselves to the hardships of campaign life . . . when they can do service in the Peninsula in much greater comfort and without risk.' Instead, he went on, Spain should be studying how to get officers to stay in Africa for as long as possible, so that they could get to know the country and the problem, and acquire a love for it, the only means whereby the High Command could be properly supported.

The bulk of Jordana's letter was devoted to the excruciating dilemma in which he said he had been placed during four years of placating Raisuni. 'The sharif is a difficult man, with a violent character and very distrustful. To deal with him and not end the meeting within five minutes, it is necessary to be armed with patience.' Were it not for Jordana's sense of duty, he would have turned his back on Raisuni, 'leaving him with his words in his mouth'. So he made out to be a good friend of the sharif when in fact he 'detested him more than anyone else'. During the period in which the status quo had to be maintained, Jordana 'was given a thousand reasons by Raisuni to break with him and it required a superhuman effort on his part not to do so', for which he was despised by his fellow officers. The result of his tolerance was that Raisuni now ruled in the west, 'perfectly convinced that we dare not break with him'. The end of the First World War now counselled a change of strategy. Raisuni must be told to respect the authority of the Mahkzen, return all the rifles and mules he stole from the Spanish troops, and commit himself to peace. Unless he did so, military action was required, 'a very limited surgical operation followed by a rapid staunching of the wound with the building of schools and dispensaries . . .'. If there was no resolute action of this kind, the Protectorate would have to be abandoned. If the government did not make a clear commitment to adopt this course, Jordana would resign.[68]

The ink had hardly dried on his signature before Jordana died of a heart attack at his desk. His death was no doubt hastened by the strain of balancing government policy, Moroccan resistance, and military belligerence. His replacement by General Dámaso Berenguer signalled the adoption of the policy he had recommended in his letter and the end of accommodation with Moroccan resistance to Spanish penetration. Now that the First World War had concluded, the Spanish government was free to pursue a more aggressive policy towards its 'colonial subjects'. In a speech in parliament in February 1919, Prime Minister Romanones made a coy but unmistakable statement of the new strategy in the west zone of the Protectorate: 'what happened with

---

[68] Jordana letter to Romanones on 18 Nov. 1918, AGPR 12956/16. See also Galbán, *España*, 128–9.

Raisuni is what happens in life with all people. A man can be useful today and, however, can be harmful tomorrow, and because he was very useful to us in some circumstances this does not mean things should continue in the same way if circumstances have changed. This has always happened, especially with Moroccan policy.'[69] His inelegant phrases put the contradictions of Spanish colonialism in a nutshell.

The problems caused by the varied responses of indigenous leaders to colonial penetration were not confined to the Spanish Protectorate. With the exception of the French in Morocco, European invasion elsewhere in Africa was equally slow and uncertain, marked by ignorance of local society and geography. Shortages of money and the irresolution of governments led to conflicts between the colonial military elites and their statesmen. Thus, like Raisuni and Mohammed Abdel Krim, Africans had the opportunity to bargain with colonial power or test its limits. Contrary to the colonialists' view of the indigenous response to their expansion, it was calculated and pragmatic, even as it moved between resistance, evasion, or accommodation.[70]

And when the colonial army exposed its own frailties, indigenous accommodation could give way to jihad, as we shall see in the next chapter.

---

[69] Speech of 19 Feb. 1919 in *Diario de Sesiones del Congreso de los Diputados* (henceforth DSCD), 1918, vol. 12, no. 126, p. 5139.

[70] Ross E. Dunn, *Resistance in the Desert: Moroccan Responses to French Imperialism 1881–1921* (London, Croom Helm, 1977), 263; T. O. Ranger, 'African Reactions to the Imposition of Colonial Rule in East and Central Africa', in L. H. Gann and Peter Duignan (eds.), *Colonialism in Africa 1870–1960* (Cambridge, CUP, 1969–73), i. 293–301.

CHAPTER THREE

A Disaster Foretold? The Spanish Defeat at Anual

THE HISTORY OF colonial campaigns is littered with military disasters suffered by the European powers. The British in particular were defeated several times at the end of the nineteenth century at the height of their expansionism in south and eastern Africa. They were routed in 1879 by the Zulu army at Isandhlwana. The Mahdi uprising in 1882 in Eastern Sudan led to the ten-month siege of British-held Khartoum and its fall in 1885 and the death of General Gordon and his soldiers. The Boers in South Africa inflicted defeat on the British army in 1881 and then during the Boer War of 1889–1902. For their part, the Italians suffered military defeat at the hands of the Ethiopians at Adowa in 1896, which led to the fall of a government and Italy's abandonment of its aim to create a colonial empire in Abyssinia.

None of these disasters, however, was as severe as that suffered by the Spanish colonial army in Morocco in July 1921, nor did they have the same depth of domestic repercussion. Indeed, this defeat became a mythical reference point in the different discourses both of Spaniards and Moroccans and of left and right in Spain. Above all, the disaster was a catalyst in the development of the Army of Africa as a ruthless and interventionist force. This chapter, therefore, will concentrate on the narration of the disaster and on an elucidation of its causes and effects.

The events leading to the military defeat began with the new Spanish offensive of March 1919, which was the renewal, after a pause during the First World War, of Spain's strategy of extending direct control over the entire Protectorate. It claimed to be doing so in the name of the Sultanate according to the role assigned to it by the Great Powers. But in much of northern Morocco the authority of the Mahkzen was a fiction, and in effect it was Spanish rule that was being imposed on the subjects of the Protectorate. Although the policy of bribing and cajoling tribes to maintain order (euphemistically described as a political strategy) was not discontinued, it was now subordinated to the task of military pacification. From the early spring of 1919, the Spanish government instructed General Berenguer to begin penetrating once again into the rebellious areas.

Spain's political leaders were keen to cut down the costs of policing the Protectorate, but they were also anxious to be seen to be keeping their bargain with the Great Powers. France was chafing at the borders of the Spanish zone, frustrated by the ripple effects in its own Protectorate of Spain's problems of law and order. French troops had already occupied a town across the south-eastern border without notifying Spain and were preparing to penetrate even further into Spanish territory. The government's primary aim was limited to subduing Raisuni and the tribes associated with him in the west and pacifying the vexatious tribes in the eastern zone. In this way, it was hoped that untroubled communication could be established between the major urban centres in the Protectorate and with the international zone of Tangier. It was estimated, rather optimistically, that this operation would take from two to three years, after which the colonial army could be trimmed down and the deeply unpopular military service cut to two years.[1]

The budget assigned to this campaign was woefully inadequate, whatever the resistance local inhabitants might make to further penetration by the Spanish army. As already noted, the numerous governments since 1898 had failed to take advantage of the Disaster to restructure and re-equip the army. During the first decade of the new century half the military budget had been devoted to salaries, mainly those of officers. In 1909, as we have seen, there was one officer for every four soldiers. Compared to the thirty-four British divisional generals in active service, there were sixty such Spanish generals who commanded less than a third of the number of troops. By 1918 the ratio of officers to men had improved, but not enough to provide the army with the weapons and infrastructure it needed.

In any case, the lion's share of the budget went to the metropolitan army, most of which just sat in offices and paraded in barracks to no apparent purpose. The Artillery and the Engineering and Communications corps learnt what they could about new technology and trained their troops to use the equipment. But when the metropolitan army went on exercise, which it did rarely, it trained to repel another European army rather than prepare for a colonial war. Thus, on the eve of the new campaign the colonial army's fortunes rested on sheer luck and the acquiescence of the rebellious tribes of the west and east to Spanish penetration. The weapons, vehicles, and supplies it had available were insufficient for a prolonged and combative campaign. In case it needed to call on the help of the metropolitan army, there was only a thin line of conscripts and reservists that could be mobilized, and they were totally unprepared for the unorthodox war of the Rif.

The single most vexatious problem for the military authorities was the evasion of call-up. After the introduction of an obligatory but lenient military

---

[1] 'Notas reservadas sobre Marruecos', 9 Oct. 1919, in AGPR caja 15.765/15 and 'Informe político-militar sobre la zona Marruecos 1920' in ibid., caja 15.510/12. For the French connection, see the latter report and caja 15.509/5 and in SHM R100, leg. 27, carp. 1. A British emissary to Morocco in February 1919 noted that the Spanish army was now convinced that negotiations with Raisuni were no longer advisable and that co-operation with the French was vital: PRO FO 371 3843.

service in 1912, agencies (nicknamed the 'desertion agencies') had sprung up to help young men evade it, mainly by emigrating for a while to Spanish America. Another method of evasion was paying for a medical certificate that would earn exemption, or, for those families who could not afford such a bribe, self-mutilation or starvation. In 1912, 27 per cent of potential conscripts were exempted on medical grounds and in 1914, 22 per cent deserted.[2]

In the Moroccan Protectorate the most troublesome resistance to Spanish penetration had been led by Raisuni. So it was to the western zone that Berenguer and his staff devoted their closest attention. The sharif's efforts to safeguard his own power against colonial encroachment had led to an obsession amongst Spanish advocates of military action to destroy him. The option of peaceful penetration was beginning to lose credibility among colonial officers. One of Berenguer's progressive officers explained to a French diplomat in Tangier that their aim was to detach the tribes from Raisuni, forcing him to seek retirement in the Spanish-controlled zone, which they promised to make luxurious. However, their attempts to win over tribes merely drew these colonial officers into the labyrinthine feuds of local factions.[3]

Without totally discounting the previous methods of political work, Berenguer embraced a military strategy based on the French colonial military model. Drawing on close observation of the methods of generals such as Lyautey, he called for greater flexibility and speed in the formulation of tactics. The Moroccan war was totally unpredictable, the enemy's response frustrated traditional expectations, and resources were often impossible to anticipate, giving rise to excesses or deficiencies and creating indecision and division. Any advance had to employ the French 'oil-stain' tactic of ensuring the protection of the rearguard. Vital to success was an understanding of the enemy and of his ways of making war.[4] Berenguer's definition of the problem was accurate and his proposals were sound. But once again, through tradition, poor training, and lack of resources, the Spanish Army of Africa failed to meet the challenge.

Publicly, the colonial army would admit only to the lack of means given to them as the source of their difficulties. Their complaint was entirely justified. The campaigns in Morocco were so unpopular that Spanish governments were loath to raise the military budget, especially at a time when the economy

---

[2] Bachoud, *Los españoles, passim,* and Margarita Caballero Domínguez, 'La cuestión marroquí y su corolario de Annual como causa y consecuencia de la crisis del sistema restauracionista', *Investigaciones Históricas* (1997), 219–42.

[3] Richard Pennell, 'The Responsibility for Anual: the Failure of Spanish Policy in the Moroccan Protectorate, 1912–21', *European Studies Review,* 12 (1982), 74. The French source is the Report of ministre plénipotentaire of the French Consulate to the French minister of foreign affairs, 6 May 1919 in Archives Diplomatiques du Ministère des Affaires Etrangères, Maroc (henceforth ADMAE), vol. 221, pp. 38–9.

[4] 'Nuestra acción africana en pleno laberinto', cyclostyled report of 1919 in AAFAMM Mortera, caja 4; General Dámaso Berenguer Fusté, *La guerra en Marruecos. (Ensayo de una adaptación táctica)* (Madrid, n.p., 1918), 17 and 40–3.

was suffering from the effects of peace in Europe, having profited immensely from neutrality in war. Military expenditure in Morocco for the financial year 1919–20 was below that of each of the first three years of the First World War period, despite the fact that the military action envisaged was far greater and that prices had been driven up by wartime inflation.

Some of the military outgoings during the First World War, in fact, had been devoted to bribing Raisuni to keep the peace by providing everything he asked for: rifles, artillery, munitions, and supplies. In 1919–20 military costs (in both army and navy) in the mainland amounted to 447 million pesetas, while only 133 million was spent on the colonial army, although a new war had just been launched in Morocco. The inadequacy of colonial military resources was matched by the paucity of the budget for civilian projects with which Spain was supposed to bring civilization and woo the 'natives'. In the same year the Ministry of Development spent 3 million pesetas in Morocco and the Ministries of State and Government some 6.7 million, a total, that is, of less than 10 million. The British in India spent three times more on their army than on civilian projects in their colony, yet their investment in education, famine relief, and irrigation was far greater than anything spent by the Spanish government.[5]

The amount available to Berenguer for his military campaign was thus completely inadequate. The commanders of the three military zones had put forward calculations for the 1920 campaign that Berenguer had reduced to a minimum in his proposals to the government. The cabinet had then cut these even further. For example, for the immense task of building fortifications in the newly occupied areas, the commanders had asked for 1 million pesetas, which Berenguer had reduced to 900,000 and for which the government conceded only 300,000. No extra funds were granted until the general's first successes in the autumn of 1920 and after the visit of the minister of war, Viscount Eza, to the Protectorate. The cabinet then approved a rise of just under 2 million pesetas, enough, according to an opposition paper, to buy a dozen tents and build 2 kilometres of road.[6]

The colonial army was therefore in no condition to undertake a major campaign covering the three zones into which Spain had divided the Protectorate. In a long letter Berenguer himself explained to Eza the state of the Army of

[5] Figures for the Spanish military budget are taken from Comisión Preparatoria de la Conferencia de Génova, 'Estados que se mencionan en la ponencia de la subcomisión de Hacienda Pública', 8 Apr. 1922, AFAMM 382/20. For Britain in India, see David Omissi, *The Sepoy and the Raj: The Indian Army, 1860–1940* (London, Macmillan, 1994), 192–3.

[6] *El Sol*, 31 Oct. 1921. Figures for the campaign are in Berenguer's letter to Eza of 12 June 1920, in Vizconde de Eza, *Mis responsabilidades en el desastre de Melilla como Ministro de Guerra* (Madrid, Gráficas Reunidas, 1923), 363–5. The inadequacy of supplies is well illustrated by the experience of a captain of the Melilla General Staff who was in charge of establishing two outposts. Needing a minimum of 8,000 sandbags, he was supplied with only 2,000: Sigifredo Sainz Gutiérrez, *Con el General Navarro en operaciones y en el cautiverio* (Madrid, Sucesores de Rivadeneyra, 1924), 4.

Africa. A large proportion of the rifles needed calibrating, the machine-guns were so defective that many broke down after the first few bursts, the artillery was in a bad way and lacked sufficient shells, there were very few aircraft that could fly and their munitions were scarce and defective, and the army medical service lacked supplies and modern medicines. As for the conditions of the troops on campaign, they were often given cold rations with biscuits rather than bread and had to sleep in the open. In winter they only had a poncho with which to cover themselves, even when surrounded by snow. Their footwear was espadrilles, which in winter got stuck in the mud and often disintegrated so that the soldier had to carry on barefoot. 'This is the sad reality', wrote Berenguer, 'which everyone feels and which cannot be missed by anyone who sees this Army at close quarters. It is the result of years of failure to meet its needs; it is not the result of lack of foresight but lack of resources. And nevertheless we have to act as if everything was in good order; we have closed our eyes to the realities in order to carry out the mission that we have been charged with; have we had any other choice?'[7]

The inadequacy of the colonial army for the task of occupying the most rebellious areas of the Protectorate encouraged the idea amongst some circles in Spain of a technological quick-fix that might solve the Moroccan problem without further labour costs or mobilization. The lure of a chemical war against the Moroccan foe became irresistible for close observers of the colonial campaign, such as the king. Toxic weapons like mustard gas had been used, to apparent deadly effect, in the front lines of the First World War. Withdrawing troops and dousing the enemy with chemicals seemed a splendid idea to many officers and politicians. The Romanones government had already attempted to obtain chemical bombs from France in January 1919, while the king began to use his contacts in Germany in an effort to acquire the latest weapons, including toxic gases. Chapter 5 deals in greater detail with the secret measures taken to prepare for the chemical war against the Moroccans.

A more immediate problem was expanding the number of troops employed in the new offensive and improving their quality. The illiterate Spanish labourer did not form the basis of an effective army, while the middle classes could still evade military campaigns by paying money to the state and completing a short spell in barracks in the mainland. Worse still, military service in the colonial war continued to be deeply unpopular in Spain. This had been recognized all along by the military command, and Spanish troops had often been used for building roads rather than fighting battles. Instead, it was the Regulares and the native police who had been deployed as the shock troops of

---

[7] Letter of 4 Feb. 1921 in Eza, *Mis responsabilidades*, 210–12. Berenguer may have exaggerated somewhat the conditions of the army to convince Eza of the need for more resources, but his description is echoed by reports from British and French sources, e.g. Colonel Tisseyre's report to the French minister of war, 'Situation militaire dans la zône du Maroc Espagnol', on 31 July 1919, in ADMAE Maroc, vol. 221, pp. 107–17, and Lord Herschel's report of Feb. 1919 in PRO FO 371/3843.

the Spanish Army of Africa. All European colonial powers had discovered the advantage of hiring indigenous armies to fight their wars in Africa for them, and it was their mobilization rather than superior technology that had won victories.[8] The problem with Spain was that their native soldiers belonged to the land where they fought and were deployed against people they could identify with. The native troops often disappeared with their guns when the harvest season began or when they had settled scores with their internal enemies. Reliance on local mercenary soldiers had already proved inadvisable, when a battalion of Regulares defected to the enemy.

The best Regulares recruits had come from the French zone, many of whom were Christians and therefore unlikely to identify with the predominantly Muslim population of the Spanish sector. But the rise in demand for labour as a result of increasing French investment in public works meant that recruitment to the Regulares was falling.[9] As for the officer class, the elimination of incentives in 1917 meant that the recruitment of professional colonial officers had slowed down, and posts in Morocco were being filled by officers without any colonial vocation who were merely doing an obligatory spell in the Protectorate.

The much-wafted idea of creating a Spanish equivalent of the French Foreign Legion now took shape. It was the brainchild of the slightly dotty colonel, José Millán Astray, a veteran of the colonial war in the Philippines at the end of the previous century. He had been posted for a while to French Algeria, where he was able to observe the operations of the French Foreign Legion. The formal proposal for the launching of the Spanish Legion or Tercio (named after the sixteenth- and seventeenth-century mercenary troops employed by the Spanish kings) was made in October 1919. It envisaged the recruitment mainly of foreigners, especially veterans of the First World War who had failed to settle down to civilian life, and others with 'an uncertain past' who might be attracted by the anonymity of the legionnaire's life; in other words, emotionally scarred ex-soldiers and men with criminal records or psychological problems of one sort or another. The aim of the Legion would be to take the brunt of military action and liberate the ordinary soldier from everything except defence and rearguard duties.[10]

The plan was given royal approval and launched on 4 September 1920. Foreign recruits were not required to provide any documentation, and if considered suitable were given a permit to enter the country by their local Spanish embassy. Similarly, the recruitment offices set up in provincial capitals in Spain

---

[8] Vandervort, *Wars*, 29.

[9] 'Notas reservadas sobre Marruecos', 9 Oct. 1919, AGPR 15.765/5. Berenguer had reported unrest among the native troops to the minister of war at the end of August of that year because of the availability of better-paid work elsewhere, and had managed to persuade him to raise their wages by a small amount: ibid.,15.509/5.

[10] 'Proyecto de creación de una legión extranjera en África', Oct. 1919, AGPR 15.621/11.

asked few questions and promised good pay and conditions. The ease of enlistment worried the minister of state, who wrote to Eza warning him about the danger of recruiting secret Bolsheviks. Eza himself had written to Berenguer before the launch of the Legion expressing his concern that foreigners might import 'modern anarchic' ideas into the Army of Africa. Initial reception to the recruitment drive was enthusiastic in many capitals of Europe. The Spanish ambassador in Prague reported numerous volunteers among Austrians, Hungarians, Poles, and Czechs, many of them First World War veterans who could not find work and were struggling to survive.[11] Some officers in Morocco were less than keen about the recruitment of foreigners. Four months after the creation of the Legion Berenguer advised Eza that no more foreigners should be taken on, because they were not producing results and indeed some were deserting. Silvestre was always opposed to the idea, not least because when he took over command of the Melilla region he found the recruitment in Ceuta of the first Legion was attracting many of his own veterans away from his side.[12]

Just as vital to the new offensive as creating a professional army was keeping the supposedly pro-Spanish tribes on Spain's side. Colonial officers in the Army of Africa were at a distinct disadvantage compared with their French counterparts. Unlike the French zone, the Spanish Protectorate contained no great tribal leaders or Caids whose domain extended over large areas. On the contrary, Spanish colonial officers of native affairs had to deal with a myriad of small chieftains in a complex, fluid, and highly fragmented society.[13] It is very unlikely that any of the chieftains who collaborated with Spain welcomed Spanish colonialism, despite their protestations. The most co-operative amongst them, such as Abdel Krim's family, the al Khattabis, hoped that Spain would help to modernize their backward society without imposing the direct colonial rule characteristic of the French.

However, Spain had brought few benefits to northern Moroccan society. It is true that under the colonization programme considerable areas of land had been planted with wheat, maize, olive trees, vineyards, and market-garden produce, irrigated by newly constructed canals. But they were cultivated mainly by Spanish settlers from Algeria.[14] The budget for public works, education, and health, on the other hand, was abysmally low set next to the needs

[11] Letter to the minister of state on 31 Jan. 1921, AGMAE leg. 2883. For the latter's letter of 4 Oct. 1920, see ibid. For Eza's letter of 2 June 1920, see *Mis responsabilidades*, 358–9.

[12] Berenguer's letter to Eza of 4 Feb. 1921, including the reference to Silvestre, in Eza, *Mis responsabilidades*, 203. Eza also mentions on p. 358 that colonial staff had expressed their opposition to the project in the first place. Vincent Sheean, *Personal History*, 3rd edn. (London, Hamish Hamilton, 1969), 97. For further discussion of the Legion see Chs. 6 and 8.

[13] As argued by Colonel Patxot in a conversation with a British officer on 30 Mar. 1920, in PRO FO 371/4525.

[14] Augusto Vivero, *El derrumbamiento. La verdad sobre el desastre del Rif* (Madrid, Caro Raggio, 1922), 27–31; Francisco Gómez Hidalgo, *Marruecos. La tragedia prevista* (Madrid, n.p., 1921), 228–30.

of a poor society. Eza claimed that Spain had done much for the people of its Protectorate in a newspaper interview in the summer of 1920. But British diplomacy reported that very little attempt had been made to overcome illiteracy, and that while Spanish army doctors had done some good, their efforts to improve public health had been hampered by a dearth of medicine, medical instruments, and modern surgeries. Many of the public-works projects had a military purpose, and when the works were not carried out by Spanish troops, Spanish workers in the area were often employed rather than local Moroccan labourers. Under the general in charge—an 'admirer of Prussianism', according to the British chargé d'affaires in Tangier—tribesmen were subjected to unpaid forced labour using their own pack animals.[15]

Rather than on anything of lasting benefit to northern Morocco, Spain relied on bribes and gifts to keep tribal chiefs on its side. Records of the handouts are somewhat fragmentary, but it is clear that they accounted for a sizeable portion of the money the Army of Africa received from the state for its colonial work. In 1916, for example, four chieftains based near Al Hoceima alone received a total monthly handout of 20,000 pesetas. By 1921 monthly payments of 44,729 pesetas were being made in the eastern zone to chiefs and individuals in tribes near the troubled area of the Beni Urriaguels (of which the al Khattabis received 500 pesetas a month), as well as in the south-east, where French incursions were upsetting the tribes. Some idea of the value of these handouts can be gauged from the price of wheat, which oscillated at around 2 pesetas per pound weight. Only a tiny amount of the money available was devoted to grants for education and medicine. A lieutenant-colonel claimed that the vanguard of all military advances was the Bank of Spain.[16]

The effect of these so-called pensions could not have been more divisive. They were not allocated on the basis of need but of utility. Tribal chieftains near rebellious areas got more than those in the rearguard, irrespective of the degree of their collaboration. So it became more profitable to be rebellious than submissive. The amounts paid out were negotiated on the hoof by local colonial officers and ratified by high command, and were subject to great disparities, even within the same area. Tribal chiefs in one region, for example, got anything from 250 to 1,000 pesetas monthly. Tribal subjects saw their leaders make money and fail to pass on the benefit to them. As the new Spanish offensive began, these chiefs were under even greater pressure from their people to renounce the bribes and resist. Often they kept the money and made promises to the Spanish that they had no intention of fulfilling. Many officers were deeply unhappy about the system of bribes and kept warning their commanders about its bad effects. A captain of the native police complained in

---

[15] Clark Kerr to Lord Curzon on 8 June and 28 1920 in PRO FO 371/4525; Eza's interview in *El Sol*, 28 July 1920.

[16] Fernández Tamarit's testimony in *De Anual*, 420. The figures are from SHM R738, leg. 1, carp. 5. For 1916, ibid., leg. 2, carp. 2.

1921 that the exorbitant pensions being given out were merely 'awakening the appetites and greed of the natives', and proposed common rates of payment for first-rank chiefs on the one hand and second-rank chiefs on the other.[17]

Also, unlike the French, the Spanish colonial army could not guarantee the protection of pro-Spanish or neutral tribes. These were often subjected, without regard to their allegiance, to looting or the molestation of their women by the native police or the Regulares, for whom pillage was an important supplement to low pay. Sometimes villages were attacked by mistake. According to British diplomatic sources, a caid in the western zone, who had been acting on behalf of Spain, complained to Berenguer that villages that had submitted to him had been bombed by Spanish aircraft from Larache aerodrome. He also complained of the dishonesty and tyranny of some colonial officers. Throughout 1920, the British Vice-Consul in Tetuan also reported frequent attacks on the collaborators with Spain by rebellious tribes. 'How can the Spaniards hope to make the natives contented with their rule where those who submit to them are harried by them by day and left unprotected, and without hopes of compensation, to be raided by their own unsubdued brethren by night?'[18] Although there were some enlightened colonial officers who had taken the trouble to learn Arabic and the local shelja language as well as local laws and customs, there were many others who knew little about the tribes they had to deal with, and were happy to let their native police loot and rape at will.[19]

Berenguer's western offensive was halted before it had got very far and after the colonial troops had suffered severe casualties. Raisuni gathered together his resources, including arms provided by Spain and Germany during the First World War, and launched a fierce attack against the Spanish in July. His soldiers seized the road linking Tetuan to Tangier and cut land communication between the two cities. A second Spanish push in September 1919 compelled Raisuni to retreat into his mountain stronghold. Casualties in the Spanish army were high in this second offensive alone, but the success of the operation blunted their political repercussions. In recognition of the new policy of unadulterated military penetration, Berenguer's responsibilities as high commissioner were enlarged by royal decree to include control over native police, aviation, transport, and the funding of military campaigns. At a stroke, he became the virtual pro-consul of northern Morocco.[20]

The most important target of the new campaign that autumn was the small town of Chauen, a holy shrine for all Muslims in Morocco. Some 95 kilome-

[17] SHM R759, leg. 16, carp. 4. For evidence of pressure from tribal subjects and the chiefs' reactions see Silvestre's report of 20 May 1920 in SHM R100 leg. 27, carp. 1.

[18] Atkinson to Clark Kerr (report on bombing was written on 8 June 1920) and to Herbert M. White re looting on 2 Feb. 1920 in PRO FO 371/4525.

[19] According to the evidence of MPs Lazaga and Solano in DSCD 20 Oct. 1921, 3674–9. For further discussion of the colonial officer see Ch. 6.

[20] Real Decreto, 24 Aug. 1919, Documento número 28, *Acción de España en Marruecos*, 94–5.

tres south of Tetuan, the town is high up in the hills and built at the foot of a tall and rocky mountain that hinders access from two sides. The choice of Chauen as the main objective of the operations in the west was the result of a political and not a strategic decision. Its occupation would represent a blow to the confidence of the anti-Spanish jihad. But it was a difficult place to reach and an even more difficult place to hold.

The extraordinary story of its surrender has been omitted in many accounts of the operation. The leading Africanist in western operations, Colonel Alberto Castro Girona, who had become well known among Arab chiefs for his close knowledge of that part of Morocco and his willingness to negotiate peace, went alone into the town disguised as an Arab charcoal-burner. He walked into a meeting of the town's elders and persuaded them to surrender on the main grounds that the town was surrounded by Spanish columns. This was not entirely true, because of the three columns that were supposed to be converging on the town from north and west, only one had managed to fight its way to the outskirts. Hence the invasion of the town by Spanish troops was not accompanied by any occupation of the surrounding region, with the result that they were almost besieged by Raisuni's irregular troops. The difficulty of pacifying the outlying area around Chauen can be gauged from the fact that the second column only battled its way into the town some weeks later in November and the third column never managed to get to Chauen at all.[21]

Nevertheless, Berenguer rode in triumph into the holy city and shortly afterwards was ennobled with the title of Count of Xauen (the Spanish version of Chauen). The symbolic importance of the holy town was recognized by the decision to stage in the near future a second triumphal entry, this time of King Alfonso XIII. The only people in the town who seemed genuinely to welcome the Army of Africa were the descendants of the Jews expelled from Spain in 1492. Apparently speaking a very old form of Spanish, they brought out into the streets huge iron keys that they said were the keys to the houses and synagogues of their ancestors in Granada. It may be that their welcome was also to do with the opportunities for trade offered by the arrival of Spanish troops. Spanish failure to hold on to Chauen must have been a devastating blow to the small Jewish community, who were forced to leave the town and probably suffered terrible privations and violence, a story that seems not to have been recorded or researched.

As commander-in-chief of the eastern zone from 1920, Silvestre would soon face a new and even more formidable foe than Raisuni: the Abdel Krim brothers. After their difficult relationship during the First World War, the Spanish had rehabilitated the Abdel Krim family. Yet Spanish compliance with French demands that Moroccans in the Spanish Protectorate who had agitated on behalf of Germany during the war should be handed over to them, led the

---

[21] *L'Afrique Française* (Nov. 1920), 336 and (Dec. 1920), 376.

Abdel Krim family to withdraw their co-operation, even though they were not directly threatened. By mid-1920 the Spanish knew from their own intelligence that Mohammed Abdel Krim was gathering troops to oppose their penetration into the Rif.[22] What they seemingly did not know was the amount of money his family had accumulated from German funds during the First World War and from the sale of mining rights to companies such as the Spanish firm Setolázar. Without this knowledge, the Spanish army critically underestimated Abdel Krim's potential. With the help of his money, the Rif leader and his brother would soon begin to weld together what had been until then local and sporadic resistance against the Spanish into a comparatively well-armed force under a single command.[23]

Silvestre's confidence, understandably, was based on past experience. The Rif tribes seemed always to have been disunited and there appeared to be no leader of the calibre of Raisuni to lead a concerted resistance against the Spanish advance. For a long time the Abdel Krim family had been patronized by the Spanish and had provided information vital to military security about anti-Spanish activities in the surrounding tribes. While he was building up his forces, Mohammed Abdel Krim (henceforth Abdel Krim) continued to correspond with his Spanish contacts, assuring them of his loyalty to Spain, and indeed continued to do so even after the army had begun to suffer military disasters at his hands. He sent a letter to one of his Spanish contacts just sixteen days before his attack on the post of Anual, which would lead to the Spanish military debacle of late July 1921.[24]

The most significant thing about these letters is that many of them were written to representatives of the Setolázar mining company. While Abdel Krim was attacking Spanish forces, he was negotiating the exploitation of new mines with Spanish businessmen. Alongside him, other Rif chieftains were in contact with mining companies and entrepreneurs such as the Basque millionaire Horacio Echevarrieta. In negotiations with them, Abdel Krim had been willing to concede the creation of Spanish military posts to protect the mines.[25] This apparent contradiction was in fact consistent with what we know of his objectives. His family had hoped that, as a result of Spain's weakness as a colonial power, northern Morocco would be the recipient of neo-colonial benefits without suffering the oppression of a full-blown colonialism. Keen to modernize the immensely backward region of the Rif while maintaining or even intensifying its religious life, they nurtured the illusion that Spain would bring education, health services, technology, and public works to northern Morocco without insisting, like the French, on running their lives. They had even backed

---

[22] Gabriel Morales, 'Memoria de la situación política', 19 July 1920, in SHM R100, leg. 27. For the relationship between the Abdel Krims and the local Spanish command, see Riquelme's testimony to the Comisión de Responsabilidades in *De Anual*, 117–22.
[23] Galbán, *España*, 7–8.   [24] Copies of the letters can be found in AAFAMM leg. 278/7.
[25] Victor Ruiz Albéniz, 'La leyenda de Al Hoceima', *El Sol*, 2 Nov. 1921.

repeated plans for a seaborne invasion of the Rif heartlands via Al Hoceima, calculating, in all likelihood, that the benefits of a potentially brief occupation outweighed the disadvantages.[26]

Their disillusionment with this model was patent by late 1919. Not only had Spain failed to make an impact on the Moroccan economy and infrastructure, it was beginning to invade their own tribal lands. In a letter to a colonial official in August 1919, Abdel Krim had reiterated his interest in the joint development of the natural wealth of the Rif but complained that Spain had so far failed to invest significantly. Spanish colonial practices were also having a damaging effect on relations between the tribes. He pointed out that the Spanish policy of pensions had created deep divisions among his people. The result of both was that local chiefs were turning against Spain. Repeatedly, the family had suffered hostile actions from other chieftains. Now the family's long association with the Spanish was under increasing pressure from their own people.[27] A year later his father was poisoned to death, probably by an anti-Spanish faction. Nevertheless, the Abdel Krim brothers still hoped to continue attracting Spanish capital to the Rif mines, with or without Spain's backing.

Hence, like Raisuni and so many other Moroccan leaders who collaborated with the Spanish, the Abdel Krim family were not supporters of Spanish colonialism nor 'traitors' after they broke relations, as many in Spain later argued.[28] Their collaboration with the Spanish authorities was driven by pragmatism, so that their ambiguities were the ambiguities of Spanish colonialism. The price of resistance to colonialism was war. As long as Spain failed or neglected to impose direct rule, collaboration might have far greater benefits than fighting back. For Raisuni, those benefits were the preservation of tradition, religious and social, and local power. Abdel Krim had a much more ambitious and progressive vision, the liberation of his people and their emancipation, not just from hunger but from their own backwardness.

None of this was understood by Spanish ministers or most colonial officers. The Spanish minister of state was shocked by Abdel Krim's letter of August 1919. He accused him of ingratitude and insolence, and suggested merely that he had been prompted to complain by an enemy agent. Silvestre, however, was more sensitive to the issues raised by Abdel Krim. In a letter to Berenguer in

---

[26] In his later testimony to one of the committees investigating the disaster of July 1921, Berenguer claimed they had always put up last-minute objections that had led to its repeated cancellation, implying that they were playing a double game. But this unverifiable claim is more likely to have been part of Berenguer's efforts to defend his actions than a true reflection of the Abdel Krims' intentions (*De Anual*, 328). For the only sophisticated interpretation of the Abdel Krims, see Madariaga, *España*, 397–439. Ch. 7 below examines the theme of local resistance and collaboration in greater depth.

[27] Letter to Manuel Aguirre (Secretario de la Sección de Marruecos), 15 Aug. 1919 in SHM R738, leg. 1, carp. 5. For Abdel Krim's own rather distorted a posteriori account of his disillusion with the Spanish, see Roger-Matthieu (ed.), *Mémoires*, 71–82.

[28] A close Spanish associate of Abdel Krim claimed, rather improbably, that he broke with the colonial administration out of resentment that the local commander at Al Hoceima had turned against his family, just as his predecessor had in 1915: evidence of Riquelme in *De Anual*, 119–20.

February 1921, he admitted that some of Abdel Krim's complaints were not without reason and that he would be happy to welcome him back into the Spanish fold. One area in which they might have agreed was the divisive effect of the pensions. But rather than rationalize them, Silvestre abolished the payments as he advanced and refused to make new ones.

The sudden withdrawal of a monthly stipend cannot have endeared Spain to the Abdel Krims. The general was approached by businessmen hoping to engineer a reconciliation between them. Silvestre was not prepared to contact them, however, because they 'would make too many demands', the implication being that his conditions for renewed collaboration was their acceptance of his offensive.[29] Communication with Abdel Krim was maintained by Silvestre's second-in-command, the enlightened colonial officer Gabriel Morales, through various intermediaries such as a Spanish businessman who had been trading with the Rif tribes. As late as May 1921 Abdel Krim was still protesting his loyalty to the Spanish cause.[30]

Yet given Morales's report that he was building up his forces in the summer of 1920 and his separate dealings with Spanish mining companies, the available evidence would suggest that the Abdel Krim brothers broke with Spanish colonialism when Silvestre crossed the Rubicon of the Kert river in mid-1920. The elder brother's protracted communications with Morales and others were probably an attempt to allay Spanish suspicions that he was raising a *harka* (irregular troops from a tribe or fraction of a tribe fighting for money on the Spanish side) to resist the Army of Africa as it moved towards the heartlands of the Rif. Abdel Krim needed time to negotiate with the chiefs of other clans and tribes and overcome the resentment caused by his family's collaboration with Spanish colonialism over many years.[31]

By the beginning of 1921 Silvestre's troops had penetrated far into the eastern zone. On 15 January the general established a forward position at Anual, an abandoned, desolate village surrounded by Mt. Izumar, at some 100 kilometres distance from Melilla, most of it along a stony, tortuous path through craggy mountains. His objective was to hold on to all the strategic positions in the rearguard and penetrate by land into the heart of the anti-Spanish resis-

---

[29] 10 Feb. 1921 in SHM R738, leg. 1, carp. 5. Silvestre expressed his opposition to the pensions system in an interview with a Spanish journalist: Eduardo Rubio Fernández, *Melilla. Al margen del desastre (mayo–agosto 1921)* (Barcelona, Cervantes, 1921), 43.

[30] Ruiz Albéniz, *Ecce homo*, 256–64.

[31] Pando asserts that the Abdel Krim brothers sought continued collaboration with Spain right until the spring of 1921 (*Historia secreta*, 42–3), but this ignores evidence of military build-up on their part and takes their statements of loyalty to Spain too literally. Moreover, the letters between them and the mining company do not necessarily denote continued support for Spain, as I have tried to suggest above. Indeed, there was a precedent for the separate interests of Spanish mining capital and the military. The Minas del Rif company had made a secret deal with El Roghi in 1907 that undermined Spanish military strategy—see Ch. 1. For Abdel Krim's own later admission that he had had to work hard to overcome the suspicion among the Rifians caused by his collaboration with the Spanish, see Roger-Matthieu (ed.), *Mémoires*, 85–6.

tance in the territory of the Beni Urriaguels some 30 kilometres away, a desire long cherished by advocates of military action in Spanish Morocco. The minister of war, Eza, had insisted that any further operations should receive his approval in order to ensure that their costs were commensurate with the military budget. Silvestre was fully conscious that Berenguer, as commander-in-chief and high commissioner, had also to sanction the final offensive. Twice Berenguer had rapped Silvestre over the knuckles for going behind his back and informing the minister of war without informing him. But he had also sensibly given Silvestre a margin of discretion in the choice of tactics.[32]

For all his military dash, Silvestre was a traditionalist who respected the hierarchy of command. He was also aware of some of the risks that lay ahead. In a report six months before he had been warned by Morales of the danger of leaving the unconquered Beni Said tribes in his rearguard as his troops moved towards the Beni Urriaguels. 'Not one step can be taken westwards if we are leaving behind our backs a strong enemy with a high morale who could give us serious trouble, since their frontier is only 32 kilometres from Melilla.'[33] Yet, when faced with a balance of choices, he was more likely to rely on audacity than on caution. He was encouraged in this choice by the apparent absence of the enemy. The advance to Anual had met with little resistance. He was also animated by the king, with whom he had had a special relationship for some years. Alfonso's influence over his decision to push forward was well known, but documents implicating the king in the military disaster that followed were hidden or destroyed.

What also impelled Silvestre to advance further was a colonial zeal backed by humanitarian concern. Like his fellow-Africanists, he was convinced that Spain was bringing the fruits of European progress to a backward society torn by feuds, not realizing that much of the instability in northern Morocco was due to the penetration of Spanish capital and the Spanish military. As we saw in his dealings with Raisuni, he was shocked by the injustices of Moroccan society and was impatient to set them right. His sense of mission was intensified in the winter of 1921 by the continued drought in the north-eastern part of the Spanish zone, whose people were beginning to die of starvation. In a letter to Berenguer in February 1921 he wrote:

The bright hopes for the future of the labourers are in horrible contrast to the misery that now reigns in all the territory . . . anything I can tell you is little next to reality and I simply cannot begin to describe to you the picture of hunger and of horror that confronts us all, not only in the countryside but even here in Melilla where the native police have had to find and prepare a place in which over 200 women, children, and old people, who are milling around in the streets in a pitiful state, can shelter and sleep

---

[32] Pando, *Historia secreta*, 91. Eza's letter to Berenguer, 16 Jan. 1921 in SHM Legado Silvestre, apéndice 55, and Berenguer's letters to Silvestre of 9 May and 8 July 1920 in SHM R100, leg. 27.

[33] 'Memoria de la situación política', 19 July 1920 p. 12, in SHM Legado Silvestre, apéndice 56.

under a roof; not a day goes by without natives dying in the territory for lack of food and here there are many who go into hospital only to die the next day.

Silvestre attacked the meanness of the government, which had authorized a gift of barley to the starving that was so small it hardly made any difference. Charity on the right scale was all very well, but what mattered was work. State investment in roads and railways could provide the jobs that Moroccans needed so badly. In an exchange of letters three weeks earlier, Berenguer had authorized Silvestre to advance to the limits of the 'elasticity' of his forces to bring relief to the starving people. A people weakened by famine were of course an easier target for military occupation, and Berenguer's later testimony made it clear that this strategic consideration played an important part in the decision to advance, but this does not contradict the humanitarian sentiments privately expressed by both generals.[34]

The picture of Silvestre that emerges from these documents, which are still held in a confidential file in the military archives, is very different from that of traditional post-disaster literature. He was not a prudent soldier, but nor was he driven merely by impetuosity and ambition, though these were features of his complex personality. He was careful on most occasions to get the agreement of his superiors before launching military operations and, like Berenguer, he had a paternalistic and public-spirited concern for the people that he believed he had a duty to colonize. Although he defended the primacy of military solutions, unlike some of his more progressive fellow-officers, he recognized the value of investment and public works in convincing the 'natives' of the value of colonial rule.

Silvestre presented his plan for the final assault against the enemy to Berenguer in March 1921. They had already consulted each other about strategic options. The commander-in-chief had been undecided, torn between the option of a concentrated offensive along the coast or one spread across a wider front of coast and mountains.[35] Neither conformed to his own strictures about the 'oil-stain' strategy. Yet Berenguer left his subordinate to make up his own mind. Silvestre chose the second. With some modifications by Berenguer, the plan was put to the minister of war. It was agreed that a defensive line would first be established stretching some 40 kilometres from the coast southward. A land offensive would then be launched towards Al Hoceima through the territory of the Temsaman and then the Beni Urriaguel tribes. It would consist of a three-pronged attack along a 32-kilometre front near the coast and through the mountains. The columns would converge as the offensive reached the Beni Urriaguel territory before sweeping into the Al Hoceima area and dispersing the enemy (see map on p. 107). Having agreed in principle with the plan, Berenguer took

---

[34] Berenguer testimony in *De Anual*, 330. The Silvestre letter of 28 Feb. and the Berenguer letter of 21 Jan. are in SHM Legado Silvestre, apéndice 56. See also Pando, *Historia secreta*, 95–6.

[35] Letter from Berenguer to Silvestre, 21 Jan. 1921, in SHM Legado Silvestre, apéndice 56.

time off from his offensive in the west against Raisuni to visit the eastern front at the end of the month. He gave his final seal of approval to the coming operation and wrote to Eza expressing confidence that it would be successful.[36]

Historical narratives can easily become *ex post facto* rationalizations, when in fact individual or collective behaviour or unforeseen occurrences can tip a finely balanced situation in one direction or another. The outcome of Silvestre's offensive cannot be described as a predictable disaster, as many texts would claim.[37] Yet the manner of his advance was decidedly imprudent. Silvestre's own experienced officers expressed considerable doubts about the advisability of the offensive, and above all about the available resources in arms, supplies, and men. Morales counselled Silvestre to wait until the new front was consolidated and the Spanish troops were properly trained.[38] By the standards of conventional war, the operation was far too risky. Of the 25,720 or so troops based in the eastern command, many were on leave or off sick or had to be stationed in the rearguard.[39] The result was that Silvestre only had some 12,000 troops available. This meant that the advance positions and the offensive columns would be thinly distributed.

In fact, the front extended for some 80 kilometres and was 92 kilometres away from the main base in Melilla. The only railway link with Melilla stretched only 50 kilometres to Tistutin, a long way from the front line. Dotted about the intervening mountains and plains were 130 positions (or block-houses), some defended by handfuls of soldiers and many situated at some distance from a water supply. A military position in the southernmost point of the eastern zone, for example, was supplied with water from 38 kilometres away by two lorries, and the twenty-one small positions surrounding the base were then supplied by camel.[40] There were no columns linking the various positions nor reserve columns near the front line. Yet for each soldier in a blockhouse, up to three or even four other military personnel were needed to provide medical back-up and manual labour, as well as to ensure the supply of ammunition, food, and water. In contrast, the Moroccan muhayeddin were 'marvellous conjurors of their own bodies', needing nothing more than a bush, rock, or tree trunk to hide behind and figs and bread in the hood of their jellaba.[41]

It is true that in the peculiar conditions of warfare in northern Morocco the reaction of the adversary was hard to predict. But Morales had received

[36] Eza quoted from this letter in a parliamentary debate on 29 Nov. 1922, in DSCD p. 4402.

[37] One such book, written immediately after the Anual disaster, was Gómez Hidalgo, *Marruecos*.

[38] Morales, report of 16 Feb., in SHM Legado Silvestre, apéndice 56. For another officer's report see Pando *Historia*, 139–41.

[39] Of the total number (in round figures), 13,000 were Spanish infantrymen, 1,000 cavalrymen, 3,000 artillerymen, 1,500 engineering corps, 1,200 quartermaster-stores personnel, 600 medical staff, and 5,300 native troops: ACD leg. 650, Negociado de Marruecos, Estado de fuerza de la Comandancia General de Melilla, July 1921.

[40] Fernández Tamarit testimony to the Picasso hearings in *De Anual*, 418.

[41] Antonio Azpeitua, *Marruecos. La mala semilla: ensayo de análisis objetivo de cómo fue sembrada la guerra en África* (Madrid, n.p., 1921), 124–5 and 141.

intelligence reports that chiefs who had previously supported Spanish administration were having trouble with their own people. He had earlier warned Silvestre that, however bad the effect of the pensions was, it was worse to withdraw them altogether. Moreover, he echoed the fear that the allegiance of the most pro-Spanish of all the clans, the Abdel Krims, was now unclear. An attempt to intimidate the rebellious Rifians by the shelling of a town from the nearby Spanish-held island off the coast at Al Hoceima on market day on 13 April had the opposite effect, and helped to sway many into joining a common resistance against the Spanish.[42]

Nevertheless, Silvestre decided to go ahead with the offensive, even though he had received new information in May suggesting that his adversaries were successfully gathering together contingents to oppose his advance. Casting aside his doubts and the advice of several of his closest confidants, he ordered a unit on 1 June to establish a forward post in enemy territory at the top of Mt. Abarrán, which could be seen in the distance from Anual. As most of the unit began the return journey to Anual, leaving a small garrison to defend the makeshift post, a combined force of local tribesmen and men from the Beni Urriaguel tribe fell upon the new position and killed most of its defenders. They were helped by the defection of the handful of native police in the post, who turned their guns on their officers. An old Moroccan of 90 remembers that, as a 10-year-old boy from the village further down the slope, he watched the muhayeddin cut the barbed wire of the camp and rush the position. He saw seven Spanish soldiers killed as they tried to flee.[43]

The capture of the Abarrán position had an enormous psychological impact on the surrounding tribes. The mountain had a deep religious significance for the local tribes and its occupation by Spanish troops had been a new affront in an unending succession of casual or critical offences by the Spanish against their beliefs. The artillery pieces captured in the position were displayed in triumph in nearby towns, and the remaining Temsaman clans joined the jihad.[44] The chieftains who had collaborated with the Spanish for many years now found themselves under pressure from their own people to break with the invader. Aware of the new situation, the colonel of one of the many fortified positions in the Beni Said territory, with the blessing of Silvestre, threw a party for the local chieftains at which he presented each of their wives with the gift of a silk handkerchief. Their leader, however, told the colonel that if the Spanish did not bring more forces into the area they would have to move out, because the pressure from the new jihad would oblige him to revolt with his clan.[45] But Silvestre failed to take heed of the many warning signs. The bombing offensive by the Spanish was stepped up and the few aircraft of the eastern zone began to drop explosives

[42] Pando, *Historia secreta*, 110 and 104–5. For Morales's concerns about 'pensions', see his report of 19 July 1920 in SHM R100, leg. 27.

[43] Interview with Mohammed Saleh Faraji on 23 Apr. 2001.   [44] *De Anual*, 18–27.

[45] Testimony of Captain Araújo y Soler in ibid., 581–3.

on towns in enemy territory. The bombs aroused even greater hostility, as Abdel Krim warned the military governor of the island of Al Hoceima by letter, probably in his continued efforts to throw the Spaniards off the scent.[46]

Desperate for more troops and arms, Silvestre met with Berenguer on board a warship on 5 June. The high commissioner claimed he could not send any more for the time being and, oblivious to the mounting crisis on the eastern front, sent a report to Eza the next day claiming that the situation there was under control.[47] Silvestre constructed a further four positions in the hope of reinforcing his lines of defence. One of these was a forward post built on the slopes of Mt. Igueriben, some 6 kilometres south of Anual. Like many other positions, it was exposed, vulnerable, and of little use in the mobile conditions of colonial warfare. The only water supply for the 300 soldiers was 4.5 kilometres away and required an arduous daily trip with mules and buckets along terrain that seemed designed for ambushes. Repeatedly the mules and the military detachment were shot at, with a resulting high level of casualties in men and animals.[48] Several weeks passed without further attack, but Spanish intelligence knew the tribesmen were busy bringing in the harvest. In the meantime, Abdel Krim was beginning to negotiate a united *harka* under his leadership. Morales met with the few chiefs who remained collaborators with Spain, but was no longer able to extract any further commitment from them.

Abdel Krim's forces struck on 17 July. Igueriben was surrounded. For four days the garrison held out amidst increasingly desperate conditions. According to one of the few survivors, the water supply ran out almost immediately and they were forced to drink whatever liquid was available, from ink to urine. Dead mules piled up at the entrance to the camp and their carcasses burst in the terrible heat of the Rif summer, releasing such putrefaction that soldiers stopped up their noses with cotton wool soaked in iodine, but to little effect. Vain attempts were made to relieve them, but the Rifian forces had dug a trench across a wide front between the two positions and manned it with their fighters to prevent any convoy getting through. Silvestre gave the garrison an order to surrender, which they refused to do, knowing they would not survive anyway. On 21 July the commander of the post sent a heliograph message asking for the Spanish artillery to fire on the position after they had shot their twelfth and last shell. Some of the survivors then committed suicide, while others tried to charge out of the post and were cut down in a hail of bullets.[49]

[46] Ruiz Albéniz, *Ecce homo*, 264.

[47] *Información gubernativa instruido para esclarecer los antecedentes y circunstancias que concurrieron en el abandono de las posiciones del territorio de la Comandancia General de Melilla en el mes de julio de 1921* (Madrid, Consejo Supremo del Ejército y Marina, 1922), 319.

[48] Luis Casado y Escudero, *Igueriben. IV de junio a XXI de julio, MCMXXI. Relato auténtico de lo ocurrido en esta posición* (Madrid, 1923), 49–50.

[49] Ibid., 180–204; another eyewitness account of an artilleryman who took part in a failed convoy can be found in Eduardo Ortega y Gasset, *Annual. Relato de un soldado e impresiones de un cronista* (Madrid, Rivadeneyra, 1922), 28–44.

Silvestre now knew that he had to order a retreat from all the positions on the front line. The problem was that the adversary was so mobile that the line of retreat towards Melilla could be cut off, especially because Silvestre had left the hostile Beni Said and Beni Ulichex tribes uncontested in his rearguard. He sent a telegram to the king requesting that he use his influence to mobilize the air force to bomb villages near Anual in the hope that this might divert the enemy from their siege. The minister of war ordered that ships in Cadiz be requisitioned to steam to Ceuta, pick up troops, and transport them to Melilla to prop up the front lines. Silvestre dismissed this measure as totally inadequate.

Desperate to save the situation, Berenguer proposed the landing of troops in the Bay of Al Hoceima, accompanied by a massive bombing campaign by air and from battleships against the Beni Urriagel villages, but he must have been aware that it would take many days to put together such a force.[50] A plan to retreat from Anual to the coast was shelved because the navy could not provide a sufficient number of vessels to transport so many soldiers to the port of Melilla. All Silvestre could do was to mobilize the few reserves left in Melilla to reinforce as many positions as possible. Then he drove to Anual to take charge. As the Rif fighters gathered around Anual after taking Igueriben, Silvestre ordered a retreat for the next day along the track that led up through the nearby pass towards a defensive position a few kilometres away.

What happened on 22 July and over the following eighteen days became a national tragedy on a much greater scale than any other military defeat suffered by Spain, including the war of 1898 that led to the loss of the remnants of the Spanish American Empire. The reasons are several. The scale of casualties for such a short period was huge (calculations have varied from around 8,000 to 12,000 dead). Popular opinion was largely against the war, and therefore the loss of life fuelled the already acute social protest against call-up. In popular imagination the lurid myths of Moorish savagery and cruelty built into Spanish culture over centuries were reactivated. And unlike in 1898, the press and to a lesser extent the radio were now mass media that could be mobilized to arouse popular feelings. The 'Disaster of Anual', as the events of 22 July to 9 August began to be called (misleadingly, because the defeat extended over most of the eastern part of the province), entered into the collective imagination and became polarized around conflicting myths, such as heroism or cowardice, military genius or incompetence, according to different political ideologies. Any reconstruction of the events is therefore bound to be coloured by these ideologies, just as it has to rely to some extent on the fractured accounts of survivors, on their 'texts of trauma'.[51]

[50]   Telegrams from Berenguer to Eza and Silvestre to the king (Jefe Casa Militar SM) and order from Eza, all on 21 July 1921 in AGPR Marruecos 1921, caja 15510/10.

[51]   Joanna Bourke, *An Intimate History of Killing: Face-to-Face Killing in Twentieth-Century Warfare* (London, Granta Books, 1999), 8–10. The main sources on which I have relied for the following

Silvestre's order for retreat covered not just the position of Anual but a string of front-line positions. In the main camp in Anual there were some 194 officers commanding approximately 5,000 troops. Surrounding them were some 8,000 to 10,000 Rifian guerrillas. The camp occupied the undulating slopes of a promontory, from where the hills fell away into valleys on either side before rising into a massive mountain range. From the highest points of the camp the Rifian fighters could be seen making their way from these mountains into the valley in preparation for their assault. Berenguer had been made aware of the deteriorating situation in the eastern zone and had ordered two battalions each of the Legion and the Regulares to be detached from the western campaign and to sail for Melilla.

Silvestre's stress over the pending attack was such that he began to lose control of the situation. Under pressure from some of his officers, he changed his mind and ordered the defence of Anual, only to rescind the order after a violent quarrel with other officers. In theory the position could have been held for a while. It was well placed, commanding the slopes on all sides of the promontory. Its small artillery pieces could have caused the assailants problems. But there was only one narrow pass through which reinforcements could be sent, if any could be shipped over from the western zone in time. The track that led to and from the nearest base snaked its way through the pass and up and down mountain slopes, offering ideal opportunities for ambush. A journey of some 18 kilometres took four hours. But if they decided to stay in Anual, water and food might run out before a sufficient number of troops could be deployed from Melilla to rescue them. Silvestre also had to think of all the other positions surrounding the camp.

As the Spanish prepared for the retreat once again, Rifian guerrillas could be seen gathering for the assault. The influence of Abdel Krim and his lieutenants had been evident for several weeks already. In an operation in June, the Spanish had noticed that the Rifians now carried out a staggered retreat when they abandoned positions.[52] Silvestre's boldness had been due largely to an underestimation of the capacity of the Rifian fighters to become organized. Their traditional tactics were based on guerrilla warfare waged by small groups drawn from the same tribe. They would fire on the enemy from close cover, and only charge on horseback at the enemy positions when confident of success. The Rifian soldiers surrounding the Anual position could now be seen organized into compact columns marching on the camp from the surrounding valleys.

summary of the disaster are, for primary sources: the archives of SHM; *De Annual: Información gubernativa*; José María Arauz de Robles, *Por el camino de Annual. Apuntes y comentarios de un soldado de África*, 3rd edn. (Madrid, Voluntad, n.d.); and for secondary sources: *Historia de la Campañas*, vol. 3; Pando, *Historia secreta* (the most complete reconstruction based on all available and some private sources); Manuel Leguineche, *Annual. El desastre de España en el Rif, 1921* (Madrid, Alfaguara, 1996), and numerous eye-witness and journalistic accounts. Sources will be given in the footnotes only where specific information or analysis is referred to.

[52] Ortega, *Annual*, 20–1.

One of the most interesting of the many accounts by the survivors of the Anual disaster (and perhaps the least known) was given to a newspaper by a military doctor attached to the Regulares.[53] His narrative vividly re-creates the confusion of the Spanish retreat. It also highlights the crucial moment when Moroccans who fought on different sides met and joined forces to kill the Spaniards. The doctor and a small detachment were posted on a hill 200 metres from the entrance to the camp to cover the retreat of the troops. From there, although fired on continuously, he had a panoramic view of events at the camp. He saw the troops leaving and the enemy advancing rapidly towards them. At the entrance of the camp, the pro-Spanish harka were joined by soldiers as they filed out:

at first in formation and very slowly; then in confused and motley groups and finally in irregular file into which the Rifian bullets opened numerous gaps. Already Moors and soldiers were mixing together on the track. Uniforms and jellabas became jumbled together in that crowded mass and in the bright sun amidst the bare reddish hills they scrambled down the narrow track with shouts, moaning, swearing, contradictory orders, curses, groans, and blasphemies. The soldiers of the friendly *harka* were going back to their villages along the same track as our battalions. And the soldiers went along trustfully beside them. They thought the other Moors were behind them. But the others then came down the hills like avalanches; rose up from ravines and stream-beds to join the strange column retreating in confusion and discord. And suddenly, it was impossible to tell who were the Kaddur's Rifians [Kaddur had been a Spanish ally] and who were Abdel Krim's. Almost automatically, the races divided. On one side the victims, the Christians. On the other, the executioners, the Moors. I waited for the order to retreat that did not come. They had forgotten us.

With his binoculars the doctor watched Silvestre standing at the entrance of the camp gesticulating and shouting. Some Moors ran up onto the track shouting and firing their rifles. 'The general walked a few paces as if offering himself to the cruel, implacable enemy. I saw him vacillate, raise his hands to his chest, then to his head, and then fall face-down.' Two other witnesses nearby, on the other hand, saw Silvestre walk back to his tent, and from 50 metres away they heard a shot fired in the tent and concluded he had committed suicide.[54]

The morale of the retreating soldiers had not been improved when they saw officers leaving the camp in cars filled with luggage, nor when others tore off the insignia of their rank so that they would not be singled out by the Rifian soldiers. Panic seized them when the native troops began to turn their guns on them. The artillery pieces were abandoned and the wounded were pushed off stretchers to allow the horses and mules to be used for escape. Weapons, money, clothes, munition boxes, first-aid kits, documents, and all manner of military and personal objects lay strewn about, 'the material substance of a

---

[53] Testimony of Dr Carlos Puig in 'De la tragedia de julio', *El Sol*, 2 Jan. 1922.
[54] Mentioned in Pando, *Historia secreta*, 170, from SHM Legado Silvestre.

whole army abandoned'.[55] As they reached the Izumar pass and started to climb up through 6 kilometres of ravine, the massacre of Spanish soldiers began in earnest. Stragglers had to climb over mounds of bodies of their fellow-soldiers as they tried to escape. Local Moroccans, including old men and women, joined in the slaughter, working their way through the dead and wounded in the rearguard with their long knives in search of loot. Groups of officers and men put up desperate resistance, including Morales and Manella, and most met their deaths in the valley and on the slopes of the Izumar.

The victory of Anual transformed the sporadic resistance of the Rifian tribesmen into an insurrection. According to Abdel Krim, 'having progressed so rapidly, our warriors had trouble believing in the reality of their victory, of the catastrophe into which the enemy was falling'. The authority of Abdel Krim was immeasurably strengthened and he was able finally to impose some organization on the motley tribes and their factions. Having had only some 300 warriors under his command during the attack on Abarrán, according to his own admission, he now had thousands.[56] His financial reserves also played an important part in the consolidation of his power. He offered 5 pesetas for each artillery shell delivered to his headquarters, shells that could be fired from the artillery pieces the Rifian fighters were suddenly acquiring in great numbers. He also created a professional police force paid out of his funds. Abdel Krim insisted that all booty be divided equally and, according to a Spanish prisoner, this order was respected. However, his instruction that prisoners should not be maltreated was not obeyed in the killing at Anual and in its aftermath.

Abdel Krim soon set up a government in the Tensaman territory with a 200-strong military guard. There he met with tribal chiefs and administered justice according to the Koran law while his brother took charge of foreign affairs. In the same place, Spanish prisoners were kept in caves awaiting ransom. A holy war against the infidel invader was declared throughout the region, and contingents were sent out to destroy the numerous Spanish positions across the whole of the eastern zone.[57]

The survivors of the Anual disaster were joined by troops fleeing from the intermediate positions. A cavalry regiment made several charges at the advancing Rifian soldiers and managed to hold them back briefly, at the cost of many casualties. The next garrison along the route of retreat towards Melilla was abandoned because its commander claimed he had received no orders. The largest munitions dump in the eastern zone was blown up, sending plumes of smoke into the sky and alerting the Rifian fighters of the movement of Spanish troops. The arrival of increasing numbers of fugitives in the camp at Dar Drius further along the route eastwards, 'a mass of distraught

---

[55] Ortega, *Annual*, 55.   [56] Roger-Matthieu (ed.), *Mémoires*, 93 and 100.
[57] Testimony of Captain Soler in 'Lo que cuenta el capitán Soler' in *El Sol*, 9 Oct. 1921.

men, with large numbers of wounded, without any sign of organization or command', sent a wave of panic through the small garrison.[58] On 23 July, the day after the Anual debacle, General Navarro, who had replaced Silvestre as Commander-in-Chief of the eastern zone, gave the order to abandon the camp and its surrounding positions. But yet another blockhouse was not notified, and of its 604 soldiers only thirty-seven survived the overwhelming attack by Rifian fighters.

An order to hold a new line of defence by Berenguer, who arrived in Melilla by ship on the same night, was overtaken by the revolt of local tribes who had decided to join the spreading uprising. That same night, too, advance contingents of the Rifian army reached the Gurugú mountains overlooking Melilla, to which hundreds of Spanish settlers and mining personnel were fleeing. While the reinforcements from the western zone were still sailing to Melilla, the town had only 1,800 soldiers to defend it. Just as the main garrisons fell in the occupied areas, the 4,000 soldiers spread out in small positions between Anual and Melilla abandoned their posts or made a stand against hopeless odds. The main body of fleeing troops made their way towards the railway station at the end of the line from Melilla, where they hoped a train might carry them to safety.

Eyewitnesses reported Dantesque scenes during the flight. Soldiers fought amongst each other to get horses and mules to carry them away. Others pretended to be wounded. More officers tore off all insignia and clothing that could identify their rank. Ambulances and lorries were so full that they broke down or their axles snapped. The cavalry regiment made repeated charges until most of its troops had been killed or wounded. That day, two Spanish fighter planes flew over the area and reported seeing a trail of bodies, artillery pieces, and abandoned lorries all the way from Anual to the railway station, and plumes of smoke arising from dozens of positions throughout the eastern zone.[59]

The first reinforcements from the western front reached Melilla on the morning of 24 July. Made up of Legion battalions, they had been ordered to abandon the siege of Raisuni's headquarters late on 21 July without any explanation. In a forced march, the up-and-coming young major and second-in-command of the Legion, Francisco Franco, covered the 96-kilometre journey to Tetuan with his battalion in seventeen hours with only a three-and-a-half-hour break. From there, they went by train to Ceuta and then by boat to Melilla. Eza had offered to send troops from Spain, but there were virtually no trained reserves on the mainland and Berenguer rejected the offer on the grounds that reinforcements could not be thrown into battle without training. Since many of the native police and Regulares had gone over to the enemy, he

---

[58] Testimony of Lt. Fernando Gómez López in *De Anual*, 573.

[59] For the scenes of retreat, ibid., 478–80, 573–6, and other pages.

would have to rely largely on the Legion.[60] But by the time the troops from the west were ready for combat, most of the eastern Protectorate had fallen to Abdel Krim. The garrisons along the railway line to Melilla fell one by one in rapid succession.

The major base at Monte Arruit held out in desperate conditions until 9 August. Besieged by thousands of Rifian fighters, the 3,000 defenders of the fort under Navarro's command waited for a counter-attack from Melilla that never came, despite numerous efforts by senior officers to put together a relief column. Abdel Krim's contingents had brought up the artillery they had captured and fired constant salvoes into the fort. Inside, soldiers were driven mad by thirst; some died of gangrene from their wounds and a few committed suicide. By 9 August the scarce water supply had been exhausted, despite efforts by Spanish planes to drop food and ice by air.

Navarro sent two officers separately to discuss the terms of surrender, and one was shot down. Meanwhile word had reached Berenguer from an envoy of Abdel Krim that the besiegers of Arruit were not obeying his orders, implying that he could not guarantee the safety of the besieged. Finally terms appeared to have been agreed. Led by Navarro and his general staff, and with the injured in the front ranks, the Spanish troops began to march out of the garrison. But the Rifian soldiers fell on them immediately and a new massacre began. Navarro and his top-ranking officers were kept apart, because they could fetch a big ransom while the ordinary soldier was valueless. A few soldiers managed to reach safety, but the overwhelming majority of unarmed officers and men were slaughtered on the spot.[61]

With the fall of Monte Arruit, the whole of the eastern zone of the Protectorate, except a small area around Melilla, was lost to Spain. In eighteen days almost 10,000 Spanish soldiers were killed. Thousands of others were wounded and many had been taken prisoner. The shock-waves set up by the disaster radically changed the political climate in Spain. Scepticism, indifference, and ignorance about the military enterprise in Morocco gave way among many sections of opinion to anger against those responsible for the disaster and a spirit of revenge against the enemy. Four days after the fall of Monte Arruit, the government resigned and a government of 'national concentration' was formed among several parties, with Maura once again at the helm in his fifth term as president.

One of the first and unavoidable tasks Maura faced was to address the domestic repercussions of the disaster and satisfy the clamour for retribution, justice, and clarity. The previous administration had begun the process by appointing General Juan Picasso, a much-decorated veteran of the late-nineteenth-century colonial war in Morocco (and a relative of the youthful Pablo Picasso), as examining magistrate. His brief consisted of drawing up a

---

[60] Berenguer to Eza on 26 July 1921 in AAFAMM 442/6.   [61] Pando, *Historia secreta*, 253–7.

government report on the basis of which legal proceedings could be initiated against those responsible for the events in the eastern zone up to July 1921. Successive royal decrees in August and September, however, exempted the High Command in Morocco from any investigation. Thus, when he arrived in Melilla in late August to begin his inquiry Picasso found himself deprived of those documents vital to any determination of responsibility for the disaster. Neither Berenguer nor Eza were obliged to give him any papers, and Silvestre's archive had been secreted away.

From the beginning, Berenguer had insisted that any investigation should be limited to 'partial actions'. In a letter of mid-August, Picasso had appealed to him, arguing justifiably that the chain of events in the eastern zone could not be understood without reference to the military plans that had lain behind Silvestre's advance. Berenguer had complained to the new minister of war, and the king had duly obliged once again by ordering that Picasso's investigation should have nothing to do with the high commissioner.[62] All that Picasso could do, therefore, was to hear evidence from officers and soldiers and refer individual cases to military judges for action according to normal military legislation. Acting in these extremely difficult circumstances, Picasso produced a lengthy report in April 1922 that painted a devastating picture of inefficiency, incompetence, and corruption among officers in the eastern zone. Some of the evidence he produced will be examined at greater length in Chapter 6.

As a result, five military judges were appointed to begin proceedings against soldiers and officers picked out by the Picasso report. Yet their investigations were systematically obstructed. Documents crucial to their inquiry were made unavailable. Both Berenguer, as high commissioner, and the commander-in-chief of the eastern zone, with the connivance of other colonial officers, made it impossible for the military judges to investigate senior officers. A well-known native officer, accused by Picasso of fraud, was shielded so effectively by his fellow-officers that no evidence could be produced to put him on trial. The result was that, with few exceptions, only junior officers, probably those with no 'godfathers', could be put on trial. The judges' efforts to question eyewitnesses were repeatedly hampered. Obligingly, the king granted a royal decree in November 1922 whereby officers were only required to leave their posts to appear before the judges in exceptional circumstances, the exception being determined by the High Command.

The dingy military offices where the judges worked almost had their electricity supply cut off because the bill had not been paid by the Melilla command. Documents they requested were not sent, officers they had received permission to interrogate often failed to turn up, and their work was subjected to constant delays by the bureaucratic manoeuvring of the local authorities. One of the five military judges, Colonel Domingo Batet, had been arguing all

---

[62] *De Anual*, 604–6.

along that he should not be there at all and only officers from the legal corps of the army should be evaluating the cases they were investigating. The sole official response to his plea to be replaced was an accusation that he was taking his time to complete the inquiry.[63]

A perusal of some of the cases reveals the extraordinary constraints placed on the military judges' investigation. As in Picasso's case, their inquiry was limited to the ten days or so of the disaster of July 1921 and the actions of individual officers, rather than the strategies and orders of the High Command that had led up to it. Batet wrote that he felt 'tortured' by the injustices of his task, punishing subaltern officers for a crisis created by their commanders, whom he could not prosecute.[64] Some of the cases in front of the judges were similar to those brought against individual soldiers during the First World War for cowardice in conditions only recently acknowledged as being unendurable. No such revision has ever been undertaken in Spain. Of the fifteen cases he had to deal with as a result of the Picasso report, Batet appears to have demanded the prosecution of only six. Several of the other cases he dismissed out of hand.

One of the cases, for example, was manifestly unjust. A young second lieutenant newly arrived in Morocco had been posted to Anual on 20 July. During the retreat from Anual he had remained in command of his detachment, and when they arrived at Monte Arruit in a state of exhaustion he was told by a superior that they were in no condition to fight so he returned with them to Melilla by train. But he went back to the front almost immediately after he had reached Melilla and was wounded twice in the course of the next few weeks. Nevertheless, he was charged with desertion. Batet commented that his 'disastrous' flight to Melilla was due above all to the vacuum of authority. In the pell-mell confusion of Monte Arruit, there were no officers giving orders and assigning tasks in that great 'mix of corps and units'.[65]

Other cases involved officers with respectable military credentials but proven records of illness. An infantry colonel claimed he had suffered a mild stroke in the stressful conditions of the retreat and had to return to Melilla from Monte Arruit by car. He had a record of strokes, and witnesses testifying in his defence claimed he had all but fainted, but others brought in by Batet's prosecution declared that he had appeared to be in normal health. Mainly on this basis he was sentenced to six years military detention and dismissal from the army. In a more bizarre case, a lieutenant with a good military record was charged with desertion when he had been manifestly ill. He had been in Anual and had taken over as commander of his company when his captain had had a serious attack of piles. Suffering himself from acute bronchitis brought on by pneumonia, Fontán was given a written order to return to Melilla by his

---

[63] Archivo Batet (AB), caixa 1, exp. 4.1 and 4.2.   [64] 'Mi confesión', in ibid., 4.1.
[65] Ibid., 4.3.

lieutenant-colonel. At least in this instance, it is clear that the prosecution under Batet dropped its case of desertion.[66]

In an even less excusable incident, another guiltless officer was made a scapegoat for the disaster. A lieutenant much respected by the men under his command was in charge of a besieged blockhouse (later nicknamed the 'death blockhouse') on the new front line near the Wolf Ravine, where the 1909 Disaster had occurred. The Moroccan guerrillas had reached the walls of the fortification and were throwing hand grenades through the slits of its walls. Deciding that they would not survive by remaining inside, he gave the order to evacuate the blockhouse. According to one account, his sergeant refused to abandon the site, in an unusual reversal of roles, and persuaded some of the soldiers to stay with him. The lieutenant fought his way out with the rest of his men and he and some of the soldiers reached safety, while those who remained behind were all killed. When word of these circumstances reached his commanding general, the lieutenant was arrested in front of the troops and court-martialled.

Imprisoned in the fortress in Melilla, he was handed a revolver by his fellow officers in order to shoot himself but bungled his suicide. An order reached the hospital where he was dying not to operate on him. Shortly after his death, an application was made for the sergeant to be awarded posthumously the highest military award in Spain, the *Laureada*. But later, for fear that a case in the lieutenant's defence might be opened revealing the complicity of his fellow officers in his death, the application was changed and the posthumous award was in fact given to him and not to the sergeant.[67] These four incidents contrast sharply with the many accounts of officers abandoning their posts, tearing off their insignia, and requisitioning getaway cars for no reason other than self-preservation, the vast majority of whom were never brought before a military court.

At the same time as the military investigations in Morocco, the Supreme Council of the Army and Navy, formed largely by veteran generals unsympathetic to the colonial military, had also set up its own investigation in 1922 following the Picasso report. In June it published an impassioned exposé in which the trial of thirty-nine officers was proposed, from a second lieutenant up to Berenguer himself. In this document, the Supreme Council appealed to the Senate to overrule the protection given to the general by the royal decrees, following the government's ruling that any public investigation of Berenguer could only be conceded if a petition were put to and approved by Parliament.[68]

---

[66] Ibid., 4.4 and 4.5. For more on the Jiménez Arroyo case, see Pando, *Historia*, 209–12.

[67] Most of the information on this incident is taken from J. M. Prous i Vila, *Quatre gotes de sang. (Dietari d'un català al Maroc)* (Barcelona, Llibrería Catalana, 1936), 99–100. Pando's account in *Historia Secreta*, 285–6, based on a parliamentary speech by the MP Ramón Solano, differs on a number of points terminating with the lieutenant's apparently successful suicide.

[68] *Información gubernativa* (op. cit.) This came to be known as the *Suplicatorio de Berenguer* (the Berenguer petition).

Two parliamentary commissions were set up in 1922 and 1923, and lengthy debates were held in the Congress of Deputies in which the discussion of the military campaign in the eastern zone and the disaster itself gave rise alternatively to sweeping denunciation and passionate defence of the Army of Africa.[69] In the course of the second commission, Berenguer was forced to defend his actions, bringing to the investigation a number of documents that he claimed exonerated him because none suggested he had supported Silvestre's offensive. On 13 September 1923 sixteen days after the Senate agreed to the military petition to put Berenguer on trial, the coup of Primo de Rivera brought to an end all efforts to define the responsibilities for the disaster.

Eighty years later, the disaster of Anual still stirs controversy. While it continues to capture the imagination of historians, it remains a mythical reference-point for many old inhabitants of the Rif, for whom Anual had been the crowning victory of a holy war.[70] From the evidence that has been pieced together over these years (though some, like Silvestre's papers, have still not surfaced), a more balanced picture is emerging of causes and responsibilities. The disaster cannot be adduced as proof that Spain was exceptional. Amongst colonial powers, defeat at the hands of their colonial subjects was common, as we have seen. Like the British disaster at Isandhlwana in 1879 and the Italian defeat at Adowa in 1896, the debacle at Anual was the result above all of resistance to colonial penetration, which had not only disrupted the local economy and social relations but also challenged religious beliefs and traditions. Those who collaborated with Spain had done so for pragmatic reasons or out of self-interest, not because they welcomed its domination of their country. However, that small portion of land that Spain was expected to control for the benefit of the international community of colonial powers was amongst the most unyielding in the world.

Beyond military causes, the most important origin of the disaster was thus a political one. Spain failed in its naive bid to control its Protectorate peacefully through the existing networks of rank and prestige. Following, as always, the model of French colonialism and under French pressure, Spain resorted to trying to impose its own power. Colonial invasion was not accompanied by any significant investment in infrastructure. With some exceptions, the officers and administrators appointed to run the Protectorate lacked the vocation and training to do it competently and tactfully. Thus, the numerous governments since Spain moved into Morocco must share the responsibility with the colonial military. They must take the blame for failing to stand up to the metropolitan military in order to carry out a radical reform of the army in Spain when they had the opportunity. They also failed to provide sufficient resources to the colonial army in Morocco, fuelling its consequent inefficiency.

---

[69] DSCD 1921 to 1923 (27 vols.).   [70] For further discussion, see Ch. 7.

The main repercussion in Morocco of this political failure from above was the growing antagonism of the Moroccans. The more progressive elites, which had cherished the illusion that the country would grow through Spanish investment, had their expectations frustrated, as we have seen. The increasing hostility was largely hidden behind manifestations of friendship, compliance, or even complicity towards Spanish rule, because these were the only means available to survive colonialism. It was a Spanish misreading of this acquiescence that contributed to the disaster. The errors and abuses of colonial officers provoked, in the words of one of Picasso's witnesses, 'a profound disruption in some communities and a certain latent malaise, waiting to break out at the slightest setback of our forces'. The troops under their command, both native and Spanish, were responsible for widespread mistreatment, from looting and rape to the casual disregard for local customs.[71] Poor discipline was in itself a product of low pay and motivation. Thus the sudden explosion of violent brutality on the part of the Rifians in 1921 was the result of an accumulation of grievances over many years of colonial rule.

The more immediate cause of the disaster was military incompetence. The fundamental problem of the High Command's plan rested on a miscalculation of the strength of the enemy born of a lack of understanding of local society. Of course, it is only in relation to the intensity of resistance that the lack of resources on the Spanish side can be judged. Silvestre relied too much on past experience and failed to take into account military intelligence about the changes that were taking place among the opponents of Spanish colonial expansion in the Rif. He appeared to know little about the money Abdel Krim had accumulated and his growing authority among the Rifians after he had abandoned the Spanish cause. He also overlooked both the psychological transformation that occurred amongst the Rifians as a result of their victory at Abarrán and the military build-up that consequently took place in their ranks in the six weeks before the siege of Igueriben. Their new sense of confidence turned them into a far more dangerous adversary than before. On the day of the disaster, Berenguer confessed that he could never have imagined how much they would achieve.[72]

In any circumstances, Berenguer's deployment of the exiguous and poorly armed colonial army over two fronts and Silvestre's decision to stretch his forces across a wide area were militarily unsound. The Africanists were right to criticize the government for failing to provide them with sufficient resources, but they failed to take these limitations into account when devising strategies. The decision about which positions should be occupied was the result of an ill-advised mix of military and political considerations; that is, locations were often chosen in complete disregard of their logistics because of the pressure of

[71] *De Anual*, 409 (Riquelme's testimony) and 462 (Fray José Antona's testimony).
[72] Berenguer to Eza, 22 July 1921, AGPR, Marruecos 1921, caja 15510/10.

supposedly pro-Spanish local tribes to provide them with protection.[73] Silvestre's plan for advance into the heartlands of the Rif, approved by both Berenguer and Eza, lacked two of the fundamentals of military strategy— reserve troops near the front line and a secure rearguard. Indeed, in the plan there was no provision for a retreat; that is to say, Silvestre refused to imagine anything other than victory.

The accusation of military ineptitude, however, must be also directed at the Spanish military institution itself. The incompetence and laxity of garrison life in the metropolis were reproduced in the midst of a colonial war. The Junta-inspired law of 1917 abolishing campaign bonuses and creating a closed-scale system of promotion based almost entirely on length of service, as we have seen, must have dissuaded many ambitious officers from volunteering for service in the Moroccan war. Many of those who fought in the campaign were doing so simply because they had been posted there. Picasso's report revealed that many officers who were supposed to be stationed in the front-line positions at the time of the disaster were, with Silvestre's permission, enjoying a comfortable life in the rearguard. The general appeared to tolerate the transgression of his own ruling of 2 May 1920 obliging colonels to spend twenty days a month in their posts. The chronic absenteeism among officers resulted in a lack of continuity of command and a relative absence of confidence between soldiers and their superiors, a factor that may account in part for the breakdown of discipline in Anual and elsewhere, as subsequent reports suggested.[74] The antagonism between officers over the issue of promotion also caused mistrust that eroded the capacity for efficient communication and co-operation.

Another important element in the collapse of the eastern front was the over-reliance of the Spanish command on native troops. Spanish commanders were caught in a predicament. Apart from the recently created Legion, Spanish servicemen were not the best front-line troops in any war, least of all such an irregular war such as that in Morocco. So they largely remained spectators of battles. Yet without exposure to this war they were unlikely to respond adequately to critical situations such as that of July 1921. The abysmal training they received when they arrived in Morocco made them even less capable of resisting the Rif onslaught.[75] But the dependence of the Spanish army on native troops rested on a misconception about their allegiance. Both the British and the French armies used native troops from other parts of their empire in their colonial campaigns. The Spanish had little choice but to deploy troops that shared the same religion and, by and large, the same culture as their opponents. When faced with overwhelming odds, as in Abarrán or Anual, the reaction of many Moroccan soldiers in Spanish pay was not to die

---

[73] Monje y Llanos's and López Pozas's testimonies in *De Anual*, 423 and 442.

[74] Ibid., 53–4, and *Información gubernativa*, 309.

[75] Colonel Salcedo's testimony to Picasso in *De Anual*, 455–6.

for Spain but to join their brothers on the winning side and shoot the alien infidel.

Like the 1898 Disaster, Anual branded the minds of colonial officers with failure. In the prevailing military ideology, defeat was like losing masculinity. From then on, revenge and reaffirmation became obsessive goals. The Spanish state was viewed with intensified resentment. The new disaster also deepened the cleavages within the military. Paradoxically, however, the Army of Africa seemed to be backed as never before by public opinion. The middle classes responded at last by sending their sons to fight in Morocco and by raising money for new weapons. But the colonial army faced a formidable new enemy. Abdel Krim now commanded an army in which most of the tribes of north-east Morocco had united in a new jihad to eject the ancient enemy from their land.

CHAPTER FOUR

The Forging of a Colonial Army
1921–1930

THE DISASTER OF Anual transformed the meaning of the colonial war for both soldiers and civilians. The driving force of the professionals of the colonial army in the months and years that followed was a spirit of compulsive revenge. Many officers and soldiers had lost comrades in the debacle. As in all wars, the loss of close friends encouraged murderous aggression among the survivors and erased any lingering sense of guilt at the methods used to avenge their death. Those officers who had sought to make friends among Rifians of doubtful allegiance were sidelined by those seeking total war. For the new troops shipped to Morocco for the autumn counter-offensive, the discovery of the mutilated and unburied corpses of Spanish soldiers, rotting or picked clean by vultures, served to instil meaning into the colonial campaign. As in other wars, the anger and hatred felt by these soldiers helped to override fear or battle shyness and it became easier for them to face death and to kill.[1] This meaning was enhanced by a determination to rescue the prisoners held by the enemy, many of whom were comrades of the survivors. In the immediate aftermath of the disaster, the solidarity of shared defeat gave a new cohesion to the Army of Africa.

As advocates of the Prussian military model stressed, this new sense of militant purpose was militarily more valuable than any input of improved tactics and training, though without these two the troops would continue to suffer a high level of casualties. Out of the ashes of Anual a new colonial army began to be forged that had revenge as its fundamental motive power. But the defeat also forced officers to re-examine their armaments, strategies, and tactics. New weapons needed to be employed that were deadlier than the distant artillery barrages and the cavalry and fixed-bayonet charges. Proponents of the deployment of the type of chemical weapons used in the First World War began to gain adherents. A greater use would also be made of incendiary bombs as part of a more determined scorched-earth strategy. More importantly, any lingering compunction about distinguishing between civilian and military targets largely disappeared in the new climate of attrition.

---

[1] As Joanna Bourke points out in reference to the major wars of the twentieth-century in *An Intimate History of Killing: Face-to-Face Killing in Twentieth-Century Warfare* (London, Granta Books, 1999), 139–70.

The strategy of dispersing forces across the Protectorate had led to military defeat, so new methods of deploying forces were drawn up for the campaign. From the sedentary system of isolated blockhouses and temporary incursions into enemy territory, the army was going to rely on strong mobile units, often maintaining contact with each other and living off the enemy land through pillage and tribute. These same units should intensify tactics of lateral deployment and encirclement. The shock-troops of this new colonial army would remain the Legion and the native troops. But the Regulares now had to be recruited from areas outside the Rif because many of them had defected to the enemy in July.

Much of Part II will be devoted to a thematic study of the metamorphosis of the Army of Africa into an efficient if brutalized and interventionist military force. This narrative chapter will focus instead on the transformation of the colonial army through events from the aftermath of the disaster to the final conquest of those areas resisting Spanish invasion.

As in the aftermath of the 1909 disaster, the new colonial campaign was backed, if only briefly, by public opinion in Spain. Defeat can sometimes mobilize nationalism more powerfully than victory. The disaster stirred a society that had largely preferred to ignore the colonial war. The minister of war's enlistment for combat duty of the sons of middle-class families who had paid to keep them away from the battlefield was greeted with apparently universal enthusiasm. For once, the Moroccan war could be seen as a collective effort on the part of all Spanish men and their families, and not just of the poor.[2]

The Anual disaster may have aroused patriotic feelings but it did not make the purpose of Spain's military presence in Morocco any clearer to civil society. If anything, it strengthened the feeling that Spain should abandon its Protectorate. In fact, a much more important motive for civilians than the defence of national pride was the urgent need to rescue the thousands of prisoners held by the Moroccan enemy. Equally strong amongst many Spaniards in the metropolis was the desire to avenge the deaths of so many Spanish soldiers. The disaster intensified the collective anger of sections of Spanish society and unleashed a wave of racism in the media. It became possible to talk about a holocaust of vengeance. The overblown account of the war after Anual by the correspondent of a liberal Madrid newspaper went as far as to propose that 'to act against the Rifians as they acted against us would not be enough: it would be necessary to ruin the land, exterminate the race . . .'.[3]

[2] For an analysis of the urban response in Spain to the disaster, see Pablo La Porte Fernández-Alfaro, 'La respuesta urbana ante la crisis de Anual (1921–1923)', *Revista de Estudios Africanos*, 18–19 (1996), 109–24 and his Ph.D thesis, 'La respuesta urbana ante la crisis de Anual (1921–1923)', Universidad Complutense de Madrid, 1997.

[3] Alfredo Cabanillas, *La epopeya del soldado desde el desastre de Anual hasta la reconquista de Monte Arruit* (Madrid, n.p., 1922), 275. Bourke, *An Intimate History*, 160–5, also points out that civilian reactions to the enemy can sometimes be more virulent than those of the front-line troops.

The media hype surrounding the war finally gave colonial officers the national recognition many had always craved. In an effort to mobilize patriotism, the coming counter-offensive was now dubbed the Reconquest, linking it with one of the most enduring myths of Spanish history, the *Reconquista* of Spain from the Moors. The paradox was that, unlike the medieval Christian war against the infidel, there could be no pretence that the Protectorate was Spanish territory.

The new troops shipped from Spain to Melilla were in no state to undertake an immediate counter-offensive. The only corps that the military command could rely on to defend the town were the units of the Legion and Regulares brought over from the western front and what was left of the Regulares in the eastern command. The majority of the native troops had gone over to the enemy, and the only ally left among the Moroccan tribes in the east was a chieftain whose tribe was based to the north of Melilla. A week after the disaster Berenguer reported in a telegram to the minister of war that the 'conglomerate' of units at his disposal were deficient in war matériel, training, and numbers. 'This case is really extraordinary, since it is not a question of reinforcing an army with new elements but of creating an army to fight the next day.' As fresh troops arrived from Spain, the supply of tents and mattresses ran out and NCOs and soldiers had to sleep outside on the ground and search for shade during the day. Some were posted in no man's land beyond the security limits of the town's environs, where they were targeted by the Rifian fighters with cannon captured from the Spanish.[4]

The victory by the Rifian forces had catapulted Abdel Krim into the leadership of the new jihad. But the motley army he now commanded was more effective as an aggregation of mobile guerrilla forces than as an army. Traditions of war in the Rif rested on brief military engagements, not on regular warfare. When the warriors had gathered the rich and variegated booty from the towns and military posts they had ransacked between Anual and Melilla, many dispersed to carry it home.[5] The harvesting season was also approaching, requiring all able-bodied men to return to their fields. Melilla had been there for Abdel Krim's taking, but much of his army had dissolved, leaving him with insufficient forces to conquer the town. His ability to command rested on his capacity to negotiate with tribal leaders. Until he could meet with them after the victory and begin to impose some kind of order on their forces, as he later acknowledged, he had to be prudent.[6] So his inconsiderable force of warriors led a noisy and disruptive siege of Melilla without

---

[4] Prous, *Quatre gotes*, 13–14. Berenguer's telegram of 29 July is in AGPR Marruecos 1921, caja 15510/10.

[5] Mohammed Saleh Faraji (interviewed in the Ajdir region on 23 Apr. 2001) remembers that his uncle, who had been one of the muhayeddin who came close to Melilla, returned home with a handsome horse and rifle taken from the Spaniards.

[6] Roger-Matthieu (ed.), *Mémoires*, 104–5.

venturing further, attacking sentry posts all along the front line, and firing salvoes of shells into the city from the heights of the Gurugú mountains with captured artillery pieces.

Seven weeks after the fall of Anual, the Spanish counter-offensive was launched. Some 47,000 soldiers had now been massed in Melilla behind the 1909 defensive line. They consisted of twenty-five infantry battalions, five cavalry regiments, artillery units manning nine mountain batteries, twelve light batteries and three heavy fixed batteries, and companies of sappers and telegraph, railway, transport, ambulance, and stores personnel. Of the total number of troops, 22,000 were available for the counter-offensive columns, 3,500 were kept as a reserve column, while the rest were deployed for the defence of Melilla and its surroundings.[7] The new recruits shipped over from Spain had received only a rudimentary training, so the shock-troops continued to be the Legion and Regulares soldiers brought over from the western zone. These Regulares were less likely to defect than their eastern Rif counterparts, because they belonged to altogether different tribes from those of the enemy fighters.

With the Legionnaires and native troops in its vanguard, the new army began its advance on 17 September against the mobile guerrilla forces of Abdel Krim, after a massive bombardment of Rifian positions by air, artillery, and warships off the coast. Both the logistics and the tactics of the offensive were completely different from those of the pre-disaster campaigns. Under Silvestre, the army had established a string of lightly defended positions in strategic positions on hilltops or at the entrance to valleys as it advanced. This so-called blockhouse system had been criticized by a well-known military writer as early as 1909.[8] Each of these positions had posed logistical problems of supply and defence, and condemned the soldiers manning it to intense boredom and occasional terror. The whole system had collapsed when the Rifians went on a coordinated offensive for the first time.

In the new campaign the colonial army put into practice some of the lessons learnt during the disaster. The enemy was regarded no longer as a pushover but as a formidable force. In contrast to Silvestre's widespread and tentative probing into the heartlands of resistance, the army now knew intimately the land it was going to try to recapture. Its objectives were much clearer—to recapture the main positions it had lost two months previously against an enemy that could be defined more easily and that would be defending rather than attacking these same positions.

Instead of spreading out its forces, firepower was concentrated in three columns, at the vanguard of which were the shock-troops commanded by General Sanjurjo. The two other columns were deployed to provide lateral and in-depth defence, and a fourth went by ship to recapture the port 12

[7] SHM R414, leg. 264, carp. 41, and Estado Mayor, *Historia*, 496–7.
[8] Capitán X (Nazario Cebreiros), *Verdades amargas. La campaña de 1909 en el Rif* (Madrid, n.p., 1910), 26–34.

kilometres south of Melilla (where the first landing by the Spanish took place in 1908) and attack the Rifians from behind. As the Spanish army advanced from different angles seeking to employ the tactic of envelopment against the enemy, the still disorganized troops of the Rifians were forced to fall back.[9]

The campaign reports sent by Berenguer to the government were filled with rhetorical hype on behalf of an army abashed by the rout of July. While the government's failure to ensure adequate supplies and reinforcements was made much of, the operations were described as 'brilliant', 'glorious', 'sublime'. Everywhere, the enemy appeared to be in retreat and disarray. The king made his contribution to this collective self-deceit by calling for 'fresh triumphs to ennoble the virile and selfless effort of the Army'.[10]

The new army moved forward on two main fronts from the north and the east. As the troops recaptured the closest positions they were deeply distressed by the scenes of massacre and devastation left by the retreating enemy. Amid the putrefaction of the rotting bodies, it was clear that many Spaniards had been killed after surrender and many had undergone savage torture. Some had had their genitals cut off and stuffed into their mouths, or their eyes gouged out, or their ears or tongue cut out. Some bodies had their hands tied together with their intestines, and some had barbed-wire stakes shoved up the behind. Bodies were missing heads, arms, and legs. Some had been cut into two. Covered by flies, the 3000 or so bodies at Monte Arruit lay strewn about inside and outside the fort. The jackals and the crows had stripped much of the flesh off the corpses and the sun and rain had disfigured them out of all recognition. Piling the stinking bodies together, the troops, vomiting from the stench, set fire to them. Without any Moroccan enemies in sight, soldiers took it out on fields and orchards nearby and burned deserted villages whenever they came across them. The exaltation of the early days of the new offensive gave way to a darker mood; one soldier remembers that they no longer sang.[11]

Berenguer admitted to the minister of war in the new government led by Maura that, in their thirst for revenge, his troops chopped off the heads of their Moroccan enemies and carried them away as trophies. The famous story of the duchess who led a team of Red Cross women in the hospitals of the rearguard and was presented by soldiers with a basket of roses, in the middle of which were the heads of two Moroccans, was probably based on a real incident.[12] The cautionary beheading of Moroccan prisoners by General Alfau in 1913 had now become casual and routine behaviour among the colonial

---

[9] Ibid.   [10] 'Partes de guerra', SHM R101, leg. 28, carp. 1–3.

[11] José Ramón Fernández Oxea, *Crónicas de Marruecos. Tras la rota de Anual* (Barcelona, Sotelo Blanco, 1985); for the burning of fields, entry for 24 Oct. 1921 in Antonio Aguilar Fuentes, 'Libro de memorias de un soldado que estuvo en Africa', unpublished handwritten diary, 1921–2. Also Antonio Cordón, *Trayectoria. Memorias de un militar republicano*, 2nd edn. (Barcelona, Crítica, 1977), 77–82; Pando, *Historia secreta*, 289 and 292–3; Arturo Barea, *La forja de un rebelde* (Mexico, Ediciones Montjuich, 1959), 328 and 407.

[12] Ramón Garriga, *La señora de El Pardo* (Barcelona, Planeta, 1979), 40; Pando, *Historia secreta*, 294–5.

troops.[13] The brutalization induced by the disaster and the sight of tortured Spanish corpses swung even the most progressive colonial officers towards more barbaric methods of war. As we shall see later, the idea of using chemical weapons such as mustard gas against the Moroccan enemy had by now become acceptable to all the colonial officers and even to liberal politicians.

By November the Spanish counter-offensive reached the banks of the Kert river, the front line of Spanish expansion until Silvestre began his invasion of 1919. The political significance of the Kert line was that most of the Spanish mines lay behind it and could now be reoccupied and defended.[14] It also had strategic importance because the Kert riverbed, swollen in winter and almost completely dry in summer, provided a natural line of defence at the foothills of the virtually impenetrable mountain range where Silvestre's troops had been defeated. To the intense chagrin of colonial officers, it was there that Maura brought the offensive in the east to a virtual halt. In a speech to parliament on 10 November, he explained that the operation had been undertaken only to ensure the security of Melilla. Spain was in Morocco to guarantee the authority of the Mahkzen, not to impose its own rule, as both the Spanish government and the Army of Africa had mistakenly tried to do until then. Once pacification had been completed in east and west, the army would occupy coastal positions only and indeed would be withdrawn altogether from Morocco as soon as possible.[15] The disgruntlement of officers was also fed by the failure of efforts to ransom their fellow officers who were held prisoners by the Rifian army. Maura had blocked efforts to pay the ransom money of up to 4 million pesetas demanded by Abdel Krim on the grounds that it would strengthen the enemy.

But in Maura's government of 'national concentration' opinions differed about the future of operations in Morocco. A conference between the cabinet and leading generals and admirals reached a compromise agreement typical of the contradictions of Spanish Moroccan policy: pacification without occupation. The word 'irradiation' was used to describe this operation, referring presumably to the old tactic of flying columns that sought to bring about peace through bribing tribal chieftains. However it was done, pacifying the east and west zones could not possibly be accomplished, as Berenguer argued, from the positions currently occupied by the Army of Africa. Yet the government was under pressure to limit any further military expansion. Once again, the mirage of an amphibious landing at Al Hoceima was conjured up as a solution, but

[13] Decapitating the enemy seems to have been a more-or-less common practice among French colonialists: the frontispiece of Weiskel's *French Colonial Rule* displays a photo of the decapitated head of an Ivory Coast man stuck on a sword or spear of three Frenchmen as they pose for the camera.

[14] And indeed, the mining of iron was renewed shortly afterwards. While total production fell from 419,700 tons in 1920 to 101,200 in 1921, it rose again to 300,800 tons in 1922 and to 403,700 in 1923: Ministerio de Trabajo, Dirección de Estadísticas, *Zona de protectorado de los territorios de soberanía de España en el Norte de Africa, Anuario estadístico, 1941* (Madrid 1942), 112.

[15] Antonio Maura, *Transcendental discurso pronuciado por D. Antonio Maura* (Madrid, n.p., 1921).

the date of the operation was left open, postponed to sometime in the summer when climatic conditions would be more propitious. Meanwhile, the bombing campaign was to continue in preparation for the retreat of the army to the coast once pacification was completed, and for the repatriation of many of the troops to Spain.[16] It was a strategy with little coherence. It also wildly under-estimated the military capacity of the Rifians under their new leader Abdel Krim. He was now free to create a virtual state in the Rif, raising taxes, nego-tiating with tribal leaders, and putting together an army.

The results of the outburst of collective solidarity in the autumn and winter of 1921–2 appeared meagre by the spring. Resigning from his post in March, the minister of the navy drew up a bleak balance-sheet of the campaign. It had taken seven months, 160,000 men, and 700 million pesetas to advance 35 kilo-metres. The prisoners had not been freed, the Protectorate had not been reim-posed, the repatriation of the troops had not begun, and nobody had been taken to court for the events of July.[17] Rent by internal contradictions, the multi-party government of Maura fell.

Successive administrations were caught between two fires: the determina-tion of the colonial army and its civilian supporters to step up the military cam-paign, and the pressure from civil society to free the prisoners by whatever means possible and to repatriate the troops. Repeatedly governments sought and failed to satisfy either constituency. The army was allowed to continue lim-ited military action while it was bursting for an all-out military offensive, and at the same time peace-feelers were put out to both Moroccan leaders.

Once again, Raisuni was wooed in yet another Spanish volte-face. He had been about to be defeated by Berenguer in July 1921 when the Anual disaster had forced the High Command to move the bulk of its troops to Melilla. Castro Girona and a team of civilians were sent to negotiate with him in early August 1922. Raisuni's diplomatic skills and his lavish treatment of the Spanish visitors convinced them of his intention to keep the peace with Spain. They were right, but only to the extent that Raisuni's efforts had always been directed at keeping Spain out of the area where he maintained hegemony.[18] In fact, he had been in close touch with Abdel Krim since the autumn of 1921 and had asked the Rifian leader for reinforcements so that he could attack Spanish positions in the north-east.[19] As a result of the truce the Spaniards concluded with him after repeated negotiations, Raisuni was given back land seized by the Spanish army and generously compensated. He was also awarded a stipend, his troops were able to return to their villages, and his sacked palace

[16] A summary of the Pizarra Conference is in AFAMM leg. 351 no. 17, and Berenguer's reactions are in a letter of 25 Feb. to La Cierva in ibid., leg. 277, no. 6.

[17] *La Libertad*, 16 Mar. 1922.

[18] Letter from diplomat Vicente Ramírez to Emilio María Torres, 1922, AGPR caja 15599/16.

[19] Abdel Aziz Temsamani Khallouk, 'Lectura en el archivo de Jebala: sobre las correspondencias entre Raisuni y Jattabi', *Al Alam Athakafi*, 10 Sept. 1988, 4–5.

was rebuilt at the Spanish taxpayers' expense. At his insistence, the Spanish named several of his relatives to positions of power in the Protectorate.[20]

The minister of war and many of the colonial officers were appalled at the terms of the peace proposal. His colleague, the minister of state, had conducted the negotiations behind his back. Tribal leaders who had collaborated with Spain would be exposed to reprisals as a result of the agreement, and indeed the whole notion of collaboration would be seriously devalued. Equally serious would be the effect of the proposal on the colonial officers, many of whom had fought against Raisuni's forces for years. In a report in December 1922, a captain of the native police stationed in the west exclaimed: 'we don't even thank he who has exposed his life in our cause, and instead we splendidly reward those who have remained our enemies; is there anything more odious? Is there anything left of our ancient and traditional chivalry?'[21] The sense of bitterness among the colonial military against civilian governments and the apparent fickleness of public opinion can only have been strengthened.

In the east, efforts were made to bribe tribal factions close to Spanish-controlled areas to abandon Abdel Krim's cause. 'Peseta diplomacy' was accompanied by the continued aerial bombardment, and a new offensive was launched to restore the front line to where it had been just before the disaster.[22] But the ambition to reach the heart of the Rif through a combination of bribery and war was, like Silvestre's, based on a serious underestimation of the Rifians' capacity to resist. It also relied on support at home that was rapidly dwindling. By the autumn of 1922 the backing of the establishment and the middle classes for continued military action in Morocco had fallen away. Popular organizations that had sprung up as a result of the disaster, such as the pro-prisoners' committee, were now mobilizing huge support against the war from the trade unions and student and neighbourhood associations up and down the country.

The colonial officers' bitterness towards civilian rule was intensified when the government began appointing civilian high commissioners. The first of them wrote a scathing report about the ten years of misrule in the Protectorate by military administrations. The direct rule imposed by the Spanish military in Morocco had been a gross reversal of the role Spain had been given by the European Powers, he wrote. Spain was there to ensure the rule of the Moroccan government and its local representatives. The only change Spain should have sought was economic, that is, to spread the benefits of European economic progress to Morocco. Cultural assimilation was misguided and the

[20] Report of 24 Sept. 1923 in AGA Africa, Serie Política, caja M16, exp. 1. Details of negotiations with Raisuni can also be found in the Picasso Report, vol. 2 of the 1931 edition, pp. 356–61.

[21] BN Africa, Documentos Raisuni, leg. 2 exp. 6; Tessainer, El Raisuni, 221–3; for the minister of war's reactions see AGPR caja 12956/7.

[22] Francis Koerner, 'La Guerre du Rif espagnol vue par la Direction des Affaires indigènes française (1921–1924)', Revue Historique, 287 (1992), 148.

Spanish army should respect local culture. The most urgent reform was to remove the power of political decision-making from the commander-generals and install civilian politics in the pacified areas.[23] These plans did not endear him to the Army of Africa.

New efforts were made to negotiate the ransom of prisoners held by Abdel Krim since July 1921. On 27 January 1923 the progressive Basque millionaire and entrepreneur Horacio Echevarrieta, who had had dealings with the Rifian leader in the past over mining concessions, oversaw the release in the Bay of Al Hoceima of 326 survivors of the 534 Spanish soldiers held in tough conditions by the Rifian army.[24] The ransom money of 4 million pesetas went to pay for further contingents and arms for the army Abdel Krim was painstakingly building out of the scattered forces of the Rif. Legend has it that, on learning of the ransom price, the king remarked how expensive chicken meat had become. Whether it is true or not, the legend illustrates the scorn felt by Alfonso XIII for the Spanish Tommy and the impatience of the colonial military, with whom the king closely identified, over the government's priorities.

Meanwhile, under a new civilian high commissioner, Luis Silvela, an informal ceasefire was put into effect in the early spring of 1923. Secret negotiations for peace, led by the same people who had concluded a truce with Raisuni, were held with Abdel Krim on a naval launch in the Bay of Al Hoceima. The Rifian leader, well versed in the culture of the mining companies, hoped to use the freedom of Spanish commercial penetration as bait for the recognition of his republic by Spain. But the Spanish would not give way over the question of the territorial integrity of the Sultanate and the negotiations broke down.[25] The high commissioner's parallel efforts to set up an alternative pro-Spanish regional government in the Rif were immediately destroyed by Abdel Krim's men, and by May the new Rifian army was beginning to assemble for a fresh offensive. Launched at the end of the month, it rapidly spread to most of the front line.

New talks were held, again in secret, with the help of a pro-Spanish chief, who was promptly murdered for his pains in mysterious circumstances.[26] This time the negotiations were more formal, involving both the Spanish consul and a minister of the Caliphate. Fresh offers were made on both sides. Spain volunteered to recognize Abdel Krim as the caid of the Rif and offered economic help and military protection, but insisted on his acceptance of the

---

[23] AGA África, caja M24, exp. 1.

[24] Madariaga, España, 515–16; Pando, Historia secreta, 338. A bold visit to Abdel Krim by the editor of the liberal newspaper La Libertad revealed that at least the officers were treated reasonably well, although many of them appeared to be desolate after one-and-a-half years in captivity without any news: Luis de Oteyza, Abdel Krim y los prisioneros (Madrid, Mundo Latino, n.d. [1925]).

[25] Castro Girona's talks with Abdel Krim are reported in SHM R742, leg. 4, carp. 9.

[26] Madariaga's suspicion in España, 517–28 that it was ordered by Martínez Anido is not far-fetched, because the militarist wing of the colonial army had no interest in coming to an agreement with Abdel Krim.

Sultanate. The Rifian leader agreed to accept the Protectorate but maintained that the independence of the Rif was not negotiable. Recognition of a Republic of the Rif, however, was not something that the most liberal of Spanish governments could reconcile with Spain's international obligations. The talks were called off once again. A letter from Abdel Krim's foreign minister brought the negotiations to an end. 'We are astonished', he wrote,

> how you can feign to ignore that it is in the interests of Spain herself to conclude peace with the Rif, to recognize its rights and its independence, to respect the links of neighbourhood, and to cement a union with the Rifian people, instead of treading on it, humiliating it, and attacking its legitimate human rights, [a recognition that would be] in accordance with the code of civilization and the Treaty of Versailles which ended the First World War.[27]

Faced with the realities of the Moroccan situation, the pacific intentions of the liberal government and its civilian high commissioner gave way to a reluctant strategy of aggression. The cabinet itself was deeply divided between a minority who preferred to abandon Morocco altogether and those willing to renew the war. Silvela petitioned the minister of state for the purchase of toxic-gas shells to fire at Abdel Krim's forces. The minister replied giving his and the president's approval. One of the seeming attractions of chemical weapons was that they might take the place of thousands of soldiers who would otherwise have to be mobilized for war. As we have stressed, the government was under huge popular pressure to end the war and repatriate the troops. But a committee set up by royal decree in August 1923 advised against the rhythm of repatriation envisaged by the cabinet.[28] In these circumstances, any further mobilization for a new offensive would upset the fragile political balance.

For all his acceptance of war as a necessary evil in Morocco, Silvela found himself increasingly shunned by the military. In an interview with a French journalist, he described the garden of his Tetuan residence as the 'Vatican Garden'. 'M. Silvela's phrase', the Frenchman reported to the French Foreign Office, 'describes exactly and spiritually the isolation in which the civilian high commissioner is held.' Silvela confessed to him that Ceuta and Melilla, the basis of all operations, were 'conquered lands, subjected for centuries to an exclusively military regime, where interests of all kinds have been created that need the war to continue'. This indirect reference to the culture of war and the corruption of many officers reveals the depth of his disillusion with his post.[29] The continual problem he faced trying to persuade the government to provide

---

[27] Madariaga (ibid., 543–5) reproduces the letter in full. See also Cándido Pardo González, *Al servicio de la verdad* (Madrid, n.p., 1930), 121–36, and for further negotiations in June 1923, see Francisco Hernández Mir, *Del Desastre a la victoria (1921–26). Del Rif a Jebala* (Madrid, n.p., 1927), 143–50.

[28] Report of 23 Aug. 1923 in AGPR caja 15511/2.

[29] Léon Rollin, 'Voyage a la Zone Espagnole Septembre 1923. Notes', ADMAE Maroc 1917–40, vol. 197, pp. 12–13.

the resources necessary to carry out military operations, added to the hostility of the colonial officers he had to deal with, finally persuaded him to resign.

Silvela probably knew he had little choice. He tendered his resignation on the day of General Miguel Primo de Rivera's coup, 13 September 1923. It was an open secret that the army in Spain was about to seize power. Of the four main co-ordinators of the coup, two were veterans of the colonial war. The king was also closely involved, having considered taking executive power himself earlier in the year.[30] The support of the majority of colonial officers for Primo de Rivera's coup might seem paradoxical. The general had been the most decided supporter in the army of withdrawing from Morocco altogether. The latter part of his career had been based exclusively in Spain, so he did not form part of the Africanist coterie. Unpardonably for many colonial officers, he had backed the Juntas de Defensa, the corporatist movement among officers in Spain. Yet they shared his determination to end what they saw as the civilian government's persecution of the military for the disaster of Anual. The second Responsibilities Committee was due shortly to pronounce its verdict on the causes of the disaster. Primo's coup brought the whole juridical process to a halt, and among his first initiatives was an attempt to confiscate the Picasso report from the parliamentary archive. Only the prescient action of one of the members of the committee saved the document.[31]

Colonial officers also backed Primo's coup because they shared his disgust for the Restoration system. Apart from its inability to impose law and order in an increasingly restless society, the regime had failed to provide the resources to restore the prestige of the colonial army and avenge the deaths of their comrades. It had allowed the press to attack the army when they believed it should be applauding the patriotic and heroic self-sacrifice of the military in the bloody war in Morocco. The liberal and left-wing press were given the freedom to accuse the army of incompetence and corruption, as in the press campaign to expose the fraudulent practices of the quartermaster stores in Larache.[32] The 'decadence' of Spanish society was epitomized by industrial unrest, Catalan 'separatism', and the demonstrations of opposition to the war by soldiers embarking for Morocco and their relatives. Incidents took place in Valencia and Malaga in August 1923. The most serious was the mutiny of a group of soldiers in Malaga who had been bound for service in Morocco. The government's repeal of the death sentence imposed on the ringleader of the mutiny added to the colonial officers' sense of alienation from Restoration politics.[33]

[30] As he confided to Maura's son Gabriel: Javier Tusell, *Antonio Maura. Una biografía política* (Madrid, Alianza, 1994), 250.

[31] Pando, *Historia secreta*, 312–13.   [32] See Ch. 8 for further details of military corruption.

[33] The Malaga incident was widely reported in the press. Reports consulted include *El Liberal*, *La Correspondencia de España*, and *El Globo* on 24 and 25 August. The mutiny in Malaga and the incident in Valencia were analysed at length by the French diplomatic sources in ADMAE Maroc 1917–40, vol. 226, pp. 49, 127–8, and 166.

But they had every reason to harbour mixed feelings about Primo de Rivera. He was a typical soldier from the Silvestre mould—a no-nonsense man, brave, genial, generous, and authoritarian to the core. In fact he was an outsize figure in more ways than one, with a large paunch and a Rabelasian lifestyle that led to all-night carousing in brothels.[34] Yet he had spoken out in no uncertain terms against the whole Moroccan enterprise. In his new modernizing discourse, colonialism was a thing of the past. Less than two years before his coup, he had publicly stated: 'No one should believe in all that nonsense that Spain's future and security lie on the other side of the Straits . . . for all those who have known how to and been able to (and not simply wanted to) throw off that colonial atavism (worse still in those sterile lands, inhabited by fanatical mountain people armed with Mausers) the future lies in the internal reconstruction of Spain, in agrarian development, in industrial progress, in culture . . .' In complete contradiction to the foreign policy of earlier statesmen, he exclaimed in the senate that the Spanish Protectorate actually endangered the defence of Spain.[35] Such a discourse was anathema to officers who had invested so much in the colonial endeavour. Over the years they had accumulated wounds, medals, and the memory of dead comrades, all of which had been woven into an epic narrative of heroism and patriotic sacrifice. Primo de Rivera scornfully dismissed the war as a series of 'skirmishes, surprises, aggressions, and ambushes.'[36] The disaster of 1921 had seen an overwhelming consolidation of the Africanist narrative. Giving up the Protectorate now, without overturning their defeat and taking revenge on the enemy, meant abandoning their dead comrades and ridiculing their heroic past. Colonel Castro Girona, the enlightened Arabist officer whose whole professional life was built around colonial service, now confessed he could not bear living in Morocco any more. 'I am going through a black period too,' he wrote to a friend, 'and I'll also do what I can to leave Africa.'[37]

Yet colonial officers were among the new dictator's most important constituencies. Primo's programme of internal regeneration had to be balanced against their wishes. Nor could he easily withdraw Spain from the commitments she had taken on in the various international treaties. His hope of persuading Britain to exchange Gibraltar for Ceuta and using this diplomatic triumph as a decorous means of withdrawing altogether from Morocco was dashed by Britain's lack of interest in the deal.[38] Primo de Rivera therefore

[34] According to the British consul in Tetuan, 11 Oct. 1924 in FO 636/8.

[35] The quote is from Rodrigo Soriano, 'Ayer y hoy', El Liberal, 24 Nov. 1921 and the reference to the speech in the senate from 'Marruecos en el Senado', ibid., 26 Nov.

[36] José Manuel and Luis de Armiñán Odriozola (eds.), Epistolario del Dictador. La figura del General Primo de Rivera, trazada por su propia mano (Madrid, Javier Morata, 1930), 43.

[37] Pardo, Al Servicio, 402–3; both Mola and Franco later confirmed the colonial officers' lack of confidence in Primo: Emilio Mola Vidal, Obras Completas (Valladolid, Santaren, 1940), 1024, and Francisco Franco Salgado-Araujo, Mis conversaciones privadas con Franco (Barcelona, Planeta, 1976), 136.

[38] Susana Sueiro Seoane, España en el Mediterráneo. Primo de Rivera y la 'cuestión marroquí', 1923–1930 (Madrid, UNED, 1992), 134–5.

found himself following a policy in Morocco that was just as pragmatic as that of the government he had overthrown. But it was neither Machiavellian nor completely improvised, as historians have differently argued. The suggestion that he planned to withdraw the troops to a defensive rearguard so that Abdel Krim's men would expand towards the French lines, thereby provoking the French into intervening alongside the Spanish, is not borne out by the primary sources. But nor was he making up his policy as he went along.[39]

The evidence suggests, on the contrary, that he was following a secret strategy marked by two stages. The first involved attempts to negotiate peace with Abdel Krim and Raisuni while the colonial army maintained its existing lines of defence. If negotiations failed with the former, the hope was that the latter could be persuaded to mobilize his *harkas* against the Rifian leader. After all, Raisuni had sent a letter of congratulations to Primo de Rivera on his seizure of power, hoping perhaps that he would be designated caliph under the new regime.[40] The second stage was conditional on the failure of the first. If Abdel Krim persisted in his offensive, the colonial army would retreat to a new defensive line. Behind this fortified line the Spanish would impose a fierce blockade preventing arms, munitions, and food from reaching the enemy.

They would also carry out a massive bombing campaign with TNT, incendiary bombs, and the poisonous chemicals whose supply had begun to be built during the previous administrations. Dropping the toxic bombs while Spanish troops were still engaged in battle would expose them to their terrible effects; navigational errors and mistaken targeting might have devastating results on the Spanish side, news of which would quickly reach Spain. Primo de Rivera's secret enthusiasm for the rapid manufacture and supply of mustard-gas bombs must be seen in the light of this strategy of retreat. It also explains the 'unfathomable mystery' to which a French journalist alluded, as to how the dictator could pacify those areas in enemy hands by withdrawing from them.[41]

So while he intensified the build-up of stocks of chemical weapons, Primo de Rivera first sought a peace deal with both Abdel Krim and Raisuni. Less than two weeks after his coup he authorized talks in Paris and Madrid with a friend of Abdel Krim. His secret offer to the Rifian leader went well beyond the framework of the international treaty of the Protectorate. He proposed an

[39] For the first argument, see e.g. María Teresa González Calbet, *La Dictadura de Primo de Rivera. El Directorio Militar* (Madrid, Ediciones el Arquero, 1987), 198 and 127. For the 'improvisation' thesis, see Sueiro, *España*, 132–4.

[40] Temsamani Khallouk, 'Lectura', 4–5. In fact, France blocked Primo de Rivera's support for Raisuni's candidature on the grounds that he had been pro-German during the First World War: Ibn Azzuz Hakim, *Armed Resistance*, 199.

[41] Quoted in Sueiro, *España*, 137–8, though Sueiro has no answer to the 'mystery'. Cordón, in *Trayectoria*, also argues that Primo de Rivera saw chemical warfare as a cheerful but not cheap way of ending the war without sacrificing any further Spanish soldiers, though he offers no evidence (p. 128). Primo de Rivera's repeated reference in his speeches to the bombing campaign must be seen in this light; e.g. his speech to the Zaragoza Chambers of Commerce in autumn 1924 (Hernández Mir, *La Dictadura*, 149). See Ch. 5 for further details of the chemical war.

organic statute for the Rif whereby the region would enjoy virtual autonomy from the Sultanate. Under its terms Abdel Krim would be free to form a regional government with a council of notables and Spanish representatives of the high commissioner. The Rifian leader would have the right to command an army of 3,000 soldiers led by his own and Spanish officers. Spain would bear the cost of both and would in addition cover any deficit in the Rifian government budget and pay for a programme of public works in the new autonomy (whose geography would be determined by a mixed Rifian–Spanish commission). In exchange, Abdel Krim should suspend all hostilities, release the prisoners, hand over all his weapons to the Spanish (who would pay for each item), and allow the Spanish authorities to visit the battlefields of 1921 to bury their dead. A token of the Spaniards' relative ignorance of Moroccan customs was that the position of emir offered to Abdel Krim was not one he was entitled to according to Koranic law because it could only be awarded to descendants of the Prophet.[42]

Bearing Primo de Rivera's offer of a peace deal, Abdel Krim's friend went to the Rifian leader's headquarters while his French wife was paid a generous maintenance allowance by the Spanish authorities, which she used to live an extravagant life in Málaga. But he disappeared in the Rif, probably detained there against his wishes by Abdel Krim.[43] Primo de Rivera then utilized the services of the Basque millionaire Echevarrieta, but to no avail. Well versed in the colonial subjects' strategy of surviving colonial rule, Abdel Krim sought to keep Spain guessing about his intentions. Under the previous government, Spanish intelligence had intercepted a letter he had written to his brother, whom he had sent to Paris to seek international support, in which it was clear that Abdel Krim's apparent willingness to consider a truce was a manoeuvre to gain time before his new offensive.[44] Emboldened by his military successes, the Rifian leader was not prepared to accept anything else but recognition by Spain of the complete independence of the Rif.

Primo de Rivera had more success in his efforts to reach a deal with Raisuni. Indeed, four days after his coup the chieftain had sent an open letter offering to help in the fight against the Rifian enemy. The dictator's high commissioner, Luis Aizpuru, negotiated a new pact with Raisuni in October 1923 (the third such agreement) in which the sharif was recognized as the supreme authority of the Moroccan government in the Jebala. As such, he was authorized to pacify the insurgent parts of north-west Morocco with the aid of Spanish forces. In exchange, Raisuni agreed to recognize the Mahkzen and the caliph of the Spanish Protectorate. But in a secret verbal agreement he was offered the position of pasha of Tetuan, which would make him the de facto caliph because the incumbent had just died.

[42] José Manuel y Luis de Armiñán Oriozola, *Francia, el dictador y el moro. Página históricas* (Madrid, Javier Morata, 1930), 84–90.
[43] Sueiro, *España*, 142–4.   [44] AGA AE, caja 6296.

Primo de Rivera's worries about the French reaction to the unilateral desig-
nation of one of their old enemies as caliph were overcome by Aizpuru's passionate defence of the advantages of having him on their side.[45] In further
talks, Raisuni was assured that the retreat of Spanish troops to a new line of
defence was only temporary. A new advance would take place later after the
employment of other resources, which would have 'positive and immediate
results'—no doubt an oblique reference to the coming use of mustard-gas
bombing.[46]

Compromise with Raisuni deeply offended the proponents of war, the militarist Africanists. In a report to the dictator, three leading officers made a vit-
riolic attack on Aizpuru and his 'pacifist' colleagues. Peace with either
Moroccan leader was pure self-deception, they said. While talks were going
on, Spanish allies in both areas were being robbed, persecuted, and killed. By
negotiating with Raisuni, the Spanish had lost all dignity and 'national superiority'. Many officers, it was claimed, had left the colonial army in disgust as a
result. These mediators should be sacked and replaced with 'apolitical' personnel.[47] The notion that seeking peace through negotiations was merely
advancing a political cause reveals the self-image of colonial officers as custo-
dians of the national interest.

But Raisuni was no longer of much use to Spain. He was seriously ill with kid-
ney disease and, although repeatedly treated by Spanish medical officers, could
not move from his bed to take up his new position in Tetuan. His dealings with
the Spanish must have been by now well known to his fellow countrymen, and
many were turning to Abdel Krim for leadership. The campaign he now tried
to launch against the Rifian leaders' adherents in the west did not attract much
support. As the British consul in Tetuan observed: 'The call to arms, unpopular
as it generally was, was tolerated when Raisuni wielded real power and the
enemy was the Spaniard. But when Raisuni is only a stalking-horse of the
Spaniard and the enemy are fellow Moslems, there will either be refusals, or
frightened obedience which will only produce the scum of the villages to make
mock war. "When Moslem fights Moslem, many bullets go wide." '[48]

Nevertheless, Raisuni was in a position to provide the Spanish army with
useful intelligence reports. He was too deeply imbued with the prevailing culture of inter-tribal rivalry to feel a common solidarity with his traditional rivals
against the Spanish invader. Thus he was happy to inform the Spanish
military authorities of a local concentration of Abdel Krim forces and went as
far as proposing that Spanish planes should bomb them.[49] The claim by his

[45] Tessainer, *El Raisuni*, 232–53.

[46] 'Síntesis de las conversaciones sostenidas entre el Cherif Raisuni y el Señor Cerdeira, en Tazrut,
desde el 8 al 12 de junio', 13 June 1924, AGA Africa, caja M12, exp. 2.

[47] Report of 18 Apr. 1924 in AGA Africa, caja M24, exp. 10. See also Mola, *Obras*, 16.

[48] Hope Gill to consul-general in Tangier on 31 July 1924, PRO FO 636/6.

[49] 5 Dec. 1923, SHM R120, leg. 49, carp. 13.

contemporary supporters that he was deeply patriotic and religious must be weighed against evidence that he was willing to betray other Moroccans fighting against foreign penetration.

Primo de Rivera's decision to withdraw the troops to a new line of defence was agreed by his cabinet, the so-called Directorate, on 30 May 1924. No mention was made in the agreement of the use of mustard gas, but in a telegraphic communication with Aizpuru a few days before the dictator made it clear that the timing of the retreat was connected with the arrival of the first mustard-gas bombs for use by the air force.[50] The new front line would be a crooked line of defensive positions in the extreme east and west of the Spanish Protectorate. In the west it was designed above all to protect the rail-link between Tangier and the capital of the French Protectorate, Fez, as well as the road-links between Tangier, Tetuan, and Ceuta. In a later operation in the east, the troops would fall back some 15 kilometres to a new front line, abandoning a string of positions along the battlefields of 1921. But the most significant retreat would be in the west, and in particular from the holy city of Chauen, whose capture in 1920 had cost the lives of many Spanish soldiers and native troops.

Primo de Rivera hoped that the withdrawal to the new front line would mean a substantial reduction of military expenditure and of deployed Spanish troops. The Directorate calculated that of the approximately 125,000 soldiers on duty in Morocco, no more than 50,000 would be needed to defend the line once it had been established, and that the cost of the Protectorate would not exceed 100 million pesetas.[51] However, these financial calculations did not take into account the huge expense of buying chemical weapons and the materials to make them. The retreat was in itself dangerous because it meant exposing large columns of soldiers and equipment such as cannons to the highly effective ambushes of Abdel Krim's partisans. Yet many of the existing garrisons in the present front line were under repeated siege, and without retreat the risk of one or more new disasters seemed imminent.

Abdel Krim's movement in the area had been immeasurably strengthened by the support of two key leaders of the local Jebala tribes, who had abandoned Raisuni's cause and brought their guerrillas over to Abdel Krim's army. One of them, the youthful Jerirou, had been a sergeant of the Regulares in Tetuan and so had an intimate knowledge of Spanish military habits. A token of the Rifian leader's new level of organization was that, from his capital in Ajdir he was in direct contact by telephone and telegraph with his followers in Jebala via cables supported by poles that stretched for miles through forest and over the top of mountains.[52] The most important telephone-exchange system was based at his headquarters, an advance position in the south from where his

[50] 24 May 1924, AGA Africa, caja M12, exp. 2. [51] Ibid.
[52] Interview on 18 July 2000 with Jerirou's son and son-in-law, Hach Med Ben Ahmed Jerirou and el Hach Abdel Krim Ben Ahmed Ben Ali; further information about Jerirou from Léon Rollin, 'L'Espagne au Maroc', Bulletin du Comité de L'Afrique (Nov. 1926), 528–9.

supporters in the west could be warned about Spanish bombers approaching them from the eastern airfields. Once the message had been communicated, his soldiers in the west would fire rifles into the air to advise civilians to take refuge in caves.[53]

The dictator was less bothered about the likely international repercussions of the retreat. Under the existing treaties Spain was under no obligation to occupy the land. The only part of Morocco he was really interested in maintaining under Spanish control was Ceuta and the adjoining coastal strip. The acquisition of Gibraltar was one of Primo de Rivera's most cherished ambitions, and he hoped to be able to barter Ceuta for the Rock in some future deal with Britain.[54] In any case, France had always maintained the principle of the utility of some parts of the territory and the futility of occupying others. Nevertheless, the French government had already expressed deep concern to the Directorate about the threat posed to the security of her Moroccan Protectorate by a Spanish retreat. It would allow Abdel Krim's forces even greater access to tribes across the Franco-Spanish border, where their call for a jihad against the invaders was already being echoed.[55]

The militarist Africanists may well have known about the dictator's intention to retreat behind a defensive line in order then to use blanket bombing with mustard gas as a weapon of submission. Although they took care not to express their views about chemical war either in public or in their correspondence, there is no doubt that they supported the principle of toxic bombing. Paradoxically, the officers who seemed to have the greatest enthusiasm for such methods were the enlightened Africanists, such as Aizpuru. As we shall see in Chapter 5, chemical bombing was regarded by some as a more humanitarian form of warfare. A short, sharp, and devastating onslaught, it was thought, would force the enemy to capitulate quickly and thereby save lives in the long run. Probably for the militarists, on the contrary, revenge and the redress of defeat had to be gained by combat rather than by remote control. Using the latest newfangled weapons, such as mustard gas, would keep them away from the action. It would deprive them of the opportunity to shine in battle and earn promotions and medals.

The pressure on Primo de Rivera to launch a new and traditional offensive and abandon his idea of a retreat was intensified by the publication in January 1924 of a new journal representing the views of the militarist Africanists, the *Revista de Tropas Coloniales*. In successive issues, his policy of seeking peace negotiations was indirectly but bitterly criticized. In the fourth issue, in April, an

---

[53] Oral evidence given by one of these soldiers on 1 Jan. 1991 in Yassin El Habtí, 'La resistencia de Chauen contra el colonialismo español (1920–1956)', Ph.D Thesis in Arabic, DES, University of Tetuan, 1999, pp. 104–5.

[54] Armiñán (eds.), *Epistolario*, 43. Seven years earlier Primo de Rivera had made a highly polemical statement on this theme in *La cuestión del día. Gibraltar y Africa* (Cadiz, n.p., 1917).

[55] Sueiro, *España*, 146–53.

article by Lieutenant-Colonel Franco attacking the supposed passivity of Moroccan policy led to the confiscation of the journal. But since the dictator needed the support of the colonial army, the journal was allowed to resume publication a month later. In the May issue the founder of the Spanish Foreign Legion, Millán-Astray, wrote a passionate article defending Spain's presence in Morocco. The king added his support to the colonial militarists by receiving a group from the journal and, during his audience, enquiring not so innocently whether the April issue with an article by 'Franquito' had come out yet. He was quoted as saying: 'I cannot hide the fact that the desires of my colonial troops coincide with my own.'[56]

By June 1924, Primo de Rivera had become seriously concerned about the agitation among the front-line officers against any retreat. He had received warnings from his commanders-in-chief in Ceuta and Melilla and from his friend General Sanjurjo, who was quite open about his opposition to the dictator's plans. Primo de Rivera cautioned the officers to maintain discipline and respect the unanimous opinion of the nation that the retreat was necessary.[57] Judging that he should try to convince them in person, he made a trip to the garrisons and front lines between 11 and 21 July. Everywhere he went he was confronted by signs of hostility bordering on insubordination. Notices proclaiming 'Viva Berenguer' were even found on a cruiser taking him along the coast. Taking the salute at a march-past in Ceuta, Primo de Rivera may have noticed that a company of the Legion were ordered to cast their eyes left in the direction of their founder and extreme militarist Colonel Millán-Astray, rather than at the dias on the other side where the dictator was standing.[58]

A dinner offered in his honour at the Legion's headquarters turned into an open expression of opposition to his plans. Legend has it that, as the lieutenant-colonel commanding the garrison, Franco ordered a meal to be served consisting mainly of eggs because the Spanish word for eggs, 'huevos', also means 'balls', and Primo was being reminded that he had none. But, given Franco's care to cultivate his superiors, it might well have been the result of an a posteriori joke based on the fact that eggs happened to be on the menu, which was then turned into a legend by the Legion's and Franco's hagiographers.

In the customary speech proposing a toast to the visitor, Franco openly attacked the idea of any retreat to a new defensive position and called for a new offensive. His words, as reconstructed later by an officer present at the occasion, suggest that the thirst for revenge, direct action, and old-fashioned mili-

---

[56] The article by Franco is 'Pasividad e inacción' (April 1924), no pp.; by Millán-Astray, 'Necesidad de permanecer en Africa' (May 1924), no pp., and in the same issue, 'Su Majestad el Rey y la "Revista de Tropas Coloniales" '. For further discussion of the journal, see Ch. 6.

[57] Telegrams and letters 16–17 June 1924 in SHM R70 (no leg. or carp.) and SHM R573, leg. 403 carp. 8.

[58] Hernández Mir, *La Dictadura*, 155.

tary honour were more important in his mind and those of his fellow Africanists than military strategy, even if this included the devastating use of poisonous bombs:

We would like to take the flag where honour and the memory of our brothers demand it . . . who spilt their blood on these lands . . . We want, General, to reach the last crag of the Rif, to make us worthy of the affection of our motherland and to extol those who died in the furrow . . . We want whoever commands us not to lead us to defeat. We want to go forward bare-chested (*a pecho descubierto*), facing glory, and, as we want the honour of Spain to come before the convenience of the government, the Legion awaits your words with anxiety and concern.

Primo de Rivera replied explaining his reasons for retreat and insisting on the officers' 'blind discipline'. Another phrase of his speech revealed his awareness of the emergence of the Africanist military as an exclusive caste that might pose a danger to his rule. 'You have no right', he exclaimed, 'to think that you yourselves have a monopoly of patriotism.' The dictator's speech was greeted with open, occasionally violent, expressions of disagreement.[59] He responded to this growing insubordination by typical and successive gestures of exemplary chastisement and reconciliation.

The unrest among the colonial officers was noted by the British consul in Tetuan:

The solidarity of the army, which the Marquis de Estella [Primo de Rivera] repeatedly proclaims, is noticeably lacking in Morocco. The army of occupation, judged even by Latin standards, more nearly resembles a Greek debating society in its passion for politics than a fighting instrument; internal criticism is freely indulged in and its energies are dissipated in advocating this policy and condemning that . . . he [the dictator] cannot have failed to observe the distinctly anti-Directory atmosphere. In the military casino officers have been heard even to inveigh against the king.[60]

By September the Africanist discontent was such that secret talks were being held about staging a military coup against the dictator. According to his own account, General Queipo de Llano, one of the officers demoted by Primo de Rivera and now reinstated, met Franco on 21 September to discuss the uprising. But like many such previous plots, the plan failed to materialize. Once again, the impetuous general was sacked by the dictator.[61] Instead, it was Primo de Rivera who seized the initiative. From 5 September he had taken

[59] Ramiro Gómez Fernández, *La dictadura me honró encarcelándome* (Madrid, Javier Morata, 1930), 116–22; Paul Preston, *Franco: A Biography* (London, HarperCollins, 1993), 44–5; Hernández Mir, *La Dictadura*, 163; 'Incidente de Ben Tieb', Archivo Varela, vol. 3.

[60] Hope Gill to the consul-general in Tangier, 21 July 1924, PRO FO 636/6.

[61] Queipo de Llano, *El General Queipo de Llano perseguido por la dictadura* (Madrid, Javier Morata, 1930), 105 (for his criticism of fellow officers, see pp. 42–3, 67–8, and 77–81); Preston, *Franco*, 45–6; General Gonzalo Queipo de Llano, 'Relación detallada de mi actuación en la zona de Ceuta', AR 58/38; for Primo de Rivera's paternal tolerance of Queipo de Llano's agitation, see Armiñán (eds.), *Epistolario*, 87–90.

KINGSTON LEARNING RESOURCES CENTRE COLLEGE

over command of the Army of Africa and had been overseeing operations led by Aizpuru to prepare for the retreat. His sense of alarm at the deteriorating military situation can only have been intensified two days later when he and his General Staff found themselves surrounded in a position they were inspecting. They only escaped by hiding behind bales of straw on a military train that happened to be passing by.[62]

The initial stage of the retreat was to relieve the garrisons and innumerable outposts that were being besieged near the coast and in the Teutan area. The second stage was to gather the troops deployed throughout the area, together with the civilians who had supported Spanish rule, and bring them back safely to Tetuan. For this purpose Primo de Rivera brought new troops over from Spain and got the Directorate to award extra war credits of over 61 million pesetas to bump up the artillery, air force, and medical services.

A large garrison on the coast was successfully evacuated in a naval operation. Columns of troops set off to relieve other positions in the interior in early September. In cases where the besieged posts could not be rescued, Primo de Rivera was prepared to pay the ransom demanded by Abdel Krim's local forces. Soldiers under siege for thirty-eight days were freed on payment of a ransom of half a million pesetas.[63] A large column set off on 23 September to relieve Chauen and battled its way to the holy city by 2 October. In the hills on either side of the road leading there from Tetuan, bloody engagements took place with Abdel Krim's forces, during which the Spanish army suffered enormous losses.

French military intelligence reported that between August and mid-October Spanish casualties amounted to some 18,000 (including the sick), with some 3,000 soldiers made prisoner. Another contemporary calculation, based on Spanish sources, put the number of war casualties at 12,800 for the same period, of which some were medical staff and the quartermaster corps. Three months later the American journalist Vincent Sheean, accompanied by one of Abdel Krim's captains, visited some of the positions fought over and lost by the Spanish. He saw the blackened and half-eaten bodies of Spanish soldiers lying everywhere, sometimes piled one on top of another. In one place he calculated there were 600 bodies or more in a space no larger than the courtyard of the Ministry of War in Madrid.[64]

The fall or abandonment of positions also resulted in the loss of large amounts of ammunition, arms, and equipment, all of which fell into the hands of Abdel Krim's army. The operations and the losses of men and matériel,

---

[62] Handwritten report by Sr. Aranda, 'Datos de Marruecos', 21 Oct. 1924, AR leg. 63, carp. 44.

[63] Hernández Mir, *La Dictadura*, 218–24.

[64] Spanish calculations in Aranda, 'Datos'. The French report is from P. de Cuverville to the minister of war, 15 Oct. 1924, in Service Historique de L'Armée de Terre (SHAT) 7N 2754; Vincent Sheean, *Adventures among the Riffi* (London, George Allen & Unwin, 1926), 313–14 (an American edition of the same year entitled *An American among the Riffi* was published in New York).

according to the French, were costing the Directorate 100 million pesetas a week. There were scenes of terrible pathos. In one position, lost and then recovered by the Spanish, a dead soldier was found with a note he had written attached to his clothing, reading: 'I die abandoned.'[65]

Despite the triumphant accounts of military communiqués, the retreat was badly planned and executed. A general killed in the operations complained in a letter to a friend five weeks before his death that Primo de Rivera's strategy was a fiction, and that his own column had been utterly abandoned, without food, animal fodder, or even cartridges. The lack of co-ordination between the different units was illustrated by an incident near Chauen. The town notables had approached Castro Girona, as commander of the troops in the area, to seek permission to negotiate a guarantee with Abdel Krim's men that there would be no reprisals once the Spanish troops had left. For his part, Castro Girona had asked the notables to offer money to the muhayeddin besieging Chauen in exchange for allowing his troops to leave and for announcing to the Rifian partisans that they were abandoning the town for lack of water. He backed up this offer with a threat to shell the town from a nearby Spanish position if their evacuation of Chauen were impeded. With Primo de Rivera's agreement, the 100 or so Moroccan leaders went to a town close by to meet representatives of Abdel Krim. To Castro Girona's alarm, Spanish pilots, uninformed of this meeting, bombed the town with TNT while it was taking place. Nevertheless, the negotiations appeared to have been successful and the Chauen notables returned with a promise from the Rifian commander to allow the troops to leave.[66]

The retreat from Chauen began on 18 November. Leaving dummies filled with straw and dressed in the uniform of the Legion along the parapets of the town, a huge convoy made up of thousands of exhausted troops and truckloads of wounded and sick soldiers set out in the direction of Tetuan.[67] Accompanying them were Jewish and Arab civilians and their families who had collaborated with the Spanish. With Castro Girona as overall commander, the rearguard was led by Franco and consisted of three companies of the Legion and a battalion of Spanish troops. Beset by rain and cold and bogged down in the spreading mud, the convoy took almost a month to reach its destination. Ferocious engagements took place all along the itinerary. The level of casualties became so high that on 30 November Primo de Rivera issued an order forbidding all officers and soldiers to speak of the campaign upon pain of death. On 13 December the convoy finally reached Tetuan, completing the

[65] The detail of the dead soldier is also from Aranda 'Datos'. For a vivid and partisan eyewitness account of one siege, see Emilio Mola, 'Dar Akkoba. Páginas de sangre, de dolor y de gloria', in *Obras Completas* (Valladolid, Librería Santarén, 1940), 10–219.

[66] Mola, *Obras*, 232–5; details about the negotiations, based on an interview in 1988 with one of Abdel Krim's wartime leaders in Chauen, are taken from Habtí, 'La resistencia', 92. For General Serrano's letter see Hernández Mir, *La Dictadura*, 229–30.

[67] John Scurr, *The Spanish Foreign Legion* (London, Osprey, 1985), 15.

retreat to the new front line in the western zone. A Spanish officer put the number of deaths for the whole operation in the west at 15,000, almost double the losses suffered in the Anual disaster.[68] After so many casualties, it was difficult for Primo de Rivera to claim that the withdrawal of the troops would save Spanish lives. The novelist Blasco Ibáñez described Primo de Rivera as the most defeated general in the world.[69]

Yet these operations revealed that the colonial army had become a far more efficient fighting machine than that of the pre-disaster years. It was not only imbued with a new sense of purpose, but was also better trained and co-ordinated. A more effective balance had been established between the use of the professional and conscript units. The latter were usually deployed as back-up forces and were often shielded by the shock-troops. Thus, in the retreat from Chauen units of the Legion and the Regulares were placed in the vanguard and rearguard while the metropolitan troops occupied the centre. When operations allowed it, the servicemen were used to construct roads or blockhouses. The accumulation of battle experience had helped to bond the Legionnaires and native troops to their officers. As we shall see in Part II, the uniforms, the rituals, and the liturgy of songs and chants amongst Legionnaires reinforced their sense of collective identity. The organization, supplies, and weaponry of the colonial army had also improved. Primo de Rivera had his fingers on the purse-strings and was not under the same pressure as the previous governments to placate the civilian lobby against the war.

However, his combined strategy of retreat and chemical bombing was not producing the results he and his advisers had hoped for. The massive doses of mustard gas, incendiary bombs, and TNT that the expanded Spanish air force had been dropping on the population of the Rif did not seem to have deterred Abdel Krim's advance. His soldiers were now at the gates of Ceuta and were shelling Tetuan from the mountain heights above the city. The tribes of the extreme north-west of the Protectorate had risen against the Spanish despite their long record of collaboration. As a result, communications were cut between Tetuan, Tangier, and Ceuta.

On 24 January 1925 Abdel Krim's men besieged Raisuni's headquarters. With misplaced confidence, the ailing leader had declared to his supporters a few days earlier in reference to his holy palace that 'heaven was far from the barking of dogs'. Once the siege began he sent a message to the Spanish asking them to stop bombing the area because some of the bombs were hitting his headquarters. Instead, he requested a daily air campaign with 'bombs, gases, and poisons' against those tribes nearby who had passed over to Abdel Krim's army. The following day Raisuni was captured by the local commander of the Rifian army and taken in a box carried by sixteen men on a long, seven-day

[68] Hernández Mir, *La Dictadura*, 241–3.
[69] Quoted in General E. López Ochoa, *De la Dictadura a la República* (Madrid, Zeus, 1930), 60.

journey to the Rifian headquarters in Ajdir. He died there in captivity in April. With his capture and death western indigenous resistance to Abdel Krim faded away and the Spaniards lost their last important, though utterly unreliable, ally. Abdel Krim's forces, on the other hand, gained in strength from the large amounts of money and arms accumulated by Raisuni that fell into their hands.[70]

The failure of his strategy led Primo de Rivera for the first time to take seriously the options put to him by the militarist Africanists. There can be little doubt that through his daily contact with them he began to be influenced by their pressure. It had long been their aspiration to strike at the heart of the Rifian resistance by staging a landing in the Bay of Al Hoceima, only a short distance from Abdel Krim's headquarters. The attraction of such an operation for Primo de Rivera was that it might force the Rifian leader to divert many of his troops from their siege of the front lines in east and west. Unlike the Africanists, however, he was deeply worried about the international repercussions of Abdel Krim's ascendancy. Totally ignoring the nationalist and religious aspirations of the Rifians, he feared that Al Hoceima might become a Bolshevik or Communist base. Almost as serious in his view was the threat that the French might reach an understanding with Abdel Krim and establish a base opposite the coast of Spain, an outcome that Britain had entrusted Spain with preventing.[71]

Primo de Rivera's espousal of their strategy, however, did not signal his conversion to the Africanists' desire for a massive invasion of the Rif. He still laboured under the misapprehension that some agreement could be reached with Abdel Krim before or after a landing. This was surely the result of the Rifian leader's continuing ability to sow the illusion that he was keen to strike a deal. Like Raisuni and other Arab leaders, he had acquired remarkable skills in his dealings with the Spanish military, among which was the ability to keep them guessing about his intentions. As late as March 1925 Primo de Rivera could write to his presidential deputy in Spain about the 'eagerness and haste felt in Ajdir [Abdel Krim's home town] to reach an understanding with us'. Yet the gap between Abdel Krim's aspiration for independence and Primo de Rivera's inability to concede more than a vague autonomy to the Rif was well known and too wide for any agreement.[72]

Even in June, Primo de Rivera was hoping to negotiate a deal through a new meeting between Echevarrieta and the Rifian leader. He asked the Basque millionaire to offer the Rifians money and food in exchange for their acceptance of a Spanish landing in the Bay of Al Hoceima. Such a proposal responded more to the dictator's international policy concerns than to a wish to defeat the

<hr/>

[70] Interviews with a man who helped to take Raisuni to Ajdir, Hach Med M'Hauesh, Tetuan, 24 July 2000, and with Jerirou's son, Hach Med Ben Ahmed Jerirou, on 18 July 2000; Vincent Sheean witnessed the arrival of Raisuni: *Adventures*, 278–82; Tessainer, *El Raisuni*, 306–17.

[71] Letter to Magaz, 21 June 1925, in Armiñán (eds.), *Epistolario*, 227–31.

[72] Letter to Magaz, 23 Mar. 1925, ibid., 55.

enemy. Once Al Hoceima was occupied, he clearly believed, the Bolshevik or French danger could be averted and the Rifians could be denied their only significant maritime staging-post. Once again, the offer revealed the naivety of Primo de Rivera's understanding about the nature of the Rifians' struggle. Echevarrieta went to meet Abdel Krim's representatives with a different but equally naive proposal, to give mining and commercial concessions in exchange for his submission and the release of the Spanish prisoners. The Rifian leader accepted neither offer, and Primo de Rivera finally set in motion the preparations for the oft-postponed seaborne invasion.[73]

His planned operation had been given an enormous boost by the French offer of joint action against Abdel Krim. Until the rise of the Rifian leader's power in northern Morocco, the French authorities had pursued a successful policy of divide and rule in their Protectorate by exploiting traditional rivalries between the tribes. But after Anual Abdel Krim's influence had begun to penetrate into the French zone, and in the summer of 1922 he had begun to collect subsidies and raise fighting units among a number of tribes in the area. On a trip to the zone, the editor of a Spanish liberal newspaper noticed Moroccans wearing items of Spanish uniforms under their jellabas, taken from the bodies of soldiers and officers killed in the 1921 disaster.[74]

Primo de Rivera's retreat had angered the French. Their high commissioner, Marshal Lyautey, now found he had to bear the consequences of Spain's failure to keep order in its own Protectorate.[75] By the end of 1923 the French authorities had become sufficiently worried about the spread of his rebellion to the tribes that occupied land on both sides of the frontier that they tried to establish contact with Abdel Krim to seek an understanding with him. As with the Spanish, the Rifian leader gave repeated assurances to the French of his friendly intentions, though they could not have felt reassured given Abdel Krim's well-known sympathies towards the Central Powers during the First World War.

In early 1924 French troops were sent across the Franco-Spanish border into a region where Abdel Krim's supporters were beginning to gain ascendancy over the pro-French faction. The frontier between the two Protectorates had been drawn on the basis of topography rather than the tribal composition of the local population, so that the local tribe was split in two. This was also an area crucial to the Rifians' war effort. The fertile grain belt of the surrounding area helped to feed their regular troops, and they needed also to secure their southern front. Abdel Krim also owed a debt to the local tribe for supporting his uprising against the Spanish.[76]

[73] Letter to Magaz, 21 June, ibid.   [74] Oteyza, *Abdel Krim*, 181–2.

[75] Lyautey, *Paroles d'action. Madagascar–Sud–Oranais–Oran–Maroc (1900–1926)* (Paris, Armand Colin, 1927), 424–5; Koerner, 'La guerre du Rif', 147.

[76] Rupert Furneaux, *Abdel Krim: Emir of the Rif* (London, Secker and Warburg, 1967), 147–51.

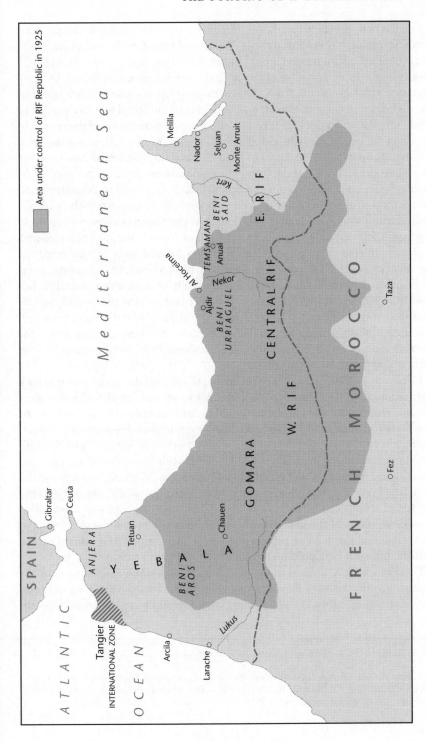

MAP 2   Spanish Morocco

The French, on the other hand, hoped to stop the spread of the jihad by installing military posts throughout the area. One of their emissaries made contact with the Rifian government in February 1925 and warned its ministers against any further agitation in the area the French now controlled. Lyautey requested reinforcements from France to prop up his lines of defence, but before the new troops reached them Abdel Krim launched an offensive on 12 April. The Rifian leader's later protestations that it was the rebellious tribes in the area who began the war with the French without his consent are less than convincing, the result of his need to justify his actions after his surrender to the French. Abdel Krim wanted to force the colonial powers out of Morocco. His extraordinary successes against the Spanish had given him the confidence to spread the resistance to colonial rule to across the Franco-Spanish border.[77] Abdel Krim's attack on French positions had the French troops reeling back. Between April and June some forty-three out of sixty-six forward posts fell and his forces inflicted some 2,000 casualties on a scattered army of 25,000 men, a rate of 8 per cent.[78] Taza and Fez were now threatened and communications with Algeria disrupted. Abdel Krim might even have been able to take Fez, but as with Melilla in 1921 he held back, probably because the defence of the city against a powerful French counter-attack would have been difficult and would have immobilized troops he needed to deploy elsewhere. French scorn for Spanish military incompetence was now tempered by direct experience of the ruthless skill of the Rifian army.

The French military disaster of the spring of 1925 led the government to seek negotiations with the Spanish for a joint operation to defeat Abdel Krim. First contacts were established at the end of May, and crucially the Spanish agreed that French troops could move even further into their Protectorate. A final agreement for a joint military operation was reached in August. The Spanish would stage a landing in the Bay of Al Hoceima with French naval support and move inland towards Abdel Krim's headquarters at Ajdir. After pacifying the south, the French would advance directly northwards towards the Rif and the two forces would catch the bulk of the Rifian army in a pincer movement. According to one of the generals who would lead the landing at Al Hoceima, the French had taken some persuading before they agreed to it, the disastrous British landing at Gallipoli in 1915 still fresh in their memories.[79]

The French were able to draw on considerably greater resources than the Spanish for the coming offensive. Troops from the French army of the Rhine were diverted to Morocco, where they were joined by new units of Algerian

---

[77] Roger-Matthieu (ed.), *Mémoires*, 121–40; David S. Woolman, *Rebels in the Rif: Abd-el-Krim and the Rif Rebellion* (Stanford, Stanford University Press, 1968), 164–73; Armiñán, *Francia*, 119–21.

[78] Roger-Matthieu (ed.), *Mémoires*, 142.

[79] Pedro Pascual, 'Así fue el desembarco de Al Hoceima', *Historia 16*, Año XXIII, n. 282, pp. 65–6; Mohamed Kharchich, 'La alianza franco-española contra el movimiento rifeño', *Fundamentos de Antropología*, vols. 4 and 5 (Granada, 1996), 71–7.

and Moroccan mercenaries. Altogether, the French colonial army in Morocco now totalled some 120,000 men, twice the number previously employed. A large proportion of these could be deployed in mobile columns in the coming invasion of the Rif.[80] In contrast, the Spanish army was tied down in defensive actions throughout the Protectorate. Nor could Primo de Rivera easily mobilize large numbers of additional troops from Spain, where the war remained unpopular. The plan for the landing at Al Hoceima envisaged the deployment of 18,000 soldiers. But the logistical support for the seaborne invasion—navy, air force, munitions, transport, first aid, water, food, and so on—required a massive organization and concentration of resources.[81]

Abdel Krim's intelligence service was so effective that he knew about the coming landing even before it began to be prepared. Moroccan spies in Spanish pay reported that as early as June 1925 the Rifians were building defences around and on the beach in Al Hoceima Bay. One night that month sentries had seen lights at sea and Abdel Krim's officers were able to assemble a large force, though it turned out to be a false alarm. Information reached Primo de Rivera that the defensive works were being supervised by a German army captain who had deserted from the French Foreign Legion. Cannons with a range of 10 kilometres captured from the French had been transported to the Bay and were firing at the nearby Spanish-held island and at the beach every day for target practice.[82]

Abdel Krim was also preparing a diversionary operation near Tetuan. Unnoticed by the Spanish, his forces in the west built a defensive system of trenches and underground tunnels during August that was to serve as the launching pad for an attack on the outer defences of Tetuan. Primo de Rivera could later barely disguise his admiration for their 'skill and audacity'. In a letter to the deputy president two days after the first landing in September, he described their 'tangle of underground positions covered by stones, superior in number to our own, and completely shielded from the effects of the air force, because they are a kind of cave protected along the slopes of the mountains where our positions are based and very close to them at dead angles, which also makes the use of gases extremely dangerous'.[83]

Indeed, Abdel Krim must have been aware of the projected date for the Al Hoceima invasion, because he launched his attack on the most forward position in the Tetuan defences just a few days before the landings took place at the other end of the Protectorate. It was timed also to coincide with the diversion of troops from Tetuan to the invasion force. His local commander, Jerirou, led

[80] Armiñán, *Francia*, 140–2.

[81] See Primo de Rivera's letter of 11 May to the chief of the General Staff, Ignacio Despujols, who had been involved in drafting Al Hoceima invasion plans since 1923: AGA caja M7 81/03.

[82] 'Confidencias', 20 June 1925, SHM R777, leg. 29, carp. 1–19. Letter from Primo de Rivera to Marqués de Magaz on 18 June in Armiñán (eds.), *Epistolario*, 206–7.

[83] Letter to Magaz, 10 Sept., ibid., 265.

the assault on an outpost that was so fierce that Primo de Rivera had to rede-
ploy 4,000 of his crack troops from the Al Hoceima force to counter the
offensive, and admitted he expected a 25 per-cent casualty rate.[84]

However, the Rifians could not be certain on which beach or beaches the
landing would take place in the Al Hoceima area. The operation was preceded
by an intense aerial bombardment of the whole region by seventy-six aircraft,
using TNT and mustard gas. Abdel Krim's headquarters at Ajdir continued to
suffer a deluge of poisonous bombs, and all the villages on the heights surrounding Al Hoceima and beyond were targeted, as well as cannon emplacements known to the Spanish. A few days before the projected landing,
thirty-two Spanish and eighteen French naval vessels anchored at sea pounded
at Abdel Krim's defences, their targeting guided by a Spanish observation balloon that hung above the bay.[85] Diversionary tactics were also employed.
Columns were sent out from the front line in the east to engage Rifian forces
in an effort to divert them from the coast. A rumour was deliberately spread
that the landing would take place to the east of Al Hoceima. On the night
before the landing some ships gathered near a beach at another part of the
coast with their searchlights lit, to give the impression the operation was going
to take place there. Not even the officers knew where they were supposed to
land until they were allowed to open secret instructions given to them in an
envelope once they were on board ship.[86]

The first landings finally took place on 8 September, after two cruisers and
160 planes had bombarded the Rifians' positions. The landings have been portrayed as the first combined air and naval operation in history.[87] This may
have been so, but they occurred on the wrong day, at the wrong places, and at
the wrong time. They had been planned for the day before, but to Primo De
Rivera's intense annoyance mist and the dispersal of dozens of ships by the
strong currents prevalent in the Straits had delayed the action. The landings
were supposed to happen before dawn but took place in mid-morning. And the
two advance parties landed on beaches different to those they had been
assigned. This may fortuitously have helped the Spanish to surprise Abdel
Krim's forces. The Rifians had expected the landing in the Bay of Al Hoceima,
and instead it took place on beaches some 9 kilometres to the west. Of all the
tactics the Spanish employed in the invasion, this turned out to be the most
effective. Nevertheless, luck played an important role. The beach where the
first party landed had been mined by the Rifians with unexploded Spanish
bombs equipped with detonators, and above it they had positioned a machine-
gun nest whose fire covered most of the beach. By chance, the Spanish land-

---

[84] Letter to Magaz, 10 Sept., 268.
[85] SHM R633, leg. 449, carp. 3; ibid., leg. 514, carp. 1, and R635, leg. 451, carp. 1–9.
[86] Interview with Manuel Gutiérrez de Tovar y Beruete on 26 Mar. 1999.
[87] e.g. Riesgo, 'La guerra', in n.a., *La campaña*, 50.

ing craft ran aground at the extreme western corner of the beach, away from the mines and far from the machine-guns.[88]

The columns of soldiers had waited forty-eight hours, pitched about in the rough sea and packed together in armoured landing craft like the tinned sardines they were carrying as provisions. These vessels, called K-landing craft, used in the Gallipoli landings and bought from the British in Gibraltar, showed their age when several broke down as they approached the shore.[89] On one beach the landing craft ran aground on the stony bed of the sea at a metre's depth. The craft's commander radioed the news to High Command, which ordered him to withdraw. But Franco ignored the order, and he and his Legionnaires and Regulares leapt into the water up to their necks, holding their arms and munitions above their heads, and like the troops that had launched the first military action of the war in 1908, waded to the beach under desultory fire. This was far from the military efficiency depicted in the Bertuchi drawing that became part of the iconography of the Franco dictatorship, in which the first troops are portrayed running down the ramp of a K-boat onto the beach.

The inability of the landing craft to approach closer to the shore made it impossible to disembark the ten light tanks that were meant to take part in the operation. The three artillery batteries had to be transported to land in pieces, while munitions, water supplies, food, and so on had to be carried to land by the soldiers who followed in successive waves. Mules could not be put ashore, so men had to take the place of beasts of burden. Cattle were pushed out of the craft, but some turned away from the shore towards the sea and drowned. Because there were no pack-animals water became scarce, and with less than a litre each per day the soldiers on land suffered severe thirst in the extreme heat of the summer. Many of the troops could not be disembarked at all, and some ships waiting at sea ran out of water and food and had to return to Ceuta.

The Spanish landings on two beaches led to the occupation of some 6 square kilometres on the peninsula at the western end of Al Hoceima Bay. From an eyewitness account, it appears that the Moroccan fighters who were captured were treated without compunction. A pilot involved in the toxic-gas bombing was horrified to watch through binoculars from one of the ships in the bay as the Legion threw two Moroccan prisoners off the cliff.[90] Yet Spanish troops were under constant fire from the Rifian artillery and snipers. With their forces now installed near Al Hoceima, the High Command had to be careful about bombing operations. Although many troops were equipped with

[88] Pascual, 'Así fue', 68–9.

[89] The ensuing brief account of the Al Hoceima operation is based on the following sources: SHM R635, leg. 451, carp 1–11, and R26, leg. 58, carp.1; SHAT 3H 100; interview with Gutiérrez de Tovar; Pascual, 'Así fue'; Benito Artigas Arpón, *La epopeya de Al Hoceima (Los alicates rotos)* (Madrid, n.p., 1925); Eduardo Álvarez Varela, 'Desembarco de Al Hoceima', *Aeroplano*, 8 (Nov. 1990), 5–24.

[90] Ignacio Hidalgo de Cisneros, *Cambio de rumbo* (Bucharest, n.p., 1961), 216–17.

gas-masks, chemical bombs might still cause them damage. If the planes flew too high, they risked bombing their own troops; if too low, they might be brought down by enemy fire.[91] Abdel Krim's men also chained their Spanish prisoners to artillery pieces in an effort to deter the bombing of their cannon, just as they had earlier placed them in front of targets the Spanish navy were attempting to hit. It is likely, therefore, that after the landings toxic-gas bombs were only dropped further inland while TNT continued to be used in the Al Hoceima area, and it is possible that some stray TNT bombs hit Spanish positions.

Because he had had to spread his troops across the length of the Al Hoceima area and beyond, Abdel Krim could not ensure that the Spanish troops became pinned down on the beaches and so lost the advantage of the heights above the coastline. By 10 September the Rifians had gathered their forces for a counter-attack. Abdel Krim threw his most battle-hardened muhayeddin against the Spanish positions. Hundreds were killed as they hurled themselves at the front lines. Although the Spanish positions were held, the high level of casualties (just under 500 soldiers) and the thirst and fatigue of battle were beginning to lower the morale of even the crack mercenary troops in Spanish pay.

The French military were critical of Sanjurjo as commander-in-chief for his seeming obsession with waiting until everything and everyone had disembarked before advancing beyond the positions already occupied. Yet for the first time they grudgingly admitted that the Spanish colonial army had improved its military effectiveness. Indeed, it had overturned the old system of advance by day and retreat by night. Well supplied by a more efficient stores, the columns were now able to bivouac on the spot and continue their advance in the morning. Co-ordination between the forces had improved significantly, so that the path of any advance by the infantry was first bombed and shelled by the air force and artillery. General Pétain's chief liaison officer attached to Spanish military headquarters reported to him:

I believe we must completely modify the sometimes severe judgements made in France of the Spanish army. Helped by the long months of semi-armistice that followed the retreat of the troops and the organization of the present lines of resistance, the army has been through a complete overhaul owing above all to the authority of General Primo de Rivera. The officers have learnt from the hard lessons of the defeat. A great enterprise of organization and training has been accomplished and the first impression I have of this army is that it is a solid and perfectly tested instrument.[92]

The change in French military opinion was not unconnected with their own harsh discovery of the effectiveness of Abdel Krim's troops.

---

[91] Sanjurjo to Primo de Rivera, 22 Sept.: SHM R63, leg. 451, carp. 1–9.
[92] Report of 16 Sept. in SHAT 3H 100.

Primo de Rivera finally decided to go onto the offensive on 23 September. On 1 October Spanish troops descended into the plain of Ajdir and captured Abdel Krim's home town. There they found large quantities of artillery pieces, munitions, and supplies abandoned by the Rifian fighters. The Rifian leader's headquarters and the caves where he and his General Staff sheltered had been turned into rubble by prolonged bombing. Amidst the ruins lay innumerable twisted bomb propellers, many of which had undoubtedly been fixed to the mustard-gas bombs.[93]

Retreating southwards, Abdel Krim's irregular army of some 20,000 men now faced two armies totalling 90,000 men (with many more in the rearguard), equipped with the latest military technology, including chemical weapons, tanks, and 150 warplanes. The French and Spanish columns advanced from all directions into the heartlands of the resistance to colonial invasion. Having abandoned the old tactics of blockhouses and front lines, the Spanish pushed their forces forward in a swift and co-ordinated movement. The offensive halted at the end of October when autumn storms suddenly turned the tracks into a sea of mud, driving the French and Spanish troops into winter quarters. The unusual ferocity of the rain and the snowstorms that followed also largely immobilized the Rifian forces.[94] The lull in the fighting gave the European allies the opportunity to pressurize local tribes into surrendering by bribery, bombing, and shelling. The so-called 'political work' consisted of threats of further violence combined with promises of money if resistance were ended. On the Spanish side, 'politics' involved the regular use of shelling. Amongst artillerymen, the term 'tiro político' (or 'political shot') referred to the shell that they would fire into villages that appeared still to be uncertain about surrendering. Artillery officers were told to use these shells sparingly because they cost a lot of money, but they were unlikely to have been chemical shells because Spanish troops would be moving in shortly afterwards. The Spanish air force also continued to target civilians on a mass scale. Some of the French military were shocked at the degree of devastation caused by the bombing. General Armangaud reported that one minute's bombing on a market caused 800 victims.[95]

The simultaneous land offensive was renewed in early spring 1926, following a further Franco-Spanish agreement about joint operations. Abdel Krim's forces were burdened with new problems. The war had prevented their people from sowing seed, so that once the reserves of the previous harvest had been consumed, they faced starvation. Also, their support in the rearguard was now

---

[93] Capitán Andrés Sánchez Pérez, *Acción decisiva contra Abdel Krim. Operaciones en el Rif central en colaboración con el Ejército francés* (Toledo, n.p., n.d. [1930]), 114.

[94] 'Abd-el-Krim's Power', *The Times*, 20 Dec. 1925.

[95] *Quelques enseignements sur la campagne du Rif en matière d'aviation (1925–1926)*, quoted in Kharchich, 'La Alianza', 80, n. 45; Luis Cerdó, 'La artillería de la zona Ceuta–Tetuán en las últimas operaciones', *Memorial de Artillería* (1927), 1038, in Afr GF, caja 79-J.

severely diminished owing to the pressure of the enemy, with the result that insufficient arms were being passed on to the front-line troops.[96] Efforts to negotiate a peace settlement through intermediaries, such as the Englishman Gordon Canning, secretary of the London-based Rif Committee (an organization set up in July 1925 in solidarity with the Rifian movement, with the support of a German mining trust keen on exploiting the local mines[97]), had failed to persuade the French or Spanish governments to halt their offensive. So Abdel Krim himself sued for peace.

Prior to the negotiations that followed, the French were adamant that operations should be suspended while they took place. Primo de Rivera thus ordered the suspension of shelling and bombing for the duration of the conference. The French reassured the Spanish commander-in-chief that any anti-Spanish declarations made by their emissary to Abdel Krim's headquarters were a cover for his intelligence-gathering on behalf of both countries.[98] Yet the French were far keener than the Spanish for a deal with Abdel Krim. Knowing this, the Rifian leader hoped to engineer a split between the two. However, the April conference between Abdel Krim's representatives and the Franco-Spanish team soon broke down. No doubt because of Spanish pressure, the allies demanded the return of all prisoners still held, the unconditional surrender of the Rifian forces, their renunciation of the Rif Republic and acceptance of the authority of the Sultan. In addition they insisted on the exile of Abdel Krim and his advisers.[99] In exchange, the Rifians were promised some vague form of autonomy within the Moroccan state. These were not conciliatory terms.

The renewed offensive from all sides placed Abdel Krim in an impossible situation. Rather than submit his family and those who continued to support him to a suicidal struggle, he contacted the French to discuss terms of surrender. Unaware of these secret negotiations, the Spanish bombed the marketplace of the town on the day two French officers went there to make final arrangements. To the stupefaction and anger of the Spanish, the Rifian leader gave himself up to the French at Targuist on 27 May 1926.[100] Unlike the Spanish military, the French evidently respected Abdel Krim. The naval captain who had been sent to negotiate with him before the conference wrote after Abdel Krim's surrender of his 'dignity' and 'nobility of sentiment', and how he, as captor, felt a profound esteem towards the defeated enemy leader 'who remains great'.[101]

[96] SHM R635, leg. 451, carp. 10 re Abdel Krim's problems and SHM R680, leg. 496, carp. 24 for the negotiations.

[97] Francisco Hernández Mir, *Del desastre a la victoria (1921–26): El Rif por España* (Madrid, n.p., 1927), 29–30.

[98] Communications between Sanjurjo and Primo de Rivera in Apr. 1926 in SHM R680, leg. 496, carp. 24.

[99] Hernández Mir, *El Rif*, 61–85.   [100] Sánchez Pérez, *La acción decisiva*, 121 and 140–1.

[101] Quoted in Kharchich, 'La Alianza', 89.

With his surrender, the surviving Spanish prisoners were finally released. Most of them were in a sorry state. They had been treated well at the beginning of their captivity, when the promise of ransom money had encouraged their captors to keep them in good health. But when that promise evaporated and the bombing campaign became lethal, their Moroccan guards began to deal with them harshly. They were usually deployed in appalling conditions to build tracks in mountains or to dig silage pits. They were frequently beaten, some were executed for attempting to escape, dozens died of typhus, and the injured were usually not treated. The food they were given was totally inadequate, although the Moroccans did not have much to eat either. The prisoners occasionally received provisions sent from the Spanish military, but when these did not get through or were taken by the Moroccans for themselves they had suffered extreme privation and cold.[102]

Abdel Krim's surrender did not signal the end of resistance to the Franco-Spanish offensive. The Rifian command structure appointed one of its members to replace him as commander-in-chief. But the Rifian fighters were retreating all the time, and as they did so they began to lose their modern communications system. Throughout the summer of 1926 the tribes of the Rif heartlands began to lay down their arms as the Spanish columns advanced until most of the eastern rebel territory was in their hands. Close observers from the French colonial army were highly critical of the 'pacification' methods used by the Spanish military. They recognized that the Army of Africa had made remarkable improvements to their organization and supplies. Soldiers on the move now had tents to sleep in, the medical services were well equipped, telegraphic communications functioned efficiently, food was much improved, and the weapons deployed by the army were as good as in the best European armies. But the brutal tactics of submission practised by Spanish officers, according to their French counterparts, continued to be counter-productive and had the effect merely of provoking further resistance.

The French officer in charge of native affairs in the Fez region was shocked to find that, rather than seek peace, the Spanish sought to 'punish, disarm, and dominate'. Their brutality, he claimed, took the form of the summary execution of prisoners, the prolonged detention of hostages, and the eviction of local chiefs from their houses to accommodate officers. They allowed their own partisans from the same area to pillage the villages and take away animals and crops. He also gave a much more critical picture of the military tactics of the Spanish colonial army. As if the post-disaster campaign had still not taught them the need to study topography and logistics lessons, the French officer remarked that his Spanish equivalents continued to site fortified positions

---

[102] According to a French doctor, French prisoners were treated more benevolently: Hernández Mir, *El Rif*, 206–14. For a recent account given by one of the survivors, see Alfredo Bosque Coma, 'Prisionero de Abd el-Krim', *Historia 16*, 206 (June 1992), 23–8, and for a contemporary eyewitness account of the prisoners' conditions, see Oteyza, *Abdel Krim*, 89–106.

without regard to the security of the rearguard, to the proximity of roads or tracks, or even to the supply of water. 'In sum, the occupation carried out by the Spanish resembles infinitely more that of the Sharifian mehallas [troops in the pay of the sultans] . . . than a rational occupation and organization of the country.' His superior remarked on the total ignorance of Spanish officers of the local geography and society. Of the commanders he met, only one appeared to have a map.[103]

Resistance to the Franco-Spanish offensive continued in the north-western area, led by Abdel Krim's lieutenant Jerirou. For a while his men controlled the pass between Chauen and Tetuan, preventing any link-up of Spanish troops from the eastern and western theatres of operation. From their strongholds, Jerirou's guerrillas attacked Spanish fortified positions and observation posts. With a Bertha artillery piece captured from the French and dragged to a mountain by their Spanish prisoners, they had shelled Tetuan while Abdel Krim was still in command. Spanish artillery and air force had tried to destroy the dug-out from which the cannon was operating with bombs and mustard gas, but it was only two large columns of infantry that had finally managed to dislodge Jerirou's position.[104] There was an added reason for the Spanish to crush this local resistance. The High Command was anxious to establish control of the route between the east and west of the Protectorate for fear that the French might take it over in their own rapid advance northwards and split the Protectorate in two.[105]

Resistance against the crushing forces of the Franco-Spanish alliance was now fragmentary and local.[106] Unusually, the allies' offence continued throughout the autumn and winter of 1926–7, when in the past military actions had been suspended because of the rain and snow. The operations of the column led by Osvaldo Capaz Montes in the south-east became thereafter a model for military strategists in Spain. Capaz stood out from many of his colleagues through his ability to speak Arabic, his close knowledge of the social organization and culture of the tribes, and his acquaintance with some of their leaders. His column, made up of a thousand-strong harka, lived off the land, exacting food and fuel as it made its way at breakneck speed from village to village. In each of them, Capaz forged pacts with local authorities (or replaced them if they had been prominent in the resistance) and took hostages with him

[103] Reports by Lt.-Col. Dubuisson on 2 May 1927 and by Col. Strohl in ADMAE Maroc, 1917–1940, pp. 102–9 and 122–3. Mola himself was happy to admit later that in his 1926 operations in the Larache area the Regulares troops he commanded devastated the fields and burnt huge areas of elm and olive trees: José María Iribarren, *Con el General. Escenas y aspectos inéditos de la Guerra Civil* (Zaragoza, Librería General, 1937), 214.

[104] *Bulletin du Comité de l'Afrique Française* (Mar. 1926), 148–9; interviews with Hach Med Ben Ahmed Jerirou and El Hach Abdel Krim Ben Ahmed Ben Ali on 18 July 2000.

[105] Telegram from Sanjurjo to Jordana, 12 June 1926, in SHM R682, leg. 500, carp. 3.

[106] Sometimes it was conducted by tribal fragments grouped around leaders who, like the Jebalan Danfil, had refused to join either Raisuni or Abdel Krim: interviews with his niece and nephew, Hacha Oum Koulthoum Ahmed Kasem Al Amrani and Med Maati Al Amrani, on 22 and 24 July 2000.

to ensure the pacts were kept. He maintained wireless contact throughout, and aircraft were deployed on his instructions to make bombing and machine-gunning raids against recalcitrant villages. His earlier experience as flight observer in the air force made these contacts even more effective.[107] This model of military strategy became the basis of the actions of the Army of Africa in the early part of the Civil War.

The success of these operations, however, was also due to the demoralization of the muhayeddin after the surrender of Abdel Krim. The speed with which the columns operated made it difficult for local leaders to reconstruct resistance against the combined offensive of the French and the Spanish. Rather than archetypal military actions, these mopping-up operations were, as a French commentator put it, a 'campaign of legs and lungs'. The overwhelming force of the colonial armies made further defiance expensive in lives, livestock, and crops. The Spanish artillery and air force would pound villages and their fields into dust. The result was that many people fled to the French zone, leaving the areas where resistance had continued virtually empty of inhabitants, though there were repeated flare-ups.[108] When the last remaining leaders, such as Jerirou, were killed or captured (Jerirou himself was shot in the back by one of his own men[109]), resistance petered out in early summer and the Spanish army seized the whole of the rebellious area in an iron grip.

The Spanish General Order of 10 July 1927 declaring the end of the war was predictably oratorical in its triumph. 'The end has come of the campaign of Morocco, which for eighteen years has constituted a problem for the Governments, producing at critical moments serious worries for the Nation, which, prodigally, has shed its blood and its moral energies to maintain the legacy of pride and valour left us by our ancestors, the conquerors of a World.'[110] For all its wilful rhetoric, the commander-in-chief's statement made a curious implication about the nature of the Moroccan campaign. Eschewing the parallel frequently made with the Reconquest against the Moors, he implicitly compared the Moroccan wars to the conquest of the New World, which, in traditional discourse, was the struggle to convert the pagan and barbarous peoples of the Americas to the true faith. Thus mixing traditional and modern images, he implied that the army had had to conquer an ignorant and semi-savage people in order to bring them the benefits of civilization.

It is at this point that a curtain of silence falls on all the accounts of the colonial campaign. Since the war was over, the opportunities for medals, promotions,

---

[107] General Manuel Goded, *Marruecos. Las etapas de Pacificación* (Madrid, Compañía Ibero-Americana de Publicaciones, 1932), 330–7.

[108] Léon Rollin in *L'Afrique Française* (July 1927), 284. Telegram from Steeg to minister of war, 27 Mar., and État Majeur de L'Armée report of 11 Apr. 1927 in ADMAE Maroc, 1917–40, vol. 228, pp. 75 and 84–7.

[109] Hach Med Ben Ahmed Jerirou (son of Jerirou) and El Hach Abdel Krim Ben Ahmed Ben Ali. 18 July 2000.

[110] Goded, *Marruecos*, 433–5.

and press coverage dropped away. The prying eyes of foreign diplomats and military intelligence services turned in other directions. The so-called pacification campaign that followed over the next few years can only be glimpsed fragmentarily. I have had to read between the lines of the military reports and rely on interviews with Moroccans who remember what it was like to live in those areas reconquered by the Spanish. Official discourse talked about the need for reconciliation among Moroccans who had warred amongst themselves, as if an unwilling Spain had found itself caught in the midst of a civil war. According to this discourse, Spain had been acting all along on behalf of the Moroccan government and the international community. Spain was in Morocco to civilize its people. Ignorance and fanaticism had finally been defeated, the Spanish texts asserted, and at last an era of peace and work could begin.[111]

Pacification campaigns after anti-colonial struggles or the suppression of colonial dissidence have usually been marked by the use of terror by colonial powers. Recently unearthed documents reveal that the British authorities in India imprisoned over 80,000 Indians in a penal colony on the Andaman Islands between 1858 and 1939, and there inflicted torture, medical experiments, and forced labour on its inmates, during which many died and many survivors remained crippled for life.[112] Eight years earlier, the French had instituted their brutal penal colony on Devil's Island off Guyana. And amongst the most notorious cases in recent years was the French army's repression of supporters of the Front de Libération Nationale in neighbouring Algeria thirty years after the Spanish colonial war in Morocco.

The Spanish army did not conduct its campaign with the same level of brutality as the British in the Andaman Islands or the French paratroopers and Foreign Legion in Algeria. Amongst the native officers there was some concern to woo back the rebellious population and create new complicities.[113] The 1928 handbook of the native officer stressed that his primary mission was to ensure peace and security in the villages of erstwhile rebellious areas, so that families, communities, and local authorities could be rebuilt. But it also insisted that no efforts should be spared to obtain information so that the 'bad seed' of dissidence could be rooted out.[114] Disarmament and the punishment of those who failed to submit thus became the most important task of the 'pacifiers'.

From the evidence I have gathered, it seems that many officers charged with pacification behaved with the same brutality they had practised in the war. Interrogation centres were set up, such as in a house still standing by a road

[111] Statements by Sanjurjo in *ABC* (July 1927), and Gómez-Jordana (as the new high commissioner) in *Revista Hispano Africana* (May 1927), both reproduced in n.a., *Acción de España en África* (Madrid, Ministerio del Ejército, 1935), 251–3; n.a., *Manual para el servicio del oficial de intervención en Marruecos* (Madrid, n.p., 1928), 6.

[112] Cathy Scott-Clark and Adrian Levy, 'Survivors of Our Hell', *Guardian Weekend*, 23 June 2001.

[113] Tomás García Figueras, 'Intervención militar de Beni Arós', report of 13 July 1926 in Archivo García Figueras.

[114] n.a., *Manual para el servicio del oficial de intervención en Marruecos* (Madrid, n.p., 1928), 5–9.

near Chauen and another in the centre of the town itself, where people suspected of having information about hidden arms were tortured. A man who
fought for the Spanish and was a guard in the second house remembers that
most of the people taken in had been betrayed by fellow Moroccans. He asserts
that the interrogators and torturers were pro-Spanish chiefs, though no other
sources exist to verify this claim.[115] The most common method of torture used
by the interrogators was whipping the suspect's body with a rope soaked in
water and applying salt to the resulting wounds.[116] Many people were beaten
up and had their legs or arms broken, or were forced to carry hot objects that
burnt their hands. Some committed suicide before they could be tortured, with
knives they had hidden in their robes. Known muhayeddin who were caught
were imprisoned without trial. Many were executed. Others were taken off to
do forced labour.[117] Young ex-fighters were prevented from learning skills such
as building or driving cars, skills which might have helped them integrate into
the colony. Instead they were employed as labourers, digging ditches or building roads for the Spanish.[118]

Yet undoubtedly there were victims of torture who had done nothing unto-
ward. Whippings were administered on the mere suspicion of harbouring
arms. In one case at least, a man was tortured because of a misunderstanding.
The military authorities intercepted mail as part of their drive to uncover hidden arms. A Moroccan had written a letter to a friend or relative asking him
to obtain a *barred* or teapot. The word for explosive powder is *barud* and the
Arabic-speaking Spanish officer who read the letter thought the reference was
to this; the man was arrested and whipped until he convinced his torturers of
their mistake.[119]

Without any prospect of reconciliation, thousands of the ex-combatants of
the war of resistance chose to live in exile. One man lived in Casablanca for
seventeen years, returning clandestinely from time to time to visit his family. In
1944 he finally gave himself up and was imprisoned and then transferred one
month later to Tetuan gaol. He died there, according to his fellow-inmates, in
mysterious circumstances, and the family received no letter or report from the
Spanish authorities nor was his body ever given to them.[120]

The Spanish army continued to employ the elaborate methods of the war
to build networks of paid informers. The handbook of the native officer

---

[115] Second interview with Enfeddal Oulad Ben H'mamou Zeruali on 7 May 2001 in Chauen. His
openness about the participation of Moroccans in the repression springs from his belief that they were
combating bandits rather than fighters of resistance against Spanish military penetration.

[116] Interviews with Med Maati Al Amrani, Mohammed Saleh Faraji, and Hadou El Kayid Omar
Massaud (the latter on 23 Apr. 2001 in Ajdir region).

[117] Interviews with Hach Med M'Hauesh, Mohamed Amar Hammadi, Mohammad Ben
Hammou, on 17 July 2000, and Mohammed Sosse Alaoui on 21 July 2000, both in Tetuan, and Ali
Raisuni in Chauen. Testimony of the continued executions can be found in a French military report
by Capt. Jourdan: ADMAE Maroc 1917–40, vol. 228, pp. 186.

[118] Hadou El Kayid Omar Massaud.   [119] Ali Raisuni.

[120] Information supplied by his granddaughter, Souhaila Riki, on 20 Apr. 2001.

recommended Jews (referring presumably to Sephardic rather than Berber Jews) as the most useful sources of information, since they had not been involved in the resistance against colonial penetration and indeed had suffered when the muhayeddin took over towns such as Chauen. Moroccan informants were employed in surveillance operations in markets, teashops, on pilgrimages, and at crossroads and mountain passes.[121] The army was also relentless about collecting all pieces of shrapnel and metal from the bombs dropped over the rebel areas. Moroccans were offered money if they handed in any of these pieces. Units of the army scoured the countryside to gather any fragments they could find.[122] The implication of this campaign is clear. The military authorities wished to eliminate all evidence of the use of chemical bombs and shells.

A French military delegation sent to the Spanish Protectorate in August 1928 to meet their counterparts produced a sympathetic report on the Spanish colonial authorities for their superiors, yet recognized the contradictory practices of the officers. They found that Spain had undertaken many public works since the war, such as the provision of roads, housing, waterworks, electricity, and railways. They also found that the garrisons and hospitals were now being properly equipped. But they were puzzled by the contradictions of 'native' policy. 'Their method is a mix of very modern humanitarian principles and tendencies towards the most brutal violence. This incoherence is evident in all domains and it deforms their attitude and makes it very difficult to form an overall judgement.'

However, their report made it also very clear that the Army of Africa had become a powerful new military machine, staffed by young officers burning with ambition. The French military attaché confirmed this in a report of April 1929 after he had paid a visit to the Spanish Protectorate. But he was aware of one outstanding feature of the Army of Africa: 'The troops of Morocco form something of a separate army where the mentality is quite different to that of the Metropolitan Army and much more military.'[123] This sense of a separate identity was to form the basis of the military insurrectionism of the 1930s.

---

[121] *Manual*, 11–16.

[122] Interview with Mohamed Amar Hammadi, 23 Apr. 2001; also with Mohammed Saleh Faraji and Hadou El Kayid Omar Massaud.

[123] The first report by Capt. Jourdan is from ADMAE Maroc 1917–1940, vol. 228, pp. 160–88; the second, sent to the French minister of foreign affairs, Aristide Briand, is in ibid., 190–220. A German military observer told Mola in 1929 that the military forces in Madrid were a caricature of an army but that the Army of Africa demonstrated that Spain could create a great army: Mola, *Obras Completas*, 1031.

PART II

The Brutalization of Colonial War

CHAPTER FIVE

The Secret History of Chemical Warfare Against Moroccans

FOR ALL THE horrors of the First World War, the European powers still officially clung in the post-war period to what might seem to us today the antiquated notion that there were moral standards in warfare. In the codes of the time, the conduct of the belligerent parties was meant to be limited by the moral boundaries of Western civilization. Thus, for example, war was still regarded as an affair between men enrolled in professional armies. As late as 1938, the British prime minister Chamberlain declared that the bombing of civilians was unlawful. The problem was that technology was outstripping these inherited moral values. The most important advance in the technology of war was the development of long-range bombers with a capacity to inflict huge damage on the enemy. From the beginning of the Second World War, the old moral standards were quickly ditched and the two sides increasingly engaged in a war of attrition directed above all at the urban civilian population, as the bombing of London, Dresden, or Würzburg attested.

Yet even before the total war of 1939–45, a distinction was made by all colonial powers between the treatment of fellow Europeans and that of colonials who resisted European advance. The standards of warfare that could be applied to the colonial enemy were different because these opponents were not 'fully civilized'. Thus, in addition to bombing the civilian population in parts of Africa or the Middle East, the colonial powers turned to chemical warfare, aimed not just at soldiers, as in the First World War, but against old men, women, and children in the recalcitrant parts of would-be colonies.

Spanish military values of conduct in warfare had already been deeply undermined by the colonial wars in Cuba and the Philippines between 1895 and 1898. In addition to military engagements, the Spanish colonial army had used economic warfare to starve out the enemy. In Cuba, civilians had been herded into badly resourced concentration camps, leaving Spanish troops a free hand to burn crops, plantations, and villages, and kill whomsoever they came across. The savagery of the Spanish response to the struggle for independence by ex-colonial subjects was rationalized as a temporary measure sanctioned by the exceptional conditions of the colonial war and the barbarity of the enemy. It was not, of course, among the worst cases of colonial brutality, such as the mass extermination practised by the German army in South-West Africa in 1904–7.[1]

Similarly, the war in Morocco was marked by a progressive descent into brutal methods of military engagement and repression, accelerated by two defining events, the disaster of 1909 and above all the Anual disaster of 1921. As we saw in Chapter 2, colonial officers were already careful by 1912 to be secretive about the growing brutality of their methods. A common practice such as beheading prisoners was rightly judged to be too fierce for public consumption in Spain. The relative failure of the 'enlightened' colonial strategy of winning tribes over by bribes and by token respect for local authorities led to the hegemony of the militarist discourse by 1919, whereby the defeat of the enemy by whatever means should precede the march of civilization.

The resources available for this strategy were shown to be totally inadequate during the disaster of 1921. A poorly equipped army operating on difficult terrain in climatic extremes was no match for increasingly well-armed and competent guerrilla units. The army's reliance on native soldiers as part of the front-line shock-troops fell apart at Anual when large numbers of them went over to the enemy. On its own the Legion could not undertake a war on both fronts against an enemy brimming with confidence. Nor was the massive mobilization of military-service recruits from Spain a practical solution. Most of them were barely trained and lacked motivation. They could be used to build roads, lug sandbags onto parapets, and provide back-up for the shock-troops, but they were not the stuff of a successful colonial army. Thus the notion that expensive and technologically advanced chemical weapons could replace the reluctant foot-slogging soldier as the main weapon against the enemy began to seize the imagination of colonial officers and politicians alike.

Highly effective chemical weapons had been developed and tested on the killing fields of the First World War. The most basic of these weapons, hand grenades filled with tear gas, had been used from the beginning by the French, while the Germans had fired T shells filled with another kind of tear gas on the Polish front at the beginning of 1915.[2] By early spring the Germans had developed a more lethal weapon, the choking agent chlorine gas. Released from cylinders, it was first used at Ypres in April 1915 against unprotected Algerian and French soldiers, provoking the collapse of the front they were defending. Later that month Canadian troops suffered a similar assault, against which their only defence was wet handkerchiefs and cotton masks.[3] German research produced a new, even more lethal, chemical shortly afterwards, another choking substance called phosgene, which had the advantage of being almost

---

[1] Balfour, *The End*, ch. 1; Vandervort, *Wars*, 196–202.

[2] John Keegan, *The First World War* (London, Hutchinson, 1998), 214; Niall Ferguson, *The Pity of War* (London, Allen Lane, 1998), 290; L. F. Haber, *The Poisonous Cloud: Chemical Warfare in the First World War* (Oxford, Clarendon, 1986), 23–6.

[3] Martin Marix Evans, *Passchendaele and the Battles of Ypres 1914–18* (London, Osprey, 1997), 27–32.

impossible to detect. It was first used against the Russians on the Carpathian front at the end of May. Soon it was improved by being mixed with chlorine. For their part the British began to use chlorine gas in the autumn of 1915, with a poisonous cloud attack at Loos in September. The problems both sides faced in the new chemical war were the inadequacy of the masks provided to protect their own troops against the chemicals and the frequent inaccuracy of the poisonous clouds, in particular when the wind changed and blew the chemical back at their advancing soldiers.[4]

The turning-point in chemical warfare in the First World War was the introduction in 1916 of projectiles filled with poisons and fired by the artillery. It enabled a more accurate targeting and a choice of chemicals to suit the conditions. Several new substances had been developed in the course of the first two years of the war that were many times more virulent than their earlier versions. Among these were diphosgene and chloropicrine. The most lethal of the new chemicals, the vesicant poison called sulphur mustard gas (or dichlorethylsulphide), was first used to great effect by the Germans in the Ypres sector on 12 July 1917 (hence its French nickname Iperite, or its Spanish equivalent Iperita). Two thousand five hundred soldiers were gassed, of whom 87 died shortly afterwards. Over the next three weeks the deployment of mustard gas resulted in a further 14,726 victims, 500 of whom died.[5] People who were close to the explosion either died quickly or suffered agony for hours, their body burnt inside and out. But the deadliness of mustard gas was that for those at some distance its effects were imperceptible at first, causing intense damage to the body and contaminating the environment. A slow-acting, thick-flowing liquid rather than a gas, it burnt the body, killed the nerve cells, polluted water, and penetrated clothing and shoes. It also clung to buildings, ground, and vegetation. Without treatment of the environment, it could remain active for many days if not weeks.[6]

The delayed effect of mustard gas for those who had not been within the zone of its explosion made it very difficult to evade its consequences. Over several hours, it provoked temporary blindness, conjunctivitis, blisters, skin rashes, gangrene, bronchitis, lung inflammation, and where exposure was prolonged, death. For survivors, its long-term effects included depression, fibrosis, TB, laryngitis, asthma, disordered action of the heart, neurasthenic disablement, eventual blindness, and cancer.[7] After overcoming technical problems in

[4] Haber, *The Poisonous Cloud*, 34–6.   [5] Marix Evans, *Passchendaele*, 60.

[6] Haber, *The Poisonous Cloud*, 189–92; The Medical Department of the United States in the World War, vol. XIV, *Medical Aspects of Gas Warfare* (Internet).

[7] For the estimated figures of deaths during the war, see Tim Cook, '"Against God-Inspired Conscience": The Perception of Gas Warfare as a Weapon of Mass Destruction, 1915–1939', *War and Society*, 18: 1 (May 2000), 58; for long-term effects: Constance M. Pechura and David P. Rall (eds.), *Veterans at Risk: The Health Effects of Mustard Gas and Lewisite* (Washington DC, National Academy Press, 1993); Haber, *The Poisonous Cloud*, 195, 225, and 257–8; Stockholm International Peace Research Institute (SIPRI), *Delayed Toxic Effects of Chemical Warfare Agents* (Stockholm, SIPRI, 1975); Robert Harris

its use, the Allies started to fire mustard-gas shells in the summer of 1918. One of the casualties of a British shell filled with this chemical was a young runner attached to a Bavarian Reserve Regiment, Adolf Hitler. He was practically blinded, and invalided out of the war.[8]

The potentially devastating effects of mustard gas, however, were attenuated by technical difficulties in the two years in which it was employed. The use of chemical weapons was still confined to artillery, limiting their action to the range and accuracy of guns. Politicians such as Churchill were calling for their development for use by the air force. As secretary for war and air in 1919, he proposed that bombs filled with chemicals should be dropped by air behind the enemy lines. British air chiefs, however, were reluctant to take up his proposal because they could not guarantee that the bombs would hit their targets and might not instead affect the civilian population, revealing the continuing concern not to use poisonous bombs against civilians.[9] The effects of chemical offensives were also being limited by the development of more sophisticated protection against them. Rubber suits and respirators were produced that gave better defence, even though they hindered the mobility of troops. The number of casualties from chemical weapons fell dramatically as a result. Before masks and respirators were introduced, the mortality rate among those on the receiving end of toxic gases was some 40 per cent; by 1918, this had fallen to 2.5 per cent, despite the introduction of more lethal chemicals.[10]

Indeed, an overall evaluation of the effect of chemical weapons in the First World War suggests that they played a far less crucial role in the balance of military power than their notoriety would suggest. Estimates of the number of casualties on both sides vary from 500,000 to 1.3 million, but the vast majority were Russian soldiers, the least prepared for chemical war. Of those affected by the poisoning, only a small percentage died in the short term.[11] It is true also that 'gas' became an important psychological weapon. Soldiers were haunted by the memory of the chemical poisoning of the early years of the war, and obsessed by the fear of becoming contaminated by the invisible agent mustard gas.[12]

Thus the use of chemicals caused a far greater outcry than the butchery of the machine-guns and artillery barrages. It was easier perhaps to express the horror of war by focusing on new rather than traditional weapons. Civilian reactions were also coloured not just by the unusual sufferings of those wounded by the poison, but also by widespread apprehension about the power of science and technology, exacerbated by popular science-fiction.[13] On the

---

and Jeremy Paxman, *A Higher Form of Killing: The Secret Story of Gas and Germ Warfare* (London, Chatto and Windus, 1982), 34–6; 'Toxicological Effects of Vesicants', Mitretek Systems, http://www.mitretek.

[8] Haber, *The Poisonous Cloud*, 203–4.   [9] Ibid., 224–5.

[10] G. Laghaux and P. Delhomme, *La guerre des gaz 1914–18* (Paris, Hegida, 1985), 155–7.

[11] Ibid., and Haber, *The Poisonous Cloud*, 245–8 and 278.

[12] Cook, ' "Against God-Inspired Conscience" ', 51–7.

[13] For a typical report on the effects of chlorine in early 1915, see 'Poison Gas', *The Times*, 1 May 1915; on science fiction, see Haber, *The Poisonous Cloud*, 17–18.

other hand, the experience of chemical poisoning of front-line soldiers deepened their sense of hatred against the enemy. As a Canadian soldier who saw
some of his comrades killed by poison gas wrote, 'we who inhaled less of the
filthy noxiousness grew black with a deadlier hate. Then, with what strength
we could gather, did we kill and kill and kill. More, we butchered savagely.'[14]

The public outcry against the use of poison chemicals was reflected in a wel-
ter of international treaties in the aftermath of the war. Earlier conventions,
such as the first and second Hague Peace Conferences of 1899 and 1907, which
had explicitly banned chemical weapons, had failed to prevent their use in war.
Indeed, all the belligerents of the First World War except Italy had ratified the
conditions of the Second Conference on the eve of hostilities. In the post-war
period, Articles 169–72 of the 1919 Treaty of Versailles imposed an absolute
ban on German manufacture, importation, and use of chemical weapons and
extended the prohibition to all signatories, one of which was Spain. This was
followed by further negotiations leading to a draft treaty, drawn up under the
auspices of the League of Nations, the Geneva Gas Protocol, which excluded
the use of chemical and bacteriological weapons (though it did not ban their
research and development). It was signed in 1925 by twenty-six states, including Spain, Germany, and Italy. However, the nations signing the Geneva
Protocol agreed only to ban the first use of chemical weapons against other signatories, thus giving themselves a free hand to deploy them against other
nations and peoples and to respond in kind against another signatory that had
broken the agreement. Nevertheless, neither Spain, the United States, nor
Japan was willing to ratify it. Spain did so only in 1929, two years after the end
of the colonial war.

These treaties were clearly Eurocentric. In the colonial wars that followed,
the new chemical weapons were used to deadly effect and with little compunction against soldiers and civilians in African, Middle Eastern, and Asian countries fighting against the continued penetration of colonial powers. The British
were the first to use them in the post-war period. In support of the Russian
White Army, the British air force used arsenic smoke generators against the
Red Army in Murmansk and Archangel in the summer of 1919. Later that year
they dropped phosgene and mustard gas against Afghans and hill tribespeople
on the north-west frontier. In Iraq in 1920 the British artillery launched shells
filled with mustard gas at Arabs fighting against the British occupation of most
of the country. Referring to the British cabinet's initial reluctance to use chemical weapons, Winston Churchill, now secretary of state for war and air,
declared: 'I do not understand this squeamishness about the use of gas. I am
strongly in favour of using poison gas against uncivilised tribes.'[15]

[14] Bourke, An Intimate History, 230.
[15] David E. Omissi, Air Power and Colonial Control: The Royal Air Force 1919–1939 (Manchester, MUP,
1990), 160; Geoff Simons, Iraq: From Sumer to Saddam (London, Macmillan, 1994); Harris and Paxman,
A Higher Form, 43–4.

There is a general but mistaken belief that Italy under Mussolini was the second (if not, as popularly believed, the first) power to use chemical weapons in the post-First World War period.[16] Italy shelled and bombed Libyans with phosgene and mustard gas in 1923–4 and 1927–8 in air raids against tribes resisting Italian colonial expansion. Eight years later the Italians moved vast quantities of chemical warheads to Eritrea and Somalia in preparation for their invasion of Ethiopia. During the four years of the Italo-Ethiopian war Italy dropped at least 500 tons of phosgene, mustard gas, and the poisonous blood agent arsine on unprotected soldiers and civilians. Although the Italian state did not admit its use of banned chemical weapons until 1996, the fact was well known throughout Europe during the war and details were frequently passed on to journalists by Red Cross workers and foreign observers. At the end of 1935 the Ethiopian emperor Haile Selassie complained to the League of Nations about the Italian use of chemical bombs and the League obtained proof of casualties from these weapons among Ethiopian soldiers and civilians. Having admitted the evidence against her, Italy walked out of the League in May 1936.[17]

Less well known is the fact that Spain used chemical weapons against the tribes of northern Morocco between 1921 and 1927, and in vast quantities between 1924 and the beginning of 1926. Both the British and the French knew of this. France in particular kept a close watch on the bombing campaigns across her colonial border, and when the Franco-Spanish alliance got under way France co-ordinated closely with the Spanish military authorities over the campaign. For all their brutality against anti-colonial resistance in their own area of influence, the French do not seem to have used chemical warfare in Morocco, or at least I have found no evidence of this in either French, British, or Spanish military archives. Indeed, in the middle of the Franco-Spanish offensive in autumn and winter of 1925 the Rifians appealed to international opinion against the Spanish deployment of poisonous gases but made a point of stressing that the French had not used it.[18] However, both France and Britain refrained from publicizing Spain's chemical warfare, and only in the last few years have British intelligence documents referring to it been released for consultation.

In Spain itself great care was taken to cover up the use of chemical weapons. Until recently, almost without exception, books and memoirs about the war

---

[16] Thus the *Times* correspondent, G. L. Steer wrote of the mustard-gas air raid by Italy on 22 Dec. 1935: 'For the first time in the history of the world, a people supposedly white used poison gas upon a people supposedly savage': *Caesar in Abyssinia* (London, Hodder and Stoughton, 1936), 233.

[17] Angelo Del Boca et al., *I gas di Mussolini. Il fascismo e la guerra d'Etiopia* (Roma, Riuniti, 1996), 17–18, 33–44, and 53–4; by the same author, *Gli italiani in Africa Orientale. La conquista dell'Impero* (Roma-Bari, Laterza, 1979), 490–1, and *L'Africa nella coscienza degli italiani. Miti, memorie, errori, sconfitte* (Roma-Bari, Laterza, 1992), 71–2; Christopher Hollis, *Italy in Africa* (London, Hamish Hamilton, 1941), 225–6; and Haber, *The Poisonous Cloud*, 307–8. The latter also mentions the sporadic use of mustard gas by the Japanese against China in Manchuria and elsewhere from 1928.

[18] 'Abd-el-Krim's Power', *The Times*, 29 Dec. 1925.

omitted all reference to their use despite the fact that everyone involved in the war knew about it intimately. Records of meetings by politicians and military to discuss chemical weapons were either not taken or were destroyed or hidden.[19] It is likely that the war correspondents of the Spanish newspapers were also aware of the campaign, but kept quiet in the 'national interest' or because they depended on military sources for their information.

Nor was the news of the chemical war directed against Moroccans ever publicized in Morocco itself. As we have seen, the war in the Rif was a struggle for the independence of the Rifians from both Spain and Morocco. Until recently, the Moroccan state was reluctant to admit that the war took place at all. Only in the last year or so, under the administration of the new king, has there been a cautious recognition of Abdel Krim, though his struggle is represented as part of the nationalist struggle for the independence of Morocco. The attempt by the Moroccan Association for the Defence of Victims of Toxic Gas in the Rif to hold a conference in April 2001 in Al Hoceima, the capital of the area most hit by chemical bombs, was cut short at the eleventh hour by a government ban. The reluctance of the Moroccan state to publicize the devastation meted out to its citizens in the Rif in the 1920s was probably due above all to fear that it might worsen relations with Spain in the new millennium. But it was also the result of the continued marginalization of the Rif by the dominant political elites in Morocco.

Among Spaniards, the confidential reports and correspondence between the High Command and the government, and even those within the military itself (now housed in the military archives in Madrid), were usually careful to refer to chemical bombs only in code or, more carelessly, by alluding to them as 'those bombs', the 'special bombs', or the 'X bombs'. The military headquarters of the Army of Africa in Tetuan issued a code for the nomenclature of bombs in June 1923 and ordered that any reference to chemical weapons in future should use only that code.[20] Such was the care that the military took to

[19] Thus, for example, there is no record in the Maura archives of his meeting with the German engineer awarded the contract to supply mustard gas to the Spanish army (see below). Felipe Acedo Colunga's book on the Spanish air force between 1922 and 1928, *El alma de la Aviación española* (Madrid, Espasa-Calpe, 1928), makes no mention of the chemical air raids by the Spanish air force in Morocco. Eduardo Álvarez Valera's more recent and detailed study of Spanish aviation in the Al Hoceima landing gives details of the size of bombs but fails to mention what kind were used: 'Desembarco de Al Hoceima', *Aeroplano*, 8 (Nov. 1990), 5–25. Lt.-Gen. Jorge Vigón, in his 3-vol. book on the history of Spanish artillery, discusses the technical detail of the casing of toxic-gas shells without mentioning once that they were used massively by Spanish cannons in the colonial war: *Historia de la Artillería española* (Madrid, n.p., 1947), ii. 386–7. In another striking example, Francisco Hernández Mir makes no reference, in all his books on the colonial war and Primo de Rivera, to the use of chemical bombs and the dictator's enthusiasm for this new technology of war. Nor do the authors of a book on the air force in the Moroccan war published in 1990 by the Spanish Museo del Aire, A. Flores, and J. M. Cicuéndez, *Guerra aérea sobre el Marruecos español (1913–1927)*. The list of such deliberate omissions would be endless.

[20] SHM R139, leg. 80, carp. 7, 5 June 1923. This was necessary, according to the communication 'in order to avoid naming them using words that would make manifest their special nature'. A more complete classification of bombs was issued on 24 May 1924: SHM R599, leg. 421, carp. 3.

conceal evidence of their use as the bombing campaign progressed that reports often referred only to the number of bombs dropped without reference to their classification or size. Many articles were written about chemical warfare in the press and in specialist military journals, but none acknowledged that Spain was about to employ, was employing, or had employed such methods. This of course gave Spanish military specialists an enormous advantage over foreign experts in that, without ever admitting it, they were able to base their discussion of chemical warfare on first-hand experience.[21]

Occasional news about the chemical bombs launched against Moroccans trickled out during the campaign. An article in 1921 in the French-language paper in Tangier, *La Dépêche Marocaine*, referred to toxic gas bombing in the Rif. Brief mention of the chemical war was made in a handful of books and articles at the time, mainly by non-Spanish observers. One of the pilots who dropped mustard-gas bombs later wrote an autobiography in which he narrated very briefly his part in the chemical campaign.[22] More recently, a study of the German connection to the equipping of the Spanish army and air force with chemical supplies was made in 1990, using German sources almost exclusively. In the last two years three books have brought fresh evidence based on a variety of sources. The first two contain only fragments of information about the chemical war, while the third, by the Spanish historian Angel Viñas, brings together German and Spanish diplomatic evidence in a short but searching narrative.[23] But no attempt to reconstruct the chemical offensive has ever been made, because until now no researcher has been able fully to penetrate the almost inaccessible military reports of the Army of Africa.

What follows is the first, inevitably fragmentary, reconstruction of this war using all available sources in private and public archives in Spain, France, and Britain. Recently declassified documents in British and French military archives reveal a considerable amount of new information, suggesting that the military in both countries followed the chemical war in Morocco with close attention. Above all, the narrative below is based on a lengthy and painstaking

[21] e.g. José Giménez Bueso, 'Los gases de combate', *Memorial de Artillería*, Jan. 1926, ano 81, serie VII, vol. 1, pp. 615–40; see also the issues of *La Guerra y su Preparación*, of Jan. and Feb. 1921, Oct. 1923, Dec. 1923, Apr. 1924, and July 1924. For the post-war absence of reference to their use, see e.g. the minister of war, the Duque de Tetuán's article in *La Nación* on 3 Dec. 1927 about chemical warfare; E. Estévez-Ortega, 'La legítima defensa. El Dios Marte se hace alquimista', *Nuevo Mundo*, 29 Nov. 1929; and Senen del Oso, 'El arma química', *Ejército*, 14 (March 1941), no pp.

[22] *La Dépêche Marocaine*, 27 Nov. 1921: copy in AMAE España, Fondo Manuel González Hontoria, caja 4, Marruecos (1910–22), Hoja 2. A French observer, Léon Rollin, for example, mentions the chemical war in *L'Afrique Française*, 1 (Jan. 1923), 40. The daily paper *La Correspondencia de España* appears to back the use of mustard gas in an article on 16 Aug. 1923, 'Cartas de un soldado'. The Spanish pilot's book is Hidalgo de Cisneros, *Cambio de rumbo*, 193–7.

[23] Rudibert Kunz and Rolf-Dieter Müller, *Giftgas gegen Abdel Krim: Deutschland, Spanien und der Gaskrieg in Spanisch Marokko 1922–1927*, Einzelschriften zur Militargeschichte, vol. 34 (Freiburg i. Breisgau, Rombach, 1990); Juan Pando, *Historia Secreta*; Carlos Lázaro Ávila, 'La forja de la Aeronáutica Militar: Marruecos (1909–1927)', in Mesa *et al.*, *Las campañas*, 164–93; Angel Viñas, *Franco, Hitler y el estallido de la Guerra civil. Antecedentes y consecuencias* (Madrid, Alianza, 2001).

trawl I undertook over several years through the labyrinthine Spanish military archive (where all military documents referring to the colonial war are housed). It relies also on interviews with Moroccans who experienced and survived the chemical bombs. No complete account of the chemical offensive will ever be possible, however, because no overall figures are available covering the whole period of the campaign, least of all the number of casualties caused among Moroccans by the bombing.

The earliest reference to Spanish interest in chemical weapons was a request in 1918 by Alfonso XIII to the German military authorities for samples and information about their manufacture.[24] It is probable that the king was considering their use in Morocco, though the military situation there was relatively calm at the time. It may be that he was also expressing his penchant for new gadgets. As a military man and an admirer of Wilhelmine Germany (and of Austrian descent through his mother), the king liked to keep abreast of the latest technology of warfare (as well as the latest racing cars). He was clearly unmoved by the horror that the use of chemicals had provoked among millions of people in Europe. Unsuccessful attempts had been made by the Spanish government as early as January 1919 to obtain chemical bombs from France.[25] The king, probably with the support of his advisers, sent an envoy to Germany in August of that year in an abortive attempt to negotiate the acquisition of war matériel, of which chemical weapons were likely to have been the most important. The envoy's letter clearly implies that Alfonso had taken this initiative behind the back of his finance minister, who was likely to resist the high costs involved.[26]

An undated report in the king's archives, probably written in the same year, recommended the use of toxic-gas cartridges for machine-guns mounted on aircraft (of which the only make recommended was the German Junkers) and of mustard-gas bombs dropped from the same aircraft.[27] As we shall see shortly, his interest and that of his generals in the deployment of poison gas in Morocco was revived, and for some first awakened, by the 1921 disaster. The brutal events converted what might have been considered a weapon of last resort into what they hoped would be the principal weapon for the repression of the colonial rebels. This weapon had to be obtained from whatever source could be found.

It would appear that other military men, such as the enlightened Africanists, who had been reluctant to contemplate the use of chemical weapons in Morocco were swung over by the Anual disaster. In a telegraphic exchange on

[24] Kunz and Müller, *Giftgas*, 59.

[25] Spanish government requests to Paris were for both chemical bombs and gas masks: ADMAE (Paris) Europe 1918–1940, Espagne, chemise 19.

[26] Letter from Antonio Tovar to the king on 21 Aug. 1919, AGPR 15.510/9.

[27] 'La guerra de Marruecos y el aeroplano': AGPR 15.621/14.

12 August 1921 with the minister of war, the Vizconde de Eza, Berenguer acknowledged: 'I have always been opposed to the use of asphyxiating gases against those natives, but after what they have done, and their treacherous and dishonest conduct, I have to employ them with real effectiveness.' Two months later the king told him, 'It's a pity that we could not have sent you a squadron of bombers with gases to devastate the Rif countryside and quickly make them feel our strength in their land. Using all our planes at once, the effect would multiply and I don't think more than seven or eight groups would have resisted before they were violently dissolved.'[28]

Borne along by the public outcry, voices calling for the deployment of chemical weapons were raised in parliament and in the media, and the government began secretly to seek their supply from another source.[29] Of all the belligerents in the First World War, Germany had produced by far the largest quantity of chemical substances (over three times the amount of mustard gas made by the Allies). The process of dismantling the weapons factories and destroying the stocks of war chemicals under the conditions of the Versailles Treaty was a lengthy one. The post-war German high command, the Reichswehr, and some individual producers of chemicals, such as the entrepreneurial chemical engineer Hugo Stoltzenberg, who had been director of the German chemical war service, were both seeking to hinder or delay disarmament. Given the failure of the efforts of Spain's military and government to obtain such substances from the Allies, and the continued attraction among some Spanish officers for the Prussian military model, it was unsurprising, although a somewhat risky enterprise, that they should secretly approach both. Stoltzenberg was hoping to set up as a dealer in second-hand war chemicals and for that purpose would soon rent a site in Hamburg in 1923. At the same time, the Reichswehr was keen to continue commissioning toxic substances and was hoping to negotiate a deal to produce them for the Russians, with Stoltzenberg as manufacturer.[30]

Secret Spanish contacts with the Reichswehr were established on 20 August 1921, a month after the Anual disaster. In November, with the Reichswehr's agreement, Stoltzenberg flew to Madrid and held secret meetings with the prime minister Antonio Maura, and his finance minister, Francesc Cambó.[31] In June 1922 a contract was drawn up with the Germans for the construction of a chemical arms factory on a site near Madrid and Aranjuez called La Marañosa. To facilitate his cover, Stoltzenberg was given Spanish nationality. At the same time, other German firms were approached to construct a factory for gas masks and another for hand grenades and bombs. A number of very

---

[28] Telegraphic communication on 8.10.21 in AFAMM leg. 364/4. The first quote can be found in Pando, *Historia secreta*, 263, and is from AFAMM leg 442/9.

[29] One of the most vociferous proponents was the MP and ex-artillery officer Crespo de Lara, who published an article in *La Correspondencia Militar* on 10 Oct. 1921, calling for their use in Morocco.

[30] Haber, *The Poisonous Cloud*, Table 11.1, p. 261; on Stoltzenberg and the Reichswehr, see ibid., 304.

[31] No record of this meeting can be found in the Maura archives but it is clear from German sources that it took place.

modern hydroplanes to carry the bombs were also ordered. Stoltzenberg carried out a study of conditions in Morocco and, with the backing of the Reichswehr, concluded that mustard gas was the most appropriate chemical to be used since it would penetrate into the rough terrain of northern Morocco and impregnate the fields and the scarce water supplies of Abdel Krim's supporters.[32]

A year after the contract, production at the factory in La Marañosa (called, rather rashly, the Alfonso XIII factory, reflecting presumably the king's passion for chemical weapons) was under way and the first bombs were tested there on 26 June 1923, the day after Stoltzenberg had been given an audience by the king. By the following year the progress registered in the production of chemical weapons in collaboration with the Germans was such that the government decided to drop its request for related material from the French and disband the committee it had set up for this purpose.[33]

While the bombs were being prepared for testing, Spain, with the blessing of German aviation, had been negotiating with Stoltzenberg in June 1923 the purchase of further mustard-gas bombs for use by its air force. The German engineer informed the military envoy from Spain that fifty of these bombs of the 50 kilo variety would be sufficient to 'clean out' an area of 20 square kilometres. Apart from the bombs constructed under German supervision in La Marañosa, the Germans insisted that those Spain wished to purchase should be made in Germany because of the dangers involved in their production. The Spanish envoy was assured that there would be no problem in getting them to Spanish Morocco. A combined operation by the German Ministry of Foreign Affairs and the Spanish embassy in Berlin would ensure that the dispatch of the bombs would evade the international committee watching over German affairs. Their transport, apparently, did not constitute a problem. They would be shipped to Melilla via Denmark, Holland, or Italy, presumably without the knowledge of these countries and in conditions of extreme security.[34]

In the same month as the contract was signed with the Germans, and long before the first mustard-gas bombs were let loose on the Moroccans, toxic weapons were being assembled by the Spanish artillery in a jerry-built workshop in Melilla. With equipment and materials bought from the French, and under the supervision of French experts from the Schneider armaments firm, the factory began to produce shells filled with poison gas from June 1922. The chemicals included a range of substances such as phosgene and tear gas or

[32] Kunz and Müller, *Giftgas*, 74–90; Viñas, *Franco*, 93.

[33] AMAE, Madrid Archivo Histórico, Correspondencia 1543, Francia (1924–5); in the royal diary for June 1923 there is no record of the king's meeting with Stoltzenberg, though only official meetings and engagements were normally entered (except for the almost daily film that Alfonso had shown in the palace): AGPR, Registro 6052.

[34] 'Bombas de aeronave', F. Mohor to Despujol 14 June 1923, SHM R139, leg. 80, carp. 7.

chloropicrine, but not yet mustard gas.[35] They were designed for use at first by the artillery, despite the fact that artillery officers had no experience or training in chemical warfare. If we are to believe the French colonial newspaper, *La Depêche Coloniale*, the first onslaught of these toxic-gas weapons had taken place earlier in November 1921 near Tangier, probably using phosgene- or chloropicrine-filled shells bought from France. The newspaper attributed the unusual success of Berenguer's campaign in the western part of the Protectorate from that date to this first use of toxic gases. The report claimed to be based on correspondence and declarations received by the newspaper from the areas affected by the gas.[36]

Aircraft bombs filled with phosgene or chloropicrine made probably in the Melilla factory appear to have been in use by November 1923. Since these chemicals may have been vulnerable to heat, the air force was required to bomb its targets at dawn or even during night raids. The pilots also had to fly low to ensure that toxic gas was not dispersed by the wind before falling on its target. An order from the High Command at Melilla on 9 November makes it clear that not many of these bombs were yet available, so there was all the more reason to use them selectively. Thus strategic bombing became a skill developed early by the Spanish air force.[37]

Before looking any further at the Spanish chemical war campaign, it is worth considering how the use of poison chemicals was rationalized by its protagonists and defenders. There was much international polemic in the post-First World War period about 'poison gases'. World public opinion was decidedly against their use. While the Versailles Treaty and earlier conventions had explicitly condemned them in war, many politicians and military officers and some scientists (among them the progressive British scientist J. B. S. Haldane) openly justified their use on the grounds that there was no such thing as a humane war and that chemical weapons were no different from conventional ones. Defenders of the international ban, by far a majority of those who made public declarations on the issue, argued that they were indeed different

---

[35] Kunz and Müller, *Giftgas*, 58–9; telegrams between Berenguer and Eza, 6 and 8 June 1922: SHM Caja 53, carp. 6 'Explosivos'. Some of the equipment in the Melilla factory, such as empty shells for the insertion of chemical poisons, is listed in SHAT 7N 2126 Ministere de la Guerre, Direction de Contrôle, Cessions de matériels, Sept. 1921.

[36] Quoted in *La Depêche Marocaine*, 27 Nov. 1921. I have not found any evidence in Spanish archives of the use of chemical shells by artillery at that time: a communication between the minister of war and General Hernando about the state of the artillery two-and-a-half months earlier makes no mention of toxic weapons: AGPR 15510/10.

[37] SHM leg 386, carp. 6, quoted in Lázaro, 'La forja', 186. The author of this article believes the toxic bombs referred to in this document were mustard-gas bombs. In fact, as we shall see, mustard-gas aircraft bombs were not used until the summer of 1924. His confusion, understandable given the complexity of the documentation in the military archives, arises from the fact that he did not have the full details of the bomb codes. Thus he refers to all C bombs as mustard gas, whereas in fact C3 bombs are phosgene and C4 are chloropicrine.

in that they had a far greater potential to maim and kill non-combatants and they caused far greater physical torture than conventional weapons.[38]

We now know that the poisonous substances also had long-term effects, such as cancer, as will be discussed later in this chapter. The moral qualms of those who disapproved of the use of toxic weapons but accepted the validity of war might seem quaint to us. Since the Second World War, war has become synonymous with all forms of brutality directed at combatants and non-combatants alike. But we should not judge the standards of warfare of the past with those of the present. Until the 1920s at least, the only acceptable stage for war was the battlefield and the only actors allowed on that stage were male soldiers.

Another matter, as I have already suggested, was whether such standards of warfare should be applied to people considered uncivilized. In some circles, especially military ones, deeply influenced by the prevalent positivist discourse on the inevitability of Western civilization and technology, it was held that those people who had rejected the opportunity to become civilized deserved to be treated in an uncivilized manner. Wing-Commander Gale of 30 Squadron RAF, operating in Kurdistan at the same time as British artillery was bombing Iraqis with chemical shells, declared: 'If the Kurds hadn't learnt by our example to behave themselves in a civilised way then we had to spank their bottoms. This was done by bombs and guns.'[39]

The same brutal racism was displayed in Spain in private by those officers and politicians who called for a purely military solution to the Moroccan war. The king, closely identified with the militarist Africanists, as we have seen, was quite prepared to convey his extreme views on this issue privately to the French authorities. In an interview with the French military attaché on 15 June 1925, he stated that the most violent means possible should be employed against Abdel Krim, without the embarrassment of 'vain humanitarian considerations'. A combination of blockade leading to starvation and the 'intensive and continuous bombing' of the tribes in the heart of the Rif, 'with the aid of the most harmful of all gases', would save Spanish and French lives. 'The important thing', the attaché reported the king as saying, 'is the extermination, like that of malicious beasts, of the Beni Urriaguels and the tribes who are closest to Abdel Krim . . .' Overlying this genocidal racism was an extreme right-wing discourse increasingly shared by Alfonso's coterie of militarists. The Rifians' offensive, the king went on, 'was but the sketch (amorce) of a general

---

[38] For a summary of the arguments, see Haber, The Poisonous Cloud, 291–5. In his efforts to open up the debate about this hushed-up subject, Giorgio Rochat wondered recently why chemical weapons should be considered worse or morally different from the effects of a hand grenade or a 'bayonet in the stomach' (in Del Boca, I gas, 50). But he does not take into account that it was used in Ethiopia and in Morocco to a large extent against civilians and that its long-term effects on survivors can be qualitatively worse than conventional wounds.

[39] Quoted in Simons, Iraq, 180.

uprising of all the Muslim world at the instigation of Moscow and international Jewry . . .'[40]

It may seem surprising that the supposedly progressive colonial officers were also calling for the use of chemical weapons against the Moroccan enemy. But they employed a different rationale. Many liberal circles in the late nineteenth and early twentieth centuries saw science and technology as progressive in themselves. Improving the environment and the human race in accordance with the Western model meant adopting measures that were harsh but indispensable. Eugenics, for example, attracted widespread support in Europe. Like eugenics, chemical warfare was, in the opinion of enlightened Africanist military opinion, the regrettable but necessary corollary of civilization. For example, the second-in-command of the commander-in-chief's General Staff in Morocco, Colonel (later General) Ignacio Despujols, as convenor of a military committee studying a projected landing in Al Hoceima Bay, wrote a report on 28 July 1923 to his immediate superior recommending the use of vast quantities of chemical bombs. These bombs were to be dropped directly behind the HQ of the enemy in preparation for the landing (which finally took place in 1925, as we have seen, using smaller amounts of chemicals). He argued that their use should be preceded by an intense day-long artillery bombardment with conventional shells so that the enemy would know the coming offensive was for real and would therefore gather together the greatest number of their forces. After this an 'incessant and continuous action over twenty-four hours' by bombers should take place, dropping 'a veritable flood of bombs with gases in a proportion ten times greater than that which Von Tschudi, president of the German Air Force, advises is necessary to annihilate all living beings in the 80 or 100 square kilometres of the rich, fertile, and populated area contiguous to the Bay of Al Hoceima . . .'. Nobody should remain alive, therefore, but anybody who did would be completely disabled. This, he wrote, would be the 'best pacifist propaganda amongst the rebel tribes'. He continued ingenuously: 'What beautiful horizons would then open up in this now completely pacified territory for the educational work of Spain.'[41]

Enlightened Africanists saw the use of chemical weapons as the most effective way of bringing the war to a rapid end. Borne along by wishful thinking, they envisaged that the intense bombing of the enemy with mustard gas would bring about their immediate surrender without conditions. The first civilian high commissioner, Luis Silvela, consulted both his militarist and enlightened Africanist generals, such as Martínez Anido, Castro Girona, and Montero, and

[40] SHAT 3H134. I am indebted to Jean-Marc Delaunay for bringing this document to my attention.

[41] In both AR 58/37 Informe reservado and AGPR 15.511/3. Despujols' reference to Von Tschudi's advice was almost certainly the result of the visit to the latter of his envoy F. Mohor, who reported that he had agreed with the Germans that chemical warfare might appear inhumane at first sight but was, on the contrary, very humanitarian because of the speed of its results: Pando, *Historia*, 264.

all apparently saw chemical warfare as a panacea. It would avoid the military defeats which had so inflamed public opinion, save Spanish lives, bring the war to an end, and enable the repatriation of the troops to Spain.[42]

Another progressive Africanist officer maintained, after negotiating the purchase of mustard-gas bombs with Stoltzenberg in Berlin in June 1923, that the purpose of the intense chemical bombing of the 'natives' was not to punish them but to frighten them, 'so these procedures which at first seem inhumane are, on the contrary very humanitarian, because of the rapidity of their results'.[43] The colonel in charge of drawing up plans in 1923 for the invasion of Al Hoceima called for the massive use of toxic and incendiary bombs before the landing on the grounds that, 'although it may appear paradoxical, the successes derived from this procedure will always be more humanitarian than those achieved by fighting between men, because the total casualties will always be fewer than those of any operation using shock-troops, above all for us.'[44]

Behind this woolly thinking lay a wilful evasion of the fact that the casualties were going to be mainly among civilians. The use of the word 'humanitarian' probably rested on the belief that, since poison gas was a casualty agent rather than a mass killer, it would not be as harmful as military action. Yet such reasoning ignored the widely publicized evidence of the devastating effects of mustard gas during the First World War. Its use in Morocco would inflict unspeakable pain on children, old people, and women, as well as young men. This rationalization of its use was an effort to reconcile the residue of nineteenth-century military values with the brutalization of war since 1914. The ease with which enlightened military Africanist opinion embraced the most violent methods of warfare perhaps also testified to the ascendancy of militarist Africanist thinking in the aftermath of Anual.

Looking back over the events of the chemical war some thirty-five years later, one of the pilots responsible for dropping the most lethal of the mustard-gas bombs, Ignacio Hidalgo de Cisneros, condemned the campaign as 'truly despicable' (verdaderamente canallesca). 'I have to confess', he wrote in 1961, 'that not for one second did it occur to me that the mission I had been given was an abomination or a crime; I have to say also that I do not remember having had the slightest remorse over what I was doing. It is incredible how naturally one can commit the greatest barbarities when one has a certain mentality.' He admitted that he only began to realize the enormity of what he and his fellow pilots had done when he heard about the Italian chemical war against the Abyssinians in 1935. His first reaction was a sense of indignation at the atrocity the Italians were committing, until it dawned on him that he had taken part in the same sort of atrocity in Morocco. The 'mentality', as he describes it, or the moral codes shaped by the Church and the army, with which he and his

[42] Alto Comisario a Ministro Guerra y Estado, 15 July 1923, SHM R139, leg. 80, carp. 7.
[43] F. Mohor to Despujol, 14 June 1923 in ibid.   [44] Pardo, Al servicio, 162–3.

fellow officers conducted their lives, implicitly excluded the Moroccans against whom they were fighting. This was not only because the Moor was felt to be a secular enemy of Spain, as Hidalgo acknowledges, but also because he was seen as racially inferior, like the colonial subjects of Britain, France, or Italy.[45]

Mustard gas (as opposed to other chemicals, such as phosgene) appears to have been used for the first time during the battle of Tizzi Azza on 15 July 1923, and it was fired by the artillery.[46] Luis Silvela seems to have been delighted by the results. To the commander-in-chief of Melilla, Martínez Anido, he promised the prompt dispatch of 'X bombs' (mustard-gas bombs dropped by plane), 'which I do not tire of requesting, and in which I have so much faith'. His enthusiasm was reflected in his improbable request to the ministers of war and state for the immediate purchase of at least 50,000 mustard-gas bombs for warplanes. By early September, shortly before Primo de Rivera's coup, the government was promising to send 400 of these bombs every week.[47]

His successor, General Luis Aizpuru, as Primo de Rivera's first high commissioner, was equally committed to the massive use of chemical weapons. But he first made efforts to secure peace through negotiations with Abdel Krim and Raisuni. The strategy envisaged by the dictator and himself was for the withdrawal of troops from the battlefield to well-defended positions in the rearguard, where Spain could administer what remained of her Protectorate effectively and with fewer personnel.[48] The retreat to the new line of defence would be followed by a general dousing by aerial bombardment of the whole area in enemy hands with mustard gas, TNT, and incendiary bombs. A telegram to military commanders from the commander-in-chief in Melilla on 1 May 1924 called for 'a highly intense and continuous campaign of bombing and destruction of the enemy's cattle and crops . . . bombs of all types especially the incendiary bombs and those others . . .'.[49] This was far from the policy of abandoning Morocco with which Primo de Rivera has been credited.

---

[45] Hidalgo, *Cambio de rumbo*, 193–5. His denunciation is not unconnected with the fact that he fought for the Republic in the Civil War, though this does not mean that other veteran airmen who remained loyal to the Republic ever talked about the chemical campaign. See Ch. 6 for more discussion on this issue. See also Ch. 7 for a discussion of the Moorish Other.

[46] In his novel *Imán*, 5th edn. (Madrid, Destino, 1995), 78, the veteran of the colonial war Ramón J. Sender mentions that the mustard gas was blown by the wind into the Spanish line of blockhouses, seriously affecting the soldiers. However, he gives the date of 5 July and suggests that they were dropped by planes; military sources, on the contrary, indicate they were fired by cannon.

[47] For Luis Silvela's communication with Martínez Aido, see SHM R742, leg. 4, carp. 11; Pando, *Historia*, 263–4; for his request, see SHM R139, leg. 80, carp. 7, and for the government's dispatch of bombs, SHM R534, leg. 373, carp. 1. Hernández Mir (*La Dictadura*, 11–12) quotes the minister of state Alba's letter to Silvela approving of his proposal to use toxic gases and confirming PM García Prieto's knowledge of it. French diplomatic sources reported artillery barrages using toxic shells (probably filled with phosgene) in the battle over Tifaruin in August: ADMAE Maroc 1917–40, vol. 226, pp. 125–7; this is corroborated by Pardo, *Al servicio*, 283.

[48] 'Acuerdos adoptados por el Directorio', 30 May 1924, AGA, Africa, caja M12, exp. 2.

[49] SHM R602, leg. 424, carp. 5. The strategy is also confirmed in an accurate and detailed report by the French military attaché: SHAT 3H 134.

What is clear from these communications is that there was no longer any compunction about distinguishing between enemy combatants and civilians. The coming campaign could not be only a precision-bombing exercise, nor would it be effective to drop bombs on the highly mobile guerrillas of the Moroccan resistance. Instead it was to be directed at densely populated areas—villages, markets, and districts under intense cultivation. These had been the targets, in any case, of the TNT bombing campaigns until then. For example, an order from the commander-in-chief to the air force in Tetuan on 1 October 1923 had instructed the airmen to bomb an important market town with explosives on the day and at the time when most people would be milling about in the market.[50] Apart from killing, injuring, and maiming men, women, and children, mustard gas would have an advantage over both TNT, incendiary bombs, and other toxic bombs such as phosgene and chloropicrine in that it would infect the land and the water supplies for many days. Given the ignorance of local people about chemical poisons and their treatment, its effects were no doubt expected to be all the more devastating. Phosgene and choloropicrine had already been revealed as fairly ineffective.[51]

However, a strike in Hamburg and the flooding of the factory in La Marañosa after the River Tajo overflowed its banks delayed production of mustard gas even further. Expecting to start the bombing campaign in February, the air squadrons in Morocco were still awaiting the arrival of the bombs in May. Tactical problems were also holding up the start of operations. The first area targeted for the mustard-gas bombing, the Beni Urriagel territory, was at some distance from the airport at Nador near Melilla from where the planes would fly, making the operation more hazardous. Moreover, the air force in the eastern zone of the Protectorate had only between thirty-five and forty planes available for this operation (out of the eighty-eight listed in a report of 4 March 1924). Impatiently, the under-secretary of war, General Correa, insisted that the campaign had to begin as soon as possible, 'so that the enemy will begin to suffer the extraordinary punishment which is going to be inflicted on them'.[52]

Also impatient at the delay, Primo de Rivera asked the Melilla commander on 20 May to explain why he had not used the 'special bombs' yet. But the latter had already sent the government a telegram announcing that the first batch of mustard-gas bombs being made in the Maestranza factory in Melilla under the supervision of German technicians would be ready in a week. Finally, in a communication with the high commissioner General Aizpuru on 24 May, Primo de Rivera promised that they were about to be unleashed.[53] As we saw

[50] SHM R920, leg. 4, carp. 275–399.

[51] Transcript of telegraph communications between General Correa and the chief of staff in Melilla on 3 May 1924 in SHM R120, leg. 50, carp. 1.

[52] Ibid., 5 May 1924. Ibid. for the report on plane numbers.

[53] Telegram of 19 May 1924 in ibid. For Primo's communication: SHM R602, leg. 424, carp. 5. For the telephone conversation between Primo and Aizpuru: AGA Africa, caja M12, exp. 2.

in Chapter 4, the timing of his announcement in July of the withdrawal of troops to the new line of defence called the Estella line was closely connected with the coming on stream of the new weapons. The retreat would enable the blanket bombing of the enemy with mustard gas without danger to his own troops.

The key unit in the new operations was the air force. The first air squadron had been sent to Morocco in 1913. Operations began in November of that year, and the first Spanish casualties of the air war occurred when Moroccans brought down a light plane with their Mauser bullets.[54] Since then, the pilots had also provided valuable information for the army by taking aerial photographs of the largely unknown terrain of the Rif interior, thus replacing the service previously supplied by hot-air balloons. In the new-born Spanish air force planes had not been allowed to bomb at an altitude of less than 500 metres, in order to avoid exposing them to enemy gunfire, so that casualties tended to be few amongst the pilots and were usually the result of inexperience or mechanical failure. The number of aircraft available for military action had been considerably boosted after the First World War, when the government acquired aircraft at bargain prices that had seen action on the Western Front and that France and Britain no longer required.

After Anual, aviation tactics changed completely. The technology of warplanes had been transformed by the First World War. While bombs continued to be dropped by pilots by hand as they leant over the edge of their cockpits, the newest planes had a bomb-release gear that made for greater accuracy and safety. In all aircraft, the pilot was accompanied by a co-pilot, a lieutenant or sergeant, whose role was to man the machine-gun, or drop the bombs by hand or release them with a lever when he received a signal from the pilot.[55] Machine-guns could be installed on the back cockpit of many planes facing the rear, allowing them to carry 1,000 cartridges in four drums in addition to six bombs. Machine-gun fire was particularly effective just before troops advanced across terrain defended by the enemy. It was also used to deadly effect against the souks or markets, so much so that the Moroccans soon only held them at night when they could not be strafed. Pilots were also expected to drop supplies to the dozens of positions besieged after the Anual disaster. The air fleet had been augmented by the purchase of many new planes thanks to collections organized in different parts of Spain by the provincial authorities. Amongst them were the De Havilland 4 fighter-bombers, the agile Bristol F-2B fighters, and the heavy De Havilland 9A bombers. The heaviest of the

[54] Coronel José Gomá, *La guerra en el aire (vista, suerte y al toro)* (Barcelona, AHR, 1958), 21–2.

[55] The Italian air force in the Eastern African campaign from 1936 evidently used different techniques for mustard-gas bombing. According to evidence by Hailè Selassie, the planes at first dropped barrels filled with the liquid, to no satisfactory effect. So spraying equipment was attached to planes and the chemical was then sprayed over a large area of land by successive waves of planes, creating a thick and deadly mist: Del Boca, *Gli italiani*, 490–1.

new planes were a fleet of four French Farman F60 Goliaths, the first airbus in aviation history, which had been ferrying small groups of passengers across the English Channel since 1919.[56]

The new operations required pilots to swoop low over the enemy, and this exposed them to the accurate rifle-fire of the Moroccans. Indeed, the muhayeddin would try to shelter in caves or dug-outs when the planes arrived, then would start to count the number of bombs that were dropped on them. If nine bombs fell from a plane they could be sure that it was not equipped with a machine-gun, and they would immediately come out of their shelters to shoot at it after the ninth. When only six had fallen they could expect machine-gun fire and were therefore more circumspect.[57] The new tactics caused a sudden rise in casualties, as the muhayeddin began to score hits on the low-flying planes with rifle-fire and brought many down.[58] By early 1924, despite the pilots' reluctance to cramp their space further, High Command insisted they carried lifebelts in the cabin so they could ditch their planes in the sea when hit and await a rescue launch. They were also issued with a letter in Arabic and a cheque for 5000 pesetas, redeemable when they were delivered safely to a Spanish position.

Nevertheless, some pilots were unwilling to expose themselves to these sorts of risk. An American observer reported that the Spanish bombing campaign he witnessed over many days during his stay with the Metalsa tribe in 1924, was 'a curious sort of comic-opera affair'. The planes always arrived at exactly the same time morning and afternoon, give or take ten minutes. On Sunday only one aircraft came, and during the rest of the week two planes flew over daily except on the market-day, Thursday, when three were sent. 'The bombs were thrown with such evident lack of effort to do any damage that one supposed the Spanish aviators must be rather like boys distributing hand-bills.'[59]

It would appear, however, that most pilots were committed to the new low-flying tactics, not least because they needed to drop supplies to colleagues in the beleaguered outposts, where pinpoint accuracy was crucial. These low-flying tactics owed a lot to the British model of aerial TNT bombing in Iraq. Indeed, the new strategy of mass bombing was derived from the experience of the RAF. Like the British, the most intensive part of the campaign was to take place during the harvesting season, which in Morocco fell between mid-April and mid-May. During those four to six weeks the planes were to undertake 'systematic, persistent, and methodical bombing', in particular of the strongholds of the enemy. But their action would continue until the complete submission

---

[56] Flores and Cicuéndez, *Guerra aérea*, 37–8; Hidalgo, *Cambio de rumbo*, 180–1.

[57] José Paramo Godoy, 'Aeronautique militaire', report of 4 May 1922 (trans. into French) in AGA Asuntos Exteriores, caja M34.

[58] Riego, 'La guerra aérea', 42–5.

[59] Sheean, *Adventures*, 81–2. Sheean observed the same cursory style among the pilots bombing the area of Abdel Krim's home town of Ajdir: p. 128.

of the 'rebels'. Unlike the British, however, the Spanish air force was about to unleash toxic gases.

In order to ensure that there would be no Spanish casualties, such bombing had to take place at some distance from the troops. It was calculated that the 127 fighters and bombers available for the campaign (including thirteen planes based in Seville) would be sufficient to drop some 1,680 bombs daily.[60] This new type of warfare placed a huge responsibility on the shoulders of the pilots. Used to TNT and incendiary bombs, they had no experience of the danger-ous mustard-gas projectiles. One of the pilots involved in the new campaign, Hidalgo de Cisneros, claims that he was the first to release such a bomb from a supply of a hundred bombs of the heaviest kind available, the 100-kilo model, and he seems to suggest he did so before the summer of 1924, although he gives neither date, month, or year. Purchased from post-war Allied stocks and deliv-ered with great care to the chemical factory in Melilla, they could only be car-ried by a Farman F60 Goliath since they were too heavy for the other planes.[61] There is no reason to doubt his testimony, and the operations involving the 100-kilo bombs may have been a one-off venture that preceded or coincided with the main bombing campaign. However, the archives otherwise make it clear that mustard-gas aircraft bombs were first used only in June 1924.

In fact, the first supplies reached the Nador aerodrome on 20 June. Officially designated as C1 bombs weighing 50 kilos each, they were made up of mustard gas and a few kilos of TNT to explode their contents. The first sortie was made on 22 June. Sixteen bombs were dropped on Abdel Krim's headquarters at Ait Kamara, another twenty on his house nearby, twenty on the banks of the lower Guix river, twelve on the village of Tizimoren, nine on the villages between the Nekor and Guix rivers, eighteen on Abdel Krim's home town of Ajdir, and four on the village of Zoco el Hadh, a total of ninety-nine C1 bombs or almost 5,000 kilos of mustard gas.[62] Next day 101 C1 bombs were dropped. Subsequent waves of air strikes on an almost daily basis deposited more mus-tard-gas bombs alongside TNT and incendiary bombs. By 23 July the smaller C2 or 10-kilo mustard-gas bombs were also beginning to be deployed, and by December C5 or 20-kilo bombs were being used. French intelligence, which closely monitored the military campaign of the Spanish army, reported that the bombing raids carried out in June using mustard gas and incendiary bombs had no 'appreciable results', but it was difficult to know how they could calculate their effects so soon.[63]

[60] 'Informe sobre la Actuación de la Aviación en el Protectorado', 4 Mar. 1924, AGA Africa, caja M12, exp. 2.

[61] Hidalgo, *Cambio de rumbo*, 193–4.

[62] Telegram of 22 June 1924 in SHM R120, leg. 50, carp. 1.

[63] SHAT 7N 2754. French military intelligence reported the use of 'asphyxiating' bombs bought from Germany in a massive air offensive during April 1924 (ibid., 3 and 30 Apr.) but this is not borne out by documents in the Spanish military archives.

The use of chemical bombs was more problematic in the west. Spanish troops were being deployed in parts of the western Protectorate and it was difficult, according to a military report, to convince them of the dangers of penetrating too soon into an area contaminated by chemicals. It was also quite possible, the report went on, that their commanders were not even informed as to where the bombs had been dropped. Judging from military sources, the lighter C2 bombs were initially used in greater profusion in the west than the 50-kilo C1 bombs because they contaminated a smaller area.[64] However, in the campaign in Anjera in the northernmost part of the Protectorate in December 1924, an onslaught of chemical bombs similar to that in the east was unleashed on the people of the area. Between 15 and 30 December some 184 C5 bombs, seventy-five chloropicrine (C4) bombs, and 110 TNT bombs were dropped in the western zone, including Anjera (aside from the 559 unspecified bombs dropped on 11 December on the town of Zoco El Arbaa alone).[65]

The continued resistance by some tribes in Anjera led to a stepping up of the bombing campaign in the area. An order from the General Staff dated 30 May 1925 called for the 'harshest possible punishment that must be felt with the greatest intensity . . . it is necessary not only that the action of the air force should not stop even for one day, but that the bombing should be carried out with the maximum intensity and with the greatest possible number of planes and bombs'. Thus, over a twenty-five-day period 3,000 C5 bombs, 8,000 150-kilo-TNT bombs, and 2,000 incendiary bombs were to be dropped over Anjera.[66] Evidently, the targeting of the Spanish aviators was sometimes haphazard. Anjera was next to the international zone of Tangier, and bombs started to land across the frontier. An international committee representing the European Powers visited the area accompanied by Spanish officers, and to the presumably intense embarrassment of the latter witnessed further inaccurate bombing.[67]

Anjera's proximity to the international enclave of Tangier caused further problems. Thus, the first news that came out of Moroccan casualties from chemical bombing was based on observations by the international community about the bombing campaign in that area. From his headquarters in French Morocco, Lyautey wrote to the French president that the Spanish air force 'had severely hit the rebel villages, frequently using tear gas and asphyxiating bombs, ravaging the peaceful population. A large number of women and children came to Tangier to be treated, where their presence provoked pity amongst the Muslim population as well as indignation against the Spaniards.' The French marshal did not miss the irony that Spain claimed at the same time

---

[64] SHM R120 and R920, leg. 4, carp 400.   [65] SHM R120, leg. 50, carp. 2.
[66] SHM R126, leg. 58, carp. 5.
[67] Walter B. Harris, *France, Spain and the Rif* (London, Edward Arnold, 1927), 150.

to be bringing the benefits of civilization to the inhabitants of northern Morocco (yet his own methods were not especially civilized).[68]

The SIS reported that 'gas' (almost certainly mustard gas) was also used against the inhabitants of the Larache district in the westernmost part of the Protectorate, after Spanish troops had evacuated the area, with an estimated 25 per cent of fatal casualties (though again, how these calculations were made is not clear). The US military attaché reported to the British that he had been told by Spanish artillery in January that the results of mustard gas were marked on both people and animals. 'The practice of Spanish airmen was to drop gas bombs in villages where markets were being held, either the day before this gathering or while the market was going on.' Numerous reports in the military archives attest to this strategy of seeking the most populated areas and periods for chemical bombing.[69] But it can be inferred also that many mistakes occurred, and that villages which had tried to keep on the right side of the Spanish army were bombed by mistake. A circular went out on 31 March to all commanders and pilots strictly prohibiting the bombing of any area without an express order from the General Staff, based on advice given by the colonel in charge of relations with the 'natives', who had specialist knowledge of the allegiance of the tribes.[70]

Two German officers disguised as aviation mechanics were sent in 1925 to Spain and then Morocco by the Reichswehr to report on the Spanish chemical offensive. On their return, they produced an account that heavily criticized the Spanish army and air force. Like French and British military observers, they could not conceal their disdain for their Spanish counterparts. Although they witnessed the devastation that the toxic gases had caused during flights arranged for them by the Spanish High Command, they reported that the campaign was deficient, above all because Abdel Krim had not surrendered. The confidence that mustard gas, if used with German efficiency, could bring any enemy to their knees, shines through their report. They found the whole operation was badly organized, from the conditions of the Melilla chemical factory to the targeting of the pilots and the insufficiency of the amounts of chemical bombs used.[71]

By March 1925, nevertheless, all areas in the hands of the enemy were reported by the Spanish military command to have been bombed with mus-

---

[68] For Lyautey's comments, see ADMAE Maroc 1917–40, vol. 201, p. 87. See also v. 202, p. 48. *The Times* reported on 5 Jan. 1925 that Spanish airmen had dropped bombs on the market of Sok el Jemis in Anjera, but without specifying which kind. The fact that Primo wrote a letter two days later thanking the newspaper for its reporting and attacking the 'absurd notices' printed elsewhere testifies to the sensitivity over leaks about the use of chemical weapons.

[69] A telegraph communication of 14 Dec. 1925 records the native officer or interventor recommending the bombing of a village all day because it was market day: AGPR 15599/16; for the SIS Gas Report and the US military attaché's report, see PRO WO 188/765.

[70] SHM R126, leg. 58, carp. 4.   [71] Kunz and Müller, *Giftgas*, 199–214 and 144 ff.

tard gas.[72] But Primo's change of strategy in mid-1925, from withdrawal to reconquest, made the use of chemical bombs difficult. Troops could not be sent into areas contaminated by mustard gas unless they were kitted out with masks, special clothing, and dousing equipment. According to a report of November 1925 by the British controller of chemical warfare research, the Spanish military command had not shown sufficient care about protecting their own troops. 'It would appear . . . that chemical warfare tactics have not been closely studied with the Spanish army. A persistent gas such as mustard gas should seldom be used on ground over which an advance is shortly to be made as it will interfere with the movements of the attacking forces . . . Mustard gas should be reserved for targets which it is not intended to occupy for at least a week.' Thus, for example, the contingents used in the suppression of the Anjera uprising were affected by some of the gas (probably chloropicrine) dropped earlier by the air force because the wind blew it back in their faces.[73] A British air force officer, H. Pughe Lloyd, on an official visit to Spanish Morocco, reported to the War Office in a secret memorandum that the use of chemical weapons was unpopular with the soldiers because they were not provided with respirators and thus suffered casualties. 'One Colonel explained to me at great length that Yperite (or mustard gas) and gas were no good as when his troops attacked a village that had been shelled with gas three weeks previously, he lost a number of men as casualties from it.'[74]

It may well be for this reason that Despujol's recommendation for the use of massive amounts of mustard gas in the taking of Al Hoceima was not adopted when the landing finally took place, at least not on the scale he had proposed. But a considerable amount was fired in preparation for the landing. Villages on the surrounding heights and beyond, including the already devastated Ajdir, were targeted.[75] Spanish troops were also equipped with masks. A thousand of them were bought from the British and were deployed in the aircraft carrier *Dédalo*, which took part in the landing in Al Hoceima Bay. The British visitor learnt that a considerable amount was also fired during the landing. Reports on Spanish chemical casualties, if any, are not available. On the other hand, Abdel Krim's men were clearly affected. Pughe Lloyd wrote that: 'The Riffs had learnt a thing or two, and when gas was fired they went up into the hills. However, a lot of them were killed and a considerable number gave themselves up in quiet sectors hoping to be cured. They were mostly half blind or their lungs were very badly affected.'[76]

[72] SHM R602, leg. 424, carp. 5.

[73] J. Davidson Pratt, report on 7 Nov. 1925 in PRO WO 188/765; re. Anjera, report by Major W. W. Torr on 20 May 1925 in ibid.

[74] H. Pughe Lloyd, letter to J. Davidson Pratt, 30 Jan. 1926 in ibid.

[75] SHM R633, leg. 449, carp. 3; ibid., leg. 514, carp. 1, and R635, leg. 451, carp. 1–9.

[76] Re the masks, report of 25 May 1925 and Pughe Lloyd's report both in PRO WO 188/765. A Spanish military source also confirms the use of chemical weapons during the landing: SHM R538, carp. 6.

The Spaniards also suffered a relatively high number of casualties in the workshops where the chemical bombs were being assembled, largely through negligence. But the mustard gas they were making in both Spain and Morocco was of a very basic, undistilled kind and therefore could be neither easily controlled in the production process nor stored for any length of time. Over eight months of production in the chemical-weapon factory in Morocco, the Maestranza y Parque de Melilla, some ten officers and eighty-two soldiers had been injured in the assembly of the mustard-gas bombs, even though fifty of the workers there were sappers specially trained in chemical warfare.[77] Judging by Pughe Lloyd's observations to the head of the British chemical warfare centre in Porton, little care was taken to protect the workers. 'I saw them charging shells. It was rather an antiquated and dangerous practice after the one you have at Porton, but the fellows seemed to be fairly handy in getting out of the way when it was spilt.'[78] Shortly after his visit the factory had to suspend production for a week, despite the huge demand for chemical bombs, because so many of the personnel had been affected by the poison. On one occasion, a 100-kilo mustard-gas bomb stored in the Melilla aerodrome started to leak badly and twenty people were severely injured, including the head of the chemical-warfare unit himself, Captain Planell. On the same or another occasion, a Spaniard was so badly burned by mustard gas in an accident that, after nine months of treatment, military doctors had to amputate the limb affected.[79]

A similar level of casualties no doubt occurred in the other chemical-weapons assembly plants in Spain, but details of these appear not to be available, probably because the plants were largely in private hands. We know from fragmentary and sometimes contradictory accounts in French and British military sources that several factories and workshops were set up in addition to the plants in La Marañosa and Melilla. According to the British, a workshop existed in the Ministry of War building in Guadalajara in 1925, where chemical bombs were put together with the help of German and Austrian technicians. Several other plants were being reconverted or extended to

[77] According to a letter from the director to the Melilla commander-in-chief on 27 Feb. 1925 in SHM R602, leg. 424, carp. 5. An earlier letter of 12 Jan. (ibid.) also gave details of the technical problems encountered in the production of mustard gas. The detail about the sappers is from PRO WO 188/765, report of 22 July 1925. Many years after the colonial and civil wars, a Spaniard from Melilla recalls bicycling frequently past the hangar where the factory was housed, on which the words 'Chemical War' (*Guerra Química*) were written in huge letters. It was subsequently removed. Conversation with Vicente Moga Romero on 16 March 2001.

[78] Pughe Lloyd, letter. The fact that the Spanish military authorities were happy to show the British officer around the factory attests to their well-placed confidence that his observations would not be made public. Indeed, the documents of which his report forms a part were not released for public scrutiny until 1 Oct. 1997.

[79] 'Chemical report', 23 Jan. 1928, PRO WO 188/781; Hidalgo, *Cambio de rumbo*, 197. For the suspension of production in the Melilla factory see SHM R694, leg. 14, carp. 1, 12 Feb. 1926 and ibid., R633, leg. 514, carp. 1, 2 Feb. 1926.

accommodate the production of mustard gas. One was an electrochemical plant at Flix on the River Ebro in the province of Tarragona, and another an explosives factory called the Fábrica de Pólvoras y Explosivos in Granada. A factory in Mallorca called La Puebla was producing chlorine gas. Close to the Alfonso XIII plant at La Marañosa, a factory in Aranjuez was making a modest fifty shells a day, which were then sent to Melilla for the installation of mustard gas. French military intelligence also reported that mustard gas was being made in factories in Puig and Denia, both of them close to Valencia. A later report by their British counterparts mentioned a munitions factory in Vizcaya, the Talleres de Guernica S.A., part of which appeared to have been converted to accommodate the manufacture of mustard-gas bombs.[80]

Given the fragmentary nature of the evidence in the Spanish military archives (the only source from which a full picture of the chemical war could be drawn, were it possible), it is extremely difficult to calculate how many chemical weapons were made. Piecing together the scant evidence, it would appear that large supplies of mustard gas for installation in bombs began to be built up during 1924. Some were shipped to Spain and Morocco from Stoltzenberg's Hamburg factory and others were made in the La Marañosa and Melilla factories. According to telegrams from Primo de Rivera to his military commanders in Morocco in October, 30 tons or 30,000 kilos of mustard gas had been ordered from Germany and two boats were transporting the first consignments from Hamburg. Supplies of the chemical were possibly also being obtained from private sources in France. The new supplies would enable daily production in the Melilla factory to be raised from 300 kilos to 1 tonne.[81] Given that the factory near Madrid almost certainly had a higher production capacity than that in Melilla, overall production of mustard gas from the end of 1924 must have reached impressive figures. The German officers' calculation that some 400 metric tons of mustard gas were manufactured between 1923 and 1925 does not take into account production from the last quarter of 1925 until the end of the war. Nor does it take on board the substances for the production of all toxic-gas bombs and shells that were bought from the French and the Germans.[82]

The size of the bombs has already been considered. Secret RAF reports suggest the size of the aircraft bombs ranged between 2, 5, 10, 12, 20, and 25 kilos, of which the majority were between 12 and 25 kilos.[83] Larger mustard-gas bombs, like the 100-kilo type, were employed briefly, but it is unlikely that the massive 280-kilo bombs (the C500 T) dropped by the Italians on the

[80] PRO WO 188/765 and /781, and SHAT 7N 2616.

[81] SHM R545, leg. 382, carp. 1, 3–5 Oct. 1924. References to French supplies of mustard gas can be found in the Davidson Pratt report of 7 Nov. 1925 and another unsigned report of 25 May 1925, both in PRO WO 188/765.

[82] Kunz and Müller Giftgas, 199–214.

[83] Unsigned report of 25 May 1925, PRO WO 188/765 and another of 23 Jan. 1928, reporting on unused stocks after the end of the war, in PRO WO 188/78.

Ethiopians in the 1930s were ever bought or used by the Spanish. A Moroccan eyewitness described to me the small size of an unexploded bomb that he examined, which gave out the typical odour of mustard gas and was likely to have been a C2 10-kilo bomb.[84]

Even more hazardous is any estimate of how many were actually used. There appears to have been some difficulty at the beginning in persuading pilots (rather than artillery officers) to begin the massive use of chemical bombs. The commander of the two air force squadrons in Tetuan in 1923 had complained that they had never stored nor used the mustard-gas bombs before, while the phosgene bombs supplied to them at the Larache aerodrome previously had not been 'stable', according to the commander of the latter. The implication was that unless the chemical bombs of whatever type were properly tested, they were too risky for them to use. Technical problems may also have delayed the massive employment of the bombs. Given the enormous risks involved in their transport and storage, the aerodromes of Ceuta, Tetuan, and Larache needed to be properly equipped before receiving supplies from Melilla. Moreover, the delicacy of the firing mechanism on some aircraft was such that if the bombs were not installed correctly they could be activated by contact with other parts of the aeroplane, or could simply get stuck in the bomb-release mechanism.[85]

The storage of the bombs was also a major headache. Given their undistilled composition, they posed a severe risk if they remained unused for even a short period. They contained a rudimentary system for the detection of leakages but had no fail-safe mechanism that could prevent their detonation. Worried about the accumulation of bombs in the Maestranza factory in Melilla, the local commander-in-chief ordered the transfer in May 1925 of 400 of the 1,200 C5 bombs stored in the factory to the two other chemical bomb depots in Tetuan and Larache.[86]

It is also likely that only certain aeroplanes, such as the Farman F60 Goliath, were fitted out with a bomb-release gear and that the pilots flying them needed to be trained to use it. The bomb releases seem to have involved a claw acti-vated by the pilot, enabling the bomb to drop clear of the aircraft. The bombs themselves were detonated by a fuse that was fitted, on the bigger models, only when they had been installed on the undercarriage of the wings. Their down-wards path seems to have been controlled by a propeller inserted at the back of the shell just before the flight (unlike the more sophisticated mechanism

---

[84] Interview with Mohammed Ben Ayache El Amraní H'mimed on 22 July 2000. A report from the Melilla factory on 25 Feb. 1925 registered 915 mustard-gas bombs in its stocks (size unspecified), together with 9,388 incendiary bombs of different sizes (though these were invariably smaller than the chemical bombs) and 114 chloropicrine bombs: SHM R. 602, leg. 424, carp. 5.

[85] 'Instrucciones para el manejo de las bombas cargadas con Iperita', SHM R694, leg. 14, carp. 1; for transport and storage, see also SHM R139, leg. 80, carp 7, Comandancia General de Ceuta, 5 Nov. 1923; Cuartel General del Ejercito de Espana en Africa, 7 Nov.; and Ingenieros del Ejercito, 23 Nov.

[86] Letter to Primo de Rivera on 7 May 1925 in SHM R126, leg. 58, carp. 8.

adopted by the Italians in Ethiopia, in which the bomb was activated by an internal propeller). The bombs were designed to explode in mid-air, spraying drops of mustard-gas liquid over as large an area as possible in accordance with their size. Thus, the height, angle, and timing of their release as well as a correct calculation of the prevailing wind-speed were essential to their success.[87]

A Moroccan whose family was the victim of three consecutive mustard-gas bombs showed me the contraption used for carrying the bombs on what was clearly a type of plane used by the Spanish without any bomb-release mechanism. It had fallen into his courtyard from the plane when the last bomb had been released. His family kept it hidden while Spanish troops scoured the countryside at the end of the war for all material evidence of their weapons. It is a steel device shaped like a carousel with simple 'S'-shaped hooks on which six bombs could be hung, and it is likely that the co-pilot had to unhook the bombs from the device and drop them manually onto the target.[88] The primitive nature of the installation would suggest why some pilots might have been reluctant to use toxic bombs in the first place.

Indeed, it is clear that in the early stages of its use, pilots and their commanders had little knowledge about the bombs and how many they could use. Even as late as January 1926 the air force appeared to be deploying only a fifth of their planes for chemical bombing. Pughe Lloyd reported: 'Only 2 machines out of 10 carry gas bombs, not because they don't believe in gas, but simply because they don't know how to use it.' Also, many of the early sorties may well have failed because of the inexperience of the pilots. Fragmentary evidence also suggests that both the bombs and artillery shells fitted with chemicals often failed to explode. Unexploded mustard-gas bombs were collected by the Moroccans, carried in hay sacks, and then thrown by hand at Spanish positions after the fuses were lit by fire. Abdel Krim was apparently offering 2 pesetas for every unexploded one handed in.[89] The variety of aircraft used by the Spanish military, against the advice given earlier to the king that only Junkers should be acquired, must also have hindered the effective use of the bombs. In 1925, twenty Breguet planes and thirty Fokker planes, both of 450 horsepower, were bought, alongside two Savoia and one Dornier hydroplanes.[90]

The use of chemical weapons by the artillery is far less well documented. Reports of shelling hardly ever referred to the kind of missiles used, and instead mentioned only the calibre of the artillery pieces. Some scant evidence does exist that gives an idea of the number of chemical shells employed. Incomplete

[87] 'Instrucciones', ibid.; Del Boca, *I gas*, 65, 95–6, 163.

[88] Interview with Mohamed Amar Hammadi. I am grateful for the advice on this matter of Peter Elliot, senior keeper of the Department of Research and Information Services of the Royal Air Force Museum in Hendon, London.

[89] SHM R694, leg. 14, carp. 1, 13 Feb. 1926 and SHM R772, leg. 25, carp. 1–2. For discrepancies over numbers of chemical bombs see Cuartel General del Ejército de Espana en África, 7 Nov. 1923, ibid. Pughe Lloyd's report in PRO WO 188/765.

[90] AGPR 15.511/9, 5 Sept. 1925.

inventories of the stock of munitions held by the artillery in 1926 suggest a high turnover of what is referred to as 'gas bombs' in the Melilla and Ceuta sectors. In February the Melilla stores had 228 of these shells and Ceuta 183. By April the Melilla stocks had fallen to eighty and those in Ceuta had risen to 293. The following month the first registered 594 shells and the second had used up all its stocks. In September Melilla had 328 shells but two months later its stocks had fallen to zero. The weight of these shells is not clear from the records, but the fact that they were fired exclusively from the largest of the artillery pieces, whose calibre was 15.5 centimetres, might suggest they were equivalent to the C5 plane bomb.[91]

As with the projectiles fired from the air, Abdel Krim's fighters used to retrieve unexploded shells of mustard gas launched by Spanish cannons and fire them back at the enemy's lines. They fired some against Tetuan from an artillery piece captured from the French, but the shells failed to explode or even reach the town. A Spanish artillery lieutenant was ordered to gather them and have them thrown into the sea, but instead he attempted to fire them once again against the Moroccan positions, without success.[92] The Rif fighters also used their ingenuity to invent their own bomb. In the absence of the chemicals available to the Spanish, they put together shells filled with chilli powder in the hope that on explosion it might also affect the vision and breathing of their Spanish foe.[93] The chilli bomb is emblematic of the military encounter between the West and the Third World in the early twentieth century. Against the deadly technology of industrial Europe, the Moroccans deployed all the weapons they could lay their hands on, including one made from a vegetable.

The chemical offensive in 1926 and 1927 is more difficult to piece together than that of the two preceding years. Increasingly, military reports failed to specify the kind of bombs that were used. Judging from the regular reports on the number of weapons held in the aviation stores, however, it is evident that C5 bombs continued to be employed, but in ever-smaller numbers. The new aerodrome in Drius was equipped with 200 C5 bombs in April 1926, while at the beginning of the year the Nador aerodrome had 114 of these bombs. Military files report the use of 160 C5s by Nador planes during January and February, but throughout the period of May to August 1926 the number of C5 bombs at the Nador aerodrome remained stationary at 353, suggesting they were not used at all. On 21 August their number was increased to 5,000, and given the dangers of storing the bomb for any length of time, this may have coincided with a new offensive against the Temsaman people because an earlier suspension of bombing had not led to their surrender.[94] Yet the blanket bombing of the first chemical air raids seems to have given way two years later

[91] AGPR 15.511/9; 15621/10 and 12953/13.
[92] Interview with Juan-Francisco Díaz Ripoll, 26 Mar. 1999.
[93] Habtí, 'La resistencia', 108. I have found no evidence of this bomb in Spanish archives.
[94] SHM R779, leg. 30, carp. 19 and R694, leg. 514, carp. 1–3.

to a more sparing use of the weapon. The occasional reference to their use suggests that mustard-gas bombs were used mainly against fortifications and cannon emplacements, though some villages continued to be scourged.

The most important reason for the reduction in the use of mustard gas was almost certainly the penetration of Spanish and French troops into the insurgent areas. As we have seen, any advance by colonial troops would have to be held up for weeks until the effects of the poison wore off. There were the additional problems of co-ordination and military intelligence. Pilots or their commanders made mistakes and conventional bombs were frequently dropped on or near allied troops. The French army complained on 28 May 1926 that Spanish planes had dropped bombs in an area where a French column was operating and Capaz's column similarly narrowly escaped bombing by one of its own pilots in September.[95] In such conditions, the use of mustard gas was obviously inadvisable.

Similarly, its use against villages that were showing signs of a desire to surrender was probably not considered appropriate. Villages in the heart of the Rif and Jebala resistance were beginning to lay large white pieces of cloth on the ground to indicate their surrender and avoid being bombed. Officers of the native police (Servicio de Intervención) were increasingly able to convince their commanders-in-chief to suspend the bombing of villages when they received rumours that they might surrender.[96] Moroccan oral sources, on the other hand, suggest the Spanish air force and artillery continued to use mustard-gas bombs against very specific targets right to the end of the war, in particular in the last areas to resist their advance around Chauen in the western zone.[97]

An overall calculation of the effectiveness of the Spanish chemical-warfare campaign is difficult to make because of the patchiness of evidence on both sides. One claim that can be completely ruled out is that it had little effect. From his cockpit, it appeared to Hidalgo de Cisneros that the 100-kilo bombs he was dropping did not disturb the Moroccans one bit. After he and his fellow pilots had dropped sixty of the 100 bombs they had at their disposal, they thought they observed the same Moroccans occupying the same place. It seemed, he wrote, 'as if the Moors were gargling with the mustard gas'. Such was the sense of its ineffectiveness that one wag at the aerodrome suggested that instead of gas, they should drop bottles of 'gaseosa', or the fizzy lemonade they were provided with in Melilla, because this drink was so poisonous the enemy would fall ill with a stomach bug.[98]

In any judgement about the effects of the toxic bombs, the number that was dropped does not necessarily give an indication of the likely damage. It is clear

[95] SHM R694, ibid.   [96] Ibid.
[97] Interviews with Hach Abdel Krim Ben Ahmed Ben Ali, El Ayache Sellam El Amraní, and Mohammed Ben Ayache El Amraní H'mimed.
[98] Hidalgo, *Cambio*, 197.

that huge numbers of chemical bombs often had to be used for very small targets, in particular, the emplacement of a piece of enemy artillery. Thus, in a very specific campaign, 100 mustard-gas aircraft bombs of unspecified size were deployed to destroy a single enemy cannon.[99] In other words, the quantity of chemical bombs used is not necessarily a measure of the extent of casualties. However, the mustard-gas bombing of villages and crowded markets undoubtedly resulted in high numbers of dead and injured because of the concentration of people over a wider area. We have already considered reports from different sources about the effects of mustard gas in Anjera and Al Hoceima. Abdel Krim had posters made in January 1925 about the Spanish chemical campaign, which were displayed in different parts of the Protectorate and in which he accused the Spanish government of 'raining down suffocating gases over the whole area on innocent people, women, children, and animals, who have committed no fault . . . We have sent a certain number of women and children to the hospital in Marshan [in the French Protectorate], to the French doctor Forraz. Some are dead and have appeared before their Master with their liver burned by poison.'[100]

Some idea of the effects of the chemical bombing and shelling can be gauged from reports of the Spanish military based on information supplied by Moroccan informers in their pay. In addition to those killed because they were close to the bomb's impact, the effect of the mustard gas was evidently devastating over a wide area. The earliest report dates shortly after the first chemical-bombing sorties in late June 1924. People in the Beni Tuzin district were said to be suffering from burns and sickness. Some had been completely blinded, others had serious problems with their eyes. Even those who arrived a few hours later had burning feelings all over their body. The overwhelming reaction among the people affected, according to the report, was panic and fear that the bombing would continue. On 3 July some informers saw thirty Beni Urriaguels whose bodies were covered with lacerations.

On 16 July the informers reported a new and strange illness among the Moroccans of the interior, in particular the Beni Urriaguel and the Temsaman people. It was characterized by streaming eyes and nasal catarrh, clearly the effects of mustard gas at some distance from the explosion. They had also discovered that their agricultural produce, like the fruit on the trees, could not be eaten because they had become contaminated.[101] Since the Moroccans had no knowledge of the advanced technology of war, it became common to call the strange symptoms of gas bombing a 'plague of the countryside'. Orthodox Spanish and European narratives of the war, which do not mention the use of chemical weapons because they rely on official or secondary Spanish sources, make much of the spread of typhus in this period as an important factor in the

[99] SHM R694, leg. 14, carp. 1, Comandancia General de Melilla, 10 Apr. 1926.
[100] ADMAE Maroc 1917–40, vol. 201, p. 173.
[101] SHM R772, leg. 25, carp. 1–2, 29 June 1924.

weakening of the Rif resistance.[102] Among the symptoms of typhus is the eruption of purple spots on the body as well as fever and prostration. The darkening blisters and exhaustion caused by mustard gas may well have been mistakenly interpreted as symptoms of typhus. Considering their determination to cover up the use of mustard gas, it may also be true that the Spanish authorities encouraged that interpretation.

Almost as much as the deaths and illnesses that descended on them, the inhabitants appeared to be shocked by the death of their animals and the contamination of their orchards and fields by the chemical poison. These could not be protected like humans. An order came from Abdel Krim in mid-July for all Beni Urriaguels to build caves to shelter from the bombing, threatening severe punishment to those who failed to obey. He himself had abandoned his house and gone to live with his family in a cave. Many sought to protect themselves from the effects of toxic gas by burning hay at the entrance of the tunnel where they were sheltering. Local people began to change their daily routines to cope with the new Spanish campaign. The fields began to be cultivated under the protection of darkness and the souks or markets were held at night. Yet by August an increasing number of Abdel Krim's fighters had to abandon the war because of disabilities caused by the mustard gas.[103]

After noting the impact of the first wave of chemical bombing, the Spanish military command seemed to lose interest in reporting subsequent effects. The files usually fail to distinguish between conventional bombing and the use of poison gases. But their reports, based on information from their Moroccan spies, of an increase in emigration from June 1924 from areas affected by the bombing to the French Protectorate, would suggest that the chemical weapons were intensifying the suffering caused by TNT and incendiary bombs. 'The morale of the enemy has become depressed,' wrote one report. 'They fear the gases and we believe it advisable to use them intensively.' In September 1925 informers reported seeing large numbers of blind people in the villages.[104] By the end of the war (although the frequency of chemical bombing dropped considerably between 1926 and 1927) hundreds of Moroccans had been killed and probably thousands severely affected by the deadly chemical dropped on them over a four-year period.

A vigorous oral tradition still exists in northern Morocco about the toxic effects of Spanish bombing. Eyewitness accounts made to me in recorded interviews recall the consequences—blindness, permanent and temporary, boils, sores, respiratory and gastric problems, blood in the lungs, and severe burning of the skin and lungs. In areas contaminated by mustard gas, witnesses reported that the animals died quickly, vegetation would not grow for months, the water, or the stones used by Muslims in their frequent daily ablutions when

---

[102] The latest example is Álvarez, *The Betrothed*.
[103] Interview with Hadou El Kayid Omar Massaud; SHM R772, leg. 25, carp. 1–2, 29 June 1924.
[104] SHM R772, ibid. and R777, leg. 29, carp. 19.

there was no water (a ritual known as Woudou), tore off the first layer of skin 'like potato peel'.[105] For many Moroccans, chemical bombs were amongst many different types of weapons being used against them, albeit the strangest and most pernicious. Witnesses remember people going around immediately after a bombing sortie with garlic held to their noses to ward off the unpleasant and garlicky smell of mustard gas, without realizing the damage being done to their bodies. Cloth masks were made in a vain attempt to keep the gas from the inside of the body. Others saw the muhayeddin returning from action blinded and crippled, using their rifles as crutches. Yet others remember continued shelling by Spanish artillery using chemical weapons, even during the last campaigns of the war against villages near the town of Chauen in the Jebala.[106]

Unknown to the Spanish and other nations that used mustard gas at the time, the chemical had serious long-term effects as well. In those areas most hit by chemical bombs, probably thousands of people have died of cancer as a result. In two villages near Abdel Krim's home town of Ajdir, people told me of the injuries and deaths in their family caused by what they called 'sim', or mustard gas. Many of their relatives were wiped out. The dominant forms of cancer they reported, that of the lungs, the respiratory tract, and leukaemia, are symptomatic of one of the effects of mustard gas.[107] A peasant from the village of Tafrast recounted how three mustard-gas bombs fell into his family's backyard several years before he was born. His two elder sisters were blinded for life and died later of cancer, his elder brother was left without hair, and his mother suffered from respiratory problems all her life until she too died of cancer of the lungs. Another man from the same village reported how his grandfather, father, mother, aunt, and sister all died of cancer 'in the throat and chest' because they had been near the explosion of a 'sim' bomb. A third man from a nearby village said that where vegetation had been abundant, nothing grew for five to six years after a bomb had fallen in the area. A friend of his lost his voice forever, and after an attack he himself saw blackened bodies lying everywhere.[108]

The list of such victims would be endless if the Moroccan government had not prohibited the Association for the Defence of Victims of Toxic Gas in the Rif (many of whose members suffered similar losses in their own families) from conducting a survey. Long before the Association prepared its questionnaire,

[105] Interview with Hach Med M'Hauesh, Tetuan, 24 July 2000.

[106] The above information is taken from interviews with id.; Mohammed Ben Hammou; Hach Abdel Krim Ben Ahmed Ben Ali on 18 July 2000; Hacha Oum Koulthoum Ahmed Kasem El Amrani on 22 July 2000; Abdessalam Abdessalam Ben Husain Rian and Med Maati Al Amrani, both on 24 July 2000; Mohammed Ben Ayache El Amraní H'mimed and El Ayache Sellam El Amraní, all in the Jebala region; and Mohammed Saleh Faraji on 23 Apr. 2001 near Ajdir.

[107] Pechura and Rall, *Veterans*, 4–5.

[108] The first interview with Mohamed Amar Hammadi, the second with Akkou Mar Zook Abdeslam, and the third with Hadou El Kayid Omar Massaud, all on 23 Apr. 2001.

however, those affected by mustard gas had died without leaving any record. The poorest peasants never went to hospital or consulted a doctor, so no trace exists of their illness except the oral evidence of their descendants. The only centre of oncology that collects figures for cancer victims is located in Rabat, the capital of Morocco, and it does not break these figures down into regions. However, it has privately admitted, according to members of the Association, that 60 per cent of cancer patients in Rabat are from the El Hoceima and Nador regions alone, both of which suffered heavy chemical bombing. Yet these account for only a small percentage of those who died of cancer in the areas most hit by mustard gas.[109]

There is also *prima facie* evidence in Morocco that mustard gas might have caused mutation of the genome and that cancer may have been genetically transmitted from those affected by the chemical bombing of the 1920s to their descendants.[110] Experiments on animals in the United States and elsewhere have indicated that the substance causes genetic damage and can induce heritable mutations in germ cells in the offspring.[111] Again, insufficient figures are available for this evidence to be properly tested in Morocco. The only statistics I have had access to are based on far too small a sample from which to draw a sound hypothesis. But they strengthen the suspicion that the chemical bombing has affected new generations of northern Moroccans. Out of 2,624 children treated for cancer in the Rabat cancer hospital between 1986 and 1998, 49 per cent came from the north, although the vast majority of parents from that region would not have been able to send their children to the capital for treatment. That is, the proportion of children in the north suffering from cancer is likely to be considerably higher.[112]

Another untested theory is that large doses of mustard gas may have permanently damaged the environment. There are regions such as Baquiwa, Ben Bu Ifrah, and Ajdir (near the Ghis river) where no plants grow or where the plants that do grow have abnormal botanical forms. The man in whose backyard three mustard-gas bombs fell assured me that nothing has grown there since, and indeed the area is desert-like, while similar soil nearby supports considerable vegetation.[113]

Genetic and environmental damage has hardly figured in the research on the effects of mustard gas. Indeed, the literature on the long-term consequences to health of exposure to this poison is meagre. A committee set up by the American Institute of Medicine in the early 1990s discovered that there was

---

[109] Interviews with Dr Fouad Ouyahya, Al Hoceima, 24 Apr. 2001 and Dr Abdel Wahab Tadmor, Tangier 23 Feb. 2001.

[110] Dr Ouyahya, interview.   [111] Pechura and Rall, *Veterans*, 184–9.

[112] 'Childhood Cancer in Morocco. A Single Institution Retrospective Epidemiological Data. Experience of the Cancer Ward of the Children's Hospital of Rabat, Morocco, 1996–1998'. Unpublished document of the Ministère de Salut Publique, Institut National d'Oncologie, Rabat, n.d. [1999?].

[113] Dr Abdel Wahab Tadmor and Mohamed Amar Hammadi, interviews.

'an atmosphere of lingering secrecy' in the United States Department of Defence about the effects of mustard gas and Lewisite. At least 4,000 US servicemen were exposed to the substances in the Second World War, in both war and in laboratory and outdoor tests. Tens of thousands of military personnel and civilians worked in US arsenals producing mustard agents. Yet the soldiers continue to obey their original instructions to keep quiet about these tests. No long-term follow-up was carried out to provide medical care or monitor the results of exposure.[114]

Undoubtedly, the chemical war against Abdel Krim's supporters severely weakened their resistance. On top of the casualties of conventional battle and the starvation provoked by war and incendiary bombs, the chemicals caused extreme suffering and want amongst Moroccan soldiers and civilians. However, it did not have the effect that its apologists naively expected—the immediate surrender of the enemy. Indeed, it may well have strengthened the resistance of the Moroccans to Spanish penetration. The eventual victory over this resistance was the consequence above all of Franco-Spanish collaboration. The failure of chemical warfare to live up to Spanish expectations was thus due not just to technological and strategic ingenuousness, but also to an underestimation of the capacity of the enemy to continue resisting. The lure of a brief and devastating onslaught of chemicals, similar to that of the Central Powers in the First World War, turned out also to be a mirage. Officers were drawn into a prolonged chemical war in which any remaining codes of military conduct towards the enemy were deeply eroded.

Moreover, the close co-operation between the German and Spanish military over the chemical offensive can only have strengthened their ties. Successive generations of Spanish officers had already seen the Prussian military establishment as a model of ruthless efficiency and professionalism, as compared with the French model of the citizen army. The gratitude and admiration felt by the militarist Africanists towards their German counterparts may well have encouraged their later identification with the Third Reich.[115] Collaboration over the war against the Moorish Other laid the groundwork for the even more crucial aid given to the Army of Africa by the German military in the Civil War.

---

[114] Pechura and Rall, *Veterans*, 1–4.   [115] Viñas, *Franco*, 109.

CHAPTER SIX

A Divided Army:
Military Castes and Factions

THROUGH THE SPANISH Army of Africa rode a variety of military castes and factions whose composition and balance changed radically over the eighteen years of the colonial war.[1] The castes could be broadly defined by the arm or branch of the military forces to which officers belonged but they were by no means hermetic. Factions, on the other hand, represented political or ideological divisions within or across the castes. At a more individual level, officers were also divided by allegiances to powerful figures high up the military command, on whom they depended for appointments and promotions. Informal coteries gathered around the top generals like cliques at the court of the Bourbon monarchs. Indeed, as we have seen, the king (a Bourbon himself) liked to be surrounded by his favourite officers, such as Silvestre. Franco also received powerful support from the king, who was, after all, the commander-in-chief of the army. The fact that Franco was in addition a protégé of Sanjurjo accounts in some measure for the rapidity of his ascent into the top ranks of generals during the Primo de Rivera dictatorship.

However, this chapter is concerned above all with the broader collectivities within the Army of Africa that I have defined as castes and factions. In theory, there were not meant to be professional differences of this kind among the officers. All those who served in the Moroccan Protectorate were expected to behave like model colonial officers. The Spanish archetype of the colonial officer never varied much throughout the colonial war. He was supposed to be a paragon of Spanish military virtues, whose main role was to preserve order in the Spanish sphere of influence on behalf of the Sultanate and the European powers so that the supposed benefits of civilization could reach the remotest regions of northern Africa.[2] In practice, officers of the Army of Africa departed from the ideal to an increasing degree as the sporadic clashes with unsubdued tribes turned into full-scale war. Their effective control over civil society in the Protectorate led them to adopt increasingly uncivil and

---

[1] Some of the ideas in this chapter first appeared in Sebastian Balfour and Pablo La Porte, 'Spanish Military Cultures and the Moroccan Wars, 1909–1936', in *European Historical Quarterly*, 30: 3 (July 2000), 307–32.

[2] For a typical portrait see Tebib Arrumi (Ruiz Albéniz), 'Palabras de un optimista. Psicología de la oficialidad colonial', *Revista de Tropas Coloniales*, 1 (Jan. 1924), 8–9.

authoritarian practices towards Moroccan and Spanish civilians alike. At the same time, the military discords of the metropolitan army were exported to the colonial army, with the result that officers were sometimes at each other's throats.

In the early period of Spanish colonial expansion in Morocco between 1909 and 1912, rather than well-defined military castes there were tendencies represented by individuals. The growing confrontation between France and Germany, and then the First World War itself, exacerbated a primary divide in Spanish military culture between the French and the Prussian models. The heterogeneity of the Army of Africa was at its most acute between 1917 and 1921, and the differences were played out in the midst of the Anual disaster. But in its aftermath, as we have already argued, a more professional colonial corps was forged which came to dominate the colonial army and indeed distinguished itself increasingly from the metropolitan army. Its culture, which I have defined as militarist Africanism, formed the foundations of the military insurrectionism of the 1930s.

Amongst the earliest generation of officers who served in Morocco were those with a strong colonial vocation. This group had had a close relationship with the former Spanish colonies overseas. Most had been born or brought up there (like many who have already appeared in Part I, such as Mola, Berenguer, Silvestre, Morales, Castro Girona, Cavalcanti, Capaz, and Kindelán), and some of them had mothers from long-standing pro-Spanish colonial families, like Mola, or were married to Spanish women from these families. Many of them had also fought in the wars against the creole rebels and then against the United States in 1898 to defend Spanish sovereignty in the colonies. Their cultural references were, therefore, a mix of colonial and metropolitan, although all had completed their military training in Spain. This dual identity or expatriate culture tended to set them apart from their Spanish contemporaries, so much so in some cases that they regarded themselves or were regarded as outsiders within Spain. This may explain the enthusiasm with which they embraced a new colonial vocation when the Spanish military enterprise in Morocco began in 1907.

The new culture of militarist Africanism, therefore, had its roots in the overseas colonial experience of the late nineteenth century. The tactics and mentalities deployed by the army in Morocco from the earliest stages were deeply influenced by the values of the war in Cuba and the Philippines and the experience of the defeat by the United States. After Europe had stood aside to allow the crushing victory of the Americans and the dismemberment of the old colonies, the military was imbued with an unfocused *revanchisme*. The enterprise in Morocco offered opportunities not only to restore the image of the Spanish army in Spain and Europe, but also for promotion and prestige unavailable at home. It also renewed an imperialist vocation for military expansion based on a myth of the martial virtues of the Spanish race that was strongest in the army. For some officers, a new empire in Africa, where Spain in any case was supposed to have a historical vocation, was there to be conquered. Colonial war was good for everyone, including the 'primitive races' that had to be confronted.[3] As we saw in Chapter 1, this bellicose instinct was balanced by a half-digested assimilation of Western rationalizations for colonial rule rooted in a positivist belief in the inevitability of progress according to the European model.

Military experience in the overseas colonies had been dominated by irregular warfare. Neither the Cuban or Filipino guerrillas nor many of the American troops, such as Theodore Roosevelt's Rough Riders, were conventional enemies. Apart from the naval battles, there had been no set-pieces of standard warfare. The most efficient units of the Spanish army had been the counter-guerrilla groups. This experience provided a tactical model that might have been applied with some success in Morocco. Yet there appears to have been no systematic reflection among Spanish military thinkers on the lessons of the colonial war overseas. Instead, it remained at the level of an instinctive response to military events. This was in marked contrast to the French. The theories of General Thomas-Robert Bugeaud, who successfully defeated Algerian resistance to French penetration in the 1840s, became a major influence on all French colonial campaigns in the nineteenth and early twentieth centuries. Having gained his first experience against the Spanish irregulars in the Napoleonic Wars, Bugeaud set about incorporating the tactics of guerrilla warfare into conventional military doctrine.[4] No doubt those Spanish officers deeply influenced by the French military, such as Berenguer, imbibed many of his lessons, but they fought alongside an officer corps that showed little interest in military theory.

Yet the colonial war in Morocco in addition posed severe problems of logistics and strategy that required a level of training and organization conspicuously absent in the Spanish army. It is true that some of the specialized corps, like the artillery and engineers, were highly trained and technical elites, but in the mobile conditions of war in both the colonies and in Morocco they had a less prominent role to play than the cavalry and infantry. The admiration many colonial officers felt for the Prussian military model was not reflected in the staff work of the Army of Africa. Had the Spanish combined the efficiency of Moltke's army with the tactical ruthlessness of Bugeaud's Armée coloniale, they might not have suffered so many military disasters in Morocco. Yet they were also hamstrung by the top-heavy officer–soldier ratio and the abysmally low military budget that left them underequipped until at least 1922.

In the new Moroccan campaigns the cavalry and infantry officers, who led most of the actions, tended to value bravery and boldness of action over tactics

---

[3] Typical expressions of this tendency are Isaac Muñoz, *Política colonialista* (Madrid, n.p., 1912), and Narciso Gibert, *España y África* (Madrid, n.p., 1912).

[4] Vandervort, *War*, 62–9.

and organization. Burguete, one of the leading exponents of this vitalist current, argued in 1907 for the supremacy of willpower over strategy in war. Even his critic, the well-known military writer Modesto Navarro, asserted in the following year that the quality of an army depended above all on the character and energy of its commanders.[5] For Burguete and others, the model officer was not the man who took care to study the terrain, tactics, and firepower and sought to survive battle to ensure continuity of command, but one who set an example to the troops by leading the action. This cult of the bayonet and cavalry charge led by officers, behind which was an even more antiquated cult of honour, was rife in the first actions of the Army of Africa (just as it was true of the French army in the early days of the First World War). Its negative consequences were illustrated by the high level of casualties amongst officers in the 1909 campaign. A very critical account by an eyewitness of that campaign characterized the officers as cultural illiterates who disdained military science and sought heroic status. Given the kind of enemy they faced, according to this journalist, the Rif was the least appropriate place for bayonet charges.[6]

Silvestre was a typical product of this culture (and his own reported suicide was yet another symptom of it). Impulsive, loyal, chivalrous, macho, and generous to the men under his command, he was imbued with the military values of late nineteenth-century Spain, relying on action over strategy and honour over pragmatism, with fatal consequences. As we saw in Chapter 2, his relations with local Moroccan chiefs soured him against the collaboration required by the politics of the Protectorate. The straight-talking soldier was disgusted by the sinuous behaviour of Moroccans, failing to understand that it was a means of surviving colonialism. He was equally impatient with the efforts by some of his native officers to continue discussions with the 'deceitful' Moroccans. According to one of his friends, Silvestre's closest associates gave up trying to persuade him to respect the authority of the Moroccan chieftains. 'The brave Fernández Silvestre, a man who took to heart the problem of Morocco like few others, never saw it as a Protectorate regime. Sharing power with the Moroccan authorities irritated and upset him . . . For him, the Moroccan problem was one of conquest and absolute domination; he had reached such mistaken conclusions after long-standing experiences in Africa. His position was unjust but sincere.' Other militarist advocates of conquest in the early days of the Protectorate were less scrupulous than Silvestre. The Spanish army was dealing with a backward and barbarous community that would only bow to reason by the use of force.[7]

[5] Robert Geoffrey Jensen, 'Moral Strength through Material Defeat? The Consequences of 1898 for Spanish Military Culture', *War and Society*, 17: 2 (Oct. 1999), 31–7; Modesto Navarro, 'De táctica', *Ejército Español*, 20 Jan. 1908.

[6] Eugenio Noel, *Lo que vi en la Guerra. Diario de un soldado* (Barcelona, n.p., 1912), 252–4.

[7] *Un africanista más, La guerra y el problema de África. Unas cuantas verdades por un Africanista más* (Burgos, n.p., 1914). The comment by Silvestre's friend Manuel Aznar is in 'España en África. El protectorado y la opinión de los militares', *El Sol*, 19 Oct. 1921.

Other officers of Silvestre's generation, many of whom shared the same colonial background, believed on the contrary that the most appropriate strategy in Morocco was one of subordinating military action to the assiduous task of winning over its tribes by peaceful means.[8] The equivalent of the Arabists of the British army such as T. E. Lawrence, or those of the French colonial army like Galiéni and Lyautey, these enlightened Africanists played an important role in the earlier stages of Spanish colonial penetration in Morocco, in particular under the regimes of Marina and Jordana, between 1913 and 1918. Like their comrades, many were formed by the expatriate culture of the overseas colonies or owed their position to long service in the colonial wars. The attraction of the Moroccan enterprise was that it gave a new focus to their colonial identity, albeit in a radically different environment. Seduced by a Western reading of Arab culture, many of them found mystery and exoticism in the land and the people of Morocco. As part of their work as native officers, they also began to integrate aspects of this culture into their own. Some learned Arabic and shelja (the language of the Rif), studied the Koran and the local customs and laws, and often wore the local dress, the jellaba. A few even took to living with unorthodox Moroccan women in a Moroccan house, eating and sleeping like a local inhabitant. This assimilation of local culture distanced them even more from their own culture.[9]

They came with an almost impossible mission—to balance colonial penetration with respect for local cultures and hierarchies. Like Silvestre, they were unhappy at the injustices of Moroccan society, but unlike him they advocated the slow, methodical, and peaceful penetration of Western values through the work of the local colonial offices. They were much influenced by the Spanish civilian organizations of the first decade of the century which were advocating closer ties with Morocco. Representing businessmen, intellectuals, and aficionados of Arab culture, these organizations were pushing for a neo-colonial relationship with Morocco on the basis of a common geo-strategic interest and a shared historical past. As a youngish captain, Berenguer had expressed the somewhat naive but probably quite genuine view that Spain was not in Morocco to conquer or impose its authority but to uphold a legally constituted government, with its laws, customs, and religions: '. . . we limit ourselves to being mandated by Europe to bring the civilization that we enjoy to these semi-savage regions.'[10]

The enlightened Africanists took the French colonial enterprise in Morocco as their model. From the moment of their first penetration into Moroccan territory in the twentieth century, they kept the French constantly in their sights

---

[8] Thirteen years older than Silvestre, Ricardo Donoso Cortés was an officer who helped to shape the enlightened Africanism of this generation. An influential book of his was *Estudio geográfico político militar sobre las zonas españolas del Norte y Sur de Marruecos* (Madrid, n.p., 1913).

[9] Cordón, *Trayectoria*, 98. For further treatment of this theme see Ch. 7.

[10] Berenguer, *El Ejército*, 7.

to see how they were handling their own problems of colonial penetration. Outside their military campaigns, the French relied on the 'oil-stain' approach, based on a slow permeation of French colonial influence during which they claimed to respect the local authorities. Military action was supposed to be used only *in extremis*, except that the French found themselves launching frequent offensives and massacring Moroccans. As high commissioner, Berenguer freely admitted his debt to them, having several years previously spent a period in the French sphere studying their actions, as we have seen. During a visit by Marshal Lyautey to the military base in Larache in the summer of 1919, he declared that the French *oeuvre coloniale* was his model, adding somewhat bizarrely that the long-term aim of both colonial powers was the restoration of the ancient Arab civilization.[11]

The enlightened colonial officers felt a genuine attraction towards Moroccan culture and immersed themselves in it. Some fell in love with Moroccan women and adopted the customs appropriate to their wooing. As in the British colonies, the practice of interracial sexual liaisons was widespread amongst all the troops even though it was largely clandestine.[12] But the more the enlightened officer penetrated into Moroccan culture, the more his contact with homeland culture became tenuous, and the more a multicultural identity emerged inside him that made him feel different or even uncomfortable in Spain.

Despite their fascination with Arab culture, however, there was no doubt in the minds of the enlightened Africanists that the Moroccans had to be dragged out of backwardness by the 'benevolent, patient, paternal treatment appropriate to a superior race', in the optimistic words of another representative figure of the first generation of enlightened colonial officers in 1913. Yet their paternalist vocation, like that of many of their British counterparts, also conflicted with the imperative of securing and extending control over the Moroccan Protectorate so as to maintain their nation's status in the international order.[13]

For all their wishful thinking, many of these enlightened colonial officers gained the respect of the Moroccans they worked closely with. This respect was probably the result less of their identification with Arab and Berber culture, than of the benefits some Moroccans, like the Abdel Krim family, hoped to gain from the Spanish presence. Nevertheless, more than any of the other

[11] *L'Afrique Française* (July–Aug. 1919), 249.

[12] One such officer wooed the daughter of the caid of Buhafora and was received regularly in his house. When he was made prisoner during the events of the 1921 disaster, the caid's family helped him to escape disguised as an Arab: Díaz Ripoll interview. For the British colonial officer, see Barbara Bush, *Imperialism, Race and Resistance: Africa and Britain, 1919–1945* (London, Routledge, 1997), 88–9, and Richard Hyam, *Empire and Sexuality: The British Experience* (Manchester, Manchester UP, 1990).

[13] Comandante Cogolludo, 'Algunas consideraciones sobre la organización del Majzen en el bajalato de Tetuán', *Boletín Oficial de la Zona del Protectorado Español de Marruecos (BOZPEM)*, Oct. 1913, p. 30; for the parallel with the British colonial experience, see Bush, *Imperialism*, 71.

colonial officers, they cemented the bonds that proved so important in the creation of Moroccan units that would fight on the Nationalist side in the Spanish
Civil War. Even after the Abdel Krims and other Moroccan collaborators had
turned against Spain in 1920, they still felt sympathy for those military men
who had tried to establish a peaceful Protectorate. This was evident in the
treatment the Rif leaders gave to Morales' body after the battle at Anual.
Abdel Krim ordered that it should be returned to the Spaniards dressed in full
regalia and with full honours. In contrast, Silvestre's corpse disappeared, and
his grave—if indeed he was ever buried—was never discovered amidst the rubble and the skeletons picked clean by vultures when Anual was recaptured in
1926. According to a survivor who was taken prisoner, the muhayeddin had
sliced off Silvestre's upper lip with its long moustache to carry around as a tro-
phy. He had seen the mutilated body of the general and had marked the spot
with a stone, but on his return it had vanished.[14]

The enlightened colonial officers always remained a minority within the
Army of Africa. They were employed mainly in the native bureau (or Servicio
de Intervención) or as officers of the Regulares and the native police, the
Mehal-las. Those working in the bureau or police were only able to come to
the fore at times when government policy sought to restrain military expansion
and impose a policy of collaboration with Moroccan chieftains (as during the
First World War, the seven-month spell of Luis Silvela as high commissioner in
1923, and the pacification campaign after the last resistance ended in 1927).
Apart from these brief periods, their work was increasingly overshadowed by
the more spectacular activities of the militarists. The commanders of the earliest campaigns in Morocco were joined during the second decade by a new
generation of colonial officers, who imbued the traditional Prussian militarism
of their elders with a new right-wing and nationalist mystique. Many had been
trained in the Toledo Infantry Academy, where these Prussian values were supplemented by new myths about war as a vitalizing force and codes or cults of
military conduct drawn from contemporary right-wing sources. Millán-Astray,
a passionate devotee of the Bushido code, gave lessons to the cadets there in
1911–12, one of whom was the youthful Francisco Franco.[15]

The relationship between the two Africanist tendencies was uneasy, yet this
tension was never openly expressed. There was no clear dividing-line between
the two, of course. Avowing interest in Arab culture was an obligatory part of
the curriculum of all colonial officers. Even after the militarists established
their hegemony over the Army of Africa, it was still the done thing to give an
enlightened gloss to the colonial enterprise, even while officers were busy
killing Moroccans and burning their villages and fields. Spanish intervention

[14] 'Las espantosas escenas del hambre', *La Correspondencia de España*, 30 Jan. 1923.
[15] He wrote the preface to the Spanish edition of the Bushido: Carlos Blanco Escolá, *La Academia General Militar de Zaragoza (1928–31)* (Barcelona, Labor, 1989), 238–9.

in Morocco, as one military publication wrote in 1926, was not about conquest but 'fraternal rapprochement' (*fraternal aproximación*).[16]

But those who cultivated such intimate links by adopting Arab habits and making friends amongst Moroccans were regarded with suspicion by the new generation of colonial officers. Aping Moroccan culture, like showing off one's knowledge of Arabic and sitting cross-legged on a mat drinking mint tea, was going too native. Sinking to the level of a backward society was failing to set the example of a higher civilization, and indeed betraying a lack of patriotism. The occasional Arab gestures of these colonial officers, such as the wearing of the jellaba, were merely a symbol of status that marked them out from their fellow Spaniards and gave them an identity they found hard to achieve on their home ground.

The case of Juan Yagüe, who joined the Regulares as a young lieutenant in 1914, is a good illustration of the intolerance of the new generation of colonial officers. If we are to believe his hagiographer, Yagüe, as a 'patriotic, Castilian patrician . . . would behave in such a Spanish way in his conversations that instead of speaking to the native in the Islamic language, even though he knew it, he preferred to make himself understood in the language of Cervantes. "Why the devil", he would protest, "does a Spanish soldier have to become a foreigner and why should it not be the other way round, that the Moor speak our language? For us that is much more useful and patriotic."' In fact, it is doubtful that Yagüe spoke more than a few words of Arabic. A confidential report critical of the colonial military sent to ex-president Romanones in 1924 asserted that in the western front only six officers spoke the language. In contrast, all Moroccans who had dealings with officials or soldiers of the Protectorate spoke some Spanish.[17]

Despite their differences, the two branches of the Africanist family were united in their distrust of the Junteros. As we have seen, the Juntas arose in 1916, partly in response to the effects in Spain of the inflationary pressures of the First World War. Their immediate objective was to halt the growing inequality of pay between officers in the metropolitan garrisons and those serving in Morocco as a result of monetary rewards for officers on active duty. Inflation in Spain had risen some 50 per cent, drastically eating into the value of their salaries. Colonial officers, on the contrary enjoyed higher rates of pay that were not so vulnerable to inflation. Another source of grievance was the promotion system. Promotion through merit had been a long-standing source of division within the Spanish army since the mid-nineteenth century. The system fostered nepotism and favouritism and, before the twentieth-century Moroccan campaigns, had also benefited the careers of officers of the technical corps because they enjoyed special status.

---

[16] n.a. *Ensayo de historial del tercer Grupo de Fuerzas Regulares Indígenas* (Ceuta, n.p., 1926), 35.

[17] Handwritten report by Sr Aranda, 'Datos de Marruecos', 21 Oct. 1924, AR leg. 63, carp. 44. Yagüe's biographer is Juan José Calleja, *Yagüe: un corazón al rojo* (Barcelona, Editorial Juventud, 1963), 35.

From 1909, however, merit promotions and bonuses became the dividend for those, in particular in the infantry and cavalry, who were engaged in military action in Morocco. Such rewards were often abused. Promotions and medals were usually awarded on the basis of heroism measured by wounds rather than on military results. The system was regarded as deeply unjust by many officers of the artillery and engineering corps, the General Staff, and those involved in the interface with the Moroccan authorities, because they had few opportunities to display the heroism in military action that so favoured their colleagues. The least acknowledged of these officers were the medics and military doctors. In the aftermath of the 1921 disaster a young medical lieutenant called Manuel Miranda Vidal was entrusted, with his team of six soldiers, with collecting 5,000 bodies, sometimes at the risk of their own lives. With other medical teams, they were also expected to clean up the military posts recaptured during the counter-offensive or carry out surgery near the front line. Such people received none of the adulation or the rewards enjoyed by their embattled colleagues in infantry and cavalry but they did much to maintain morale and restore the health of the soldiers.[18]

As we have seen, the revolt of the Junteros in Spain brought down one government and forced the next to introduce a closed scale whereby promotion and pay were largely determined by seniority and length of service. Promotion on the basis of merit displayed in war was now subject to a rigorous procedure whose final stage was a parliamentary ballot. The measure dismayed and angered many of the Africanists. As they saw it, they were no longer going to be rewarded for the risks they were taking to life and limb, while those who lived a tranquil life in garrisons throughout Spain would enjoy the same salary and promotion opportunities. Their views ignored the many colleagues serving in Morocco, such as the medics and the artillery officers, who took part in actions but had little opportunity to win promotion.[19]

The presence of Junteros in the Spanish Army of Africa has largely been ignored; indeed, the assumption is often made that they were exclusively based in Spain and that 'Africanist' is therefore a generic term denoting the colonial officer.[20] Yet membership of the Juntas was obligatory for all officers in Morocco, and committees representing each unit were set up in the colonial army in 1917 in both the eastern and the two western zones. It was true that most of the Junta supporters in the Army of Africa were normally based in the metropolis and were doing a compulsory term of service in Morocco. Yet there were professional officers serving in Morocco who were Junta activists or sympathizers and Africanists at the same time; that is, they considered themselves

---

[18] Fernández Oxea, *Crónicas*, 62–3. For other anecdotal evidence of the bravery and skill of the medical teams see Manuel Bastos Ansart, *De las guerras coloniales a la Guerra Civil. Memorias de un cirujano* (Barcelona, Ariel, 1969), 92 and 162–4.

[19] The bitter reaction of colonial officers is palpable in *El Telegrama del Rif*, 12 Nov. 1918.

[20] e.g. in Payne, *Politics and the Military*.

colonial officers whilst they also supported the corporatist values of the Juntas.[21] The tension between the Africanists and the Junteros was not, therefore, necessarily the result of a different identity but focused initially on a discrepancy over professional military structure.

Thus, José Riquelme, as president of the Melilla Infantry Junta (or Comisión Informativa, as the Juntas were later called), could be described as both an enlightened Africanist and a Juntero. Having completed many years of service in the infantry in Morocco, he was appointed in 1916 as second-in-command to Morales in the colonial agency, the Oficinas de Intervención, where Abdel Krim worked under his direction. In June 1921 he became head of the indigenous police, the post he held when the Anual disaster occurred a few weeks later.[22] Had the Juntas not imposed a closed scale in 1917, Riquelme's work amongst the tribes of the Rif would have gone relatively unrewarded in contrast to his fellow officers in the front-line units. At the same time, through his work in the colonial agency, he was committed to the objective of the enlightened Africanists of maintaining a balance of military and civil action and delegating the administration of the Protectorate as much as possible to the local Moroccan authorities.[23] Riquelme's case demonstrates that, at least for two or three years, the differences between Junteros and Africanists were reconcilable. Just as Africanists were posted to garrisons in Spain, so Junteros fought in Morocco. It was possible to share the corporatist aspirations of the latter and the strategic aims of the former. And, of course, there were many officers, possibly a majority of those posted in Spain, who had no strong feelings about either side of the military divide.

The tension between the two castes was particularly acute in the western zone in the period leading to the Anual disaster. Legion officers and others commanding the native troops, such as Millán-Astray, Orgaz, and the hotblooded Varela, led such a vociferous campaign against the closed scale that the Madrid-based Infantry Junta sent a committee of inquiry to Morocco in early July 1921. As the leading anti-Juntero in the area, Varela was hauled away from the front to face interrogation. It was a particularly sensitive moment for Varela, because an application had gone in for his promotion from lieutenant to captain following the exceptional route allowed by the 1917 law. During his interrogation Varela declared defiantly that he would resign from the infantry corps if there were no restitution of the open scale. On his return to the front a short distance away, following the first meeting, he was shot twice by a

---

[21] For details of the Juntas in the Army of Africa in July 1917, see SHM Archivo de la documentación de la Guerra de Liberación Nacional, R271, leg. 72, carp. 13. Junteros activists or sympathizers serving in Africa included Generals Burguete, Aizpuru, Tuero, and Navarro and officers such as Nuñez del Prado, Lacanal, Muñoz Grandes, Sirvent, Jiménez Arroyo, Salcedo, Fontán, Ros Hernández, Alcantara, García Esteban, Ugarte, Pardo, and Alzugaray.

[22] Though, according to his testimony, he was on sick leave at the time: Picasso, *Expediente*, 400–11.

[23] See Tomás Borrás' interview with Riquelme in 'La opinión de Riquelme. ¿Qué política debe seguir España en su zona?', *El Sol*, 20 Sept. 1921.

Moroccan guerrilla in the left thigh and lay there 'thrashing about like a rabbit', as he later wrote to his mother. Rather than take him to first aid, his fellow officers bore him by stretcher back to the tent where the inquiry had been taking place. There the Africanist general, González Carrasco, picked up one end of the stretcher and asked a member of the committee to pick up the other end and bring Varela back into the tent. The anecdote reveals the strength of feeling amongst the many Africanists but it also says a lot about their concept of the criterion for promotion. According to one of the Africanist protagonists of the incident, they had carried Varela into the tent 'to demonstrate to the Tribunal [the Junta committee] what campaign life was like and the nature of the heroic acts that gave rise to promotions . . .'[24]

The 1921 disaster turned the deeply felt professional differences between many Africanists and Junteros into profound antipathy. So tense were their relations that a pro-Junta military paper saw in them 'the germs of a fearful civil war'.[25] The Junta lobby in Spain sought to discipline the leading officers of the Army of Africa for the defeat. The Africanists, on the other hand, blamed the Juntas for the disaster on the grounds that they had diverted resources away from the Army of Africa and imposed a system of pay and promotion that prevented the creation of a professional colonial army. They also claimed that the Junteros in Morocco had tried to evade military engagements, fuelling the myth equating the Juntas with battle-shyness and bureaucracy.[26] It is true that not one member of the Regional Junta in Melilla suffered death or injury throughout the disaster; also that the artillery corps, deeply involved in the Juntas, lost only one senior officer and abandoned dozens of artillery pieces. Similarly, disciplinary proceedings were taken against several leading representatives of the Juntas for incompetence and desertion.[27]

But while the Africanists were right to see the closed scale as part of the problem they were wrong in attributing the disaster to the Juntas. The weakness of the Army of Africa was due in great measure to the failings of the army in Spain as a whole, and beyond that, the failure of the government to reform the fractious and politically interventionist military when it had the opportunity after the 1898 Disaster.[28] What the Picasso report revealed in shocking detail was the reproduction in Morocco of the military culture of the

[24] 'Herida grave en Larache en relacion con la Juntas de Defensa', n.a., July 1921, Archivo Varela (AV), vol. 1. In the same volume are further details of the case: José Varela, 'Proposición a la Junta Superior del Arma', 8 May 1920; the untitled minutes of the hearing, 19 June 1921; and notes written by General González Carrasco entitled 'Junta de Defensa', n.d.

[25] 'En defensa de la verdad. Sobre las Juntas de Defensa', *La Correspondencia Militar*, 21 Oct. 1921. This should not be regarded, however, as a case of extraordinary prescience, because the press was much given to dire presages.

[26] The most outspoken attack on the Juntas by General Miguel Cabanellas was published in a number of newspapers, including *La Correspondencia Militar* on 24 Oct. 1921 ('Momentos dificiles'), to which a spokesman of the Juntas replied in the same edition. For other press attacks on the Juntas, see *El Liberal* (Leopoldo Bejarano, 'El espíritu de la campaña') on 25 Aug. 1921 and *ABC*, 7 Jan. 1922.

[27] La Porte, 'La respuesta', 311–13.   [28] Sebastian Balfour, *The End*.

metropolis, as I will examine in Chapter 8. The disaster, in any case, was the result, as we have seen, of a much broader problem that also embraced the Africanists themselves.

Relations between Africanist and Juntero officers who had forged their careers in the Moroccan campaigns became irreconcilable divisions amongst their leading members after a leading Africanist general, Miguel Cabanellas, published a ferocious letter in the national press blaming the Juntas for the disaster.[29] The aversion intensified when officers associated with the Juntas indirectly criticized the Africanists in the Picasso hearings. The Africanist witnesses, such as Dávila, refused, on the contrary, to wash the colonial army's dirty linen in public. Even mainland-based officers with no axe to grind were caught up in the growing division. Colonel Batet, no supporter of the Juntas, displays such an aversion to the Africanists in his private documents, perhaps as a result of their attempts to block his Anual investigation, that he was prepared to accept dubious rumours about their wrongdoings as facts. Thus, he claims that Francisco Franco caught venereal disease and used it as an excuse to stay away from military operations for four months, but that this did not prevent him from frequenting the bars and the officers' mess.[30] For all his faults, this would have been uncharacteristic behaviour on the part of Franco.

The antipathy between the two castes would remain at an individual level right through to the Civil War, and would play a part in the support given to the Republic by the leading Junteros such as Riquelme when the bulk of the Africanists rose in revolt in 1936. The differences thus increasingly took on an ideological dimension. The leaders of the first Juntas in Spain had declared a rhetorical commitment to the overthrow of the old Restoration system, whilst they had really been concerned with professional grievances. From 1921 Juntero activists moved hesitantly towards progressive politics.

The fissure between Junteros and Africanists was part of a wider breakdown of the link between the Army of Africa and civil society in Spain. Both army and civil institutions in Spain needed root-and-branch reforms. But the unstable governments of the Restoration system were in no position to carry them out. The Africanists' scorn for civilian politics at home was intensified by their experience in Morocco. Colonial officers had been given almost absolute authority in the affairs of the Protectorate. Some had even taken over commercial activities to supplement their salary. The largely militarized society of Spanish Morocco had given them a sense of power and impunity. A Spanish judge in Tetuan complained to one of Maura's politicians, Angel Ossorio y Gallardo, that officers 'were accustomed in Morocco for all civilians in Morocco, amongst whom public spirit is not very developed, to bend to their demands and excesses'.[31]

[29] *La Correspondencia Militar*, 24 Oct. 1921.
[30] AB caixa 1, exp. 4.1. The document is reproduced in Raguer, *El General Batet*, 329–41.
[31] Letter to Manuel Ferrer to Angel Ossorio, 24 Aug. 1915, AM Fondo Documental Mortera, caja 4.

After Anual the scorn felt by colonial officers towards civil society turned to animosity. They felt betrayed by the government and wrongly accused by much of the media. The charges levelled at them by the leftist press and the parliamentary left further alienated the Africanists from the barely developed democratic culture in Spain. They turned inwards, seeing in their own culture the seeds of a renovated Spain. They saw their fellow officers, the Junteros, as part of the problem, too concerned about rank and bureaucracy to fight the enemy.

At a collective level, however, the divisions were subordinated to the task of reconquering the territory lost in July and avenging the death of thousands of comrades-in-arms. With the retreat of the Junteros, and in the new spirit of *revanchisme* in Spain, the post-Anual campaign helped to consolidate the militarist caste as the hegemonic force in the Army of Africa. It was increasingly dominated by the new generation, which reached the highest posts in the African army during its course.[32] Many of its members had cut their teeth on the western front of the Spanish Protectorate in the campaigns against Raisuni and now led the shock-troops transferred to the eastern front. Except for a brief period, the enlightened Africanists were swamped by the murderous intentions of their fellow officers towards the Moroccans who had risen against them. When circumstances permitted, the former tried to apply the pacific methods of the pre-1919 days, without much success.

Of all of them, Castro Girona continued to be the most decided advocate of combining military action with civil initiatives. In cyclostyled instructions in 1923 to the Spanish colonial agency, he ordered that it should carry out all its work through the medium of the 'natural' authorities, ensuring that they were the ones entrusted directly with the execution of the Mahkzen's orders. 'It is a general rule of conduct that we should not appear as dominators, since that is not our mission.' Spain's policy in Morocco, he went on, was that of attracting and creating a rapport with its inhabitants.[33] Yet surrogate colonialism was anathema to his militarist colleagues.

Castro Girona's favourable response to a confidential proposal made to him in December 1922 by the new Liberal government to appoint Luis Silvela as high commissioner did not endear him to them either. In the secret negotiations for peace with emissaries of Abdel Krim in April 1923, Castro Girona had his hands tied by the opposition of his *revanchiste* fellow officers to any deal that did not entail the surrender of the Moroccan rebels. Later he, and other enlightened officers like Riquelme, came under fire once again for renewing

---

[32] Defined by Julio Busquets as the generation of 1915 in *El militar de carrera en España. Estudio de sociología militar* (Barcelona, Ariel, 1967).

[33] A. Castro Girona, 'Instrucciones sobre la organización y funcionamiento de las oficinas de intervención', 28 Apr. 1923, Tetuán (García Figueras archive), 2–3. For the views of another enlightened officer, see Manuel del Nido y Torres, *Marruecos. Apuntes para el oficial de intervención y de tropas coloniales* (Tetuán, Editorial Hispano Africana, 1925).

efforts to seek peace with Raisuni.[34] As 'Raisunists', as the enlightened Africanist faction was now contemptuously described, they were regarded with deep suspicion. Castro Girona, in particular, was reputed to be a personal friend of the Jebala chieftain. His intimacy with the Pig, as Raisuni was nicknamed by many officers, was regarded with scorn by the more racist of his colleagues.

Differences within the Africanist caste, of which these were the most serious, were now largely stored in the family larder or dealt with internally. Dávila's reticence in giving testimony to the Picasso hearings was part of the increasing hermeticism of the Africanists. The values they shared and needed to defend on all sides were more important than their differences. Unfortunately for the historian, these discrepancies were rarely written down or voiced for posterity. In some cases the source of division might be mere professional rivalry and clashes of personality. Differences of strategy were often translated into mutual accusations of careerism or jealousy, just as political differences became expressed as attacks on military competence. Few of the militarists forgave the enlightened Africanists such as Castro Girona for their 'pacifism', even though they all supported the chemical bombing of the Moorish enemy.

The vicious attack many years later on Castro Girona by his fellow Africanist Gómez-Jordana, who shared his fascination for Arab culture, gives a good idea of how strong feelings could run within the caste and how personal the antagonisms could become. Queipo de Llano's attack on Castro Girona's and Riquelme's supposed pacifism, on the other hand, was disguised as a criticism of their military capabilities. In the drastic circumstances of the retreat in the autumn of 1924, all commanders could be accused of failure because of the high level of casualties suffered by the troops under their command. But Queipo's singling out of these two was the expression, above all, of their primary division over relations with the Moroccans.[35]

Africanists greeted the Primo de Rivera coup with mixed feelings, as we saw in Chapter 4. Although it brought to a halt the 'witch-hunt' against the Africanists, the new president was openly committed to scaling down military operations in Morocco (though his real intentions, as we have seen, were to withdraw the troops from the front in order to douse the enemy with mustard gas). Moreover, as a Junta sympathizer, he had always advocated the closed scale of promotions. For all his backing by Africanist generals, Primo drew up his Military Directorate entirely from brigadier-generals representing the military regions in Spain. His manifesto was couched in the language of the

[34] Gómez-Jordana, La tramoya, 46–8, 51; Castro Girona's favourable response to the government proposal to appoint a civilian high commissioner, Luis Silvela, is in AGA M11, 81/3, 1922, sección 15: Africa. For the negotiations with Abdel Krim see Hernández Mir, El Rif, 121–4.

[35] Queipo de Llano, 'Relación detallada', AR 58/38; id., El General Queipo de Llano, 42–3, 67–8, and 77–81. See also Gómez Jordana, La tramoya, 19. On the other hand, the attack by General Joaquín Fanjul against Sanjurjo as a general with little standing and preparation for military command is more likely to have been a personality clash than an ideological or strategic feud: AFAMM leg. 394, carp. 7.

Juntas. A leading militarist Africanist, General Emilio Mola, wrote that the Juntas had died, but not the Junteros. The latter 'could be seen to re-emerge with their egoistic spirit as a result of the coup d'état, sometimes landing marvellous civil posts through their political connections, or posts in the secretariats created by the dictator and also the best posts in Africa when the war appeared to die down . . .'.[36] The bitterness and alienation of the Africanists from the Spanish political system of whatever hue were intensified and their burgeoning sense of mission to redeem Spain from the outside was given a new impetus. Primo de Rivera's conversion in late 1924 to undiluted military action in Morocco was seen as a result of their efforts. The new strategy strengthened the hold of militarist culture in both Spain and Morocco.

The Africanists' missionary zeal towards Spain was reflected in the first issue of the colonial military journal, the *Revista de Tropas Coloniales*, published a few months after the Primo de Rivera coup. In the editorial, Queipo de Llano, as a leading militarist, wrote that Spain's 'progressive fall into an abyss of anarchy' under the Restoration regime had been halted by 'a few men of heart who, risking everything, confronted the arduous task of resurrecting the spirit of Spain dulled by Muslim fatalism . . . to guide it onto the path worthy of its glorious history'.[37] His 'men of heart' no doubt embraced the colonial officers and the new dictator, whom they presumably hoped would have a change of heart.

The self-importance and the myth-making propensity of the Africanists can be seen already in these words. Although inflated rhetoric was characteristic of the journalism of the time, Queipo de Llano's language went beyond the most baroque of contemporary styles. Even if we allow for the exaggeration typical of the man, the words suggest a monumental delusion over the significance for Spain of the colonial war in Morocco. The Africanists were fighting a largely marginal and irregular war against tribesmen in a remote part of the world. There were, of course, some large-scale confrontations between the two sides. But on the whole, the war was asymmetric, mobile, and unorthodox. Occasionally, the officers' narration of events lets slip that different reality. A particular attack by Regulares on Rif forces was described as: 'More than a battle, it seemed at certain moments like a game of football between two well-trained teams. To make it even more similar, there were rowdy fans, who miraculously escaped being hit by the ball.'[38] Living in this hermetic universe of bloody skirmishes and isolated garrisons, the Africanists came to believe their own propaganda about the historical and military transcendence of this war. By a cruel irony they were the least aware of, the war became important in Spain only for brief periods, because of the military disasters for which the colonial officers were in part responsible.

[36] Quoted in Guillermo Cabanellas, *La guerra de los Mil Días: nacimiento, vida y muerte de la II República Española*, 2nd edn. (Buenos Aires, Heliasta, 1975), i. 118, n. 36.

[37] 'Nuestro propósito', Jan. 1924, año 1, número 1.   [38] Sánchez Pérez, *La acción decisiva*, 63.

Queipo de Llano's discourse gives us a clue to the meaning of these transcendent myths. His reference to Spain's 'glorious history' can only refer to its history of conquest, and in particular to Isabel the Catholic's testament calling on Spain to continue the Reconquest beyond Spain and into the Arab world. And indeed, in subsequent issues of the journal militarist Africanists such as Millán-Astray argued quite openly that Spain's historical destiny lay in the conquest of Morocco as the first stage in the construction of a new empire. The tacit imperialism of the militarists was able to surface in the new dictatorship. Their discourse was strongly reminiscent of Italian fascism, not only with reference to historical destinies but also to the nature of war. For Millán-Astray, a passionate admirer of Mussolini, war was a source of vitality and national regeneration. For another military contributor to the journal, colonial officers were 'priests of the heroic cult' fighting an 'obscure' war of sacrifice and duty, despising death. The words convey the sense of elitism among the Africanists and the growing feeling of belonging to a military caste linked fancifully to the myth of the Christian knights of medieval Spain. His description hardly corresponds to the spasmodic and messy skirmishes of much of the colonial war, and the drinking and womanizing habits of many officers in their leisure time. But the militarists were less concerned with historical narration than with the creation of myths, and the words they used were more important for their emotional resonance than for their meaning.[39]

Queipo de Llano's article in the second issue of the *Revista de Tropas Coloniales* displayed once again the profound sense of alienation of the colonial military from life in Spain. He repeats his view that the Spanish people were suffering from a 'truly Muslim indolence', implying that they could not be the agents of regeneration. Nor could the government claim to represent Spain, since it was divorced from the people. According to him, the Army of Africa was the target of vicious attacks by the multitudes. It had been abandoned by the state, subjected to the hostility of the intellectuals, criticized by the press, and undermined from within by the Juntas. The feeling of victimization underlying these words is accompanied by a sense of mission. Spain could only be regenerated from the outside by an army untainted by the flabbiness and corruption of metropolitan culture.[40] The article points to the early consolidation amongst militarist Africanists of an interventionist and right-wing nationalism. Although it shared the myth of national identity celebrated by Menéndez Pelayo in the nineteenth century, this new nationalism was modernizing and expansionist rather than rural and clerical. The importance of the colonial

[39] José Millán-Astray, 'Necesidad de permanecer en África', *Revista de Tropas Coloniales*, 5 (May 1924), no pp., and Baldomero Argente, 'El desprecio a la muerte', ibid., 2 (Feb. 1924), 3. See also Francisco Bastos Ansart, *El desastre de Annual. Melilla en julio de 1921* (Barcelona, Minerva, 1921), for a reflection of these views.

[40] 'El problema de Marruecos. Al aparecer la "Revista de Tropas Coloniales"', *Revista de Tropas Coloniales*, 2 (Feb. 1924).

campaigns to the Africanists becomes clearer in the light of this discourse. In their minds, that 'obscure' war was the forge shaping a new military elite that would regenerate Spain.

The king openly identified with the journal's message. He claimed to read every single issue and looked forward to the next. With good reason, he had been popularly nicknamed the 'Africanist'. 'I will not hide the fact that the wishes of my colonial troops coincide with mine,' he declared to journal representatives visiting him on his thirty-eighth birthday. 'The colonial troops are more than just an embryo, they are a corps that is developing vigorously and will soon reach—I hope—the height of efficiency, and with it the corresponding satisfaction of its ideals.'[41] The vague words of the king should not disguise the tenor of his statement. He had been a close friend of Silvestre and an open admirer of the Africanists. These allegiances, combined with his praise for the journal, denoted support for further military expansion in Morocco and intervention in Spain by the Army of Africa.

The fact that the *Revista de Tropas Coloniales* published several articles by enlightened Africanists does not disguise its predominant militarism. Ambitious officers felt obliged to mouth the canonical reasons for the presence of the army in Morocco. Cultivating the image of a progressive officer bringing civilization to a backward society on behalf of Europe was a useful way of advancing one's career. In the official discourse of Spanish colonialism, officers were expected constantly to be studying Morocco and its people.[42] Franco was particularly adept at weaving between militarist and enlightened Africanism, depending on the circumstances. In the first issue of the journal, at a time when Primo de Rivera had still not been converted to military action in Morocco, he waxed lyrical about the need for identification with its people. 'In this country of light and mystery, we must not walk about in the dark, we have to raise the veil by identifying ourselves with Moroccan feelings; the military and political leaders cannot live in continuous divorce; we cannot turn our backs on the feelings of a people we have to educate.' Elsewhere he held up the French model of colonialism and recommended that his fellow officers study its texts.[43]

Yet when the new military campaign in Morocco got under way in 1925, Franco, now editor of the journal after the sacking of Queipo de Llano as commander-in-chief of the Ceuta zone, began to publish increasingly militarist articles. After Primo de Rivera wrote a piece for the journal in July 1925 admitting his change of strategy towards military conquest, Franco contributed

[41] Victor Ruiz Albéniz, 'Su Majestad el Rey y la "Revista de Tropas Coloniales"', ibid., 5 (17 May 1924).

[42] E. Bonelli, 'Actuación militar del Protectorado', ibid., 2 (Feb. 1924), 4. Another example of the enlightened discourse is Carlos Muñoz, 'Intervenciones indígenas', ibid., 1 (Jan. 1924), 24–5.

[43] The extract of the article in the *Revista de Tropas Coloniales* is on p. 6 of issue no. 1. Franco's recommendation is published as 'Una obra necesaria' in *Papeles de la Guerra de Marruecos* (Madrid, Fundación Nacional Francisco Franco, 1986), 27–9.

another article asserting the primacy of military over political methods (though avoiding, like all his colleagues, any reference to chemical weapons). He advocated that in the joint campaign with France: 'Blockade, hunger, lack of resources, weariness, constancy and time have to be our best allies; and meanwhile, to maintain offensive action in the rebel territories, constant punishment, and combined political action by the two nations, without showing any desire for prompt peace. There's nothing like desiring war to bring peace closer.'[44]

It is significant of the militarist bias of the journal that one of the most outstanding of the enlightened Africanists, Castro Girona, did not or was not invited to contribute and that his name appears only once, in unavoidable circumstances, in the whole series from 1924 to 1926.[45] The frustration felt by progressive colonial officers at the failure of their comrades to respect the local hierarchies is evident in the attempt by one of them to explain it as a genetic propensity among Spaniards to command. 'We Spaniards have been born to command, so much so that we cannot conceive of doing anything in life, not even the most insignificant thing, without ordering someone about, and as a result, it is almost impossible to rule second hand, that is, to let the native authority face the music and be the one who, in the eyes of the natives, orders and disposes.'[46]

The most brutal expression of this militarist strategy was the Spanish Legion. Within the Africanist family the Legion was the most awkward and eccentric relative. By 1925 its numbers had grown to 219 officers and 7,497 NCOs and soldiers.[47] Millán-Astray had instilled the corps since its foundation in 1920 with the trappings of the fascist condottieri. Like its Italian equivalent, the alternative name for the corps, the Tercio, was drawn from a mythologized Middle Ages, when the corps of professional soldiers called by that name fought in defence of the Spanish Empire in Europe. The officers of the Legion formed a caste whose identity was forged through elaborate ritual and liturgy. Their uniforms, emblems, parades, and symbols all encouraged a fierce esprit de corps and elitism. The political messages they imparted were drawn from an extreme right-wing nationalism, the equivalent of Italian fascism and German Nazism. Like their counterparts in those countries, their metaphysics were based on the cult of violence, redemption, death, and machismo.[48] Millán-Astray wore his numerous wounds with their accompanying medals like trophies of masculinity.

[44] 'Sistemas rifeños', *Revista de Tropas Coloniales* (1925), 2.

[45] After the second occupation of Chauen when he was second-in-command to Berenguer: ibid., época 2, no. 2 (Oct. 1926).

[46] Nido y Torres, *Marruecos*, 292.

[47] Report by C. G. Hope Gill to R. H. Clive, British consul-general in Tangier, 7 Mar. 1925, PRO FO 636/9.

[48] Vicente Blasco Ibáñez, *Alfonso XIII Unmasked: The Military Terror in Spain* (London, Eveleigh, Nash and Grayson, 1925), 94–6.

1. Anonymous photograph taken in the early 1920s showing Legionnaires in Morocco holding up the heads of Moroccans they had captured and beheaded. The right-wing Falange published the photo during the Civil War claiming it showed communist International Brigaders with the heads of Spanish 'patriots'.

2. Photograph of 1922 of the Rifian leader Abdel Krim meeting a Spanish envoy to negotiate the repatriation of Spanish prisoners.

3. Photo taken by the author of a post in Anual with a portrait of Abdel Krim on it marking a spot close to where General Silvestre died.

4. Photo of Franco and Millán Astray taken by the photographer Bartolomé Ros as they sang during a ceremony in February 1926 transferring command of the Legion to the latter shortly after Franco's promotion to the rank of Brigadier General.

5. Moros amigos. Photo of the Moroccan Native Police fighting on the Spanish side that appeared on the front cover of the popular Spanish magazine *Blanco y Negro* in 1921.

6. A cover photograph of *Blanco y Negro* in 1921 showing Spanish soldiers writing letters. Inadvertently, the photo also shows another soldier behind them searching his shirt for fleas in a characteristic pose nicknamed 'reading the newspaper'.

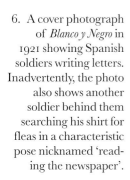

7. Photo taken by the author in 2000 of El Hach Mohammed M'hauech on his death-bed in Tetuan. He fought against the Spanish in the colonial war and for the Nationalists in the Civil War.

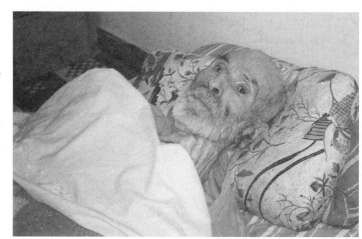

8. Photo taken by the author in 1998 of Josep Campa Ginot, who on the contrary fought for Spain in the colonial war and against the Nationalists in the Civil War.

9. Photo taken by the author in 2001 of Hadou El Kayid Omar Massaud, a 103 year old veteran of the colonial war (and member of Abdel Krim's wider family) who witnessed Spanish chemical bombing raids. In the photo he is reaping the wheat in his fields.

10. Photo taken by the author of Isidre Balada, a Spanish veteran of the colonial war who almost died of hunger and thirst in the siege of an isolated position. He fought in defence of the Republic in the Civil War.

11. 1998 photo (taken with the author) of Pau Masferrer Fontanella, a 100 year old Spanish veteran of the colonial war who was sent to Morocco for the post-Anual offensive in October 1921.

12. Photo taken by the author of Mohammed Salah Faraji, a 91 year old Moroccan who witnessed the Spanish defeat at Abarrán and survived the chemical war.

13. Photo taken by the author of Mohammed Amar Hammadi, who is holding a Spanish bomb carrier that fell (before he was born) into the back yard of his family home with the mustard gas bombs it was carrying. His family hid it. Later his mother and his two elder sisters (who were blinded by the bombs) died of cancer.

14. Photo of his backyard where he claims no vegetation has grown since the mustard-gas bombs fell.

15. A photo of Mohammed Ben Ayache el Amrani H'mimed from a village near Tetuan who survived the chemical war as a young boy (photo by the author).

16. A Moroccan from a village near Ajdir whose parents and elder relatives all died of cancer as a result of the chemical war (photo by author).

17. Photo taken by the author of Hacha Oum Koulthoum Ahmed Kasem el Amrani, the niece of Danfil, the last Moroccan leader to resist the Spanish in 1927.

18. A posed photo on the front cover of a 1921 issue of *Blanco y Negro* showing a rare picture of a 'cantinera', a Legion camp-follower or travelling prostitute. She is seen here helping a wounded officer off the battlefield.

19. A 'pagan virgin'. In her eyes, 'with their infinite gaze, with the depth and darkness of an abyss ... was a cynical and horrifying stare in which could be seen for a instant all the ferocity of these wild women, hunters of men.' The words of a Spanish journalist about a young Moroccan woman. The photo is of a nude Arab woman taken by the photographic team of Lehnert and Landrock in the early part of the twentieth-century. Postcards of naked Arab women such as this were among the possessions carried around by Spanish soldiers in Morocco.

20. A pro-Nationalist drawing depicting Moroccan troops boarding a plane in Morocco to fight in the Spanish Civil War.

21. A poster by the famous artist Bertuchi, part of a recruitment drive in 1929 for the Spanish Legion and appealing to Spaniards and foreigners to join at higher wages.

22. A photo taken by the author of Husain Ben Oulad Ali, a Moroccan veteran of the Army of Africa in the Civil War from Tetuan.

23. A Republican poster made during the Civil War warning citizens of the danger of chemical bombardment by the Nationalists.

NORMAS PARA LA DEFENSA ANTI-GAS DE LA POBLACION CIVIL

EDITADO POR EL COMITÉ NACIONAL DE DEFENSA ANTI-GAS (MINISTERIO DE SANIDAD Y ASISTENCIA SOCIAL)

Many of the officers who chose to serve in the Legion, like Franco, were probably attracted to it by the sense of security afforded by its rigid codes and hierarchy. It also provided an external identity that many found difficult to locate within themselves. The discipline it imposed on officer and soldier alike minimized emotional conflict and legitimized brutality. The pleasure some derived from bullying and inflicting punishment on their soldiers was adorned by the Legion's apologists with a patriotic mystique that made it feel acceptable. According to one of these, the relationship between the officer and the recruit in the Legion was 'a struggle between the subliminal powers of two forces that meet face to face: the leader, who incarnates in those moments the whole of military discipline and spirit and virile vigour and energy, and on the other hand, men who want, falteringly, to shake off from their shoulders the imponderable weight of the decadence of a race.'[49] These words, written in 1922, are distinctly fascist in tone and suggest that the Legion's enthusiasts saw it as the shock-troops for the regeneration of a decadent Spain.

The culture of the Legion, especially that of its rank and file soldiers, will be examined more closely in Chapter 8. For the purposes of this chapter, it should be stressed that the Legion's elitism and detachment from the rest of the Army of Africa created deep tensions therein. Among the other officer elites there were mixed feelings of admiration for the reckless bravery of the Legionnaires and scorn, if not anger, for their collective egotism and bad behaviour off the battle-field. Such was the group spirit within the colonial army once the Junteros had been seen off that internal complaints about relations between the different corps are hard to find. So we have to rely on memoirs critical of the Legion and observations by foreign diplomats to form some idea of their behaviour.

A report by a British diplomat in Tetuan in 1924 gives a shocking portrait, not just of the Legionnaires but also of their officers during off-duty moments. He reported that the high commissioner himself tried to restore order when a bunch of drunken Legionnaires invaded the main square of the town. Having failed to get them arrested, 'he turned on the groups of officers sitting in the surrounding cafes and harangued them. Then seeing Major Villalba of the Legion, a notorious character against whom the Moors have a detailed list of rapes committed in the Melilla area, he called him forward but the Major strolled away through the crowd advising them not to listen to the "old man". Villalba led his drunken bandera up the Gorgues track next morning and was severely wounded.' The 'old man' was none other than Luis Aizpuru, one of the most competent veterans of the Army of Africa war, who had been withdrawn for a while from Morocco in 1919 and replaced by Silvestre, a soldier closer to Berenguer's heart.

The British diplomat further reported that: 'The officers make no attempt to control their men and conceal their incapacity to do so by affecting to

[49] Carlos Micó, *Los caballeros de la Legión* (Madrid, Sucesores de Rivadeneyra, 1922), 31.

encourage their martial spirit and freedom from discipline imposed on common troops.' Thus, while their troops looted stores in Ceuta, Legion officers stood by without interfering, even when a shopkeeper was stabbed. 'The Legion has consequently been fined the value of the goods, which the officers publicly decry as an indignity to such heroic saviours of Spain.'[50] Even taking into account the British diplomat's obvious antipathy towards the Legion, it is clear from his account that, as a privileged caste, the Legion felt itself above the discipline of the Army of Africa. The officers' inability to deal with the rowdiness of their men suggests also a rule of thumb in the Legion whereby strict discipline on parade or in the battlefield was rewarded by the absence of control during their free time. Franco, for example, ordered the execution of a Legionnaire who had refused to eat his food and had thrown the contents of his plate at an officer while on parade.[51]

Another military caste imbued with a strong sense of collective identity in the Army of Africa was the officers of the Regulares. Between the creation of the corps in 1911 and that of the Legion in 1920, the Regulares provided ambitious officers with the opportunity to command professional mercenary troops rather than the raw and reluctant recruits from Spain on military service. Until the emergence of the Juntas in 1917, service in the Regulares also gave them frequent opportunities to rise in the ranks and to earn bonuses, because native troops were used as front-line units and saw repeated military action. Officers with a strong colonial vocation had the further opportunity of training Moroccan fighters skilled in individual guerrilla warfare into highly effective and disciplined units.

Amongst the first commanders of the Regulares were several of the enlightened Africanists and others who shared some of their interest in Morocco. As we have seen, the more committed amongst them took the trouble to learn Arabic and the shelja, the local language of the Rif, and it became customary among many to wear jellabas and take part in some of the Moroccan customs.[52] This was true also of other colonial officers similarly inclined who volunteered to command the sultan's troops, the *mehal-las*, or lead a harka, or work in the native bureaux or police. Their adoption of local culture, however superficial, developed amongst them a sense of colonial identity that separated them from the Legion and the metropolitan units of the colonial army.

The expansion of the Regulares and the creation of the Legion led to a dilution of the quality of officers commanding native troops. The Regulares grew from one battalion or *tabor* on its foundation to sixteen infantry *tabors* and one cavalry *tabor* by 1925, with a total of 13,537 men. Of these, eighty-eight were commissioned officers, of whom only twelve were Moroccan. Ambitious officers such as Franco were drawn away from the Regulares to the Legion when

---

[50] C. G. Hope Gill to W. M. Codrington, 5 Sept. 1924, PRO FO 636/17.
[51] Franco Salgado-Araujo, *Mis conversaciones*, 184–5.   [52] Mola, *Dar Akkoba*, 147.

it was founded, above all because it offered greater opportunities for promotion. There had also been a serious depletion of the numbers of the Regulares when many of its soldiers had deserted to join Abdel Krim's troops. Thereafter, service as an officer of the Regulares became less attractive. By 1925 the British diplomatic representative in Tetuan reported that the quality of the officer corps was no longer up to its previous standard. 'The native material is good,' he recorded, 'but it is poorly handled by officers who have no knowledge of the country or the language and seldom acquire it. The disparity between numbers of Spanish and native officers is noticeable. Properly led these troops have given good account of themselves, but the operations of last year showed up a lack of confidence between officers and men which has resulted in a general feeling of untrustworthiness.'[53]

French military reports of the same period were even more scornful of the officers of the native troops and those in charge of native affairs (or *Intervención*). Combined operations between French and Spanish forces in May and June of 1926 had given the divisional French general E. Dosse a close view of the culture of his Spanish counterparts. He had dined at Sanjurjo's table along with the 'Duchess of Victory', the titled Spanish woman who oversaw the administration of the hospitals in the eastern zone. During their conversation, the French were chided for their lack of understanding of the Berber character and for their 'inordinate softheartedness towards such savages'. All the officers present at the table corroborated this view, according to Dosse, and the general opinion was that 'the maximum number should be destroyed in order the better to terrorize'. No Spanish officer, he went on in his report, wanted to learn Arab or Berber. The liaison officer attached to him often expressed his amazement when the French general agreed to shake the hand of an Arab.[54]

Like their fellow officers in other colonial units, the Regulares officers made a cult of bravery or audacity, subordinating military tactics and intelligence-gathering to heroism in action. With the typical sense of superiority of the French officers towards their Spanish counterparts, General Dosse commented that officers were 'above all sporty (*sportifs*) rather than military'. An official Spanish report on the battle of Tifaruin in August 1923 comments approvingly that the commander of a Regulares *tabor* led his troops in an attack against the enemy, during which, 'without taking into account their number nor judging the difficulties that the nature of the terrain put in the way of their advance, the Regulares group threw themselves into the assault again and again'.[55] For this action the officer was awarded a military medal. It is difficult not to draw the conclusion from this and many other examples that the greater the number of losses of soldiers, the greater was the opportunity for military decoration and career advancement.

[53] C. G. Hope Gill to R. H. Clive, 7 Mar. 1925, PRO FO 636/9.
[54] General Dosse, 'Note de Service', 24 June 1926, SHAT 3H 100.
[55] García Pérez, *Historial*, 22 and 52–4.

Between officers of the Legion and those of the native troops there existed both complicity and competition. They shared a scorn for metropolitan politics and a growing mystique about their own potential to transform it. But they also competed for the prizes of military success. The major problem in their relations was the overt racism of the Legion against Moroccans. While some of the Legion officers, such as Franco, had established a good rapport with native soldiers, there were others who treated all Moroccans with disdain and often cruelty. The solidarity between both castes has made it difficult to find examples of the tension that undoubtedly existed between them as a result. But we know that the High Command tended to keep the two corps apart from each other except in battle.[56] The advice of one of the enlightened Regulares officers, Capaz Montes, about relations with Moroccans hardly corresponded to the typical attitude of the Legionnaire officer. The most important virtues of the officer of native troops, he wrote, were 'to be an Arabist, honourable, clever, discreet, well educated, and understanding of the indigenous soul, looking on the Moor, not as an inferior being, but as a friend or rather a younger brother who has to be guided and given advice, leading him by the hand until it is convenient to let it go'.[57] Legionnaire officers like Major Villalba were unlikely to be impressed by such recommendations.

Another military caste, one that has received little attention in the recent literature of the colonial war, was the pilots. Many saw themselves as a privileged caste, surrounded by a mystique of high technology and daring. Emulating British military officers, they were allowed to carry swagger-sticks when in uniform, unlike fellow officers of the same rank in other units of the army. During their training they were treated lavishly. The military school in Albacete in Spain where some were trained had tennis-courts, swimming-pools, and drawing-rooms and the local bourgeoisie held soirées for them in their homes and invited them to picnics.[58] Like the more technical units, they tended to look down on the infantry, but they were in turn regarded as cocky and conceited. In his private notes during his investigation of the 1921 disaster, Batet expressed scorn for their lack of discipline: 'The pilots have always done whatever they wanted, with the complaisance, acquiescence and applause of the Generals and Commanders.' He remembered a particular occasion when they threw a party to celebrate the patron saint of the air force while a convoy was struggling without their aid to get to Tizzi Azza.[59]

Since they formed a relatively new branch of the army and navy, the pilots were allowed considerable latitude in their flying operations. In comparison to

[56] The Regulares' camps were also kept separate from those of the metropolitan troops: Arbolí, 'Ligeras', 7–8 and 85.

[57] Osvaldo Capaz Montes, 'Modalidades de la guerra de montaña en Marruecos. Asuntos indígenas', *Conferencia del coronel Capaz*, Archivo García Figueras (n.d, n.p.), 41.

[58] According to the wife of one of the pilots: Carlota O'Neill, *Los muertos también hablan*, 2nd edn. (Mexico, La Prensa, 1973), 93; Hidalgo, *Cambio de rumbo*, 116.

[59] From Batet's private notes in Raguer, *El General*, 338.

the rigid discipline of their French counterparts, Hidalgo de Cisneros wrote later, 'we seemed more like the FAI' (the anarchist federation set up in 1927). 'We were never given a particular altitude to fly at; each flew at that which suited him best, according to the conditions in which the flight took place.' And he insisted that this was in fact more effective than the academic style of the French, which drew its inspiration from the European war.[60] Yet the fragmentary reports about the effects of the bombing suggest that the pilots were sometimes wildly inaccurate in their targeting. During the offensive in the north-west towards the end of 1924, Spanish planes dropped TNT bombs by mistake in the international zone of Tangier, prompting a committee of inquiry to visit the area where the stray bombs had fallen, only to witness further inaccurate bombing on the day of their visit.[61]

Nevertheless, the High Command needed the goodwill of the pilots more than that of any other officers because they played a key role in harassing the enemy. When preparations for the chemical bombing campaign were under way, the pilots were treated with kid gloves. A report of March 1924 by the commander-in-chief, Sanjurjo, urgently recommended that before it began all means possible should be used, 'for the humanitarian and moral effect on the aviators', to rescue one of the pilots who had been in Abdel Krim's hands for many months rather than the hundreds of other prisoners.

Among the pilots themselves, however, there were also divisions of caste, personality, and politics. Many of the pilots who flew the hydroplanes were naval officers and followed a different etiquette of war to their colleagues in the army. They were extremely reluctant, as Sanjurjo readily admitted, to become involved in the coming toxic-gas bombing. There were frequent clashes of opinion about strategy and tactics between the aeronautical commander and that of the army's air force, Lt.-Colonel Alfredo Kindelán, until one day their quarrel led to the former's arrest.[62] One pilot, Virgilio Leret, told his wife how in incendiary bombing campaigns against villages he used to give the signal to his co-pilot sergeant to release the bombs too late so that they landed in the fields beyond. It is quite likely that he tried to avoid using chemical bombs, but there seems to be no evidence of his opposition to their use. He later became a Republican and was shot by Franco after trying to defend the Melilla aerodrome against the military rebels in July 1936.[63]

Efforts by the Africanists to gather support for their opposition to Primo de Rivera's supposed abandonism were spurned by a substantial section of the pilots. Kindelán called a meeting of pilots in Melilla and asked them for their backing for a policy of resistance. According to Hidalgo de Cisneros, who was

---

[60] Hidalgo, *Cambio de rumbo*, 213–14.   [61] Harris, *France*, 150.

[62] n.a., *Historia de la aviación española* (Madrid, Instituto de Historia y Cultura Aérea, 1988), 100; Sanjurjo's report: 'Informe sobre la Actuación de la Aviación en el Protectorado', 4 Mar. 1924, AGA Africa, caja M12, exp. 2, p. 15 and handwritten note at the end of the report.

[63] O'Neill, *Los muertos*, 97.

present at the meeting, there was a long silence after his speech and then one of his colleagues openly refused support and Kindelán was forced to drop the issue.[64]

On the other hand, the pilot who flew Sanjurjo over the besieged position of Monte Arruit in 1921, Captain Sáenz de Buruaga, was a close friend of the militarist Africanists and would become a deep admirer of Franco and one of the leaders of the military rebellion in Morocco in 1936. In contrast, his colleague Ramón Franco, the future dictator's brother, would become a freemason and a Republican (until the Civil War broke out in 1936, when he sided with his brother). Unlike Sáenz de Buruaga, Ramón Franco was notorious for his boisterous lifestyle. According to the general investigating the causes of the Anual disaster, a drunken Franco once got onto the stage in a variety show in Melilla and tried to sing a duo with the female artist while doing a striptease. Two of his companions managed to overpower him and escorted him out of the cinema. He then took off in his hydroplane with a journalist and had to crash into the sea when it developed a mechanical fault. For this indiscipline he was given a sentence of a month in prison by his commanding officer, who then commuted it to two to three days of arrest.[65]

The divisions over the two castes among pilots were thus not only about methods of warfare. The navy pilots tended to avoid contact with army pilots because, as naval officers, they considered themselves more of an elite. Kindelán made a major effort to break down the barriers. Army pilots, such as Hidalgo de Cisneros, were posted to the aeronautical fleet to share their experiences of combat and technology. The latter's negative judgement of the quality of the navy pilots, however accurate or biased, reveals the gap between the two. Unlike their adventurous colleagues in the army, he writes, the navy pilots appeared to lack any enthusiasm and volunteered for few flights. Imbued with a sense of class superiority, they looked down on the non-commissioned officers and sailors they commanded, so much so, 'it was as if they belonged to two different races'. Yet these very people were in fact better trained and knew more about the planes than the navy pilots.[66]

This diversity of castes within the Army of Africa puzzled foreign military observers. A French military delegation on a visit to their Spanish counterparts found a 'mixture of very modern humanitarian principles and tendencies towards the most brutal violence. In all areas, one can note this incoherence, which deforms their attitude and makes it very difficult to reach any overall

---

[64] *Cambio de rumbo*, 163–4.

[65] Ibid. In his own account of Franco's crash, Riesgo, in 'La guerra', does not mention the episode in the cinema nor the eccentricity of Franco's flight. Instead he maintains that the plane was brought down by enemy action. Batet's private judgements were often based on rumour and coloured by his dislikes. Yet Riesgo's essay, which appeared in 2000, fails to mention the key fact of the chemical-bombing campaign, a fact that no historian of Spanish aviation can ignore. It therefore has also to be treated with caution.

[66] Hidalgo, *Cambio de rumbo*, 171–6.

appraisal.'[67] Nevertheless, the camaraderie of war in Morocco, especially in the offensive of 1924–6, helped to erode the divisions within and between the different corps of the military on active service. This was true even of the highly technical artillery, engineering, and communications corps, and the elite officers of the General Staff, all of whom had regarded themselves as separate castes in the Army of Africa and were still treated as such in the mainland army.

The General Staff, for example, tended to be the organic intellectuals of the army, students of military theory responsible for logistics, planning, map-making, and so on. They looked to the experience of armies in other countries as models. But within their ranks there were two very different castes, the Operational Unit, made up of battle-scarred officers, and the General Affairs Unit, whose officers had a more limited experience of war but were strong on theory and organization.[68] Yet all these castes, including the small and prestigious group of army pilots and officers of the Civil Guard (charged with law and order in the rearguard, but also mobilized in military operations) mixed socially with infantry and cavalry officers in camp and garrison life, a synergy impossible to find in garrison towns in Spain.[69] Their collaboration on the fields of battle after the Anual disaster imbued officers of the different corps with a common hatred of the enemy and a common purpose of retribution. They were also bound together by the secrecy of the chemical war in which the vast majority participated to one extent or another.

In stark contrast to garrison life at home, service in the Moroccan war, in whatever corps, provided officers with opportunities for the excitement of combat, for the display of heroism, for fame, promotion, good pay, comrade-ship, male bonding, affirmation of machismo, extra-marital sex in the numer-ous brothels, and, for the deeply brutalized, rape of young women from an 'inferior race'. In war the culture of machismo was such that the pressure to appear brave rather than cowardly often won over the professional evaluation of tactical choices.[70] Through war and leisure, officers posted in Morocco in the 1920s for any length of time developed a collective culture, an elite identity believed by them to be superior to any other in Spain.

Alongside them, there were officers stationed in Morocco throughout the colonial war who had no special vocation for military service in the colony and who brought to the garrisons and campaigns in Morocco the values and prac-tices of military life in Spain.[71] Many had gone to Morocco unwillingly and

[67] ADMAE Maroc 1917–40, vol. 228, p. 185.

[68] Interviews with veterans of the artillery corps, Juan Francisco Díaz Ripoll and Manuel Gutiérrez de Tovar y Beruete, on 26 Mar. 1999: Goded, *Marruecos*, 49.

[69] For a detailed and uncritical narrative of Civil Guard actions in the colonial war, see Jesús Narciso Núñez Calvo, 'La Guardia Civil en las campañas de Marruecos', in Mesa, *Las campañas*, 256–300.

[70] Mola, *Dar Akkoba*, 202.

[71] This tendency within the Army of Africa could not be defined as a caste or faction yet it played an important role in the self-definition of the Africanists. It will be discussed more fully in Ch. 8.

counted the days till they had completed their obligatory two-year service there. Some stayed longer with as little enthusiasm, simply because they came from poor families and needed to accumulate the savings that colonial military service made possible. Many were willing to take on paid work on the side despite the repeated ban on part-time jobs by the Spanish high commissioners in Morocco.[72] A confidential report of 1923 to the French Foreign Office even suggested there were two different armies in Spanish Morocco, the metropolitan army and the colonial army. In the first, officers were ready to 'pack their bags at the shortest notice' and 'lived uneasily in the inhospitable Melilla and Ceuta'.[73] The sudden collapse of the front line in July 1921 was not unconnected with the ennui of these 'peninsular' officers.

The post-Anual *revanchisme* and the reconstruction of the colonial army after 1924 ensured the eclipse of this culture and the hegemony of that of the professional colonial officer. This *revanchisme* also gave a sense of purpose and unity among its different castes for a war that could not otherwise be easily justified. They were not exposing their lives in defence of the fatherland, nor, as in the case of the British colonial officers, in defence of the empire, since, officially at least, they were acting as the agents of the sultan. The new purpose was revenging the deaths and torture of their comrades and overcoming the humiliation of defeat. The unity mitigating their divisions was a tribal loyalty against the criticism or indifference of civil society.

Nevertheless, the victory against Abdel Krim and the pacification of Morocco in 1927 raised the status of the Africanists to that of national heroes. Under their ascendancy, the new unitary spirit informing the army led to the creation in 1927 by the dictator of the Academia General Militar (AGM) in Zaragoza, with Franco as director. Dominated by Africanist officers, the AGM broke with traditional military corporatism. Its mission, as the royal decree made clear, placed more emphasis on the psychological preparation for combat than on military technique. The model of warfare in the teaching of the AGM was not based on the lessons of the First World War nor on the strategic inferences of new military technology, but on the entirely irregular colonial war in Morocco. The values that were transmitted were drawn from the mystique of the Legion, with its characteristic glorification of violence, struggle, and death.[74] At the same time, the Junta-dominated Escuela Superior de Guerra, previously manned by the more technocratic General Staff, was replaced in same year by the Escuela de Estudios Superiores Militares under the auspices of the AGM and therefore dominated by the militarist Africanists.

Whilst many of the militarists went on to new posts on the mainland, enlightened Africanists such as Castro Girona, Gómez-Jordana, and Goded

---

[72] See e.g. AAFAMM Fondo Documental Mortera, caja 4; also Rafael López Rienda, *El escándalo del millón de Larache* (Madrid, n.p., 1922), 144–7.

[73] Léon Rollin, 'Voyage à la zone espagnole', 1 Oct. 1923, ADMAE Maroc 1917–40, vol. 197, p. 19.

[74] Blanco Escolá, *La Academia*.

played an important role for a brief period between 1927 and 1931 in the renewal of links with the subjugated tribes and the re-establishment of Spanish control in northern Morocco.[75] Though they were separated after 1927, both tendencies of the Africanists and their brother officers in other units were bound together by powerful ties of camaraderie and loyalty forged during the military campaigns. As in the First World War, the experience of war in itself was highly disjunctive, setting veterans apart from those officers who had stood outside it because they had been too old or too young or had managed to evade it.[76] Their long service in the Army of Africa and their sporadic contact with Spain had turned them into an elite of officers alienated from civilian politics at home and imbued with a strong sense of mission to redeem Spain from its supposed decadence. Their hegemony over the Spanish army was evident in the latter half of Primo de Rivera's dictatorship and during Berenguer's brief tenure in his place.

Ortega y Gasset's famous phrase that 'Morocco turned the scattered soul of our Army into a closed fist' is certainly untrue of the peninsular army.[77] A large number of its officers remained loyal to the Republic in 1936, especially the Juntero supporters. But even of the Army of Africa the statement is only partially true. Until the 1930s there were a number of military factions and castes that saw their colonial roles and their military identities differently. Most of them were united around a common core of authoritarian and nationalist values, a shared ideology of authoritarian regenerationism whose chosen instrument was the colonial army. What they lacked, however, was a common political strategy. Politics among the elite of Africanist officers ranged from fascism to monarchism to authoritarian republicanism. The declaration of the Republic in 1931, therefore, found them disunited. Nevertheless, they began to draw on a shared stock of myths about the colonial war and a common hatred of the Left that were more important than their political and professional differences. Five years later the vast majority of them would unite to overthrow the Republic.

---

[75] These generals, assisted by other enlightened colonial officers such as Asensio, commander (later general) Capaz Montes, and Captains Cebollino and Cogolludo, were involved in most of the pacification plans for the territory.

[76] Eric J. Leed, *No Man's Land: Combat and Identity in World War I* (Cambridge, CUP, 1979), 74.

[77] *España invertebrada*, 15th edn. (Madrid, Revista de Occidente, 1967), 82.

CHAPTER SEVEN

The Moorish Other

THE SOCIAL ORGANIZATION and culture of northern Morocco baffled most of the Spanish colonial military. Its fluid, segmented society was not easy to understand for Europeans brought up in a codified, class-based, and at least formally democratic system. The structures of the Sultanate held sway over most of the towns but exercised little control over the countryside, despite the presence of the sultan's representatives. Before the colonial penetration of the early twentieth century, the sultan's government or Mahkzen had tried to exercise a measure of control through giving favours to local, often despotic, agents such as the caids. When that failed to raise the taxes on which the Moroccan state depended, the sultan tried, often with poor results, to send troops into the recalcitrant areas to exact the tribute by devastation. However, the traditional European view of a dichotomy between lawful and lawless areas (*bled es Mahkzen* against *bled es siba*) always overstated the difference. Even in the remote regions of northern Morocco, people were linked to other areas by trade routes, markets, and networks of religious brotherhoods and saint cults.[1]

Outside the political structures of the Mahkzen, however, social organization was highly segmented, fusing and splitting along fault-lines, in ascending order, of family (father, one or more mothers, and their children), lineage (male descent from a historically significant ancestor), sub-clan, clan (a subdivision of tribe), tribe or *kabyle* (the largest grouping of related people), and tribal confederation. The extended family was called the *adem*, a community that could include men without land or family. The fundamental component of the society was the male individual, a combined warrior and worker, who entered into competition for resources and power often with his own family. Thus brother sometimes fought brother, but both could unite to oppose cousins or join with cousins to confront lineages and so on along a horizontal line of association and conflict.[2] Tribal confederations were controlled by the *yemaa*, a committee of notable elders from the different tribes, who would be chosen and sustained by collective decision-making among males. The *leff* was a political alliance formed by segments within a tribe or among tribes as a whole to protect themselves from internal or external threat.

[1] Seddon, *Moroccan Peasants*, 45. For a recent statement of the traditional view see Tessainer, *El Raisuni*, 15–17.
[2] David Montgomery Hart, *The Aith Waryaghar of the Moroccan Rif: An Ethnography and History* (Tucson, University of Arizona, 1976).

Mediating these alliances and confrontations were representative councils set up at each level from lineage group to tribe, as well as Mahkzen spokesmen or religious figures from holy lineages exempt from warrior status, such as the young Raisuni. Violence in the area was a result mainly of blood feuds, quarrels over access to water and pasture or the possession of livestock, and disputes over honour and reputation. Petty tyrants often created a state within the state because they were favoured by the sultan and appointed as an official of the Mahkzen. Though private property was not highly developed, embryonic class divisions had emerged at the beginning of the century between flock-owners and labourers; the latter had attached themselves to the wealthy to work or receive food and protection.

As we saw in Chapters 1 and 2, European penetration exacerbated the tensions between the Mahkzen and the tribes as well as rival groupings in the same area. Even before the Spanish military began to invade Moroccan territory, social relations had already been distorted by European commerce. For most of the nineteenth century contact with European traders had been mainly indirect. Because it was difficult for Europeans to go into the interior, they sold goods to Moroccan traders who then took them inland to sell on. The highly profitable arms contraband from the 1880s opened up trade routes for foreigners, and the rapid increase in firepower in northern Morocco began to upset the delicate balance of power. Foreign investment in mines and land led to the emergence of powerful tribal councillors or *amghars* favoured by the Spanish and bribed with monthly payments or 'pensiones'. Other chiefs emerged through their control of a strategic site, such as a mountain pass along a trade route. The purchase of land for colonization by Europeans, especially where there was no clear ownership, also heightened tensions by depriving pastoral workers of land used for grazing and profiting local chieftains who seized the opportunity for self-enrichment.

The extent of the penetration of European mining capital into Morocco has not been fully appreciated in Western texts. By 1921 nineteen Spanish companies had taken over more than 41,000 hectares of territory, mainly in the northeast of Morocco, of which three, the Abraham Pinto company, the Sindicato Minero del Nordeste de Marruecos, and the Compañía Española de Minas del Rif, accounted for 19,000 hectares. At the same time, ten non-Spanish European companies, three French, three British, and four Dutch, controlled over 14,000 hectares of land. To these 136,000 acres should be added the unquantified land devoted to the transport of minerals by rail to the ports on the coast for shipment to Europe.[3]

European encroachment gave rise to a whole spectrum of responses among Moroccans, from collaboration to armed resistance. These responses have not

---

[3] Figures taken from 'Las Minas de Marruecos. El trabajo de la Comisión Arbitral', *Revista Hispano Africano* (Mar. 1923), año 2, número 3.

been understood in any of the Spanish historiography. Some very recent military histories still churn out the old clichés about the 'xenophobic', 'deceitful', and 'criminal impulses' of the Moroccans who resisted the Spanish invasion of their lands. Other, more sophisticated, histories nevertheless swallow the military myths of the past that portray the Moroccans who resisted Spanish military expansion as rebels and those who collaborated as affectionate friends of Spain.[4]

Probably for the vast majority of northern Moroccans, the Spanish were the traditional Other, the most ferocious opponent of Islam, who had expelled their ancestors from Spain, had continued to wage a sporadic war against them, and were now invading their territory. Collaboration was often a means of survival or, as in the case of Raisuni, a strategy for evading confrontation and maintaining local power. Few can have accepted the Spanish legitimization of their occupation of Moroccan soil, especially when it became clear to those, such as the Khattabi family, who had collaborated at the beginning of colonial rule, that Spain was not introducing the economic benefits they had expected.

Beneath the flow of fine-sounding intentions voiced by Spanish politicians and military chiefs lay the reality of colonial culture. In those areas that did not resist Spanish penetration, Moroccan minerals were being extracted at the lowest possible cost for the highest possible profit to investors in Europe. Spanish workers were given preference over Moroccans in jobs in the mines. Olive trees that took a decade to grow were being chopped down to provide fuel for the troops, when officers could easily purchase wood. Land was being taken over or sold by their chieftains to the Spanish company La Colonizadora at knock-down prices, for resale to Spanish settlers at much higher prices.[5] Houses belonging to Moroccans were 'borrowed' for the better comfort of officers. The colonial war and the presence of a huge army were beginning to destroy the local subsistence economy based on land and herds and the trading of goods across northern Morocco.

Despite the efforts of enlightened officers like Marina, the Spanish took little heed of the sensibilities of the culture they were expropriating. According to the Abdel Krim brothers, a Christian church built for the fifty or so Spanish inhabitants of Nador displayed a sculpture of the patron saint of Spain, St James or Santiago, killing Moors. The effect of Spanish colonialism on the 'natives', as a Catalan rank-and-file veteran of the post-Anual campaign later wrote, was of 'civilized barbarity'. The civilized Moroccans were those who

---

[4] e.g. Flores and Cicuéndez, *Guerra aérea* (this publication has cartoon illustrations in which caricatures of the Moorish enemy are accompanied by accurate drawings of planes and their equipment that are useful to the historian), and José Luis De Mesa Gutiérrez, '1919–1927, casi una década de sangre', in Mesa *et al.*, *Las campañas*.

[5] See e.g. Pando, *Historia*, 85–6.

had learnt to hurl insults in impeccable Spanish as they shot at the Spanish troops.[6]

One day when his battalion had been given the day off, the Catalan soldier was standing on a cliff-top overlooking the Mediterranean when a Moroccan approached him and pointed out the snow-capped peaks of the Sierra Nevada in Andalusia that could be discerned in the distance. 'There Spain,' he said, 'that is your land . . . you want to go there . . . why come here? Spain is big.' In their subsequent conversation, the Catalan learnt a simple truth. For this particular Moroccan, who had become a labourer in the employ of Spaniards, Spain had not brought progress. 'Before, I have house, have land, now everything like this,' he said, pointing to some ruined villages nearby. 'I earn little, eat bad, have little ones. But I do not want to go to mines because I earn same there and work more: twelve, fourteen hours a day. Mineral dust cover throat and eyes: blood come out of mouth. Many die inside, in the mine . . .' 'This was the key to it all,' wrote the Catalan soldier. 'They submit to us and fear us, they only show themselves to be our friends because they can't do anything else . . . This same man, whose hand I have just shaken, could just as easily have stood up to me face to face and we could be killing each other.'[7]

Like the Catalan, a military driver on service in Morocco called Juan Sánchez showed a subtler understanding of the Moroccans' reaction to the presence of Spaniards than that of many officers. He had twice asked friendly young Moroccans who spoke Spanish if they would like to go to Spain, expecting them to be enthusiastic. One said yes, 'with such a special smile that I was left not knowing whether he wanted to go to Spain or not'. The other, 'without saying anything, lowered his head and smiled'.[8] Sánchez's delicate implication was clear. They disliked the presence of the Spanish but had to ingratiate themselves with them in order to survive. Yet they could not break faith with their own feelings.

In contrast, officers sent reports in which, probably quite genuinely, they expressed their satisfaction at the affection and admiration of the 'natives' towards them. One of these reports, written less than seven months before the Anual disaster, noted that 'the homage of the subjugated tribes is loyal and sincere; submission is complete and the confidence that they place in Spain is absolute'.[9] Yet after Anual, many Spanish officers learnt to see the friendly gestures of many Moroccans as deceitful. Pilots who flew over the barley fields during the cease-fire of 1923 witnessed the spring harvesting and the 'more or less friendly greetings' of the reapers. But when the harvest was over that year, according to a report by the commander-in-chief in the spring of 1924, the peasants changed their tools for rifles and began to send bullets at the planes

---

[6] J. M. Prous i Vila, *Quatre gotes de Sang. Dietari d'un català al Maroc* (Barcelona, Llibreria Catalonia, 1936), 218 and 123; for the sculpture see Oteyza, *Abdel Krim*, 68–9.

[7] Prous, *Quatre gotes*, 212–14.   [8] Sánchez, 'Diario', 23 and 33.

[9] 'Informe político-militar sobre la zona. 1920 Marruecos', AGPR caja 15510/12.

rather than greetings. What needed to be done, he concluded, was to destroy their crops or prevent the harvesting, exchange, and sale of the produce, thereby depriving the villages of their only means of living.[10]

The violent response of most officers to Morrocan resistance had widely different sources of self-justification, stretching from simple racism to the reluctant adoption of brutality for the eventual good of its victims. Behind all these lay an implicit assumption, typical of colonial ideology and based on a crude Darwinist model, that Western civilization was the highest stage in the progression of mankind. The poverty and backwardness of Moroccan society was thus the consequence of a lack of contact with the West. In fact, as I have argued, some of the features of this society that the Spanish disliked were precisely the result of the penetration of European colonialism.

The intellectuals of the movement of anti-colonial resistance, such as the Abdel Krim brothers, were keenly aware of the profound shortcomings of the society in which they lived. But they turned against Spain because it was not bringing the benefits that they had expected from a more developed nation, nor was it adapting to the environment of the colonized society. Abdel Krim himself declared to a French journalist: 'My brother and I lived ten years amongst them and with them, enough time by far to convince us of their weakness and their total incomprehension not only of Rifian politics but also of the Muslim soul.'[11]

Indeed, the movement of resistance in the Rif was united only by its opposition to colonial invasion. The nucleus of leaders around the Abdel Krim brothers had a very different vision of the cause they were fighting for to that of the vast majority of their supporters. From what we can gather from the interviews they gave to the Western media and from published sources, they were seeking to create a modern Islamic state embracing a Western model of modernization while retaining some of the features of local religion, culture, and social organization.[12] The Abdel Krim brothers and some of their closest advisors had worked for the Spanish (the younger brother had completed his university education in Spain) and were conscious of the economic benefits of more developed nations. They wished to transform their society by an intelligent use of the Western tools of development. Their movement was therefore a modernizing Islamic nationalism.

They thus opposed many of the traditional customs of Moroccan life that they regarded as backward and barbaric. Amongst these were the feud, the

---

[10] 'Informe sobre la Actuación de la Aviación en el Protectorado', 4 Mar. 1924, AGA Africa, caja M12, exp. 2, p. 2.

[11] Roger-Matthieu (ed.), *Mémoires*, 71.

[12] The main sources for the following analysis are, 'Mohammed Ben Abdel Krim el Jatabi', *Fundamentos de Antropología*, nos. 4 and 5 (Granada, 1996); *Abd-el-Krim et la république du rif. Actes du colloque international d'études historiques et sociologiques, 18–20 janvier 1973* (Paris, Maspéro, 1976); Madariaga, *España*; C. R. Pennell, *A Country with a Government and a Flag: The Rif War in Morocco 1921–1926* (Wisbech, Cambs, Middle East and North Africa Studies Press, 1986); Woolman, *Rebels*; Roger-Matthieu (ed.), *Mémoires*.

vendetta, and the death penalty, which involved beheading or stoning to death (though Abdel Krim chose to retain the death penalty during the war period). Of the many reforms they carried out, the system of tribal alliances called the *leff* was abolished, as well as the custom of the collective oath whereby the family and supporters of someone accused under Koranic law could join the accused in a collective defence by oath. These reforms were driven in great measure by Abdel Krim's support for the Salafiya movement, a reformist religious current advocating a return to a purer, less mediated practice of Islam. In a society in which men hardly ever prayed and women not at all, Abdel Krim made the saying of prayers obligatory five times a day. Failure to do so merited a fifteen- to twenty-day service on the front for men, while women had to give a hen as a penalty.[13]

Europeans misread the term with which the leaders of the new movement designated the new state they had created in the Rif. The so-called Republic of the Rif rested on a Moroccanization of a European political term. The word *ripublik* had two meanings in Moroccan parlance. The first was equivalent to *siba* or rebellion against the Mahkzen, while the second merely denoted groups of people living or working together. In the latter sense, Abdel Krim described the Spanish military Juntas as a *ripublik*, just as groups of soldiers in each company of his army were a *ripublik*. Where it was used to designate such groups, it corresponded to the Moroccan word *Al Ashra*, given to the circle of four or five comrades in the battalions who ate and drank tea together, a practice that continued amongst the Regulares in the Civil War in Spain.[14] In the first meaning of the term, *ripublik* indicated a rejection of the sultan and his government, not as institutions, but in their current policy of collaboration with the colonial powers. Thus, Abdel Krim would admit to the authority of the sultan only if he were independent of the colonial powers and not, as he claimed, their prisoner.[15]

The progressive discourse of the Abdel Krims and their immediate entourage was remote from the culture of the vast majority of their supporters, for whom the war against the Spaniard was a traditional and bloodthirsty jihad. In any case, the mass harkas were usually provisional, dependent on instant success, and likely to disintegrate at any moment simply because cooperation across all the tribes was normally shunned.[16] Abdel Krim had only managed to gather together the fragmented dissidence of the Rifian people by

[13] David M. Hart, 'Dos resistentes bereberes al colonialismo franco-español en Marruecos y sus legados islámicos: Bin 'Abd Al-Krim y 'Assu U-Baslam', in 'Mohammed', *Fundamentos*, 51–5.

[14] The example of the Juntas was given to the American journalist Vincent Sheean in an exceptional interview in early 1924: Sheean, *Adventures*, 179; the 'Al Ashra' analogy was made to me in interviews with Abdessalam Abdessalam Ben Husain Rian and Mohammed Maati Al Amrani.

[15] Madariage, *España*, 275–84 and David Montgomery Hart, 'De "Ripublik" à "République": les institutions sociopolitiques rifaines el les réformes d'Abd-el-Krim', in *Abd-el-Krim*, 33–45; Sheean, *Adventures*, 179–80.

[16] Dunn, *Resistance*, 270–1.

virtue of the Anual victory, which had catapulted him into the leadership. Before 1921, as we have seen, he and his family had been distrusted or attacked because of their collaboration with the Spanish. The American journalist who managed to interview him after being smuggled through French and Spanish lines became keenly aware of the wide gap in the Rif movement between the rural muhayeddin and the urbanites at the centre of the government. He also noticed two distinct parties at the makeshift 'court' of the Abdel Krims, the war party and the civilian advisers who had served in French or Spanish institutions and were keen to seek independence through negotiation.[17]

An anecdote recounted by a Spanish ex-prisoner speaks volumes about the gap among the Rifians between the urban elite and the rural muhayeddin. He had been on a chain-gang building a track when a Ford car appeared bearing, according to the Spaniard, none other than Abdel Krim. He and other prisoners had to help push the car as it laboured up a slope. When it reached the top, the Rifian leader got out to thank them. He asked the prisoner what he thought of Primo de Rivera, to which he replied that he had not had any news from Spain for months. A few days later the guards delivered to the prisoners various issues of the French Moroccan newspaper *L'Écho d'Oran*.[18]

In order to ensure some degree of unity in the movement, Abdel Krim and his advisers had scrupulously to maintain a system of alliances with tribes and fragments of tribes, even within the army they were organizing. Thus, in the harka or guerrilla forces that backed up the front-line troops, they made sure that positions of equal distinction were given to leaders of tribal factions that had previously warred with each other. At the height of his power, Abdel Krim had 60,000 harka soldiers at his disposal, two-thirds of whom were from the Rif and the rest mainly from Jebala and Gomara. At the core of this army were his own elite troops, drawn almost entirely from his own tribe and organized along the lines of the Mahkzen army.[19] All his able-bodied male supporters were supposed regularly to give their services free under a system called *idala*, serving either on the front or as labourers. Those who could not were obliged to pay for a substitute. The rest of the population, on the other hand, was expected to feed and supply the muhayeddin.[20]

With the help of German mercenaries and deserters from the Spanish and French Foreign Legions, the Rifian regular army began to acquire some of the technological skills of a modern army. Thus, it was able to deploy the Hotchkiss machine-guns captured from the Spanish and the Schneider cannons seized or bought from the French. Led by Abdel Krim's Spanish-trained

---

[17] Sheean, *Adventures*, 134 and 182. Pennell also identifies a technocratic elite amongst the Abdel Krims' advisers: *A Country*, 100.

[18] Bosque, 'Prisionero', 26. The only doubt about this anecdote is that the chauffeur acted as interpreter between the prisoners and Abdel Krim when in fact the Rifian leader spoke very good Spanish. It may be, however, that he insisted on communicating only in *shelja* in his own sphere of influence.

[19] Hart, 'Dos resistentes', 53.   [20] Habtí, 'La resistencia', 108 and 208.

brother, some young Rifians acquired a thorough knowledge of the telephone and telegraph system that spread from their headquarters to most of the area they controlled. They were quickly able to install and operate the exchanges and keep the lines repaired. The poles that held up the lines were inserted deep into the soil to resist the strong winds that often blew in the region. Until then, the only long-distance communications system amongst the muhayeddin was shouting from mountain-top to mountain-top. The 6,000-strong regular Rif army adopted some of the organization of European armies. The grades of the caids who commanded its units were distinguished by coloured stripes on bands of green cloth worn as turbans. The army also adopted the German goose-stepping march, like its most ferocious enemy, the Spanish Legion. The effectiveness of this new force was noted by General Goded, who wrote that it brought 'a taste of European war' to the colonial struggle, 'the sensation of fighting against a regular and organized army, obedient to a single, skilled command'.[21]

Despite the huge haul of Spanish arms of July 1921 and the fact that the French appeared to do little to prevent arms trade across their Moroccan frontier, the Rif military command needed to acquire considerably more arms and munitions from wherever they could. Their fighters were expected to provide their own arms and munitions. Some sold a possession like a cow and bought a rifle and bullets in the souk with the money. One supporter who asked Jerirou for a weapon was told he could only get one by joining barehanded in an attack on a Spanish position with the armed muhayeddin.[22]

Given the paucity of arms, the Rifian leaders sought support abroad as well. One of their apparent backers in Europe, an Englishman called Charles Alfred Percy Gardiner, turned out to be something of a charlatan. He and Abdel Krim's brother M'hammed (as vice-president of the Republic) signed an agreement on 30 April 1923 whereby the former would raise a loan of 1 million pounds sterling for the Rif government in exchange for generous commercial concessions in the new Republic. But the Rifians never received a penny from Gardiner, who was not in a position to raise such a loan in the first place.[23]

Another contract appears to have been drawn up between the same parties in the preceding month for the purchase of £300,000-worth of arms, munitions, and supplies and the hiring of instructors and mercenaries. It may well have been an earlier version of the same contract. Apart from the sums involved, the only difference is that the contract was accompanied by a list of the goods required. This makes extraordinary reading. Gardiner agreed to buy 30,000 rifles, 2 million machine-gun rounds, a submarine and its crew twelve planes, 500 incendiary bombs, 14,500 airplane TNT bombs, and so on. The

[21] *Marruecos*, 205; Sheean, *Adventures*, 140–7; 'Abd-el-Krim's Power', *The Times*, 29 Dec. 1925.

[22] Hach Mohammed M'Hauesh and El Hach Abdel Krim Ben Ahmed Ben Ali, interviews.

[23] Madariaga, *España*, 535.

total number of men to be hired, among pilots, artillery instructors, weapons specialists, mechanics, and radio engineers, amounted to 146. More surprisingly, Gardiner committed himself to purchasing fifty gas shells, that is to say, shells filled with toxic chemicals of an unstipulated kind for use by the Rifian artillery. Given that mustard gas had not yet been used in the Moroccan war, it is conceivable that the gas referred to was phosgene or chloropicrine, first used by the Spanish in November 1921, rather than mustard gas.[24]

Needless to say, nothing came of this contract, and the Rifian army had to rely almost entirely on the weapons they were able to smuggle into their territory by boat or across the French Moroccan frontier, and on those captured from the Spanish forces. When France entered the war an important source of arms dried up. As for 'gas shells', it appears that the only toxic weapons the Rif fighters ever tried to use were the shells and bombs that failed to explode when they fell in their land, as we saw in Chapter 5. For obvious reasons, they were not the most effective of their arms. So the Abdel Krims' efforts to equip themselves with modern weapons were repeatedly frustrated. And as the French and Spanish forces advanced into the heart of the Rifian resistance in late 1925, local muhayeddin held on to the weapons they would normally have supplied to the Rif army in order to defend themselves. Thus, the success of the Franco-Spanish offensive was due in part to the declining firepower of Abdel Krim's army. A French quartermaster-sergeant captured and later released by the Rifians told his officers that he had witnessed Abdel Krim 'weep from discouragement', quite possibly the result of this dwindling of his military capacity.[25]

Before examining the Spanish military's images of the Moorish Other, we need to look briefly at the reasons that led many Moroccans to fight on their side. The earliest Moroccan unit created by Spain was the native police force, based on the French model and led by Spanish officers. As we saw in Chapter 2, resistance against colonial expansion led the Spanish to create the Regulares in 1912, who soon became their front-line troops alongside the Legion. Like the Indians who fought for the British in India, the Moroccans joined the Regulares largely to supplement the income of their families. Their enlistment was often based on the seasonal calendar, and many simply drifted off when the sowing or reaping seasons came round. Huge numbers of men were driven to join when the rainfall had been insufficient. Drought played a crucial role, as we shall see later, in the fortunes of the military insurrection of 1936. But like the Indians also, enlistment in the Spanish army was an assertion among many Moroccans of a martial self-image. The sense of identity as a warrior was deeply rooted in the mountain tribes of the Rif, and it must have influenced their choice of economic strategy when confronted with poor harvests. Many sought agricultural work in Algeria or in French Morocco. But enlistment in

[24] AGA Asuntos Exteriores, caja M-34.
[25] Report of 15 Dec. 1925 in SHAT 7N 2763; for the decline in the supply of arms see SHM R635, leg. 451, carp. 10.

the Regulares provided an opportunity to assert martial skills and awarded a higher status than that of a labourer.[26]

After the Anual debacle, the Spanish command tried to complement the Regulares with more dependable units. They established irregular guerrilla units based on tribes or tribal fragments, called the 'harkas' from the Arab term originally denoting the expeditionary forces of volunteer fighters organized by the sultan or his government to quell internal dissidence. The first harka funded by the Army of Africa was raised by Abdel Malek, a caid from the southern part of the Rif in the Spanish Protectorate who had been opposed to the Khattabi family for some time. Unlike the Regulares, the harkas were made up of men from the same village or grouping of villages, and each battalion or *mía* was led by the local caid, so that indigenous authority remained strong. They tended to be used in their own territory and, knowing the terrain by heart, were more mobile, more united, and less subject to privation than the Regulares.[27] Used in some of the fiercest engagements, the harkas played an important role in defeating the Rifian army. Their casualties were correspondingly high. Abdel Malek himself was killed in action and was replaced by the up-and-coming colonial officer Enrique Varela, who gave a new name to the unit, the Melilla Harka, and reorganized its structure. This harka maintained a force of about 850 native troops, replacing the dead and wounded with new recruits. Of its total number over the three-year campaign from 1924 to 1927, 255 were killed and 703 wounded.[28]

From this brief history of Abdel Malek's harka it should be clear that these irregular units fought on the Spanish side for very different reasons to the Regulares. They were conscripted by their chiefs, who had a long history of paid collaboration with the Spanish authorities. They were also mobilized to fight against tribes or tribal sections with which they had long-standing disputes. They thus tended to be more reliable than the Regulares, which were composed of individuals from different parts of Spanish Morocco and from French Morocco, who joined for mainly economic reasons and therefore deserted frequently when they had accumulated some money or booty. While the French could enrol mercenary soldiers from different parts of their empire to fight in their Moroccan Protectorate, the Spanish had to rely almost entirely on Moroccan troops. In certain circumstances, like the events of July 1921, the Regulares were susceptible to the enticement of the muhayeddin to desert and join their brothers on the other side. Uncertainty about the loyalty of front-line troops contributed to the stress of the Spanish colonial officer's life.

Indeed, the response of officers to their colonial environment was ambivalent. The contrast between Spanish values and those of a complex non-European society such as northern Morocco gave rise to contradictory

---

[26] For the Indian experience, see Omissi, *The Sepoy*, 51–2.

[27] n.a., *Historial de la Harka de Melilla. Campañas Años 1924–1926* (Melilla, n.p., n.d.), 27–33.

[28] Ibid., 154–5.

reactions—insecurity and attraction, racism and mimicry. Even before the new colonial penetration, Spanish culture was already imbued with myths about the identity of the Moroccan or Moorish Other, and colonial officers as well as soldiers must have brought these perceptions with them in their mental baggage. Popular images of the Moor were embedded in Spanish culture and imbibed through children's games, popular expressions, songs, and festivals, such as the completely distorted annual re-enactment of the Christian defeat of the Spanish Muslims. The landscape in many parts of Spain was dotted with Moorish symbols, from the great *mudéjar* architecture of Andalusia to the coastal watchtowers built after the defeat of the Moors in 1492 to maintain vigilance against their return. Amongst the brief written communications sent by soldiers to their families were postcards with traditional caricatures of the Moor on the front, representing them as either cruel or stupid.[29]

Official discourse had reconstructed the shared past of Spanish, Muslims, and Jews into a conflictive relationship, when in fact they had lived in harmony for several centuries. Cultural exchange, intermarriage, and political alliances across ethnic and religious boundaries had constantly taken place during this period.[30] Such was the interpenetration between the three cultures that after the expulsion of practising Muslims and Jews many Spaniards felt insecure about their genetic origins in the new conditions of ethnic cleansing carried out by the Inquisition from the sixteenth century onwards.[31] Cultural traditions shared by Muslim and Christian Spaniards, especially those who inhabited the south and the east of the peninsula, must have persisted for centuries despite their separation, and might account for part of the attraction felt by many colonial officers to the Moroccan environment. Indeed, the enlightened Africanist officer may well have thought of the Moroccan as a younger brother, a descendant of the inhabitants of Spanish Islam.[32] To these contradictory images of repulsion and allure were added the nineteenth-century romantic projections of Moorish culture influenced by the 'textual universe' of European orientalism and the recent rediscovery in Spain of the border ballads of the sixteenth century.[33]

At the same time, the Moor was seen as the archetypal Other of Spanish national identity. The enmification of the Moor was reinforced by the experience of soldiers in the nineteenth-century military engagements in Morocco.

[29] Henk Driessen, 'Images of Spanish Colonialism in the Rif: An Essay in Historical Anthropology and Photography', *A Critique of Anthropology*, 7: 1 (1987).

[30] María Rosa de Madariaga, 'Imagen del moro en la memoria colectiva del pueblo español y retorno del moro en la Guerra Civil de 1936', *Revista Internacional de Sociología*, 46 (1988), 575–99.

[31] Cervantes's short play, *El Retablo de las Maravillas*, depicts the uncertainties amongst Spaniards about whether they had any Jewish origins. The concept could extend to Arab descent.

[32] Josep Lluís Mateo Dieste, *El 'moro' entre los primitivos. El caso del Protectorado español en Marruecos* (Barcelona, Fundación 'La Caixa', 1997), 85.

[33] Edward Said, *Orientalism: Western Conceptions of the Orient*, 2nd edn. (Harmondsworth, Penguin, 1995), 50–3. See also Juan Goytisolo, 'Cara y cruz del moro en nuestra literatura', in *Revista Internacional de Sociología*, 46 (1988), 607–16.

Popular culture identified him with war. The target in the fairground firing-range was often a Moor, while soldiers' matchboxes had an outlandish portrait of a Moor on the cover. Both officers and men, therefore, arrived in Morocco for the first time with deeply rooted prejudices against its people. Overlaying the typical racism of European colonizers was that special antagonism against the Arab created over several centuries by the myth-makers of Spanish history.

In his private diary, an officer confessed that when he arrived for the first time in Morocco in 1919 he responded to its inhabitants quite irrationally according to the racist stereotypes he had imbibed in Spain. As the tug taking him to the port of Larache moored by the dock: 'With what astonishment I see a huge Moor blacker than pitch reach out his arms to help me disembark; I stay rooted to the spot looking at him, not daring to accept his protection because I thought at the time that all Moors were enemies, and that this one would seize the opportunity of having me in his arms to throw me into the water.'[34]

The insecurity underlying the relationship with Moroccans was reflected in the colonizing zeal of the early twentieth century that sought to dismiss the complicities between Spanish and Moroccan cultures and emphasize the essential difference between the civilizing agent and the backward recipient of progress.[35] This new layer of colonialism overlaid the traditional discourse of the unfinished religious crusade against the infidel. The military saw itself as the trail-blazer of civilization in a primitive and largely innocent society, that would welcome progress with open arms once its initial resistance was overcome. '[A]rms will plough the virgin soil,' wrote a military newspaper in 1909, 'so that agriculture, industry, mining should flourish in it, so that through it roads will open that will be the arteries of commerce.'[36] Yet the same newspaper implicitly acknowledged the special historical relationship between Spain and Morocco. In a burst of rhetoric coloured by the exotic projections of nineteenth-century romanticism, it wrote that Morocco represented 'a fatal attraction, an irresistible urge, a mysterious calling, whose voice of enchantment is heard, from time to time, leading us fatally and irredeemably, shackling our will, forcing us sometimes against our own desires, towards the fields of Africa . . .'[37]

The tenacious opposition of many Moroccans to Spanish penetration encouraged a new, more complex picture of the Moroccan Other. In the intermittent colonial war that followed, the Spanish army mobilized Moroccan versus Moroccan. The ease with which they were able to pay Moroccans to fight against their fellow countrymen was a reflection of the hardship of life in the countryside, which had driven many landworkers in the past to look for

[34] Francesc Arbolí Nadal, 'Ligeras memorias e impresiones de mi permanencia en Africa (territorio de Larache). Años 1919–20 y 21', unpublished diary, p. 3.
[35] Madariaga, 'Imagen', 585.   [36] *El Ejército Español*, 7 Aug. 1909.
[37] Ibid., 'España en Africa', 24 July 1909.

harvest work in Algeria. But it also reflected the segmented nature of Moroccan society. Spaniards could draw on old antagonisms between tribes and clans to deploy members of one against another. A dominant fault-line among Moroccan tribes was the primary opposition between tribes of the plains and those of the mountains, but even amongst the latter there were long-standing enmities that were continually being renewed. The razzia, or exemplary partial destruction of villages accompanied by looting, was a traditional form of punishment or revenge exacted by one tribe or tribal segment against another, and this became a common form of attrition sanctioned by Spanish officers among their native troops. Many of the atrocities of the colonial war were committed by Moroccans serving in the Spanish army against the people of other tribes.[38]

Yet who the enemy of the Spanish was never became very clear, because Spain's policy of divide and rule encouraged tribes to change allegiance. Moroccan soldiers fighting for Spain sometimes went over to the enemy of Spain, their fellow Moroccans. This created great problems, because enmification or the construction of the Other is vital to military effectiveness in war. War often provides a rallying-point for elite-based, traditional notions of national identity. In certain contexts it helps to assert an identity that is either not deeply ingrained or has become increasingly problematical. It does so, above all, by creating an external and caricatural Other, against which a unicultural and one-dimensional national identity can be more safely portrayed; one grotesque caricature against another. What people are invited to fight against often becomes more important than what they are supposed to be fighting for. The invention of the enemy involves a high degree of self-dehumanization, a switching off of empathy for other people.[39] This process of disassociation with the enemy also leads to a simplification of complex identities at home and an uncritical acceptance of the official discourse of war. Soldiers fight better against an enemy they think they know than for principles that are often quite hazy, none more so than in a colonial war. Indeed, the strength of nationalism or colonialism is often not so much a sense of a shared identity as a sense of what you are all against.

The spectacular military disasters of 1909 and especially 1921 facilitated the elaboration of the Moroccan Other as ignorant, primitive, and fanatical and therefore a source of legitimation for the war. The 'civilizing mission' of the early discourse of Spanish colonialism gave way, in the prevailing mood of jingoism, to a spirit of revenge against those Moroccans who had resisted it, the bad Moroccans. Neither the dislocation of Moroccan life by European penetration, nor the brutality of the French and Spanish armies of occupation were

---

[38] Arbolí, 'Ligeras memorias', 101–2, 106–7, and 115. See also Mola, *Dar Akkoba*, 153–6.

[39] Robert W. Reiber and Robert J. Kelly, 'Substance and Shadow: Images of the Enemy', in Robert W. Reiber (ed.), *The Psychology of War and Peace: The Image of the Enemy* (London and New York, Plenum Press, 1991), 3–39.

heeded or even known about. In the widespread racist discourse of the time, the enemy was portrayed as, in addition to being ignorant and fanatical, barbaric, bestial, degenerate, deceitful, indolent, and so on. Conversely, the Moroccans who collaborated with Spanish rule were also racially inferior because they were duplicitous, pliant, and submissive, as their acceptance of colonialism seemed to demonstrate.[40]

These two alternative identities, of course, conformed to the typical racist stereotypes of Western colonialism that posited pseudo-scientific justifications for colonial oppression. The Victorian British had fondly imagined in the early nineteenth century that Westernization would transform 'natives' into English gentlemen. The resistance of these natives to Western acculturation gave rise to a rationale of racial inferiority that denied cultural difference and stressed the need for the subjugation of colonial peoples into the categories of the West.[41] In fact, the behaviour of the 'natives', however caricatured, was a response to colonial power. To take two contradictory characteristics, fanaticism and duplicity were part of a distorted Western reading of the colonial subjects' ways of surviving or opposing colonialism. For example, the violence that the Beni Bu Yahi tribe meted out on the survivors of the Monte Arruit siege derived from the accumulation of appalling injustices they had been subjected to by colonialism.[42]

For its part, the colonial military had a vested interest in hyping up the ferocity of the Moroccan enemy. An emphasis on the prowess of the rebellious tribes helped to strengthen demands for promotion and medals and more arms. Thus, in military reports and accounts sympathetic to officers, battles became epic encounters with indomitable tribes. In fact it was at first a war fought by a minor colonial power, with scarce and antiquated weapons and deeply reluctant, relatively untrained soldiers doing military service, against peasant and shepherd communities used to occasional skirmishes and sometimes token raids against their local rivals. The inadequacy of the Spanish conscript led to the recruitment of a mercenary army from Moroccan tribesmen seeking extra money to survive in an environment made even harsher by colonial penetration. Both they and the fellow Moroccans they fought against became adept at the war they were forced to fight. Nevertheless, it remained a peripheral war,

[40] Fernando de Urquijo, *La campaña del Rif en 1909. Juicios de un testigo* (Madrid, n.p., 1910); A. Serra Orts, *Recuerdos de la Guerra del Kert de 1911–12* (Barcelona, n.p., 1914); Federico Pita, *La acción militar y política de España en África a través de los tiempos* (Madrid, Publicación de la Revista técnica de Infantería y Caballería, 1915); Arsenio Martínez de Campos, *Melilla 1921* (Ciudad Real, El Pueblo Manchego, 1922); Bastos Ansart, *El desastre de Anual*; Goded, *Marruecos*. Even accounts critical of the military tended to show the same lack of sympathy and understanding of the impact of Spanish colonialism on Rif culture; thus Juan Guixé, *El Rif en sombras. (Lo que yo he visto en Melilla)* (n.p., n.d. [1921]), 164–75.

[41] Ronald Robinson, John Gallagher, and Alice Denny, *Africa and the Victorians: The Official Mind of Imperialism* (London, Macmillan, 1961, p. 10; Homi K. Bhabha, *The Location of Culture*, London, Routledge, 1994), 66–84.

[42] Pando, *Historia*, 85–6.

cut off from many of the strategic, tactical, and technological advances of the European armies in the post-First World War period.

Just as nineteenth-century European culture gained in identity by setting itself off against the Orient, finding in Orientalism a sort of surrogate and even underground self, so Spanish identity and purpose in Morocco were heightened by the intense enmification of the Moroccan rebel.[43] The invention of the enemy's identity also served to arouse subterranean sexual fantasies among the literate supporters of the war. A journalist present in the post-Anual campaign wrote the following description of a young Rifian woman: 'Beneath her jellaba . . . it was easy to guess the perfection of her bodily form, with the shape and the firmness of pagan virgins. I observed her uncovered, olive-skinned face; her eyes, with their infinite gaze, with the depth and darkness of an abyss, and her plump, sensual, carmine lips . . . [But in her eyes] was a cynical and horrifying stare in which could be seen for an instant all the ferocity of these wild women, hunters of men . . .'[44] That is almost incitement to rape, combining lust with hate.

The caricature of the Moroccan Other was at times so exaggerated that it resembled the noble savage in an opera by Handel or Rameau, modulated by the erotic texts of the time. Thus, according to the same report, the Rifian chieftain El Chadly had various wives, but one in particular, 'a divine Circasian, his favourite, who fights alongside him. The two love each other tenderly and this savage idyll is not interrupted even in the clamour of battle and defeat nor in the midst of the roar of cannons. A day of blood and defeat ends for them in a truce of darkness, an epilogue of lovemaking.'[45]

The problem, as I have mentioned, was that it was often difficult to identify who were 'good' Moroccans and who were 'bad'.[46] The slipperiness of the concept of the Moroccan Other was exemplified by the wily sharif Raisuni, who professed to welcome an alliance with the Spanish while ignoring the terms dictated by the military. As we saw in Chapter 2, he managed for a year or so to persuade the bluff Colonel Silvestre of his good intentions, but then continued to raise through the use of force the taxes he had agreed to end. He also acquired land through illegal means, treated his prisoners savagely, and dealt secretly with German companies. The reaction of some colonial officers like Silvestre was to dismiss the ambiguities and half-tones of the Moroccan Other. You could not trust a Moroccan out of your sight. Their natural duplicitousness meant that tolerance and half-measures were unproductive. Only military action would instil respect for civilization.

But Spain needed Moroccan soldiers to crush the Moroccan rebels, and they needed to display the supposedly Spanish virtue of dependability. An attempt to resolve the dilemma was the attribution of a latent nobility to the Berber race,

[43] Said, *Orientalism*, 3.   [44] Urquijo, *La campaña*, 17–19.   [45] Ibid., 39.

[46] Madariaga, 'Imagen', *Revista Internacional de Sociología*, 46 (1988). See also Goytisolo, 'Cara y cruz', in ibid.

similar to that of the archetypal Spaniard. In this discourse, they both shared a glorious past, an ancient and advanced Iberian civilization that spanned the Mediterranean, uniting Berber and Spaniard. This latent nobility could be brought to life only if the benefits of Spanish civilization were properly appreciated.[47] So a Moroccan who embraced the Spanish cause was acceptable. Complicities were built between Spanish colonial officers and the Moroccans who collaborated. Both began to acquire characteristics of each other's culture, as I have mentioned, and that set them apart from their co-nationals. On the other hand, those Moroccans who refused to collaborate were bad.

Yet the frontier between good and bad Moor was always being crossed. It was often unclear to one side or the other who the real enemy was. In the difficult conditions of colonial war, Moroccans frequently adopted mimicries of resistance or complicity. As we saw in Chapter 1, El Rogui had made a pretence of firing at the Spanish army invading his territory. And so later did a *kabyle* in the far south-west of the Spanish Protectorate, which reached an agreement with the Spanish troops to pretend to fire at them in order to convince their fellow Moroccans that they were resisting the enemy.[48] Perhaps the greatest feat of parody took place in the brothel. There were, of course, many European prostitutes working in Morocco, but there were also Moroccan prostitutes and all of them had to mime attraction and affection or whatever else the client desired. Some Moroccan women were kept by Spanish officers and had to pretend also that they were in love. The contact the Spanish soldier had with Arab women was thus charged with ambiguity. They were either compliant but cold and indifferent, or equivocally loving, or 'slender white silhouettes, that evaporated into doorways as if they were merely the subtle fabric of the atmosphere'.[49]

This ambivalence about the Moroccan Other persisted throughout the colonial war. As we have seen, the leaders of the new concerted resistance to Spanish penetration in 1919, the Abdel Krim el Khattabi family, had been among Spain's closest collaborators. They had worked closely with the Spanish mining companies in Morocco. The younger son had studied mine engineering in Madrid with a grant from the Spanish authorities. There he had met the king, who had urged him to help make Morocco prosperous under Spain's tutelage.[50] Abdel Krim himself had worked for Spanish firms in Alhucemas and had qualified as a teacher in an examination in Malaga. As a political adviser to the Spanish authorities in north-east Morocco, he had been decorated with two awards, one of which carried a stipend. Later he had been

---

[47] n.a., *Ensayo de historial*, 23; F.R., 'Los Askaris voluntarios', *El Telegrama del Rif*, 7 Jan. 1917.

[48] Arbolí Nadal, 'Ligeras memorias', 101.

[49] José Díaz-Fernández, *El blocao* (Madrid, Ediciones Turner, 1976; 1st edn. 1928), 50. A very different picture of Moroccan women is given in the post-Anual narratives. According to a Spanish prisoner, the pro-Abdel Krim women were 'beasts of burden and they felt affection as would a cow, a mule, a pig . . .', Sainz Gutiérrez, *Con el General*, 644.

[50] Roger-Matthieu (ed.), *Mémoires*, 68–9.

a judge in Spanish pay with special jurisdiction over native judges, and editor of the section in Arabic of the Spanish newspaper *El Telegrama del Rif.*

The problem of distinguishing between friend and enemy became particularly acute as a result of the Anual disaster of 1921. The disaster was caused above all by the fact that most of the Moroccan soldiers fighting for Spain deserted to join the enemy. Anual also removed any lingering doubts about methods of colonialism. Within the colonial army, the spokesmen of military action already dominated over those that still toyed with pacific methods. Anual reinforced their position. The brutal methods practised since 1909 were intensified, and with them, a corresponding degree of enmification. That is, the degree of brutality was linked to the degree of resistance, or rather to the extent of the casualty rate among Spanish soldiers. Thus, the use of chemical weapons, an idea toyed with in 1918 by the king, was first essayed in 1921 and then became routine from 1924.

In the midst of the debacle of July 1921, a general and ex-minister of war wrote in a private communication passed on to the king:

The Rif Moor is completely irreducible and uncivilizable . . . the present generation lacks moral and even physical qualities . . . their rapacity, their ignorance, their apathy, appear in all the actions of their lifetime; they recognize no other law but that of their weapons, nor any friends but those of their village, not even those of their tribe. They despise all the advantages of civilization. They are hermetic to benevolence and fear only punishment. As a race they are made degenerate by the disease of avarice and tuberculosis.

In a reference to enlightened colonial opinion, the general went on: 'This is the person whom people want to tame with fine speeches and modern laws as if he was a citizen of Madrid or London.'[51]

Racist diatribes against the Moor were openly and prolifically expressed in newspapers and publications. *El Sol* quoted an officer as saying that Moroccan resistance to colonial expansion was caused by the 'atavistic hatreds stored in the savage instincts of this race'.[52] The most brutal expression of these new values was the book of a major of the engineer corps who had served in the colonial war and retired to become a right-wing deputy. For Bastos Ansart, the Moroccan people were 'the most bestial and barbaric people on earth'. Amongst their barbarous customs, he mentions their treatment of women but also their habit of 'making a horrible noise when they suck their hot mint tea through their teeth'. After Anual, he went on, 'there must be no other solution than their extermination'.[53]

Nevertheless, many officers also found Moroccan culture and people seductive and were barely able to disentangle their contradictory responses in their own heads. Morocco was filled with beauty and mystery (read: exoticism) and

---

[51] Jose Villalba, 'Notas sobre la accion de Espana en Marruecos', 21 July 1921 in AGPR 15599/16.

[52] Comandante Lopera in T. Borrás, 'El fanatismo moro', *El Sol,* 16 Oct. 1921.

[53] Bastos Ansart, *El desastre,* 29–41 and 53.

Spaniards and Moroccans shared a belief in God and destiny, though Moors were not deeply religious.[54] The lone survivor of the Igueriben massacre wrote that the Moors were a 'superbly brave race with indomitable instincts', though at the same time they displayed 'a primitive mind respecting only savagery'.[55] Amongst those officers most in contact with Moroccans as commanders of native troops or in charge of relations with natives (the *Interventores*), there developed over the years a more balanced picture of the Moorish Other. According to one, those characteristics most decried by the Spanish racist discourse were the result of years of war, oppression, invasion, disease, poverty, hunger, and lack of hygienic conditions. He made the point also that the atrocities committed by the Moroccans against the Spaniards were not used against their own people.[56] In a recent interview with the author, a Spanish veteran who had been an artillery lieutenant during the colonial war recognized how alike Moroccans and Spaniards were. 'I have never seen a Moor', he insisted, 'who could not have passed for a Spanish peasant.'[57]

Among the most respected of the Africanista officers, Colonel Capaz Montes implicitly rejected the racism of many of his fellow officers. He claimed that there was in fact no essential difference between the two races except five centuries of progress. So Moroccan society was like medieval Castile, and the caid was the equivalent of the feudal Castilian lord. His lecture to a new generation of colonial officers taking up their posts at the end of the war painted a more complex picture of Moroccan life and customs than most previous accounts. Attacking 'our adulterated orientalist writers', he dismissed the racist generalities of the discourse of the Moroccan Other and drew an altogether more sympathetic portrait of the different cultures in northern Morocco, although he was adamant that there was no democracy in Morocco and that women, especially outside urban areas, were denied basic human rights.

Like his progressive colleagues, however, Capaz Montes failed to understand that the Moroccan culture that he professed to know so well was acutely conditioned by the presence of Spanish colonialism. The evasiveness, untrustworthiness, deceitfulness, vanity, avariciousness, and cruelty that he considered common characteristics of Moroccan culture were no doubt largely a response to the demands of an arbitrary and mainly racist colonialism that had radically distorted their environment. The Moroccan 'cult of lying', he argued, 'is the defence of those of below against the arbitrariness of the powerful', without realizing that the most powerful people in colonized Morocco were Spanish officers like himself.[58]

[54] Mola, *Dar Akkoba*, 20 and 27. [55] Casado, *Igueriben*, 63.
[56] Nido, *Marruecos*, 45–6 and 277. For similar views, see Capaz Montes, 'Modalidades'.
[57] Díaz Ripoll interview.
[58] Fernando Capaz Montes, 'Usos y costumbres marroquíes en las ciudades, en el campo, sedentarios, nomadas árabes y bereberes', Tetuan, Alta Comisaría de España, 1928, in Archivo García Figueras. For his detailed knowledge of local tribes, see also his 'Cabecillas rebeldes en Gomara desde 1915 a 1927', an unpublished report of April 1928 in ibid.

As we saw in Chapter 6, their identification with their own narrative of Moroccan life alienated Africanist officers from the culture of their own homeland. In a conceptual transposition of the Moorish Other to a Spanish internal Other, Africanists began to see their fellow citizens as imbued with Muslim fatalism, treachery, and indolence.[59] The experience of the colonial war had been so powerful that events in Spain were often viewed through its lens. When General Echagüe was sacked by the civilian government as commander-in-chief in Melilla in 1923, his friend, another general, exclaimed that in Spain, 'there were many Moors dressed as Christians', an old expression referring to those Arabs who had stayed behind after the expulsion of Muslims in 1492 but had secretly continued to practise their religion. Thus also the veteran general of the war and head of the Civil Guard in 1932, José Sanjurjo, dismissed the incident in which his men killed demonstrating workers in the Andalusian village of Castillblanco by describing the protestors as a 'foco rifeño', a Rif nucleus.[60]

Yet the harsh landscape of northern Morocco, the sobriety, toughness, and valour of the enemy, and their apparent acceptance of death and destiny all resonated with the ideal values of the Spanish colonial military. The most widespread cultural symbols of this identification were the wearing of the jellaba, drinking mint tea, and sitting cross-legged on a mat. Thus, Spanish officers of the native troops tended to wear Moroccan dress instead of their uniforms.[61] During the Civil War, Franco expressed that sense of a separate identity shaped by the colonial war. He wrote: 'My years in Africa live within me with indescribable force . . . Without Africa, I can scarcely explain myself to myself, nor can I explain myself properly to my comrades in arms.'[62] Indeed, the origin and development of the Civil War itself cannot be understood without the experience of the colonial war.

[59] Queipo de Llano, 'Nuestro propósito' and 'El problema de Marruecos', in *Revista de Tropas Coloniales*, 1 (Jan. 1924) and 2 (Feb. 1924).
[60] For the first anecdote see Pardo, *Al servicio*, 300. For the second see 'Habla Sanjurjo', *El Debate*, 5 Jan. 1932.
[61] Mola, 'Dar Akkoba', 147, 211, 216.
[62] From Francisco Franco Bahamonde, *Palabras del Caudillo 19 abril 1937–31 diciembre 1938* (Barcelona, Ediciones Fe, 1939), 314.

CHAPTER EIGHT

Cultures, Conditions, and Corruption

OF ALL THE themes addressed in this book, that of the everyday life and mentality of the soldier in the colonial war is the least documented and the least subject to verification. It has always been difficult for combatants caught up in the worst moments of war to represent it to those who have not undergone its barbarism, physical suffering, and deep comradeship, and even to explain that experience to themselves. For it lies beyond discourse and even identity.[1] Most of the veterans of the colonial war in Morocco interviewed during the preparation of this book could only highlight the absurdity of their experience. It is something they find hard to make sense of, a passage of time that seems to stand outside the continuity of their own life's history, a period of exile in an unbridgeable, alien space.

The historian's task is made more difficult by the unreliability and patchiness of available data. Officers were required to produce records of casualties, war matériel, supplies, and so on for the General Staff. But where these records can be traced, they give little idea of conditions on the battlefield. Commanders sought to hide or gloss over the realities of war in their dispatches. Defeats were turned into exemplary actions, demoralization among the troops into the virtue of perseverance. Eyewitness accounts of the time tended to reflect the polarization of opinion in the metropolis: the Army of Africa was either flawless or useless. Cases of brutality, abuse, incompetence, and corruption brought to the military courts were variously interpreted, according to different ideological persuasions, as persecution by the authorities, exceptions to the rule, or part of a universal culture in the colonial army.

In contrast to the vast number of personal testimonies of the First World War, few veterans wrote about their experience in the colonial war in Morocco. Most Spanish soldiers who served there were illiterate anyway. If they could write, their letters were censored by officers. A semi-literate Catalan soldier sent garbled letters to his parents in Catalan because his officer only spoke Spanish, and if he dared write the truth about the war in Spanish he knew he would be charged. Like so many other veterans of the colonial war who could put pen to paper, neither he nor his family kept the letters sent from

---

[1] Leed, *No Man's Land, passim.*

the front, because at the time they did not think they had any historical impor-tance.[2] Indeed, most of the written communications were only postcards of the 'your son sends you much love' variety.

It is true that the 1921 disaster produced a flurry of books, but most of them were distorted by the need for self-justification or condemnation and, as we have seen, all of them sought to rationalize what was to some extent a sponta-neous and unpredictable event. The influx of more educated soldiers after the disaster resulted in a number of autobiographical or semi-autobiographical accounts or novels, some of which have become masterpieces of Spanish liter-ature.[3] But as historical evidence they have to be treated with caution, espe-cially those written as novels. Similarly, the oral evidence of veterans some seventy-five years later has been conditioned by the passage of time and the transformation of values. All the historian can do is to draw together this scat-tered and often somewhat distorted evidence, attempt to disentangle it from ideological narratives, and propose a dispassionate interpretation of the sol-dier's life in the colonial war.

Given the richness of the soldier's experience, there is a great temptation to describe rather than analyse. In this chapter I am concerned to go beyond description and attempt to evaluate how the colonial war affected the soldier who suffered its terrifying reality, how it changed him. This is an area that has not been explored in any of the literature. Even the First World War has left historians grasping for proof that it altered the character of the participants. A major obstacle in establishing the effects of such an evidently transformative experience was the profound sense of discontinuity suffered by veterans of the Great War between life in war and peace.[4] Most of this book seeks to trace the continuity of culture among the professional colonial officers between the war in Morocco and in the Civil War. This chapter, on the other hand, attempts to evaluate the effects of the colonial war on the post-war lives and attitudes of soldiers (as well as officers posted briefly to Morocco), through an examination of the cultures and conditions that surrounded them.

By culture, I mean the values and their related practices among the Spanish protagonists of the colonial war. Such was the multiplicity of corps, social classes, and regional origins of the soldiers, that there was no common culture binding them together except that of war. A number of officers and soldiers posted to Morocco managed to evade combat through family connections, ill-ness, or other means, but even they were caught up in life in the rearguard that was deeply conditioned by war. For the combatants, war meant the effacement of self. Except for brief periods of leave in Morocco, the soldier was isolated from the world with which he was familiar. Exposed to discipline, death, pain, hunger, thirst, fear, and boredom, in no particular order, his sense of identity

---

[2] Interview with Pau Masferrer Fontanella on 28 July 1999. None of the veterans I interviewed had kept any letters.

[3] e.g. Sender, *Imán*, and Barea, *La forja*.   [4] Leed, *No Man's Land*, pp. x and 2.

was constantly challenged. His sensory universe was replaced by a completely new and more intense one, fraught with menace. Yet at the same time he experienced an unprecedented comradeship with fellow soldiers and officers across barriers of social class and regional culture. And he managed to preserve some continuity with his civilian past through humour and stoicism.[5]

Within that common experience, there were differences over time and among the corps. Before 1919 the only Spanish soldiers fighting in the colonial war were from poor families who could not afford to buy them out of military service. Canalejas's law of 1912 had forced the sons of richer families to do a spell of military service, but it was short enough for them to evade service in the Moroccan war. The royal decree of August 1919, however, finally abolished the system whereby the middle classes enjoyed effective exemption from war, to the dismay of many.[6] The huge mobilization of conscripts after the 1921 disaster saw the first large-scale deployment of middle-class men in the Moroccan war.

Unlike their richer counterparts, the poor soldiers tended to regard their posting as bad luck, to be endured stoically, yet another imposition by an unfair or oppressive state, or simply the heaviest of life's normal burdens. The most courageous response, according to the novelist Ramón Sender, who did military service in Morocco post-Anual, would have been to refuse to go to war and pay for the consequences by emigrating illegally or going to prison. But few took this option, moved by a 'diffuse cowardice', or, as among the French peasants mobilized in 1914, a resigned compliance. Among those who had gone as far as volunteering for the war, many appeared profoundly to regret their decision.[7] Immediately after Anual, on the other hand, the war was imbued with a greater sense of purpose, in particular for those who had been in Morocco during the events. This was not the result of any absorption of the official discourse of war, but of a spirit of revenge for the massacre of their fellow soldiers and a determination to rescue those who were being held captive.

This spirit was especially common amongst the new recruits from middle-class families. But it was by no means the equivalent of the enthusiasm of the 'community of August' of the Western Front in 1914. Jingoism was largely absent among the Spanish soldiers in Morocco, because the aims of the war were so remote from their concerns. The civilizing of the Moor or the defence of the interests of the international community were not issues likely to make sense to the soldier. A Catalan veteran of the war told me in an interview in 1998: 'We didn't think anything. There was no cause. They spoke about the

---

[5] As among troops in the First World War: J. G. Fuller, *Troop Morale and Popular Culture in the British and Dominion Armies 1914–1918* (Oxford, Clarendon Press, 1990), 159; Leed, *No Man's Land*, 24.

[6] See e.g. the readers' letters in *El Liberal*, 29 Aug. 1919.

[7] According to a letter in 1914 to the MP Angel Galarza from the captain-general of the Valladolid Region: AR 6 (2) 8 (21); Sender, *Imán*, 60; for the French peasant recruit, see Eugen Weber, *Peasants into Frenchmen: The Modernization of Rural France 1870–1914* (London, Chatto & Windus, 1979).

"patria" but the patria of what? We all thought alike.' During his three years of military service, he did not remember any officer ever explaining the purpose of the war to him and his fellow soldiers.[8] Another veteran, an ex-building worker from Catalonia, told me that he and his fellow soldiers had nothing to do with Morocco. They were there because they had been forced to go. Generals made speeches to them while they stood at attention in the heat of the day, but none of them listened. A third veteran, an old Galician fisherman, said to me: 'It was a war that had no meaning. Nothing mattered to us. We just wanted to go home.'[9]

To an impoverished Spanish land labourer in the 1920s, the conditions suffered by Moroccans cannot have seemed very different from his own, so it was not clear what civilization he was bringing with him. The recruits who disembarked in Morocco were so thin and feeble-looking that a captain-general recommended to Maura that they should not be seen by the Moroccans; knowing some Arabic, he had already heard some local people making derogatory remarks.[10] Nor can there have been much idea among the numerous illiterate recruits from remote regions in Spain of what they were doing there or the meaning of the 'national interest' or of the 'patria' itself. The hero of Sender's autobiographical novel *Imán* asks another soldier what the 'patria' is, to which the latter replies: 'The sergeant told us when we were called up; but I can't remember.' However, many other soldiers clearly felt a strong attachment to country and flag. In his unpublished diary, a Catalan lieutenant recalls that the recruits he was training were very moved at the ceremony of the swearing-in of the Spanish flag.[11]

The negative sense of purpose of the war—revenge and rescue—probably began to evaporate among many ordinary soldiers (if they had ever felt it in the first place) soon after the positions lost in July 1921 were recovered and most of the Spanish prisoners were released eighteen months later. Only the notion of the Moorish Other may have helped to give a limited meaning to war but even that, as we have seen, was undermined by the difficulty of distinguishing between friends and enemies among Moroccans. The primary drive among soldiers continued to be survival and therefore evasion of war, though attachment to an exemplary officer may have driven some to fight more enthusiastically.

Yet the culture of war was different from corps to corps. Companionship and solidarity did develop across barriers of military institutions both in battle

---

[8] Isidre Balada interview, 18 Apr. 1998.

[9] Jesús Cotelo interview, 15 Mar. 1998; Josep Campa Ginot interview, 20 July 1999.

[10] Barea, *La Forja*, 306; letter to Maura from Captain-General Ochando on 6 Apr. 1914 in AFAMM leg. 351 no. 6.

[11] Juan Sánchez Rodrigo, *Diario de un soldado en la campaña de Marruecos 1921–1922* (Serradilla, n.p., n.d.), 13; Sender, *Imán*, 121; Arbolí, 'Ligeras memorias', 68. The lack of enthusiasm for colonial war seems also to have been prevalent among British soldiers in the Boer War: Richard Price, *An Imperial War and the British Working-Class: Working-Class Attitudes and Reactions to the Boer War 1899–1902* (London, Routledge & Kegan Paul, 1972).

and in the rearguard, but the experience of war varied according to the status and function of each corps. The infantryman, the sailor, the medical orderly, the soldier attached to the engineering corps or to telecommunications all worked within different military cultures. These differences were kept alive by the efforts of the military High Command to maintain the distinction between elite corps, peninsular infantry, and native troops. Even the unskilled conscript posted by chance to a technical corps like the artillery learnt to regard the less skilled troops as beneath him. Artillerymen called infantrymen the *pipiolos* or 'pipsqueaks'.[12]

Of all the elite troops, the Legion was the most self-consciously exclusive, as we have seen. Its aristocratic identity was fostered by elaborate ritual and by physical separation from the rest of the army. Yet most of its recruits came from the most marginal social groups in Spain and abroad. Enlistment required no prior documentation, with the result that many men with criminal records who had difficulty finding gainful employment were taken on with no questions asked and paid an immediate bounty of 500 pesetas (some £25 at the time) if they joined for three years or 700 pesetas for five years. Many of the foreigners attracted to the Legion were veterans of the First World War who had failed to settle down to civilian life or had been unable to find work. Post-war unemployment drove many ex-soldiers in Britain, France, Germany, Austria, Hungary, Poland, Czechoslovakia, and elsewhere to flock to the Legion's recruitment offices. Volunteers from as far away as Cuba, South Africa, the United States, and Canada, and even white Russian soldiers exiled in Tunis and Prague, responded in great numbers to the apparently generous enlistment terms offered by the Legion. The immediate payment of a bounty was by far the most enticing offer. This ragbag of men included Count Alexander Tolstoy, and a British army captain, a relative of the Duke of Connaught, who told a military newspaper that he had joined because hunting Moors was the only sport he had not yet taken part in.[13]

The Legion was kept rigorously separate from the rest of the troops because of fear on the part of the High Command that the ideologies some Legionnaires brought with them, such as the unemployed anarcho-syndicalists from Barcelona, might contaminate the other troops. The Spanish War Ministry expressed its concern that the lack of proper screening of foreign candidates for the Legion might let in 'propagators of pernicious doctrines', such as Bolsheviks. Contact with other units was also discouraged on the grounds that the culture of the conscript garrisons or camps, where enthusiasm for the

---

[12] Cordon, *Trayectoria*, 49.

[13] AMAE leg. 2883; *Ejército y Armada*, 7 Oct. 1921. The American journalist Vincent Sheean observed that the German recruits he saw making their way to Morocco looked 'pale, discouraged . . . woebegone': *Personal History*, 97. A French agent called Camile Fossion signed an agreement with the army in 1924 to recruit several thousand soldiers from France and Belgium, claiming he would have no problem because unemployment there was so high: SHM caja 86/3.

war was at its lowest, might induce the Legionnaires to desert. When, for logistic reasons, the Legion had to share the same camp as other units, mayhem would sometimes break out. A Legion battalion in Larache was responsible for constant friction with the other troops. On one occasion Legionnaires were said to have deliberately knocked over the food being served to the artillerymen, and were ordered as a consequence to camp outside at some distance.[14]

A major problem for the Legion in its efforts to attract foreigners was that many of its recruits were used to better pay and conditions. The generous salary they thought they were getting was made far less attractive when they found on arrival that large deductions were going to be made to cover their outfits and their daily rations. An international incident arose when twenty-six British recruits, including the nephew of the British consul in Spain, decided to tear up their contracts in November 1921 after experiencing the harsh conditions of campaign life. Accustomed to the compliance of the Spanish soldier, the High Command was nonplussed. Berenguer was unhappy that the minister of war was prepared to let them go, on the grounds that they might spread propaganda. The founder of the Legion, Millán-Astray, had even suggested to him that, rather than be released to go where they wanted, they be 'sent in a ship to where it is convenient that they should go', leaving both the minister and ourselves guessing as to what sort of 'destination' Millán-Astray had in mind.[15] After the worldwide enthusiasm for enlistment in the Legion, the number of foreigners joining its ranks began rapidly to tail off. By 1923 only one-fifth of Legionnaires came from abroad. As one, later famous, recruit wrote, rather than a 'Tercio de extranjeros' or Legion of Foreigners, it had become a 'Tercio de extranjis' or Legion of weirdos.[16]

Some idea of the social origins and culture of the Spanish recruits may be gathered from the many reports of violent incidents and desertion on their part. During the early period of recruitment in 1920, absconding with the enlistment bonus was so rife that one of the regional military commanders in Spain recommended that all recruits should be accompanied by a platoon of soldiers. A report in October 1920 also recounted the odyssey of a group of rough Legion volunteers travelling by train to one of the training camps. En route, one of the military escort accompanying them had his wallet stolen by a recruit, and such was the rowdiness of the future soldiers of the elite corps that the train was halted. The recruits disembarked and started stoning the engine. When the train finally arrived in Ronda, a squad of soldiers was waiting for them on the platform to escort them to the garrison. Desertion was not con-

[14] SHM caja 86/4, 17 Aug. 1921; Cordón, *Trayectoria*, 103.

[15] AFAMM leg. 364, no. 6, 1 and 11 Nov. 1921; Howard to Curzon, Anual Report on Spain for 1921, BD Series F, vol. 25, pp. 69–70; AMAE leg. 2883.

[16] E. Giménez Caballero, *Notas Marruecos de un soldado* (Madrid, n.p., 1923), 60; John H. Galey, 'Bridegrooms of Death: A Profile Study of the Spanish Foreign Legion', *Journal of Contemporary History*, 4 (1969), 47–63.

fined to the Spanish volunteers. Instructions from the military commander of
the port of Gijón, where German recruits were repeatedly disembarking, stipulated that they should be transported to the training camps under military
guard and by the shortest route possible.[17]

Desertion was more difficult for Legionnaires once they were integrated into
fighting units in Morocco. Nevertheless, by the end of 1923 increasing numbers
were deserting because of the conditions of war. A royal decree in December
1923 admitted that it had become an endemic disease, and offered to amnesty
the deserters if they came forward because the cost of bringing them to justice
was prohibitive. At the same time recruitment was falling. Alongside the
Regulares, the Legion supplied the shock-troops of the army and was expected
to take the brunt of the fighting in order to avoid the disasters caused by
deployment of the reluctant Spanish soldier. Veteran Legionnaires recaptured
by the army after attempting to desert reported that they could no longer stand
the constant fatigue and hardship, the lack of hygienic conditions, the discomfort of the camp, and the absence of leisure time.[18] Another report by the
Legion command suggested that continued desertion was the result of the poor
leadership of the new Legion officers who had replaced those many officers
killed or severely wounded. Also blamed for helping desertion were 'the Jews,
people from low life', and the peddlers of food and drink who hung around the
camps, as well as the Moroccans who ran cafés where the Legionnaires went
to drink.[19]

The high commissioner at the time, Luis Aizpuru, recommended that the
Spanish Legion should be treated, like the French Foreign Legion, with kid
gloves. They needed 'special autonomy' if their spirit of aggression, discipline,
and sacrifice were to be sustained. 'Everybody is aware of the thousand incidents that arise in the daily life of the camps and lead as a necessary corollary
to inquiries and trials . . .' Thus, their camps and barracks should be sited far
from those of other troops, and they should be given lighter sentences and for-
given the crimes of the past.[20] The Legion command was more forthright in
its recommendations. The Legionnaires needed regular breaks in comfortable
accommodation where they would have access to bars, cafés, and women,
'women who will divert them from the interminable hours of rest'. They also
needed a special hospital, particularly because it would make it more difficult
for them to continue the frequent practice of simulating illness and injury to
avoid battle.[21] So, a few years after the creation of the Legion, the headquarters in Dar Riffien was equipped with more comfortable accommodation than
that of other troops, water was piped down to a reservoir from a mountain
stream, and workshop and recreational facilities were set up. The inadequate

---

[17] The report about German recruits is from SHM Africa caja 86/3, 11 July 1924, while the other
reports are a telegram of 5 Oct. 1920 and letter of 11th of same month in ibid., caja 86/1.
[18] SHM R119, leg. 48, carp. 65, 11 Jan. 1924.   [19] SHM caja 86/2, n.d.
[20] SHM R119, leg. 48 carp. 65.   [21] SHM caja 86/2, n.d.

and sometimes inedible army rations were supplemented by fresh meat, vegetables, and fruit raised on the Legion's farm.[22]

Amongst Moroccans and the other Spanish troops, the Legion was notorious for its rowdy drunkenness when off duty. Most soldiers drank too much, but Legionnaires seemed to get through more alcohol than most, perhaps because they were paid more. They were also rumoured to take cocaine. But unlike the ordinary soldier, the Legionnaire's depredations seemed to be out of control. The British consul in Tetuan, whose views were admittedly skewed by prejudice (he described the Legionnaires as mostly 'Spaniards of the more criminal class, small and vicious'), was shocked to find the military police unable to cope with the Legion. The people who suffered most were Moroccan men and women. Legionnaires, combining the 'swagger of Australians with the appearance of sewer-rats', would walk through the shopping area in the Moroccan quarter of Tetuan armed with sticks, maltreating local people simply because they were Moroccan. The grand vizir made an official complaint to the military authorities to little avail.[23]

The racism of many rank-and-file Legionnaires was by no means shared by all their officers. But there was a tacit agreement of the kind mentioned by Aizpuru that the application of a strict moral code outside that of martial discipline would blunt their military effectiveness. As we saw in Chapter 7, any fine distinctions between good and bad Moors were thought to diminish the Legion's aggression on the battlefield. In an incident in Melilla, a soldier and his mates on military service tried to intervene when they saw Legionnaires maltreating a young Moroccan girl selling water. They were throwing stones at her and had broken her jug. One of the Legionnaires forced her to kiss him. When the other soldiers tried to stop them, the Legionnaire turned on them (as the soldier remembered many years later), shouting: 'What the fuck are you complaining about! How many Spaniards *she* must have killed, the dirty pig! She looks just like the one we paraded about on the end of our bayonets after she kept firing at us with her rifle! We might well do the same to all of them . . . !' The incident he was referring to was the capture of a female muhayeddin who had resisted arrest and whose decapitated head had been paraded about in Melilla on the end of a Legionnaire's bayonet.[24] Among other things, the anecdote reveals the extent to which the rank-and-file Legionnaires learnt to see all Moroccans as covert or open enemies.

Aizpuru's reference to the 'thousand incidents' that daily affected barrack life no doubt included cases of the abuse and rape of young Moroccan women.

[22] Scurr, *Spanish Foreign Legion*, 5.

[23] Hope Gill to W. M. Codrington, chargé d'affaires in Tangier, 5 Sept. 1924, PRO FO 636/17. The culture of the Legion also offended the sensibilities of the French. In his report to the French Foreign Office after a visit to the Spanish front line, the correspondent of *Le Matin* and *Le Temps* described the Legion as a 'plague': Leon Rollin, 'Voyage à la zone espagnole. Notes', ADMAE Maroc 1917–40, vol. 197, p. 20. For more on the Legionnaires' 'leisure' see Fernández Oxea, *Crónicas*, 90–2.

[24] Prous, *Quatre gotes*, 92–3.

Unfortunately for the historian, these cases are difficult to trace because the military authorities, in particular the Legion command, did their best to keep them in the 'family'. On the other hand, their efforts to ensure a supply of prostitutes and clean brothels subject to regular medical examination did not prevent the maltreatment of the prostitutes themselves.[25] The theme of sex and sexual abuse will be considered in greater detail later in this chapter, when the soldiers' conditions are discussed.

The brutality of many Legionnaires in the rear was a pale reflection of their conduct on the battlefield. English volunteers in the Legion complained to their consul in Tetuan about the behaviour of their Spanish counterparts during raids on villages abandoned by the Rifian fighters. They witnessed old men, women, and children being shot down or pushed back into the flames of burning buildings.[26] The fact that one or two of these English soldiers may have been veterans of the First World War makes their outrage all the more striking. The savagery of the Legion suggests that the moral restraints built into normal cultural patterning were deeply eroded among many of its soldiers. It may have reflected the dysfunctional socialization among those recruits who joined because they could not cope with civil society.

More than most other military units, the Legion demanded the complete integration of the individual into the collective as well as the subordination of this collective to a ferociously strict hierarchy of command. The martial qualities most cherished in the Legion were obedience and courage, perhaps even in that order. A postcard from a captain to one of his Legionnaires praised him for his 'subordination and bravery'.[27] Strict obedience minimized emotional conflict and legitimized aggression. The Legion offered an escape from a problematic self and the acquisition of a new and elite identity. It gave a sense of security and an opportunity, enticing for many, of a surrender of self-responsibility. Without any residual burden of individual guilt, it was easier to derive pleasure from hurting and killing the enemy, all the more so because they were held responsible for atrocities committed against buddies. Many may well have felt like the GI in Vietnam who confessed that: 'For every one that I killed I felt better. Made some of the hurt went away.'[28]

These values were reflected in the Legion's battle hymns and litanies. Modelled on a medieval Christian liturgy, they celebrated suffering, pain, death, and redemption. The so-called Credo of the Legion was a paean not to military professionalism but to 'blind and ferocious aggressiveness'. The only military action envisaged was to get as close as possible to the enemy and charge him with bayonets fixed. The official hymn of the Legion implicitly recognized the dysfunctional background of the recruits:

[25] Guixé, *El Rif*, 152.
[26] Hope Gill to Codrington, 25 Sept. 1924, PRO FO 636/7.
[27] Aguilar, 'Libro de memorias'.
[28] Bourke, *An Intimate History*, 227.

> A painful Calvary weighs down my soul
> Seeking redemption in the fire of battle.

It also acknowledged their dubious past:

> We are all unknown heroes,
> Nobody seeks to enquire who I am;
> A thousand tragedies of different kinds
> Have marked the passage of my life.
> When you become what you want
> The previous life no longer matters.[29]

The bravery that was encouraged among Legionnaires was not military but martial, or rather, gladiatorial. It was less to do with moral valour than with physical daring. Unlike modern mercenaries, they were more ruthless than efficient. There can be little doubt that the culture of war among the Rifian tribesmen influenced that of the Legion. The Rifian ritual of war cries, military charges, and galloping horsemen raising clouds of dust was meant to intimidate the enemy into retreating, to establish military hegemony by a show of force rather than provoke mutual mass killing. The Legion adopted the war cries, the charges with fixed bayonet against hidden foes, the decapitation of bodies. But their culture of war to the death, epitomized by their hymn, the 'Bridegroom of Death', served only to multiply the casualties on both sides.

Indeed, like gladiators, ritual was an important part of the Legionnaire's life on the battlefield and in the camp or garrison. The ceremony of the Legionnaire Saturday or Sábado Legionario, in which the effigy of 'Christ of the Good Death' (el Cristo de la Buena Muerte) was placed between the flags of Spain and the Legion, promoted the idea that the violence practised by the Legion was part of a sacred liturgy.[30] Their goose-stepping and arm-swinging march (so different from the rather untidy drill of the Spanish recruit on military service), the strange uniform with its beret capped by a dangling tassel, the barked orders, the chants and hymns were complemented by a fetishization of the bodily parts of killed enemies. Severed ears and noses were worn on the body hung from string, and decapitated heads were carried on the end of bayonets, all of them trophies of war characteristic of more ritualized pre-modern societies, including, and indeed influenced by, those of northern Morocco. The practice of cutting off parts of the enemy's body and wearing them or collecting them as mementos also strengthened the Legionnaires' warrior macho

---

[29] Federico Ramos Izquierdo, *La Legión. Historial de Guerra (1 Septiembre 1920 al 12 Octubre 1927)* (Ceuta, Imprenta África, 1933), 393–4. The lines in Spanish are: 'pesa en mi alma doliente calvario | que en el fuego busca redención'; 'Somos héroes incognitos todos | nadie aspira a saber quien soy yo | mil tragedias de diversos modos | el correr de la vida formó. | Cada uno será lo que quiera/nada importa mi vida anterior.'

[30] Mateo Dieste, *El 'moro'*, 94, n. 93.

identity and helped to sanction the violence meted out against a diminished and objectified enemy.[31]

The same soldier who had protested against their treatment of a young Moroccan girl saw Legionnaires returning from battle singing songs and covered with sweat and blood from the heads of two-dozen Moroccans, whose ears and noses had been cut off, stuck on the end of their bayonets as if they were returning from an orchard with 'a bunch of grapes and figs on the end of a stick'.[32] Even Primo de Rivera was shocked to see the heads, arms, ears, and other bodily parts of dead Rifian warriors carried on Legionnaire bayonets and about their bodies as they marched past him in Tetuan in September 1925.[33]

The culture among peninsular troops, that is, amongst those officers and men doing a spell of military service in Morocco, was much more complex and tends to defy simple generalization. Before the Anual disaster probably the most common culture among officers in the colonial army was that of the metropolis. Many officers posted to Morocco who had no special vocation for colonial service merely reproduced the values and practices of military life in mainland Spain. Most of the officers associated with this culture had technical and organizational knowledge but little training for military operations in Morocco. They tended to be wedded to the fulfilment of orders and regulations and more wrapped up with the technical aspects of military life than interested in winning honours or promotion in the battlefield. Many had accumulated years of experience in Spain in pursuit of these bureaucratic aims. Even after 1919, bureaucracy continued to plague the expeditionary army. For example, every munition dispatched to the front had to be accompanied by a receipt, and this had to be signed by the commanding officer of the troops receiving it. The continued dependency on the slow procedures of peacetime, even when officers were under fire, considerably reduced the efficiency of the army.[34]

The pressure on the officer posted to Morocco to transform himself into a warrior for a cause he did not identify with must have created enormous strains. According to a report sent to the French Foreign Ministry, he started counting the days to his return to Spain as soon as he arrived in Morocco, and this became the major topic of conversation. Those who had contracted to serve for more than the standard two years did so only because they needed

---

[31] This trophy-collecting was common practice among soldiers in the two World Wars and in the Vietnam War: Bourke, *An Intimate History*, 37–41.

[32] Prous, *Quatre gotes*, 112–14; lest the lurid incidents involving the Legion be thought of as exaggerations by its critics, a book by an American Legionnaire of Catalan descent celebrates the brutality and fetishism of its soldiers: Luys Santa Marina, *Tras el águila de César. Elegía del Tercio 1921–1922* (Barcelona, Editorial Yunque, 1939), 23–34. For another, more critical, eyewitness account, see Cordón, *Trayectoria*, 71 and 77–9.

[33] Azpeitua, *Marruecos*, 135.

[34] Arbolí, 'Ligeras memorias', 68.

money.[35] The collapse of the front line at Anual had much to do with this absence of combativeness and war experience. Indeed, it became clear in the subsequent inquiry, as we have seen, that some of the officers commanding positions on the front line only occasionally visited them and spent the rest of the time in town. Nor did such officers identify to any great extent with the work of the Africanists and many sought to avoid the more onerous duties attached to the Protectorate.[36] Relations with Moroccans were not cultivated, and few of these officers bothered to study their language or customs. Dealings with tribal chieftains were considered a torture to be avoided at all costs.[37]

Apart from the flurry of the campaigns of 1909 and 1912–15, colonial rule between the beginning of military intervention in Morocco and the offensive of 1919 was dominated by this culture. It was marked by a lack of co-ordination between military commanders and the absence of any clear military objectives. Its relative incompetence derived not just from an earlier lack of restructuring and reform but from Spain's neutrality in the First World War, which had not given officers the opportunity to learn its strategic lessons and technological implications. There were frequent disagreements between Africanist officers armed with the new colonial values of military intervention and officers recently posted to Morocco who were imbued with metropolitan culture. What exacerbated these problems was the fundamental contradiction of government policy over Morocco. Maintaining control in the Protectorate was considered vital for Spanish foreign policy, but the cost of military operations had to be kept to a minimum because of domestic pressures on the state budget. The result was almost endemic indecision or delay in decision-making.[38]

The consequent lack of resources and the ambiguity of instructions sent to the high commissioners in Morocco consolidated a culture of relative apathy among many officers, at least until 1919.[39] Even the fulfilment of garrison duties tended to be casual. From 1913, military campaigns involving potential loss of life were entrusted to native troops, while non-combatant expeditions into the field were considered onerous and therefore evaded when possible through feigned illness, special leave, bribery, or alternative postings arranged through *amiguismo* (mainly family contacts).[40]

---

[35] Léon Rollin, 'Voyage à la zone espagnole. Notes', 1 Oct. 1923 in ADMAE Maroc, 1917–40, vol. 197, p. 19.

[36] Harris, *France*, 79 ff. Carolyn Boyd's view that 'the dedicated Africanists were overshadowed by an unedifying majority of opportunists and malcontents' is somewhat exaggerated: *Praetorian Politics in Liberal Spain* (Chapel Hill, University of North Carolina, 1979), 40.

[37] In a letter written shortly after the Anual disaster, Abdel Krim himself denounced this attitude towards the local tribes prevalent, in his view, amongst a majority of Spanish officers: Mohammed Tahtah, *Entre pragmatisme, réformisme et Modernisme. Le rôle politico-religieux des Khattabi dans le Rif (Maroc) jusqu'à 1926* (Leiden, n.p., 1995), 140. A typical portrait of these officers is painted in Barea, *La Forja* and Sender, *Imán*.

[38] Allendesalazar, *La diplomacia*, 186.

[39] Miguel Alonso Baquer, *D. Manuel Azaña y les militares* (Madrid, Actas, 1977), 45.

[40] See e.g. the testimony of Guixé in *El Rif*.

Another characteristic of metropolitan culture among many officers in Morocco was the practice of moonlighting. Many sought to make up for the paucity of their salaries, as officers did in Spain, by seeking extra work as company administrators or managers, despite the repeated ban on part-time jobs by the Spanish high commissioners in Morocco.[41] The opportunities for work on the side were far greater in Morocco than in a garrison town in Spain. Huge amounts of trade and military supplies were being channelled through the colony, and officers carried much influence in their handling and distribution because the Protectorate was run largely by the army.

The temptation to become involved in corrupt practices was especially seductive because they were not subject to the admittedly feeble scrutiny of pre-1923 Spanish democracy. Small-scale corruption was endemic in the Army of Africa, just as it was in Spain. It was far more extensive among metropolitan officers and non-commissioned officers than among their dedicated colonial colleagues, although some military Africanists and Junteros may have been tempted to pocket some of the funds they were handing out to chieftains in the countryside. Indeed, the committee investigating the 1921 disaster uncovered claims for payments to chieftains who simply did not exist.[42]

The ease with which these practices were adopted was a reflection not just of the low pay of all involved but also the alienation of professional soldiers from the state. The state was an instrument controlled by social elites with which few of them could identify, so there was little moral compunction about cheating it of a few pesetas. The problem was that the opportunities for defrauding the state in the Protectorate were so great that the amounts of money thus obtained became colossal. Huge quantities of subsistence goods and arms were shipped from Spain to the military authorities in Morocco, who had exclusive control over the adjudication of contracts for their distribution. During the early part of the Protectorate, according to a confidential report sent to Maura, food supplies destined for the troops in the eastern zone were diverted and sold in French Algeria by a team of officers including the general in charge of its distribution, Federico Monteverde Sedano. In the post-Anual climate of moral cleansing, the embezzlement of some 1 million pesetas (or $140,000) by officers in Larache became a national scandal. But it was the tip of an iceberg of corruption.[43]

Since most officers and NCOs knew about these practices, it became easier for many of them to indulge in similar practices, although the scale of embezzlement diminished in proportion to the level of command. Substantial sums of money were made by selling rifles and ammunition to Moroccans; it should not have been a surprise when the same rifles were used against Spaniards in

[41] 'El contrabando de subsistencias en Melilla', AFAMM Fondo Documental Mortera, caja 4; López Rienda, *El escándalo*, 144–7.

[42] *De Anual*, 58; ADMAE vol. 202, p. 116 (b).

[43] 'El contrabando', AFAMM; López Rienda, *El escándalo*; Woolman, *Rebels*, 97–100.

1921.[44] One of the commonest frauds was to divert a small percentage of public funds earmarked for the construction of roads and barracks and the supply of equipment and food into the pockets of the officer in charge and the colleagues and NCOs who worked for him. The quartermaster stores were often party to these scams, while the rank-and-file soldiers were usually their victims. Soldiers were sometimes served even worse food than that foreseen by the military suppliers, because the NCOs in charge of catering would buy cheap, poor-quality food and pocket the difference. According to a veteran of the colonial war, NCOs tended to be far more corrupt than officers were.[45]

Another of the rackets victimized the soldiers by a simple expedient. According to the bureaucratic regulations of the colonial army, each soldier was provided with a free pair of espadrilles every three months, the only footwear most of them could afford to wear (apart from some of the middle-class soldiers, whose families could buy them boots). Since he was usually on the move, the espadrilles would wear out long before the three months had elapsed. He would therefore be obliged to seek another pair from the stores, and the price of this pair would be deducted from his pay. When he then requested his new free pair he was told that he was no longer entitled to it, having acquired one already within the regulatory period. Thus, the free espadrilles would accumulate in the stores and the NCOs in charge would order fewer pairs from the producers in the next financial year while declaring that they had received the full number. The money thus saved would be shared out among the military staff in the store, while the accounts would appear to be above board.[46]

Other common scams included the acquisition through seniority, bribery, or family connections of monopolies in the supply of food and other goods. There were cases of officers who would set up a business run by their family and award it an exclusive contract for the supply of goods to their battalion or regiment or award this contract to a business for which members of their family worked.[47] Spanish culture was permeated by nepotism and favouritism, but these practices were even more rife in Morocco because the needs or opportunities for profit among officers were greater. During the period 1910–20, the Melilla town-hall was filled with relatives of officers who absorbed over

---

[44] A 1919 report lodged in the archives of the royal palace in Madrid suggested that the most efficient way of ending local resistance in Morocco was to change the make of rifle and machine-gun used by the Spanish troops so that Moroccans could no longer buy ammunition from them for their old Mauser weapons: 'Notas reservadas sobre Marruecos', 9 Oct., AGPR caja 15.765/5.

[45] Balada interview. Pau Masferrer Fontanella and Josep Campa Ginot also confirm widespread corruption in their interviews. For the diversion of canteen resources into officers' pockets see also 'Cartas de un soldado', *La Correspondencia de España*, 12 Sept. 1923.

[46] Barea, *La Forja*, 365–6 and 299. For other scams of this kind see ibid., 255–9, 290, 295; Ciges Aparicio, *Entre la paz*, 128–55; and Leguineche, *Anual*, 142–3 and 167–8.

[47] A case of this kind is mentioned in a letter to Primo de Rivera from the commander-in-chief at Melilla, 25 Apr. 1925, SHM R126 leg. 58 carp. 8.

600,000 pesetas annually, some five times the amount received by town-halls of similar-sized towns in Spain. Yet public services in Melilla were very poor.[48]

Like all politicians with influence, Maura received countless letters from friends and supporters asking for favours. A Legionnaire who was a member of his party wrote several letters to him complaining that many of his comrades were being relieved from service in Morocco because they had political connections. Having registered his opposition to this practice, he then requested that Maura do the same for him, clearly failing to realize the implicit contradiction. Promotions were also the focus of much corruption. Officers in positions of power were able to recommend the promotion of soldiers, NCOs, and other officers in exchange for favours or for cancelling debts, or because of political or family connections.[49]

Other and lesser forms of venality may not even have been recognized as corruption by their practitioners. Many of these were exposed in the aftermath of the 1921 disaster. Members of parliament, such as the Socialist Indalecio Prieto, drew the parliament's attention to the common practice among officers of using official cars for their family excursions or cavalry horses for their wives' and daughters' leisure, or, as Prieto had claimed three years previously, of detailing soldiers for duty as servants in their houses. In the climate of recrimination after Anual, these accusations may well have exaggerated the extent to which these practices were universal. But the earlier assertion by high commissioner Gómez-Jordana senior in 1918 that the accusations of corruption were all based on unfounded rumours was unconvincing in the light of his own constant edicts to officers urging them to behave according to the strict moral codes of the army.[50]

The victims of all this corruption included not just the rank-and-file soldiers but also local people, both Spanish workers based in Ceuta and Melilla and Moroccans living in Spanish-controlled areas. The latter could be coerced or encouraged to buy dearer goods from illegal military sinecures or forced to pay taxes that ended up in the local commander's pocket. According to the report written for Maura, Moroccan producers of barley, without any alternative outlets, were forced to sell their crops to the local Spanish quartermaster stores at a far lower price than the market rate, while the latter then sold them on to their counterparts in Spain, pocketing a profit of 30 per cent.[51]

Corruption and venality may have been widespread in the Spanish Protectorate before 1921, but it was by no means universal. Anual, in any case, brought with it a substantial clean-up of military practices. Establishing the

[48] 'El contrabando', AFAMM, ibid.
[49] Queipo de Llano, *El General*, pp. 128–9. Maura, more principled than most politicians, refused to answer the letters of the Legionnaire: AFAMM leg. 302/3.
[50] SHM Africa, caja 52/6; AR 58 37/1; for the post-Anual parliamentary denunciations see DSCD, 1921, vol. 7, pp. 3674–84 and 3826–7, *inter alia*.
[51] 'El contrabando', AFAMM.

extent of corruption is extremely difficult, because officers tended to keep quiet about the behaviour of their fellows as long as they kept to proportions deemed acceptable. With the limited knowledge available, it can be surmised that corruption of one sort or another was least practised by dedicated colonial officers and those from the technical corps such as artillery, engineering, and telecommunications, whose cultures were considerably more professional than that of the infantry or the quartermaster stores. Officers of these units started off with a higher status than their colleagues in infantry and cavalry, although as the war progressed, the latter two increasingly enjoyed the limelight. They also tended to be more professional in their dealings with the lower ranks, even though their own soldiers were usually unskilled (recruits attached to the engineers, for example, spent a lot of their time filling sandbags and lugging them on to parapets).[52]

The unit least recognized in the hagiographic accounts of pro-Africanist writers was the medical corps. Their bravery and dedication gained little acknowledgement because of the gladiatorial culture of the colonial army, in which wounds won on the battlefield were regarded as the true measure of courage. But doctors, medical orderlies, and stretcher-bearers had to pick up or tend to the wounded, often under fire. They had to deal with soldiers dying in agony, their insides ripped out or their brains oozing out of their heads. The medical supplies they were given were often utterly inadequate, and the strain of seeing men die who could be saved with simple drugs or surgical tools that were not made available must have caused deep distress to trained medics.[53]

Those soldiers and officers least exposed to fire were often those who were able to use their contacts to obtain posts in the rear. Most sought-after were posts in the offices, where life could be fairly leisurely, or in the stores, where there were opportunities to make money on the side. Without this influence, conscripts could try to win the officer's favour over time by being serviceable. Their comrades would dislike them for sucking up to authority and be happy if they were posted elsewhere.[54] But there were others who were posted to the rear because they had skills needed there by the military, like Arturo Barea, whose knowledge of topography got him posted to the General Staff.

As for those Spanish soldiers mobilized for combat, most were based in the infantry units. We know from many autobiographical accounts, and indeed from interviews with veterans, that there was little eagerness amongst them for the war. For a start, they had very little training. Unlike the British soldiers of the First World War, who were given up to one year's instruction at home,[55] the Spanish soldier was shipped immediately to Morocco where he tended to

[52] Interviews with Balada and Manuel Soto Meizoso, the latter on 15 Mar. 1998.

[53] For a portrait of one such doctor see Giménez Caballero, *Notas*, 52–8.

[54] Sender, *Imán*, 107–8.

[55] Gloden Dallas and Douglas Gill, *The Unknown Army: Mutinies in the British Army in World War One* (London, Verso, 1985), 29.

get a few weeks of rather desultory training. As we have seen, the brief enthusiasm for revenge and reconquest after the 1921 disaster, stronger among the more educated soldiers arriving from Spain than among the poor, gave way soon to a common culture of stoical endurance. This may have had much to do with the static and defensive strategy adopted by the High Command after the Spanish government brought the initial counter-offensive to a halt in November. Equally, the disastrous retreat from the front-line positions in the west in 1924 can only have lowered the morale of soldiers. What kept them going was solidarity and comradeship in the collective struggle for survival. In some cases, their willingness to fight was motivated by a respect for, even devotion to, their commanding officers.

Nevertheless, soldiers devoted much rational and creative energy to the evasion of danger. What appeared most sought-after among the front-line troops was the 'tiro de suerte', the lucky shot that wounded a soldier in the least vulnerable part of his body but gave him months off combat duty or maybe a trip back home (or even a promotion).[56] When they became desperate, soldiers would surreptitiously raise a leg above the parapet in the hope it would be shot by a Moroccan marksman. Officers knew of this ruse and would arrest any soldier they suspected of trying it out. But it was also common, at least in the early part of the military campaign, to shoot oneself in the hand. According to a general in 1914, a rifle would go off almost every day through an act of self-mutilation, leaving one soldier after another wounded in the right hand.[57] Other techniques of evasion involved putting chopped nettles into scratches, that would swell up alarmingly the next day, or heating a coin and sticking it to the skin to provoke an ulcer, or twisting mustard paper used for the treatment of catarrh into a thin tube and pushing it into the penis to create a drip effect typical of gonorrhea, or sticking the tongue into milk just before the doctor's examination.[58]

Humour and swearing were less painful ways of coping with the stress of war and discipline. Unpopular officers or the uncomfortable conditions of campaign life were enrolled into scenarios of raillery or irony that made them more bearable and strengthened the sense of solidarity among the soldiers. As we shall see later, one of the greatest enemies of soldiers on campaign was the flea. A joke circulating the camps and outposts was that the flea and the Moor had reached an agreement whereby the flea would attack the Spanish troops and weaken them before battle. The craving for sex was made less intolerable by swearing and jokes. A visitor to Melilla was shocked by the intensity of the

---

[56] Sender, *Imán*, 36; Barea, *La Forja*, 309.

[57] Confidential letter from General Federico Ochando y Chumillas to Angel Galarza, 2 May 1914, passed on to Romanones: AR leg. 6 (2), carp. 8 (21).

[58] Ibid., 307; Sender, *Imán*, 88; Masferrer interview. In December 1921 the minister of war was so concerned about simulated diseases and wounds he called on Berenguer to investigate and punish these evasions: 3.12.21 in AFAMM leg. 364/8.

erotic language of the soldier, claiming it went far beyond that of any town in Spain. He suggested that this 'dirty eroticism . . . saturating conversations and general concerns' should be dealt with by the imposition of hard work and study.[59]

The most difficult question to address is the soldiers' attitude to the enemy. As we saw in Chapter 7, they were encouraged to see the Moorish Other as an archetypal enemy that needed destroying. Most would have imbibed the implicit or explicit racism of Spanish culture. Yet there were subtle differences in the intensity of prejudice. An artilleryman went to a Muslim wedding and found the dance performed after the ceremony 'grotesque'. On the other hand, a military driver heard the chanting at a Moroccan funeral and noted in his journal simply that they were not keeping time, 'just like kids at a Spanish school singing a lesson'.[60] In the first case, the soldier derived a racist judgement from a cultural difference; in the second, the other soldier merely registered the difference without seeking to judge it.

In any case, the discourse of the Other was unlikely to draw recruits into a lethal hatred of 'bad Moroccans' unless they had been severely hurt by them. The vast majority of soldiers did not see the atrocities of Anual, Monte Arruit, and other places and so were less likely to be moved by anger and thirst for revenge. The narratives of the colonial war are filled with contradictory anecdotes of cruelty, indifference, and generosity towards the enemy on the part of the rank-and-file soldier on military service. In his memoirs of war, a Catalan soldier remembers seeing a Moroccan prisoner being dragged down a slope head-first by rope, to the approval of some soldiers and the indifference of others.[61] One of the veterans I interviewed admitted that it was common practice to torture prisoners with a bayonet to obtain information. On the other hand, Sender's autobiographical hero comes across a corporal surreptitiously using the first-aid kit he carried for himself to treat the wound of an old and dying Rifian enemy.[62]

Another of the veterans I interviewed claimed that he often shot into the air when his officers were not looking, because he had nothing against the Moroccan enemy.[63] Clearly no soldier would do this if his life were at risk. The Catalan soldier mentioned earlier wrote: 'I really did not want to kill any of them but nor did I want any of them to kill me. I am thinking this yet I carry on firing. There's no way round.'[64] The natural suspicion that the veteran's claim was one of the involuntary distortions of memory caused by time and changing values must be set against evidence from the two World Wars that soldiers on military service were reluctant to kill the foe when they could see him. Testimonies painstakingly collected by S. L. A. Marshall in the Second

[59] Guixé, *El Rif*, 154; the joke about the flea is in Prous, *Quatre gotes*, 40.
[60] n.a., *La Bateria*, 16; Sánchez, 'Diario', 29.   [61] Prous, *Quatre gotes*, 46.
[62] Díaz Ripoll interview; Sender, *Imán*, 282.   [63] Campa Ginot interview.
[64] Prous, *Quatre gotes*, 33.

World War indicate that even battle-hardened veterans rarely shot directly at the enemy, because they were too deeply socialized by the values of civilized society.[65] In the Moroccan war it appeared to be easier for officers to order the killing and maiming of thousands of men, women, and children with poisonous chemicals dropped from a great height than for some soldiers on military service to kill a single enemy in front of them.

As for the conditions of the soldiers' life both on the front line and in the rear, there can be no quantitative or systematic study given the absence of data. While the First World War has been subjected to an intense scrutiny of conditions and their effects on soldiers, no such effort has been made in the case of the colonial war in Morocco. Like the combatants of the First World War, life at the front in Morocco forced the soldier to mobilize new resources and transform the way in which he interpreted the environment. The life-skills he had acquired as a civilian were no longer appropriate in war. The physical conditions that surrounded him required new responses and changed the meaning of everyday actions. He was obliged to reconfigure all his sensory instincts. The war was an onslaught against all the senses. Hearing and vision became vital to survival, while smell, taste, and touch were assaulted and brutalized.

In the small and remote fortified positions (or blockhouses), for example, the reflex act of defecation was transformed into an existential act, a problem of life or death, the centre of conversation. Unable to shit within the position because the accumulated smells of urine, sweat, and dirt were bad enough without that of faeces, the soldier was forced to seek a convenient place outside to do his business. But when he ventured out of the position and lowered his trousers, he became a squatting target for the skilled Rifian snipers who lay waiting for just such an opportunity.[66] Fear or a bad diet could paralyse the act of defecation, but they could also stimulate it. Advances were often held up by soldiers squatting on both sides of the road or stopping frequently to urinate. Often soldiers urinated or defecated in their pants out of terror.[67]

Unlike the First World War, which was characterized largely by static fronts, trench warfare, heavy artillery barrages, and slow advances across devastated terrain, the colonial war presented a wide range of scenarios. Soldiers could be posted to small, isolated posts, deployed on long marches across barren landscapes by day or night, mobilized for bayonet charges or landings by sea. The Rifian fighters seldom attacked frontally. Instead, the war featured repeated ambushes, encirclement, constant shifts of the point of attack, and more often than not, an almost invisible enemy that harassed columns and positions and could not be distinguished from the surrounding rocks.

In the small fortified Spanish posts, long periods of excruciating boredom were punctuated by moments of intense fear. The absence of action was almost

[65] S. L. A. Marshall, *Men Against Fire* (New York, 1966), 78, quoted in Leed, *No Man's Land*, 9–10; for evidence from the First World War, see ibid., 105–14.

[66] Barea, *La Forja*, 297.   [67] Mola, *Dar Akkoba*, 91 and 93.

worse than the terror of attack. It seemed sometimes as if 'the Moors preferred we suffered the martyrdom of monotony', as if the High Command had forgotten the existence of the outpost. The boredom was only interrupted every fortnight or so by the arrival of a convoy carrying supplies and mail; in the meantime soldiers would dream about the letters they might get from home.[68] In an outpost more exposed to enemy action, vision and, above all, hearing became essential. Ambivalent signs permeated the landscape at night. Sentries had to maintain their alertness to distinguish the effect of the wind and the noise of wild animals, like rats and jackals, from the stealthy approach of Moroccan fighters. In many outposts soldiers hung empty tin cans on the barbed wire, and if they started to clang the sentries fired some rounds in the direction of the noise.[69]

Sentry duty was decided by lottery; the worst times were during the night or at midday in the heat of the sun. If they were allotted a good time, some soldiers traded it for money or goods they could later sell. During the daytime, also, simple operations like fetching water from a nearby well required a sharp sensory vigilance, even the development of a sixth sense. Yet death and injury were usually haphazard. As one veteran wrote: 'Here life and death is always a surprise for everyone. Death can surprise you just as easily as remaining alive. Everything is fortuitous.'[70]

Marches were equally exposed to attack. Yet such were the conditions soldiers were subjected to that at night they usually marched shoulder to shoulder, somnolent, their ears covered by the collars of their uniforms, their weapons unready for combat. An American journalist passed a platoon of soldiers 'plodding along in makeshift sandals'. Primo de Rivera was thus prompted to describe his soldiers as docile, resistant, disciplined, honest, but too inexperienced and too trusting.[71] Columns on the move often lacked sufficient tents to accommodate the soldiers, while the officers had to cram into small spaces in the few tents available. The soldiers slept on the ground with only a blanket to protect them from the cold and rain. During the day, the marching soldiers were assailed by insects and broiled by the sun or soaked by the rain.

In the larger and more permanent front-line camps, life over twenty-four hours was dominated by the search for a minimum level of comfort. Sleep was difficult at night, even though tents and sacks filled with hay were provided for the soldiers. The changing of the guard repeatedly disturbed sleep, mosquitoes and rats went about their work in profusion, jackals howled, the cots of the mobile brothel creaked, and Rifian fighters hurled insults and fired their guns to provoke a waste of ammunition and exacerbate sleeplessness.[72] If there were

[68] Díaz-Fernández, *El blocao*, 32 and 102.   [69] Bosque, 'Prisionero', 24.

[70] Prous, *Quatre gotes*, 31; Sender, *Imán*, 52.

[71] *Bulletin de Comité de L'Afrique Française* (Jan. 1925), 38–9. Sheean, *Personal History*, 101.

[72] Sender, *Imán*, 82; Prous, *Quatre gotes*, 120–7.

no fighting or sorties to be made that day, the soldier was obliged to work in the heat of the sun, carrying sandbags, building tracks, or doing sentry duty or any of the numerous other tasks assigned by the officers and NCOs. One veteran remembers an excruciating day in 1926 when he and his fellow soldiers had to stand in military formation from nine in the morning till four in the afternoon; the purpose was to await the arrival of the recently promoted Brigadier-General Franco.[73] Another recalls the obsessive metal-button polishing he was forced to carry out even though all the soldiers' jackets were filthy. Discipline was frequently harsh. A third veteran remembers a sentry being shot to death by his commander for negligence. Maltreatment of recruits was so rife that Gómez Jordana issued an order in 1914 threatening severe punishment for any officer or NCO guilty of such a charge.[74]

Off duty, the soldier spent time dealing with the animals and insects that surrounded him. There were a thousand insects and vermin, recalls one soldier, from flies to scorpions: 'this is the land of creepy-crawlies'. 'Reading the newspaper' was the ironic term for the morning habit of raising a shirt in the air with arms outstretched to look for the lice that had accumulated in its folds during the night. Another of the occupations on the front line was killing rats. The army offered money for the tail of each rat, until it was discovered that so desperate were some soldiers for pennies that they would forge rats' tails. From then on the whole body had to be handed in. But some soldiers bred rats to get extra money. Other animals, such as monkeys and birds, were kept as pets. Some kept dogs and cats tied up in case food ran out. At least one soldier collected fleas and kept them in a box.[75] With their pennies the soldiers could buy snacks and drinks, such as dried figs, wine, and brandy from the peddlers that followed the columns everywhere, even on their marches. Many of these were poor Spaniards from the south eking a living off the soldiers rather than the officers and senior NCOs, who would shun the shoddy goods they sold.

Such purchases were not luxuries. Hunger and thirst dominated life at the front. Worst of all was the lack of drinkable water. Barrels of water were transported by lorry or carried with the marching columns on the backs of donkeys. But there was never enough. Wells along the route were often contaminated, while fortified positions were built regardless of the proximity of sources of water. One of the veterans interviewed for this book was part of a unit that had to supply water every day to an isolated position on the western front.

[73] Campa Ginot interview.

[74] Order of 29 Jan. 1914, SHM R273, leg.125, carp. 1; Prous, *Quatre gotes*, 38; Masferrer Fontanella interview; Noel, *Lo que vi*, 115. Many officers continued to treat NCOs and soldiers harshly in the 1920s but they were subject to greater control. In 1925 an infantry officer was suspended briefly for ordering a sergeant to spend the night outside their position exposed to the enemy because that sergeant had failed to obey orders to advance on the grounds that he had considered the operation too dangerous: AHN (Salamanca), Sección Político-Social, Madrid, leg. 722.

[75] 'La Batería', 31; Mola, *Dar Akkoba*, 64; Sender, *Imán*, 75, and Cordón, *Trayectoria*, 100–1; Fernández Oxea, *Crónicas*, 104–5.

Eventually he was invalided out of the war after twenty-six months' service with malaria he had caught from a well he had been detailed to clean.[76] Spanish planes often tried to drop blocks of ice for besieged soldiers, but more often than not these broke as they landed or fell into the hands of the attackers. According to the Socialist MP Indalecio Prieto, the Spanish government had bought a huge and expensive tanker in 1921 to bring water to the front line in the east. But its hull was too deep to moor close to the coast and no hoses or small boats had been provided to carry the water to land. So 6,000 tons of water lay unused in the tanker, 'breeding frogs.'[77]

Lack of water drove besieged soldiers crazy. When they had consumed all the water and alcohol, they would lick the rocks at dawn or drink their own urine. Even here, distinctions of class and rank played an important role. The officers usually had access to a supply of sugar and were able to sweeten their urine, while ordinary soldiers had to drink it 'straight'. A veteran artilleryman told me that during the siege, in which he almost lost his life through thirst and hunger, the Moroccan besiegers would come close to his position and swish containers filled with water to encourage the soldiers there to surrender.[78]

Thirst was exacerbated by the cold rations served to soldiers on campaign. The typical food carried on the back of mules or in the soldiers' knapsack was smoked sausage (or chorizo) and tins of sardines, both heavily salted, accompanied by dry bread or often stale biscuits. According to one wag, these biscuits were so old they dated from the Spanish War of Independence of 1808, if not before. At least in the early part of the Moroccan campaign the biscuits were truly old, part of the supplies left over from the Cuban war of 1895–8, and they had to be cut in half with a machete on a stone or soaked in water, if that was available. Another soldier claimed that some of the sardine tins were so old they were rusty inside and the oil had evaporated. Occasionally they were given raw herrings, but they could not always find wood to make a fire so these had to be eaten uncooked. Chickpeas were also sometimes part of the campaign rations, and when they could not be cooked they also had to be eaten raw, causing intense indigestion to the soldiers.[79]

Food in the camps was of course better, as long as they had mobile kitchens. Soldiers tended to get a stolid diet of beans, chickpeas, rice, meat, and salted cod, with a glass of very rough wine a day. The more technical corps, like the artillery, usually served better meals because they were more stationary and their officers were more concerned about the soldiers' conditions than, for

[76] Campa Ginot interview.

[77] Indalecio Prieto, *Con el rey o contra el rey* (Mexico, Ediciones Oasis, 1972), 106.

[78] Balada interview; Sender, *Imán*, 121.

[79] Masferrer interview; Prous, *Quatre gotes*, 45. Commenting on the saltiness of the campaign rations, the Socialist Deputy Indalecio Prieto wrote: 'To which wise men in our magnificent quartermaster stores did the idea occur that tinned sardines should be the basis of cold rations, in a country lacking water and where thirst is the constant torment of the troops?': *Con el rey*, 105.

example, their colleagues in the infantry. The occasional raid against a village might also yield a supply of cows and sheep, and all the soldiers would get fat for a while on the meat. But the cattle kept by the units were usually in poor condition because of the lack of feed, and some could hardly walk.[80]

Another source of constant suffering for the troops was the lack of suitable clothing and footwear. In the extremely volatile climate of the Rif mountains, their uniforms gave protection from neither heat nor cold. Worse than the clothes they wore was the footwear. Espadrilles (or *alpargatas*) were the standard footwear for most of the soldiers, as we saw earlier. They were, of course, of little use in the campaigns. They would fall to pieces quickly or become sodden in the mud. Artillerymen carrying heavy pieces of cannon up a mountain were obliged to abandon their espadrilles when the rain started to fall, and to drag the pieces up the hillside barefoot. First-aid centres were filled with soldiers suffering from sore and swollen feet after long marches.[81]

One of the worst aspects of camp life was the smell. Unlike their middle-class colleagues or the officers, most soldiers were from poor families living in slums or the countryside and had grown up among bad odours and dirt. But the smells of the colonial war were probably much worse than they had ever encountered, only exceeded by those of the rotting corpses that lay strewn about in the battlefields of the summer of 1921. The blockhouse smell or the all-pervading stench of the camp was an assault on the olfactory sense. It seemed to stick to the skin, as one veteran remembers. It was like the smell of dirty clothes left for weeks in a damp corner, only a hundred times worse. Body odours were almost as bad. In the early campaigns, many soldiers were expected to wear the same uniform for up to a month, stiffened by dirt, discoloured by rain and sun, and smelling putrid. The latrines close to the tents or blockhouses gave off a putrefying odour. The stale bacon that was often one of the 'delicacies' served up in the canteen had a whiff of burnt rubber and the rice smelt like sweaty shirts treated with starch. For those who enjoyed war, like Mola, the mixture of sweat, used leather, stables, and cheap cooking could be a heady perfume. But he was prepared to admit that other odours, such as faeces and urine and the smells emanating from the bodies of dirty soldiers, were not so pleasant.[82]

The poor conditions of campaign life were reflected in the high level of casualties due to illness or stress. For many years of the war illnesses far exceeded war injuries. In 1912, for example, the number of wounded soldiers in the Melilla hospitals was one-tenth of those interned with illnesses. In 1915 reports

[80] Arbolí, *Memorias*, 58–9; 'La Batería', 29–30; Arauz de Robles, *Por el camino*, iii. 79.

[81] Arbolí, *Memorias*, 151; Prous, *Quatre gotes*, 69; Eliseo Vidal Gallego, *El joven del Rif. ¡¡¡Los muertos de Annual ya son vengados!!!* (Madrid, Gráfica Administrativa, 1932), 74; for an eloquent description of campaign life during the rainy season, see 'Es una sangría para España', *El Socialista*, 22 Mar. 1912.

[82] Barea, *La forja*, 296; Arauz, *Por el camino*, 45; Urquijo, *La campaña del Rif*, 93; Sender, *Imán*, 39; Mola, *Dar Akkoba*, 61 and 185.

from the same area made it clear that there was an excessive number of soldiers down with malaria, typhus, typhoid, anaemia, and rheumatism.[83] Five years later epidemics of bubonic plague and typhus broke out. A report indicated that forty-two veterans being repatriated to Spain were so sick and hungry that the Red Cross had to intervene to treat them. Other more common ailments included ulcers (a typical symptom of stress), diarrhoea, TB, and scabies, the latter a condition so wretched that it 'incites you to commit suicide or to throw yourself into a pot of boiling oil'.[84]

The most widespread illness of all was venereal disease of one sort or another. On its own, it was probably responsible for more casualties than the war. In a Melilla military hospital in July 1920, for example, 200 out of 546 patients suffered from venereal diseases such as gonorrhoea and syphilis, while fewer than twenty-six were interned with injuries caused by war or the use of weapons.[85] Prostitutes, both Spanish and Moroccan, were available almost always, even during military campaigns. Many of the poorest of them had caught venereal disease. They would follow the troops, along with the peddlers and hangers-on seeking to make a few pennies. In the temporary camps mobile brothels were set up consisting of a tent or two and some cots. The prostitutes would sometimes get caught up in the military action and thus experienced the horrors of both war and sexual abuse.[86]

With the exception of the Red Cross hospitals, which all commentators agreed were well staffed and supplied, conditions in the other hospitals were very poor. The staff–patient ratio there was not bad except when military campaigns were intense. A year before the disaster at Anual, for example, the two military hospitals in Melilla had between them nineteen doctors for 1,191 patients, that is, one for every 62.7 patients.[87] After Anual, the number of injured and sick outstripped the capacity of whatever extra staff could be mustered from Spain. The statistics for 1922 make extraordinary reading. In the eastern zone, of the 65,075 troops based in the area, 49,323 were admitted to hospital and 15,494 were treated in the first-aid centres in the barracks, making a total of 64,817. Of these, 544 died during treatment, but the vast majority were able to return to service. The proportional statistics indicate that each soldier had to be treated in hospital or in first-aid centres on an average of almost ten times during 1922. But if we count the sick and injured already in hospital on 1 January 1922, that is, those who were still being treated for injuries resulting from the post-Anual events, the figures are truly shocking. On this

[83] SHM R241, leg. 92, carp. 22 and R309, leg. 159, carp. 2 and 5.
[84] Details for 1920 in SHM caja 53, carp. 3 and caja 52, carp. 6, 16 Nov. 1920 and 12 and 13 Dec. 1920; Masferrer interview; Micó, *Los Caballeros*, 275.
[85] AGA Sección 15: Africa, caja M360 81/3.
[86] SHM R656, leg. 465, carp. 10; Giménez Caballero, *Notas Marruecas*, 187; Sender, *Imán*, 82; Mola, *Dar Akkoba*, 97–8.
[87] AGA Sección 15: Africa, caja M360 81/3, report of 4 July 1920.

count, the total number of people who were treated in the hospitals during that year was 1,221,968.[88]

Medical services in the Melilla zone already suffered from a bad reputation. A detailed report by an army captain in 1915 had denounced the state of the local hospitals. Pay for the medical staff was very low and medical supplies were totally inadequate. The lunch served to the patients was made up of watery soup with noodles, some of which, according to the captain's ocular estimate, were less than 3 centimetres in length. The meat that followed smelt bad, weighed as little as 15 grams, and was so tough it could hardly be torn apart with the fingers. The indignant captain painstakingly counted the chickpeas that accompanied the meat and found there were only between thirty-five and forty-three on each plate. Extraordinarily for a hospital filled with feverish patients, there was a shortage of water.[89] Berenguer himself complained to the minister of war, Viscount Eza, in 1920 about the state of the military hospital in Tetuan, 'a repulsive place made of wood filled with all types of parasites and microbes, built in 1913 as a provisional structure to cope with the situation at the time'.[90]

The worst hospitals appeared to have been those for infectious diseases, such as one in Melilla named after the high commissioner Gómez Jordana. When infections were rife the hospital could not accommodate all the patients, so they were put in tents outside in the heat. But the medical personnel were too few to deal adequately with the patients, so they were left unattended for hours in the midst of dirt, smells, and swarms of flies. An inmate of the Tetuan hospital for infectious diseases remembers a soldier attached to the medical team doing the rounds of the patients putting a thermometer in the mouth of one patient, then wiping it and putting it in the mouth of the next.[91]

The military authorities made strenuous efforts to improve medical services and the level of hygiene. If they were willing to study it, they had a model of hygiene and preventive medicine in the neighbouring French colony of Algeria. In very similar conditions, the French had adopted measures that kept their soldiers by and large healthy. Unlike the Spanish, they were all vaccinated against typhus and were only served food that could survive the heat, at least for a short while.[92] For the duration of the colonial war the Spanish military archives are filled with orders emanating from the top, urging proper measures to be taken to improve sanitation, conservation of food, cleanliness, the location of latrines, and so on. The authorities went as far as to intervene in the drinks consumed by soldiers. The alcohol and bottled water served by the

[88] 'Movimiento general de enfermos por Cuerpos de Ejército, África, Melilla y plazas menores', *Instituto Nacional de Estadística* (1924), 534.

[89] SHM R309, leg. 159, carp. 1.   [90] Eza, *Mi responsabilidad*, 365.

[91] Arauz, *Por el camino*, 133–8; Barea, *La forja*, 331.

[92] Justo Larios de Medrano, *España en Marruecos. Historia secreta de la campaña* (Madrid, n.p., n.d.), 110–11.

pedlars and bar owners were tested by their laboratories and often found to be adulterated, leading the authorities to impose severe fines on the guilty parties.[93]

Hygienic measures were considerably improved over the years. Semi-official brothels became subject to strict controls, and the prostitutes who worked in them had to undergo regular medical inspection. By 1926 strict orders had been issued to ensure the cleanliness of bars and toilets, the draining of pools and puddles, and the destruction of rats, fleas, and mosquitoes. Soldiers were once again urged to wash as often as possible.[94] Yet for all their efforts, the overall level of sanitation and hygiene remained abysmally low. This was largely because the resources set aside to improve these services were inadequate. For example, water was often not available for daily ablutions. The environment of the front line did not encourage healthy practices, and in any case, most officers were not bothered about such niceties.

The conditions of war, therefore, drove many soldiers to despair. The culture of evasion, as we have seen, was widespread. But the most drastic form of escape from the terrible environment of war was suicide. In February 1922 the Congress of Deputies became so concerned about rumours that many soldiers had killed themselves that they requested statistics from the military authorities in Morocco. The figures sent to them did not correspond completely to the period they had specified and only covered suicides between March 1920 and January 1922. Over this term, three officers and nine soldiers were registered as having killed themselves; except for one officer, whose suicide was attributed to a chronic illness, all were reported to have done so for an 'unknown reason'. However, the figures clearly did not include those, like Silvestre, who may have killed themselves to avoid capture. That is, the data supplied by the military appear to have excluded suicides during military action and only registered rearguard suicides. It was, of course, much easier to disguise suicides on the front line as casualties of war. The fact that the Army of Africa declared that other information requested by the deputies about expulsions and internal prosecutions was not available suggests how little it was prepared to co-operate with the civil authorities.[95] We are left with the strong suspicion that there were indeed suicides on the front line that were never declared.

On the rare occasions when troops were given time off from the campaign, life in the rear was a welcome relief. But it represented a challenge of a very different kind. The rank-and-file soldier sought during his rare days of leave to forget briefly the terror of war and the utter boredom of camp life. Unlike the soldiers in the First World War, leave did not usually mean a spell back home.

---

[93]   Thus e.g. SHM R309, leg. 159, carp. 2 and 3 and R241, leg. 92, carp. 22.

[94]   SHM R656, leg. 465, carp. 10; Ramón Castejón Bolea, 'Los médicos de la higiene: medicina y prostitución en la España contemporánea (1847–1918)', *Bulletin d'Histoire Contemporaine de l'Espagne*, 25 (June 1997), 85; SHM R694, leg. 513, carp. 15, 24 and 28, order of 24 Aug. 1926.

[95]   SHM Africa, caja 85/16.

It may be that, like the Allies in the First World War, the authorities did not wish the soldiers to see the hardships suffered by their families. In the Spanish case, indeed, they may have feared that soldiers would become aware of the relative indifference of most Spaniards towards the colonial war, creating an even greater demoralization amongst them.[96] A more likely reason was simply that the military authorities could not release any soldier for more than a few days. So for three years or so the Spanish conscript stayed in Morocco, unless he was severely wounded or incapacitated. Posted to garrison towns like Melilla or Tetuan for brief periods, he was supposed to have the opportunity to let off steam. However, with the 15 céntimos he earned daily (in around 1922), he had little chance to do much more than see a film or a show and drink the cheapest alcohol available.[97]

Those who could afford it, like the Legionnaires, drank massive quantities of alcohol both on leave and at the front. 'We all smoked kif in pipes and we drank alcohol whenever we could. Shit, did we drink!' recalls one veteran. It did great damage to the effectiveness of the colonial army. The wine and brandy drunk all day in the towns by better-off soldiers on leave impaired the body and gave rise to murderous quarrels and gratuitous violence. The cheap wine was often adulterated by the addition of chemicals to prevent too rapid a fermentation.[98] Drinking was regarded by the macho officer as the necessary price of war. It was the easiest way to let off steam. By drowning themselves in drink, they could, in the vivid Spanish idiom, undrown themselves of war (*desahogarse*) or let off steam.

Apart from drinking, the most popular activity was almost certainly sex. Holed up for months in the outposts, according to Díaz-Fernández's autobiographical novel, soldiers passed the time playing cards or talking about sex in 'obscene dialogues'. His protagonist would spend hours staring through a telescope to try to catch sight of Moroccan women in a nearby village. 'I looked for women. Sometimes, a white silhouette, evaporating often among the fig trees, would give rise in me to a rare anguish, the tender anguish of sex.' A 15-year-old Moroccan girl would venture near the blockhouse during the day selling eggs and figs. Despite her cold, indifferent stare, the stare he knew betokened hatred, she became the focus of his sexual fantasies. Then one day she turned up at dusk and, against his better instincts, he went out to meet her. In fact she was the bait used by the muhayeddin to ambush the soldiers in the outpost, and four of them were killed before the assailants were driven back.[99]

Opportunities for sex, on the other hand, were numerous in the rearguard. The towns were filled with brothels. Many of the prostitutes had come from Spain or were from Spanish families who had settled in the area. Others were Moroccan, from both Spanish and French Morocco. In garrison towns not far

---

[96] Fuller, *Troop Morale*, 72–4.
[98] Barea, *La forja*, 312–14; Soto Meizoso interview.
[97] Isidre Balada interview.
[99] Díaz-Fernández, *El blocao*, 35–9.

from the border with the French Protectorate, such as Chauen, there were many French prostitutes. One of the best districts of Melilla was given over almost entirely to prostitution. Of course, the brothels repeated the social divisions of rank and class. In the better-class brothels for officers, only a well-respected sergeant with an educated background might gain admission.[100] For those rank-and-file soldiers who had saved some money cheap brothels were available but many of their prostitutes had venereal disease.

For those who could not afford a prostitute, on the other hand, masturbation was a common means of coping with sexual needs. According to Moroccan sources, it was so open among the soldiers that it was sometimes done in a group. The habitual public arena where group masturbation took place was the cinema. Seated in the darkness in the cheapest seats, consisting of stools, soldiers would openly masturbate as they watched what was, by modern standards, an only mildly erotic film. A Moroccan soldier who fought for the Army of Africa claims that masturbation was very common among Spanish soldiers, particularly on the front lines. He also asserts that prolonged service in the blockhouses or the theatres of war led soldiers to have sex with each other.[101] For many such soldiers, these experiences were more likely to have been the product of bisexuality. However much it was practised, bisexuality or homosexuality was such a taboo subject among soldiers, writers, and journalists that not even the most oblique reference to it seems to have been made in reports or memoirs, leaving the historian unable even to guess at its dimensions. Nevertheless, a strong aura of latent homosexuality hangs over the portrayal of male bonding among colonial officers in the Francoist film *Harka*.[102]

There were also many bookshops in the towns given over entirely to pornography. If they could afford the magazines, Spanish soldiers would buy them and take them back to the front line. Officers were apparently not bothered about the pornographic hobby of their soldiers. Many of them probably indulged in it themselves. Instead, they were deeply concerned about the presence of any left-wing literature, which they sought to confiscate.[103] Striptease shows were also available for soldiers. To see real women on the stage must

---

[100] As a sergeant of the engineering corps, Barea managed to frequent one of these: *La forja*, 276; for a vivid picture of a brothel see Vidal, *El joven*, 160–4. Renewed efforts were made by the authorities in 1927 to bring prostitution under control to avoid the high levels of venereal diseases among soldiers: Dirección de Intervención, Inspección de Sanidad, *Instrucciones provisionales reglamentando el ejercicio de la prostitución en las ciudades de la Zona de Protectorado de España en Marruecos* (Tetuan, Editorial Hispano Africana, 1927).

[101] Second interview with Enfeddal Oulad Ben H'mamou Zeruali ; interview with Ali Raisuni on 22 July 2000 in Chauen.

[102] Peter Evans, 'Cifesa: Cinema and Authoritarian Aesthetics', in Helen Graham and Jo Labanyi (ed.), *Spanish Cultural Studies: An Introduction* (Oxford, OUP, 1995), 218–19. In contrast, there appears to be considerable evidence of widespread sexual contact between males in the case of the British Empire: Hyam, *Empire*, 212.

[103] Barea, *La forja*, 352–3.

have been a novel change in itself, after the drag shows soldiers put on in the camps in an effort to find some entertainment. One veteran recalls seeing a soldier dressed up as a young woman in one of these shows who had a voice made deep and hoarse by brandy (*la señorita de la voz aguardentosa*).[104]

Again, the shows in town were socially segregated. Officers frequented café-cabarets, where striptease of a 'more sophisticated kind' was performed. Many also had kept women, who were usually high-class prostitutes, some of them Moroccan. Other officers had Moroccan sweethearts who had largely broken from local traditions and lived like Spaniards. On the other hand, some officers who lived with their Moroccan girlfriends ate and slept like Moroccans. All these women would mix freely with the wives of senior officers (junior officers were not normally expected to bring their spouses) and civilians in the many social venues of the town where they lived. This social promiscuity across barriers of race, class, and convention was unthinkable in Spain.[105]

Another very popular pastime, both on the front and more especially in the rearguard, was gambling. Judging by the many references in the archives and in literature, gambling was, for those who got caught up in it, more an all-consuming obsession than an occasional flutter on the cards. The towns had separate gambling casinos for officers and sergeants, and soldiers could bet money on cards at almost every street-corner where a table or a drum was set up. While gambling in the casinos was regulated by military codes, open-air gambling was controlled by professional card-sharps, some of whom also monopolized prostitution.[106] A common pastime among Spanish men of the day, betting on baccarat or *rouge et noir*, became a passion, even a compulsion, amongst soldiers driven by boredom or the flight from battle. It often ended up in street disturbances, or in accumulated debt and despair.

In the culture of opprobrium that followed the 1921 disaster, gambling became one of the targets of those seeking to identify its causes. The words of Primo de Rivera's brother, Lt.-Colonel Fernando Primo de Rivera, killed in the disaster, were brandished in the Congress; one of many people turned into *ex post facto* prophets, he had warned that gambling could result in a military catastrophe. The parliamentary deputy Crespo de Lara attributed the military debacle in part to the widespread vice of gambling, which undermined discipline and attention to duty, and fostered demoralization among officers and men. In one of his sonorous parliamentary speeches, Indalecio Prieto declared: 'gambling has been one of the blights that has most broken the morale of the Army of Africa, turning men, impelled by the enthusiasm of their military devotion to those battles, into repulsive delinquents that cheat and rob the Nation at a time when gambling is a nightmare in all of Spain.'[107]

---

[104] Arbolí, 'Ligeras memorias', 46.
[105] Cordón, *Trayectoria*, 98 and 107; Díaz Ripoll interview.
[106] Barea, *La forja*, 257, 276, and 387.
[107] Crespo de Lara on 6 July 1922 in DSCD 3460–1 and Prieto on 21 Nov. 1922 in ibid., 4191.

'Repulsive delinquents' or not, the veterans who returned to Spain after their military service in Morocco had ended were deeply marked by their experience, at least those who had seen action on the front line. That much is obvious. What precise effect this experience had on them is much more diffi-cult to ascertain. Compared to the copious literature of war neurosis in post-First World War Europe, there is nothing in Spain about the individual aftermath of the Moroccan war. No book has studied the problems experi-enced by soldiers in their effort to integrate into society. Yet it can be surmised that the war must have controlled their everyday lives for some time after their demobilization.

In Chapter 6 I tried to analyse the significances of the war for the profes-sional colonial officer. There are very few sources on which to judge the same for the officers, NCOs, and rank-and-file soldiers simply doing military service in Morocco. The best-known accounts, such as Barea's and Sender's autobio-graphical novels, weave personal recollections of the war into an implicitly political narrative. For both writers it was one of the most formative experi-ences in their political development. Barea saw his spell in the war as part of the forging of his rebelliousness (*la forja de un rebelde*).

It would be a lot to expect of other, less literate veterans that they make the same sense of the war, of its nightmarish absurdity, its utter disconnection from the usages of everyday life. So removed was the experience of the war from the normal world that it must have been difficult to integrate the two experiences into a coherent memory. But from unpublished diaries and memoirs, and the interviews used in this book, some tentative hypotheses can be made about its effects. Among the abiding memories of the war were the comradeship and solidarity of the front line and the camps. That sense of community could not be easily reproduced in civilian life, and so demobilization generated a sense of loss, compounded by that resulting from death in battle of close friends.

Another striking characteristic of the soldiers' memory of the war is the absence of enmity towards the Moroccan Other. It is possible again that more politically correct attitudes have filtered through into the memories over the years and transformed them. Yet the lack of a convincing cause for fighting the enemy, and the apparent friendliness of most Moroccans, attenuated any anger at the violence they inflicted on the soldiers. Two of the veterans I interviewed quite separately used the same phrase: 'the Moors were like us', and one of them went on to explain that in Morocco only the chiefs of the villages live well, implying that things were not especially different in Spain.[108] Moreover, the reaction of many soldiers to the scenes of desperate poverty they saw all around them was one of pity. The same two veterans remembered with sorrow the plight of Moroccan women carrying great weights on their shoulders or pulling a plough by a rope lashed to their bodies.

---

[108] Interviews with Isidre Balada and Josep Campa Ginot.

The rank-and-file soldiers also came back from the war with a diffuse sense of injustice at the fact that they had had to undergo so much terror, horror, and discomfort for so little purpose. Like Barea and Sender, that injustice politicized some of the veterans. One of those I interviewed said that for all the years of military service he had performed in Morocco, he had accumulated only enough money to buy a suitcase, four packets of tobacco, and a handkerchief for his girlfriend. When he and his fellow soldiers arrived in Spain after demobilization, the customs police or *carabineros* ordered them to line up and open their suitcases. The soldiers then did what they would never have done before the war, which was to refuse to obey the police, and had to spend three days in jail as a result.[109] Another veteran admitted that he had been changed a lot by the war and had also become deeply anti-militarist. In a note appended to his diary, a friend of the driver of the quartermaster stores, Juan Sánchez, wrote that Sánchez 'had drawn the following lesson, among others: that the army is the greatest school of anti-militarism there is in Spain; and I saw him on the day of his demobilization, a bit beside himself, a bit drunk with a strange and double happiness: that of going to his village, that of leaving jail, a really sad state of affairs if we think of how those who run the country pay those who serve it.'[110]

Yet for that sense of injustice to become identified with a political discourse, the veteran needed contact with a political environment. It is probably no coincidence that among those I interviewed the Catalan building worker, for example, was more likely to draw political conclusions from the experience of the colonial war than either the Galician fisherman or agricultural labourer. For the latter two the war was amongst the inevitable burdens of an unjust and unchanging world that had to be borne stoically. On the same day as the fisherman had to leave for Morocco, his father had died. His reaction some seventy-seven years later was to remark that 'these things have to happen'.

Tracing their lives after the war, the Catalan veterans tended to be supporters of the Republic and brought their experience of the colonial war to the Republican army. The Galicians, on the other hand, fought on the Nationalist side, not necessarily out of any conviction in its cause but because, like so many other Spaniards, they happened to be in an area that fell to the Nationalists when the uprising took place in 1936. Similarly, the experience of the colonial war did not significantly influence the decision of the officers who had served briefly in Morocco over which side they supported in the Civil War. Their decision was often the result simply of where they found themselves in the first days of the insurrection.[111] Thus, the experience of the Moroccan war was internalized by the soldiers who survived its challenges in ways that defy simple generalization.

[109] Isidre Balada interview.
[110] Sánchez, *Diario*, 64; Campa Ginot interview.
[111] As Stanley Payne stresses in *Spain's First Democracy: The Second Republic, 1931–1936* (Madison, University of Wisconsin, 1993), 365.

PART III

The Colonial Army from Republic to Civil War, 1931–1939

CHAPTER NINE

Repression and Conspiracy

THE PROCLAMATION OF the Republic on 14 April 1931 was greeted with deeply contradictory responses within Spain. For many Spaniards, the Republic represented the first real democracy in a country hitherto ruled by an oligarchy backed by a reactionary clergy and a repressive military establishment. Primo de Rivera had resigned in January 1930 after his regime had become discredited and died two months later in exile in Paris. He was replaced by General Dámaso Berenguer, whose aim had been to engineer a return to the pre-dictatorship constitutional monarchy. But neither he nor his military successor were able to overcome the shift in popular opinion against the monarchy that had gathered pace since Primo de Rivera seized power with the king's blessing in 1923. When the left scored a victory in the municipal elections of April 1931, Alfonso XIII fled the country into exile and the Republic was established. The more conservative and traditional sections of Spanish society, however, viewed the new Republic with distaste and disquiet. Conservative military officers saw the regional autonomy promised by the new government as the beginning of the break-up of Spain. They were also alarmed at the prospect of a restructuring of the army leading to mass redundancies. Only among an extremist fringe, however, were there plans at such an early stage to overthrow the Republic by military force.

To some foreign observers, the colonial army appeared to receive the news with indifference. A British army officer on an official visit to Morocco reported that the changeover to the Republic 'took place so quietly that officials dozing in their offices were not disturbed'.[1] French military intelligence was less sanguine, however, because it was better informed about Spanish colonial military opinion. Shortly after the coming of the Republic, it reported a riot among the Legionnaires, who 'had been trained to be fiercely royalist and an embodiment [of the monarchy]'.[2] According to another source, there were also royalist demonstrations in Melilla. The fervent monarchist Colonel Osvaldo Capaz Montes was arrested as a result, but later released when it appeared that he had in fact tried to order the protesters to return to their barracks. Small-scale anti-Republican protests also took place in the Legion

---

[1] Capt. F. H. Mellor, *Morocco Awakes* (London, 1939), 99. [2] SHAT 3H 139, 8 May 1931.

garrisons in Dar Riffien, Xauen, and Larache.[3] These pockets of protest augured badly for the Republic.

General Sanjurjo, regarded by the new government as a friend of the Republic because he had refused to mobilize the Civil Guard to defend the king, was sent briefly to Morocco to restore order. As the new high commissioner and commander-in-chief of the Army of Africa, he made a pointed speech to his fellow Africanists equating patriotic duty with discipline and loyalty to the new government.[4] Yet, despite the rumblings of discontent in the Army of Africa, the new government appeared to be more worried about other problems. It was concerned about burgeoning labour agitation among Spanish workers in Morocco and the unrest among Moroccan nationalists, who were launching demonstrations in the hope that the Republic could be induced to abandon the Protectorate.

No evidence is available, however, that at this stage Africanist officers intended to plot against the Republic. Only a handful were close to the intransigent right in Spain. The new government gave no indication that it would radically alter colonial policy. Indeed, the Republican movement had a solid colonialist tradition stretching back to the early nineteenth century. 'Traditional republican doctrine is Africanist', contentedly declared a newspaper close to the Africanist officer opinion.[5] In any case, the majority of colonial officers were on the defensive. Closely identified with the king, the dictator, and Berenguer, they no doubt felt implicated in the political failure of all three. Their bitter rivals within the army, the Junteros, on the contrary, imagined they were the beneficiaries of the Republic.

Also, despite the power of their common *esprit de corps*, there was a wide range of political cultures amongst the Africanists, from republicanism to monarchism, which prevented a coherent response to events in the metropolis.[6] The relative isolation from Spain of officers serving in Morocco hindered immediate contact with anti-Republican forces. Most colonial officers had little in common with the best-organized of these forces, the Carlists (supporters of an alternative monarchical dynasty), because the army had fought them repeatedly in the nineteenth century in defence of the Alfonsine monarchy. Indeed, unlike the monarchical loyalty of the officer corps in other armies in Europe such as the Austrian or British, most Spanish officers were not wedded to the monarchical dynasty in Spain, whether Alfonsine or Carlist.

---

[3] *El Telegrama del Rif*, 15 and 18 Apr. 1931; Joaquín Arrarás, *Historia de la Segunda República española* (Madrid, Editora Nacional, 1956–68), i. 62–3.

[4] *El Telegrama del Rif*, 26 April 1931; *Ejercito y Armada*, 27 Apr. 1931.

[5] Santos Fernández, 'La República y Marruecos', *El Telegrama del Rif*, 14 Apr. 1931. Under Franco's editorship the *Revista de Tropas Coloniales*, now renamed *África*, seemed to accept the eventual independence of Morocco: A. M. de Escalera, 'Ceuta, Melilla y el abandono', July 1931, pp. 137–41.

[6] Miguel Alonso Baquer's view in *D. Manuel Azaña y los militares* (Madrid 1997), 60–1, that most were apolitical, however, is only sustainable if this implies support for a political party. As we have seen, Africanist officers were strongly ideological.

What began to polarize military opinion against the new Republican government was its seeming determination to intervene in the army's affairs, even though officers had done nothing to prevent its inauguration. Since the early nineteenth century the military had become accustomed to see itself as the ultimate guarantor of the national interest. It had stepped aside to allow the politicians of the Restoration to run the state, but in its own unarticulated self-image it was above politics rather than below. Used to special privileges and the flattery of politicians, the military was unlikely to accept its subordination to the state gracefully. For many officers this was tantamount to victimization. In the typical discourse of the military, politicians were once again showing their lack of appreciation for the patriotism of the army.

The first issue that inflamed the sensibilities of colonial officers at home and in Morocco was the determination of the radical left members of the governmental coalition to exact retribution for what they saw as the injustices of the past. The attorney-general, the Radical Socialist Angel Galarza, began a judicial enquiry into the Anual disaster and the collaboration of military officers and civilians with the Primo and Berenguer dictatorships. Berenguer and Mola were arrested and imprisoned, along with some of Primo's civilian collaborators. Leading members of the cabinet, including Manuel Azaña as minister of war, opposed the policy of retribution. Yet the so-called Responsibilities Commission was set up by parliament in August, empowered to investigate military and civilian offences since 1919.[7] Further arrests were made, including those of twelve of Primo's ageing generals. Although in the final outcome in December 1932 the sentences affected few veterans, relations between the military and the government were severely damaged.[8] Instinctively unfriendly towards the Republic, the colonial military were encouraged as a result to see the new regime as vindictive and hostile to their institution.

Alongside the Responsibilities issue, Azaña's military reforms were also bound to upset officers. Despite his perennial fatigue, Azaña threw himself into the task of restructuring the army. Like most Republicans, he was aware that military reform was essential for the survival of democracy. Rather than wait for the lengthy processes of parliament, he issued a series of decrees in rapid succession that set out to transform the military. Their extent and the speed with which they were issued must have taken the officers' breath away. Deeply influenced by the military reforms of the French Third Republic, Azaña set out to create a small and well-equipped army whose fundamental purpose was to defend the nation from external rather than internal foes. In a parliamentary speech in 1931, he pointed out that, unlike other nations, Spain had failed to reduce its armed forces after concluding a major war. The result was that the

[7] Carolyn P. Boyd, ' "Responsibilities" and the Second Spanish Republic 1931–6', *European History Quarterly*, 14 (1984), 151–82. For Azaña's unhappiness with the Commission see his *Obras Completas* (henceforth *OC*) (Mexico, Ediciones Oasis, 1968), iv. 115.

[8] *Marte*, 5 Dec. 1932.

army was ill-equipped, and the officers were poorly paid, had few prospects, and were understandably unhappy, prone therefore to intervene in political life.[9]

Few officers could dispute the need for cuts in the military budget and the restructuring of the army, least of all the colonial officers and the veteran Africanists. In 1930 there had been 163 generals and 21,996 officers on active service (and many more on the reserve list still receiving pay), while the troops (excluding non-commissioned officers) totalled some 115,930; that is, there was a general for every 711 privates and a commissioned officer for every nine. There were cavalry regiments without horses. In the Army of Africa, on the other hand, there were five generals and 2,300 officers for almost 45,000 troops, a much more balanced ratio.

Azaña's reform envisaged a dramatic reduction in the number of officers serving in the metropolis and only a moderate reduction in the colonial army.[10] His cuts in the military budget were designed not only to release funds for much-needed social reform but also to begin to improve the poor level of arms and equipment of the armed forces. He was also determined to depoliticize or at least tame the military elites. By increasing the number of non-commissioned officers in both armies he hoped to foster a lower layer of officers more sympathetic to the Republic. He thus envisaged the metropolitan army as a conscript army led by well-paid and trained professional officers drawn from different social classes, 'the nation en masse under arms', as he declared in another parliamentary speech in March 1932.[11]

Azaña had no illusions about the reaction of officers to his measures. He had never been unduly impressed by the quality of the generals. His own account of the colonial war had stressed the inefficiency and poverty of strategy of the military command.[12] He was aware also of the culture of nepotism, rife in both the metropolitan and colonial armies. In his diaries, Azaña frequently expressed frustration at the prima-donnaish sensibilities of the officers with whom he had to deal.[13] But the oft-repeated accusation that he packed the Ministry of War with Republican cronies and promoted senior officers thought to favour the Republic above the heads of more senior commanders was only partly true.[14] Azaña made great efforts to keep the goodwill of well-known right-wing and Africanist officers, as long as they accepted the Republic, by giving them important positions and maintaining frequent dialogue. It was

[9] Quoted in Santos Martínez Saura, *Memorias del Secretario de Azaña* (Madrid, Planeta, 1999), 152–6.

[10] Victor Morales Lezcano, 'L'exèrcit d'Africa i les reformes militars: 1931–1936', *L'Avenç* (June 1980), 41–6.

[11] Michael Alpert, *La reforma militar de Azaña (1931–1933)* (Madrid, Siglo XCXI 1982), 332; Santos Juliá, *Manuel Azaña. Una biografía política* (Madrid, Alianza, 1990), 98–9.

[12] 'Memorial de Guerra', *España*, 378–86 (July–Aug. 1923).

[13] Azaña, *OC* iv. 117–18 and 415–18.

[14] Nazario Cebreiros Curieses, *Las reformas militares. Estudio crítico* (Santander, n.p., 1931), 111–12; Diario Oficial del Ministerio de la Guerra, 17 Apr. 1931; *Informaciones*, 12 June 1931.

also the case that Azaña was determined to avoid undue pressure from his Republican military advisers, who formed what the right called the 'black cabinet'.[15]

The myth of Azaña's overt distaste for the military was largely the creation of the right-wing press. It deliberately misquoted a speech he made in June 1931 in which he said he was intent on crushing the power of *caciquismo* (the old system whereby parties could secure elections through their local elites), claiming he had said instead that he would crush the army.[16] This was totally uncharacteristic of Azaña's careful public utterances about military issues. In his dealings with officers, he tried to be circumspect and courteous (though it is clear from his diaries that this was quite an effort, given his instinctive and understandable distaste as a democrat for many of them). He was thus alarmed and disgusted when, some eight months after he became prime minister, the minister of justice, Sánchez Albornoz, was reported to have declared in a public meeting in June 1932: 'During the monarchy, it was enough for a general to sneeze to make the upper echelons of power tremble. Now the generals no longer sneeze . . .' Such a remark, wrote Azaña in his diary, could destroy in fifteen minutes everything he had achieved over one year.[17]

The Francoist interpretation of the restrained reaction of 'patriotic' officers to Azaña's reforms suggests a unity of purpose that simply did not exist at that stage. Indeed, what preoccupied them more than anything else was their careers. Well-known officers were happy to curry favour with Azaña, plead their special cases with him, or seek the appointment of relatives or friends. Some treated him with an obsequiousness that Azaña abhorred; in his diary, he recounts how the Africanist hero Castro Girona kissed his hand when he took his leave in a gesture of submission and gratitude. Some, like Queipo de Llano, were even prepared to run down their colleagues in tête-à-têtes with the minister of war.[18]

The method Azaña chose to carry out the reduction in personnel divided military opinion. His law on retirement offered full pay for life to officers who chose within thirty days to retire or be placed on the reserve list. Those who did not take up the offer, on the other hand, faced dismissal without

[15] Azaña, *OC* iv. 65 and 415–18.

[16] Paul Preston, *The Coming of the Spanish Civil War: Reform, Reaction and Revolution in the Second Republic*, 2nd edn. (London, Routledge, 1994), 51. Unfortunately, this myth persists despite easily available evidence to the contrary: e.g. Carloyn Boyd, 'Violencia pretoriana: del Cu-Cut! al 23-F', in Santos Juliá (ed.), *Violencia política en la España del siglo XX* (Madrid, Taurus, 2000), 316, assumes Azaña was referring to the army and writes that it was typical of Azaña's 'rhetorical excesses'. Miguel Alonso Baquer, in *D. Manuel Azaña y los militares* (Madrid, Actas, 1997), also exaggerates Azaña's irascibility and contempt towards the military.

[17] Quoted in Arrarás, *Historia*, i. 429. For Azaña's reaction, see his *Memoria políticas y de guerra 1931–39* in *OC* iv. 406–12. Sánchez Albornoz claimed that the conservative paper *ABC* had wrongly quoted his words. Azaña remained unconvinced by his protestations. In the end, under pressure from Azaña, the minister got *ABC* to reword the quotation.

[18] *OC* iv (in numerical order), pp. 24, 39, 116, 120.

compensation if they were found to be superfluous. Many officers were shocked at having to make such a decision without knowing their chances of retaining their posts if they failed to take up the offer. But Azaña could not determine the future size of the officer corps until he knew how many officers were prepared to retire under his generous terms.[19] Azaña also calculated that, by allowing self-selection for redundancy, he was less likely to incur accusations of political persecution.

Whatever method he chose, it was bound to anger sections of the military. However, those who felt more secure in their posts, in particular colonial officers, welcomed his decision on the grounds that the cuts would affect the Army of Africa much less than the metropolitan army. Privately, few Africanist officers felt sympathy for the army in Spain and some were even delighted with Azaña's evident determination to turn it into an efficient fighting body.[20] What upset many of them was not the retirement law itself but the effect that the subsequent cuts in personnel would have on the careers of those who chose to remain. By drastically reducing the number of posts, Azaña's reform might narrow their promotion prospects. In the event, out of 20,576 officers, 7,613 took up Azaña's offer, some 36.9 per cent of all officers. Many did so calculating that their chances of promotion were slim owing to their advanced age or the low position they occupied in their scale. We do not know how many colonial officers opted for redundancy, but it is clear that Azaña's offer was taken up by colonial, monarchist, and Republican officers alike and did not form part of the dichotomies that led to the Civil War.[21]

Rather than the issue of redundancy, it was Azaña's decree of June 1931 announcing a review of promotions, rewards, and decorations awarded during the dictatorship that most incensed colonial military opinion. It appeared that few colonial officers would be exempt from the risk of demotion, although in the end the vast majority were reinstated after examination. They were enraged by the implication that the Republic failed to appreciate the bloody victory they had achieved against the Moroccan foe at a huge cost to lives and limbs. The promotions had been won on the battlefield, and the nature of the regime in power at the time was felt to be irrelevant.[22] But Azaña's point was that promotion should be the result not merely of courage in battle but of efficient command. He was not against promotion on war merit

---

[19] Alpert, *La reforma*, 140–1.

[20] Castro Girona found Azaña's method both generous and efficient: see his prologue to Cándido Pardo González, *Desempolvando legajos. El problema militar en España. Su resolución más racional económica y nacional* (Madrid, AEL, 1934), 13–14. A military colleague of Varela wrote to him (and we can surmise that Varela shared his feelings) that a surgical operation on the army, however cruel and painful, was necessary and that Azaña was doing a good job: Antonio Lago to Varela, 1 June 1931, AV vol. 11. Even Franco recognized in retrospect that the law was not as bad as officers thought at the time, because the best ones stayed on: Franco Salgado-Araujo, *Mis conversaciones*, 397.

[21] Alpert, *La reforma*, 150–77.

[22] 'La revisión de ascensos', *Ejército y Armada*, 18 June 1931. Varela wrote to Azaña on 10 June 1931 to complain about the effects of the law on his own career: AV vol. 11.

in principle, but wished to ensure that the promotions of the past had been just, a sort of retroactive quality assurance.

The list of officers who faced the threat of demotion was long and distinguished. Brigadier-generals such as Franco and Millán-Astray risked becoming colonels once again or at least being demoted to the bottom of their rank.[23] Likewise, the colonel who had most distinguished himself in the last operations of the colonial war, Capaz Montes, felt he was now menaced with demotion to captain. Returning immediately to Tetuan from the Rif, where he was exercising his function as delegate of native affairs, Capaz made furious statements against the decree and intimated that he had the support of the tribes of the Rif and in Gomara.[24] It was the first warning that the Army of Africa might mobilize the colonial subjects against the Republic.

In fact, the review of promotions did not hit the colonial military severely. There were no significant demotions. Out of 500 cases of promotion examined, 365 were invalidated, as in the cases of Franco, Goded, Orgaz, and Varela, but this usually meant a drop of a point or two in their respective rank rather than demotion to a rank below.[25] Nevertheless, given the extent of Azaña's other reforms, it was a gratuitous exercise and further soured the colonial veterans' attitude towards the Republic.

Azaña's strategy for the Spanish Protectorate also aroused mixed feelings among colonial and ex-colonial officers. They probably welcomed his purge of civilian administration, since the military had always seen it as their role to run the Protectorate. Azaña wrote in his diary that, 'if in Spain we tend towards a certain superabundance of personnel in public administration, in Morocco this has reached the limits of fantasy in all senses in terms of numbers and equipment'.[26] Although the military cuts were not as severe as in the metropolis, they nevertheless hurt. The budget was cut by 14.5 million pesetas and the number of troops stationed in Morocco was reduced from a total of some 57,000 to just over 45,000 soldiers and 1,873 officers.[27] The Legion was purged of individuals that Azaña and his advisers considered dangerous. He cut its

[23] For a list of the possible effects of the law on colonial officers promoted during the dictatorship see Tebib Arrumi (Ruiz Albéniz), 'La Reforma militar', *Informaciones*, 12 June 1931.

[24] 'Coup d'oeil d'ensemble sur l'évolution de la situation en zone espagnole', SHAT 3H 139, 25 Sept. 1931. Capaz, described by Azaña as 'militarist, authoritarian, brave they say, and a cacique', had been in danger of losing his post since the beginning of the Republic because he was known for his anti-Republican views. His resignation was accepted by the new civil high commissioner, López Ferrer, in April 1931. As part of his efforts to placate individual officers, Azaña then promoted him to general and transferred him to Las Palmas, 'to get rid of him': Azaña, *OC* vol. iv. 215–16, 241. Under Azaña's successor as minister of war, Diego Hidalgo, Capaz was brought back to the colonies in 1934 to command an expedition to seize and colonize the territory of Ifni, where he was named governor.

[25] Alpert, *La reforma*, 223–4.

[26] Azaña, 'Marruecos: orientación de la Política del Gobierno', in 'Una política (1930–1932)', *OC* ii. 232.

[27] 'Orden circular del 12 de junio de 1931', *Diario Oficial del Ministerio de la Guerra* (1931), ii. 24. These numbers were further reduced in March 1932 to approximately 30,000 soldiers and 1,600 officers: ibid., 'Orden circular de 28 de marzo de 1932', i. 29.

ranks by 1,500 men and reorganized its units. In addition, Azaña made new appointments to the Army of Africa of officers judged to be loyal to the Republic. The majority of these had already served in Morocco and knew the colonial army well. Many came from an older generation than those officers who formed part of the 1915 generation of right-wing Africanists, and many were based in the technical corps such as the artillery, in which support for the Republic was greater than in the infantry.[28] Azaña also named the former Spanish consul in Tetuan, López Ferrer, as the new high commissioner. His appointment was the first stage in the process of substituting civilian for military administration.

Few of these measures pleased the colonial officers. Mola had been furious at the seeming 'docility' with which his fellow officers greeted Azaña's reform. He was also deeply concerned at the cuts in the colonial military budget, on the grounds that they would seriously weaken the Army of Africa.[29] French military sources reported that further mutinies broke out amongst the troops and that some officers and NCOs were killed.[30] The new mixed civilian-military regime in the Protectorate got off to a bad start when Capaz resigned after disagreeing with López Ferrer's appointment of a Moroccan to an important post. The new commander-in-chief of the colonial army, Cabanellas, chosen by Azaña to replace Sanjurjo because he also professed Republican sympathies, quarrelled with the high commissioner over the division of responsibilities, on the reasonable grounds that experienced colonial military officers such as Capaz were more suitable than civilian novices as intermediaries with the tribes.[31] It was yet another legacy of the two decades of military ascendancy over colonial matters that the Republic would find hard to overturn.

In his diaries, Azaña appears confident he could keep the recalcitrant colonial officers in line. He was more worried about the spread of communist and nationalist agitation in Morocco. Decolonization was not on the agenda of the new government, for all its progressive liberal programme at home. For Azaña, any further weakening of the colonial army raised the spectre of Moroccan, not military, revolt. Morocco was the 'Achilles heel (*el talón vulnerable*) of the Republic' because of the threat of indigenous nationalism and the feebleness of civilian colonial authority.[32] This might explain why a report on extremists in the Spanish army drawn up by military intelligence in September 1932, one month after an attempted military coup in Spain, was concerned, in its section devoted to the colonial army, solely with communists and Moroccan national-

[28] Balfour and La Porte, 'Spanish Military Cultures', *European History Quarterly*, 325; Miguel Alonso Baquer, 'La selección de la élite militar española', in Mario Hernández Sánchez-Barba (coord.), *Historia social de la Fuerzas Armadas españolas* (Madrid, CESEDEN, 1986), v. 65.

[29] Mola, 'El pasado, Azaña y el porvenir', in *Obras Completas*, 1060 and 113–18.

[30] In the absence of corroboration elsewhere, however, the killing of officers seems unlikely. SHAT ibid.

[31] Ibid., 12 and 18 Nov. 1931. Morales Lezcano, *España*, 120–1.

[32] Manuel Azaña, *Diarios, 1932–1933. 'Los Cuadernos Robados'* (Barcelona, Crítica, 1997), 125.

ists.[33] Thus, Azaña's democratic project to turn the Spanish army into a largely conscript army was not extended to the colonial army. The failure of conscripts to deal with the jihad had been a harsh lesson of the colonial war. So the Army of Africa remained a largely mercenary army, based on the Legion and the Regulares, backed up by some Spanish units and the sultan's troops under Spanish command.

Moreover, Moroccan hopes quickly faded that the Republic might take the first steps towards the withdrawal of Spain from their country. On the contrary, they were encouraged by the government's policies to see the new state as equally unsympathetic to Moroccan independence as the previous one.[34] The appointment of Sanjurjo as the first high commissioner of the Republic was evidence of the Republic's lack of sensitivity towards Moroccan nationalist opinion, since Sanjurjo had commanded the colonial army at the close of the colonial war. These policy omissions proved to be the most serious weakness of the Republic.

As I have stressed throughout, Spain was under pressure by the French to maintain order in her Protectorate. Like their predecessors, Republican politicians were caught in the colonial dilemma typical of the less developed European powers. Spanish colonialism had caused enormous disruption to life in northern Morocco, distorting social and economic relations and depriving many of the tribes of their traditional lands. Yet unlike French Morocco, no significant investment had been made in the Spanish Protectorate. The resulting unrest had meant that only the army could guarantee law and order. Azaña thus proposed investing some of the money saved by the military cuts into colonial development.[35] His 1932 law also provided incentives for army veterans to become settlers in Morocco. Yet the generous redundancy terms offered to officers choosing retirement made a chimera of significant colonial investment.[36]

Azaña's belief that he could keep the lid on officer disgruntlement was perhaps over-confident. His measures, rather than exploiting the differences among officers, helped to throw together the more conservative amongst them. They were also beginning to share a common alarm at the rise of popular and regional nationalist agitation.[37] The changing climate of opinion among Africanist officers is well illustrated by vivid accounts in Azaña's diaries of long conversations with his chief of staff, Manuel Goded. In an exchange on 22 July 1931 Goded appeared content with his position, even though he openly

---

[33] 'Gráfica esquemática de los militares extremistas descubiertos en el Ejército, septiembre 1932', SHM, Archivo de la Documentación de la Guerra de Liberación Nacional, R270, carp. 11. The figures for 'extremists' in the colonial army was higher than in any region in Spain, except for Galicia and Zaragoza.

[34] Mohammad Ibn Azzuz Hakim, *La actitud de los moros ante el Alzamiento* (Málaga, Algazara, 1997), 19–20.

[35] Azaña, *Diarios, 1932–1933*, 125.

[36] Morales Lezcano, 'L'exèrcit d'Africa'.

[37] Alonso Baquer, *D. Manuel*, 75–9.

disagreed with the law on retirement. The openness with which he confided his doubts to Azaña at this stage does not suggest he was yet conspiring against the Republic, as his son later claimed.[38] He was prepared to go as far as criticize some of his Africanist comrades who had been given 'scandalous' awards by Primo in what he called a 'binge', but he begged Azaña not to pass on his remarks to them. He also confessed that he was under some pressure to break with the government but had counselled 'calm and silence' to his more militant colleagues.[39]

Less than a year later he was involved in a public row with a pro-Republican officer that almost descended into blows. Goded had ended a speech to infantry officers and cadets from the military academies with a cry of 'Long Live Spain! And nothing else', explicitly omitting the customary accompanying call of 'Long Live the Republic!' The Republican lieutenant-colonel, Julio Mangada, had kept quiet when the audience repeated Goded's cry to show his disapproval, and Goded's challenge led to a violent argument between the two. In a long night-time conversation with Azaña, Goded defended himself, pretending unconvincingly that his omission of any reference to the Republic had no significance. But at the same time, he confessed that he was now uncomfortable as Azaña's chief of staff and asked to be relieved of his post, to which Azaña reluctantly agreed.

Azaña wrote in his diary, 'I have tried to reconcile Goded to the regime and to the overall politics of the Republic, an endeavour I would not have attempted with others, who are pure oafs. With this small, bright, and rather cantankerous man, the attempt seemed useful and a good move on my part. I thought I had achieved a lot, as Goded himself let on. But he obviously carries within him inextinguishable grudges.'[40] Goded's increasing discomfort over his collaboration with the left-wing Republican government was a measure of the growing pressure he was under from his Africanist colleagues as Azaña's military measures began to bite.

Knowing through his security apparatus and his numerous contacts that many officers were meeting to discuss action against the Republic, Azaña took measures to keep them separate. For the time being, these manoeuvres, by dispersing well-known anti-Republican officers, appointing loyal officers to key positions, and throwing a *cordon sanitaire* around Morocco, made it difficult for officers inclined to conspire against the Republic to make plans. Further to his appointment of supposedly trustworthy officers, Azaña sent three men to Morocco separately in August 1932 to report on rumours of unrest in the army.[41]

It was one of his own appointees, José Sanjurjo, who made the first serious attempt to overthrow the government. The fact that Sanjurjo had been an

---

[38] Manuel Goded, *Un "faccioso" cien por cien* (Zaragoza, Heraldo, 1938), 15–16.
[39] Azaña, *OC* iv. 39.   [40] Ibid., 415–18.   [41] Ibid., 49.

unlikely supporter of the Republic in the first place and an unlikely opponent a year later demonstrated the ambiguity of his political allegiances. The son of a Carlist officer, he had been closely associated with the king and the Primo de Rivera dictatorship. So it had surprised and shocked many of his fellow officers, in particular Franco, that, as director-general of the Civil Guard under the monarchy, he appeared to jump on the Republican bandwagon in 1931.[42] But as a close friend of Primo de Rivera he had been angered by the king's withdrawal of confidence from the dictator. He was also suspected of a secret deal with Republican leaders whereby he would be rewarded with an important position in the new order in exchange for not mobilizing the Civil Guard.[43]

Later, as head of the Civil Guard under the Republic, he had confessed to Azaña that nobody knew which side he was on (or, to quote literally the Spanish expression he used, 'on which foot he was limping').[44] His lukewarm support for the Republic disappeared when he was forced to take the blame for the killing of some demonstrating workers by one of his detachments. His demotion to the post of head of the Carabineros turned him against the centre-left government. But what he intended to replace it with was not clear. Like many of his fellow Africanists he could not identify closely with any of the political ideologies on offer in Spain. His point of reference was the Army of Africa and his loyalties were based on the comradeship forged in the colonial campaign. Like many of his comrades, he saw the elite of colonial officers as the catalyst for a new Spain. He had confided to his old friend and confidant Sainz Rodríguez that 'the State is like a limited company; if the management is good then that's fine; if management is bad, then change it'.[45] The remark revealed a naive technocracy and a powerful streak of military interventionism.

His attempted coup of 10 August 1932 was ill planned and lacked support. It was carried out in the traditional style of the nineteenth-century *pronunciamiento* or military uprising, relying on personal prestige and 'virile contagion' rather than on organization.[46] Republican police had monitored his preparations from the outset. From Azaña's own account, it was clear that Sanjurjo enjoyed support from a few of his ex-comrades in the Moroccan campaigns, such as Cavalcanti, Goded, and Cabanellas. He also had some backing in the existing Army of Africa for his plans. A coded telegram was sent from the general's headquarters in Seville to Tetuan on the day of the uprising. But, as Azaña wrote, 'there is an indisputable fact and that is that nobody in Africa moved'.[47]

---

[42] Salgado-Araujo, *Mis conversaciones*, 88–9 and 120. Republican leaders, according to José María Pemán, had confused 'his ill-tempered passivity over the 14th of April with a heart-and-mind loyalty towards the new regime': *Un soldado en la Historia. Vida del capitán general Varela* (Cádiz, Escelicer, 1954), 111.

[43] Preston, *Franco*, 70 and 77–8.   [44] Azaña, *OC* iv. 35.

[45] Pedro Sainz Rodríguez, *Testimonio y recuerdos* (Barcelona, Planeta, 1978), 326.

[46] Pemán, *Un soldado*, 112.   [47] Azaña, *OC* iv. 49.

Sanjurjo also had the backing of Varela, the impetuous Africanist colonel confined to Cadiz by the Azaña government as a danger to the Republic. The self-exculpatory notes Varela made during his arrest for complicity in the so-called *Sanjurjada* give a rare insight into the mentality of the anti-Republican military.[48] While implausibly denying any part in the conspiracy, Varela makes wild accusations against the government. Beneath his passionate language, filled with emotive words and multiple exclamation-marks, lies a contradictory discourse that became a feature of the self-justifications of the July 1936 uprising. Varela wrote that the problem lay not with the form of government, the Republic, since that had been chosen by the people, but with the government itself, which had betrayed the values of the Republic. In the hands of ministers, the Republic had become a civilian dictatorship and the Constitution a myth and so also had liberty and fraternity. Communists had penetrated into the heart of the army. Spain was in the throes of moral destruction. Mixing political and corporate resentments, Varela accused the government of insulting the army, and society of forgetting the patriotic heroism of the colonial war. 'I continue to dream of, to want, to desire a brave and efficient army, filled with companionship, with international prestige, which it does not have today, apolitical, which it is not today, and nothing of this contradicts [the notion of] liberty, which in Spain is reserved for only one sector.'

The implication of Varela's text was that the government should be overthrown in order to uphold those very values on which the Republic was based, liberty, fraternity, and democracy, and the subjection of the army to the discipline of the state. How these values could be reconciled with the coup and the military dictatorship sought by the fervent monarchist Varela and his anti-Republican colleagues was resolved by an appeal to a conceptualization of Spain and Christianity that overrode rational discourse and democratic processes. Eventually, when this true Spain and the true religion were restored, those values could be addressed, or so Varela implied.

Varela's text reaches heights of abstraction when he compares the plump, squat bon viveur, Sanjurjo, to Christ. 'In the street they are asking for the head of Sanjurjo. Do you not remember the voices of the mob? Who do you want to condemn, Christ or Barrabas? Christ, Christ! How many truths are contained within the doctrine of the Crucified!' Varela thus represents the military conspiracy within a Christian liturgy of persecution, sacrifice, and redemption. Sanjurjo, persecuted by the Communist hordes and condemned by the alien power represented by Azaña's government, would redeem Spain by his sacrifice. The image of Sanjurjo as a new redeemer sits ill with the fact, well known among his brother officers, that he spent most of the time during his visits to the capital in a brothel.[49]

---

[48] 'Copia de los apuntes manuscritos del General Varela sobre el complot de agosto de 1932', AV vol. 2.

[49] Sainz Rodríguez, *Testimonio*, 252.

In fact, Sanjurjo was not the most appropriate figurehead for a monarchist movement against the Republic since he was credited with Republican sympathies. Nor were the monarchists pleased that he was also conspiring with right-wing republican politicians seeking to replace the centre-left government with a conservative one. Sanjurjo's failure to mobilize his comrades in the Army of Africa was also due as much to the problems of communication as to the uncertain outcome of his risky plans. While he was able to hold conspiratorial meetings in Spain (some, in restaurants and other public places, were closely monitored by Republican security), it was more difficult to conspire at a distance with fellow officers in Morocco.[50] The abortive coup made it clear to other would-be conspirators that any uprising required greater consensus and had to be more carefully planned.

Measures taken by the government during the *Sanjurjada* further polarized military opinion. The only military paper still published after Azaña's decree of 1932 closing down the military press reacted furiously to its suspension for four months, and by the end of 1933 was talking of civil war between left and right.[51] Azaña's review of promotions obtained during the Primo dictatorship completed its course at the end of the year, and on 28 January 1933 a new decree sanctioned the promotion to higher ranks of most officers, including those of the leading Africanists. Most were thus allowed to count the intervening years of service since their promotion towards their position on the seniority scale. Though there is no evidence of the private feelings of the colonial officers, such a measure probably did little to assuage their growing disenchantment with the Republic.

Azaña's centre-left government fell in the autumn of 1933, and after several administrations a new centre-right government was formed at the end of the year with the backing of the largest party in parliament, the right-wing Confederación Española de Derechas Autónomas (CEDA). The new administration began to nullify the progressive legislation of the first two-and-a-half years of the Republic. Its measures created the conditions for closer contact between old colonial comrades in arms. Azaña's policy of dispersal was reversed, and officers who had been displaced or sent to remote postings were brought back to enjoy the prestigious positions they felt entitled to. Diego Hidalgo, appointed as minister of war in early 1934, rescinded the measure that had put 149 officers in a situation of semi-retirement. He would claim later in a Francoist court that 'all my work was designed to cauterize the wounds and correct the mistakes of military policy carried out by Sr Azaña'.[52] The

---

[50] Three officers and a sergeant of the Legion were arrested for complicity in the 'Sanjurjada', according to *Telegrama del Rif*, 15 Aug. 1932. For an analysis of the Sanjurjada on the mainland, see Emilio Esteban-Infantes, *La sublevación del General Sanjurjo*, 2nd edn. (Madrid, n.p., 1933), Goded, *Un 'faccioso'*, and Mariano Aguilar Olivencia, *El ejército español durante la Segunda República: claves de su actuación posterior* (Madrid, Econorte, 1986), 306–16.

[51] 'Los culpables de la guerra civil', *Marte*, 15 Nov. 1933.

[52] From the transcript of his trial in 1939 in Archivo Diego Hidalgo (ADH).

new government's reinstatement of generals like Goded and Fanjul dampened the activities of the clandestine junta of anti-Republican generals.

Yet the 'two black years' (or *bienio negro* in the words of the left) that followed polarized opinion to such an extent that many officers who had remained aloof from politics began to commit themselves to the growing anti-Republican movement. Until then party politics had engaged only a minority of officers, from the pro-Republican Junteros, strongly represented in the technical corps, to the Alfonsine and Carlist 'catastrophist' fringe that believed in the overthrow of the Republic. Most uncommitted officers shared a contempt for professional politicians. This in itself was a political ideology of sorts, because behind it lay an unarticulated belief that the military culture of order and hierarchy was best for Spain, as opposed to the inefficiency and corruption of civilian rule (though the recent experience of military dictatorship had somewhat dented this conviction). But while there was no clear and united project for an alternative political system to the Republic, the vast majority of colonial officers, whether they were based in Morocco or Spain, were too concerned about their careers and salaries to run the risk of clandestine engagement in politics. Promotions and postings depended on cultivating the right political contacts, or at least, as in the case of the determinedly ambitious Franco, keeping options open whilst being seen to be scrupulously professional.[53]

Anti-Republican agitation in the metropolitan army was conducted mainly by right-wingers amongst the lower ranks of commissioned officers. At the end of 1933 the clandestine organization closely linked to the fascist Falange, the Unión Militar Española (UME), was set up amongst younger officers, many of whom had accepted the redundancy offer of Azaña's law. Despite its rapid permeation among garrisons and military academies throughout Spain, there appears to be no evidence that it made any inroads into the Army of Africa. Only towards the end of 1934 did UME leaders begin to make contact with the most militantly anti-Republican veterans of the colonial war, Goded and Fanjul among others, but these were now based in Spain.[54]

Just as the reactionary and repressive measures of the centre-right governments of 1934–6 undermined the faith of many working-class people in democracy, so the upsurge of labour and political protest began to persuade conservative and right-wing officers that they had to seize power once again. Two popular and violent uprisings in 1933 and 1934 provided them with the training ground for their attempted coup of 1936. The first was the anarchist revolt of December 1933, which was put down eventually by the deployment of metropolitan troops. The second was the uprising of October 1934, which

[53] Preston, *Franco*, 72–3. See also Azaña's comments on Cabanellas in *Diarios, 1932–1933*.

[54] A semi-official history of the UME, written in 1940 and therefore with every reason to highlight its links with the Army of Africa, mentions no such contacts: Antonio Cacho Zabalza, *La Unión Militar Española* (Alicante, Egara, 1940). Nor does Gil Robles, though he stresses that by the end of 1934 the UME embraced a broad spectrum of officers: *No fue posible*, 708.

used as its rationale the formation of a new right-wing government with three ministers from the CEDA party. Unlike the first, the October uprising was widespread and had the backing of both Socialists and anarchists. Its epicentre was Asturias, where the most militant and best-organized workers, the coalminers, seized control of the region. The response of the government was to mobilize the Army of Africa, because it could be trusted to crush the revolt more efficiently and was less likely to feel any sympathy with the rebels. Colonial troops had already been brought over twice for action in Spain. Berenguer had sent for a unit of the Legion from Morocco in December 1930 to join metropolitan troops in suppressing the pro-Republican insurrection of Galán and Hernández, and units of the Regulares had been used to suppress the *Sanjurjada* in 1932.

It was perhaps more than a coincidence that the mainland army under General López Ochoa had been on manoeuvres in the region of Leon, contiguous to Asturias, just before the uprising. The government clearly expected trouble and the military exercise was almost certainly a precautionary measure to get the troops ready for domestic action. No sooner had they returned to barracks than the first national actions by the left, the trade unions, and the Catalan nationalist movement took place. Easily suppressed in most of Spain, the revolt was soon confined to Asturias, where the trade unions, armed with dynamite, the odd piece of artillery, and arms and ammunition looted from an arms deposit, seized the main towns and the mining valleys. The minister of war, Diego Hidalgo, had wanted to appoint Franco as commander-in-chief of the forces that were about to be mobilized to crush the Asturian uprising. Aware that the appointment of a veteran of the colonial war would be unpopular among many sections of public opinion because of the Army of Africa's reputation for brutality, President Lerroux insisted on naming the more liberal peninsular general López Ochoa to lead the military action.

Instead, Hidalgo managed to get Franco as his adviser, and from the Buenavista Palace in Madrid Franco was able to play a decisive role in the suppression of the revolt. Most sources, including Hidalgo himself, agree that it was Franco's suggestion that contingents of the colonial army consisting of the Legion and the Regulares should be mobilized, and that they should be led by the grizzled veteran of the Moroccan war, Colonel Yagüe.[55] In response to objections over the use of colonial troops, the minister of public works later declared, referring to the miners: 'For those who committed so many acts of savagery, there weren't enough Moors because they deserve Moors and something more.'[56] The historical irony of using Moors to fight a war against Spaniards was not lost on spokesmen of the traditionalist discourse. It was even

[55] Diaz Nosty, *La comuna asturiana*, 242–3; Diego Hidalgo, *¿Por que fui lanzado del ministerio de la guerra? Diez meses de actuación ministerial* (Madrid, Espasa-Calpe, 1934); Francisco Aguado Sánchez, *La revolución de octubre de 1934* (Madrid, San Martín, 1972).

[56] Quoted in Díaz Nosty, *La comuna*, 359.

more significant that this war was being fought in precisely that area where, according to this discourse, the Reconquest of Spain against the Moors had begun. The contradiction was resolved by referring to a new Reconquest for Christian civilization against a modern foe, the Soviet Union, which the Spanish left was supposed to see as their fatherland.

This inverted logic was taken to convoluted extremes. Asturias was now described as a new Rif that had risen just when Spain, under the new centre-right government, was starting to recover her true identity, just as she had been at the beginning of the century before the troublesome Rif tribes revolted. In a later interview with a journalist, Franco declared that the action in Asturias was a 'frontier war', implying that the miners were foreigners and that the use of Moroccans was therefore justifiable. Indeed, I would argue that colonial officers no longer saw Moroccan volunteers as foreigners but as part of the same Spanish military community.[57] The disassociation of Asturians from the category of Spaniards enabled the uncaring repetition of the brutalized behaviour of the colonial war in their repression.

Detachments of the Legion and the Regulares were transported by boat from Ceuta to Asturias, and the first units arrived on 10 October, almost a week after the uprising, at El Musel, a port on its northern coast near Gijón. En route, the lieutenant-colonel of one of the battalions was ordered to disembark and was immediately arrested, after word had reached the minister of war and Franco that he had declared to friends that his troops would not fire on fellow Spaniards.[58] Led by Yagüe, the first units were transported by lorry to one of the rebels' strongholds in Asturias, the adjacent port of Gijón, and were joined there by colonial reinforcements on 12 October. Together they made up a column of some 2,000 mercenaries out of a total force of 15,000 soldiers deployed to suppress the uprising. Yagüe's troops recaptured Gijón after bitter hand-to-hand fighting and then moved on to Lugones, to link up with López Ochoa's column and prepare for an assault on the Asturian capital, Oviedo. The extent to which the operations as a whole were controlled by Franco is evident from López Ochoa's observation that he had been agreeably surprised to see the Regulares approaching his position, because he had not been told they had been sent. With his local troops now stiffened by veterans of the colonial war, the general changed his strategy and decided to employ only the professionals for the attack on Oviedo.[59]

After massive aerial bombardment of rebel strongholds in the city, the units of the Army of Africa entered Oviedo, encountering fierce pockets of resistance. What they did as they made their way through the city and the sur-

---

[57] Significantly, it was a well-known right-wing Africanist who made most of these parallels: Tomás Borrás, 'La Federación de Maestros Nacionales de Asturias publica un manifiesto condenando la criminal revolución socialista', *ABC*, 1 Nov. 1934. For Franco's comment see Claude Martin, *Franco, soldado y estadista* (Madrid, Fermín Uriarte, 1965), 129–30.

[58] Arrarás, *Historia de la Segunda República*, ii. 611, n. 1.   [59] López Ochoa, *Campaña*, 119.

rounding mining towns has been the subject of much polemic. The right has always kept quiet about the methods used by the colonial columns, while some of the propaganda of the left has suffered from considerable exaggeration.[60] Nevertheless, the atrocities committed by the colonial troops in Asturias had been part of the culture of war on both sides in the colonial war, a fact that the Spanish public had been kept ignorant of. The difference was that for once the behaviour of the Army of Africa was subject to, albeit limited, public scrutiny and accountability.

The colonial units in Asturias were responsible for several kinds of atrocities: the execution of prisoners after summary interrogation, the murder of civilians, the rape of women, and the looting of houses. The government, the right-wing press, and accounts written by military commanders denied any wrongdoing.[61] Yet the detailed evidence accumulated by left-wing MPs and others in the aftermath of the events and supported by personal testimonies is overwhelming. According to this evidence, up to 200 men and women were executed in the patio of the Oviedo hospital after summary interrogation by one of Yagüe's officers. Similarly, some 100 were shot and their bodies burnt in the Pelayo barracks. Rebels were often killed immediately upon capture.[62] Long after the revolutionaries had retreated and arms inspections had been carried out, the colonial troops went through some of the streets in the outskirts of Oviedo and in the mining towns nearby on a spree of shooting, looting, and wanton destruction. Information collected by Socialist deputies and journalists from survivors of the atrocities willing to testify point to the random killing by both the Legion and the Regulares of men and teenage boys who had been uninvolved in the insurrection and of women and children taking refuge in their homes. The rape of women undoubtedly took place but seemed to be less frequent than accounts on the left suggest. Some of the victims of the violence were local shopkeepers as well as families who had been in hiding from the revolutionaries, because many of the rebels' families had been evacuated before the bombing.[63]

[60] One of the accounts on the left was constructed on the evidence of a Foreign Legion deserter (n.a., *Los crímenes de la reacción española. La represión en Asturias. La verdad sobre octubre* (Madrid, Ediciones de la Sección Española del Socorro Rojo Internacional, 1935), 42–4 and 49) who claimed, among other things, that the Legionnaires chopped off the heads of rebels and the Regulares their hands. The former story may well have originated from the famous photograph of Legionnaires with the heads of Moroccans taken during the colonial campaign, which was to be used to very different effect by the Francoists in the Civil War (see Ch. 10).

[61] e.g. *ABC*, issues for Oct. 1934 and López Ochoa and Yagüe's own accounts (for latter see Luis Madero, *El octubre español* (Mexico, Ediciones de 'El Nacional', 1935), 49–56).

[62] n.a., *La represión en Asturias. Reporte sindicalista* (n.p., n.d.), n. pp.; N. Molins i Fábrega, *UHP. La insurrección proletaria de Asturias* (Madrid, Editorial Júcar, 1977; 1st edn. 1935), 185–6.

[63] Evidence on these events and those further below is drawn from reports by MPs Marco Miranda, Felix Gordón Ordás, Julio Álvarez del Vayo, and Fernando de los Ríos, in Margarita Nelken, *Por qué hicimos la Revolución* (Barcelona, Paris, and New York, Ediciones Sociales Internacionales, 1936), 172–255; also from Felix Gordón Ordás, *Mi política en España* (Mexico, n.p., 1962), ii. 253–312; Álvarez del Vayo, *Documents historics* (n.p, Edicions de la U.S.C., n.d.); Luis Araquistáin *et al.*, *La Revolución*

As in the colonial war, the main objective of the Regulares and Legionnaires appeared to be loot. Money, jewellery, ornaments, cutlery, clothes, shoes, and bedclothes were among the many objects carried off to be kept or sold. An officer who had bought a Longines watch off a Moroccan soldier advised a fellow officer to go to Oviedo. 'You can get the most extraordinary bargains . . . You only have to go to a company of Moors, or, better still, the Foreign Legion. They were almost giving the stuff away!'[64] For the Moroccan soldiers, such behaviour was part of the culture of inter-tribal warfare in the Rif and Yebala and loot was an important motive, in addition to the wages they were being paid, for undertaking such dangerous work in a foreign country. But Legionnaires and Regulares had been encouraged by their officers to feel such hatred for the local population that they systematically destroyed or mutilated what they could not or did not want to take with them. Furniture and crockery were smashed, soldiers defecated on the floors and mattresses in order to soil the homes they pillaged, and graffiti was painted on the walls. One of the graffiti was signed by a certain Corporal Valdés and read:

> THIS HOUSE WAS OCCUPIED BY THE LEGION.
> LONG LIVE SPAIN
> LONG LIVE THE REPUBLIC
> LONG LIVE THE ARMY . . .
> DOWN WITH COMMUNISM.

In another incident, the photograph of a couple was torn in two to separate them symbolically.

That not all officers of the Legion and the Regulares approved of such behaviour is suggested by the occasional anecdote in reports by the left. Survivors witnessed a lieutenant-colonel tearing a strip off a captain for allowing atrocities to be committed. Some officers also seem to have intervened occasionally to stop human-rights abuses, though the evidence suggests that they approved of looting.[65] A measure of the attitude of officers towards the local population can be gained from another anecdote, in which an officer was about to order the execution by his Moroccan troops of twenty-five people when he recognized his own cousin amongst them. Halting the execution, he was then persuaded by his cousin to save a further fifty people, who had been selected for similar treatment. The sense of alienation against the Other encouraged by war and propaganda suddenly came face to face with literal familiarity and disappeared briefly.[66]

española de octubre: documentos sensacionales inéditos (Santiago, Occidente,1935); n.a., *Los crímenes*; n.a., *La revolución de Asturias. (Documentos)* (Mexico, Ediciones Defensa Roja, 1935); and n.a., *La represión en Asturias. Reporte sindicalista* (n.p., n.d.). For reports of rape, see Molins i Fábrega, *UHP*, 205, and Marco Miranda in Nelken, *Por qué*, 174–5.

[64] José Martín Blázquez, *I Helped to Build an Army: Civil War Memoirs of a Spanish Staff Officer* (London, Secker & Warburg, 1939), 17.

[65] *La represión*; Nelken, *Por qué*, 176.   [66] *La represión*.

As is often the case in the history of atrocities, it took the murder of a journalist to gain the attention of the media in Spain.[67] An independent journalist, Luis Vigón Rosell, known by his pen name Sirval, had been collecting information in Oviedo about military abuses for a newspaper. Evidently, he had managed to get eyewitness details from three legionnaires of the murder by the Legion of a revolutionary female combatant. It is possible that rightwing civilians sharing his hotel in Oviedo overheard his interview with the legionnaires and reported the fact to officers of the Legion. In the meantime, Vigón, along with other left-wing journalists, was arrested and imprisoned. Three Legion officers, led by the Bulgarian lieutenant Dimitri Ivanov (an officer with an appalling record of desertion, brutality, and the rape of a Moroccan girl during the colonial war), went to the prison and took Vigón into an adjoining patio. There they tried to get him to give them the names of his three Legion informers. Failing to do so, they shot him dead, a murder witnessed by residents living above the patio. His executioners seized Vigón's papers and destroyed all reference to their actions in the battle for Oviedo (although Vigón's brief but detailed notes about other atrocities were left untouched and largely confirm other accounts). An absurd judgement by a Supreme Tribunal dominated by right-wingers later absolved the three officers, claiming they had acted in self-defence.

The arrest of left-wing journalists and the tight censorship imposed on the media meant that the news of the operations was that released by the military authorities or the government. According to these sources, the only atrocities were those committed by the revolutionaries. The *Chicago Daily Tribune* was happy to repeat on 28 October the minister of public works' accusation that they had chopped off the legs of a monk and then boiled him alive. But when censorship of the foreign press was lifted the next day, news of the depradations of the colonial troops began to filter through. The same paper began to report some of their atrocities, dismissing many of the stories published hitherto in right-wing newspapers as 'figments of the excited imagination published by newspapers with an axe to grind'.[68]

After the liquidation of resistance in Oviedo on the night of 12 October, the troops moved southwards towards the town of Mieres, reaching the outskirts on the 17th. Unable any longer to justify the huge casualties they were suffering, the leaders of the revolution arranged a meeting between the miners' leader Belarmino Tomás and López Ochoa. The general's conditions were that the revolutionaries should lay down their arms, hand over prisoners, and surrender a quarter of their leadership. The only condition requested by

---

[67] The following account is drawn primarily from two sources: a report by Eduardo Ortega y Gasset in legal representation of the journalist's family published in M. Álvarez Portal, *Sirval* (Barcelona, Ediciones Adelante, 1936), and an eyewitness account by a fellow journalist in n.a., *¡Acusamos! El asesinato de Luis de Sirval* (Valencia, Ediciones del comité 'Luis de Sirval', n.d.).

[68] *Chicago Tribune*, 29 Oct. 1934.

Tomás was that the Legion and the Regulares should be withdrawn because their behaviour 'was not worthy of a civilized nation'.[69] That the left should make this their only condition is evidence in itself of the brutality of the colonial troops. López Ochoa later argued that his willingness to allow the Legion and Regulares to bring up the rearguard was a matter of expediency, but that he threatened to let them loose 'with blood and fire' if the slightest shot was fired by the revolutionaries.[70] By all accounts Yagüe was furious with the decision, and in an explosive encounter with López Ochoa pulled out his pistol and threatened him.[71] Under López Ochoa's overall command, the colonial troops were kept in the background in the mopping-up operations in the mining communities, and when the insurrection had been completely crushed they were sent back in two stages to Morocco.

López Ochoa would later claim that the atrocities that occurred in Oviedo were the responsibility of the Civil Guard under its brutal commander Major Lisardo Doval. Equipped with special powers to deal with the uprising, Doval and his lieutenant Nilo Tella were guilty of the torture of dozens of prisoners. However, the first brutalities were committed by the African troops under López Ochoa's command. Both he and Doval were put on trial for these atrocities in March 1936, after the electoral victory of the Popular Front.[72]

In retrospect, the military operation of October 1934 was a dress rehearsal for the uprising of 1936. For the first time, the colonial troops gained experience of battle in Spain. The operation was crucial for Franco and the Army of Africa. It gave them renown and raised their status among the right and right-wing military. Their decisive intervention in crushing revolution encouraged their own latent sense of a messianic mission to restore Spain to its true identity from the barracks of Spanish Morocco, uncontaminated by metropolitan politics. For the right, the events of October served as a catalyst for 'catastrophist' opinion. The conservative *ABC* paper, obligatory reading amongst most right-wing officers, openly called for military dictatorship. According to an editorial of November 1934, the left uprising indicated that there was no middle road; the dictatorship of the espadrille could only be countered by the dictatorship of the boot (ignoring the fact that the espadrille was not just the footwear of the peasant but had been that of the soldiers in the colonial war).[73]

However, preparations for a military coup were far from complete. The core of the conspiracy was formed by veteran Africanist generals based in Spain. The Organization, as it came to be called, was led by Varela, as official rep-

[69] Manuel Grossi Mier, *La insurrección de Asturias* (Barcelona, Ediciones La Batalla, 1935), 212–13.
[70] López Ochoa, *Campaña*, 162.
[71] Díaz Nosty, *La comuna*, 305, n. 183; Aguado Sánchez, *La revolución*, 301–2 and n. 23; while sympathetic to Yagüe, Arrarás (in *Historia*, ii. 637), confirms that he threatened López Ochoa with his pistol, though he also quotes Yagüe's rather unlikely version of the argument on p. 614.
[72] For López Ochoa's claim see *Campaña*, 180–4; for the trial see *ABC*, 13 Mar. 1936.
[73] Adolfo Marsillach, 'Las dos dictaduras', *ABC*, 21 Nov. 1934.

resentative of Sanjurjo in exile in Spain, and appeared to have the backing of the CEDA leadership. At a clandestine meeting in November 1934 to discuss the proposed resignation of CEDA ministers from the Lerroux government, Varela, wearing his general's sash and almost bathed in tears, announced: 'It is not possible to do anything. It [the planned coup] is still not ready . . . We must wait . . . Do not leave the government.'[74] His words implied that many right-wing officers still needed to be persuaded. The abject failure of the *Sanjurjada* no doubt cautioned many of them to hold back. The formation in May 1935 of a new government dominated by the CEDA, with Gil Robles as minister of war, must also have inhibited the spread of the conspiracy. As long as the right could now dominate policy-making through its control of three key ministries, cautious officers like Franco did not respond to the blandishments of their more militant colleagues.

Probably the bulk of military opinion was willing to give the centre-right government a chance. The issues that had polarized opinion amongst colonial officers could now be addressed. Gil Robles, cultivating military opinion assiduously, immediately began to roll back Azaña's reforms. The highly unpopular law of promotions was returned to the right-wing dominated parliament for reconsideration. The regiments that had been disbanded under Azaña were now reconstituted with their original 'imperial' names. Some of the Africanist generals who were to lead the 1936 uprising were brought into the centre of decision-making. After his service under Hidalgo as overall commander of the operations in Asturias in 1934 and then as commander of the colonial army in Morocco, Franco was brought back to Madrid to be chief of the general staff under Gil Robles. General Fanjul, who had never ceased to conspire against the Republic, was named undersecretary of war, while Mola was posted to replace Franco in Morocco. Some eighty other right-wing officers were appointed to key positions from where they could prepare the planned coup. Some were promoted for entirely political purposes above the heads of more senior officers.[75] On the other hand, generals closely associated with the Republic or known to be liberal freemasons, such as López Ochoa, were sacked from key posts by Franco. Of these, only one, José Riquelme, was a veteran of the colonial war. According to a right-wing journalist close to Africanist military opinion, the generals seemed satisfied.[76]

The highly distorted *ex post facto* accounts of preparations for the uprising by Francoists suggest a unity of purpose and strategy among the conspirators. In fact, the divisions amongst the right were almost as great as those between liberal republicans and the far left. Right-wing republicans, Alfonsine

[74] Unsigned report, probably written by Gil Robles in March 1937, in 'Preparación del Movimiento, José María Gil Robles', AV vol. 13.

[75] *El Sol*, 25 May 1935.

[76] Tebib Arrumi, 'El Ejército, satisfecho' and 'Los nombres de los antiguos Tercios y Regimientos de la España imperial, vuelven a su vigencia': *Informaciones*, 14 May 1935 and 26 June 1935.

monarchists, Carlists, the fascist Falange, and authoritarian military officers, among other ideologues, had to negotiate amongst themselves the terms of common action against the democratic Republic and its replacement. These same divisions existed among Africanist veterans. Varela, for example, had joined the Carlists in 1934; Yagüe, a friend of José Antonio Primo de Rivera, joined the Falange as soon as it was formed in 1934; Cabanellas had been a freemason; he, Queipo de Llano, and Mola were republicans; and Kindelán and Orgaz were Alfonsine monarchists. Relations between Africanist generals and right-wing politicians were sometimes tense. In the Ministry of War, Goded and Fanjul were exasperated with Gil Robles's continued attachment to the constitution and his vacillations about sacking politically dubious officers and replacing them with others committed to end the Republic. Many officers sympathetic to the idea of overthrowing the government remained highly cautious about committing themselves. According to Goded himself, Franco, as chief of staff in the Ministry, remained somewhat aloof from the conspirators in an effort to hedge his bets.[77]

Nevertheless, where it was possible to remain within constitutional legality, the ditherers on the military right were happy to support the groundwork for action against the Republic. In the summer of 1935 military manoeuvres were held in Asturias. The claim by a Francoist apologist that they were a covert preparation for the coming coup is not far-fetched and it cannot have been far from the minds of those who took part.[78] After all, the León manoeuvres of 1934, as we have seen, were not unconnected to intelligence reports of the danger of an uprising among miners. Although the conspirators' plans for a coup at this stage did not involve action in Asturias, there could be no doubt in their minds, after the experience of October 1934, that a violent military operation would once again be necessary in that region if the coup were successful.[79]

Little can be deduced about opinion in the colonial army. Reports about military opinion in Morocco from the high commissioners and commanders-in-chief, if these documents still exist, are not available for scrutiny.[80] The colonial officers were subject to much greater pressure to keep out of politics than their colleagues in Spain because of the political tensions of the Protectorate. This was reflected in the contents of their only mouthpiece, the periodical *Revista de Tropas Coloniales* (renamed *África*), edited until 1932 by Franco himself. Resolved to avoid closure, it remained a determinedly apolitical publication, and many of its pages in the early 1930s were incongruously devoted to the

---

[77] Goded, *Un 'faccioso'*, 23–4.   [78] Beltrán Güell, *Preparación*, 113.

[79] It is clear from Mola's instructions as 'Director' of the conspiracy on 25 May 1936 that the experience of the Asturian miners' revolt weighed heavily in the plans for the uprising: Federico Bravo Morata, *La República y el ejército* (Madrid, Fenicia, 1978), doc. no. 51, p. 266.

[80] All archives where such documents could be stored have been consulted. Their most likely location is in the dozens of boxes relating to the Protectorate in the early 1930s, still unopened in 2001 and stored in AGA under 'Presidencia del Gobierno'.

fauna and flora of Morocco.[81] A notable exception was an article in the June 1935 issue, which reveals the penetration of 'catastrophist' and indeed fascist values into the colonial army. Its discourse is rooted in the racism typical of European fascism. Spain had been about to be shipwrecked by the work of religious 'secret societies' and racial 'foreign agents', that is, freemasons and Jews. In pseudo-biological language, it argued 'the positive necessity of the cohesion of the molecule to liberate it from the effects of dissociation with which the exterior or interior agents of nature were threatening it'. In terms clear to the initiated amongst its readers, the article called for the building of a movement of 'national defence'.[82]

The fall of the centre-right government at the end of 1935 appeared to bring to an end the option on the right of a legalist road. Surrounded by his Africanist generals, Gil Robles made an emotional farewell speech in which he referred to the 'great bitternesses' he had suffered as minister of war, an implicit accusation that his efforts to work within the constitution had been blocked by the left.[83] Gil Robles wrote later that of all his military advisers only Franco now urged caution about fixing a date for a coup. The ever-impatient Goded, according to his son, accused the minister of having been too frightened to abandon legality and launch a coup from the Ministry of War, despite his and Franco's pressure. Improbably, he suggested that it was only their 'gentlemanly' feelings towards Gil Robles that prevented the military from pressing the issue. Six months after the Civil War had begun, Franco agreed in an exchange of correspondence with Gil Robles that the plans for the military uprising had not yet been in place when the latter was in office, and that 'any action at that time was condemned to failure.'[84] As if there could be any doubt about Gil Robles's position, his speeches during the electoral campaign in early 1936 called for a new constitution, a new society, and a new state. Much of his effort was dedicated to attracting support amongst the military for the barely disguised cause of dictatorship.[85]

The victory of the Popular Front in February swung many of the more diffident contacts of the conspirators towards the Cause. In the discourse of the right, the new government was the Trojan Horse of forces alien to Spain, the barely differentiated Marxists, freemasons, Jews, and the working-class rabble. Subsequent self-exculpatory accounts by Francoists drew a melodramatic and totally distorted picture of Spain before the uprising, whose imagery was sometimes similar to that of Nazi propaganda. In one text, for example, the interim

[81] Franco's replacement, A. M. Escalera, insisted in the January issue of 1932 that the paper was 'absolutely apolitical'.

[82] Fernando de Carranza, 'La Defensa Nacional', África, June 1935, pp. 104–9.

[83] ABC, 15 Dec. 1935.

[84] Goded, Un 'faccioso', 25–6. Franco's letter to Gil Robles of 4 Feb. 1937. For correspondence between Franco, Gómez Jordana, and Gil Robles on this issue: AV, 'Jose Maria Gil Robles', vol. 13.

[85] 'Todo el poder para el jefe' and 'La política subversive de la CEDA. Gil Robles y el Ejército', Heraldo de Madrid, 20 and 25 Dec. 1935.

president Martínez Barrio is described leaving Cadiz by train after an official visit with crowds of supporters on the platform. 'In the window of the coach, a smooth and masonic smile. On the platform, raised fists and hurrahs to Russia . . . And Spain in the middle, destroyed, between the aggression of those fists and the acquiescence of that smile.'[86]

Aware of efforts by the leading right-wing generals to win over more adherents, the new government again reshuffled the military commands to distance suspected or known conspirators as far away as possible from strategic posts. Franco was stationed in the Canaries, Goded was posted to the Balearic Islands, and Mola was transferred to Navarra from Morocco and replaced as commander-in-chief of the Army of Africa by a more reliable general, Agustín Gómez Morato. By now it was clear that the original plan to stage a traditional coup by seizing the parliament, the ministries, and the military headquarters in Madrid, backed up by action in provincial capitals, was fraught with risks. The inference was that insufficient support had been won in the garrisons of the capital. A decision to carry out this plan on 19 April had been shelved.[87]

A new strategy was proposed by Mola for a co-ordinated military uprising in cities within striking distance of Madrid where the right could command considerable backing and from where Madrid might be surrounded. It is unlikely that this decision was easily reached. As one of Sanjurjo's representatives in Spain, Varela had been in charge, with Orgaz, of the plans to seize power in Madrid since 1934 and seemed to cling on to the earlier scheme. In a meeting on 9 March Mola had argued unsuccessfully against Varela's insistence on staging a traditional coup in the capital, convinced it would fail. At the same meeting, Mola had insisted that the uprising should not be against the Republic but against the Popular Front. The date for the coup in Madrid had been set for 20 April, but was postponed when it became clear there was still insufficient support. Knowing that he had to get the backing of a senior general, since he was only a brigadier-general, Mola had persuaded Goded to support his plan. Varela's posting to Cadiz in April (after the government received an indication of his continued plotting) had cleared the path for the adoption of Mola's strategy by the junta of conspiratorial Africanist generals.[88]

In the new scheme, issued on 5 May by Mola from fictitious headquarters called Villa Cort, no role was assigned to the Army of Africa except as reserve troops to be deployed only if the main plan was not immediately successful. It

---

[86] 'Antecedentes y primeros días del alzamiento en Cadiz', AV vol. 14, p. 4.

[87] Ibid., 4; Felipe Beltrán Güell, *Preparación y desarrollo del Alzamiento Nacional* (Valladolid, Librería Santarén, 1939), 114–24. Francoist accounts suggest the plan was dropped merely because a key conspirator, General Rodríguez del Barrio, got cold feet at the last minute: e.g. General Francisco Javier Mariñas, *General Varela (De Soldado a General)* (Barcelona, AHR, 1956), 70.

[88] This is perhaps implied in a confidential account by Varela's widow's, 'Preparación del Alzamiento', AV, vol. 13; Roberto Muñoz Bolaños, 'La Guerra Civil Española. Una síntesis histórico-militar', in Ricardo Recio Cardona (ed.), *Rojo y Azul. Imágenes de la Guerra Civil Española* (Madrid, Almena, 1999), 12.

was also taken for granted that the uprising in Madrid would fail. Instead, the putsch would begin with a co-ordinated insurrection in cities to the north and east of the capital, which would be followed, once the control of these cities had been consolidated, by a convergent and concentric march on Madrid. Like Morocco, Andalusia was assigned a passive role in the scheme. Uprisings would take place there at the same time as in the north, but the southern garrisons would only be deployed as reserve troops. Their task would be to ensure the consolidation of bridgeheads in case the Army of Africa needed to be brought over. The plan was couched in easily decipherable code and, in a feeble attempt to evade suspicion, was written as a blueprint for the defence of Spain against an attack by an enemy that had invaded home territory. Such codes could well have helped to consolidate the feeling among veterans of the colonial war who felt estranged from Spanish culture that the Popular Front government was a foreign power, republican loyalists were foreigners, and Madrid was a foreign city.[89]

Of the bridgeheads for the hypothetical deployment of the colonial army, only Cadiz was considered feasible. It was well connected to Seville, had ample supplies, arms, and transport, and was more likely to fall to the rebels. The other two potential bridgeheads, Algeciras and Malaga, were rated as difficult. The only advantage offered by Algeciras was its proximity to Ceuta. Otherwise, its garrison was small, with insufficient supplies and ammunition for the colonial troops. Communications by road and rail were problematic and the working-class movement was strong enough in this port town to make the insurrection uncertain. Malaga, finally, was discounted as a potential landing-place for the Army of Africa. It was too far from the Moroccan coast, but more importantly the left was strong enough there and the local garrison weak enough to make the success of the uprising unlikely.[90] As commander of the Cadiz garrison, Varela was delighted that his home town should have been chosen. But his Africanist colleague Yagüe, who was expected to lead the expeditionary colonial troops across the Straits of Gibraltar if necessary, believed Algeciras was the only appropriate bridgehead for his troops. This was mainly because it was only a two-hour sea journey from Ceuta as opposed to the seven-hour crossing to Cadiz, which might well expose his troops to Republican bombers and loyalist naval vessels. The two apparently exchanged heated letters, mediated only by the cautious Franco from his post in the Canaries.[91]

As nominal head of the growing insurrectionary movement, Sanjurjo confirmed Mola as 'director' of the uprising in Spain on 25 May. As one of Berenguer's blue-eyed boys, Mola had been deeply resentful of Sanjurjo's

[89] Ejército de Operaciones, 'Instrucciones Generales', nos. 1 and 2, AV vol. 13.
[90] Ejército de Operaciones, 'Instrucciones Particulares, Zona Z', ibid.
[91] Pemán, Un soldado, 150–1. This correspondence, once housed in AV, is no longer available.

support for Primo de Rivera, the man who had let down his champion.[92] But given the continued tensions between Africanist generals, his willingness to put aside old divisions would make him an effective co-ordinator of the plot. The key position Mola occupied as commander of the Pamplona garrison and the fact that, despite being a republican, he had become the *bête-noire* of the Republic, made his selection almost obligatory. In addition, Mola displayed almost frantic energy and a talent for methodical and surreptitious organization, honed by his experience in 1930–1 as director of security. The codes he used in his correspondence were by far the most complex. While other conspirators would often use a coded language that could easily be guessed (referring, for example, to Cabanellas as the 'bearded one' and Malaga as the 'city of raisins'), Mola used a numerical code that could only be broken by a specialist.[93] He also showed greater ideological flexibility than many of his colleagues, especially Varela. The latter had blocked any approach towards two of the most prestigious Africanist generals, Cabanellas and Queipo de Llano, on the grounds that the first was a freemason and the second an active republican. Mola's more tractable stance helped to bring on board the uprising two of the key military commanders in Spain.[94]

Mola's plans for the Army of Africa of 25 May, the day he officially became the 'director', assigned it an even more passive role in the uprising. The instructions he issued extended military action to new regions and broadened the scope of the insurrection to include the right-wing militias. But it limited the Moroccan garrisons to a 'passive attitude' and only envisaged an insurrection in Morocco if the government attempted to mobilize them as shock-troops against the putsch.[95]

Mola was also careful to ensure that the insurrection was to be carried out on the terms established by the Africanist-dominated military conspirators. In a statement of 5 June, the junta laid down that once the uprising was successful the nation would be run initially by a military Directorate. The 1931 Constitution would be suspended, parliament dissolved, and a republican dictatorship installed. The separation between Church and State would be maintained. Eventually, free elections would be held to elect a new constituent parliament, presumably once the left and the working-class organizations had been destroyed.[96] The terms outlined by the junta were a reminder that the dominant political ideology among Africanists was republican, anticlerical, and authoritarian. The leading conspirators thus envisaged their revolt as part of the nineteenth-century patriotic, Jacobinist tradition.

Preliminary agreement on these principles had been reached with the Falange in a meeting on 1 June between Mola and an intermediary of José

[92] Muñoz, 'La Guerra', 14.   [93] 'Clave', AV vol. 13.

[94] 'Preparación del Alzamiento', AV vol. 13.

[95] 'Instrucciones reservadas del general Mola, director del alzamiento de julio de 1936', Bravo Morata, *La República*, document 51, pp. 266–7.   [96] Arrarás, *Historia*, iv. 499.

Antonio Primo de Rivera, the dictator's son and leader of the Falange. Negotiations with the clerical, monarchist Carlists were proving more difficult. They had tried to lay down political conditions for their participation, including the creation of a military-civilian Directorate whose two civilian members would be chosen by them. Mola and his junta had turned down their demands on the grounds that these would 'mortgage the future of the new State'; the implication was that only the Africanist military could properly represent the alliance of right-wing forces committed to the uprising.[97] Such was his suspicion of political organizations that Mola had initially refused to accept money from the CEDA. Through intermediaries, Gil Robles had offered 500,000 pesetas in June to what he called the 'Military Movement' from party funds left over from the elections of February. Mola only began to draw on the funds in July after the new date of the insurrection had been set.[98] He also insisted that all civilian militia should obey only the military commanders of the insurrection. Referring to the approach some Falangists had made to anarchists in the hope of wooing them over to a 'national revolution', he ordered that the contacts some 'madmen' had made should cease forthwith.[99]

The continued absence of documentary evidence makes it difficult to decide why the plan for the insurrection changed so radically as to make the colonial army its key player. Mola's new instruction of 24 June ordered Yagüe to await the arrival of a 'prestigious general', while preparing to embark the troops in Morocco for Spain once the uprising in the Protectorate had been successful. The vagueness of the general's identity may have been due not just to the need for security but to Franco's continued indecision about whether to join the conspiracy.[100] Disregarding the earlier decision to ship them to Cadiz, Mola's instruction ordered the colonial troops to make their way to Malaga and Algeciras. The date fixed for the rebellion was now 14 July. Having crossed the Straits, the colonial troops were then expected to march on Madrid at great speed to join up with the other anti-government forces.[101]

Three hypotheses spring to mind to explain these changes. It may be that the colonial officers based in Morocco demanded a more important role in the

[97] El Director, 'Informe reservado', 1 July 1936, AV vol. 13.
[98] 'Preparación del Movimiento. José María Gil Robles', ibid.
[99] El Director, 'Informe reservado', 1 July 1936, ibid.
[100] According to Mola's closest collaborator, José María Iribarren, Franco had met Mola in early March and since then they had gone their own ways, exchanging only one letter each that had crossed in the post. If this is true, then Franco played little part in the preparations of the insurrection until shortly before it began. Iribarren's book of 1937, from where this detail was taken (p. 15), was withdrawn from circulation. He published a new book in 1945 in which Franco is portrayed as having taken charge of the insurrection plans as early as the end of May—yet another Francoist attempt to rewrite history. The first is Con el general Mola, Zaragoza, n.p., 1937, while the second is El General Mola (Madrid, Editora Nacional, 1945): the reference to Franco's supposed early assumption of the leadership is in n. 6 on p. 51.
[101] Joaquín Pérez Madrigal, Augurios, estallido y episodios de la Guerra Civil (Avila, n.p., 1937), 308–10; José Manuel Martínez Bande, La campaña de Andalucía (Madrid, San Martín, 1986), 13 and doc. 1, and Arrarás, Historia, iv. 497.

approaching 'Crusade'. It is possible also that the military conspirators needed to mobilize the colonial army in order to keep control over their civilian allies during the process of political change following the rebellion. Perhaps more crucial, however, was Mola's and the junta's realization that they still had not won sufficient support among the metropolitan garrisons for the uprising to be successful without the support of the professional army.[102] Thus, the decision to deploy the Army of Africa in the coming action was a measure of the resistance the conspirators thought they were likely to have to overcome in the metropolitan army.

The mobilization of the Army of Africa would also mean a fundamental alteration of the balance of power among the conspirators. The head of the new state was to be Sanjurjo, and Mola, as director of the plot, would also play a key role in the regime. The two forceful politicians of the extreme right, José Antonio Primo de Rivera and José Calvo Sotelo, would be expected to figure prominently in the new state. Other high-ranking generals such as Cabanellas, Goded, and Fanjul would occupy key positions in the hierarchy of power. However, if he could be persuaded to join the conspiracy, Franco, as commander of the elite troops of the rebellion, would hold considerable advantage over his fellow generals in any dispute over leadership. The leaders of the uprising in Andalusia, especially Queipo de Llano in Seville and Varela in Cadiz, would also need to be rewarded for their role in preparing the ground for the landing, equipment, and transport of the colonial army. Moreover, the deployment of the colonial army also meant once again having to justify the use of Moroccan troops against Spaniards, one of the possible reasons why the Army of Africa had not figured in the original plans.

More detailed plans for the insurrection in Morocco were issued by Mola on 30 June. All the colonial troops were to be mobilized. Among the many drastic measures, all 'left-wing elements', including trade unionists and masons, were to be 'eliminated' and all 'suspicious' civil personnel arrested. The brutality of these plans marked the distance the conspirators had travelled since Sanjurjo's attempted coup of 1932. The *pronunciamiento* of Spanish military tradition, reliant on bravado and contagion, had given way to meticulous organization and ruthlessness, in which the experience of the colonial war must have been an important influence. It also reflected an awareness that the depth of political consciousness and the extent of mobilization among the masses were such that a nineteenth-century style uprising would almost certainly fail.

Mola's instructions also revealed a clearer grasp of the likely support for and opposition to the insurrection in Morocco than in similar documents about Spain. The leader of the Moroccan nationalists, Abdel-Kahlek Torres, was to

---

[102] This is the explanation, rather cagily given, of the Francoist military historian Martínez Bande in *La campaña*, 13.

be detained and all his followers put under house arrest. Another significant detail was Mola's order that the leaders of Moroccan resistance during the colonial war should also be arrested, a clear indication that post-war tensions had not abated. At the same time, the military rebels were instructed to begin a policy of seducing the Moroccan authorities, including the caliph and his government, as well as the religious brotherhoods.[103] They could offer only two enticements: the promise of greater autonomy for Morocco and a crusade against atheism.

The Popular Front government was aware of preparations for a coup and attempted to gather evidence against some of the conspirators. Mola was approached on behalf of the government by a loyalist fellow general, Batet, and gave his word he would not rebel, convinced that his word was less important than the Cause. He was surprised at the extent to which the government knew about plans for the uprising.[104] It would appear, however, that it knew considerably less about the preparations in Morocco, despite the appointment of loyal officers to key posts there. Moroccan nationalists had twice warned the Republic about agitation in the Army of Africa.[105] However, secrecy was much easier to maintain in a highly disciplined, barrack-based professional army than in a conscript army based in the mainland. The high commissioner, Álvarez Buylla, and the commander-in-chief of the Army of Africa, Gómez Morato, knew the names of a few conspirators but had insufficient evidence or judged it unwise to proceed against all of them.

A mutinous speech by one conspirator, the impetuous right-wing officer of the Legion, Rolando Tella Cantos, had prompted an order for his arrest in April, but Tella, helped by inside information, fled to the French zone. Before he left, he gave an even more seditious speech to his regiment in which he virtually announced the coming uprising. Spain had been corrupted and required regeneration, he announced. Only the Legion was equipped to accomplish this task, and 'will serve as a shield of good Spaniards and will save Spain, destroying once and for all the traitors to the country and the national honour'.[106] The government authorities also knew that Yagüe was conspiring and, according to a Francoist source, the minister of war, Casares Quiroga, tried unsuccessfully to tempt him with an offer of a post anywhere he desired in Spain.[107]

Without documentation, it is impossible to estimate how much the Republican authorities knew about the insurrectionary plans in Morocco. We know that the reports they received from sources in different Moroccan garrisons, probably from some of the conspirators themselves, announced, in the standard phrase of military jargon, 'an atmosphere of apparent tranquillity' as

---

[103] El Director, 'Directivas para Marruecos', 24 June 1936, Beigbeder papers in Ibn Azzuz Hakim Archive.

[104] Arrarás, *Historia*, iv. 394.

[105] Ibn Azzuz Hakim, *La actitud*, 91–7.

[106] Afr.GF.DOC, caja 25, carp. 2.

[107] Beltrán Güell, *Preparación*, 161–2.

late as five days before the uprising.[108] Unknown to them perhaps, a junta had been set up linking the main cities in the Protectorate and staffed by officers from all the military units, including the Civil Guard. Under them were grouped individuals from all the right-wing parties and organizations in Morocco.[109] One of their number, a retired colonial officer, Lt.-Colonel Seguí, who had taken early retirement under the Azaña decree, used his freedom of movement to act as intermediary between the conspirators in Morocco and Spain. In mid-May he visited Mola to report that the army in Morocco was ready to rise. The government must have received several secret reports of unrest in the Army of Africa but was unlikely to have known the plans for the insurrection.

A French report noted considerable tension between Legionnaires and pro-Republican civilians in Ceuta that broke out in an ever-increasing number of incidents, until the military authorities decided in June to move the whole garrison inland. It can be surmised from the same document that the conspirators were still not confident that they would win the support of all their fellow officers for the coming insurrection, so they fell back on rumour and forgery. Word was spread that the Legion was going to be dissolved by the Popular Front government. A forged document was also circulated, similar or identical to the one that was being used in Spain, which purported to be of Soviet origin and contained orders for a revolutionary uprising. Among its instructions, it ordered the execution of all officers above the rank of commander as well as all those below it who had shown hostility towards revolutionary ideas at any time in the past. It also ordered the expropriation and distribution of the goods of all shopkeepers.[110]

Final preparations for the uprising in Morocco were put into place in early July, during military manoeuvres in Ketama in the mid-southern part of the Protectorate. The timing of the manoeuvres, like those of León in 1934 and Asturias in 1935, was perhaps not fortuitous. It may have been the result of pressure on Gómez Morato by senior officers who were part of the conspiracy, although Mola had to delay the date of the uprising as a result. The ostensible purpose of the operation was to rehearse for a hypothetical uprising among the Ketama tribes. The manoeuvres enabled rebel officers to meet without arousing the suspicion of the Republican authorities. In their tents during the evening, officers from Melilla, Ceuta, Tetuan, and the Larache region hammered out the details of the rebellion. The typical Francoist evocation of a reigning atmosphere of unity and patriotic exultation is too far-fetched to be taken seriously.[111] In the absence of any documents or critical narratives, we have to imagine the arguments, the tension, the bargaining, the vacillations,

---

[108] 'Informes de las Fuerzas Militares de Marruecos', SHM ADGLN, R270, C 14.

[109] Calleja, Yagüe, 78–9, n. 1.

[110] 'La situation en zone espagnole', in Archives Diplomatiques de Nantes (ADN), Protectorat du Maroc, Région de Casablanca, carton 718, pp. 14–15.

[111] B. Félix Maíz, Alzamiento en España. De un diario de la conspiración, 2nd edn. (Pamplona, Editorial Gomez, 1952), 244.

and the frustration that must have existed among those who met in the tents and the officers and soldiers they tried to recruit for the rebellion.[112] According to one source, a captain from Larache had obtained the plans for the uprising in Morocco and was heading for the manoeuvres to give them to the high commissioner. Waylaid by three of his closest fellow officers, who were part of the conspiracy, he was persuaded to back down.[113]

Again according to a Francoist narrative, many officers, gathered for the open-air banquet held to celebrate the manoeuvres, shouted the abbreviated slogan of the Falange, CAFE (*Camaradas, Arriba Falange Española*). Álvarez Buylla was supposed to have been puzzled that they should want coffee with their hors d'oeuvres, but he was no fool and it would be surprising that he was not already aware of the slogan.[114] On the final day of the manoeuvres, 18,000 troops assembled in the Llano Amarillo (Yellow Plain) for inspection by the high commissioner and his staff and foreign observers. Then, for some two hours and in the heat of the Moroccan summer, they marched past a raised dais, saluting the authorities of the Spanish government. The date was 12 July, only five days before the new date set by Mola for the uprising.

The only piece missing in the jigsaw of the conspiracy was Franco. Selected to lead the uprising of the Army of Africa, he had still not overcome his almost chronic indecisiveness to commit himself fully. Some of his closest colleagues were deeply upset by his prevarication. In a conversation with Franco's brother-in-law, Serrano Suñer, Yagüe expressed his despair at the 'general's hesitations and parsimony'. In fact, in a typically ambiguous letter to the minister of war, Casares Quiroga, on 23 June, Franco had warned him of conspiracies in the army and somewhat tortuously had offered to crush them himself if he were put in command.[115]

The plotters had arranged for a private plane, a Dragon Rapide, to be flown from England to pick Franco up in the Canary Islands and fly him to Morocco. On 12 July, the same day as the Dragon Rapide landed in Casablanca on its last leg to the Canary Islands, the same day also of the march past of the Army of Africa in the Llano Amarillo, Franco sent a coded message withdrawing from the uprising. In a fit of anger, Mola threw the belt in which the young female courier had carried the message to the floor and immediately set in motion an alternative plan to divert the plane to Portugal to pick up Sanjurjo and fly him to Morocco in Franco's place. Two days later, having learnt of the assassination of the right-wing monarchist Calvo Sotelo, Franco finally threw in his lot with the conspirators.[116]

[112] One of the officers approached by the rebels was the commander of the Ceuta Regulares, Lt.-Col. Caballero, who refused to join the uprising and abandoned his post just before it began, and was later executed by the Nationalists: Jose Pettenghi, 'Los moros', *Diario de Cádiz*, 18 July 1997.

[113] Calleja, *Yagüe*, 80.   [114] Arrarás, *Historia*, iv. 394, n. 1.

[115] Ramón Serrano Suñer, *Entre el silencio y la propaganda. La Historia como fue. Memorias* (Barcelona, Planeta, 1977), 52; Preston, *Franco*, 132–3; Carlos Blanco Escolá, *La incompetencia militar de Franco* (Madrid, Alianza, 2000), 202–8.   [116] Serrano Suñer, *Entre el silencio*, 121.

CHAPTER TEN

The Reconquest of Spain

THE MILITARY UPRISING in Morocco, in contrast to Spain, was almost immediately successful. By the evening of 18 July all of Spanish Morocco was in rebel hands. The overwhelming majority of officers and soldiers of the Army of Africa supported the insurrection once it began. In comparison to their counterparts in Spain, the obstacles the rebels faced in Morocco were feeble. The balance of forces gave them a devastating advantage over Spaniards loyal to the government. Facing them were only a handful of officers appointed for their allegiance to the Republic, a comparatively small number of loyal Assault Guards and Civil Guards, and groups of Spanish workers with hardly any weapons. Between the two sides were numerous officers and soldiers whose backing for the uprising, it was hoped, might be won by audacity, pressure, and an appeal to 'patriotism'. Opinions had been secretly and intensely canvassed in the preceding months, though some of the officers approached were still undecided the day before the event.[1]

As we saw in the previous chapter, the rising had been meticulously prepared. The local Falange were primed for action and the military conspirators had managed to get them the necessary arms. The Legion had been inculcated with the ideals of its officers and drilled to obey them unquestioningly. The native troops, whose allegiance to their officers had been won over many years of fighting and training, had also probably been prepared for the event, though no evidence of this seems available. The attachment of a new generation of Moroccan conscripts to their officers stemmed largely from the fact that the latter were committed native officers who had chosen to serve in the Regulares (though many may have preferred the even more elitist Legion). They respected Moroccan culture (and several were Moroccans themselves), most spoke some words of Arabic, and some took the trouble of learning the language. Officers of the native bureaux and the Regulares, some of them Moroccan, had also secretly approached local chiefs to win their backing for the revolt. Most of the caids and pashas owed their jobs to the Spanish military for having sided with Spain in the colonial war, and so were easily persuaded to join in the conspiracy.[2]

---

[1] Maíz, *Alzamiento*, 130 and 241.

[2] Fernández de Castro y Pedrera, Rafael, *Hacia las rutas de una nueva España. Melilla, la primera en el Alzamiento. De cómo se preparó y porqué hubo de comenzar en Melilla la santa cruzada ¡17 julio 1936!* (Melilla, n.p., 1940); PRO: CO91/500/2 'Spanish Disturbances 1936'; Manuel Sánchez del Arco, *El Sur de España en*

The key to the success of the uprising in Morocco was getting the troops from garrisons scattered about the Protectorate into Melilla, Ceuta, Larache, and Tetuan before the Republic could mobilize its own forces. The first troops to be mobilized were the 5th Tabor of the Regulares, which had set out the previous night on 16 July across mountainous terrain towards Al Hoceima from the southern part of the Protectorate.[3] When the Republican authorities under General Romerales, finally alerted to the conspiracy, attempted to arrest the rebels in Melilla on the afternoon of 17 July, the revolt had already got under way. As soon as the Republican squad of Assault Guards and police was itself disarmed by the conspirators, military rebels already on alert in garrisons throughout Spanish Morocco were telephoned to begin the action immediately. The oft-postponed rebellion had been due to begin one hour later, but only that afternoon an order had come through delaying the action for a further twenty-four hours because Franco was unable to get to Morocco on time.[4] The insurgents arrested the Melilla commander, General Romerales, and brought their armed Falange supporters out into the streets.

The speed of their action took the government by surprise. The president and minister of war, Santiago Casares Quiroga, telephoned Romerales to find out what was going on and was answered by the local commander of the rebels, Colonel Solans. Casares then ordered the commander-in-chief of the Army of Africa, Gómez Morato, to fly to Melilla, where he was immediately arrested. Shortly afterwards the first rebel troops arrived in the city. The French vice-consul in Melilla witnessed people fleeing in panic before the rebels, and the Legion going around ordering windows to be closed. Supporters of the Popular Front had raided armouries and the French diplomat heard the sporadic exchange of gun and machine-gun fire throughout the night and then again the next day in the early afternoon. Some of the pilots of the Melilla aerodrome, led by their commander, a veteran of the colonial war, put up a spirited defence until they were overwhelmed. By the evening of 18 July Melilla was quiet.[5]

Outnumbered Republican loyalists also put up fierce resistance in the other cities of the Protectorate. Franco's cousin and boyhood playmate, Major Ricardo de la Puente Bahamonde, led the defence of the Sania Ramel airport of Tetuan, sabotaging the planes when he and his fellow Republicans were about to be overwhelmed by the rebels.[6] By evening, the forces of the Legion

la Reconquista de Madrid (diario de operaciones glosado por un testigo) (Seville, Editorial Sevillana, 1937); Ricardo de la Cierva, *Historia esencial de la Guerra Civil Española. Todos los problemas resueltos, sesenta años después* (Madrid, Editorial Fénix, 1996), 97–108.

[3] Fernández de Castro, *Hacia las rutas*, 315.   [4] Beltran Güell, *Preparación*, 182.

[5] ADMAE vol. 207, 'Sédition au Maroc espagnol', 18 July 1936; Enrique Arqués, *17 de julio. La epopeya de África. Crónica de un testigo* (Ceuta–Tetuan, Imprenta África, 1937).

[6] Unlike the other airmen captured by the rebels, he was not immediately shot because of his family link with Franco. After he arrived, Franco left the decision to Orgaz, who ordered his execution: Ignacio Alcaraz Cánovas, 'Marruecos y la Guerra Civil', *Cuadernos Republicanos* (Jan. 2000), 99.

and the Regulares, which had marched into the city capital earlier in the day from outlying garrisons, had taken control of the capital. The capture of Ceuta, under the leadership of overall commander of the rebels in Morocco, Colonel Juan Yagüe, was also accomplished by dawn after determined resistance from Spanish workers and pro-Republican military personnel.

In the far western part of the Protectorate, some 2,000 Regulares had marched on Larache from neighbouring garrisons and, together with the city's troops, overwhelmed loyalist defence, killing five officers and seven civilians amongst those who opposed the insurrection.[7] In the cities and garrisons, loyalist officers were executed during the course of the action or shortly after, whilst the commanders were made prisoner to await trial. One of those executed was the veteran of the Moroccan war, Luis Casado Escudero, one of the handful of survivors of the 1921 disaster at Igueriben. He was shot in Melilla because he was a sympathizer of the Republic.[8] The Africanist rebels could not claim they had a monopoly of the heroism of the colonial war.

Franco finally arrived in Tetuan on the morning of 19 July, after delaying his departure for many hours.[9] There, he took over from Yagüe as commander of the insurgent Army of Africa. One of his first actions was to set up a concentration camp on the outskirts of Tetuan called El Mogote, and this was followed by the creation of two further camps elsewhere in the Protectorate, one in Melilla and the other on the Tangier border. Hundreds of Republican supporters, workers, soldiers, members of the Masonic Lodges, and Jews were rounded up and imprisoned in appalling conditions in these camps and in the El Hacho fortress in Ceuta. Many were used as forced labour during the day, and every morning dozens were executed by Moroccan soldiers under the command of Spanish officers after the local Falange had selected the victims. A Tetuan shopkeeper remembers witnessing the executions every day at dawn as a 15-year-old Moroccan orphan recruited by the Falange. Like many others on military service in Morocco, a Spanish soldier had watched bemused as the fighting took place among rebels and loyalists, barely aware of what was going on. When his rebel officer ordered the platoon to which he was attached to load rifles, they obeyed without question. A few days later, his best friend was picked out at random and told to get ready for a parade. He polished his boots, cleaned his rifle and uniform, and shaved. He returned later that day in a pitiful state. Without having been told anything, he had found himself on an execution squad and had had to shoot a popular captain who had remained loyal to the government.[10]

---

[7] ADMAE vol. 207; 'La situation', ADN p. 27.   [8] Pando, *Historia secreta*, 330.

[9] Blanco Escolá, in *La incompetencia*, 212–22, argues that Franco's delay was a deliberate effort to ensure he would take over only when the insurrection in Morocco had been completely successful.

[10] Interview with Hach Hamaida el Filali, 21 July 2000; Alcaraz Cánovas, 'Marruecos', 100–1 and 106–7 (the article uses documentary evidence housed in the public archives of Ceuta). See also his book *Entre España y Marruecos. Testimonio de una época 1923–1975* (Madrid, Catriel, 1999), 45–50. José Llordés Badía, *Al dejar el fusil. Memorias de un soldado raso en la guerra de España*, 2nd edn. (Esplugues de Llobregat, Ariel, 1969), 46–52.

The success or failure of the military rebellion now lay in the hands of the Army of Africa. Despite the support of many officers, the uprising in Spain had been largely unsuccessful. The expected coup d'état had failed and a mere third of the territory had fallen to the rebels, including only two pockets of Andalusia opposite Ceuta. Overall, the number of rebel and loyal forces and the arms and munitions they could deploy was roughly equal. The insurgents controlled 53 per cent of the army, 35 per cent of the navy and air force, 60 per cent of the artillery, 49 per cent of the Civil Guard, but only about 32 per cent of the Carabinieros and Republican Assault Guards. A majority of the High Command remained loyal to the Republic, and of the 15,300 officers in service just under half obeyed the state. Moreover, many of the leaders of the uprising were ex-colonial officers who had been sacked or had chosen early retirement and were not therefore in command of any troops. In addition, the Republic could deploy large forces of conscripts commanded by officers loyal to the state, to which could be added the Republican militiamen, and volunteers from political and labour organizations.[11]

Indeed, mobilization in defence of democracy was so intense that the government forces of law and order were briefly overtaken by popular organizations. The failure of the coup meant that civil war seemed likely. Victory in that war was now unthinkable without the participation of the only truly professional troops in the Spanish army, the Army of Africa. It is a measure of how poorly the conspirators had judged their support in the armed forces that only two and a half months previously they had assigned a purely passive role to the colonial troops.

Moreover, after Azaña's reforms and the enormous cuts in manpower since the colonial war, the troop numbers of the Legion and the Moroccan soldiers in the Army of Africa were totally inadequate for the rebels' war effort in Spain. On the eve of the uprising the number of troops stationed in Morocco was approximately 34,000. Of the European, mainly Spanish forces, there were the two regiments of the Legion and several battalions of the Cazadores, a light infantry unit made up mainly of national service personnel and therefore not likely to be mobilized as shock-troops. Indeed, amongst them there were almost certainly many secret sympathizers of the Republic. The Moroccan units consisted of 9,000 Regulares, grouped into five regiments, a battalion of the Sidi Ifni Tiradores (almost identical to the Regulares), the military and police forces of the Mahkzen, that is, the Mehal-las and the Mejaznias, and two artillery units. Of the total number of troops in the Army of Africa on 18 July, some 18,000 were European (almost all Spanish) and 16,000 Moroccan.[12]

---

[11] Ramón Salas Larrazábal, *Historia general de la guerra civil* (Madrid, Editora Nacional, 1976), 60–4; Martínez Saura, *Memorias*, 456–69.

[12] These calculations take into account ADMAE, 'Annexe au compte rendu mensuel des renseignements', July 1936, V.208, pp. 67–80 (though the French give a higher total figure of 38,000);

But not all of these troops were available for action. Some of the Moroccan soldiers might not wish to participate in the war in Spain. Many troops would have to remain in the garrisons in Morocco, if only because the French, forever impatient with Spanish colonial administration, might be tempted to occupy the Spanish Protectorate on the grounds that it was insufficiently defended against Moroccan nationalists.[13] The Cazadores battalions also posed a security problem in that some of their soldiers might be covert supporters of the Republic. So the rebel military leaders set about integrating some of the most loyal native troops into their ranks to prevent any revolt.[14] But the most important task for the Spanish rebels was to recruit as many mercenaries to the Legion and the native troops as possible and to get them rapidly across the Straits of Gibraltar to help the faltering insurrection in Spain.

The enlistment of Moroccans was made more attractive by dramatically raising the level of pay and bonuses. Those who joined the Regulares and other native units were offered a daily rate of 5.25 pesetas, while recruits to the Legion were promised up to 7 pesetas, with an enlistment bonus of 6 pesetas for both. But both Regular and Legionnaire had small sums deducted for their meals and uniforms, and a daily sum of 1.10 pesetas was put aside as savings for the moment of their discharge. An ex-Legionnaire calculated that he in fact only received 3 pesetas daily, which rose to 3.85 on days when he saw military action.[15] Pay rose considerably during the Civil War, and both the Legion and the Regulares always earned 50 per cent more than the militiamen of the Nationalist army. In addition, two months' advance pay was pledged as well as bonuses in kind such as weapons, sugar, oil, and bread for the recruit's family.

The money offered was far in excess of the meagre wages many Moroccans obtained in seasonal labour in Algeria, and was especially attractive because of the hardship caused by the bad harvests of the previous two years. During the first months of 1936 drought had devastated agriculture in the eastern zone of the Spanish Protectorate, and Moroccan labourers had returned to their villages in a sorry state without a penny in their pockets. They and many others who lived and worked in the towns of the Protectorate were driven to join the army because they lost their jobs in the workshops and services that closed

Marcel Roubicek, in *Special Troops of the Spanish Civil War 1936–1939* (Doncaster, Athena, 1987), puts the total figure of native troops at 12,870; José Semprún, 'Del Hacho al Pirineo: el Ejército Nacional en la guerra de España', MS submitted for *Así Fue. La Historia Rescatada* (1999), 70–80; Victor Morales Lezcano, *España y el norte de Africa:el protectorado en Marruecos*, 2nd edn. (Madrid, 1986) and for Moroccan troops, José María Gárate Córdoba, 'Las tropas de Africa en la Guerra Civil española', *Revista de Historia Militar*, 35: 70 (1991), 16.

[13] On the very day of the uprising in Morocco the commander-in-chief of the French army in Morocco, General Corap, urged his minister of defence to sanction French occupation of the most rebellious parts of the Spanish Protectorate: ADMAE, 'Sédition' (n. 5 above).

[14] 'La situation', ADN p. 26.

[15] Frank Thomas and Robert Stradling, *Brother against Brother: Experiences of a British Volunteer in the Spanish Civil War* (Stroud, Alan Sutton, 1998), 48–9.

down when the uprising took place.[16] The fundamental motive, therefore, for the successful recruitment of thousands of Moroccans into the ranks of the rebel army was economic. This is borne out by each of fourteen Moroccan veterans of the Civil War interviewed in preparation for this chapter.

There were other, less crucial reasons that also facilitated recruitment. The Republican government had not promised independence to Morocco, nor had it paid any special attention to the problems of its inhabitants. An attempt to negotiate a deal with Moroccan nationalists after the outbreak of the Civil War was blocked by France.[17] Encouraged by the rebels, many Moroccans believed the Popular Front government to be dominated by Communists and atheists, *bêtes noires* of orthodox Muslims. Among the recruits, rumour had it that they were going to fight the 'rohkos', the reds. A number of caids close to the Spanish colonial army met in Ajdir on 19 July and agreed to support the military rebellion.[18]

The Republican cause amongst Moroccans was not helped when shells from Spanish warships in Republican hands firing at rebel targets hit coastal towns indiscriminately. Nor was it advanced when one of four amateurishly converted Douglas DC-2 planes dropped bombs on Tetuan the day after the uprising, missing their target, the High Commission, and hitting the Moroccan quarter instead, causing the death of three children and a further seventeen casualties. Moroccan labourers in some of the towns also resented the Republican authorities, according to the British consul in Tetuan, because Spanish trade unions had successfully persuaded them to favour the recruitment of local Spanish workers over Moroccans, breaking with the established practice of non-discrimination. When Moroccan workers in Tetuan in May 1931 had asked for equal pay and hours of work with Spanish workers in the Protectorate, the authorities had brought the troops out and killed several of their number.[19]

The rebels, on the contrary, were making all sorts of assurances in an effort to woo the Moroccans. The new high commissioner, General Orgaz, and his team of Africanists were making vague noises to sympathetic caids in the Rif about some form of future autonomy for the region. There was nothing new in this. Such offers had been made before, as we have seen, both to Raisuni and Abdel Krim. The caliph of the Spanish Protectorate, Moulay Hassan Bel Mehdi, had been won over to the rebel cause shortly before the uprising, and the grand vizir in Tetuan shortly afterwards, largely through the efforts of

[16] 'Sédition', p. 81; 'La situation', ADN, 19; interviews with Mohammad El Hassani and Mohammad Ben Hammou, 17 July 2000.
[17] Robert A. Friedlander, 'Holy Crusade or Unholy Alliance? Franco's "National Revolution" and the Moors', *Southwestern Social Science Quarterly*, 44 (Mar. 1964), 351–2.
[18] Madariaga, 'The Intervention', 77.
[19] Alcaraz Cánovas, *Entre España*, 119; PRO: CO91/500/2, 'Spanish Disturbances'; Fernández de Castro, *Hacia las rutas*, 315–16. Re the bombing see ADMAE, vol. 207, pp. 22–3 and Gerald Howson, *Arms for Spain: The Untold Story of the Spanish Civil War* (London, John Murray, 1998), 11.

Colonel Juan Beigbeder, who spoke Arabic and knew several dialects and had cultivated local contacts. An official tour of the Spanish Protectorate was organized for Moulay Hassan in September, and everywhere he was showered with honours and orchestrated public adulation. Orgaz and Beigbeder encouraged him in the illusion that he might exercise a degree of sovereignty in the Protectorate independently of the sultan.

On 12 October Moroccan representatives were flown over to join the celebrations in Seville of the Spanish 'Day of the Race', commemorating Columbus's discovery of the Americas. Mosques were opened in Sevilla and Cordoba. The grand vizir and the leader of a section of the Moroccan nationalist movement calling itself the National Reformist Party, Abdel Khalek Torres, made radio speeches in Seville supporting the Nationalist cause. All these efforts also helped in the recruitment of the Mehal-las or Caliphate troops into the Nationalist army (though they would be used not so much to fight in the Civil War as to man the positions won by regular troops). In December Franco also gave official recognition to Abdel Khalek Torres in order to appear pro-Moroccan to all Moroccans.[20] A month earlier Queipo de Llano had made a radio broadcast in Franco's name promising independence to Morocco, and as late as September 1938 Beigbeder would still be promising an entirely illusory independence to Morocco at some undefined time in the future.[21]

In marked contrast to Nationalist efforts to win over Moroccan opinion, the Republican government failed to seize the opportunity to undermine the military rebels by offering autonomy or independence to the Spanish Protectorate. President Giral did not respond to the pressure exerted for such a strategy by the future foreign minister Álvarez del Vayo, insisting that he and his colleagues were far too busy trying to contain the insurrection in Spain.[22] As we have seen, Republican leaders had shown little sympathy for the Moroccan nationalists. But the Giral cabinet's lack of interest in trying to win them over in an effort to undermine the rebels' cause was probably based on

[20] ADMAE, ibid., pp. 82 and 88; 'La situation', ADN pp. 48–52; SHAT 7N 2763; Beigbeder to Abdel Khalek Torres, 5 Aug. 1936, in Archivo Ibn Azzuz Hakim; Ramón Salas Larrazábal, *El protectorado de España en Marruecos* (Madrid, Mapfre, 1992), 210–13; *Bulletin du Comité de l'Afrique Française* (Oct. 1936), 563–4 (Nov. 1936), 599, (Dec. 1936), 597–600. For Beigbeder, see Charles Halstead, 'A "Somewhat Machiavellian" Face: Colonel Juan Beigbeder as High Commissioner in Spanish Morocco, 1937–1939', *Historian*, 37 (Nov. 1974), 46–66 and 'Un "Africain" méconnu: le colonel Juan Beigbeder', *Revue d'Histoire de la Deuxième Guerre Mondiale*, 21: 83 (1971), 31–60.

[21] Alberto Elena, 'Cine Africanista Español: "Romancero Marroquí"', in *Semencias*, 4 (Apr, 1996), 88, n. 20.

[22] According to Álvarez Vayo in the interview in 1972 in Abel Paz, *La cuestión de Marruecos y la República española* (Madrid, Fundación de Estudios Libertarios Anselmo Lorenzo, 2000), 103–4. In the absence of government action, the CNT leader Juan García Oliver established contact with one branch of the Moroccan nationalists and, as minister of war in autumn 1936, Largo Caballero sent an agent to Morocco to try to organize an anti-Francoist revolt amongst the Moroccan tribes: ibid., 106. Neither of these initiatives came to anything.

a evaluation that the Army of Africa had much closer links with the local population than the Moroccan nationalists, who were based largely in the cities.

Indeed, what facilitated the conscription of Moroccans to the rebels' cause were the intimate bonds that had been established between long-serving colonial officers and tribal chiefs. Those caids who had had close links with the officers for native affairs in the past were obliging the insurgents by providing lists of names of potential recruits. They could be assured also of continuing to receive from the rebels the generous payouts that the Spanish authorities had used for two decades to keep the Moroccan chiefs on their side. Even more important for recruitment was the bonding that had occurred between colonial officers (those of both the combat forces and military administration) and soldiers of the Regulares and the sultan's troops. During the colonial war and in the post-colonial 'pacification' campaigns they had formed a community of soldiers in which fraternity and solidarity were more powerful than ideology or politics. An anecdote reveals the strength of these bonds. A Moroccan sergeant of the Regulares, veteran of the Spanish colonial army, joined up and was sent on the first boatload of troops to Cadiz. During the voyage he was astute enough to suspect that the sailors were preparing to mutiny against their officers. As soon as he landed he went straight to Varela, his old commander in the colonial war, to warn him.[23]

There was fierce opposition in certain areas of Spanish Morocco to the enlistment drive, despite the heavy-handed tactics employed by the Spanish army against any dissent. Mola's secret instructions for the rising in Morocco had stipulated that anyone opposing it should be shot and that all those who refused to collaborate with the new authorities should be jailed. One of these instructions specifically ordered that all leaders of the resistance against the Spanish 'pacification' campaign in 1926–7 should be arrested.[24] Whilst men poured into the recruitment offices from the traditional areas of conscription, such as the eastern Rif and Gelaya, those more impenetrable regions that had been most resistant to Spanish invasion, in particular the central Rif, Gomara, and Yebala, continued to cause problems for the Spanish army. The military authorities attempted to isolate these regions for fear their opposition might spread. Rebellious Gomara tribesmen clashed with Spanish forces, and a section of the Beni Urriaghel tribe, the most militant tribe in the anti-colonial war between 1919 and 1926, rose up once again under the leadership of the caid Azirkan. Only through the deployment of native troops from other areas and the imprisonment or execution of refractory tribal chiefs was Orgaz able to impose order once again.[25]

[23] José Pettenghi, 'Los moros', *Diario de Cádiz*, 18 July 1997. According to the writer, Varela warned the captain of the boat, the *Churruca*, and suggested that he should embark a group of Regulares for the return journey. The captain refused and the mutiny took place once the boat had left Cadiz port.

[24] El Director, 'Instrucciones', Beigbeder Papers, Ibn Azzuz Hakim archive.

[25] According to *El Sol* of 19 Sept. and 1 Oct. 1936 and *La Veu de Catalunya* of 25 Sept. 1936 quoted in *Bulletin du Comité de l'Afrique Française* (Nov. 1936), 598; Friedlander, 'Holy Crusade', 353; Madariaga, 'Imagen', 592–3.

Though there were veterans of the war against Spain amongst recruits to the Regulares, the initial geography of support for the military rebels in Spanish Morocco tended to replicate the pattern of subjugation and dissidence of the colonial war. Thus, the repression of the 'pacification' campaign in the late 1920s continued during the Civil War. In October 1938 members of Abdel Krim's family, including his brother, were once again jailed on the mere rumour that the Rif leader had escaped from his confinement on the island of Réunion and had made his way secretly to French Morocco to organize an uprising against Spain.[26]

As the Civil War progressed, the extent of the rebels' need to recruit Moroccans to fight their war in Spain was reflected in their desperate bids to hoodwink or coerce potential conscripts. The son of a Moroccan soldier who had fought and died for the Spanish in the colonial war was told that he and his mother had to leave the house where they lived in Ceuta unless he joined the war.[27] The French authorities reported that recruits were often falsely promised they would not be sent to fight in Spain. Other reports suggested that they were coerced into joining or were told they were being sent to put down an uprising in Spain against the Republican government.[28] The rebel authorities used their control of food supplies and grants to reward families that had contributed soldiers to the war effort and punish those that had refused.[29] Efforts were made soon after the outbreak of war to prevent communication between the volunteers in Spain and their families for fear that news of the spiralling level of casualties might deter further recruitment. A French newspaper in Morocco related in December that 800 local workers had been hired by the military for a public-works project, but once they were about to begin they were given equipment for soldiers and told they were to receive military training so that they could join the army. Their determination to refuse, even after they were surrounded by troops, forced the military authorities to let them go.[30]

The military rebels were therefore happy also to recruit men from the Spanish Protectorates in Ifni and Western Sahara and men from French Morocco who had made their way across the frontier seeking work. The French had closed the border and were patrolling its length in an effort to prevent Spanish recruitment. An 18-year-old from Fez had paid money to be

[26] *La Presse Marocaine*, 18 Oct. 1938, in Archivo General del Protectorado de Tetuan (AGPT), leg. 3745. One of these veterans was Hach Mohammed M'Hauesh, who had fought alongside Abdel Krim: interview in Tetuan on 24 July 2000. Jose Pettenghi confirmed that several of his Moroccan soldiers were veterans of the war against the Spanish: interview in Cadiz, 2 Apr. 2000.

[27] Mohammad El Hassani interview.

[28] ADMAE, vol. 208, pp. 82 and 88; *Bulletin du Comité de L'Afrique Française* (Nov. 1936).

[29] *Boletín Oficial de la Zona del protectorado Español en Marruecos (BOZPEM)*, 21 (1937), quoted in Mustapha El Merroun, 'El Cuerpo de Ejército Marroquí en la Guerra Civil Española (1936–1939)', Ph.D thesis, Granada University (1999), 46.

[30] *La Dépêche Marocaine*, quoted in *Bulletin du Comité de L'Afrique Française* (Jan. 1937), 41–2.

smuggled into the Spanish zone to find work. The man who had helped him across advised him not to seek a job because he would be treated badly, and instead suggested he should join the troops being sent to Spain. Impelled by an irrational fear that he might be executed if he was handed back to the French, he joined up in Bab Taza and was taken immediately to Ceuta and then shipped to Cadiz.[31]

Thus, by one means or another, the Nationalists (as the rebels liked to call themselves) were able to assemble a considerable fighting force of Moroccans. Unlike the Legion, they were not all mercenaries in a strict sense, that is, professional soldiers. Rather, the majority were civilians who volunteered to do military service to earn money. It is true that the first units were made up mainly of veterans of the Spanish colonial army, many of whom had fought in the Moroccan war on the Spanish side. Indeed, age did not seem to be a barrier to military service among the Regulares. An American war correspondent who spent some time with the Army of Africa commented: 'Some of the Moors are very old. One I saw must have been well past sixty. The minimum term of enlistment is four years, and many have served in this Tabor eighteen years.'[32] But as the number of new recruits grew, the Moroccan troops were increasingly made up of people who had never seen battle and had as little training for it as the Spanish conscripts of the colonial war. Thus, the combat-effectiveness of the native troops was very uneven.

The young recruits would turn out to be particularly vulnerable to aerial bombardment. Unlike the veterans in the Nationalist army who had fought against the Spanish in the colonial war, they would find the experience of the destruction that rained down from enemy planes terrifying. Some had never seen a plane before they joined up. One position held by the Nationalists in the easternmost part of Avila province near Madrid would be abandoned after repeated sorties by the Republican air force had demoralized the mainly Moroccan defenders.[33]

Moroccan veterans of the colonial war were soon promoted to sergeant, or in a few cases to officer, to command these rookies. But as casualties mounted, in particular among these veterans, who tended to lead the action, the native troops became increasingly diluted. Nevertheless, the Nationalist army continued to need as many recruits as could be mustered from Morocco. The co-operation of the Moroccan authorities over this burgeoning recruitment was such that an official decree of the pro-Francoist caliph on 18 November, countersigned by Beigbeder as delegate for native affairs, provided over 3 million pesetas-worth of credit for the expansion of the native forces.[34]

[31] Interview with Buxta Ben Abdellah Zeruali, 7 Mar. 2001, in Rabat.

[32] H. K. Knickerbocker, *The Siege of Alcazar: A War-Log of the Spanish Revolution* (London, Hutchinson, n.d. [1936]), 62.

[33] E. Santos, *'El Secretario'. Revelaciones sobre la Guerra Civil en Badajoz* (Badajoz, n.p., 1984), 207–8.

[34] Madariaga, 'The Intervention', 77.

According to all accounts, the new recruits received only a brief military training before being sent to Spain. If we are to believe one of the veterans, some received none at all. Many of the youngsters who joined up, he claims, were deeply upset by the way the Spanish army treated them. He remembers being locked up in a garrison as soon as he joined and hearing some of the other young recruits weeping during the night. He and they were taken to the battlefields in Spain without any preparation. Instead of training they were subjected to an abusive military discipline during which they were punished for any clumsiness. Officers told them that if they did not kill the infidel they would be killed themselves.[35] Given the brutal methods of training in some units of the colonial army, such treatment may well have occurred, but it is unlikely to have been a common experience. Most officers were keen to establish a good rapport with their native troops. But it does seem true that the Moroccans who went to Spain knew it was going to be a bloody fight. One of the songs they would sing as they embarked for Spain had the following lyric:

> Guard your belt and put another one over it,
> For we are going to Spain to die.[36]

The training of Legionnaires, on the other hand, continued to be based on the practices of the colonial war. The training officers applied a whip to instil discipline, though they avoided using it on most foreign recruits. A Welsh Legionnaire also remembers how they used to kick recalcitrant recruits in the testicles. Any action during the war deemed 'misbehaviour' was punished by heavy and dirty work, such as clearing the roads of mule manure with bare hands, accompanied by physical beating if the work was not satisfactory.[37]

Three months after the uprising some 18,000 colonial troops had been transported across the Straits, and by the beginning of 1937, 31,440 were fighting in Spain whilst a further 18,000 recruits were being prepared for action. Only six months after the beginning of the Civil War a total of 50,000 Moroccans would be fighting on the Nationalist side, representing one in fourteen of the total population of Spanish Morocco and one in seven of all males. Of these, only about a third were inhabitants of the Rif, the great mountain range stretching across most of the Protectorate.[38] As casualties in the Civil War rose, so recruitment in Spanish Morocco fell and the military authorities were obliged to intensify their search for new conscripts outside the zone, from Ifni, the Western Sahara, and from French Morocco, as we have seen.

---

[35] Abdellah Zeruali interview.   [36] Hart, *The Ait*, 417.

[37] Thomas and Stradling, *Brother*, 106–7 and 134, n. 23.

[38] Gárate Córdoba, 'Las tropas', and Abdelmajid Benjelloun, 'La participation del Rifains a la Guerre Civile Espagnole', *Revue d'Histoire Maghrébine*, 87–8 (May 1997), 459–61. Fieldwork in the 1960s revealed that in one town of the Ulad Stut tribal group in eastern Rif, 26 out of the 42 heads of households had fought in the Civil War for the Nationalists (while 8 of the total number had not been eligible because they were too young): Seddon, *Moroccan*, 157.

Once again, the Spanish Army of Africa, by bribery, coercion, and old loyalties, succeeded in putting together an army of native troops to help fight its war. Its ability to maintain the morale of these soldiers depended on the strength of their relationship with the colonial officers. When casualties began to rise, new, inexperienced recruits and officers took the place of those who had fought together in the colonial war or had served together in the early 1930s in the colonial army. Accordingly, the native units began to suffer demoralization.

One of the problems was that, unlike in the colonial conflict, the Moroccan soldiers were captive on the Spanish peninsula, unable easily to desert or join the 'enemy' had they wanted to. Their families suffered because the soldiers were only allowed to go back home if they had been seriously wounded. Nor were the wives of Moroccans and Legionnaires allowed to join them in Spain. As the general of the western zone of the Protectorate wrote, it would create 'a bad effect', so that 'morally this does not interest or suit us'. Some effort was made to help the families of Moroccans killed in the Civil War. Two orphanages were set up to train some 2,000 boys in useful skills. However, families often learnt about the death of their loved ones long after it occurred from other Moroccan soldiers on sick leave rather than from the military authorities.[39] Much of the available information about these injustices or abuses derives from the concern of officers at the highest level to stamp them out in order to ensure continued recruitment.

One such document reported the despair of wives of Moroccan soldiers in Spain at their prolonged absence. Some were seeking divorce as a result. Others were reported to have been the victims of humiliating or abusive treatment. A Spanish captain of the Regulares based in Tetuan used his influential position to seduce the women he fancied among these wives while maltreating those he did not like.[40] Payment to soldiers or their families was also the subject of much injustice. The relatives of those killed in the war found it very difficult to get the payments they were due. Even veterans were cheated of their full salary when they returned from Spain. In a scam reminiscent of the corruption of the colonial war, veterans of the Tetuan Regulares were told to sign a receipt before they were given their pay. When they went to collect the money they found it was less than they had signed for, and when they complained they were threatened with jail.[41]

The offences suffered by Moroccans and their families at the hands of some colonial officers and NCOs were the reflex actions of a racist and brutalized army of occupation. How, then, could the Nationalists justify the use of

[39] Interventor Regional, Xaeun, 30 Oct. 1938 and letter of 20 Aug. 1937 from the General Jefe de la Circunscripción Occidental de Marruecos, both in Archivo General del Protectorado en Tetuan (AGPT), leg. 3745; Alcaraz Cánovas, *Entre España*, 127.

[40] Interventor Regional, Tetuan, 25 Jan. 1938 (AGPT). Cases of such abuse are also reported by the Delegación de Asuntos Indígenas, 18 Dec. 1937, ibid.

[41] Delegación de Asuntos Indígenas, Tetuan, 11 Mar. 1939, ibid.

Moroccan troops against their own people? Within the coalition of forces that rose against the Republic there were very different conceptions about national identity and national interest. It could be argued that it was kept together, not just by Franco's opportunism and lack of ideological definition, but also by the hatred of the internal Other, a hatred heightened by the experience of colonial war. What had been the external Other was mobilized against the internal Other. From a Christian war against the infidel of old tradition, the Civil War was portrayed as a religious war against atheism waged together by the two dominant religions of the Mediterranean. It could also be argued that this transposition had its class dimension. The categories attributed once to the Moroccan hordes—foreign, uncivilized, uncouth, and illiterate—were now applied to the workers and rural labourers against whom the Nationalists would be fighting.

Reshaping the discourse of the Other was necessary because the recruitment of Moroccans became fundamental to the Nationalist cause. Victory in the Civil War was now unthinkable without the participation of the only truly professional troops in the Spanish army, the Army of Africa. Thus, the mobilization against Spaniards of non-Spaniards, amongst whom were soldiers who had fought against Spain in the colonial war, now had to be rationalized.

Chapter 7 stressed that Spanish representations of the Moroccans in the colonial war had been fraught with difficulties because many local inhabitants kept crossing the frontier between who was a good Moroccan and who was bad. In the construction of the Other in the Civil War, the practice of this colonial discourse was transposed to the homeland, just as the colonial army was transported across the Straits of Gibraltar. The most striking characteristic of this discourse was the systematic inversion of roles. In the colonial war Spain had sought to 'liberate Morocco from savagery' in pursuit of common spiritual goals (this could be interpreted as an involuntary rationalization of Spain's failure to colonize effectively), while bad Moroccans had started the war to 'defend evil'. In the same way, the Spanish Other had in 1936 unleashed a war against the 'authentic' Spain. Thus, it was the Republicans who were in fact the military rebels and the Republican army was the mercenary army. The anti-fascist volunteers who joined the International Brigades were mercenaries attracted by the smell of money, while the Moroccan soldiers joined the war because they adored their officers and in gratitude for the pacification of Morocco. By fighting on the side of the 'patriots', the Moroccans had joined in the struggle to liberate Spain.[42] In doing so, they became Spaniards while those they were fighting against were ethnic or ideological foreigners. Thus

[42] Beltran Güell, *Preparación*, 158; Antonio Garrachón Cuesta, *De África a Cádiz y de Cádiz a la España imperial. Por sendas de heroismo, de justicia, de hermandad y de amor (impresiones de un periodista)* (Cádiz, Establecimientos Cerón, 1938), 119. Teniente Coronel Hartmann, 'Sobre la psicología del soldado moro' (1942), Archivo Garcia Figueras. Re the Army of Africa, see Varela's speech in Segovia on 31 Oct. 1937, quoted in Garrachón, *De África*.

Moroccans began to acquire the traditional characteristics of the 'authentic Spaniards'. They were 'gentlemen of faith and ideals'. They exhibited 'Muslim gallantry towards the beautiful young women who stroll along the streets'.[43] All this was surely part of the romanticization of native soldiery typical of an anti-modernist current in Western imperial literature, which saw the 'noble savage' in a much better light than the cheeky proletarian conscript.[44] In the Spanish case, the latter was fighting on the Republican side, thus acquiring the attributes of a foreign Marxist.

Similarly, attempts were made to overcome the religious contradiction implicit in using Muslims to fight Spaniards. In traditional discourse, the true Spain was Catholic and Spain's enemy had always been the Arab. The 'essential' identity of the Spaniard derived from the medieval struggle to liberate Spain from the Muslim infidel and install the only true religion, Catholicism. After the conquest of Granada in 1492 this meant continuing to purge the Spanish population of Muslims and Jews still covertly practising their religions. Yet in their discussions with friendly caids before the uprising, conspiratorial colonial officers would have stressed the commonality of Islam and Christianity against the anti-religious enemy.

Once the Civil War had begun, this became the leitmotif of approaches by the Nationalist authorities to Moroccan leaders. They took great care to express fraternal links with Islam because they needed to recruit mercenaries for the war effort. Franco himself went to some lengths to organize a pilgrimage by boat to Mecca, offering huge subsidies and benefits to the pilgrims that chose to go. Much was made of the fact that a Republican plane bombed the harbour in Ceuta where the ship was moored, as if its main target had been religious.[45] General Antonio Aranda was sent by Franco on a special mission to exploit the affair. During visits to different parts of the Protectorate, he met local notables, reviewed the troops, and made speeches stressing the religious links between Catholics and Muslims. In his speech in Larache, he stated: 'Those who fight against Spain on national territory wish to destroy all religions: not just Catholicism which is that of the Spaniards, but also the Muslim religion, and in general, all the religions of the world.' Improbably, he went on to state that 'never have the Spanish authorities nor the Spanish soldiers carried out the slightest attack on the prestige and respect due to the saintly Muslim religion, which has always been respected by the true Spain, always defended and protected by us against its enemies'.[46]

After the first colonial troops had been transported to the mainland, Catholic women supporters of the Nationalist cause in Seville embroidered the image of the Sacred Heart onto the tunics of Regulares mercenaries in the city.

---

[43] Antonio de Puelles y Puelles, *Por las rutas del tercio Mora-Figueroa (recuerdos de la campaña)* (Cadiz, n.p., 1939), 43; Fray González, 'Los Regulares y la población del Rif', *Telegrama del Rif*, 14 Aug. 1936.
[44] Said, *Orientalism*, and Robinson, Gallagher, and Denny, *Africa and the Victorians*.
[45] *Bulletin du Comité de L'Afrique Française* (Feb. 1937), 105–6.   [46] Ibid., 106–7.

It is possible that Moroccan soldiers, coming from a culture also steeped in superstitions, hoped the image might turn into a shield against enemy bullets just as it had always been a symbol of protection for Spanish Catholics. On the other hand, Franco is supposed to have told a small inner circle of generals and fellow officers he was having supper with that the same Moroccans had told him that a long time had gone by since they had been allowed to kill Jews. That is to say, they were happy to be wearing the emblem of the heart of a Jew because they were starting to kill them.[47] We must assume this to have been told as a joke; nor is it a surprising one in view of the close bonding between Africanists and Regulares and their shared anti-Semitism. After all, one of the main enemies of the Nationalists was the Jew, a traditional internal Other. The joke is also indicative of anti-pious (though not anti-Catholic) culture of the Africanist officer, who tended to look down on symbols of religiosity with Spanish macho scorn (a prejudice they shared with sections of the left).

However, the publication in a French newspaper of a photograph of Moroccans wearing the image upset some of the Moroccan authorities, and the Nationalists were forced to lie, claiming improbably that the soldiers in question were in fact Spaniards who had enrolled in the Regulares.[48] After witnessing the Catholic icons dangling from Spanish and Moroccan soldiers alike, an Irish officer and Catholic supporter of the Nationalists, in a letter to the Irish president, Eamonn de Valera, described the Nationalist army as a Catholic army. 'Never since the Moors were driven from Spain', he wrote, 'has there been such a Catholic army in this country as there is today . . . This is not a Civil War: it is a Holy War, a Crusade.' In an effort to square the circle, however, the Irish officer insisted that the Nationalist army was fighting 'what is worse than Islam, for Islam believes in God'.[49]

Equally, the Nationalists made efforts to play down the iconography of the Spanish medieval Reconquest in order not to offend their new allies. In Chapter 7 mention was made of a Catholic church in the Moroccan town of Nador in the 1920s which, according to the Abdel Krim brothers, had displayed a sculpture of St James (or Santiago) putting the Moor to the sword. A church that stands in the village of Castaño de Robledo in the Sierra de Aracena in Andalusia had had its large altarpiece burnt down by labourers and miners of the area in July 1936 in protest against the military uprising. After Nationalist troops had taken the village, the Bishop of Pamplona, who was born there, ordered a statue dedicated to Santiago the Killer of Moors to be built to replace the altarpiece. Instead of the customary set-piece showing

---

[47] The anecdote was recounted by one of the officers present, José María Iribarren, in the first edition of his book *Con el general Mola* (Zaragoza, n.p., 1937), 272, and suppressed in subsequent editions.

[48] *Bulletin du Comité de L'Afrique Française* (Oct. 1936), 530. Giulana di Febo, *La santa de la raza: un culto barroco en la España franquista (1937–1962)* (Barcelona, Icària Editorial, 1988), 55.

[49] Captain Francis McCullagh, *In Franco's Spain: Being the Experiences of an Irish War-Correspondent During the Great Civil War Which Began in 1936* (London, Burns, Oates & Washbourne, 1937), 40 and 88.

the saint killing the Moor, the Bishop ordered the sculptor to replace the Moor with an effigy of Lenin carrying a flaming torch in one hand and shielding himself from Santiago's sword with his other arm, like the Moor in traditional pose.[50]

The search to Hispanize pro-Nationalist foreign soldiers, as I have already suggested, was perhaps part of an effort to come to terms with the complexity of identities in the Nationalist camp. The different forces that had joined the uprising were so divided they could only agree initially on one thing, their detestation of the Popular Front government and its supporters. This was even true amongst the generals that had fought the colonial war together. According to his head of propaganda, Queipo de Llano's earliest broadcast on 18 July assured listeners that the insurrectionary movement was not against the Republic but against the government of the Popular Front, and it ended with the words 'Long Live the Republic', followed by the Republican national anthem. The veteran general had also refused to go to a ceremony replacing the Republican flag with that of the monarchy, and had tried to boycott Franco's headquarters when they were set up in Seville.[51]

The colonial army itself was also divided. As we saw in previous chapters, neither officers nor troops saw eye to eye. Thus, when troops set up camp near the port of embarkation to Spain, the officers took great care to keep the Regulares camp at some distance from that of the Legion. However, in the peculiar conditions of the war some Moroccan veterans of the colonial war were allowed to join the Legion, benefiting thereby from the higher wages paid to Legionnaires. Although there is no evidence to prove it, it is likely that these suffered problems of adaption to the culture of the Legionnaires. For a start, they were obliged under protest to shave off their beards. They were also unlikely, at least at first, to share the passion for alcohol of their fellow Legionnaires.[52]

But the new enemy was similarly complex, and here the colonial instinct helped to resolve the problem of identities. In the colonial war the Moorish Other had been a slippery enemy. Spanish easygoingness with those like Raisuni who had pretended to be a friend of Spain had led to treachery and war. Thus, the response to colonial ambiguities learnt by colonial officers was to deny them. Applying the same standards to the Civil War, the Nationalists

---

[50] During the transition to democracy in the second half of the 1970s, the Lenin figure was replaced by an effigy of the Moor with the agreement of the parish priest and the local dignitaries, because of the fear that communists might attack the church again: information from Joaquín Bustamante, supplied to the author by Enrique Carabaza Bravo.

[51] Antonio Bahamonde y Sánchez de Castro, *1 año con Queipo. Memorias de un nacionalista* (Barcelona, Ediciones Española, 1938), 26–50. Falangist officers were also anti-monarchist and favoured a right-wing republic. Thus Yagüe greeted the capture of Badajoz on 14 August with a speech ending 'Long live the Republic! Long live the Army!': R. Garriga, *El general*, 33 and Sánchez del Arco, *El Sur*, 91.

[52] ADMAE vol. 208, p. 81. However, oral testimonies suggest that by 1939 if not before some Moroccan soldiers were drinking a lot of alcohol: interview with Josep Vallés, Teresa Vallés, and Joan Saltó, 26 Apr. 2000.

may have wanted to disregard the complexities of identity among supporters of the Republic because to recognize these complexities would challenge their own sense of guilt about the legitimacy of their cause. This underlying insecurity was even more intense because amongst those loyal to the Republic were relatives and friends with whom they had been brought up or had served in the colonial war, just as Moroccan friends loyal to Spain like Abdel Krim had turned into the Moorish Other. Franco had been prepared to allow his cousin de la Puente Bahamonde to be executed for defending the airport where the general had been about to land.[53]

Reduced to its quintessential character, the Spanish 'Other' was Communist. Apart from Islam, historically 'anti-Spanish' identities—Jewishness, freemasonry, liberalism, atheism, protestantism, and so on—thus became boiled down to a single category in the rhetoric of the Nationalists. It was a useful concept for mobilizing support, not only among traditional sections of the Spanish population but also among Moroccans, for whom these identities were a threat. Moroccans and 'true' Spaniards could see themselves fighting a common enemy, whilst their divided religions became a common religiosity and their separate fatherlands became a common *patria*. The true Spain was also the Spain of Moroccans because Spanish Morocco was 'a continuation of our civilized and civilizing fatherland'. The 'soldiers of Spain', a term embracing colonial troops, were fighting *sui generis* foreigners, the Marxists. The war was a new Reconquest fought jointly by erstwhile enemies against a common enemy that had occupied their land. As the Nationalist troops advanced, wrote one hagiographer, farms, hamlets, and villages 'discovered the great happiness of being incorporated once again into Spain', a murderous euphemism for the repression and massacres that were taking place en route.[54]

By a further inversion of identities, true Spaniards could also become Moroccans. As we have seen, for colonial officers even the Moroccan enemy had been a model of military courage, however fanatical. So, according to the veteran Africanist colonel and ex-pilot Sáenz de Buruaga, who led some of the first colonial troops across the Straits, the 'soldaditos' (little soldiers) of Cadiz (mainly Falange members) became entitled to call themselves the 'Regulares of Cadiz' through their display of bravery.[55]

Spanish colonial troops had also become impregnated with the 'fatalist, terrible, and efficacious principles of Koranic justice', values which had been condemned as barbaric in the colonial war. This provided them with the justification for brutal repression.[56] As they moved through the harsh, sunbaked landscape of Extremadura, they were encouraged by Nationalist propaganda

[53] Alcaraz Cánovas, 'Marruecos'; Preston, *Franco*, 151.

[54] C. G. Ortiz de Villajos, *De Sevilla a Madrid. Ruta libertadora de la columna Castejón* (Granada, Prieto, 1937), 66; Juan Brasa, *España y la Legión*, 2nd edn. (Valladolid, Santarén, 1938), 100; Sánchez del Arco, *El Sur*, 106 and 112.

[55] Garrachón, *De Africa*, 163. [56] Ortiz, *De Sevilla*, 45.

to see in it the conditions of the Rif war, which had supposedly imbued them with the virtues of toughness and austerity. In contrast, the moral flabbiness of Spanish society was now associated with the 'phantom' columns of the Republican army. The Nationalist myth-making propensities, animated by the need to justify the rebellion, also found a link between the Army of Africa and the conquistadores of the Americas, some of whom, like Pizarro, had come from Extremadura. As they crossed the arid landscape, the new conquistadores could, it seems, discern the distant outline of Madrid, 'like the mirage of Goa'.[57]

The multiple inversion of roles and the reductionism of the discourse of the Other could give rise to confusion. Old and new enemies could occupy the same imaginative space in the Civil War. In an interview I recorded in 1999, an old Francoist general who had fought in both the colonial war and Civil War repeatedly confused *moro* and *rojo*, Moor and red, saying repeatedly that he had fought the reds in the first and the Moors in the second. Far from being a semantic slippage due to old age, this is more likely to have been a conceptual slippage because the right-wing simplification of identities encouraged a sort of metastasis between the Moorish and Spanish Others.

The military and civilian supporters of the Second Republic who had now to face the Moroccan foe also responded according to colonial stereotypes. The Moors came across the Straits with a fearsome reputation for cruelty and barbarism. The distant sight of the coloured turbans and white clothes of the Moroccan troops on board the first ships to cross the sea encouraged the civil governor of Cadiz, who had barricaded himself in his headquarters with Assault Guards and trade-union militants, to raise a white flag and give himself up. During the Civil War, whole villages would flee before the advancing colonial troops, fearing they would all be massacred.[58] Indeed, the use of Moroccan mercenaries was also a conscious attempt by the Nationalists to scare Republican resistance. They were helped by the long tradition in Spain of seeing the Moroccan Other as a bogeyman. This tradition was sustained by nursery-rhymes, ballads, and sayings. For example, the phrase 'moros en la costa' (Moors on the coast) is a popular reference to a looming danger.[59] Added to that was the popular memory of the colonial war and the horror stories recounted at length after the 1921 disaster.

So the deployment of such troops was calculated to demoralize both the miners in Asturias in 1934 and the hastily assembled militiamen and women in the south in the early days of the Civil War. The atrocities committed by the

[57] Sánchez del Arco, *El Sur de España*, 95–112.
[58] See e.g. 'Informe de la columna Delgado', Oct. 1936, AV vol. 69, and Ronald Fraser, *Blood of Spain: The Experiences of the Spanish Civil War* (London, Allen Lane, 1979), 257; for Cadiz, see Jose Pettenghi, 'Nuevos datos para su historia' and 'Tres días de julio', in *Diario de Cádiz*, 18 July 1990 and 1991.
[59] Madariaga, 'La imagen'.

Legion and the Regulares were sanctioned by their officers and the top command. There were several reasons for this. Most knew of no other war than the colonial war, in which massacre and looting against other tribes was common culture and second nature. Secondly, attrition against the civilian population was seen as a means of deterring further resistance. Lastly, looting was a cheap and traditional way of rewarding the colonial troops. The attraction of booty was almost as important as the attractive wages offered to Moroccan recruits and Legionnaires. So in the early part of the Civil War campaign the strategy and tactics of the Army of Africa repeated those of the colonial war. They were similarly unsophisticated, came unstuck in the siege of Madrid, and had to be reconstructed from the roots upwards.

The colonial war, then, had encouraged the creation of simple dichotomies of identity, and this psychological mechanism became the means whereby Francoist officers were able to overcome or overlook the complexities of the Republican Other. In Asturias in 1934 it was still possible for colonial officers to acknowledge these complexities, as we saw in Chapter 9 in the case of a Spanish officer of the Regulares who halted the execution of twenty-five people in a suburb of Oviedo when he recognized his own cousin amongst them. Such qualms seemed to have disappeared in the July 1936 uprising. As we have seen, Franco stepped aside to allow his cousin to be executed. His lack of action was also a grim reminder to his supporters that no mercy should be shown against the enemy, even if they were from your own family.

Having attempted to justify the use of foreign mercenaries against their own people, Francoist propaganda made a lot of the presence of foreigners in the ranks of the Republican army. In yet another inversion of roles, the International Brigades became the bloodthirsty foreign mercenaries fighting against Spaniards on Spanish soil, while the Legion and the Regulares had joined the Nationalists to fight for an ideal and were not motivated by pecuniary ambitions. As part of that propaganda, the Falangists published on 23 January 1938 a notorious photograph originally taken in the colonial war showing Legionnaires holding up the decapitated heads of Moroccans. The caption, though, was 'Red monstrosity' implying that it was a photo of 'Red' militiamen or soldiers of the International Brigades in the Civil War with the heads of Spanish patriots.[60] Thus, what had been common practice among the colonial troops was now attributed to the enemy. A drawing of the 'Marxist hordes' by a Francoist colonel shows a degenerate mob surging through the street with a decapitated head stuck on the end of a stick. As we saw in Chapter 8, Legionnaires in the colonial war used to stick Moroccan heads on the end

---

[60] In a further distortion, a book by an Italian fascist published in 1938 claimed that the photo was found in the pocket of a militiaman captured by the Nationalists: see Herbert R. Southworth, *Anti-Falange. Estudio crítico de 'Falange en la guerra de España, la unificación y Hedilla' de Maximiano García Venero* (Paris, Ruedo Ibérico, 1967), pp. xxi–xxii, ills. nos. 44a and b.

of their bayonets. Like the photograph, this cartoon was an implicit and involuntary acknowledgment of the barbarity of the Army of Africa.[61]

The task of transporting this now 'patriotic' army to Spain was made exceptionally difficult by the mutiny of ratings against their pro-rebel officers on Spanish ships operating off the coast of Southern Spain and Morocco. Moreover, there were only four Andalusian towns, Seville, Cadiz, Algeciras, and La Línea, where the rebels, with the help of small detachments of colonial troops, had secured a foothold; without these, there was nowhere for the Army of Africa to go. The few aircraft available—three Fokker military trimotors, two Dornier flying boats, and a Douglas DC-2—were used to fly the first troops from Tetuan to Seville on the morning of 20 July to help subdue resistance to the uprising among Sevillan workers. They then continued to shuttle small numbers of soldiers across the Straits, transporting between twelve and twenty-five passengers on each flight, depending on the size of the planes. On his own initiative, the leader of the Cadiz Falange requisitioned two feluccas and sailed over to Ceuta by night to pick up a handful of troops and bring them over to stiffen the local rebellion. An enthusiastic right-wing pilot from the Aero Club of Seville flew over to Morocco in his tiny plane countless times to pick up just one legionnaire at a time.

Meanwhile, sailors of two ships in Melilla mutinied against their rebel officers, and one of the ships, which was bound for Málaga, was forced to sail back. The troops on board were taken by land to Ceuta, and a small convoy made up of a destroyer and two steamers brought some 220 soldiers to Cadiz. But the ratings on the destroyer seized the ship immediately afterwards.[62] By 19 July almost all the naval vessels operating off the southern coast of Spain were in loyalist hands and the rebel sea-craft consisted of only a gunboat, a coastguard vessel, and a torpedo boat. Between the uprising and the end of July, the Nationalists were able to convey only 850 soldiers across the Straits. It had also become clear three days after it was launched that unless the bulk of the Army of Africa could be transported to Spain the rebellion would fail.

Mola, Queipo, and Franco had sent separate delegations to request military aid from Germany and Italy. It was only after several refusals that Mussolini finally agreed. Hitler, initially dubious about the rebels' chances of success, also conceded military aid, which he dubbed Operation Magic Fire after Wagner's opera *Siegfried*, a performance of which he had seen just before his decision on 25 July. Franco's efforts were more successful than those of his Africanist colleagues, mainly because his German contacts in Morocco managed to get greater access to the highest levels of the Third Reich. His success would strengthen his bid to become the overall leader of the rebellion. This special relationship was helped by the Nationalists' control over the economy of the

[61] The cartoon is by Colonel Lagarde, in Colonel José Fernández Ferrer, 'Guerra de España', *Ejército*, 16 (May 1941), 21.
[62] Sánchez del Arco, *El Sur de España*, 14–25.

Protectorate. The mineral wealth of the area enabled them to reward German military aid by awarding the German-Spanish company HISMA privileged access to the iron ore of the Rif mines.[63]

German and Italian military support became crucial to the fortunes of the uprising. Twelve Savaoia-Marchetti bombers were sent from Sardinia to Nador airport in Morocco (though three failed to reach their destination) and twenty Junker-52 bombers and six Heinkel-51 fighters were dispatched by different routes from Germany to Morocco.[64] By early August the first substantial planeloads of troops began to be flown across the Straits of Gibraltar. In less than a fortnight some 14,000 men, fifty-two artillery pieces, and 283 tons of war matériel were flown to Spain.[65] By 30 September the rebels had received up to 140 German and Italian military aircraft. It was the first significant airlift in history.

On 5 August, protected by German and Italian bombers, a naval convoy (later dubbed the 'Victory Convoy', whose success was attributed in the new Francoist mythology to the protection of the Virgin of Africa and the supposed boldness of Franco) crossed to Spain from Morocco, carrying large numbers of soldiers, artillery, and military equipment. Uncharacteristically, it had been Franco who had pushed for the operation against the advice of naval commanders and of Yagüe, who feared an attack by the Republican air force and fleet.[66] In fact, Franco was well aware that the Republican fleet was in a sorry state; without most of its officers and some of its specialist crew, it was suffering numerous technical problems as well as a severe shortage of fuel. Nor could the Republican air force match the new planes provided by Italy and Germany, some of which provided the air protection necessary for the successful crossing of the convoy. A government destroyer tried to halt the convoy but was forced to retire when attacked by the rebels' aircraft.[67]

A few days earlier the first units of the so-called Column of Madrid, drawn largely from reinforcements of the Army of Africa flown over by German and Italian planes, set out towards north-west Andalusia and Extremadura, from where it hoped to rendezvous with forces of the Northern Army under Mola. The decision not to take the quickest and traditional route to Madrid directly

---

[63] Shannon E. Fleming, 'Spanish Morocco and the Alzamiento Nacional, 1936–1939: the Military, Economic and Political Mobilization of a Protectorate', *Journal of Contemporary History*, 18 (1983), 34–5; Preston, *Franco*, 158–9; José Ignacio Escobar, *Así empezó* (Madrid, Ediciones G. del Toro, 1974), 55–60.

[64] The Italian bombers were grounded for five days because the high-octane fuel they used had to be shipped from Italy. Their Italian crews also had to be enrolled into the Legion as if they were volunteers since there was no one capable of flying them on the rebel side. The rebels also were awarded far more aid than they had originally asked for in maintenance facilities, anti-aircraft cannons, munitions, equipment, airmen, mechanics, engineers, medical units, instructors, etc.: Howson, *Arms for Spain*, 17–19; *L'Afrique Française* (Aug.–Sept. 1936).

[65] Alfredo Kindelán, *Mis cuadernos de guerra 1936–1939* (Madrid, Editorial Plus, 1945), 21–2.

[66] Martinez Bande, *La campaña de Andalucía*, 54–63; Preston, *Franco*, 154–5.

[67] Michael Alpert, *La guerra civil española en el mar* (Madrid, Siglo XXI, 1987), 86–96; Kindelán, *La verdad*, 176–7; Muñoz, 'La Guerra', 29.

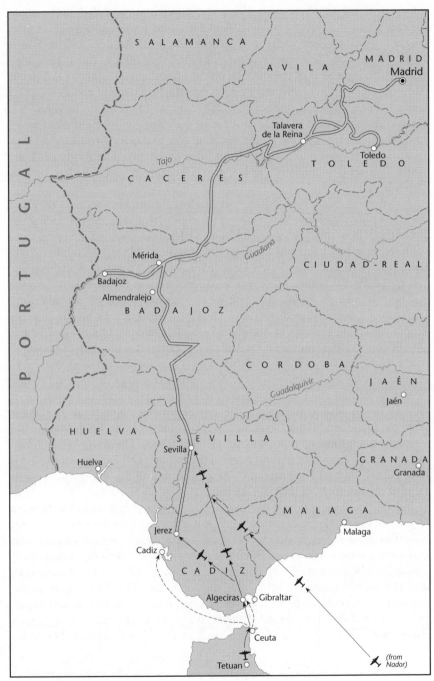

MAP 3   Route of the Army of Africa to Madrid in 1936

northwards via Cordoba and along the Guadalquivir valley, and to take instead a longer route via western Andalusia and Extremadura was entirely that of Franco, as commander-in-chief of the Army of Morocco and the South. It was typical of his cautious nature as a military officer. But it may have reflected the wariness of the colonial officer after the experience of the war in Morocco; for instance, Silvestre's march into the heartland of the dissident Rif tribes without sufficient protection of his rearguard had led to the disaster of Anual. The advantage of the western route was also that it would allow access to Portugal, from where the rebels would be able to receive direct support from the Salazar regime and supplies from Nazi Germany. The Army of Africa could also send supplies to Mola's army through Portugal if that became necessary.

The decision took both Mola and Madrid by surprise because they had expected that a lightning strike against the capital would be the overriding target of the rebels' military strategy. Mola's 24 June directive for the uprising, as we have seen, had proposed the most direct route to Madrid.[68] While units of the Army of Africa started their long colonial march through Andalusia and Extremadura, Republican defences in Madrid were at their weakest.

The offensive in Andalusia, meanwhile, was intensified by the additional mercenary troops shipped over on 5 August. A meeting in Seville between Franco and rebel generals in Andalusia on 28 July had put Queipo de Llano in overall command of the Army of Andalusia operations. Small flying columns made up of a motley array of colonial troops and local rebel units backed by armoured cars and artillery pieces had radiated outwards from rebel-held Seville, Córdoba, and Cadiz in operations to mop up Republican resistance in nearby towns and countryside. Of the provincial capitals in Andalusia, Almería, Jaén, and Málaga remained in government hands. From Málaga, the Republican air force continued to attack rebel forces. There were also numerous pockets of resistance in most parts of the region. The strategy employed in both Andalusia and Extremadura was akin to that of the small-scale expeditions of the last stage of the colonial war.

Indeed, the experience of the war in Morocco was crucial in the first few months of the conflict in Spain. The army had had no experience of European wars. On the contrary, it was more familiar with sporadic, mobile warfare, executed on a number of fronts. Such a strategy had its advantages and disadvantages. The commander of each column had a high degree of autonomy, and the overall commanders of the various fronts, like Varela and Yagüe, enjoyed the freedom to devise their own tactics. Frontal assaults on the enemy's positions tended to be avoided. Instead, the tactic of the 'indirect approach' was employed because it had worked well in the Moroccan war. The forces

[68] El Director, 'Directivas'; see also Cabanellas, *La Guerra*, 572–3 and Blanco, *La incompetencia*, 210 and 230–7.

would split into two or three smaller columns in order to encircle the enemy or engage them from different angles so as to create the impression of greater numbers and encourage their retreat. They might feint at the enemy's front to draw them out, then attack with heavy forces from the rear. The centre of gravity shifted from the central command to the wings and vice versa, enabling surprise, agility, and speed.[69]

A British military observer noted the different tactics of Legionnaires and Regulares. The Legionnaires 'are fit, alert, confident, conscious of being masters of their trade, certain of victory; and knowing that, cheerful and gay . . . In battle, the Legionnaires advance in those short baffling rushes which only the finest infantry, once down, will rise to, when under fire.' On the other hand: 'The Moors are solemn and patient . . . They are shanky, hollow-cheeked, sinewy. They are polite. They seldom smile. They walk softly, and with the forward thrust of animals that live dangerously . . . The Moors in battle work upon their stomachs and wriggle forward at a reptilian speed.'[70]

However, overall mobility was poor because, as in the colonial war, the columns had to return to their base to recoup, store or sell their war booty, and receive new orders. Both the northern and southern armies of the Nationalists were organized like old-fashioned organic divisions, responsible for order and administration in the regions assigned to them. While the Republican army had already organized flying tactical columns that could be transported to strengthen fronts or punch holes into the enemy advance, the Nationalists only began to create the first non-territorial divisions in April 1937.[71]

There was another, more important reason for the territorial organization of the rebel army. Colonial officers had learnt in the colonial war the value of systematic ethnic cleansing as a means of ensuring order. Sending punitive columns in the rearguard to punish the town and village people who had supported the Republic was necessary, not so much to secure the rearguard, as Nationalist apologists claim, but to cleanse Spain of its internal enemies. Lorry-loads of Legionnaires and Regulares would scour the villages after they had been bombed by planes, shoot all suspects, and then go back to their bases. The word *limpieza* or 'cleansing' is stressed in many of the rebel reports of operations in the south.[72] The circuitous advance towards Madrid was part of this strategy of attrition.

[69] Miguel Alonso Baquer, *Las preferencias estratégicas del militar español* (Madrid, EME, 1985), 120–1; Ortiz, *De Sevilla*, 56; Pemán, *Un soldado*, 203; Luis María de Lojendio, *Operaciones militares de la guerra de España 1936–1939* (Barcelona, 1940), 101–4; Martínez Bande, *La campaña de Andalucía*, 37–9; Knickerbocker, *The Siege*, 135; Major Geoffrey McNeill-Moss, *The Epic of the Alcazar: A History of the Siege of the Toledo Alcazar, 1936* (London, Rich & Cowan, 1937), 166–70.

[70] McNeill-Moss, *The Epic*, 166.

[71] Alonso Baquer, 'Preferencias'; Ricardo de la Cierva, 'The Nationalist Army in the Spanish Civil War', in Raymond Carr (ed.), *The Republic and the Civil War in Spain* (London, Macmillan, 1971).

[72] *The Times*, 13 Aug. 1936; Lojendio, *Operaciones*, 100; Ortiz, *De Sevilla*, 66; Martínez Bande, *La campaña*, 134 passim. The American journalist John T. Whitaker, who witnessed some of the 'cleansing', was told by one of Franco's chief press officers that its purpose was to exterminate one-third of the male

Cleansing involved the exemplary use of brutality. This was another famil-iar tactic in the colonial war. As we have seen, this had been a reflex and sys-tematic action by the Legion and the Moroccan troops, legitimated by the conventional model of strategic dissuasion drawn up by Lyautey and Kitchener. Under Franco's command, the use of terror was written into the orders issued to the Nationalist army of the South.[73] In towns and villages that had resisted the uprising or where Republican supporters were known to exist, people were rounded up and identified by informers or by the mark of a rifle's recoil on their shoulder. On his frequent tours of the area around Seville, Queipo de Llano's head of propaganda, Antonio Bahamonde, saw countless bodies of executed supporters of the Republic lying on the outskirts of the towns and villages. He also noticed that the walls of cemeteries, where many of the executions took place, were pockmarked by bullet-holes, which the rebel authorities had filled in with mortar in a futile attempt to disguise them. He was ordered to witness the execution of prisoners in Seville who had been so badly treated they had to be dragged and kicked to the cemetery where the execution was to take place. The firing squad was made up of Moroccan sol-diers, who, it seemed, had replaced the Falange squads because, being better marksmen, they wasted fewer bullets.

A more casual but no less systematic brutality was applied during the occu-pation of towns. According to Bahamonde, Legionnaires and Moroccans raped women and burnt down houses after looting their contents. The booty they obtained was piled into the lorries or coaches that took them back to Seville and reappeared on the streets as items for sale, especially radios, watches, jewellery, and cigarettes looted from tobacconists.[74] No official Francoist source would, of course, admit to such violence and pillage. But unofficial sources do suggest that this was common behaviour among colonial troops, at least in the early stages of the Civil War. This can also be surmised by a reverse reading of orders and reports. We know, for example, that the rape of women was severely punished by some of the officers in command. A Spanish officer of the Regulares confirmed to the author in an interview that in his regiment rape, when it was seen by officers or proved by evidence, was punished by instant execution. In his battalion some ten to twelve Moroccan soldiers were executed for rape during the course of the Civil War. 'There were

---

population, thereby purging the country of the proletariat and eliminating the problem of unemploy-ment at a stroke: *We Cannot Escape History* (New York, Macmillan, 1943), 108–12. No doubt many of those executed were officially reported as killed in battle.

[73] Alonso Baquer, 'Preferencias', 137; José Manuel Martínez Bande, *La marcha sobre Madrid* (Madrid, SHM, 1968), 165–70.

[74] Bahamonde, *1 año*, 96–113. Even apologists for the Nationalist cause could not disguise the real-ity of looting. The right-wing correspondent of the *Daily Mail* admitted that while the Moroccan sol-diers were 'great gentlemen', they did loot on a large scale: Harold G. Cardozo, *The March of a Nation: My Year of Spain's Civil War* (London, 1937), 114–15.

excesses. They had to be stopped, you had to be on top of them [the Moroccans], you had to run behind them when they went into villages.'[75]

Yet it seems that, unlike other Nationalist soldiers, the Legionnaires and Moroccan troops were given the freedom by some of their commanders for one hour to scour a town they had captured for booty and for women. The Nationalist authorities must bear some of the blame, because of their determined efforts to demonize the enemy, including women. But looting and rape were in any case a common feature of the colonial wars. That they took place during the Civil War can also be gathered from the instructions issued in August 1936 by Varela's chief of staff during the Andalusian operations, instructing officers to keep the soldiers in hand to prevent 'abuses and pillage'.[76] Eyewitness accounts also suggest that rape was part of the everyday culture of war amongst the Legion and the native troops. The American journalist John T. Whitaker watched as the by-now famous Moroccan officer of Regulares, El Mizzian, ordered two teenage female textile workers arrested by the army to be taken to a schoolhouse to be raped by Moroccan soldiers. El Mizzian brushed his protest aside, assuring him that the women would not live for longer than four hours, as if this made the violence more palatable.[77]

Further pieces of lateral information help to confirm looting on a large scale, an activity the Nationalists were less concerned to conceal. In November 1936 a Moroccan soldier on operations in Andalusia dictated a letter (signing it with his thumbprint) to General Varela complaining that the money he had collected during the campaign and sent to the commander-in-chief in Ceuta had not been delivered to his relatives. According to his account, most of the considerable sum he had collected had either been looted from houses or pillaged from enemy soldiers (including an International Brigader whom he had killed with hand grenades). He had made some more money by selling blankets he had taken from houses.[78] Cash was the most treasured loot, followed by jewellery and watches. Portable booty, like watches, was usually stored in the long and voluminous trousers of the Moroccan soldiers that were gathered tightly round the ankle.[79]

Another characteristic of the behaviour of the colonial troops was their casual brutality towards prisoners. An Italian fascist volunteer in the Legion

[75] Jose Pettenghi interview, 2 Apr. 2000.

[76] 'Instrucciones para las columnas en operaciones', AV vol. 68. Further instructions, drawn up at the time the Nationalists believed they were about to capture Madrid, ordered troops to show 'the greatest respect to women and children' and to put out of their mind 'any idea of razzia or lucre': Colonel Martin Moreno, 'Instrucciones que deberan observarse al ocupar Madrid nuestras tropas', 4 Nov. 1936, AV vol. 69. This concern about the behaviour of the troops is even more apparent in later instructions, ordering officers to forbid troops to enter houses and to 'speak to the heart of the soldier', enjoining him to scotch red propaganda that the Nationalist soldiers looted and raped: 'Instrucciones generales para la ocupacion de poblaciones', 17 Apr. 1938, AV vol. 80.

[77] Whitaker, We Cannot Escape, 114. Ronald Fraser's oral history of the war (Blood of Spain) also confirms that rape by soldiers of the Army of Africa was common, e.g. p. 157.

[78] AV, 'Expedientes personales', vol. 108.   [79] Jose Pettenghi interview.

witnessed the barbarous murder of four French prisoners of the International Brigades by a Moroccan sergeant. The sergeant made them kneel and then cut them with a sword on their faces and heads, finishing them off with a rifle, shouting the words, 'long live Franco, long live Spain!' and, remembering the Italian's nationality, added, 'long live the Duce and long live Italy!' Nevertheless, as the Italian was keen to stress, this sort of conduct was more typical of the early days of the Civil War. Strict orders were given not long after this incident that prisoners should not be killed, although in the midst of war this was not always adhered to, as we shall see later.[80] As the Nationalist authorities set up their war tribunals, the casual murder of prisoners was replaced by more widespread and systematic executions after summary trials.

The brutality of the colonial troops in the early days of the Civil War was most in evidence in the Extremaduran campaign. While operations continued in Andalusia, the first so-called Madrid column penetrated into Extremadura on 2 August and moved by lorry and coach north up the main road towards Mérida, encountering fierce resistance along the way from ill-armed groups of militiamen, left-wing party activists, and workers. A second column set off towards Extremadura the next day and a third on 7 August. Believing that the rebels would go straight for Madrid, the government had sent some of its main columns south across La Mancha towards eastern Andalusia. The result was that the Army of Africa initially encountered few regular troops. Backed by German and Italian bombers, the colonial troops seized town after town, carrying out numerous executions in their wake. One of the most brutal actions so far was the execution of around 1,000 militiamen (including 100 or so women) in Almendralejo on the way to Mérida, most of them farm labourers and peasants.[81]

The *razzias* the colonial troops perpetrated as they went along were deeply familiar to the veterans of the colonial war. In a letter to Mola on 11 August, Franco emphasized the need to destroy all resistance in the 'occupied zones', a Freudian slip revealing the deep influence of the Moroccan campaigns and contradicting the official Nationalist discourse of the zones liberated by the authentic Spain from the Marxists. The countryside through which they were travelling also increasingly bore resemblance to that of the Rif. The *ABC* journalist who accompanied them was reminded of some scene in the Rif, with 'its dark walls . . . over which hangs a leaden sky, burning with the August sun'.[82]

After the capture of Mérida the colonial troops turned off the road to Madrid, moving south-west to seize the provincial capital of Badajoz on the border with Portugal to where many Republican militiamen had fled before the advancing rebel troops. Like the later detour to relieve the siege of Toledo, however, the diversion allowed Madrid more time to reorganize the defence of the capital. The decision was almost certainly that of Franco rather than the

[80] Francesco Odetti di Marcorengo, *Trenta mesi nel Tercio* (Rome, M. Carra & Co., 1940), 117–18.

[81] Justo Vila Izquierdo, *Extremadura: la Guerra Civil* (Badajoz, Universitas Editorial, 1983), 38–40.

[82] Sánchez del Arco, *El Sur*, 87; Franco's letter quoted in Preston, *Franco*, 165.

overall commander of the Madrid column, Yagüe, because Franco controlled the daily operations of the Army of the South and was closely involved in the Extremadura campaign.[83] Once again, the strategy reflected the deep influence the colonial war exerted on Franco; leaving the rearguard unprotected had often led to military debacles in Morocco. The troops should not advance if they had to keep looking behind their backs.

In fact, Badajoz hardly represented a threat to the rebels. Much of its garrison had been withdrawn to defend Madrid. Confronting the professional army of the Nationalists were militiamen and poorly armed workers with no experience of war. Yet their defence of Badajoz was the first serious resistance the colonial columns had encountered in the Civil War. The war in Morocco had been almost exclusively a mobile, rural war. The veterans of the Army of Africa now faced an enemy entrenched in a city who would continue their defence by all means possible, including street fighting. But the rebels had the advantage of greater technology. The Republican air force hardly made an appearance. Instead, the Nationalists could rely on Junkers JU-52 and Savoia-81 fighter bombers operating from Portuguese airfields to pound Republican positions. In addition they had superior weapons and in greater number: mortars, machine-guns, and a battery of field artillery.

The assault began on 11 August. The Nationalist columns attacked the city from all points of the compass. Two military barracks to the east and south of the boundary walls that ringed the old part of the city were stormed over the next three days. The colonial troops in the eastern district reached one of the heavily defended gates that led into the centre. Successive waves of soldiers charged at the gate and were cut down by Republican machine-guns. The entrance was finally breached, and while they defended the streets inch by inch, Republican forces scattered. In the main square of the city the defenders had set up a machine-gun nest in the tower of the cathedral. Once again their last-ditch defence led to numerous casualties among the rebel troops, despite the constant pounding of the tower by enemy artillery. As the colonial troops tried to storm the cathedral door with hand grenades they were mown down by the Republican machine-gun. Finally the defenders ran out of ammunition. They were then killed as they surrendered or tried to hide from Nationalist troops. Sporadic fighting continued in the outlying districts of the city, but by 14 August Badajoz lay in rebel hands.[84]

[83] Preston, *Franco*, 166 and n. 98.

[84] This account of the battle for Badajoz and the repression that followed is based largely on the following sources: Jay Allen, 'Blood Flows in Badajoz', in Marcel Acier (ed.), *From Spanish Trenches: Recent Letters from Spain* (London, Cressat Press, 1937); Mario Neves, *La matanza de Badajoz. Crónica de un testigo de uno de los episodios más trágicos de la Guerra Civil de España (agosto de 1936)* (Extremadura, Editor Regional de Extremadura, 1986); Peter Wyden, *La guerra apasionada. Historia narrativa de la guerra civil española, 1936–1939* (Barcelona, Martínez Roca, 1983: the English edition, *The Passionate War: The Narrative History of the Spanish Civil War, 1936–1939*, was published in New York by Simon & Schuster in the same year); Santos, 'El Secretario'; Bahamonde, *1 año*, 116–20; Vila, *Extremadura*, 47–81; Félix Gordón Ordás, *Crímenes en la retaguardia rebelde* (Havana, Editorial Facetas, 1939), 9–15.

The violence unleashed by the Army of Africa and the local Falangists against the town and its inhabitants over the following days was the subject of much polemic at the time and continues to arouse justifiable anger because of Francoist efforts to disguise the truth.[85] The evidence now overwhelmingly corroborates the fragmentary eyewitness accounts that looting, raping, and the systematic execution of prisoners took place on a mass scale. The Moroccan troops in particular worked their way through the commercial district of the city, breaking the windows of houses, shops, and offices and pillaging the goods they found inside. What has never been explained is why no distinction was made between property owned by well-known right-wingers and that identified as belonging to Republican sympathizers. In fact rightists owned most of the shops that were looted. For example, a baker's shop owned by the local Falange was robbed of its two typewriters.[86]

A simple explanation is that looting was part of an unwritten contract between the Nationalist command and the Moroccan troops, and they were let loose on the city to compensate for the huge losses they had suffered during its siege. The damage to property of Nationalist sympathizers may have been considered a small price to pay for the capture of the city. It was a war tax they paid for salvation, one rebel officer said to the American journalist Jay Allen.[87] But perhaps the ransacking was also an expression of the alienation of the colonial army against the symbols of the urban Spain it had grown to hate.

On the other hand, the victims of the massacre that followed the seizure of the city were those identified, by one means or another, as enemies. Armed with a black book filled with names, the rebels went round the city arresting known sympathizers of the Republic, trade-union leaders, democratic politicians, civil servants who had 'failed' to join the rebellion, and so on. Men were stopped in the streets, their shirts were ripped open, and if any tell-tale mark of the recoil of a rifle was found on their shoulders, they were also hauled off for execution. As part of the cleansing operation, prisoners were brought in from towns and villages throughout the province to be executed.

On-the-spot executions took place throughout the day the city was taken on 14 August. More organized executions began at around nine that evening and continued till dawn. They were held in the bullring, where prisoners had been herded into the bull-pens. They were taken out in groups of twenty and machine-gunned. On this first night, some 1,200 were killed. Their bodies were collected by butchers' lorries and transported to a cemetery, where they were doused with petrol and burnt. A large ditch was also dug in the bullring into which bodies were thrown. Nationalist soldiers and Falangists were allowed to watch these first executions and it seems the crowds grew apace as the days went by. A Moroccan radio operator who served in the Regulares

---

[85] The most recent book on this issue, Alberto Reig Tapia, *Memoria de la Guerra Civil. Los mitos de la tribu* (Madrid, Alianza, 1999), devotes a chapter to the events of Badajoz and the Francoist propaganda.
[86] Wyden, *La guerra*, 132.   [87] Allen, 'Blood Flows', 6.

recounted to me how he would watch the prisoners being executed.[88] The squads who carried out the killings, after the machine-gun was replaced by rifles, were made up largely of Moroccans. Jay Allen, who managed to get into Badajoz on 23 August, was told that a crowd of some 3,000 people (many of them Portuguese fascists who had made the short journey across the frontier) watched and cheered as each execution took place. Efforts were made at some point to turn the killings into a human bullfight, with bayonets used as the bull-fighter's sword on the victims. Meanwhile, the spectators were entertained by a musical band playing the March Real, the monarchist march, and the Falangist hymn.[89]

As journalists began to make their way into Badajoz with passes issued to them by the Nationalist authorities, the executions came to an end. But the evidence lay strewn about. The first journalist to get wind of the events, Mario Neves, the correspondent of the Portuguese *Diario de Lisboa*, had already managed to penetrate the security defences of the rebel command on 12 August. Two days later he got a permit from the military authorities to go into the city, and his first report appeared in the paper on the 15th. Before the rebels could remove the evidence of widespread executions, Neves saw piles of corpses in the streets and smelt the stench of decaying bodies. His report alerted the international press to what was going on in Badajoz.

Neves was also able to interview Juan Yagüe, who was commanding the troops that took the city. He asked him if there had been any executions, saying that he had been given the figure of 2,000. 'They can't be that much', replied Yagüe, admitting implicitly that they had taken place. The rebel commander was more forthright in an interview with the American journalist John T. Whitaker, in which he admitted to a far higher number of victims. 'Of course we shot them', he said. 'What do you expect? Was I supposed to take 4,000 Reds with me as the column advanced, racing against time? Was I expected to turn them loose in my rear and let them make Badajoz red again?'[90]

His response revealed that the Nationalist propaganda machine had not yet been fully assembled. But it also showed that Yagüe, and probably many of his fellow colonial officers, felt no embarrassment about acknowledging the mass killing of prisoners. Such brutality had become second nature to them during the colonial war, and their lack of contact with civil society in Europe had blunted their perception of civilian sensitivities about the treatment of prisoners. But mass killings were also a crucial part of the Nationalists' strategy of dissuasion through terror, a tried and tested method employed by the army in the colonial war.[91]

[88] Interview with Mohammed Ayache Zeruali, Tetuan, 21 July 2000.
[89] Allen, 'Blood Flows', 6; Vila, *Extremadura*, 58; Wyden, *La guerra*, 135.
[90] Neves, *La matanza*, 47; Whitaker, *We Cannot Escape*, 113.
[91] Later, according to one of his hagiographers, Yagüe said he deeply regretted the executions but, as he had admitted to Whitaker, felt he had had no option because he could not take prisoners with

News about the killings finally began to appear in the international press. Even on 23 August Jay Allen of the *Chicago Tribune* could smell the blood of the executed men and women. With easy access to rebel sources (including the concession of a one-hour interview with Franco), Allen calculated in his article of 30 August that some 4,000 prisoners had been executed between 14 and 24 August. *The Times* gave a vivid, though probably second-hand, account based on Neves's first reports of the aftermath of the shooting of prisoners in the street; it was nonetheless poignant. 'When this grim work was finished the pavement in front of the military headquarters ran with the blood of the victims, it dripped into the gutters and congealed there, forming ghastly pools in which lay the caps, torn papers, and small belongings of the massacred men.' Pictorial evidence of bodies and bloodstains had been collected by a Parisian film-maker, but he was arrested and the implicating shots were destroyed. It has also been claimed that German officers took photographs of the bodies of victims who had been castrated and their genitals stuffed into their mouths, like the Spanish victims at Monte Arruit in 1923.[92]

Pro-Nationalists outside Spain leapt to the defence of the rebels. A British officer claimed the massacre was an invention and the bodies that had been seen were simply the casualties of the battle to take the city.[93] The concerted effort to cover up the atrocities in Badajoz revealed that by the end of August the Nationalist propaganda machine had begun to get its act together.

It took the colonial troops almost a week to carry out the 'cleansing' of Badajoz and the surrounding province. Had they moved northwards immediately after the seizure of the city, they would have met less resistance from Republican forces. They now faced Loyalist columns led by their erstwhile colleague and veteran of the colonial war, General José Riquelme. In the battle of the Tagus river, the greater experience and firepower of the Army of Africa rolled back the Republican columns. The government reconcentrated its forces in the key strategic town of Talavera de la Reina, further north on the banks of the river. The Communist Fifth Regiment was sent from Madrid to stiffen the defence of the town and the colonial columns were confronted for the first time by troops that were better organized and more determined to resist their advance than the militiamen and Civil Guard they had faced until then. Nevertheless, they won the battle for the town on 3 September and followed up their victory by the massacre of some 600 militiamen. By the 9th the first contact was made between Franco's Army of Africa and Mola's Army of the North, two totally distinct forces that shared little except a commitment to destroy the left.

---

him on his march northwards nor did he have the resources to keep them imprisoned in Badajoz: R. Garriga, *El general Juan Yagüe: figura clave para conocer nuestra historia* (Barcelona, Planeta, 1985), 104–5.

[92] 'Savagery at Badajoz', *The Times*, 17 Aug. 1936; Allen 'Blood Flows', 7; Reig, *Memoria*, 114.

[93] Major Geoffrey McNeill-Moss, *The Legend of Badajoz* (London, Burns, Oates & Washbourne, n.d.).

Once the two armies had linked up, columns of colonial troops began to be dispatched to stiffen battle-fronts elsewhere in Spain. The second battalion of the Legion was sent to the Basque Country. Further battalions were moved shortly afterwards to operations in the mountains north of Madrid, and later to Asturias and Aragon. All the while colonial troops were being employed in the operations in Andalusia, where Malaga continued to resist the Nationalist siege. Always regarded as the shock-troops of the Nationalist army, however, the bulk of the Legion and the native troops were almost exclusively deployed on the strategically crucial fronts. For as long as Madrid remained the primary objective of the Nationalist war effort, the Army of Africa dominated the columns marching on the capital. Now integrated into the Army of the North under Mola, the colonial troops moving towards Madrid under Varela's command were made up of four Legion battalions, seven Regulares battalions, a further eleven squadrons of native troops, and ten artillery batteries. A further two Legion battalions were being trained in Talavera for use on the Madrid front, and in Morocco more colonial troops were being recruited to augment the fighting force and to replace the increasing casualties suffered by the Army of Africa.[94]

The advance on Madrid had been delayed by the need to send troops to break the Republican siege of Oviedo in the north. More importantly, Franco had decided to change the strategy agreed with the Nationalist generals and his own commanders and make a detour to relieve the besieged fortress of Toledo. There has been much controversy over his decision. Unlike Madrid, Toledo was not a crucial military objective. The capture of the capital, on the other hand, would almost certainly have ended the Civil War sooner. The detour meant a delay of one month, during which the Republican government was able to strengthen the capital's defences. The immediate siege of Madrid might well have forced the Republicans to withdraw their troops from Toledo and enabled the defenders of the fortress to hold out longer, as none other than Yagüe had argued just before Franco's decision.[95]

Franco's numerous apologists claim unconvincingly that the relief of Toledo represented a moral and spiritual victory more important than considerations of military strategy. Franco's relief of Toledo was a symbolically charged operation because the town had been captured from the Moors in the Middle Ages by the Cid, to whom Franco would be compared in the post-war iconography. Franco's decision may well have had something to do with his talent for self-promotion. Once again, it was typical of the historical incongruities of the Francoist cause that he used Moroccan troops to defeat the Spaniards who held the city.

The most charitable rationalization of Franco's decision was that it was due to his characteristic caution: as in the earlier western operations, he found it difficult to accept the presence of enemy troops behind his back. But another

---

[94] José Semprún, 'Del Hacho', 304–9.   [95] Garriga, El general, 113.

explanation is that the relief of the fortress allowed him to consolidate his ascendancy over the other generals and secure his nomination as head of state. A few days before his decision the junta of generals had appointed him commander-in-chief, but most of them were reluctant to hand over power. Once Toledo had been taken, the junta met again and, amid an orchestrated mass campaign in favour of Franco, agreed to recognize him not only as commander-in-chief but also as head of state.[96]

The operation also coincided with the arrival in Madrid of crucial Soviet military aid. The month's delay gave the government a breathing-space to prepare the capital's defences and bring in fresh arms and troops, including the International Brigades. As a result, when the Nationalist army approached the capital at the end of October after taking Toledo, it was met by increasingly fierce and effective resistance. The original strategy of surrounding Madrid from the north and west and strangling its supplies and communications had given way to a frontal assault by the colonial columns from the south. Without support from the static front in the north, and now exposed on the east from where the Republicans could deploy their armed forces, the colonial troops came to a halt on the outskirts of Madrid.[97]

The battle for Madrid was therefore a completely new experience for the Army of Africa. The veterans had been used to the mobile and fluid operations of the colonial war, which had to some extent been replicated in the march from Andalusia to Toledo with the exception of the battle for Badajoz. Like the Moorish Other, the enemy in the south had lacked tanks and heavy artillery. They were policemen or inexperienced soldiers doing military service, or civilians who had grabbed the nearest rifle. Before the battle of the Tagus, no substantial body of professional soldiers had stood in the way of the advancing rebel troops. One of the few properly military columns previously sent by the Republican High Command to counter the colonial troops, was nicknamed the 'phantom column', because for a while it failed to make contact with the Nationalist troops and when it did was easily routed.

The colonial troops now faced conditions more like those of the First World War in northern Europe, intensified by the improved technology of the artillery, tanks, and air force on both sides. The exhilarating sweep of the Madrid column through the villages and along the roads of the south gave way to trenches, fixed positions, and heavy shelling and bombing from enemy planes, artillery, and tanks (not least from the latest and highly efficient T-26 Soviet tanks). Veteran officers of the colonial war could not rely on the experience they had gathered in the irregular warfare in Morocco, though they were tempted to apply it. Instead, like their metropolitan colleagues, they had also to take into account the textbook military strategy they had learnt in the military academies.

---

[96] Blanco, *La incompetencia*, 262–3.   [97] Ibid., 252–63 and 290–4.

To encourage the troops, distorted accounts were given by the Nationalist Information Service suggesting victory would be easy because of the 'deep demoralization' of the *madrileños*.[98] They must, therefore, have been surprised by the tenacity of the resistance. They now faced a more organized and stubborn enemy that matched the toughness of their own elite units. Very soon these would be joined by the International Brigades. The outskirts of Madrid were fought over inch by inch as the Nationalist troops advanced from the west and north-west through the Parque del Oeste and park of the Casa de Campo. As in the colonial war and in the summer campaign in the south, units of the Army of Africa exacted greater revenge on their prisoners when enemy units had put up a fierce defence and inflicted a high level of casualties. Echoing Yagüe's unguarded remark to Whitaker after the massacre of Badajoz, a military report on a fierce engagement in the village of Aravaca north of Madrid nonchalantly communicated that prisoners were shot on the spot, 'so we could carry out a counter-attack without any worries'.[99]

Military reports from commanders of units in action began to reflect the attrition of this war on the morale of the troops and on the organization of the army. In normal circumstances Nationalist officers tended to write upbeat reports that exaggerated the scale of military action of their units and the casualties they inflicted on the enemy. Such accounts were designed to raise morale but also to advance the careers of the commanders. They were sometimes accompanied by a request for a collective medal for bravery and skill. A common discourse of reporting seems to have established itself after the first disorganized campaigns of the Civil War. Adopting the terms of the official discourse of the Nationalist side, these reports and war diaries appear to be written more for posterity than for the successful prosecution of war. Inflated by a typical sense of mission and destiny, they are filled with rhetorical effects. Invariably, the enemy put up a 'tenacious resistance' and launched repeated and violent counter-attacks, which were all repulsed, and they were forced to leave their dead 'strewn about the field' (the number of enemy casualties was not subject to the same bookkeeping as those on their own side). The words 'brilliant' and 'brilliantly' littered most accounts of the actions of the Nationalist troops.[100]

This sort of hyperbole is, of course, frustrating for a military historian of the Civil War. But it was also damaging to the effectiveness of the Nationalist army. This was clearly of concern to the Nationalist High Command. An official telegram in December 1936 from Mola to Varela (now commander of the army besieging Madrid) ordered that reports in future should be a 'faithful

---

[98] 'Recopilación de noticias', 28 Oct. 1936, AV vol. 69. The Nationalists had a fifth column in Madrid that fed intelligence reports about enemy movements and the state of the civilian population, to which was added information brought across the lines by deserters.

[99] 'Columna del Coronel García Escamez', 3 Dec. 1936, AV vol. 70.

[100] e.g. Varela's 'Diario de Operaciones', in AV vol. 81.

reflection of reality', and that 'all manner of superlative qualifications should be totally suppressed.'[101]

As conditions on the Madrid front deteriorated and the casualties among colonial troops rose (among the wounded alone, 5,234 soldiers were hospitalized in one month, that is, an average between 6 and 21 November of 260.7 a day),[102] reports became more critical. One, dated 27 November, from Lt.-Colonel Asensio to Varela, warned that the degree of demoralization, exhaustion, malnutrition, and dirt among the front-line troops was such that they could not last much longer. (Indeed, one of the Moroccan soldiers on the Madrid front remembers being covered permanently in dirt and lice.[103]) The lack of water, tobacco, and candles was acute and due to inefficiency. There was not enough meat. The cold rations consisted only of a tin of sardines per man per day. Tinned meat was not provided because some contained pork and the Moroccan troops did not eat pork, so, apart from the main meal, sardines became the daily fare of both them and the Legionnaires. The former got neither the chocolate nor the dried fruit to which they were accustomed. Without proper cover, the wounded could only be evacuated during the night. Any new advance, the report went on, should only be attempted if there was certainty of success, 'in order to avoid the disastrous effects of another failure that would be felt in the columns that have already tried twice before'.[104]

Such criticism was far from the self-congratulatory tone of most contemporary reports and the subsequent military accounts by pro-Francoists.[105] The latter give little idea of the severity of conditions and the fragility of the army on the Madrid front. The comments from officers suggest that, at this stage at least, the Nationalist army was not the efficient military machine of Francoist propaganda but a hastily improvised force subject to disorganization, error, division, and inappropriate military strategy. Occasional campaign reports and confidential correspondence between the units and the High Command that I have managed to obtain and that are not normally available to the historian (combined with my interviews with veterans) help to give a more balanced account than official or semi-official historiography. While the quality of the front-line troops was not open to doubt, the rearguard, manned entirely by Nationalist militiamen, was the focus of frequent complaints by officers of the colonial troops. A weak rearguard meant the front line lacked depth and was exposed to flanking action. The anti-tank units of the Legion were also exposed to enemy fire because they were insufficiently protected.[106]

[101] 'Telegrama oficial', 22 Dec. 1936, in AV vol. 71; Santos, 'El Secretario', 209–11.
[102] 'Estado numérico de las bajas', AV vol. 70.
[103] Ben Abdellah Zeruali interview.
[104] 'Informe que da el Teniente Coronel Asensio', AV vol. 70.
[105] e.g. Manuel Aznar, Historia militar de la guerra de España 1936–1939 (Madrid, Edicionies Idea, 1940), and Martínez Bande, La marcha.
[106] Reports to Varela on n.d. and 3 Mar. 1937, AV vol. 71.

Mola himself wrote to Varela to complain that discipline in the rearguard was poor:

... in all the rearguard garrisons there are a great number of officers who wander about the streets and invade the cafes, which is evident proof that they have nothing much to do ... [T]here are many soldiers recovering from wounds who treat the hospitals like guest-houses where they go only to eat and sleep ... Many of the corps ask for clothes and then don't give them out but keep them in the stores to have spares ... with the result that clothes are ordered for the front-line troops and the units there remain naked.[107]

Details about training and logistics often suggest that officers were inadequately prepared for combat. There was insufficient firing practice and, as in the colonial war, officers sometimes knew nothing about the terrain on which they were operating and often had no maps.[108]

The increasing attrition on the front line on the outskirts of Madrid led to concern that it could not be held. The mounting casualties and the illnesses resulting from poor conditions seriously depleted the colonial shock-troops. Battalions were sometimes down to just over 100 soldiers when they should have had between 500 and 600. In early March the total number of colonial infantry on a new front to the east of Madrid in the Jarama mountains had fallen from an original 3,700 to just over 2,000.[109] Efforts to recruit more native troops and Legionnaires were stepped up as the toll of dead and wounded rose in the Madrid front. Such was the urgency that proposals were made to recruit prisoners for the Legion from the Seville and Cadiz jails, but Franco, with his customary punctiliousness, turned them down on the grounds that the suggestion was 'improper'.

Legion recruits were usually not questioned about their past. Many were volunteers from abroad, drawn by money and usually by their Catholic or right-wing ideology.[110] Trained in the camp in Talavera de la Reina, the new recruits were expected to imbibe and assimilate the brutal, macho culture of the Legion. Millán-Astray was often deployed to exhibit his war wounds and exhort the new Legionnaires. In one of his speeches to them, he declared how shocked he had been to discover that many Legionnaires had savings, not just in their wallets but in the bank. 'Death: that is your duty ... the Legion is made for brave men, not for people with savings accounts. Take your savings out and spend them tonight.' What most would spend their money on if they had any was of course alcohol, but Millán-Astray had a further suggestion. Meeting a

[107] 22 Mar. 1937, AV vol. 72.   [108] Ibid.; Pettenghi interview.
[109] Orgaz to Franco, 22 Jan. 1937, SHM ADGL R2; 'Notas sobre las operaciones en el frente de Jarama', 3 Mar. 1937, AV vol. 71.
[110] SHM ADGL R2, 11 Dec. 1936 and 9 Feb. 1937. At the beginning of 1937 2,000 White Russians, presumably sons of the exiles, applied to join.

veteran of the colonial war, he reached into his pocket and gave him 100 pese-tas, telling him to spend them on *putas* (prostitutes).[111]

As the war began to take its toll of veterans of the Legion, the quality of both officers and men in the elite unit fell. A Welsh Legionnaire remembers that the old Legion officers were replaced by ones from the regular army who had no experience of leading shock-troops and who commanded little respect from their men. 'Our old officers, such as *Teniente* Ivanoff and *Alférez* [Second Lieutenant] Blanco, led us into whatever faced us, while this new type of offi-cer is content to watch our progress from behind. This had a lowering effect on the men's morale . . . I had come to Spain willing to accept fair risk of death or serious injury, but this permanent use of the *bandera* as shock-troops con-verted the risk into certain death, which I was not prepared to accept.'[112]

But it was amongst the native troops that the greatest dilution took place. The Nationalist authorities in Morocco were having to extend their recruit-ment net ever wider as the number of available young men in the Protectorate rapidly declined. Despite strict censorship, word had evidently spread amongst Moroccans in the Spanish Protectorate about the heavy losses suffered by vol-unteers in the Civil War. The sight of Moroccan soldiers returning crippled to their homeland could confirm this, and the number of desertions among fresh troops undergoing training increased.[113] As recruitment became more diffi-cult, the army began to replace Moroccans with Spanish soldiers and NCOs, and later began a clandestine recruitment drive in French Morocco.[114] The quality of the new troops was not as good as that of the veterans of the Andalusian and Extremaduran campaigns, nor were their Spanish comman-ders. They were trained hastily and few of the officers had experience of com-bat. Complaints were sent to Varela about the low standard of the new officers. Discreetly, he suggested that the troops should not apply the same standards as in the past.[115]

Unable to pierce the Madrid defences from the south, south-west, and north, the Nationalist army multiplied the fronts around the capital in an effort to cut its communications and probe weaker, less fortified points. The units

---

[111] Odetti, *Trenta mesi*, 189–91; Santos, '*El Secretario*', 204; the Irish officer Francis McCullagh reported that the Legion was always accompanied by travelling prostitutes who dressed in Legion clothes and drank with the Legionnaires: *In Franco's Spain*, 182.

[112] Thomas and Stradling, *Brother*, 119–20.

[113] Foreign Office sources were reporting a depressed mood in the Protectorate as a result: Michael Alpert, 'The Spanish Zone of the Moroccan Protectorate During the Spanish Civil War 1936–1939', *Maghreb Review*, 18: 1–2 (1993), 36.

[114] Thus citations for bravery among the Regulares increasingly list Spanish soldiers: in actions from 2 to 8 May 1938, 8 out of 28 soldiers and corporals cited for bravery were Spanish: 'Parte de Guerra de los días 2 al 8 de mayo de 1938', AV vol. 81. For the falling standards of recruits and the recruitment drive in French Morocco, see José María Gárate Córdoba, 'Los moros en la guerra de España', *Historia y Vida*, 23: 267 (June 1990), 94–5.

[115] Telegram of 30 Oct. 1936, AV vol. 69, and 'Notas sobre las operaciones en el frente de Jarama', 14 Mar. 1937, A, vols. 69 and 71.

employed in the offensive, mostly colonial troops, had been renamed the División Reforzada or Reinforced Division on 6 December 1936 and were led by Varela under the overall command of Orgaz, his senior and another veteran of the colonial campaign. No serious reorganization of the rebel army had been carried out since Franco became commander-in-chief, and its basic units remained the columns inherited from the colonial war.[116] Their shared experience in the Moroccan war was of no avail to Varela and Orgaz in the new campaign. As the offensive ground to a halt and the toll of casualties rose, relations between the two became increasingly acrimonious. Faced by a more complicated war, their Africanist solidarity broke down. While Orgaz had preferred to accumulate forces to punch a hole through the defences to the west of the capital, Varela had argued the need to create more than one front in order to disperse the enemy. The former's strategy had prevailed, not without violent argument. Dense fog and the inexperience of the new recruits meant that the little ground finally gained on the western front was hardly worth the high level of casualties, amounting to 3,200 according to Varela's calculations.[117]

Varela's preferred option, an offensive east of Madrid, was also tried in early February. Eighteen infantry battalions, thirteen of which were colonial units now diluted by inexperienced recruits, were gathered together. But torrential rains bogged down the advance while the Republican commanders mobilized their forces in the knowledge that this was the decisive battle for the defence of the capital. Their defence, backed by greater air power, tanks, and artillery, was so fierce that the División Reforzada began to suffer severe losses. Two colonial battalions lost most of their officers and one of them half of its force. The 6th Bandera of the Legion lost control and began a disorderly retreat. Varela insisted that the offensive could only continue if more troops were deployed. Franco came to the front and, in a probably heated exchange with Varela, he and Orgaz ordered a retreat to positions on the other side of the Jarama river. The confrontation between old Africanist colleagues deepened when Varela once again opposed a new order on 7 March for a renewed offensive with the same battalions. Three days later Orgaz informed him that he had been sacked as commander of the Madrid offensive and transferred to command the Avila Division, which contained few of the elite colonial units he had been accustomed to lead since the Moroccan war.[118]

Thus the strong bonds that united colonial veterans were put under increasing strain, as new and unaccustomed strategies had to be tried. Tensions also arose between old comrades-at-arms over promotions, medals, and in the long term over the nature of the state that would replace the Republic. As Franco gained ascendancy, doubts about his ability as a statesman and indeed

[116] Blanco, *La incompetencia*, 275–6.   [117] Varela, 'Notas', AV vol. 71.
[118] Varela, 'Notas', AV vol. 71, 13–25.

scepticism about his military capabilities must have gained in strength, although as usual he kept his cards close to his chest. Mola's death in a plane crash in 1938 cleared his way to the top, leaving the leadership uncontested. Where rank was less important, primary allegiances still held. Thus, when Varela was sacked from his position as commander of the Reinforced Division, his subordinates, all Africanist veterans and comrades, showed strong solidarity.

The failure of the Madrid offensive had deeply undermined the Nationalist military cause. Varela and Yagüe had told the German military observer, Captain Roland von Strunk, that they were finished. Von Strunk, convinced also of the crisis in the rebel army and the danger of a Republican counter-attack, had relayed this information to Hitler and requested the immediate dispatch of 20,000 German infantry.[119] The combined German and Italian aid came just in time to save the rebels. The Italian general who signed the secret agreement with Franco was very scornful of the Nationalist strategy. In a telegram to the Italian minister of foreign affairs, he accused the rebels of behaving as if they were taking part in a colonial war. [120] The Germans also insisted on a reorganization of the armed forces as part of the price of further aid. The arrival of the German Condor Legion brought the most modern armed force in the world, equipped with the most recent technology of war, to fight alongside an officer elite forged in an irregular colonial war.

The failure to capture Madrid, combined with the defeat of the Italian troops in Guadalajara on 12 March 1937, shifted the focus of the Nationalist offensive to the campaign in the north. The Army of the Centre was created, and the elite-based Reinforced Division was separated into four divisions and dispersed on different fronts. After their concentration on the Madrid front, the colonial troops were split up further and began to be moved around according to the exigencies of the war on different fronts. It thus becomes difficult to trace the participation of the Army of Africa in the Civil War. But it is clear that it continued to play a crucial role as the shock-troops of the Nationalist army. For example, in the corps of the Army of Castile (the result of further reorganization in early 1938), there were only three colonial units out of twenty-two, all three of them native troops of the Regulares. Yet in six days of operations beginning at the end of March 1938, they suffered more than half the casualties of the corps as a whole.[121]

Indeed, it was the native troops that continued to bear the brunt of the fighting. John T. Whitaker gives a vivid account of the way in which the Nationalists used the Moroccan soldiers as cannon fodder:

... through field glasses, I watched the Moors clean out the six- and seven-story tenements just across that narrow and bloody little river [the Manzanares river in Madrid].

---

[119] Preston, *Franco*, 205–6; Whitaker, *We Cannot Escape*, 104.   [120] Preston, *Franco*, 206.

[121] 'Relación numérica de bajas por Unidades en este sector de Albarracín desde los días 29 de marzo hasta el día 3 de abril ambos inclusive', AV vol. 80.

A detail of fifty Moors would surround a building, silence the ground-floor defenders, and rush in. Then they would clear the second story with sub-machine-guns and hand grenades. These Moors were calm and tight-lipped, expert workmen. They would clear each building floor by floor. There was one difficulty. By the time the Moors had reached the top floor there were no Moors left . . . The Moors would clean these buildings floor by floor and the Moors would die floor by floor.[122]

Like the Welsh Legionnaire, one of the Moroccan veterans of the Regulares claims that there was much discontent among his fellow soldiers because of what they saw as their over-exposure to enemy fire. He alleges that when they were sent into action their officers would invariably follow them in the rear-guard. On one occasion, he maintains that a whole platoon of Regulares refused to advance and he saw them being executed by their officer and their NCO. This latter claim seems a bit far-fetched and I have found no evidence to corroborate it. Whether it is true or not, or an exaggeration of a smaller incident, it does testify to the sense of injustice in the historical memory of some of the veterans I have interviewed at their treatment in the war by the Nationalists.

Many others, however, remember their officers with sympathy. One Moroccan who worked in the headquarters of his battalion described his commanding officer, Lt.-Colonel Asensio, as a 'saint'.[123] In fact, the evidence suggests that the majority of colonial troops maintained their morale and fighting quality, even though they suffered extraordinarily high casualty rates. And it is difficult to explain this in any other terms than the consequence of good officer–soldier relations, as well as the martial culture to which the Legionnaires and many of the Moroccan recruits belonged, like the elite units and Gurkha troops that fought for the British.

The dispersal of the colonial troops meant that by the spring of 1937 their units were involved on most fronts. Some remained in Andalusia and in the now relatively static Madrid siege, others were in operations in Extremadura and on the northern front, first in Vizcaya and then in Cantabria. They became much more dependent on decisions of Franco's High Command rather than on divisional commanders. Thus, unlike the early days of the Civil War, they became mobile battalions, employed mainly to plug gaps created by the Popular army. But they were used also to raise morale where Nationalist militiamen suffered from Republican offensives. Battalions of the Legion and the Regulares were deployed to halt the Republican advance in Brunete on 6 July and then in Aragon in August. Colonial troops were employed the following month in operations in Toledo and Aranjuez near Madrid. Despite their high level of casualties, their numbers reached their highest level in the Civil War at the end of 1937. Out of the 640 battalions of the Francoist army at that

[122] *We Cannot Escape*, 102.
[123] Interview with Mohammed Ayache Zeruali; the claim about the execution was made by Tuhami Ben Abdeslam Ben Mohammed in an interview in Ceuta, 18 July 2000.

stage, 117 were, formally at least, colonial troops, although amongst their ranks there were now many Spaniards.[124]

However, the composition of 'native' recruits was changing. Many Moroccan soldiers returning home from front-line action were refusing to go back, so the Francoists had set up a 'Recuperation Service' to try and entice them back to the war. The high level of deaths and disabling injuries suffered by those who had first joined the Nationalist army had resulted in the withering of recruitment in the traditional areas, so the Nationalists were forced to seek new areas of recruitment in French Morocco, Algeria, Ifni, and the Spanish Sahara. The sultan, however, issued a proclamation suspending any further Spanish recruitment in the French Protectorate, regretting that his subjects 'had been carried off to become submerged in a fruitless and pitiless war'.[125] In contrast, the Moroccan authorities in the Spanish Protectorate continued to support the war. A Moroccan notary employed by the Nationalists remembers vividly the visit of the caliph to the hospital in Seville in 1938 where he was employed to help the wounded Moroccan soldiers write to their families and draw up wills.[126]

Despite the radical change in military strategy during the Civil War, there were times when experience in the colonial war became useful. The pilots who fought for the Nationalists, like the king's first cousin, Alfonso de Orleans, had acquired consummate skills in aerial war tactics in Morocco. In their earliest actions in the Civil War they had to rely on improvisation. Some planes were not fitted with bomb racks, so that the co-pilot had to drop bombs by hand.[127] When the rebel fleet heavily bombed Republican-held Málaga on 5 February 1937, thousands of refugees fled along the road to Valencia in cars, lorries, and carts and on mule-back, carrying hastily gathered possessions. The Nationalist fighters then swooped down on them with impunity, mowing down the men, women, and children with machine-gun fire and dropping bombs on them with deadly accuracy.[128]

In the more static fronts like southern Aragon in early 1938, colonial officers were able to employ some of the tactics that the Moroccan enemy had used against them more than ten years previously. In his new post, Varela instructed his troops to keep up a constant harassment of the Republican units facing them, obliging them to deploy their forces across a wide front. Repeated ambushes and surprise attacks would provide information about enemy positions, enable the capture of prisoners, and maintain insecurity among the

---

[124] Semprún, 'Del Hache', 355.   [125] Alcaraz Cánovas, 'Marruecos', 105.

[126] Interview with Abdessalam Abdessalam Ben Husain Rian, Tetuan, 24 July 2000.

[127] Captain José Larios, Marquis of Larios, Duke of Lerma, *Combat over Spain: Memoirs of a Nationalist Fighter Pilot 1936–1939* (New York, Macmillan, 1966), 26–7 and 46.

[128] Arthur Koestler, *Dialogue with Death* (London, Arrow Books, 1961), 33; Rafael Gil Bracero and Antonio Cazorla Sánchez, 'Málaga, Granada, Almería. Febrero de 1937: el desastre humano de los refugiados y sus responsabilidades políticas. Una nueva perspectiva', in *Anuario de Historia Contemporánea*, vol. 14, *1987–91* (Universidad de Granada, 1992), 195–220.

enemy troops. The alternation of short, rapid bursts of fire and slow, prolonged concentrations from small arms and artillery fire would also depress their morale, and prevent them from improving defence and supply lines, observation points, and evacuating their wounded. These methods may have been drawn from the classic textbook tactics of 'active defence', but Varela and other veterans enjoyed the advantage of having experienced them in the Moroccan war.[129]

Franco himself criticized the rigid 'Frenchified' concept of military advances of some of his generals, possibly referring to those with less experience of the colonial campaign. His own instructions emphasized the importance of flanking manoeuvres rather than frontal attacks and of preliminary contact with the enemy to gauge their strength before action. These tactics, though probably drawn up by his staff, were no doubt inspired by the experience of the Moroccan war and strengthened by the Nationalists' failure to take Madrid. In another set of orders also influenced by the colonial war, he stressed the value of surprise and rapidity of action, the need to retreat to secure positions rather than hold advanced ones exposed to enemy fire, and the usefulness of night operations. In a clear reference to the constant use of colonial forces as the shock-troops of the Nationalist army, he criticized his generals for failing to employ other units in order to spread the experience of battle as well as the casualties.[130]

Franco's reputation as an outstanding military strategist was fabricated by his supporters during and after the Civil War. He had been a brave and competent colonial officer, largely respected but also feared by the men under his command. But he had not distinguished himself as a methodical tactician and had never shown much interest in military theory.[131] The deeply formative experience of the colonial campaign, added to his innate caution, led him to rely on the tried and trusted methods of that war in the largely different circumstances of the Civil War. One of the most crucial tactics of the Moroccan war had been the use of poisonous gases against the 'uncivilized' enemy. Immediately after the military rebellion in July 1936, Franco had been tempted to use the same weapons against the new foe. According to Italian diplomatic documents, Franco asked Mussolini on 21 August 1936 to supply chemical weapons and gas masks for his troops. The Duce had ignored the request, probably fearing international opposition.

Franco made a second request to Italy for chemical weapons in January 1937, impelled no doubt by the failure of the Madrid offensive. His shopping-list included 50 tonnes of 12-kilo-mustard gas bombs, 50 tonnes of 1.5-kilo diphosgene bombs, 60,000 anti-gas masks, and 50 tonnes of calcium hypochloride

---

[129] 'Instrucción número cuatro', AV vol. 79.
[130] Franco's instructions are in 'Instrucciones para las próximas operaciones', 9 Dec. 1937, AV vol. 78.
[131] For a devastating critique of Franco's abilities as military leader, see Blanco, *La incompetencia*.

(probably for use in dealing with the contamination caused by mustard gas). This time Mussolini took his request more seriously. It was no coincidence that an expeditionary force of 45,000 Italian soldiers had just arrived in Spain. Shortly afterwards, 50 tonnes of mustard-gas bombs were sent in two separate shipments to Nationalist Spain, together with quantities of other chemical weapons such as the blood agent arsine. A large team of Italian troops trained in chemical warfare was also dispatched to Spain.[132]

It does not appear, however, that these weapons were ever used, despite the fact that manouevres took place to prepare Nationalist troops for their own deployment of them. Instead, the Nationalists made a lot of propaganda about the Republican use of toxic gases. Officers of the Chemical War Service were issued with instructions as to how to put on gas masks. Other reports claimed the enemy had bombed the airport and railway station of Talavera de la Reina with 'gases'. Yagüe asserted that Republican planes were loading chemical bombs in Madrid airport. Franco twice informed the Italian command that the Republicans had used or were about to use toxic gas against his troops.[133] There is no evidence, however, that the Republic ever deployed chemical weapons. The Nationalists might have been fed dubious information by their spies, instilled by the fear of the devastating effects of mustard gas. That they expected to be hit by chemical bombs might suggest that they saw them as an inevitable part of war and were preparing to launch such weapons themselves.[134] In Franco's case, however, his reports may have been an effort to prepare the Italians for his own use of chemicals. Because there appears to be no documentation on this issue, we can only speculate as to why the Nationalists never used any toxic bombs. One reason could be logistical. Although the type of mustard gas provided by the Italians was less dangerous to handle than the more basic, undistilled kind used in Morocco a decade earlier, it nevertheless posed considerable problems of transport and the contamination of areas over which the rebels would have to advance. The respirators that many Nationalist

---

[132] A telegram from the leader of the Italian mission, General Felipe Anfuso, to the Italian government dated 26 January 1936 contains a list of the materials requested by Franco: Ufficio Spagna (US), 24 Archivio Storico-Diplomatico del Ministero degli Affari Esteri, Roma (ASMAE), while the list of the materials supplied by Italy can be found in US 68 ASMAE. I am very grateful to Morten Heiberg for providing me with these documents. His study of the Italian intervention in the Civil War is based on meticulous research in the Italian archives. A preliminary article preceding a forthcoming longer study is: 'Nuove considerazioni sulla Guerra di Spagna: la storia secreta dell'intervento militare italiano', in Robert Mallett and Morten Heiberg, *Pensiero ed azione totalitaria tra le due guerre mondiali* (Cività Castellana ed Orte, Centro Falisco di Studi Storici, 2000), 52–6.

[133] 'Instrucciones para los oficiales afectos al servicio de guerra química (SGQ)', 10 Sept. 1936, in AV vol. 68; unsigned report entitled 'Reservados' of Nov. 1936, in AV vol. 70; Yagüe's 'Boletín de Información' of 2 Nov. 1936, in AV vol. 69; and Franco's claims in Heiberg, 'Nuove considerazioni', 54–5.

[134] A six-page report from Franco's headquarters to the various General Staffs goes into details about each chemical agent and how to deal with it: 'Información sobre los agresivos químicos y medios de contrarrestar sus efectos', in 'Instrucciones para el funcionamiento durante la batalla de los Estados Mayores', Jan. 1938, in AV vol. 78.

troops had to carry around with them may well have been provided to try to protect them from the effects of mustard gas launched against the Republicans.[135]

More important, perhaps, in staying Franco's hand was that international opinion was following events in Spain too closely for comfort. An international outcry following his use of chemical weapons would damage his reputation at a time when he needed to strengthen it. In an interview with the special correspondent of *The Times* in August 1936, Mola claimed the Nationalists had large stocks of gas but were refusing to break the international law forbidding its use.[136] This is not to say that Franco was merely flirting with the idea. As the secret Italian documents show, the Spanish and Italian military commands were discussing an ambitious future collaboration over chemical warfare. An Italian memorandum of 19 November 1937 commented on the willingness of the Nationalists to build toxic-gas factories under the direction of the Italians and envisaged their use in any future Italian war in northern Africa or in Europe. Accordingly, representatives of the Spanish chemical warfare service (Servicio de Guerra Química) visited their counterparts in Italy in 1937–8 while officers from the Italian Academy of Chemical Warfare were attached to the Spanish service at the end of 1937. The Nationalists also received chemical weapons from Germany, which had supplied Spain with the bulk of toxic war matériel in the 1920s. The Germans had made contact with the Spanish chemical service months before the Italians, and on 29 January 1937 sent 50 tons of 12 kilo mustard gas bombs and 50 tons of 12 kilo diphosgene bombs.[137]

As part of Franco's new offensive against Madrid via Guadalajara, the Nationalist army was reorganzed into three groups. One of these, under Yagüe's command, was soon nicknamed the Moroccan Corps because it had a large number of colonial troops, even though it also included Spanish metropolitan divisions and Italian artillery units. A Republican counter-offensive at Teruel in December meant rapidly moving this corps to southern Aragon to halt their advance. Failure to equip troops with proper clothing meant that the sudden snowstorms in Teruel devastated the Nationalist forces. The Republican victory at Teruel was brief, however. The overwhelming superiority of Franco's air force and artillery (whose equipment and officers were supplied largely by Germany and Italy) forced the Republicans to withdraw from Teruel after two months of bitter warfare.

The retreat of the Popular army in February 1938 was a turning-point in the Civil War.[138] The Nationalists began an offensive in Aragon the next month

[135] A Moroccan veteran of the Regulares, Husain Ben Oulad Ali, confirmed to me that he had always to carry a gas-mask: interview in Tetuan, 20 July 2000.

[136] *The Times*, 19 Aug. 1936.

[137] I am grateful to Morten Heiberg for providing this information from Italian sources. See also his, 'Nuove considerazioni', 53–6 and n. 17.

[138] Semprún, 'Del Hacho', 358–70.

covering a wide front of some 300 kilometres and involving some twenty-seven Divisions. The bulk of the colonial troops were employed in this new advance, both the Moroccan Corps, the Cuerpo del Ejército Marroquí under Yagüe (backed by the tanks and planes of the German Condor Legion), and the Cuerpo del Ejército de Castilla under Varela. In the face of their offensive, the Republican front lines collapsed, and by 15 April the Nationalists reached the Mediterranean at Vinaroz, cutting the Republic in two. Yagüe, advised by the German commander of the Condor Legion, had employed Blitzkrieg tactics and his troops encountered no serious resistance as they moved northwards. By early April they had captured the important Catalan town of Lleida. Varela's progress southwards alongside Italian and other Spanish troops, however, had met fierce opposition and the Nationalist command brought their offensive south of the Ebro to a halt in order to concentrate their forces further to the north.[139]

The injection of new Soviet aid across the French border stiffened Republican resistance in the north, and by May the two battle-fronts were static. Franco's new offensive in June against Republican lines defending Valencia ground to a halt, and once again the Nationalist command was caught by surprise on 25 July when the Republican general Vicente Rojo launched an imaginative counter-attack across the Ebro river along a wide front. With many other Nationalist troops, Yagüe's colonial soldiers were used in successive attempts to dislodge the Popular army. Only after seven Nationalist offensives were the Republicans forced to retreat in mid-November and the last serious resistance against the rebels came to an end.

It is unquestionable that the Nationalists would have been defeated had they risen without the participation of the Army of Africa. The conspirators decided to mobilize the colonial troops less than a month before 18 July because they knew they had insufficient support in the garrisons of Spain. Later, German and Italian military aid rescued the Nationalist army from defeat by the increasingly effective Republican army. But the Army of Africa remained the shock-troops of the rebel forces, their cannon-fodder. Calculations about how many colonial troops participated in the Civil War and how many died or were injured vary enormously. A reliable account based on several sources puts the total number of Moroccan troops deployed in Spain at 78,504. Of these about 11,500 were killed and 55,468 wounded, that is, one in every eight Moroccan soldiers was killed and almost every one of those who survived was injured at some time or other.[140]

The size and casualties of the Spanish Legion as a colonial force are more difficult to calculate. When the Civil War began there were only two regiments in Morocco (in which there was only a total of sixty-seven foreigners). Once

[139] Blanco, *La incompetencia*, 443–7.   [140] Gárate Córdoba, 'Las tropas', 58–61.

these were transported to Spain, the numbers of Legionnaires grew rapidly as pro-Nationalist Spaniards without any colonial experience were enrolled in Spain and volunteers joined them from many countries, especially Portugal. French volunteers were organized into a Joan of Arc company and for a brief while there was even an Irish battalion under the command of the veteran General Eoin O'Duffy. Even the Italian and German troops that came to the rebels' aid were classified as Legionnaires in an attempt to disguise their origin. Thus, the Legion suddenly acquired 'Legionnaire aviation' and 'Legionnaire submarines'. Discounting the troops from Italy and Germany, the Legion had some 14,000 troops at its highest point of recruitment. Like the Moroccan troops, it was subject to heavy casualties. According to official figures, 7,645 Legionnaires were killed and almost 29,000 were wounded, while 776 were not accounted for.[141]

Given such a high casualty rate, how was the Nationalist army able, by and large, to maintain the quality of its shock-troops throughout the Civil War? Disregarding the brutality of the colonial troops, the military achievements of their officers were remarkable. Although it suffered considerable dilution during the course of the war as its core veterans and officers were killed or disabled, the Army of Africa remained an elite force that the Nationalist command employed constantly to plug holes in defence and raise the martial quality of its other troops. The military effectiveness of the colonial troops responded to different rationales in each of the main components, the Regulares and the Legion. Many of the Moroccan soldiers came, as I have already suggested, with a martial tradition derived not just from the colonial war but from the long-standing culture of their tribes. Accompanying this tradition was a basic toughness and a greater acquaintance with pain and discomfort. As we have seen, they were moved to join up above all because of poverty. The wages were attractive but so was the promise of loot. For example, their fellow Moroccans in the Tiradores de Ifni were paid slightly less but expected to make up the difference by the money they could make from plunder. When the opportunities for pillage diminished in the late winter of 1937, some of these soldiers complained to the High Command and were dismissed for insubordination.[142]

Another factor that accounted for the military effectiveness of the Moroccan troops was the strong bonds that existed between them. The military command respected the small groups of men from the same or nearby tribe, the so-called Al Ashra, who would come together during moments of leisure to drink tea and smoke kif, the plant from which hashish is made. In contrast to the men of the International Brigades, these groups spoke the same language and

[141] Antonio Martínez de la Casa, *La Legión Española. Cincuenta años de historia. Desde 1936 hasta nuestros días* (Madrid, La Legión, 1973), no pp.; Semprún, 'Del Hacho', 72–3.

[142] SHM Avila, Cuartel General del Generalísimo, Cuartel General del Estado Mayor, febrero–abril 1937.

shared the same culture and were thus more efficient at communication.[143] The death or wounding of one of the group would stir the others to seek vengeance. Equally important was the bonding with their officers. Most of the veteran officers of the Regulares cultivated concern for the health and welfare of their men and were prepared to expose themselves to equal if not greater danger. They were also happy to let their men loot. These factors helped to create the bonds and the mutual respect that made the causes of war far less important than the primary attachment to leaders. An Italian fascist volunteer in the Legion remembers seeing Moroccan soldiers kissing the blanket of their wounded officers.[144]

Despite the abuses committed in Morocco by colonial officers mentioned at the beginning of this chapter, the troops on duty in Spain were treated relatively well when campaign conditions allowed it. For example, each office of native affairs in the campaign army had a postal service to ensure that letters and money orders reached the soldiers' families. Wounded Moroccans were sent to medical centres where they were well treated and fed, if only to ensure that they made a rapid recovery and returned to the front.[145] Confidence about their treatment in normal campaign circumstances did much to maintain the morale of the Moroccan soldiers at the worst moments, such as in the siege of Madrid.

The training of the Regulares and other Moroccan units also played an important part in their success in the battlefield. In addition to the centres in Morocco, there were seven training camps throughout the Nationalist zone where the recruits were introduced to the new environment of war, the tactics and the weapons they were expected to use. The Nationalist command conceived of the idea of using wounded Moroccan veterans to train the new recruits before they left for Spain. So 50 per cent of those allowed to go back to their country to recover from severe wounds were enrolled as military instructors of recruits in Morocco. But the rapid turnover of military personnel from late autumn in 1936 posed a serious problem for the training of recruits, because the war demanded the immediate dispatch of new troops to the front. At the best of times during the war, training lasted only two months. Sometimes the recruits were sent off after only four days and were therefore far less prepared.[146]

The training of recruits to the Legion was dogged by the same problems. As we have seen, its recruitment and training centre was based in Talavera de la Reina where a crucial battle had been won against the Republicans in September 1936. By all accounts, the iron discipline of the Legion was instilled into new Legionnaires by violent means, such as the use of the whip and the

[143] Merroun, 'El Cuerpo', 253–4.   [144] Odetti, *Trenta mesi*, 119.
[145] Merroun, 'El Cuerpo', 267.
[146] SHM Avila, Cuartel General del Generalísimo; AV vol. 72, Cuartel General del Ejército del Norte, 1 Apr. 1937.

kind of verbal abuse later famously practised by the US marines. The same methods continued to be employed once they were incorporated into the ranks. As in the colonial war, insubordination was often punished by death and misdemeanours were rewarded by a gruelling period spent in the punishment squad or *pelotón de castigo*. For recruits with problems of insecurity or identity, this fierce discipline was probably welcome, if not enjoyed.

The advantages of being a Legionnaire were the sense of belonging to an elite feared by the enemy and respected by all on the Nationalist side, and the special treatment given to the corps in the conditions of the camps and barracks. The efficacy of the Legion also derived from a powerful *esprit de corps* boosted by the fetishism of uniforms, side-whiskers, hymns, and tattoos. The discourse of the hymns, chants, and harangues by the officers appealed to the mythical resonances of death, love, sex, religion, and patriotism. As in the colonial campaign, the brutalization of the training instilled a pleasure in killing and the thrill of combat. The battle against Russian tanks was defined as a form of bullfight in the new 'revolutionary theory of the Belmonte school' (after the famous bullfighter), in which the Legionnaires were the bullfighter and the tank the bull. The morale of the Legion, like that of the native troops, also derived from the bonding between officer and soldier. The veteran officer of the Legion was a ruthlessly efficient disciplinarian, feared but respected for his competence and courage.[147]

Thus, despite the dilution caused by new and rapid recruitment and despite the radical overhaul of the strategy and tactics of the Nationalist army, the colonial troops remained its backbone throughout the Civil War. Their discipline, commitment, small-unit loyalty, and post-Madrid tactical flexibility made them a formidable force far superior to any other units on the Nationalist side, with the exception of the German Condor Legion. Only the International Brigades could match them on the Republican side, and they too suffered devastating losses.

To conclude, the colonial experiences of other powers, such as the British and French, had a profound impact on their respective metropolises, but none more so than the Spanish colonial war. Its deep imprint meant that throughout the Civil War the Africanist officers conceived of their struggle in terms of their experience in Morocco. They were forced to transform the military tactics and strategies they had learned in the colonial war by their failure to take Madrid. Subsequently, their military thinking was reshaped by their contact with German and Italian troops. But they continued to see the war in the same ideological light. It was a means of purifying a degenerate Spain from the outside. Backed by colonial troops forged in the harsh landscape of North Africa, they saw themselves as leading a movement to restore Spain to its true identity,

---

[147] According to a British veteran, Peter Kemp, *Mine Were of Trouble* (London, Cassell, 1957), 80–6 and 111–12; for the fetishism of the Legion, see the Italian veteran Odetti's *Trenta mesi*, 89–97; and for discipline, the Welsh veteran Thomas, *Brother*, 50–6.

which only they, as outsiders, could guarantee. Their mission had been to reconquer Spain from the new enemy, some 450 years after the Moors had been driven out.

Some of the older generation of Africanists, such as Mola himself, had been outsiders from the start, having been born in the overseas colonies and brought up in a colonial military family. But the most formative years of the younger generation of colonial officers like Franco had been spent in the war against Moroccans, and their sense of identity was moulded by it. That colonial exclusiveness was expressed, for example, in Franco's chosen symbolic bodyguard, the *Guardia Mora* or Moorish Guard, the flamboyant squadron of Moroccan troops on horseback, dressed in flowing robes and carrying native pennants, which he chose to accompany him on march-pasts after the war. It was meant to be a constant reminder to the Spanish people that they had been saved by the Army of Africa. The sycophantic tributes to the dictator hailed him as the reincarnation of the medieval Christian and Castilian hero El Cid. The name El Cid derives from the Arabic *sayyid* or master because, like Franco, the original figure, Rodrigo Díaz del Vivar, surrounded himself with Moroccan mercenaries and fought against his own people with a mercenary Moorish *mesnada* or legion.

What Franco and his fellow Africanist officers set out to do was to rechannel Spanish colonialism internally towards the homeland. The dictatorship that followed was intended as a continuation of that colonial crusade, whose incarnation was now Franco. With his Africanist officers, he would colonize Spain, ridding it of internal enemies, decontaminating the minds of those who had been poisoned by them, and installing their own myths, just as they had tried to do in Morocco.[148] The military was the great beneficiary of the victory and its Africanist generals now controlled political life under their 'maximum leader'. Two years after the end of the Civil War, the army absorbed 45 per cent of the state budget and kept half a million men under arms.[149] Within it, the Nationalist officers who had made their previous career on the mainland enjoyed little of the prestige of the Army of Africa, which dominated the iconography of the new regime.

Nevertheless, Franco's men had to come to terms with the other right-wing elites who had risen with them against the Republic. So the irreverent Africanist machismo now had to display piety to keep the Church happy. Equally, the Falange and the Carlists had to be recognized because they provided troops and helped to marshal the rearguard. But they were brought under the control of Franco and his army under the Decree of Unification of

---

[148] Much of the literature on the Civil War and the Francoist dictatorship underestimates the influence of the colonial experience. A recent example is Pedro Carlos González Cuevas, 'Política de lo sublime. Etiología de la violencia en la derecha española', in Juliá, *Violencia política*, 105–43.

[149] Gustau Nerín and Alfred Bosch, *El imperio que nunca existió. La aventura colonial discutida en Hendaye* (Madrid, Plaza & Janés, 2001), 30.

the spring of 1937, which swept away any autonomy they had previously enjoyed.

The Africanist officers looked outwards as well. With the collapse of the French Army in 1940 and the siege of Britain, the mirage of a new empire for the new Spain seized their imagination. The vague offers of autonomy made to the Moroccans in 1936 in order to gain their support for the uprising were forgotten. The satisfaction of seeing the humiliation of their French counterparts, who had almost always treated them with contempt during the colonial war, was matched by the hope that Spain could take over French Morocco as part of the spoils of an Axis victory. Indeed, secret plans were drawn up for an invasion of the French Protectorate by the Army of Africa.[150] The redeemed Spanish race could now expand into the whole of north-west Africa at whose gates it had halted in the Middle Ages. Beyond that lay a million square miles of British and French colonies in West Africa that appeared to be there for the taking. This imperial fantasy was driven by an incongruous mix of Spanish traditionalism, European fascism, and the Africanist culture forged in the colonial war. A text of the nineteenth-century right-wing politician Donoso Cortés was dusted down and brandished in support of the new imperialism: 'Give unity to Spain, extinguish the discords that madden its children, and Spain will be what it once was . . . and we will encircle Africa with our arms, that daughter caressed by the sun, who is the slave of the Frenchman and should be our wife.'[151]

The prospects for Africa could not be pleasant. The Africanists' love affair with Morocco had turned, in the 1920s, into a deadly embrace.

[150] I am grateful to Morten Heiberg for providing this information extracted from Italian secret military sources.

[151] Ibid., 28, taken from J. L. Massa, *Economía marroquí* (Tetuan, n.p., 1942). The passage is also quoted in Instituto de Estudios Africanos, *África en el pensamiento de Donoso Cortés* (Madrid, Consejo Superior de Investigaciones Científicas, 1955), which also claims that any speech by Donoso Cortés could be used by the current minister of foreign affairs: pp. 11 and 44–5. For a statement by the enlightened Africanist officer Castro Girona to a similar effect, that Spain would become the centre of the world because of its closeness to Africa, see his preface in Pardo, *Desempolvando legajos*, 37.

Appendix: Interviews Conducted Between 1998 and 2001

Moroccan Protagonists and Witnesses of the Colonial War

Abdessalam Abdessalam Ben Husain Rian
El Ayachi Sellam el Amraní
El Hach Abdel Krim Ben Ahmed Ben Ali
El Hach Mohammed M'Hauech
Hacha Oum Koulthoum Ahmed Kasem El Amraní
Hadou El Kayid Omar Massaud
Hammadi Mouh Hamich
Mohammad Ben Hammou
Mohammed Ben Ayache El Amraní H'mimed
Mohammed Maati El Amraní
Mohammed Saleh Faraji
Sidi Enfeddal Ould Ben H'mamou Zeruali
Two anonymous interviewees

Testimony of Children of Moroccan Protagonists

Ahmed Omar Amzaouri
Akkouh Marzook Abdeslam
Aziz Benazzouz
Hach Mohammed Ben Ahmed Jerirou
Mohamed Amar Hammadi

Moroccan Protagonists of the Civil War

Abdessalam Abdessalam Ben Husain Rian
Ahmed Mohammed Shaara
Ahmed Omar Amzaouri
Husain Ben Oulad Ali
Buxta Ben Abdellah Zeruali
El Hach Mohammed M'Hauech
Hach Hamaida El Filali
Mohammad El Hassani
Mohammed Ayachi Zeruali
Sellam Ayad
Sidi Enfeddal Ould Ben H'mamou Zeruali
Tuhami Ben Abdeslam Ben Mohammed
One anonymous interviewee

Moroccan Doctors

Dr Abdel Ouahab Tadmori
Dr Fouad Ouyahya

Spanish Protagonists of the Colonial War (corps and rank in brackets)

General Juan-Francisco Díaz Ripoll (artillery lieutenant)
General Manuel Gutiérrez de Tovar y Beruete (artillery lieutenant)
Isidre Balada (soldier in the communications corps)
Jesús Cotelo (sailor and medical orderly)
Josep Campa Ginot (infantry soldier)
Manuel Soto Meizoso (soldier in the engineering corps)
Pau Masferrer Fontanella (infantry soldier)

Testimony of Children of Spanish Protagonists

Amadeo Cortes Porta (son of sergeant of quartermaster stores (Intendencia))
José Álvarez Álvarez (son of infantry soldier)
Juan Juárez Virgili (son of carabinero survivor of Anual)

Spanish Protagonists and Witnesses of the Civil War

Florentino Herrera (soldier in Tiradores de Ifni)
General Gutiérrez del Tovar (Nationalist artillery)
General Juan-Francisco Díaz Ripoll (Nationalist artillery)
Isidre Balada (Republican carabinero)
Jesús González del Yerro Martínez (lieutenant of 4th Bandera of Legion)
José Pettenghi (Regulares officer)
Josep Campa Ginot (Republican infantry soldier)
Manuel Solsona Ibañez (soldier in Republican Durruti column)
Pau Masferrer Fontanella (Republican infantry soldier)
Vicente Ibarra Berge (lieutenant of Nationalist 4th Division of Navarra)
Joan Saltó (civilian)
Josep Vallés Vallverdú (civilian)
Teresa Vallés Vallverdú (civilian)

Sources

PRIMARY SOURCES

Unpublished Sources

Official and Public Archives

Archives Diplomatiques de Nantes (ADN).
Archives Diplomatiques du Ministère des Affaires Etrangères (ADMAE), Paris.
Archivo Batet (in Archivo Tarradellas), Monasterio de Poblet (AB).
Archivo de la Biblioteca General de Tetuan.
Archivo de la Fundación Antonio Maura Montaner (AFAMM), Madrid.
Archivo de la Real Academia de la Historia (Archivo Romanones, AR), Madrid.
Archivo del Banco de España, Madrid.
Archivo del Congreso de los Diputados (ACD), Madrid.
Archivo García Figueras, Biblioteca Nacional (Documentos Raisuni *et al.*) (BN GF), Madrid.
Archivo General de la Administración (AGA), Alcalá de Henares.
Archivo General del Cuartel de la Región Militar Sur, Sevilla (AGCRMS).
Archivo General del Ministerio de Asuntos Exteriores (AMAE), Madrid.
Archivo General del Palacio Real (AGPR), Madrid.
Archivo General del Protectorado en Tetuán (AGPT).
Archivo General Militar, Segovia (AGM).
Archivo Histórico del Aire, Madrid.
Archivo Histórico Nacional (Madrid and Salamanca).
Fundación F. Largo Caballero, Madrid.
Fundación Pablo Iglesias, Madrid.
Public Records Office, Foreign Office (PRO FO), and War Office (PRO WO), London.
Service Historique de L'Armée de Terre, Versailles (SHAT).
Servicio Histórico Militar (Documentación de la Guerra de Liberación Nacional; Ponencia de África, and Legado Manuel Fernández Silvestre) (SHM), Madrid and Ávila.

Private Archives and Collections

Archivo Diego Hidalgo Durán (ADHD), Madrid.
Archivo José Enrique Varela Iglesias (AV), Cádiz.
Ibn Azzuz Hakim, Tetuan.
Mustapha El Merroun, Tetuan.

Official Publications

Acción de España en África, 3 vols. (Madrid, Ministerio del Ejército, 1941).
Anuario Militar (Ministerio de la Guerra, Madrid).

Boletín Oficial de la zona del Protectorado Español (BOZPEM).

British Documents on Foreign Affairs: Reports and Papers from the Foreign Office Confidential Print (University Publications of America, 1991) (BD).

British Documents on the Origins of the World War, 1898–1914, ed. G. P. Gooch and Harold Temperley, vol. 1, *The End of British Isolation* (London, HMSO, 1927).

Consejo Supremo del Ejército y Marina, *Información guberuatiura* (Madrid, 1922).

De Anual a la República. La Comisión de Responsabilidades (Madrid, Javier Morata, 1931).

Diario de Sesiones del Congreso de los Diputados, 1904–36, (Madrid) (DSCD).

Diario Oficial del Ministerio de Defensa Nacional, 1937–39.

Diario Oficial del Ministerio de la Guerra, 1931–36.

Dirección de Intervención, Inspección de Sanidad, *Instrucciones provisionales reglamentando el ejercicio de la prostitución en las ciudades de la Zona de Protectorado de España en Marruecos* (Tetuán, Editorial Hispano Africana, 1927).

Documentos presentados a las Cortes en la legislatura de 1911 por el Ministro de Estado (D. Manuel García Prieto) (Libro Rojo) (Madrid, 1911).

Documents Diplomatiques Français (1871–1914) (Ministère des Affaires Etrangères).

Estado Mayor Central del Ejército, *Enseñanzas de la campaña del Rif en 1909* (Madrid, Talleres del Depósito de la Guerra, 1911).

Estado Mayor Central del Ejército, *Historia de las campañas de Marruecos (1859–1927)*, 3 vols. (Madrid, Servicio Histórico Militar (SHM), 1947–81).

Estado Mayor Central del Ejército, *Organización de las fuerzas del Ejército de operaciones en Melilla* (Madrid, SHM, 1909).

Instituto Nacional de Estadística, 1915–30.

Manual para el servicio del oficial de intervención en Marruecos (Madrid, n.p., 1928).

Ministerio de Fomento, *Expansión comercial de España en Marruecos* (Madrid, 1906).

Ministerio de Trabajo, Dirección de Estadísticas, *Zona de protectorado de los territorios de soberanía de España en el Norte de África, Anuario estadístico, 1941* (Madrid 1942).

Real Sociedad Geográfica de Madrid, *Exposición al Excm Sr. Presidente del Congreso de Ministros*, 30 Apr. 1904.

Documents, Memoirs, Diaries, Speeches, and Other Works by Protagonists

¡Acusamos! El asesinato de Luis de Sirval (Valencia, Ediciones del comité 'Luis de Sirval', n.d.).

ACIER, MARCEL (ed.), *From Spanish Trenches: Recent Letters from Spain* (London, Cressat Press, 1937).

AGUILAR FUENTES, ANTONIO, 'Libro de memorias de un soldado que estuvo en Africa', unpublished handwritten diary, 1921–2.

ALCALÁ-ZAMORA, NICETO, *El expediente Picasso. Discursos de Don Niceto Alcalá-Zamora pronunciados en el Congreso de ls Diputados los días 24 y 28 de noviembre de 1922* (Madrid, n.p., 1923).

ÁLVAREZ DEL VAYO, JULIO, *Documents històrics* (n.p, Edicions de la U.S.C., n.d.).

ÁLVAREZ, MELQUÍADES, *Discursos de Melquíades Álvarez* (Valencia, Prometeo, n.d.).

ARAQUISTÁIN, LUIS et al., *La Revolución española de octubre: documentos sensacionales inéditos* (Santiago, Occidente, 1935).

ARAUZ DE ROBLES, JOSÉ MARÍA, *Por el camino de Annual. Apuntes y comentarios de un soldado de África*, 3rd edn. (Madrid, Voluntad, n.d.).

ARBOLÍ NADAL, FRANCESC, 'Ligeras memorias e impresiones de mi permanencia en Africa (territorio de Larache). Años 1919–20 y 21', unpublished diary.

ARMIÑÁN ODRIOZOLA, JOSÉ MANUEL and LUIS DE (eds.), *Epistolario del Dictador. La figura del General Primo de Rivera, trazada por su propia mano* (Madrid, Javier Morata, 1930).

AZAÑA, MANUEL, *Estudios de política francesa contemporánea. Política militar* (Madrid, Saturnino Calleja, 1918).

—— 'Memorial de Guerra', *España*, nos. 378–86 (July–Aug. 1923).

—— *Diarios, 1932–1933. 'Los Cuadernos Robados'* (Barcelona, Crítica, 1997).

—— *Obras Completas* (Mexico, Ediciones Oasis, 1968).

BAHAMONDE Y SÁNCHEZ DE CASTRO, ANTONIO, *1 año con Queipo. Memorias de un nacionalista* (Barcelona, Ediciones Española, 1938).

BASTOS ANSART, MANUEL, *De las guerras coloniales a la Guerra Civil. Memorias de un cirujano* (Barcelona, Ariel, 1969).

BELTRÁN GÜELL, FELIPE, *Preparación y desarrollo del Alzamiento Nacional* (Valladolid, Librería Santarén, 1939).

BERENGUER FUSTÉ, GENERAL DÁMASO, *La guerra en Marruecos. (Ensayo de una adaptación táctica)* (Madrid, n.p., 1918).

—— *El Ejército de Marruecos* (Tetuan, Editorial Hispano-Africana, 1922).

—— *Las campañas en el Rif y Yebala 1919–1922*, 2 vols. (Madrid E. Arés, 1948).

—— *De la Dictadura a la República*, 2nd edn. (Madrid, Tebas, 1975).

BONO, EMILIO DE, *La preparazione e le prime operazioni*, 3rd edn. (Roma, Instituto Nazionale Fascista di Cultura, 1937).

BURGUETE, General RICARDO, 'El problema de Marruecos', *Memorial de Infantería* (García Figueras Archive, Biblioteca Nacional).

CABANELLAS FERRER, MIGUEL, '¿Quién es el Raisuni?', *Memorial de Caballería* (September 1919), 228–37.

CABANELLAS, General VIRGILIO, *De la campaña de Yebala en 1924. Asedio y defensa de Xauen* (Madrid, Renacimiento, n.d.).

CALVO, Teniente Coronel GONZALO, *España en Marruecos (1910–1913)* (Barcelona, Maucci, n.d. [c.1914]).

CAPAZ MONTES, FERNANDO, 'Usos y costumbres marroquíes en las ciudades, en el campo, sedentarios, nomadas árabes y bereberes' (Tetuán, Alta Comisaría de España, 1928, García Figueras Archive).

CAPAZ MONTES, OSVALDO, 'Modalidades de la guerra de montaña en Marruecos. Asuntos indígenas', *Conferencia del coronel Capaz* (n.d, n.p., Archivo García Figueras).

CASADO Y ESCUDERO, LUIS, *Igueriben. IV de junio a XXI de julio, MCMXXI. Relato auténtico de lo ocurrido en esta posición* (Madrid, 1923).

CEBREIROS CURIESES, Capitán NAZARIO, *La guerra de Marruecos* (Valladolid, Colegio Santiago, 1910).

—— *Las reformas militares. Estudio crítico* (Santander, n.p., 1931).

Comandante X.Y., *Marruecos. La espada rota. Impresiones de campaña* (Burgos, n.p., 1922).

Congreso Africanista, *Primer Congreso Africanista* (Barcelona, n.p., 1907).

CORDÓN, ANTONIO, *Trayectoria. Memorias de un militar republicano*, 2nd edn. (Barcelona, Crítica, 1977).

DÍAZ DE VILLEGAS, Comandante, *Lecciones de la experiencia. (Enseñanza de las Campañas de Marruecos)* (Toledo, n.p., 1930).

DÍAZ-FERNÁNDEZ, JOSÉ, *El blocao* (Madrid, Ediciones Turner, 1976; 1st edn. 1928).

DONOSO CORTÉS, RICARDO, *Estudio geográfico político militar sobre las zonas españolas del Norte y Sur de Marruecos* (Madrid, n.p., 1913).

ESCOBAR, JOSÉ IGNACIO, *Así empezó* (Madrid, Ediciones G. del Toro, 1974).

EZA (MARICHALAR MONREAL), Vizconde de, *Mis responsabilidades en el desastre de Melilla como Ministro de Guerra* (Madrid, Gráficas Reunidas, 1923).

——*El desastre de Melilla. Conferencias dadas en el Ateneo de Madrid, abril de 1923* (Toledo, n.p., 1928).

FERNÁNDEZ OXEA, JOSÉ RAMÓN, *Crónicas de Marruecos. Tras la rota de Anual* (Barcelona, Sotelo Blanco, 1985).

FERRAGUT, JUAN (pseud. JULIÁN RODRÍGUEZ PINERO), *Memorias de un Legionario*, 2nd edn. (Madrid, Saiz Hermanos, 1925).

FRANCO BAHAMONDE, FRANCISCO, *Palabras del Caudillo 19 abril 1937–31 diciembre 1938* (Barcelona, Ediciones Fe, 1939).

——*Diario de una bandera* (Madrid, Doncel, 1976; 1st edn. 1922).

——*Papeles de la Guerra de Marruecos* (Madrid, Fundación Nacional Francisco Franco, 1986).

FRANCO SALGADO-ARAUJO, FRANCISCO, *Mis conversaciones privadas con Franco* (Barcelona, Planeta, 1976).

——*Mi vida junto a Franco. Guerra de África, Monarquía, República, Guerra Civil y posguerra* (Barcelona, Planeta, 1977).

GABRIELLI, LÉON, *Abdel Krim et les événements du Rif (1924–1926)* (Casablanca, Editions Atlantides, 1953).

GALLEGO RAMOS, Capitán EDUARDO, *La campaña del Rif (1909): orígenes, desarrollo y consecuencias* (Madrid, n.p., 1909).

GARCÍA ÁLVAREZ, M. and GARCÍA PÉREZ, A., *Diario de las operaciones realizadas en Melilla a partir del día 9 de julio de 1909* (Toledo, n.p., 1909).

GIL ROBLES, JOSÉ MARÍA, *No fue posible la paz* (Esplugues de Llobregat, Ariel, 1968).

GIMÉNEZ CABALLERO, E., *Notas Marruecos de un soldado* (Madrid, n.p., 1923).

GODED, MANUEL, *Un 'faccioso' cien por cien* (Zaragoza, Heraldo, 1938).

GODED, General MANUEL, *Marruecos. Las etapas de Pacificación* (Madrid, Compañía Ibero-Americana de Publicaciones, 1932).

GORDÓN ORDÁS, FÉLIX, *Crímenes en la retaguardia rebelde* (Havana, Editorial Facetas, 1939).

——*Mi política en España*, 2 vols. (Mexico, n.p., 1962).

GROSSI MIER, MANUEL, *La insurrección de Asturias* (Barcelona, Ediciones La Batalla, 1935).

HIDALGO DE CISNEROS, IGNACIO, *Cambio de rumbo* (Bucharest, n.p., 1961).

HIDALGO, DIEGO, *¿Por que fui lanzado del ministerio de la guerra? Diez meses de actuación ministerial* (Madrid, Espasa-Calpe, 1934).

Il Conflitto Italo-Etiopico. Documenti, 2 vols. (Milan, Istituto per gli studi di politica internazionale, 1936).

Información gubernativa instruido para esclarecer los antecedentes y circunstancias que concurrieron en el abandono de las posiciones del territorio de la Comandancia General de Melilla en el mes de julio de 1921 (Madrid, Consejo Supremo del Ejército y Marina, 1922).

Intereses de España en Marruecos (Madrid, Instituto de Estudios Africanos, 1951).

IRIBARREN, JOSÉ MARÍA, *Con el General Mola. Escenas y aspectos inéditos de la Guerra Civil* (Zaragoza, Librería General, 1937).

—— *Mola. Datos para una biografía y para la historia del alzamiento nacional* (Zaragoza, Librería Nacional, 1938).

—— *El general Mola* (Madrid, Editora Nacional, 1945; 2nd edn. of the above).

KEMP, PETER, *Mine Were of Trouble* (London, Cassell, 1957).

KINDELÁN DUANY, ALFREDO, *Mis cuadernos de guerra 1936–1939* (Madrid, Editorial Plus, 1945).

—— *Ejército y Política* (Madrid, M. Aguilar, 1946).

—— *La verdad de mis relaciones con Franco* (Barcelona, Planeta, 1981).

La represión en Asturias. Reporte sindicalista (n.p., n.d.).

La revolución de Asturias. (Documentos) (Mexico, Ediciones Defensa Roja, 1935).

LARIOS, JOSÉ, Captain, Marquis of Larios, Duke of Lerma, *Combat over Spain: Memoirs of a Nationalist Fighter Pilot 1936–1939* (New York, Macmillan, 1966).

LEÓN Y CASTILLO, F. de, *Mis tiempos*, 2 vols. (Madrid, Librería de los Sucesores de Hernando, 1921).

LIZARZA IRIBARREN, ANTONIO DE, *Memorias de la conspiración, 1931–1936*, 4th edn. (Pamplona, Editorial Gómez, 1969).

LLORDÉS BADÍA, JOSÉ, *Al dejar el furil. Memorias de un soldado raso eu la guerra de España*, 2nd edn. (Esplogues de Llobregat, Ariel, 1969).

LOBERA GIRELA, CÁNDIDO, *Notas sobre el problema de Melilla* (Melilla, Telegrama del Rif, 1912).

—— *Problemas del Protectorado. Los bienes Majzen* (Melilla, Telegrama del Rif, 1916).

LÓPEZ ALARCÓN, ENRIQUE, *Crónica de un testigo: Melilla 1909. Diario de la guerra escrita durante las operaciones militares en el Rif* (Madrid, Hijos de R. Álvarez, 1911).

LÓPEZ MUÑIZ, Teniente Coronel, *La batalla de Madrid* (Madrid, Gloria, 1943).

LÓPEZ OCHOA, General E., *De la Dictadura a la República* (Madrid, Zeus, 1930).

—— *Campaña Militar de Asturias (Narración táctica-episódica)* (Madrid, Ediciones Yunque, 1936).

Los crímenes de la reacción española. La represión en Asturias. La verdad sobre octubre (Madrid, Ediciones de la Sección Española del Socorro Rojo Internacional, 1935).

Los Regulares de Larache en el Alzamiento Nacionalista de España (Madrid, n.p. [1940]).

LYAUTEY, Maréchal HUBERT, *Paroles d'action. Madagascar-Sud-Oranais-Oran-Maroc (1900–1926)* (Paris, Armand Colin, 1927).

—— *Lyautey L'Africain. Textes et lettres du Maréchal Lyautey presentés par Pierre Lyautey*, 4 vols. (Paris, Plon, 1955–7).

MARTÍN BLÁZQUEZ, JOSÉ, *I Helped to Build an Army: Civil War Memoirs of a Spanish Staff Officer* (London, Secker and Warburg, 1939).

MAURA GAMAZO, GABRIEL, *La cuestión de Marruecos desde el punto de vista español* (Madrid, M. Romero, 1905).

MAURA, ANTONIO, *Transcendental discurso pronuciado por D. Antonio Maura* (Madrid, n.p., 1921).

MELGAR MATA, ALFREDO and RUIZ FORNELLS, ENRIQUE, *Organización militar de España y algunas potencias extranjeras*, 18th edn. (Toledo, Rafael Gómez-Menor, 1915).

Memoria sobre la Kabila de Anyera (n.p., n.p., 1927).

MIR BERLANGA, FRANCISCO, *Con el viento de la historia* (Melilla, n.p., 1993).

MOLA VIDAL, EMILIO, *Obras Completas* (Valladolid, Santaren, 1940).

MOLINS I FÁBREGA, N., *UHP. La insurrección proletaria de Asturias* (Madrid, Editorial Júcar, 1977; 1st edn. 1935).

MULHACÉN, Marqués de, *Política mediterránea de España, 1704–1951* (Madrid, Instituto de Estudios Africanos, 1952).

NAVARRO Y GARCÍA, MODESTO, *Importancia militar de Gibraltar y medios de que dispone España para anularla* (Madrid, n.p., 1896).

NELKEN, MARGARITA, *Por qué hicimos la Revolución* (Barcelona, Paris, and New York, Ediciones Sociales Internacionales, 1936).

NEVES, MARIO, *La matanza de Badajoz. Crónica de un testigo de uno de los episodios más trágicos de la Guerra Civil de España (agosto de 1936)* (Extremadura, Editor Regional de Extremadura, 1986).

NIDO Y TORRES, MANUEL DEL, *Marruecos. Apuntes para el oficial de intervención y de tropas coloniales* (Tetuán, Editorial Hispano Africana, 1925).

NOEL, EUGENIO, *Lo que vi en la Guerra. Diario de un soldado* (Barcelona, n.p., 1912).

ODETTI DI MARCORENGO, FRANCESCO, *Trenta mesi nel Tercio* (Rome, M. Carra & Co., 1940).

OTEYZA, LUIS DE, *Abdel Krim y los prisioneros* (Madrid, Mundo Latino, n.d. [1925]).

PARDO GONZÁLEZ, CÁNDIDO, *Al servicio de la verdad* (Madrid, n.p., 1930).

—— *Desempolvando legajos. El problema militar en España. Su resolución más racional económica y nacional* (Madrid, AEL, 1934).

PÉREZ DE SEVILLA Y AYALA, VICENTE, *Recuerdos imborrables* (Segovia, n.p., 1972).

PÉREZ ORTIZ, EDUARDO, *De Annual a Monte-Arruit y diez y ocho meses de cautiverio. Crónica de un testigo* (Melilla, Artes Gráficas Postal-Exprés, 1923).

PICASSO GONZÁLEZ, General JUAN, *Expediente Picasso. Documentos relacionados con la información instruída por el señor general de división D Juan Picasso sobre las Responsabilidades de la actuación española en Marruecos durante julio de mil novecientos veintiuno* (Mexico, Frente de Afirmación Hispanista, 1976: facsimile edition of the above report as submitted to the Supreme Council of War in July 1922).

PRIETO, INDALECIO, *Con el rey o contra el rey* (Mexico, Ediciones Oasis, 1972).

Primer Congreso Africanista (Barcelona, n.p, 1907).

PRIMO DE RIVERA, MIGUEL, *La cuestión del día. Gibraltar y África* (Cadiz, n.p., 1917).

Prontuario alfabético de las disposiciones oficiales más importantes relativas a la Legión (Ceuta, n.p., n.d.).

PROUS I VILA, J. M., *Quatre gotes de sang. (Dietari d'un catalá al Maroc)* (Barcelona, Llibrería Catalana, 1936).

PUELLES Y PUELLES, ANTONIO DE, *Por las rutas del tercio Mora-Figueroa (recuerdos de la campaña)* (Cadiz, n.p., 1939).

QUEIPO DE LLANO, *El General Queipo de Llano perseguido por la dictadura* (Madrid, Javier Morata, 1930).

R. DE A. Y L., *La batería de montaña de Tenerife en África, 1921–1922. Cartas de un artillero* (Laguna de Tenerife, n.p., 1923).

RAMOS IZQUIERDO, FEDERICO, *La Legión. Historial de Guerra (1 Septiembre 1920 al 12 Octubre 1927)* (Ceuta, Imprenta África, 1933).

REPARAZ, GONZALO DE, *Política de España en África* (Madrid, Calpe, 1907).

—— *Aventuras de un geógrafo errante* (Barcelona, Librería Sintes, 1922).

RIENZI (MANUEL GÓMEZ DOMINGO), *¡Guerra!* (Valladolid, Librería Santarén, n.d.).

RIERA, AUGUSTO, *España en Marruecos. Crónica de la campaña de 1909* (Barcelona, Maucci, 1909).

ROGER-MATHIEU, J., (ed.), *Mémoires d'Abd-el-Krim* (Paris, n.p., 1927).

ROMANONES, Conde de, *El ejército y la política* (Madrid, Renacimiento, 1921).

—— *Las responsabilidades políticas del antiguo régimen. 1875 a 1923* (Madrid, Renacimiento, 1925).

—— *Notas de una vida, 1912–1931*, vol. 3 (Madrid, Espasa-Calpe, 1947).

SAINZ GUTIÉRREZ, SIGIFREDO, *Con el General Navarro en operaciones y en el cautiverio* (Madrid, Sucesores de Rivadeneyra, 1924).

SAINZ RODRÍGUEZ, PEDRO, *Testimonio y recuerdos* (Barcelona, Planeta, 1978).

SÁNCHEZ PÉREZ, CAPITÁN ANDRÉS, *Acción decisiva contra Abdel Krim. Operaciones en el Rif central en colaboración con el Ejército francés* (Toledo, n.p., n.d. [1930]).

SÁNCHEZ RODRIGO, JUAN, *Diario de un soldado en la campaña de Marruecos 1921–1922* (Serradilla, n.p., n.d.).

SANTA MARINA, LUYS, *Tras el águila de César. Elegía del Tercio 1921–1922* (Barcelona, Editorial Yunque, 1939).

SENDER, RAMÓN J., *Imán*, 5th edn. (Madrid, Destino, 1995).

SERRA ORTS, A., *Recuerdos de la Guerra del Kert de 1911–12* (Barcelona, n.p., 1914).

SERRANO SUÑER, RAMÓN, *Entre el silencio y la propaganda. La Historia como fue. Memorias* (Barcelona, Planeta, 1977).

SILVELA, FRANCISCO, *Artículos, discursos, conferencias y cartas* (Madrid, Mateu Artes Gráficas, 1922–3).

TAGÜEÑA LACORTE, MANUEL, *Testimonio de dos guerras* (Barcelona, Planeta, 1978).

THOMAS, FRANK and STRADLING, ROBERT, *Brother against Brother. Experiences of a British Volunteer in the Spanish Civil War* (Stroud, Alan Sutton, 1998).

TORCY, General de, *Los españoles en Marruecos en 1909* (Madrid, Adrian Romo, 1911).

Un Africanista más, *La guerra y el problema de África. Unas cuantas verdades por un Africanista más* (Burgos, n.p., 1914).

VARELA, JOSÉ, *Ensayo de historial del 3er grupo de fuerzas Regulares Indígenas* (Ceuta, n.p., 1926).

VEJOTA, *Los soldados de infantería de Tenerife en campaña. Cartas de Marruecos* (Laguna de Tenerife, n.p., 1925).

VIDARTE, JUAN-SIMEÓN, *Todos fuimos culpables. Testimonio de un socialista español* (Mexico, Tezontle, 1973).

—— *El bienio negro y la insurrección de Asturias* (Barcelona, Grijalbo, 1978).

VIGÓN, Lt.-General JORGE, *Historia de la Artillería española*, 3 vols. (Madrid, n.p., 1947).

Newspapers and Periodicals

ABC.
Al Alam Athakafi.
Bulletin d'Histoire Contemporaine de l'Espagne.
Bulletin du Comité de l'Afrique Française.
Chicago Tribune.
Correo Militar.
Diario de Cádiz.

Diario Mercantil.
Diario Oficial del Ministerio de la Guerra.
Ejército.
Ejército y Armada.
El Debate.
El Ejército Español.
El Globo.
El Heraldo de Madrid.
El Imparcial.
El Liberal.
El Protectorado Español.
El Sol.
El Telegrama del Rif.
El Trabajo Nacional.
España.
España en África.
Informaciones.
L'Afrique Française.
La Correspondencia de España.
La Correspondencia Militar.
La Dépêche Coloniale.
La Dépêche Marocaine.
La Época.
La Guerra y su Preparación.
La Libertad.
La Nación.
La Presse Marocaine.
La Vanguardia.
Marte.
Memorial de Artillería.
Memorial de Caballería.
Nuevo Mundo.
Revista de Tropas Coloniales (later *África*).
Revista Hispano Africana.
The Times.

SECONDARY SOURCES

Books and Unpublished Theses and Manuscripts

Abd-el-Krim et la république du rif. Actes du colloque international d'études historiques et sociologiques, 18–20 janvier 1973 (Paris, Maspéro, 1976).

ACEDO COLUNGA, FELIPE, *El alma de la Aviación española* (Madrid, Espasa-Calpe, 1928).

AGUADO SÁNCHEZ, FRANCISCO, *La revolución de octubre de 1934* (Madrid, San Martín, 1972).

AGUILAR OLIVENCIA, MARIANO, *El ejército español durante la Segunda República: claves de su actuación posterior* (Madrid, Econorte, 1986).

ALCOFAR NASSAES, JOSÉ LUIS, *La aviación legionaria en la Guerra Civil española* (Barcelona, Euros, 1976).

ALESSI, MARCO, *La Spagna dalla monarchia al governo di Franco* (Milan, Istituto per gli studi di politica internazionale, 1937).

ALLENDESALAZAR, JOSÉ MANUEL, *La diplomacia española y Marruecos, 1907–1909* (Madrid, Ministerio de Asuntos Exteriores, 1990).

ALONSO BAQUER, MIGUEL, *El Ejército en la sociedad española* (Madrid, Movimiento, 1971).

——'La selección de la élite militar española en el primer tercio del siglo XX (1898–1931)', in *Sistemas militares y políticas de defensa del Mediterráneo, Coloquio de Toulouse* (Madrid, CESEDEN, 1980).

—— *Las preferencias estratégicas del militar español* (Madrid, EME, 1985).

—— *D. Manuel Azaña y los militares* (Madrid, Actas, 1997).

ALONSO, JOSÉ RAMÓN, *Historia política del Ejército español* (Madrid, Editora Nacional, 1974).

ALPERT, MICHAEL, *La reforma militar de Azaña (1931–1933)* (Madrid, Siglo XXI, 1982).

—— *La guerra civil española en el mar* (Madrid, Siglo XXI, 1987).

ÁLVAREZ, JOSÉ E., *The Betrothed of Death. The Spanish Foreign Legion During the Rif Rebellion 1920–1927* (Westport Conn., Greenwood Press, 2001).

ÁLVAREZ JUNCO, JOSÉ, *El Emperador del Paralelo. Lerroux y la demagogia populista* (Madrid, Alianza, 1990).

ÁLVAREZ PORTAL, M., *Sirval* (Ediciones Adelante, Barcelona, 1936).

ÁLVAREZ PUGA, E., *Historia de la Falange* (Barcelona, Dopesa, 1970).

ANTÓN DEL OLMET, LUIS, *Marruecos. De Melilla a Tanger* (Madrid, n.p., 1916).

ARCE, CARLOS DE, *Los generales de Franco. Memoria de un pasado dramático* (Barcelona, Seuba, 1984).

ARQUÉS, ENRIQUE, *17 de julio. La epopeya de Africa. Crónica de un testigo* (Ceuta-Tetuán, Imprenta África, 1937).

Armamento del Museo del Aire. Catálogo de armamento aéreo en el Museo (Madrid, Museo del Aire, 1991).

ARMIJO, Coronel JACOBO DE, *España y las rutas del aire* (Madrid, Instituto de Estudios Políticos, 1944).

ARMIÑÁN ORIOZOLA, JOSÉ MANUEL Y LUIS DE, *Francia, el dictador y el moro. Página históricas* (Madrid, Javier Morata, 1930).

ARRARÁS, JOAQUÍN, *Historia de la Cruzada española*, 8 vols. (Madrid, Ediciones Españolas, 1937–43).

—— *Historia de la Segunda República española*, 4 vols. (Madrid, Editora Nacional, 1956–68).

ARTIGAS ARPÓN, BENITO, *La epopeya de Al Hoceima. (Los alicates rotos)* (Madrid, n.p., 1925).

ASENJO ALONSO, *¡¡¡Los que fuimos al Tercio!!!* (Madrid, Miguel Albero, 1932).

AYACHE, GERMAIN, *Les Origines de la guerre du Rif*, 2nd edn. (Paris/Rabat, Publications de la Sorbonne, 1986).

AYENSA, EMILIO, *Del Desastre de Annual a la presidencia del consejo* (Madrid, Rafael Caro Raggio, 1930).

AZNAR, MANUEL, *Historia militar de la guerra de España 1936–1939* (Madrid, Edicioníes Idea, 1940).

AZPEITUA, ANTONIO, *Marruecos. La mala semilla: ensayo de análisis objetivo de cómo fue sembrada la guerra en África* (Madrid, n.p., 1921).

BACHOUD, ANDRÉE, *Los españoles ante las campañas de Marruecos* (Madrid, Espasa-Calpe, 1988).

BALFOUR, SEBASTIAN, *El fin del Imperio español (1898–1923)* (Barcelona, Crítica, 1997); English edn. *The End of the Spanish Empire 1898–1923* (Oxford, OUP, 1997).

—— 'Spain and the Great Powers in the Aftermath of the 1898 Disaster', in Sebastian Balfour and Paul Preston (eds.), *Spain and the Great Powers in the Twentieth Century* (London, Routledge, 1999).

BASTOS ANSART, FRANCISCO, *El desastre de Annual. Melilla en julio de 1921* (Barcelona, Minerva, 1921).

BENZO, EDUARDO, *Al servicio del Ejército. Tres ensayos sobre le problema militar de España* (Madrid, Javier Morata, 1931).

BERENGUER, JUAN, *El Ejército es el pueblo. Nuestras glorias por los campos de África* (Melilla, Postal-Expres, n.d. [1922]).

BHABHA, HOMI K., *The Location of Culture* (London, Routledge, 1994).

BIDWELL, ROBIN, *Morocco under Colonial Rule. French Administration of Tribal Areas 1912–1956* (London, Frank Carr, 1973).

BLANCO ESCOLÁ, CARLOS, *La Academia General Militar en Zaragoza (1928–31)* (Barcelona, Labor, 1989).

—— *La incompetencia militar de Franco* (Madris, Alianza, 2000).

BLASCO IBAÑEZ, VICENTE, *Alfonso XIII Unmasked: The Military Terror in Spain* (London, Eveleigh, Nash and Grayson, 1925).

BONO, EMILIO DE, *La preparazione e le prime operazioni* (Roma, Istituto Nazionale Fascista di Cultura, 1937).

BOURKE, JOANNA, *An Intimate History of Killing. Face-to-Face Killing in Twentieth-Century Warfare* (London, Granta Books, 1999).

BOYD, CAROLYN P., *Historia Patria. Politics, History, and National Identity in Spain, 1875–1975* (Princeton, Princeton University Press, 1997).

—— *Praetorian Politics in Liberal Spain* (Chapel Hill, University of North Carolina, 1979).

BRASA, JUAN, *España y la Legión*, 2nd edn. (Valladolid, Santarén, 1938).

BRAVO MORATA, FEDERICO, *La República y el ejército* (Madrid, Fenicia, 1978).

BUENO y NÚÑEZ DE PRADO, Major EMILIO, *Historia de la acción de España en Marruecos desde 1904 a 1927* (Madrid, n.p., 1929).

BUSH, BARBARA, *Imperialism, Race and Resistance. Africa and Britain, 1919–1945* (London, Routledge, 1999).

BUSQUETS, JULIO, *El militar de carrera en España. Estudio de sociología militar* (Barcelona, Ariel, 1967).

CABANELLAS, GUILLERMO, *La guerra de los Mil Días: nacimiento, vida y muerte de la II República Española* (Buenos Aires, Heliasta, 1975).

—— *Cuatro generales*, 2 vols. (Barcelona, Planeta, 1977).

CABANILLAS, ALFREDO, *La epopeya del soldado desde el desastre de Anual hasta la reconquista de Monte Arruit* (Madrid, n.p., 1922).

CACHO ZABALZA, ANTONIO, *La Unión Militar Española* (Alicante, Egara, 1940).

CALLEJA, JUAN JOSÉ, *Yagüe: un corazón al rojo* (Barcelona, Editorial Juventud, 1963).

CAMPOAMOR, JOSÉ MARÍA, *La actitud de España ante la cuestión de Marruecos (1900–1904)* (Madrid, n.p., 1951).

CANALS, SALVADOR, *España y la cuestión de Marruecos. Análisis de un debate parlamentario* (Madrid, n.p., 1915).

Capitán X (Nazario Cebreiros), *Verdades amargas. La campaña de 1909 en el Rif* (Madrid, n.p., 1910).

Cardona, Gabriel, *El poder militar en la España contemporánea hasta la guerra civil* (Madrid, Siglo XXI, 1983).

Cardozo, Harold G., *The March of a Nation. My Year of Spain's Civil War* (London, Right Book Club, 1937).

Carr, Raymond, *Spain 1808–1975*, 2nd edn. (Oxford, Oxford University Press, 1982).

——(ed.), *The Republic and the Civil War in Spain* (London, Macmillan, 1971).

Carral, Ignacio, *Por qué mataron a Luis de Sirval* (Madrid, n.p., 1935).

Casas de la Vega, General Rafael, *La última guerra de África (campaña de Ifni-Sáhara)* (Madrid, Servicion de Publicaciones del EMI, 1985).

——*Seis generales de la guerra civil. Vidas paralelas y desconocidas* (Toledo, Fénix, 1998).

Cierva, Ricardo de la, *Historia esencial de la Guerra Civil Española. Todos los problemas resueltos, sesenta años después* (Madrid, Editorial Fénix, 1996).

Ciges Aparicio, M., *Entre la paz y la guerra (Marruecos)* (Madrid, n.p., 1912).

Connelly Ullman, Joan, *The Tragic Week. A Study of Anticlericalism in Spain, 1875–1912* (Cambridge, Mass., Harvard University Press, 1968).

Copado, Bernabé P., *Con la columna Redondo. Combates y conquistas. Crónica de guerra* (Sevilla, Imprenta de la Gavidia, 1937).

Cordero Torres, José María, *Organización del Protectorado esapñol en Marruecos*, 2 vols. (Madrid, Editora Nacional, 1942–3).

——*El Africanismo en la cultura hispánica contemporánea* (Madrid, Ediciones Cultura Hispánica, 1949).

Dallas, Gloden and Gill, Douglas, *The Unknown Army. Mutinies in the British Army in World War I* (London, Verso, 1985).

Del Boca, Angelo, *Gli italiani in Africa Orientale. La conquista dell'Impero* (Roma-Bari, Laterza, 1979).

——*L'Africa nella coscienza degli italiani. Miti, memorie, errori, sconfitte* (Roma-Bari, Laterza, 1992).

——*et al., I gas di Mussolini. Il fascismo e la guerra d'Etiopia* (Roma, Riuniti, 1996).

Diaz Nosty, B., *La comuna asturiana. Revolución de octubre de 1934* (Bilbao, Zero, 1974).

Dixon, Norman, *On the Psychology of Military Incompetence* (London, Jonathan Cape, 1976).

Dunn, Ross E., *Resistance in the Desert. Moroccan Responses to French Imperialism 1881–1921* (London, Croom Helm, 1977).

Emilio Blanco Izaga: coronel en el Rif (Melilla, La Biblioteca de Melilla, 1995).

España, Juan de (Víctor Ruiz Albéniz), *La actuación de España en Marruecos* (Madrid, n.p., 1926).

Esteban-Infantes, Emilio, *La sublevación del General Sanjurjo*, 2nd edn. (Madrid, n.p., 1933).

Faldella, Emilio, *Venti mesi de guerra in Spagna (luglio 1936–febbraio 1938)* (Firenze, Felice Le Monnier, 1939).

Febo, Giulana di, *La santa de la raza: un culto barroco en la España franquista (1937–1962)* (Barcelona, Icària Editorial, 1988).

Ferguson, Niall, *The Pity of War* (London, Allen Lane, 1998).

Fernández Álvarez, Salvador, *Melilla, la primera en el alzamiento* (Melilla, n.p., 1939).

FERNÁNDEZ DE CASTRO Y PEDRERA, RAFAEL, *Hacia las rutas de una nueva España. Melilla, la primera en el Alzamiento. De cómo se preparó y porqué hubo de comenzar en Melilla la santa cruzada nacional ¡17 julio 1936!* (Melilla, n.p., 1940).

FIELDHOUSE, D. K., *The West and the Third World: trade, colonialism, dependence, and development* (Oxford, Blackwell, 1999).

FLORES, A. and CICUÉNDEZ, J. M., *Guerra aérea sobre el Marruecos español (1913-1927)* (Madrid, Museo del Aire, 1990).

FOSS, WILLIAM and GERAHTY, CECIL, *The Spanish Arena* (London, John Gifford, n.d.).

FRASER, RONALD, *Blood of Spain: The Experience of the Spanish Civil War* (London, Allen Lane, 1979).

FULLER, J. G., *Troop Morale and Popular Culture in the British and Dominion Armies 1914-1918* (Clarendon Press, Oxford, 1990).

FURNEAUX, RUPERT, *Abdel Krim. Emir of the Rif* (London, Secker & Warburg, 1967).

FUSI, JUAN PABLO and PALAFOX, JORDI, *España: 1808-1996. El Desafío de la modernidad* (Madrid, Espasa Calpe, 1997).

GALBÁN JIMÉNEZ, MANUEL, *España en Africa. La Pacificación de Marruecos* (Madrid, Imprenta del Servicio Geográfico de Marruecos, 1965).

GANN, L. H. and DUIGNAN, PETER, *Colonialism in Africa 1870-1960*, 5 vols. (Cambridge, Cambridge University Press, 1969-73).

GARCÍA DELGADO, J. L. (ed.), *España entre dos siglos (1875-1931). Continuidad y cambio* (Madrid, Siglo XXI, 1991).

GARRACHÓN CUESTA, ANTONIO, *De África a Cádiz y de Cádiz a la España imperial. Por sendas de heroismo, de justicia, de hermandad y de amor (impresiones de un periodista)* (Cádiz, Establecimientos Cerón, 1938).

GARRIGA, RAMÓN, *El general Juan Yagüe: figura clave para conocer nuestra historia* (Barcelona, Planeta, 1985).

GARRIGA, RAMÓN, *Juan March y su tiempo* (Barcelona, Planeta, 1976).

—— *La señora de El Pardo* (Barcelona, Planeta, 1979).

GELLNER, ERNEST and MICAUD, CHARLES, *Arabs and Berbers. From Tribe to Nation in North Africa* (London, Duckworth, 1972).

GIBERT, NARCISO, *España y África* (Madrid, n.p., 1912).

GIBSON, IAN, *Queipo de Llano, verano de 1936* (Barcelona, Grijalbo, 1986).

GOMÁ, Coronel JOSÉ, *La guerra en el aire (vista, suerte y al toro)* (Barcelona, AHR, 1958).

GÓMEZ HIDALGO, FRANCISCO, *Marruecos. La tragedia prevista* (Madrid, n.p., 1921).

GÓMEZ-JORDANA SOUZA, Teniente General, Conde de Jordana, *La tramoya de nuestra actuación en Marruecos* (Madrid, Editora Nacional, 1976).

GONZÁLEZ CALBET, MARÍA TERESA, *La Dictadura de Primo de Rivera. El Directorio Militar* (Madrid, Ediciones el Arquero, 1987).

GONZÁLEZ, FERNANDO, *Kábila* (Madrid, Debate, 1980).

GONZÁLEZ, HERNÁNDEZ, MARÍA JESÚS, *El universo conservador de Antonio Maura. Biografía y proyecto de Estado* (Madrid, Biblioteca Nueva, 1997).

GUIXÉ, JUAN, *El Rif en sombras. (Lo que yo he visto en Melilla)* (n.p., n.d. [1921]).

HABER, L. F., *The Poisonous Cloud: Chemical Warfare in the First World War* (Oxford, Clarendon Press, 1986).

HABTI, YASSIN EL, 'La resistencia de Chauen contra el colonialismo español (1920-1956)', Ph.D. Thesis in Arabic, DES, University of Tetuán, 1999.

HALSTEAD, JOHN P., *Rebirth of a Nation: The Origins and Rise of Moroccan Nationalism, 1912–1944* (Cambridge, Mass., Harvard University Press, 1969).

HANIGHEN, FRANK C. (ed.), *Nothing but Danger: Thrilling Adventures of Ten Newspaper Correspondents in the Spanish War* (London, Harrap, 1940).

HARRIS, ROBERT and PAXMAN, JEREMY, *A Higher Form of Killing: The Secret Story of Gas and Germ Warfare* (London, Chatto and Windus, 1982).

HARRIS, WALTER B., *France, Spain and the Rif* (London, Edward Arnold, 1927).

HART, DAVID M., *The Aith Waryaghar of the Moroccan Rif: An Ethnography and History* (Tucson, University of Arizona, 1976).

HERNÁNDEZ HERRERA, CARLOS and GARCÍA FIGUERAS, TOMÁS, *Acción de España en Marruecos* (Madrid, n.p., 1929–30).

HERNÁNDEZ MIR, FRANCISCO, *Del desastre al fracaso. Un mando funesto* (Madrid, Pueyo, 1922).

—— *La tragedia del cuota (una escuela de ciudadanos)*, 2nd edn. (Madrid, Compañía Ibero-Americana de Publicaciones, 1923).

—— *Del desastre a la victoria (1921–26): Alianza contra el Rif* (Madrid, n.p., 1926).

—— *Del desastre a la victoria (1921–26). Del Rif a Jebala* (Madrid, n.p., 1927).

—— *Del desastre a la victoria (1921–26): El Rif por España* (Madrid, n.p., 1927).

—— *La Dictadura en Marruecos. Al margen de una farsa* (Madrid, Javier Morata, 1930).

HERNÁNDEZ SÁNCHEZ-BARBA, MARIO (coord.), *Historia social de la Fuerzas Armadas españolas* (Madrid, CESEDEN, 1986).

HIGUERA Y VELÁZQUEZ, ALFONSO G. DE LA and MOLINS CORREA, LUIS, *Historia de la Revolución Española. Tercera Guerra de Independencia* (Cádiz and Madrid, Cerón, n.d.).

Historia de la aviación española (Madrid, Instituto de Historia y Cultura Aérea, 1988).

Historial de la Harka de Melilla. Campañas Años 1924–1926 (Melilla, n.p., n.d.).

HOISINGTON, WILLIAM A. JNR., *Lyautey and the French Conquest of Morocco* (London, Macmillan, 1995).

HOLLIS, CHRISTOPHER, *Italy in Africa* (London, Hamish Hamilton, 1941).

HOWSON, GERALD, *Arms for Spain. The Untold Story of the Spanish Civil War* (London, John Murray, 1998).

HYAM, RICHARD, *Empire and Sexuality: The British Experience* (Manchester, Manchester UP, 1990).

IBN AZZUZ HAKIM, MOHAMMAD, *Compendio de los pactos internacionales de Marruecos* (Tetuán, Editora Marroquí, 1949).

—— *Sherif Raisuni and the Armed Resistance in Northern Morocco* (in Arabic) (Rabat, Sahel, 1981).

—— *La actitud de los moros ante el Alzamiento* (Málaga, Algazara, 1997).

Instituto de Estudios Africanos, *África en el pensamiento de Donoso Cortés* (Madrid, Consejo Superior de Investigaciones Científicas, 1955).

JAMES, LAWRENCE, *Raj. The Making and Unmaking of British India* (London, Abacus, 1997).

JAVIER MARIÑAS, General FRANCISCO, *General Varela (De Soldado a General)* (Barcelona, AHR, 1956).

JENSEN, ROBERT GEOFFREY, 'Intellectual Foundations of Dictatorship: Spanish Military Writers and their Quest for Cultural Regeneration, 1898–1923', Ph.D Diss., Yale University, 1995.

JOFFÉ, E. G. H. and PENNELL, C. R. (eds), *Tribe and State: Essays in Honour of David Montgomery Hart* (Wisbech, Middle East and North African Studies Press, 1991).

JONES, DAVID, *In Parenthesis* (London, Faber and Faber, 1937).

JULIÁ, SANTOS, *Manuel Azaña. Una biografía política* (Madrid, Alianza, 1990).

—— *Víctimas de la Guerra Civil* (Madrid, Temas de Hoy, 1999).

—— *Violencia política en la España del siglo XX* (Madrid, Taurus, 2000).

JULIEN, CHARLES-ANDRÉ, *Le maroc face aux impérialismes 1415–1956* (Paris, Editions JA, 1978).

KEEGAN, JOHN, *The First World War* (London, Hutchinson, 1998).

KHALLOUK TEMSAMANI, ABDEL AZIZ, *Pais Yebala: Majzen, España, y Ahmed Raisúni* (Granada, Editorial Universidad de Granada, 1999).

KNICKERBOCKER, H. K., *The Siege of Alcazar. A War-Log of the Spanish Revolution* (London, Hutchinson, n.d. [1936]).

KOESTLER, ARTHUR, *Dialogue with Death* (London, Arrow Books, 1961).

KUNZ, RUDIBERT and MÜLLER, ROLF-DIETER, *Giftgas gegen Abd el Krim: Deutschland, Spanien und er Gaskrieg in Spanisch Marokko, 1922–1927* (Freiburg im Breisgau, Rombach, 1990).

La Campaña de África. Un encuadre aéreo (Valencia, Museu de prehistòria I de les cultures de Valencia, 2000).

La Legión. Breve resumen de los datos más interesantes acerca de su creación, organización y funcionamiento (n.d, n.p., García Figueras Archive).

La Legión Española. 50 Años de Historia, 2 vols. (Madrid, La Legión, 1970 and 1973).

LA PORTE FERNÁNDEZ-ÁLFARO, PABLO, 'La respuesta urbana ante la crisis de Anual (1921–1923)', Ph.D thesis, Universidad Complutense de Madrid, 1997.

LA PORTE, PABLO, *La atracción del imán. El desastre de Annual y sus repercusiones en la política europea (1921–1923)* (Madrid, Biblioteca Nueva, 2001).

LAGHAUX, G. and DELHOMME, P., *La Guerre des gaz 1914–18* (Hegida, Paris, 1985).

LARIOS DE MEDRANO, JUSTO, *España en Marruecos. Historia secreta de la campaña* (Madrid, n.p., n.d.).

LÉCUYER, M. C. and SERRANO, C., *La Guerre d'Afrique et ses répercussions en Espagne (1859–1904)* (Paris, Presses Universitaires de France, 1976).

LEED, ERIC J., *No Man's Land. Combat and Identity in World War I* (Cambridge, Cambridge University Press, 1979).

LEGUINECHE, MANUEL, *Annual. El desastre de España en el Rif, 1921* (Madrid, Alfaguara, 1996).

LEWIS, DAVID LEVERING, *The Race to Fashada: European Colonialism and African Resistance in the Scramble for Africa* (London, Bloomsbury, 1988).

LIÉBANA, JOSÉ MANUEL and ORIZANA, G., *El Movimiento Nacional* (Valladolid, n.p., 1937).

LLEIXÁ, JOAQUÍN, *Cien años de militarismo en España: funciones estatales confiadas al Ejército en la Restauración y el franquismo* (Barcelona, Anagrama, 1986).

LOBERA GIRELA, CÁNDIDO, *Notas sobre el problema de Melilla* (Melilla, El Telegrama del Rif, 1912).

LOJENDIO, LUIS MARÍA DE, *Operaciones militares de la guerra de España 1936–1939* (Barcelona, Montaner y Simon, 1940).

LÓPEZ, ELSA *et al.*, *Diego Hidalgo. Memoria de un tiempo difícil* (Madrid, Alainza, 1986).

LÓPEZ RIENDA, RAFAEL, *El escándalo del millón de Larache* (Madrid, n.p., 1922).
—— *Frente al fracaso. Raisuni. De Silvestre a Burguete* (Madrid, Sociedad General Española de Librería, 1923).
—— *Abd-el-Krim contra Francia: impresiones de un cronista de guerra* (Madrid, n.p., 1925).
McCULLAGH, Captain FRANCIS, *In Franco's Spain: Being the Experiences of an Irish War-Correspondent During the Great Civil War Which Began in 1936* (London, Burns, Oates and Washbourne, 1937).
MACKENZIE, JOHN M. (ed.), *Popular Imperialism and the Military* (Manchester, Manchester UP, 1992).
McNEILL-MOSS, Major GEOFFREY, *The Epic of the Alcazar. A History of the Siege of the Toledo Alcazar, 1936* (London, Rich and Cowan, 1937).
—— *The Legend of Badajoz* (London, Burns, Oates and Washbourne, n.d.).
MACORLAN, PIERRE, *Légionnaires. A la Légion Etrangère Espagnole. A la Légion Etrangère* (Paris, Editions du Capitole, 1930).
MADARIAGA, MARÍA ROSA DE, *España y el Rif. Crónica de una historia casi olvidada* (Melilla, La Biblioteca de Melilla, 2000).
MADERO, LUIS, *El octubre español* (Mexico, Ediciones de 'El Nacional', 1935).
MAESTRE, TOMÁS, *El problema de Marruecos. Polémica periodística* (Melilla, el Telegrama del Rif, 1914).
MALDONADO, EDUARDO, *El Rogui* (Tetuán, Instituto Generalísimo Franco, 1949).
MALLETT, ROBERT and HEIBERG, MORTEN, *Pensiero ed azione totalitaria tra le due guerre mondiali* (Cività Castellana ed Orte, Centro Falisco de Studi Storici, 2000).
MARÍAS, FERNANDO and BAS, JUAN, *Páginas ocultas de la historia* (Madrid, Destino, 1999).
MARIX EVANS, MARTIN, *Passchendaele and the Battles of Ypres 1914–18* (London, Osprey, 1997).
MARTIN, CLAUDE, *Franco, soldado y estadista* (Madrid, Fermín Uriarte, 1965).
MARTÍN, MIGUEL, *El colonialismo español en Marruecos (1860–1956)* (Paris, Ruedo Ibérico, 1973).
MARTÍNEZ BANDE, JOSÉ MANUEL, *La marcha sobre Madrid* (Madrid, SHM, 1968).
—— *La campaña de Andalucía* (Madrid, San Martín, 1986).
MARTÍNEZ DE CAMPOS, ARSENIO, *Melilla 1921* (Ciudad Real, El Pueblo Manchego, 1922).
MARTÍNEZ DE CAMPOS, General CARLOS, *España bélic—el siglo XX—Marruecos*, 6 vols. (Madrid, Aguilar, 1972).
MARTÍNEZ DE LA CASA, ANTONIO, *La Legión Española. Cincuenta años de historia. Desde 1936 hasta nuestros días* (Madrid, La Legión, 1973).
MARTÍNEZ DE PISÓN, IGNACIO, *Una guerra africana* (Madrid, Ediciones SM, 2000).
MARTÍNEZ SAURA, SANTOS, *Memorias del Secretario de Azaña* (Madrid, Planeta, 1999).
MAS CHAO, ANDRÉS, *La formación de la conciencia africanista en el ejército español (1909–1926)* (Madrid, n.p., 1988).
MATEO DIESTE, JOSEP LLUÍS, *El 'moro' entre los primitivos. El caso del Protectorado español en Marruecos* (Barcelona, Fundación 'La Caixa', 1997).
MAURA, Duque de and FERNÁNDEZ ALMAGRO, MELCHOR, *Por qué cayó Alfonso XII*, 2nd edn. (Madrid, Ambos Mundos, 1948).
MELGAR MATA, ALFREDO and RUIZ FORNELLS, ENRIQUE, *Organización militar de España y algunas potencias extranjeras*, 18th edn. (Toledo, Rafael Gómez-Menor, 1915).
MELLOR, Captain F. H., *Morocco Awakes* (London, Methuen, 1939).

MERROUN, MUSTAPHA EL, 'El Cuerpo de Ejército Marroquí en la Guerra Civil Española (1936–1939)', Ph.D thesis, Granada University, 1999.

MESA, JOSÉ LUIS et al, *Las campañas de Marruecos 1909–1927* (Madrid, Almena, 2001).

MESA GARRIDO, ROBERTO, *La idea colonial en España* (Valencia, Fernando Torres, 1976).

MESGHENNA, YEMANE, *Italian Colonialism: A Case Study of Eritrea, 1869–1934. Motive, Praxis, Result* (Skrifter utgivna av Ekomisk-historiska föreningen i Lund, vol. LVIII, 1988).

MICÓ, CARLOS, *Los caballeros de la Legión* (Madrid, Sucesores de Rivadeneyra, 1922).

MONTERO BARRADO, J., *Paisajes de Guerra: nueve itinerarios por los frentes de Madrid* (Madrid, Ayuntamiento de Madrid, 1987).

MORALES, GABRIEL DE, *Datos para la historia de Melilla* (Melilla, n.p., 1909).

MORALES LEZCANO, VÍCTOR, *El Colonialismo Hispanofrancés en Marruecos (1898–1927)* (Madrid, Siglo Veintiuno, 1976).

——*España y el norte de África: el protectorado en Marruecos (1912–1956)*, 2nd edn. (Madrid, UNED, 1986).

MOSSE, GEORGE L., *Fallen Soldiers. Re-shaping the Memory of the World Wars* (New York and London, Oxford University Press, 1990).

MUÑOZ, ISAAC, *Política colonialista* (Madrid, n.p., 1912).

——*En tierras de Yebala* (Madrid, n.p., 1913).

——*La Corte de Tetuán* (Madrid, n.p., 1913).

MUÑOZ TINOCO, CONCEPCIÓN, 'Diego Hidalgo. Política regional y política liberal en un período de convulsión', Ph.D Diss., 3 vols. Universidad Complutense de Madrid, 1984.

——*Diego Hidalgo, un notario republicano* (Badajoz, Diputación Provincial de Badajoz, 1986).

'N.C.', *El pánico de Anual y el socorro de Monte-Arrui a la luz de la crítica* (Santander, Librería Moderna, n.d. [*c*.1924]).

NAVAJAS ZUBELDIA, CARLOS, *Ejército, Estado y Sociedad en España (1923–1930)* (Logroño, Instituto de Estudios Riojanos, 1991).

NERÍN, GUSTAU and BOSCH, ALFRED, *El imperio que nunca existió. La aventura colonial discutida en Hendaye* (Madrid, Plaza & Janés, 2001).

NUNES, LEOPOLDO, *La guerra en España. (Dos meses de reportaje en los frentes de Andalucía y Extremadura)* (Granada, Librería Prieto, 1937).

NÚÑEZ FLORENCIO, RAFAEL, *Militarismo y antimilitarismo en España (1888–1906)* (Madrid, CSIC, 1990).

O'NEILL, CARLOTA, *Los muertos también hablan*, 2nd edn. (Mexico, La Prensa, 1973).

OLMEDO DELGADO, ANTONIO and CUESTA MONEDERO, Teniente General JOSÉ, *General Queipo de Llano. (Aventura y audacia)* (Barcelona, Editorial AHR, 1957).

OMISSI, DAVID E., *Air Power and Colonial Control. The Royal Air Force 1919–1939* (Manchester, Manchester University Press, 1990).

——*The Sepoy and the Raj. The Indian Army, 1860–1940* (London, Macmillan, 1994).

ORTEGA Y GASSET, EDUARDO, *Annual. Relato de un soldado e impresiones de un cronista* (Madrid, Rivadeneyra, 1922).

ORTEGA Y GASSET, JOSÉ, *España invertebrada*, 15th edn. (Madrid, Revista de Occidente, 1967).

ORTIZ DE VILLAJOS, C. G., *De Sevilla a Madrid. Ruta libertadora de la columna Castejón* (Granada, Prieto, 1937).

OSUNA SERVENT, ARTURO, *Frente a Abd el Krim* (Madrid, n.p., 1922).

PANDO, JUAN, *Historia Secreta de Annual*, 2nd edn. (Madrid, Temas de Hoy, 1999).

PAYNE, STANLEY G., *Politics and the Military in Modern Spain* (Stanford, Stanford University Press, 1967).

——*Spain's First Democracy: The Second Republic, 1931–1936* (Madison, University of Wisconsin Press, 1993).

PAZ, ABEL, *La cuestión de Marruecos y la República española* (Madrid, Fundación de Estudios Libertarios Anselmo Lorenzo, 2000).

PECHURA, CONSTANCE M. and RALL, DAVID P. (eds.), *Veterans at Risk. The Health Effects of Mustard Gas and Lewisite* (Washington DC, National Academy Press, 1993).

PEMÁN, JOSÉ MARÍA, *Un soldado en la Historia. Vida del capitán general Varela* (Cádiz, Escelicer, 1954).

PENNELL, C. R., *A Country with a Government and a Flag: The Rif War in Morocco 1921–1926* (Wisbech, Cambs., Middle East and North Africa Studies Press, 1986).

PÉREZ MADRIGAL, JOAQUÍN, *Augurios, estallido y episodios de la Guerra Civil* (Avila, n.p., 1937).

PICHARDO ORTEGA, MANUEL L., *España en Marruecos. El Raisuni* (Madrid, n.p., 1917).

PITA, FEDERICO, *La acción militar y política de España en África a través de los tiempos* (Madrid, Revista Técnica de Infantería y Caballería, 1915).

——*Marruecos. Lo que hemos hecho y lo que debimos hacer en el Protectorado Español* (Melilla, Artes Gráficas Postal-Exprés, 1925).

PORCH, DOUGLAS, *The Conquest of Morocco* (London, Jonathan Cape, 1982).

PRESTON, PAUL, *Franco. A Biography* (London, HarperCollins, 1993).

——*The Coming of the Spanish Civil War: Reform, Reaction and Revolution in the Second Republic*, 2nd edn. (London, Routledge, 1994).

——*La política de la venganza. El fascismo y el militarismo en la España del siglo XX* (Barcelona, Ediciones Península, 1997).

——*Las Tres Españas del 36* (Madrid, Plaza & Janés, 1998).

——*¡Comrades! Portraits from the Spanish Civil War* (London, HarperCollins, 1999).

——and MACKENZIE, ANN L. (eds.) *The Republic Besieged. Civil War in Spain 1936–1939* (Edinburgh, Edinburgh University Press, 1996).

PRICE, RICHARD, *An Imperial War and the British Working-Class. Working-Class Attitudes and Reactions to the Boer War 1899–1902* (London, Routledge & Kegan Paul, 1972).

PUELL DE LA VILLA, FERNANDO, *El soldado desconocido: de la leva a la 'mili'* (Madrid, Biblioteca Nueva, 1996).

RAGUER, HILARI, *El General Batet. Franco contra Batet: crónica de una venganza* (Barcelona, Ediciones Península, 1996); 1st edn. published in Catalan: *El general Batet* (Montserrat. Edicions de l'Abadia de Montserrat, 1994).

RAMÓN-LACA, JULIO DE, *Bajo la férula de Queipo. Como fue gobernado Andalucía* (Sevilla, n.p., 1939).

RAMOS WINTHUYSSEN, JAVIER, *Tropas indígenas y Ejército Colonial* (Seville, n.p., 1921).

RANGER, T. O., 'African Reactions to the Imposition of Colonial Rule in East and Central Africa', in L. H. Gann and Peter Duignan (eds.), *Colonialism in Africa 1870–1960* (Cambridge, Cambridge University Press, 1969–73), i. 293–301.

RECIO CARDONA, RICARDO (ed.), *Rojo y Azul. Imágenes de la Guerra Civil Española* (Madrid, Almena, 1999).

REIBER, ROBERT W. (ed.), *The Psychology of War and Peace: The Image of the Enemy* (London and New York, Plenum Press, 1991).

REIG TAPIA, ALBERTO, *Ideología e historia: sobre la represión franquista y la Guerra Civil* (Madrid, Akal, 1984).

——*Memoria de la Guerra Civil. Los mitos de la tribu* (Madrid, Alianza, 1999).

RIERA, AUGUSTO, *España en Marruecos. Crónica de la campaña de 1909* (Barcelona, Maucci, 1909).

RIVET, DANIEL, *Lyautey et l'institution du protectoral français au Maroc, 1912–1925*, 3 vols. (Paris, L'Harmattan, 1988).

ROBINSON, RONALD, GALLAGHER, JOHN, and DENNY, ALICE, *Africa and the Victorians: the official mind of imperialism* (London, Macmillan, 1961).

ROCHAT, GIORGIO, *Militari e Politici nella preparazione della campagna d'Etiopia. Studio e documenti 1932–1936* (Milan, Franco Angeli, 1971).

RODRÍGUEZ DE VIGURI Y SEOANE, LUIS, *La retirada de Annual y el asedio de Monte Arruit* (Madrid, Rivadeneyra, 1924).

ROUBICEK, MARCEL, *Special Troops of the Spanish Civil War 1936–1939* (Doncaster, Athena, 1987).

RUBIO ALFARO, PLÁCIDO and LACALLE ALFARO, MIGUEL, *Alhucemas 1925. Desembarco, asentamiento, evolución* (Málaga, n.p., 1999).

RUBIO FERNÁNDEZ, EDUARDO, *Melilla. Al margen del desastre (mayo–agosto 1921)* (Barcelona, Cervantes, 1921).

RUIZ ALBÉNIZ, VICTOR, *La campaña del Rif. La verdad de la guerra* (Madrid, n.p., 1909).

——*España en el Rif: estudios del indígena y del país* (Madrid, Biblioteca Hispana, 1921).

——*Estado actual del problema de España en Marruecos y medios prácticos para resolverlo* (Madrid, Ateneo de Madrid, 1922).

——(EL TEBIB ARRUMI), *Las Responsabilidades del Desastre. Ecce Homo. Prueba documental y aportes inéditos sobre las causas del derrumbamiento y consecuencias de él* (Madrid, Biblioteca Nueva, n.d. [1922]).

——*Tánger y la colaboración franco-española en Marruecos* (Madrid, n.p., 1927).

SAEZ DE GOVANTES, LUIS, *El africanismo español* (Madrid, Instituto de Estudios Africanos, 1971).

SAID, EDWARD, *Orientalism. Western Conceptions of the Orient*, 2nd edn. (Harmondsworth, Penguin, 1995).

SALAS LARRAZÁBAL, RAMÓN, *Historia general de la guerra civil* (Madrid, Editora Nacional, 1976).

——*El protectorado de España en Marruecos* (Madrid, Mapfre, 1992).

SÁNCHEZ DEL ARCO, MANUEL, *El Sur de España en la Reconquista de Madrid. (Diario de operaciones glosado por un testigo)*, 2nd edn. (Sevilla, Editorial Sevillana, 1937).

——*Política contemporánea. Ayer y hoy en Marruecos* (Tetuán, n.p., 1952).

SANGRONIZ, JOSÉ ANTONIO, *Marruecos. Sus condiciones físicas, sus habitantes y las instituciones indígenas* (Madrid, n.p., 1921).

SANTOS, E., '*El Secretario*'. *Revelaciones sobre la Guerra Civil en Badajoz* (Badajoz, n.p., 1984).

SBACCHI, ALBERTO, *Ethiopia under Mussolini. Fascism and the Colonial Experience* (London, Zed, 1985).

SCURR, JOHN, *The Spanish Foreign Legion* (London, Osprey, 1985).

SECO SERRANO, CARLOS, *Militarismo y civilismo en la España contemporánea* (Instituto de Estudios Económicos, 1984).

SEDDON, DAVID, *Moroccan Peasants. A century of change in the eastern Rif 1870–1970* (Folkestone, Dawson, 1981).

SEGRÈ, CLAUDIO G., *L'Italia in Libia. Dall'età Giolittiana a Gheddafi* (Milano, Feltrinelli, 1978).

SEMPRÚN, JOSÉ, 'Del Hacho al Pirineo: el Ejército Nacional en la guerra de España', MS submitted for *Así Fue. La Historia Rescatada*, 1999.

SHEEAN, VINCENT, *Adventures among the Riffi* (London, George Allen & Unwin, 1926).

—— *Personal History*, 3rd edn. (London, Hamish Hamilton, 1969).

SIMONS, GEOFF, *Iraq: From Sumer to Saddam* (London, Macmillan, 1994).

SOLDEVILLA, FERNANDO, *El año político 1921* (Madrid, n.p., 1922).

—— *El año político 1922* (Madrid, n.p., 1923).

SOUTHWORTH, HERBERT R., *Le Mythe de la croisade de Franco* (Paris, Ruedo Ibérico, 1964).

—— *Anti-Falange. Estudio crítico de 'Falange en la guerra de España, la unificación y Hedilla' de Maximiano García Venero* (Paris, Ruedo Ibérico, 1967).

—— *Guernica! Guernica! A Study of Journalism, Diplomacy, Propaganda, and History* (Berkeley and Los Angeles, University of California, 1977).

SPERBER, MURRAY A., *And I Remember Spain. A Spanish Civil War Anthology* (London, Hart-Davis, MacGibbon, 1974).

STEER, G. L., *Caesar in Abyssinia* (London, Hodder and Stoughton, 1936).

Stockholm International Peace Research Institute (SIPRI), *Delayed Toxic Effects of Chemical Warfare Agents* (Stockholm, SIPRI, 1975).

SUEIRO SEOANE, SUSANA, *España en el Mediterráneo. Primo de Rivera y la 'cuestión marroquí', 1923–1930* (Madrid, UNED, 1992).

SUERO ROCA, MARÍA TERESA, *Los generales de Franco* (Barcelona, Bruguera, 1975).

—— *Militares republicanos de la guerra de España* (Barcelona, Península, 1981).

TAHTAH, MOHAMMED, *Entre pragmatisme, réformisme et Modernisme. Le rôle politico-religieux des Khattabi dans le Rif (Maroc) jusqu'à 1926* (Leiden, n.p., 1995).

TESSAINER Y TOMASICH, CARLOS FEDERICO, *El Raisuni. Aliado y enemigo de España* (Málaga, Algazara, 1998).

TORRE DEL RÍO, ROSARIO DE LA, *Inglaterra y España en 1898* (Madrid, Eudema, 1988).

TUSELL, JAVIER, *Radiografía de un golpe de Estado. El ascenso al Poder del General Primo de Rivera* (Madrid, Alianza, 1987).

—— *Antonio Maura. Una biografía política* (Madrid, Alianza, 1994).

VALDÉS, ALEJANDRO, *¡¡Asturias!! Relato vivido de la insurrección de octubre* (Valencia, Ediciones Verdad, n.d.).

VANDERVORT, BRUCE, *Wars of Imperial Conquest in Africa 1830–1914* (London, UCL, 1998).

VEHÍ I CASTELLÓ, AGUSTÍ, 'L'orgull del sol. Cançó trista per un exercit trist', 1998, unpublished MS.

VIDAL GALLEGO, ELISEO, *El joven del Rif. ¡¡¡Los muertos de Annual ya son vengados!!!* (Madrid, Gráfica Administrativa, 1932).

VIDAL, CÉSAR, *La Guerra de Franco. Historia militar de la guerra civil española* (Barcelona, Planeta, 1996).

VILA IZQUIERDO, JUSTO, *Extremadura: la Guerra Civil* (Badajoz, Universitas Editorial, 1983).

VIÑAS, ANGEL, *Franco, Hitler y el estallido de la Guerra civil. Antecedentes y consecuencias* (Madrid, Alianza, 2001).

VIVERO, AUGUSTO, *El derrumbamiento. La verdad sobre el desastre del Rif* (Madrid, Caro Raggio, 1922).

WEBER, EUGEN, *Peasants into Frenchmen. The modernization of rural France 1970–1914* (London, Chatto & Windus, 1979).

WEISKEL, TIMOTHY C., *French Colonial Rule and the Baule People: Resistance and Collaboration 1889–1911* (Oxford, Oxford University Press, 1980).

WHITAKER, JOHN T., *We Cannot Escape History* (New York, Macmillan, 1943).

WOOLMAN, DAVID S., *Rebels in the Rif. Abd-el-Krim and the Rif Rebellion* (Stanford, Stanford University Press, 1968).

WYDEN, PETER, *La guerra apasionada. Historia narrativa de la guerra civil española, 1936–1939* (Barcelona, Martínez Roca, 1983); English version, *The Passionate War: The Narrative History of the Spanish Civil War, 1936–1939* (New York, Simon and Schuster, 1983).

YÑIGUEZ, FERNANDO, *Por tierras de Marruecos: valor agrícola de la zona española* (Madrid, Hijos de Reus, 1913).

Articles

ABDEL AZIZ TEMSAMANI KHALLOUK, 'Lectura en el archivo de Jebala: sobre las correspondencias entre Raisuni y Jattabi', *Al Alam Athakafi*, 10 Sept. 1988.

ALCARAZ CÁNOVAS, IGNACIO, 'Marruecos y la Guerra Civil', *Cuadernos Republicanos*, Jan. 2000.

ALPERT, MICHAEL, 'The Spanish Zone of the Moroccan Protectorate During the Spanish Civil War 1936–1939', *Maghreb Review*, 18: 1–2 (1993).

——'The Clash of Spanish Armies: Contrasting Ways of War in Spain, 1936–1939', *War in History*, 6: 3 (1999).

ÁLVAREZ VARELA, EDUARDO, 'Desembarco de Al Hoceima', *Aeroplano*, 8 (Nov. 1990).

ANDREW, C. M. and KANYA FORSTNER, A. S., ' "The French Colonial Party": its composition, aims and influence, 1885–1914', *Historical Journal*, 14: 1 (1971).

ASÍN PALACIOS, M., 'Por qué lucharon a nuestro lado los musulmanes marroquíes', *Boletín de la Universidad Central* (Madrid, 1940).

BALFOUR, SEBASTIAN and LA PORTE, PABLO, 'Spanish Military Cultures and the Moroccan Wars, 1909–1936', *European Historical Quarterly*, 20: 3 (July 2000).

BARCELÓ, MIQUEL, 'L'orientalisme i la peculiaritat de l'arabisme espanyol', *L'Avenç*, 25 (June 1980).

BENJELLOUN, ABDELMAJID, 'La participation del Rifains a la Guerre Civile Espagnole', *Revue d'Histoire Maghrébine*, 87–8 (May 1997).

BOSQUE COMA, ALFREDO, 'Prisionero de Abd el-Krim', *Historia 16*, 206 (June 1992).

BLINKHORN, MARTIN, 'Spain: the "Spanish Problem" and the Imperial Myth', *Journal of Contemporary History*, 15 (1980).

——'En Marruecos tras el desaster de Annual', *Historia y Vida*, 332 (Nov. 1995).

BOYD, CAROLYN P., ' "Responsibilities" and the Second Spanish Republic 1931–6', *European History Quarterly*, 14 (1984).

CABALLERO DOMÍNGUEZ, MARGARITA, 'La cuestión marroquí y su corolario de Annual como causa y consecuencia de la crisis del sistema restauracionista', *Investigaciones Históricas*, 17 (1997).

CAUSSE, J., 'Le Remplacement de general Alfau et la campagne du Djebala', *L'Afrique Francaise*, 9: 8 (Aug. 1913).

COOK, TIM, ' "Against God-Inspired Conscience": The Perception of Gas Warfare as a Weapon of Mass Destruction, 1915–1939', *War and Society*, 18: 1 (May 2000).

DELGADO, J., 'Notas sobre la campaña de Marruecos', *La Guerra y su Preparación* (Apr. 1923).

DRIESSEN, HENK, 'Images of Spanish Colonialism in the Rif. An Essay in Historical Anthropology and Photography', *Critique of Anthropology*, 7: 1 (1987).

ELENA, ALBERTO, 'Cine Africanista Español: "Romancero Marroquí"', in *Semencias*, 4 (Apr. 1996).

FERNÁNDEZ FERRER, Colonel JOSÉ, 'Guerra de España', *Ejército*, 16 (May 1941).

FLEMING, SHANNON E., 'Spanish Morocco and the Alzamiento Nacional, 1936–1939: The Military, Economic and Political Mobilization of a Protectorate', *Journal of Contemporary History*, 18 (1983).

—— and FLEMING, ANN K., 'Primo de Rivera and Spain's Moroccan Problem, 1923–27', *Journal of Contemporary History*, 12 (1977).

FRIEDLANDER, ROBERT A., 'Holy Crusade or Unholy Alliance? Franco's "National Revolution" and the Moors', *Southwestern Social Science Quarterly*, 44 (Mar. 1964).

GALEY, JOHN H., 'Bridgerooms of Death. A profile study of the Spanish Foreign Legion', *Journal of Contemporary History*, 4 (1969).

GÁRATE CÓRDOBA, JOSÉ MARÍA, 'Los moros en la guerra de España', *Historia y Vida*, 23, 267 (June 1990).

—— 'Las tropas de Africa en la Guerra Civil española', *Revista de Historia Militar*, 35: 70 (1991).

GIL BRACERO, RAFAEL and CAZORLA SÁNCHEZ, ANTONIO, 'Málaga, Granada, Almería. Febrero de 1937: el desastre humano de los refugiados y sus responsabilidades políticas. Una nueva perspectiva', in *Anuario de Historia Contemporánea*, vol. 14, *1987–91* (Universidad de Granada, 1992).

GIMÉNEZ BUESO, JOSÉ, 'Los gases de combate', *Memorial de Artillería*, año 81, serie vii, vol. 1 (Jan. 1926).

GOYTISOLO, JUAN, 'Cara y cruz del moro en nuestra literatura', in *Revista Internacional de Sociología*, 46 (1988).

HALSTEAD, CHARLES, 'Un "Africain" méconnu: le colonel Juan Beigbeder', *Revue d'Histoire de la Deuxième Guerre Mondiale*, 21: 83 (1971).

—— 'A "Somewhat Machiavellian" Face: Colonel Juan Beigbeder as High Commissioner in Spanish Morocco, 1937–1939', *Historian*, 37 (Nov. 1974).

HART, DAVID M., 'Dos resistentes bereberes al colonialismo franco-español en Marruecos y sus legados islámicos: Bin 'Abd Al-Krim y 'Assu U-Baslam', in 'Mohammed Ben Abdel Krim el Jatabi', *Fundamentos de Antropología*, nos. 4 and 5 (Granada, 1996).

JENSEN, ROBERT GEOFFREY, 'Moral Strength through Material Defeat? The Consequences of 1898 for Spanish Military Culture', *War and Society*, 17: 2 (Oct. 1999).

KHARCHICH, MOHAMED, 'La alianza franco-española contra el movimiento rifeño', *Fundamentos de Antropología*, 4 and 5 (Granada, 1996).

KOERNER, FRANCIS, 'La guerre du Rif espagnol vue par la Direction des Affaires indigènes française (1921–1924)', *Revue Historique*, 287 (1992).

LA PORTE FERNÁNDEZ-ÁLFARO, PABLO, 'La respuesta urbana ante la crisis de Anual (1921–1923)', *Revista de Estudios Africanos*, 18–19 (1996).

MADARIAGA, MARÍA ROSA DE, 'Imagen del moro en la memoria colectiva del pueblo español y retorno del moro en la Guerra Civil de 1936', *Revista Internacional de Sociología*, 46 (1988).

—— 'The Intervention of Moroccan Troops in the Spanish Civil War: A Reconsideration', *European History Quarterly*, 22 (1992).

'Mohammed Ben Abdel Krim el Jatabi', *Fundamentos de Antropología*, nos. 4 and 5 (Granada, 1996).

Morales Lezcano, Victor, 'La aventura económica', *Historia 16*, núum extra 9 (Apr. 1979).

——'L'exèrcit d'Africa i les reformes militars: 1931–1936', *L'Avenç* (June 1980).

Navajas Zubeldia, Carlos, 'La primera época de la *Revista de Tropas Coloniales*: un estudio ideológico', Separata de *Revista de Extremadura*, núm. 19 (Jan.–Apr. 1996).

Pascual, Pedro, 'Así fue el desembarco de Al Hoceima', *Historia 16*, Año 23, n. 282 (1999).

Pennell, Richard, 'The Responsibility for Anual: the Failure of Spanish Policy in the Moroccan Protectorate, 1912–21', *European Studies Review*, 12 (1982).

Rollin, Léon, 'L'Espagne au Maroc', *Bulletin du Comité de L'Afrique* (Nov. 1926).

Rosas Ledesma, Enrique, 'Las "Declaraciones de Cartagena" (1907): significación en la política exterior de España y repercusiones internacionales', *Cuadernos de historia moderna y contemporánea*, 2 (1981).

Ruiz Albéniz, Víctor, 'La carga de Taxdirt', *El Libro Popular. Revista Literaria*, 717 (Feb. 1914).

Scott-Clark, Cathy and Levy, Adrian, 'Survivors of Our Hell', *Guardian Weekend*, 23 June 2001.

Senén del Oso Romero, Comandante de Artillería, 'El arma química', *Ejército*, 14 (Mar. 1941).

Sotto Montes, Joaquín de, 'Notas para la historia de la Fuerzas Indígenas del Antiguo Protectorado de España en Marruecos', *Revista de Historia Militar*, 35 (1973).

——'Notas para la historia del antiguo Protectorado de Marruecos', *Revista de Historia Militar*, 35 (1973).

Sueiro Seoane, Susana, 'El mito del estratega: Primo de Rivera y la resolución del problema de Marruecos', *Cuadernos de Historia Contemporánea*, 16 (1994).

Torre del Río, Rosario de la, 'La política exterior española en el año de la crisis de 1911 a través de la correspondencia del marqués de Alhucemas', in *Estudios Históricos. Homenaje a los profesores José María Jover Zamora y Vicente Palacio Atard* (Madrid, Universidad Complutense, 1990), vol 1.

Ucelay da Cal, Enric, 'Els enemics dels meus enemics. Les simpaties del nacional-isme català pels "moros": 1900–1936', *L'Avenç* (June 1980).

Willoughby, C. A., 'Spanish Campaigns in Morocco', *Infantry Journal* (Aug. 1925); trans. and published in *La Guerra y su Preparación*, 18–19 (Nov. 1925).

Index